Theories of Internation

This book is a comprehensive guide to theories of International Relations (IR). Given the limitations of a paradigm-based approach, it sheds light on eighteen theories and new theoretical perspectives in IR by examining the work of key reference theorists. The chapters are all written to a common template: the introductory section provides readers with a basic understanding of the theory's genesis by locating it within an intellectual tradition, paying particular attention to the historical and political context. The second section elaborates on the theory as formulated by the selected reference theorist. After this account of the theory's core elements, the third section turns to theoretical variations, examining conceptual subdivisions and overlaps, further developments and internal critique. The fourth section scrutinizes the main criticisms emanating from other theoretical perspectives and highlights points of contact with recent research in IR. The fifth and final section consists of a bibliography carefully compiled to aid students' further learning.

Encompassing a broad range of mainstream, traditional theories as well as emerging and critical perspectives, this is an original and ground-breaking textbook for students of International Relations.

The German edition of the book won the "Geisteswissenschaften International" Prize, collectively awarded by the Fritz Thyssen Foundation, the German Federal Foreign Office and the German Publishers & Booksellers Association.

Siegfried Schieder is Acting Professor for International Relations and Foreign Policy at the University of Trier and teaches International Relations at the German-Chinese Graduate School of Global Politics (GSGP), Free University of Berlin.

Manuela Spindler teaches International Relations and International Relations Theory at the German open Business School (GoBS) and the German-Chinese Graduate School of Global Politics (GSGP), Free University of Berlin.

Theories of International Relations

Edited by
Siegfried Schieder and Manuela Spindler

Translated by Alex Skinner

Routledge
Taylor & Francis Group
LONDON AND NEW YORK

First published 2014
by Routledge
2 Park Square, Milton Park, Abingdon, Oxon OX14 4RN

and by Routledge
711 Third Avenue, New York, NY 10017

Routledge is an imprint of the Taylor & Francis Group, an informa business

British Library Cataloguing in Publication Data
A catalogue record for this book is available from the British Library

Library of Congress Cataloging in Publication Data
Theorien der internationalen beziehungen. English
Theories of international relations / edited by Siegfried Schieder
and Manuela Spindler ; translated by Alex Skinner.
pages cm
Includes bibliographical references and index.
1. International relations—Political aspects. 2. World politics.
I. Schieder, Siegfried. II. Title.
JZ1242.T47 2014
327.101—dc23

2013037210

ISBN: 978–0–415–81854–4 (hbk)
ISBN: 978–0–415–74114–9 (pbk)
ISBN: 978–1–315–79736–6 (ebk)

Typeset in Times New Roman
by RefineCatch Limited, Bungay, Suffolk

MIX
Paper from responsible sources
FSC® C013604

Printed and bound by CPI Group (UK) Ltd, Croydon, CR0 4YY

Contents

Contributors

Mathias Albert is Professor of Political Science at Bielefeld University, Germany. His publications: 2010 (ed.) *New Systems Theories of World Politics*. London: Palgrave (with Lars-Erik Cederman and Alexander Wendt); 2013 (ed.) *Bringing Sociology to IR: World Politics as Differentiation Theory*. Cambridge: Cambridge University Press (with Barry Buzan and Michael Zürn).

Andreas Bieler is Professor of Political Economy and Fellow at the Centre for the Study of Social and Global Justice (CSSGJ), School of Politics and International Relations, University of Nottingham, UK. His publications: 2006: *The Struggle for a Social Europe: Trade Unions and EMU in Times of Global Restructuring*. Manchester: Manchester University Press; 2010 (ed.) *Global Restructuring, Labour and the Challenges for Transnational Solidarity*. London: Routledge (with Ingemar Lindberg).

Hans-Jürgen Bieling is Professor of Political Economy and Economic Didactics at Eberhard Karls University, Tübingen, Germany. His publications: 2010: *Die Globalisierungs- und Weltordnungspolitik der Europäischen Union*. Wiesbaden: VS Springer; 2011: *Internationale Politische Ökonomie*, updated and revised 2nd edition. Wiesbaden: VS Springer.

Thomas Conzelmann is Professor of International Relations at Maastricht University, the Netherlands. His publications: 2012: Informal Governance in International Relations, in: Christiansen, Thomas and Neuhold, Christine (eds) *International Handbook on Informal Governance*. Cheltenham: Edward Elgar, pp. 219–235; 2012: A Procedural Approach to the Design of Voluntary Clubs: Negotiating the Responsible Care Global Charter, *Socio-Economic Review* 10(1): 193–214.

Christopher Daase is Professor of International Organizations at Goethe University Frankfurt am Main, Germany. His publications: 2010 (ed.) *Rethinking Security Governance: The Problem of Unintended Consequences*. London: Routledge (with Cornelius Friesendorf); 2012 (ed.) *Arms Control in the 21st Century: Towards a New Paradigm?* London: Routledge (with Oliver Meier).

Thomas Diez is Professor of Political Science and International Relations at the University of Tübingen, Germany. His publications: 2008 (ed.) *The European Union and Border Conflicts*. Cambridge: Cambridge University Press (with Mathias Albert and Stephan Stetter); 2011: *Key Concepts in International Relations*. London: Sage (with Ingvild Bode and Aleksandra Fernandes da Costa).

Barbara Finke is Head of Graduate Programmes at Hertie School of Governance, Berlin. Her publications: 2005: *Legitimation globaler Politik durch NGOs. Frauenrechte, Deliberation und Öffentlichkeit in der UNO*. Wiesbaden: VS Verlag. 2005 (ed.) *Europäische Zivilgesellschaft: Konzepte, Akteure, Strategien*. Wiesbaden: VS Verlag (with Michèle Knodt).

Andreas Hasenclever is Professor of International Relations and Peace Research at the University of Tübingen. His publications: 1997: *Theories of International Regimes*. Cambridge: Cambridge University Press (co-authored with Peter Mayer and Volker Rittberger); 2006: International Institutions Are the Key. A New Perspective on the Democratic Peace, *Review of International Studies* 32 (2006): 3, 563–583 (co-authored with Brigitte Weiffen).

Michael Heinrich is Professor of Economics at Hochschule für Technik und Wirtschaft, Berlin. His publications: 2013: Crisis Theory, the Law of the Tendency of the Profit Rate to Fall, and Marx's Studies in the 1870s, in: *Monthly Review* 64(11), pp. 15–31; 2013: The Fragment on Machines: A Marxian Misconception in the Grundrisse and its Overcoming in Capital, in: Bellofiore, Riccardo, Starosta, Guido and Thomas, Peter D. (eds) *In Marx's Laboratory. Critical Interpretations of the Grundris*. Leiden: Brill, pp. 197–212.

Christoph Humrich is Assistant Professor of International Relations and World Politics at the University of Groningen, the Netherlands. His publications: 2011: Facts Without Norms? Does the Constitutionalization of International Law still Have a Discourse-theoretical Chance?, in Ungureanu, Camil, Guenther, Klaus and Joerges, Christian (eds) *Jürgen Habermas*. Vol. 2. Farnham: Ashgate, pp. 323–338; 2011: Global Governance Through Legislation, in Enderlein, Henrik, Wältli, Sonja and Zürn, Michael (eds) *Handbook on Multi-level Governance*. Cheltenham: Elgar, pp. 343–357 (with Bernhard Zangl).

Andreas Jacobs is Research Advisor, NATO Defense College, Rome, Italy. His publications: 2004 (ed.) Euro-Mediterranean Co-operation: Enlarging and Widening the Perspective, ZEI Discussion paper, Bonn; 2006: Reformist Islam. Protagonists, Methods, and Themes of Progressive Thinking in Contemporary Islam, KAS policy paper, Berlin.

Adam David Morton is Professor of Political Economy, Department of Political Economy, University of Sydney, Australia. His publications: 2007: *Unravelling Gramsci: Hegemony and Passive Revolution in the Global Political Economy*. London: Pluto Press. 2011: *Revolution and State in Modern Mexico: The Political Economy of Uneven Development*. Lanham, MD: Rowman & Littlefield. Winner of the 2012 Book Prize of the British International Studies Association (BISA) International Political Economy Group (IPEG).

Andreas Nölke is Professor of International Relations and International Political Economy at Goethe University Frankfurt am Main, Germany. His publications: 2013 (ed.) The Politics of Financialization, in *Competition and Change*, 17(3) (special issue, in collaboration with Hans-Jürgen Bieling and Marcel Heires); 2014 (ed.) *Emerging Markets Multinational Corporations: State Capitalism 3.0*. London: Palgrave Macmillan.

Paul Reuber is Professor of Political Geography at the University of Münster, Germany. His publications: 2012: *Politische Geographie*. Paderborn: UTB; 2012 (ed.) *Die Politik der räumlichen Repräsentationen – Beispiele aus der empirischen Forschung. Forum Politische Geographie 6*. Münster: LIT (with Iris Dzudzek and Anke Strüver).

Siegfried Schieder is currently Acting Professor of International Relations and Foreign Policy at the University of Trier and Visiting Scholar at the Shanghai Academy of Social Sciences (SASS), Shanghai. His publications: 2011: The Social Construction of European Solidarity: Germany and France in the EU Policy towards the States of Africa, the Caribbean and the Pacific (ACP) and Central and Eastern Europe (CEE), *Journal of International Relations and Development* 14(4): 469–505; 2014: *Neue Sprachbilder und Metaphern für Europa? Grenzen der deutschen Europa- und Integrationspolitik*. Wiesbaden: Springer VS.

Niklas Schörnig is Senior Research Fellow at the Peace Research Institute Frankfurt, Germany, and visiting lecturer at Goethe University, Frankfurt am Main, Germany. His publications: 2012: Killer Drones: The Silver Bullet of Democratic Warfare? *Security Dialogue* 43(4): 353–370 (with Frank Sauer); 2013 (ed.) *The Militant Face of Democracy: Liberal Forces for Good*. Cambridge: Cambridge University Press (with Anna Geis and Harald Müller).

Manuela Spindler is Professor of International Politics at the University of Erfurt and Brandt School of Public Policy (until 2013), lecturer in International Relations and International Relations Theory at the German Open Business School and the Graduate School of Global Politics at the Free University of Berlin, Germany. Her publications: 2005: *Regionalismus im Wandel. Die neue Logik der Region in einer globalen Ökonomie*. Wiesbaden: VS-Verlag; 2013: *International Relations*. Opladen: Barbara Budrich Publishers.

Ingo Take is currently Acting Professor of International Governance at the University of Münster, Germany. His publications: 2012: Regulating the Internet Infrastructure: A Comparative Appraisal of the Legitimacy of ICANN, ITU, and the WSIS, *Regulation & Governance* 6(6): 499–523; 2012: Global Governance Put to the Test: A Comparative Study of the Legitimacy of International, Transnational and Private Forms of Governance, *Swiss Political Science Review* 18(2): Special Issue, 220–248.

Cornelia Ulbert is Executive Director of the Institute for Development and Peace (INEF) at the University of Duisburg-Essen, Germany. Her publications: 2005: Deliberately Changing the Discourse: What Does Make Arguing Effective?, *Acta Politica* 40(3): 351–367 (with Thomas Risse); 2013: How to Hit a Moving Target: Assessing the Effectiveness of Public-Private Partnerships, in Hegemann, Hendrik, Heller, Regina and Kahl, Martin (eds) *Studying "Effectiveness" in International Relations: A Guide for Students and Scholars*. Opladen: Barbara Budrich Publishers, pp. 101–120.

Günter Wolkersdorfer was a senior lecturer at the Department of Geography, University of Münster, Germany. He died in July 2008. His publications: 2008: Geopolitische Leitbilder als Deutungsschablone für die Bestimmung des "Eigenen" und des "Fremden", in Lentz, Sebastian, Ormeling, Ferjan (eds): *Die Verräumlichung des Welt-Bildes*. Stuttgart:

Steiner, pp. 181–192; 2007: Raum und Macht: Geopolitik des 21. Jahrhunderts, in Gebhardt, Hans et al. (eds): *Geographie. Physische und Humangeographie*. Heidelberg: Spektrum, pp. 895–904 (with Paul Reuber).

Bernhard Zangl is Professor of Global Governance and Public Policy at LMU Munich, Germany. His publications: 2008: Judicialization Matters! A Comparison of Dispute Settlement under GATT and the WTO, *International Studies Quarterly* 52(4): 825–854; 2012: Between Law and Politics: Explaining International Dispute Settlement Behavior, *European Journal of International Relations*, 18(2): 369–401 (with Achim Helmedach, Alexander Kocks, Aletta Mondré, Gerald Neubauer and Kerstin Blome).

Preface

This textbook is the English translation of the German volume *Theorien der Internationalen Beziehungen*, the third edition of which was published by UTB (University Textbooks) and Barbara Budrich Publishers in 2010. The book has been thoroughly revised for the English edition, both to ensure that the individual contributions reflect the current state of the theoretical debate and to incorporate recent titles and publications into the bibliography.

Like the original German text, the English version too owes its existence to a number of individuals and institutions to whom we owe a special debt of gratitude. We are particularly grateful to Alex Skinner for his painstaking and thoughtful translation of the German edition. Beyond that we are – as always – indebted to our authors for their unwavering commitment to this textbook and their thorough revisions of the individual contributions. There would be no English-language edition without the generous support of the Fritz Thyssen Foundation, the German Federal Foreign Office, the collecting society VG WORT and the German Publishers & Booksellers Association, who collectively awarded the book the "Geisteswissenschaften International" prize. Last but not least we are indebted to Craig Fowlie, Senior Editor at Routledge, and Barbara Budrich, who have made the textbook and its approach accessible beyond the German-speaking world. Our thanks to all of you.

Siegfried Schieder and Manuela Spindler
Trier and Berlin, March 2014

Note on the text

The translation of this work was funded by Geisteswissenschaften International – Translation Funding for Work in the Humanities and Social Sciences from Germany, a joint initiative of the Fritz Thyssen Foundation, the German Federal Foreign Office, the collecting society VG WORT and the German Publishers & Booksellers Association.

Theory in International Relations

Manuela Spindler and Siegfried Schieder

1 Introduction

"Theoretical pluralism" is the term often used to describe the coexisting and generally competing theories, approaches, perspectives and concepts that try to describe, explain and understand international relations.[1] There are three main reasons for this present "state of the art" in international relations theory. The rapid growth in theoretical perspectives can, first, be seen as *the result of cumulative theory building and a process of professionalization* within an academic discipline that can now look back on a history of more than 90 years – if we consider the subject's "year of birth" to be 1919. Against the background of the Versailles Treaties, it was institutionalized as a science and as an academic discipline through the establishment of the first "chair" in International Relations (IR) – the so-called Woodrow Wilson Chair – at Aberystwyth, University of Wales. The first professorship in IR was devoted to the systematic study of the causes of war and the conditions for world peace.[2] This aspect of cumulative theory building is particularly pertinent to the discipline of IR. Even today there is no consensus on how best to understand its subject matter in conceptual and theoretical terms or its methods of knowledge production. To put it differently, there is no agreement on what international relations are and how we should study them (see Wæver 2013: 303–315). Consequently, when studying IR theory, students will come across a huge range of different and competing theoretical accounts.

Second, this broad range of theoretical perspectives in IR is the result of a process – one increasingly hard to keep up with – of the *adaptation of insights from related and neighbouring (social) sciences*. It is in fact a key characteristic of IR, in common with all social science disciplines, that it cannot be neatly separated from disciplines such as sociology or political philosophy and theory, nor even from economics, political geography, psychology or law. Drawing on the categories and concepts found in these neighbouring disciplines can often help IR achieve additional insights. This is particularly true when we consider that international relations are becoming increasingly globalized. The object of study no longer fits neatly within the boundaries of a discipline historically devoted to the study of interstate relations. It is only against this background that we can understand why the corpus of contemporary IR theory has branched off into a multiplicity of approaches, such as the huge range of critical, constructivist and postmodern theories that have proliferated since the 1990s. This has dismantled the boundaries between formerly separate academic disciplines and brought to the fore the "social" character of international relations; consequently, IR scholars now need to engage in genuine social theorizing rather than maintaining an exclusive domain of IR theories devoted to the study of interstate relations (see, for example, Albert and Buzan 2013).

Third, and closely related to the second point, because it is a social science, there is always a *close interplay between theory building in International Relations and the discipline's historical and sociopolitical context.* Progress in IR theory is closely linked with events in the "real world" of international politics, such as the development of the bipolar system following the Second World War, the decolonization of large parts of Africa and Asia in the late 1950s and early 1960s, the Vietnam War and the global economic crisis triggered by the "oil price shocks" of the 1970s, the rise of emerging powers since the 2000s and what we generally perceive as the "processes of globalization". Global political upheavals such as the end of the East–West conflict, the shift in the role of sovereign nation states associated with globalization, and the increasing impact of transnational non-state actors rooted in economy and society have exercised and continue to exercise an enduring influence on a whole generation of theory-oriented scholars, doing much to shape their theoretical ideas about international relations. The theory of IR finds itself confronted with new challenges in the light of phenomena such as "failing" or "failed states" and the resulting security and developmental tasks involved in international "state-building", the emergence of new, globally organized forces of violence resulting from the erosion of the state monopoly of power and, not least, the increasing global economic and political importance of China and other rising powers (such as India, Brazil or Turkey) and of entire world regions (above all Asia) – all of which are highly significant in their effects on the structure of the international system and in their practical political implications. Another demonstration of the link between IR theory and the real world is the increasing number of studies that review and reappraise past theoretical work in light of the global and European crises and the political processes of the "Arab Spring". While initially the end of the East–West conflict was generally interpreted – with theoretical back-up – as an opportunity to advance world peace (the key terms here being "new world order", "peace dividend", "nuclear disarmament", etc.), events such as "9/11", the fight against international terrorism, along with new international problems such as securing energy supplies, international climate protection and, not least, turbulence in the international financial and capital markets, have refocused theoretical attention on the ambivalent, transitional and conflictual nature of international politics and global order.

One thing emerges clearly from these few examples. It is inherent in the logic of the social sciences that a shift in a discipline's object of investigation, prompted by real-world social and political changes, always goes hand-in-hand with adaptation of its theoretical-conceptual toolkit. So we can understand the development of theory in IR only in light of, and in fact as an integral part of, its historical and political context.

The diversity of the theoretical perspectives in IR is by no means an entirely new phenomenon. As mentioned above, it is a basic feature of theoretical research in the social sciences. In the case of IR, however, it was above all the 1990s that generated an unprecedented theoretical spectrum. This theoretical differentiation was, however, long hidden from view because of how it was presented in the relevant textbooks. The reason for this is the still prevalent "orthodox" historiography of the discipline as a series of so-called "great debates", and the associated failure to grasp the true complexity of theory building.

"Great debates" have formed the core structure of intellectual discourse in IR and have organized IR as an academic discipline. Through their engagement in such debates, IR scholars define their particular view of the world. These "great debates" are so fundamental to IR that Ole Wæver (1998: 715) reasons that there is no other established means of telling the history of IR. In other words, "great debates" serve to reify the discipline and create a hierarchy of scientifically relevant subjects within it.[3] A constitutive feature of these "great debates" is the contrast between two competing theories or theoretical "camps"; the clash between them is claimed to provide much stimulus for the advancement of International Relations as a sub-discipline of political science. In the academic literature you will usually come across three, and in recent times four, "great debates" (Lapid 1989; Kurki and Wight 2013; Wæver 2013).

The first of these debates, occurring in the 1930s and 1940s, was between realism and idealism (Carr [1939] 1964; for an overview, see Schmidt 2012). The key bone of contention in the first great theoretical debate was the question of whether, and if so to what extent, there can be progress in the relations between states. In light of the experience of the First World War (1914–1918), the idealists cherished the hope of avoiding future wars through the establishment of international institutions such as the League of Nations (Claude 1956). Realists, meanwhile, in view of states' power politics within a world essentially viewed as "anarchic", dismissed such hopes as mere wishful thinking and utopianism. The failure of the League of Nations as an instrument for ensuring international peace and the outbreak of the Second World War seemed to indicate that the realists were right.

The argument between realism and idealism was followed in the 1960s by the second "great debate", that between "traditionalists" (defending a humanistic methodology) and "behaviourists" or "scientists", emphasizing the importance of methodological rigour to the discipline. In essence, this was a discipline-specific version of the general social scientific dispute over the question of whether human understanding (*Verstehen*) or natural scientific "explanation" should take priority. "Traditionalists" drew on the methods of intuition, experience and textual interpretation characteristic of the humanities to justify their statements about international relations. Their scientist antagonists, meanwhile, working on the premise of the methodological "unity of sciences", claimed that it was both possible and necessary to take a "natural scientific" approach to understanding the social world. The epistemological goal of a scientific approach is to obtain empirically verifiable statements and universally valid theories of international relations on the basis of systematic description and causal explanation (for a discussion of the key issues, see Kaplan 1966; Knorr and Rosenau 1969; see also Curtis and Koivisto 2010).[4] The second debate is often thought of as having been won by the "behaviourists", at least judging from how IR as a discipline is practised in the United States (Kurki and Wight 2013: 18–19). The application of natural scientific methods triggered a period of professionalization that did much to establish IR as a distinct academic subdiscipline.

Narrating theoretical development as a series of "great debates" has clearly facilitated a neat classification of IR theory. This, however, has been increasingly contested, at least since the identification of a "third debate" beginning in the 1980s. The term "third debate" is used for two very different theoretical discourses – the "interparadigm debate" between "realists", "pluralists" and "Marxist perspectives" on world politics, which originated in the 1970s and continued into the 1980s (e.g. Maghoori and Ramberg 1982; Wæver 1996), and the debate between "explaining and understanding, between positivism and post-positivism, or between rationalism and reflectivism" (Kurki and Wight 2013: 20; see also Lapid 1989; Hollis and Smith 2009) since the mid-1980s. This in itself reveals how poorly the "orthodox" historiography conveys theoretical developments in IR. The debate between positivism and post-positivism alluded to in the above quote is characterized by profound scrutiny of and disagreements about epistemological, ontological, and methodological issues, which have called into question not only many assumptions about the nature of international relations, such as the anarchy of the international system, but also the philosophy of science that underlies social scientific theorizing more generally.

Though the "third debate" – or "fourth debate" according to Wæver (2013) and Kurki and Wight (2013) – has largely run out of steam, ontological as well as epistemological issues remain important to IR (Wendt 2006; Wight 2006; Chernoff 2007; Reus-Smit and Snidal 2008b; Kurki and Wight 2013; see also Spindler 2013). In contrast to the previous discourse, recent debates tend to cut across established currents of research and theory ("grand theories" such as neorealism, institutionalism, liberalism, etc.). According to Wæver (2013: 313), after the mid-1990s the theoretical debate was transformed into a series of debates between the "boundary of boredom" (rational choice) and the "boundary of negativity" (post-structuralism). This transformation has seen the previously dominant rational choice approaches losing their key position in IR (not least due to the waning of the so-called "neo-neo debate" between neorealism and neoliberal institutionalism). Social constructivist theorizing, meanwhile, has been increasingly marked by a diffusion of theoretical foci. A process of fragmentation has seen some constructivist authors contribute to the different strands of an intraconstructivist debate while others have helped develop a post-structuralism that has tended to engage more with specific subjects (for example, migration, racism or postcolonialism) and "less with general theory debates both *vis-à-vis* the establishment and internally" (ibid.: 312).

As a result, theoretical debates within the subdiscipline have proliferated and continue to do so. The "theoretical pluralism" mentioned above looks set to become even more significant. What we find at the core of IR theory, then, is a "debate not to be won, but a pluralism to live with", as Wæver fittingly puts it (1996: 155). This will make the systematic presentation of IR theory for studying and teaching purposes even more difficult, and represents a challenge to the writing of suitable textbooks geared towards the current state of theoretical development.

2 The notion of theory in International Relations

It is inherent in the logic of the discipline's development, as outlined at the beginning of this Introduction, that there is neither a generally accepted nor an authoritative theory of International Relations. We will thus search in vain for any generally recognized concept of theory. If, despite this, we wish to clarify what we mean when we talk about theories of International Relations, we must provide at least a broad outline of the subject matter of the discipline – namely, international relations.

In terms of a "lowest common definitional denominator", international relations are understood as a web of relations made up of cross-border interactions between state and non-state actors, interactions generally subdivided into the spheres of international politics and transnational relations. The traditional concept of international politics entails a notion of international relations as a *Staatenwelt,* or world of sovereign states; here, state actors are regarded as the most crucial ones. This notion of a "world of states" is often contrasted with that of a "world society". Here states continue to play an important role but the emphasis is on cross-border activities by all kinds of social actors such as individuals and social groups, international organizations, diplomacy and international law. Key actors include economic entities (e.g. transnational corporations such as Siemens or Google Inc.), non-governmental organizations (such as Amnesty International), global social movements (e.g. the anti-globalization movements) as well as international organizations such as the United Nations and supranational arrangements such as the European Union. The notion of international relations as a "world of states" or "world society" already indicates that our conception of what international relations are is always embedded in different world-views and perspectives – from which all theory building starts.[5]

But the concept of "international relations" must be differentiated still further. If we adopt the traditional understanding of IR as a subdiscipline of *political* science, the term refers first and foremost to the "political dimension" of international relations and their content. By *politics*, we mean the authoritative distribution of material and non-material values (such as the allocation and distribution of economic wealth among a country's citizens through tax laws and welfare programmes) through the political system *qua* legitimate state authority (Easton 1965). At first sight, the application of this concept of politics to international relations appears problematic. This is because there is no authority within international relations endowed with a monopoly of power and thus with the authority to sanction (such as a world government) that sets binding rules and norms for all and ensures compliance with them. This feature of international relations is typically referred to as "anarchy". Despite the lack of such a superordinate authority in international relations, it is clear that actions taken by state and non-state actors within international relations bring about a binding distribution of values, or are at least geared towards such a distribution – and are thus "politically" relevant. The key point here is who gets what: how much security, prosperity, autonomy, etc.[6] For want of a superordinate authority, the allocation and distribution of values within international relations are mostly enforced by means of power or on the basis of voluntary coalitions anchored in common values, interests or goals – through international organizations, for example. Processes of juridification and legalization of international politics are becoming increasingly important in the allocation and distribution of values (see Goldstein *et al.* 2000).

Also politically relevant to international relations are processes of exchange that are organized primarily via markets and their central actors (above all, economic ones). Exemplary here are the activities of international companies, along with other actors in the sphere of international trade and financial relations such as ratings agencies (e.g. Standard & Poor's, Moody's or Fitch), whose assessments of the creditworthiness of companies and states are of great relevance to the allocation and distribution of welfare gains. The current global financial and sovereign debt crisis has made us all painfully aware of this. As a rule, the voluntary coordination of international politics takes place through associations or so-called networks, or may take the form of international non-governmental organizations. International human rights networks can exert pressure to help bring about changes in political systems that violate human rights, thus exercising an impact on the allocation of values (see Finnemore and Sikkink 1998; Risse *et al.* 1999). The same applies to the policies of international organizations such as the International Monetary Fund or the World Bank.

In the broadest sense, international relations thus consist of the overall framework of all cross-border interactions between state and non-state actors that result in politically relevant value allocations in the spheres of security, economy, authority and the environment. *Theories* of IR try to conceptualize and make general statements about this web of relations, which is made up of cross-border interactions and the politically relevant actions, geared towards value allocations, taken by the state and non-state actors within it. However, as indicated above, the traditional understanding of IR as a separate academic discipline and subdiscipline of political science is subject to dispute.

2.1 Three dimensions of theory: ontology, epistemology and normativity

It is important to highlight three key dimensions of theories. First, a theory makes statements about the observer's perspective on the object of investigation. This is the *ontological dimension* of IR theory ("theory of being"). The ontology underpinning a theory, its conception of "the way the world is" or "what the world is made of", refers to the substantive ideas or world-view – understood as a system of assumptions and beliefs – that a theory engenders about its object, in this case, international relations. The question here is "What *is*?" or "What is the nature of the subject matter?" In this sense, a theory of international relations formulates general assumptions about international relations, that is, the actors' sphere of action, the type or "quality" of the key actors, their goals and preferences, as well as the driving forces of international politics and its fundamental problems and developmental prospects.

A few examples may serve to illustrate this ontological dimension of IR theory. Neorealism generates a conception of international relations as relations constituted exclusively by state actors (see Waltz 1979). The emphasis here is on the lack of any superordinate authority that might impose binding norms and rules capable of preventing states from attacking one another. On the basis of material self-interest, the action of states is thus fundamentally geared towards security and power. States' action is subject to the structural constraints of the international system, which result from the distribution of power among states (see the chapter by Niklas Schörnig in this volume). Institutionalism and liberalism also work on the assumption of anarchy as the basic condition of the international system, but place greater emphasis on the possibility of cooperation in an anarchical environment and the rules of international institutions (see the chapters by Manuela Spindler and by Bernhard Zangl in this volume), and, in the case of liberal approaches, processes of preference formation within states. For liberal approaches, it is not states but individuals and social groups within the state that are assumed to be the key actors within international relations and that therefore influence the allocation of values (see the chapters by Andreas Hasenclever and by Siegfried Schieder in this volume). World-system theorists, meanwhile, take the global capitalist system or "world-system" as the central unit of analysis and starting point of their theoretical reflections (see the chapter by Andreas Nölke in this volume), while social constructivists place great emphasis on social factors such as norms, ideas, identities and discursive learning processes as factors explaining international politics (see the chapter by Cornelia Ulbert in this volume). Other IR perspectives such as postmodern approaches focus on the analysis of texts and other representations of events rather than on the events themselves and adopt a deeply sceptical attitude towards the possibility of an "objective" reality. If what we know about reality is discursively mediated and constructed, then there is more than one version of this reality (see the chapter by Thomas Diez in this volume).

In addition to its underlying world-view or ontology, every theory makes a validity claim about its object of investigation. This brings us to the second dimension of IR theory, the *epistemological dimension* ("theory of knowledge"). This relates to the different ways of obtaining knowledge of the world and the underlying conception of science. The aim here is not to clarify the nature of the world and field of study (ontology), but to explain why we consider something to be a legitimate object of study, what counts as valid knowledge, and to set out how we might obtain scientific findings. Both the epistemological and ontological dimension are often referred to as a "second-order" criterion or "metatheory".[7] Epistemological issues, however, are often poorly understood; much of the difficulty here is due to the fact that epistemology cross-cuts the ontological differences between theories. Exponents of one and the same theoretical school, who share many basic ontological assumptions, may profess partially conflicting views on the acquisition of knowledge and on what may lay claim to the status of valid "knowledge" within IR. More specifically, epistemological positions guide, in a fundamental way, how IR scholars theorize and indeed "see" the world.

To begin to get to grips with this problem, it is helpful to divide the theories of IR very roughly into "positivist" and "post-positivist" camps. For *positivist* modes of knowledge acquisition in the social sciences, the epistemological ideal is natural science.[8] Theories committed to this ideal conceive of the social reality of international relations as an "object" that can to some extent be investigated from "outside" by an external observer who makes no value judgements. The aim here (and this is regarded as fundamentally possible) is to explain the genesis of structures and the unfolding of processes within international relations on the basis of empirically "proven" causalities, and thus to formulate universally valid theories of international relations. Here the notion of "theory" is used in a strictly delimited way. Positivists always refer to theory building in a (natural) scientific sense, and what they mean by this is a definitive set of general statements about cause–effect relations. As a rule, these are conceptualized as relationships between variables (measured quantities) in accordance with the schema: effect *b*, as a change in the value of the dependent variable, is a result of cause *a*, a change in the independent variable, with *b* temporally following *a*.[9]

From such a positivist epistemological point of view, a theory always refers to a particular field of study, delimiting it and setting out its epistemological stance. Further, a theory puts forward hypotheses, identifies regularities, infers laws or develops structural models. It provides explanations of the regularities that are characteristic of its field of application and, finally, makes predictions about the occurrence of specific phenomena within it. Theories such as neorealism, regime theory, and liberalism explicitly claim to provide "scientific" explanations, up to and including predictions of specific phenomena within international politics (Elman and Elman 2003).[10]

Traditionally, the epistemological fault line in the social sciences – though this too is a crude simplification intended to gain us some initial purchase – runs between "explanation" and "understanding". As indicated above, in IR, this fault line is presented in terms of the debate between scientism and traditionalism (see also Hollis and Smith 2004). Explanatory approaches work on the assumption that knowledge about the social and material worlds can be obtained in the same way, because social phenomena are chiefly determined by objective, empirically discoverable conditions. IR approaches that emphasize the concept of human understanding or *Verstehen* postulate that social phenomena are determined mainly by subjective perceptions and attributions of meaning (see Giddens 1982). The method of obtaining knowledge thus differs as well. On this view, social scientists cannot stand outside of their object of investigation. Social science as a whole is always part of the social realities at issue. This means that for understanding-based approaches social conditions are not "objects" that we might observe from outside. We can understand what actors do within international relations only from the "inside", in light of a web of social relations, and thus only in hermeneutic and interpretive fashion, in other words, through *Verstehen*. Ultimately, then, social science is always tied to the value judgements of those who practise it.

Since the late 1980s, however, this traditional dividing line between "explanation" and "understanding" has been joined by more radical epistemological perspectives that have strengthened the post-positivist camp. Postmodern and post-structuralist approaches, for example, work on the epistemological assumption that knowledge is contingent, and at least dependent on cultural, historical and ideological contexts. "Reality" is always a social construction that takes on meaning only within a larger framework of communication and discourse. Through the way in which we produce scientific findings, we as researchers do not simply provide a convincing picture of an external world. Instead, by means of our concepts and linguistic metaphors, we depict the world without ever being in a position to know for certain whether it coincides with the "real world" – "we construct worlds we know in a world we do not" (Onuf 1989: 42ff.).

This perspective, referred to as "epistemological constructivism", distances itself from all attempts to foreshorten our forms of knowledge to a single methodological ideal (see Guzzini 2000). Further, a radical epistemological perspective does not claim to grasp changes in the world directly and thus to be able to investigate them, because knowledge about them is itself a linguistic construction.[11] Unlike exponents of epistemological constructivism, social constructivists do not utterly reject knowledge acquisition by means of positivist methods. They merely wish to supplement them with interpretive methods, thus building a bridge between rationalist-positivist and interpretive-constructivist approaches (Adler 1997; Checkel 1998: 327; Guzzini 2001; see also Risse 2002). While rationalist and constructivist theoretical approaches to the study of international relations are commonly taught as mutually exclusive, scholars have explored the common ground between the two and demonstrated that, rather than being in simple opposition, there can be both tension and overlap (Barkin 2010).

Nonetheless, the positivist concept of theory geared towards natural science still dominates, though its exponents face mounting criticisms and their supremacy is beginning to crumble. The 1990s in particular brought forth numerous critical, postmodern and normative approaches with different ontological and epistemological positions, many of them rejecting the positivist conception of science and theory more generally. They are frequently subsumed under the umbrella term *post-positivism*. The term itself indicates that these critical discussions have ushered in an era "after" the formerly predominant positivism, an era featuring a plethora of coexisting ontological and epistemological views. Many IR theorists express their critique of positivism by eschewing from the outset a causal concept of theory that aspires to the status of natural science.

Finally, we can distinguish a third dimension of IR theories, namely their often implicit, seldom explicit, *normative* function and their relevance to *social practice*. For a long time the normative function of IR theories tended to be a peripheral topic in the theoretical literature. We might think of the normative dimension as establishing the "meaning of action" or as a guide to political action. It sets out reasons for how things "ought to be". The influence of social scientific theories on the actions of political decision-makers is evident, for example, in the implementation of John Maynard Keynes' ideas through policies designed to manage post-war economic problems in the industrialized West (see Hall 1989).[12] As a practical guide to political action, theories thus take on an importance way beyond the academic field; they not only provide guidance but also help us to reflect on this very action-guiding function, in other words to investigate the "theory-guidedness" of political actors themselves. This aspect is often "forgotten" or left unconsidered, particularly by positivist theories with their primarily explanatory aspirations. These remarks point to the conclusion that the "scientific discussion" of practical policies can never fall back on "science" as a final source of authority, because different bodies of knowledge compete with one another and competing truth claims cannot be resolved in any conclusive way (Lentsch and Weingart 2011; see also Stichweh 2006).

That IR theory has important normative dimensions is also evident in the existence of "normative IR theory" as a distinct field of scholarship (Erskine 2013). More than forty years ago Martin Wight famously claimed that "domestic politics is the realm of the good life; international politics is the realm of survival" (Wight 1966: 17). In his classic article, Wight asked "Why is there no International Theory?", arguing that under conditions of anarchy there is no place for normative or ethical reasoning. But this position has now been fundamentally rethought (Snidal and Wendt 2009). The claim that international politics is a realm of existential "necessity" is more contested than ever. Scholarship in political theory (e.g.

Rawls 1971, 1999; Walzer 1977; Beitz 1979; Caney 2005), international law (e.g. Koskenniemi 2002; see also Schieder 2009) and IR (e.g. Brown 1992; Reus-Smit 1999; Erskine 2013) increasingly integrates the normative dimension not simply of traditional interstate relations, but of transnational and global politics more generally. The insight that we cannot avoid the ethical dimension of international politics has now attained canonical status. The editors of the *Oxford Handbook of International Relations* hold that the separation of the normative (or ethical) from the empirical is untenable since "all theories of international relations and global politics have important empirical and normative dimensions, and their deep interconnection is unavoidable" (Reus-Smit and Snidal 2008b: 6).[13]

2.2 The latest twists and turns in IR theory

Many of the more recent debates between "positivism" and "post-positivism" have been devoted to the search for the "right" ontology for IR theorizing. The current theoretical debate on the ontology of international relations is reflected in various, most often social constructivist works that seek to embed IR theorizing in a scientific or critical realist ontology (Wendt 1999, 2006; Wight 2006, 2013). In contrast to the substantive dimension of IR theories, scientific or critical realism are specific positions within the philosophy of science. At their heart lie ontological issues that ascribe to unobservable entities such as the structure of the international system a status as legitimate object of scientific inquiry (a status that is denied by positivist philosophy of science). Attempts to ground IR theorizing in the ontology of scientific or critical realism have mostly been inspired by the works of Roy Bhaskar (Bhaskar 1979; see also Outhwaite 1992) and indicate a general tendency for IR theorizing and social theory to move closer together.[14]

The same is true for approaches to theories of practice in IR that revolve around the works of philosophers (such as Ludwig Wittgenstein and Hubert L. Dreyfus), social theorists (such as Pierre Bourdieu and Anthony Giddens), French philosophers (such as Michel Foucault, Jean-François Lyotard and Jacques Derrida) and theorists of science and technology (such as Bruno Latour). These approaches are often referred to as part of the "cultural turn" (Jackson 2008; Lebow 2008), "practice turn" (Büger and Gadinger 2007) or "pragmatic turn" (Kratochwil 2007; Friedrichs and Kratochwil 2009; Hellmann 2009; for an overview, see Bauer and Brighi 2009) in social science because they place "practice" and hence shared, collective, recurring and patterned action at the centre of their analyses.

Other scholars have recently questioned rationalist, positivist research by emphasizing the role of emotions in international politics (Bleiker and Hutchinson 2008; Mercer 2010; Linklater 2011). Studies demonstrate that emotions such as fear and hope (Lebow 2005), humiliation (Fattah and Fierke 2009; Fierke 2012), friendship (Berenskoetter 2007) or solidarity (Boltanski 1999; Coicaud and Wheeler 2008; Schieder *et al.* 2011) offer better explanations of political decision-making than rational calculation. For example, Dominique Moïsi has investigated the far-reaching emotional impact of globalization after the terrorist attacks of 11 September 2001, showing how contemporary geopolitics is characterized by a "clash of emotions" (Moïsi 2010). With a focus on the emotional aspects of meanings and practices in international and transnational politics, which are bound up with specific historical-political periods and contexts, this literature has contributed to a vibrant debate in IR on the significance of cognitive-psychological concepts that might be read as a nascent "emotional turn" (Crawford 2000; Wolf 2011, 2012). The same is true of the incorporation of sociological concepts into the study of world politics in line with a recent "sociological turn" (Guzzini 2000; Guzzini and Leander 2001).[15]

In addition, there have been attempts to rethink IR by reinvigorating the rich tradition of systemic thought in order to analyse the structure and dynamics of the international system, drawing on the pioneering work of Karl W. Deutsch and more recently of the German sociologist Niklas Luhmann (e.g. Albert *et al.* 2010). The literature includes recent works that aim to bring sociology to IR (Albert *et al.* 2013) or formulate a "sociology of the international" (Kessler 2009; see also Albert and Buzan 2013). Based on Luhmann's theory of autopoietic social systems, a new holistic ontology has emerged that underlines the "connectivity of communication" at the heart of international relations (Kessler 2009), while other authors more generally emphasize the need to take account of the "social whole" in the study of international relations (Albert and Buzan 2013).[16] All these recent works share an understanding of IR theory as part of a broader social theory, rejecting the idea that IR is separable from other social science disciplines; in fact, they view "international relations" as inseparable from the "social" more generally.

What is striking is that these more recent discussions tend to emphasize the crucial importance of the ontological dimension to theorizing while taking a rather relaxed view of epistemological questions (see, for example, Wendt 1999, 2006, 2010, also Wight 2006). Wendt and Wight openly declare that their main theoretical interest is in ontological matters. As Wendt has emphasized, "going into the epistemology business will distract us from the real business of IR, which is inter-national politics" (Wendt 1998: 115). Without doubt, ontological issues are of prime importance. Nevertheless, epistemological issues have also been key to the development of IR as an academic discipline (Kurki and Wight 2013: 15). Both epistemological and ontological debates are likely to become not only more pluralist but also more intense in the near future.[17] The whole notion of science as a culturally embedded system of knowledge may well lie at the centre of future debates. Wendt has recently shifted focus in an attempt to develop a "quantum social science" (Wendt 2006, 2010, 2014 forthcoming). Based on the naturalist belief that all social science must conform to the natural sciences, above all physics, the goal of this endeavour is to explore the implications of quantum physics for the social sciences. So far, Wendt's new metaphysical transfer from the world of quanta to IR has been discussed only hesitantly in the IR literature (Keeley 2007; Kessler 2007; Spindler 2013). It might, however, form part of a broader discussion on the limits of IR theorizing, which has traditionally been based on the ideal of "Cartesian" science.[18]

In addition, we can expect further fragmentation of the discursive landscape as a result of Western IR researchers' increasing interest in non-Western theoretical traditions of International Relations (see Acharya and Buzan 2010), and the emergence of new IR theories embedded in ontologically different perspectives on politics, economics and society, such as recent attempts to construct IR theories with Chinese characteristics or attempts to formulate Indian and Arab theories of politics and economics (see, for example, Chan 1999; Tickner and Wæver 2009; Tickner and Blaney 2012; Ling 2013). This debate will enable a fresh perspective on the embeddedness of IR theory in Western science and the cultural foundations on which any system of knowledge production rests (see, for example, the special issue of the *European Journal of International Relations* in 2013).[19]

3 The educational concept of the present volume

The way in which knowledge about theories of International Relations is organized is a decisive factor determining the quality of textbooks; it is therefore a key criterion in choosing the "right" book. This volume has the character of a compendium that provides an introduction to important and productive International Relations theories. In addition, the book is a kind of map showing the "coordinates" of contemporary theories. In this sense it provides a "compass" indicating possible theoretical paths that theories of International Relations may go down in the near future. We thus saw it as useful and necessary to include a relatively large number of recent so-called post-positivist (or better, non-positivist) theories and approaches in all their diversity, theories that have gradually reshaped the discipline of International Relations over the last few years and will continue to do so.

3.1 Learning objectives

This volume should help readers achieve two learning goals. First, we aim to sensitize students to the theoretical pluralism of International Relations while encouraging them to reflect on what theory is and what it can and ought to achieve. Second, though, students need a comprehensive knowledge of the theories of International Relations themselves. Acquisition of this broad knowledge through the individual chapters in this volume is the second learning goal. Each chapter builds on the same educational concept, which we will now explain in detail.

In the shape of the "theories" assembled in this volume, we present theories, approaches, perspectives and concepts that make general statements about international relations in the broadest sense. The dimensions of theory set out above can also be identified in the case of concepts such as "interdependence", "world society" or "globalization", despite the fact that there is no theory of interdependence or globalization in the narrow sense, but at most theoretical reflection on the problems associated with increasing internationalization and globalization. Often, concepts are important "building blocks" for subsequent theoretical developments.[20]

3.2 The educational concept informing the chapters

The present volume aims to set out the most important International Relations theories to facilitate an overview of the various theoretical models and theorists, while avoiding any tendency to think in simplistic categories. These aims cannot be realized by the dominant view of theories, outlined at the beginning, as "sides" within "great debates". Such a perspective leads to ideal typical constructions of two distinct "rivals" or even opponents, each of which has its own theoretical views and epistemological interests, which we may then "compare". Yet it is the very process of "construction" that generates the notion of the "other", such as idealism, traditionalism or positivism – generally with the aim of legitimizing a particular perspective while delegitimizing others (Dryzek and Leonhard 1988).[21]

We take a different approach in the present work in order to avoid this view of the discipline, which tends to obscure rather than illuminate. In presenting theories we are guided by the idea of a *reference theorist*.[22] The advantage of this is that students are confronted with an internally consistent theoretical core, rather than with a general account of so-called "grand theories" such as realism, liberalism or institutionalism, which include a large number of "internal" subdivisions. It is easier, we think, to approach the nuances and debates internal to a given theory after having first been introduced to a coherent theoretical model, and this we facilitate by presenting the ideas of a key reference theorist. As a result we pay less attention to the internal subdivisions of a given theoretical current, but we believe this is justified – vital, in fact – with respect to our primary target readership of beginning students. Our decision to organize this book around reference theorists rather than established paradigms makes it possible to address a plethora of important new theoretical currents within International Relations, currents that are not amenable to a paradigm-based approach and that are not represented, or only marginally so, in popular textbooks. This applies, for example, to the broad spectrum of critical approaches such as Critical Theory, feminism and postmodern approaches, which are all too often lumped together in the relevant textbooks, as well as theories and perspectives from the field of International Political Economy.

To ensure that each chapter fulfils the demands of an introduction, the content of each adheres to a consistent structure, in which the crucial account of the given reference theorist is embedded. Each consists of five components:

1 The first part is the *introduction*. The aim here, first of all, is to give the reader a basic understanding of how a given theory came into being by locating it within an *intellectual tradition*. We provide systematic support for this goal by including cross-references to other theories presented in the volume. Second, we pay a generous amount of attention to the *historical-political context*: as in all social scientific disciplines, theory building in International Relations is closely bound up with actual historical events (such as global economic crises and military conflicts), the social environment of specific universities and research institutions and the peculiarities of academic discourse.
2 The second section *reconstructs and elaborates the theory developed by the selected reference theorist*. What is the reference theorist's basic understanding of international relations? Which issues and problems are central to the theory? How does (s)he construct her or his explanations, in other words, which explanatory factors does (s)he cite, on what analytical level and deploying which model of actor? What does the theorist see as the "laws of motion", the crucial "driving forces", of international relations?
3 In the third section, following the description of a theoretical core, we take account of the varieties and variants of theories by making space for a discussion of the *subdivisions of a given theory and conceptual overlap, further developments and internal critique*. As a rule, theory building within International Relations does not occur in isolation; theoretical innovations tend to build partly on what has been handed down. The specific theoretical currents that we link with a particular reference theorist cannot always be clearly distinguished from one another. Often, rather than being rivals, theoretical concepts and ideas are complementary. An account that set out to "review" clearly distinguishable approaches and rival theories would fail to convey much of the interest, and much of the impetus, of contemporary theory building in International Relations, which has increasingly "frayed edges" and whose internal theoretical dividing lines are becoming increasingly blurred.
4 The fourth section provides an *account and reception of external criticisms*. What are the key points of critique emanating from other theoretical currents? What is the relevance of this theory to present-day debates and how innovative is its research programme? To what extent does the theory provide points of contact for recent findings in International Relations? As a rule, when we portray or attempt to build on a given theoretical approach, we can distinguish between "external" critique that disputes a theory's basic assumptions and "internal" critique. The latter, while remaining within a given theoretical current and thus sharing its basic assumptions, identifies shortcomings and differs significantly from the reference theorist in terms of its own theory building. But there are also cases in which the line between "internal"

and "external" criticisms cannot always be clearly drawn, because the internal differentiation and development of a reference theorist's ideas are often a response to external critique. In such cases we summarize the reference figure's response in Section 4.

5 The fifth and final section provides a *bibliography designed with specific educational goals in mind.* It is intended to encourage readers to add depth to their knowledge and develop their own interests by explicitly identifying the most important primary and secondary texts.

Every systematic assessment of the modern theoretical landscape – whether it centres on paradigms or reference theorists – is in some sense subjective and thus fundamentally contestable. Our perspective on the 18 International Relations theories, approaches, perspectives and concepts presented in this book, a good knowledge of which we consider essential, must also be seen against this background. We chose these 18 theories because they are expounded and debated with particular frequency and intensity within academic discourse. There is no particular reason for the order in which the contributions appear. Each chapter is a self-contained unit linked with the other contributions through cross-references, enabling readers to get to grips with the theories in systematic fashion. In principle, then, readers may begin with any chapter. We do have one piece of advice that arises from the ordering of the various chapters on theory, particularly in the case of beginning students or readers who are not studying the book as participants in a theoretical seminar and thus as an element of a seminar programme. We recommend that readers tackle International Relations theories in four "groups": (1) realism, neorealism, interdependence and regime theory; (2) neofunctionalism, new liberalism, approaches centred on the "democratic peace", the English School, world society and globalization; (3) theories of imperialism, world-system theory, neo-Gramscian perspectives and International Political Economy; and (4) social constructivism, Critical Theory, postmodern approaches, feminism and critical geopolitics.

The first group of contributions are traditional state-centred approaches; the explanations they provide primarily emphasize the rational pursuit of the national interest. The second group of contributions covers the broad spectrum of society-focused theories of international relations. The third group comprises International Political Economy approaches, which focus on the relationship between state and market in the broadest sense.[23] The final group brings together more recent International Relations theories, which challenge the rationalistic approaches of the 1960s to 1980s with postmodern, (de)constructionist and critical ideas.

The theories of IR make up a fascinating field in which there is much to discover. We hope you will enjoy this book; feel free to contact us with any feedback.

4 Notes

1 When we refer here and in the subsequent chapters to "International Relations" (capital letters), we mean the academic discipline. When we refer to the discipline's subject matter, we use the term "international relations" (without capitals).

2 Of course, theoretical-philosophical reflection on international relations (history of ideas) stretches back much further in history and is associated with names from political theory and philosophy such as Thucydides, Aristotle, Niccolò Machiavelli, Thomas Hobbes and Immanuel Kant. On the history of International Relations from a history-of-ideas perspective, see, for example, Knutsen (1997) or Jackson (2005). For an overview of the institutionalization of International Relations as an academic discipline and as a science, see Wæver (2013). A brief overview is given in Spindler (2013: Chapter 1).

3 For an overview of the great debates and associated conceptual frameworks, we recommend, for example, Wæver (1998) and Katzenstein *et al.* (1998). On the current state of the great debates, see Wæver (2013) and Schmidt (2013).
4 The dispute over "understanding" and "explanation" later underwent a revival within the epistemological debate on "rationalism" and "constructivism" in the 1990s and hence as part of the positivism-post-positivism debate (see Hollis and Smith 2009).
5 On world society, see, for example, the "Stanford School" (Boli and Thomas 1997; Meyer, *et al.* 1997; Meyer 2010; see also the chapter by Ingo Take in this volume) or the English School (see the chapter by Christopher Daase in this volume).
6 In line with the classical definition of politics as "who gets what, when, and how" by Harold Lasswell (1958: 13).
7 Kurki and Wight (2013: 15) explain metatheory as follows:

> Meta-theory does not take a specific event, phenomenon, or series of empirical real world practices as its object of analysis, but explores the underlying assumptions of all theory and attempts to understand the consequences of such assumptions for the act of theorizing and the practice of empirical research. One way to think about this is in terms of theories about theories.

8 Positivism, first formulated by French philosopher Auguste Comte, works on the premise that only the real, factual and thus "positive" (observable) elements of experience lead to knowledge. Traditionally, because it seeks to emulate natural science, this view has also been referred to as "scientism".
9 This relationship is also called the "Humean account of causality" – drawing on the philosophical empiricism of Scottish philosopher David Hume.
10 A prime example of this conception of theory is the new liberalism developed by Andrew Moravcsik (1997, 2003); see also the chapter by Siegfried Schieder in this volume). For an overall survey, see Pittioni (1996).
11 The notion of the linguistic construction of reality was nourished by the so-called "linguistic turn" within the philosophical discourse of modernity. The essential insight here is that language constructs what reality *is*. Language no longer functions merely as a transparent medium of discourse; instead it is a reality within which knowledge itself arises. This insight not only changes traditional epistemology but also the concept of knowledge itself. For an account of the fundamental issues here, see Rorty (1967).
12 Other examples are the politics of interdependence and multilateralism – based on the policy advice of the neoinstitutionalist/neoliberal institutionalist research programme (see the chapter by Manuela Spindler in this volume) or the politics of democratization resting on the inter-democratic peace paradigm. The same is true for realist "Realpolitik" or balance of power politics (above all in international security) with theoretical back-up from neorealist theory (see the chapters by Niklas Schörnig and Andreas Jacobs in this volume).
13 To be fair, normative concerns were long present among representatives of the English School and in the rich tradition of Critical Theory. In fact, they have their roots in the work of philosophers such as Aristotle and Plato, Adam Smith and Immanuel Kant, George W.H. Hegel and Karl Marx. Normative theory preceded the evolution of modern IR but was "temporarily obscured by the birth and ascendance of 'scientific' approaches to the study of international relations" (Erskine 2013: 41); see also Smith and Light (1992; Reus-Smit and Snidal 2008b and the chapters by Christopher Daase and Christoph Humrich in this volume).
14 In line with our view that the disciplinary borders within the social sciences are becoming increasingly blurred (see Section 1), it is important to note that the metatheoretical debate between positivist and scientific realist positions is present in other social sciences as well.
15 In recent debates, the notion of "turns" seems to be the typical categorical frame used to indicate perceived trends and directions that theory building might take in future. The multitude of proclaimed turns indicates a discipline in search of "directions" and lends additional support to our argument that we will likely have to live with increasing theoretical pluralism.
16 We recommend that readers take a closer look at the contributions in the journal *International Political Sociology*.
17 We are aware that different ontological and epistemological positions are closely tied to different methodological positions. It is beyond the scope of this Introduction to provide a detailed account of these methodological implications.

18 The term "Cartesian science" (derived from the scientific world-view of French philosopher and mathematician René Descartes) usually refers to the ideal of empirical natural science (with classical physics at its core) typical of the modern Western world.
19 For an early account of the Western dominance of International Relations in general and the theoretical debate in particular, see, for example, Stanley Hoffmann, who already declared theoretical research in International Relations an "American social science" in the 1970s (Hoffmann [1977] 1987).
20 Regime theory, for example, is based on the prior conceptualization of "interdependence".
21 On the idealism–realism debate, see, for example, Thies (2002). On the critique of the "orthodox" perspective in general, see Schmidt (2002).
22 Wæver's "Figures of International Thought: Introducing Persons instead of Paradigms" (Wæver 1997) provided valuable impetus for our textbook concept. See also Andreatta (2011).
23 This account of International Political Economy perspectives is by no means exhaustive; to provide a systematic and comprehensive survey would require a book in its own right. This is largely due to the special rivalry between International Relations and International Political Economy and their claims to be "independent" academic disciplines. In any case, we believe International Political Economy perspectives should be included in a volume on International Relations theory.

5 Bibliography and recommended reading

5.1 International Relations theories

Booth, Ken and Smith, Steve (eds) 2009: *International Relations Theory Today*. Reprinted. Cambridge: Polity Press.

Brown, Chris and Ainley, Kirsten 2009: *Understanding International Relations*. 4th edn. Basingstoke: Palgrave Macmillan.

Burchill, Scott, Linklater, Andrew, Devetak, Richard, Donnelly, Jack, Nardin, Terry, Paterson, Matthew, Reus-Smit, Christian and True, Jacqui (eds) 2009: *Theories of International Relations*, 4th edn. Basingstoke: Palgrave.

Chernoff, Fred 2007: *Theory and Metatheory in International Relations*. New York: Palgrave.

Daddow, Oliver 2009: *International Relations Theory*. London: Sage Publications.

Dougherty, James E. and Pfaltzgraff, Robert L. (eds) 2008: *Contending Theories of International Relations: A Comprehensive Survey*, 5th edn. New York: Longman.

Dunne, Tim, Kurki, Milja and Smith, Steve (eds) 2013: *International Relations Theories: Discipline and Diversity*. 3rd edn. Oxford: Oxford University Press.

Elman, Colin and Elman, Miriam Fendius (eds) 2003: *Progress in International Relations Theory: Appraising the Field*. Cambridge, MA: MIT Press.

Griffiths, Martin 2007: *International Relations Theory for the 21st Century: An Introduction*. London: Routledge.

Jackson, Patrick T. 2011: *The Conduct of Inquiry in International Relations: Philosophy of Science and its Implications for the Study of World Politics*. London: Routledge.

Jackson, Robert H. 2005: *Classical and Modern Thought on International Relations*. London: Palgrave.

Jackson, Robert and Sørensen Georg 2013: *Introduction to International Relations: Theories and Approaches*. 5th edn. Oxford: Oxford University Press.

Jørgensen, Knud E. 2010: *International Relations Theory*. London: Palgrave.

Knutsen, Torbjörn 1997: *A History of International Relations Theory*, 2nd edn. Manchester: Manchester University Press.

Reus-Smit, Christian and Snidal, Duncan (eds) 2008a: *The Oxford Handbook of International Relations*. Oxford: Oxford University Press.

Schimmelfennig, Frank 2010: *Internationale Politik*. Paderborn: Schöningh.

Smith, Steve, Booth, Ken and Zalewski, Marysia (eds) 2008: *International Theory: Positivism and Beyond*. 10th edn. Cambridge: Cambridge University Press.

Spindler, Manuela 2013: *International Relations: A Self-Study Guide to Theory.* Opladen: Barbara Budrich Publishers.

Steans, Jill, Pettiford, Lloyd and Thomas Diez (eds) 2010: *International Relations: Perspectives and Themes.* 3nd edn. Harlow: Pearson Education.

Sterling-Folker, Jennifer 2012: *Making Sense of International Relations Theory.* 2nd edn. Boulder, CO: Lynne Reinner.

Viotti, Paul R. and Kauppi, Mark V. 2009: *International Relations Theory: Realism, Pluralism, Globalism and Beyond*, 4th edn. Englewood Cliffs, NJ: Prentice Hall.

Wæver, Ole 1997: Figures of International Thought: Introducing Persons instead of Paradigms, in Neumann, Iver and Wæver, Ole (eds) *The Future of International Relations: Masters in the Making.* London: Routledge.

5.2 The subject of International Relations

Baylis, John and Smith, Steve (eds) 2011: *The Globalization of World Politics: An Introduction to International Relations.* 5th edn. Oxford: Oxford University Press.

Carlsnaes, Walter, Risse, Thomas and Simmons, Beth A. (eds) 2012: *Handbook of International Relations.* 2nd edn. London: Sage Publications.

Czempiel, Ernst-Otto 1981: *Internationale Politik. Ein Konfliktmodell.* Paderborn: Schöningh.

Frieden, Jeffrey A., Lake, David A. and Schultz, Kenneth A. 2013: *World Politics: Interests, Interactions, Institutions.* 2nd edn. New York: Norton.

Goldstein, Joshua S. and Pevehouse, Jon C. 2013: *International Relations.* 10th edn. London: Pearson.

Griffiths, Martin and O'Callaghan, Terry 2008: *International Relations: The Key Concepts.* 2nd edn. London: Routledge.

Reus-Smit, Christian and Snidal, Duncan (eds) 2008a: *The Oxford Handbook of International Relations.* Oxford: Oxford University Press.

Roskin, Michael G. and Berry, Nicolas O. 2012: *IR: The New World of International Relations.* 9th edn. London: Longman.

Spindler, Manuela 2013: *International Relations: A Self-Study Guide to Theory.* Opladen: Barbara Budrich Publishers.

Wæver, Ole 2010: Still a Discipline After All These Debates?, in Dunne, Tim, Kurki, Milja and Smith, Steve (eds) *International Relations Theories: Discipline and Diversity.* 2nd edn. Oxford: Oxford University Press, pp. 297–318.

5.3 Academic journals with a special focus on International Relations Theory

Alternatives
American Political Science Review
British Journal of International Relations
Cooperation and Conflict
European Journal of International Relations
International Organization
International Security
International Studies Quarterly
International Studies Review
International Theory
Journal of Conflict Resolution
Journal of International Political Sociology
Journal of International Relations and Development

Journal of Peace Research
Millennium
Review of International Political Economy
Review of International Studies
World Politics
Zeitschrift für Internationale Beziehungen

5.4 Other texts

Acharya, Amitav and Buzan, Barry 2010: *Non-Western International Relations Theory: Perspectives on and Beyond Asia*. London: Routledge.

Adler, Emanuel 1997: Seizing the Middle Ground: Constructivism in World Politics, *European Journal of International Relations* 3(3): 319–364.

Albert, Mathias and Buzan, Barry 2013: International Relations Theory and the "Social Whole": Encounters and Gaps Between IR and Sociology, *International Political Sociology* 7(2): 117–135.

Albert, Mathias, Buzan, Barry and Zürn, Michael (eds) 2013: Bringing Sociology to IR. World, in *Politics as Differentiation Theory*. Cambridge: Cambridge University Press.

Albert, Mathias, Cederman, Lars-Erik and Wendt, Alexander 2010: *New Systems Theories of World Politics*. London: Palgrave.

Andreatta, Filippo 2011: *Le grandi opere delle relazioni internazionali*. Bologna: Il Mulino.

Barkin, Samuel J. 2010: *Realist Constructivism: Rethinking International Relations Theory*. Cambridge: Cambridge University Press.

Bauer, Harry and Brighi, Elisabetta (eds) 2009: *Pragmatism in International Relations*. London: Routledge.

Beitz, Charles 1979: *Political Theory and International Relations*. Princeton, NJ: Princeton University Press.

Berenskoetter, Felix 2007: Friends, There Are No Friends: An Intimate Reframing of the International, *Millennium: Journal of International Studies* 35(3): 647–676.

Bhaskar, Roy 1979: *The Possibility of Naturalism: A Philosophical Critique of the Contemporary Human Sciences*. Brighton: The Harvester Press.

Bleiker, Roland and Hutchison, Emma 2008: Fear No More: Emotions and World Politics, *Review of International Studies* 34: 115–135.

Boli, John and Thomas, George M. 1997: World Culture in the World Polity: A Century of International Non-Governmental Organization, *American Sociological Review* 62(2): 171–190.

Boltanski, Luc 1999: *Distant Suffering: Morality, Media and Politics*. Cambridge: Cambridge University Press.

Brown, Chris 1992: *International Relations Theory: New Normative Approaches*. New York: Columbia University Press.

Büger, Christian and Gadinger, Frank 2007: Reassembling and Dissecting: International Relations Practice from a Science Studies Perspective, *International Studies Perspectives* 8(1): 90–110.

Caney, Simon 2005: *Justice Beyond Borders: A Global Political Theory*. Oxford: Oxford University Press.

Carr, Edward H. 1964 [1939]: *The Twenty Years Crisis, 1919–1939: An Introduction to the Study of International Relations*. New York: Harper and Row Publishers.

Chan, Gerald 1999: Chinese Perspectives on International Relations, in *A Framework for Analysis*. London: Palgrave Macmillan.

Checkel, Jeffrey T. 1998: The Constructivist Turn in International Relations Theory, *World Politics* 50(2): 324–348.

Clark, Ian 1998: Beyond the Great Divide: Globalization and the Theory of International Relations, *Review of International Studies* 24(4): 479–498.

Claude, Inis L., 1956: Swords into Plowshares: *The Problems and Progress of International Organization*. New York: Random House.

Coicaud, Jean-Marc and Wheeler, Nicholas J. 2008: *National Interest and International Solidarity: Particular and Universal Ethics in International Life*. New York: United Nations University Press.

Crawford, Neta C. 2000: The Passion of World Politics: Propositions on Emotion and Emotional Relationships, *International Security* 24(4): 116–156.

Curtis, Simon and Koivisto, Marjo 2010: Towards a Second "Second Debate"? Rethinking the Relationship between Science and History in International Theory, *International Relations* 24(4): 433–455.

Dryzek, John S. and Leonhard, Stephen T. 1988: History and Discipline in Political Science, *American Political Science Review* 82(4): 1245–1260.

Easton, David 1965: *A Framework for Political Analysis*. Englewood Cliffs, NJ: Prentice Hall.

Erskine, Toni 2013: Normative IR Theory, in Dunne, Tim, Kurki, Milja and Smith, Steve (eds) *International Relations Theories: Discipline and Diversity*. 2nd edn. Oxford: Oxford University Press, pp. 36–57.

Fattah, Khaled and Fierke, Karin M. 2009: A Clash of Emotions: The Politics of Humiliation and Political Violence in the Middle East, *European Journal of International Relations* 15(1): 67–93.

Fierke, Karin M. 2012: *Political Self-Sacrifice: Agency, Body and Emotion in International Relations*. Cambridge: Cambridge University Press.

Finnemore, Martha and Sikkink, Kathryn 1998: International Norm Dynamics and Political Change, *International Organization* 52(4): 887–917.

Friedrichs, Jörg and Kratochwil, Friedrich 2009: On Acting and Knowing: How Pragmatism Can Advance International Relations Research and Methodology, *International Organization* 63(3): 701–731.

Giddens, Anthony 1982: Hermeneutics and Social Theory, in Giddens, Anthony, *Profiles and Critiques in Social Theory*. Berkeley, CA: University of California Press, pp. 1–17.

Goldstein, Judith, Kahler, Miles, Keohane, Robert O. and Slaughter, Anne-Marie 2000: Introduction: Legalization and World Politics, *International Organization* 54(3): 385–399.

Guzzini, Stefano 2000: A Reconstruction of Constructivism in International Relations, *European Journal of International Relations* 6(2): 147–182.

Guzzini, Stefano 2001: The Significance and Roles of Teaching Theory in International Relations, *Journal of International Relations and Development* 4(2): 98–117.

Guzzini, Stefano and Leander, Anna 2001: A Social Theory for International Relations: An Appraisal of Alexander Wendt's Disciplinary and Theoretical Synthesis, *Journal of International Relations and Development* 4(4): 316–338.

Hall, Peter (ed.) 1989: *The Political Power of Economic Ideas: Keynesianism across Nations*. Princeton, NJ: Princeton University Press.

Hellmann, Gunther 2009: The Forum: Pragmatism and International Relations, *International Studies Review* 11(3): 638–662.

Hoffmann, Stanley [1977] 1987: An American Social Science: International Relations, in Hoffmann, Stanley (ed.) *Janus and Minerva: Essays in the Theory and Practice of International Politics*. Boulder, CO: Westview Press, pp. 3–24.

Hollis, Martin and Smith, Steve 2009: *Explaining and Understanding International Relations*. 2nd edn. Oxford: Clarendon Press.

Jackson, Peter 2008: Pierre Bourdieu, the "Cultural Turn" and the Practice of International History, *Review of International Studies* 34(1): 155–181.

Kaplan, Morton A. 1966: The New Great Debate. Traditionalism versus Science in International Relations, *World Politics* 19(1): 1–20.

Katzenstein, Peter J., Keohane, Robert O. and Krasner, Stephen 1998: International Organization and the Study of World Politics, *International Organization* 52(4): 645–685.

Keeley, James F. 2007: To the Pacific? Alexander Wendt as Explorer, *Millennium: Journal of International Studies* 35(2): 417–430.

Kessler, Oliver 2007: From Agents and Structures to Minds and Bodies, *Journal of International Relations and Development* 10(3): 243–272.

Kessler, Oliver 2009: Toward a Sociology of the International? International Relations between Anarchy and World Society, *Journal of International Political Sociology* 3(1): 87–108.

Knorr, Klaus E. and Rosenau, James N. (eds) 1969: *Contending Approaches to International Politics*. Princeton, NJ: Princeton University Press.

Koskenniemi, Martti 2002: "The Lady Doth Protest Too Much": Kosovo and the Turn to Ethics in International Law, *Modern Law Review* 65(2): 159–175.

Kratochwil, Friedrich 2007: Of False Promises and Good Bets: A Plea for a Pragmatic Approach to Theory Building, *Journal of International Relations and Development* 10(1): 1–15.

Kurki, Milja and Wight, Colin 2013: International Relations and Social Science, in Dunne, Tim, Kurki, Milja and Smith, Steve (eds) *International Relations Theories: Discipline and Diversity*. 3rd edn. Oxford: Oxford University Press, pp. 14–35.

Lapid, Yosef 1989: The Third Debate: On the Prospects of International Theory in a Post-Positivist Era, *International Studies Quarterly* 33(3): 235–254.

Lasswell, Harold D. 1958: *Politics: Who Gets What, When, and How*. New York: Meridian Books.

Lebow, Richard N. 2005: Reason, Emotion, and Cooperation, *International Politics* 42(3): 283–313.

Lebow, Richard N. 2008: *A Cultural Theory of International Relations*. Cambridge. Cambridge University Press.

Lentsch Justus and Weingart, Peter (eds) 2011: *The Politics of Scientific Advice*. Cambridge: Cambridge University Press.

Ling, L.H.M. 2013: *The Dao of World Politics: Towards a Post-Westphalian World in International Relations*. London: Routledge.

Linklater, Andrew 2011: *The Problem of Harm in World Politics: Theoretical Investigations*. Cambridge: Cambridge University Press.

Maghoori, Ray and Ramberg, Benett (eds) 1982: *Globalism Versus Realism: International Relations' Third Debate*. Boulder, CO: Westview Press.

Mercer, Jonathan 2010: Emotional Beliefs, *International Organization* 64(1): 1–31.

Meyer, John W. 2010: World Society, Institutional Theories, and the Actor, *Annual Review of Sociology* 36(1): 1–20.

Meyer, John W., Boli, John, Thomas, George M. and Ramirez, Francisco O. 1997: World Society and the Nation-State, *American Journal of Sociology* 103(1): 144–181.

Moïsi, Dominique 2009: *The Geopolitics of Emotion: How Cultures of Fear, Humiliation, and Hope Are Reshaping the World*. New York: Random House.

Moravcsik, Andrew 1997: Taking Preferences Seriously: A Liberal Theory of International Politics, *International Organization* 51(4): 513–553.

Moravscik, Andrew 2003: Theory Synthesis in International Relations: Real Not Metaphysical, *International Studies Review* 5(1): 131–136.

Onuf, Nicholas G. 1989: *World of Our Making: Rules and Rule in Social Theory and International Relations*. Columbia, SC: University of South Carolina Press.

Outhwaite, William 1992: *New Philosophies of Social Science*. London: Macmillan.

Pittioni, Veit 1996: Theorie, in Prechtl, Peter and Burkard, Franz-Peter (eds) *Metzler Philosophie Lexikon: Begriffe und Definitionen*. Stuttgart: Körner.

Price, R. (ed.) 2008: *Moral Limit and Possibility in World Politics*. Cambridge: Cambridge

Rawls, John 1971: *A Theory of Justice*. Oxford: Oxford University Press.

Rawls, John 1999: *The Law of Peoples*. Cambridge, MA: Harvard University Press.

Reus-Smit, Christian 1999: *The Moral Purpose of the State: Culture, Social Identity, and Institutional Rationality in International Relations*. Princeton, NJ: Princeton University Press.

Reus-Smit, Christian and Snidal, Duncan 2008b: Between Utopia and Reality: The Practical Discourse of International Relations, in Reus-Smit, Christian and Snidal, Duncan (eds) *The Oxford Handbook of International Relations*, Oxford: Oxford University Press, pp. 3–37.

Risse, Thomas 2002: Constructivism and International Institutions: Toward Conversations Across Paradigms, in Katznelson, Ira and Milner, Helen V. (eds) *Political Science: The State of the Discipline*. New York: Columbia University Press, pp. 597–623.

Risse, Thomas, Ropp, Stephen C. and Sikkink, Kathryn, 1999: *The Power of Human Rights: International Norms and Domestic Change*. Cambridge: Cambridge University Press.

Rorty, Richard (ed.) 1967: *The Linguistic Turn; Recent Essays in Philosophical Method*. Chicago: Chicago University Press.

Schieder, Siegfried 2009: *Pragmatism and International Law*, in Bauer, Harry and Brighi, Elisabetta (eds) *Pragmatism in International Relations: The New International Relations*. London: Routledge, pp. 124–142.

Schieder, Siegfried, Folz, Rachel and Musekamp, Simon 2011: The Social Construction of European Solidarity: Germany and France in the EU Policy Towards the States of Africa, the Caribbean, and the Pacific (ACP) and Central and Eastern Europe (CEE), *Journal of International Relations and Development* 14(4): 469–505.

Schmidt, Brian C. (ed.) 2012: *International Relations and the First Great Debate*. London: Routledge.

Schmidt, Brian C. 2013: On the History and Historiography of International Relations, in Carlsnaes, Walter, Risse, Thomas and Simmons, Beth A. (eds) *Handbook of International Relations*. 2nd edn. Los Angeles: Sage Publications, pp. 3–28.

Smith, Karen E. and Light, Margot (eds) 1992: *Ethics and Foreign Policy*. Cambridge: Cambridge University Press.

Smith, Steve 1995: The Self-Images of a Discipline: A Genealogy of International Relations Theory, in Booth, Ken and Smith, Steve (eds) *International Relations Theory Today*. Oxford: Polity Press, pp. 1–37.

Snidal, Duncan and Wendt, Alexander 2009: Why There Is International Theory Now, *International Theory* 1(1): 1–14.

Stichweh, Rudolf 2006: Gelehrter Rat und wissenschaftliche Politikberatung: Zur Differenzierungsgeschichte einer Intersystembeziehung, in Heidelberger Akademie der Wissenschaften (ed.) *Politikberatung in Deutschland*. Wiesbaden: VS Verlag für Sozialwissenschaften, pp. 101–112.

Thies, Cameron G. 2002: Progress, History and Identity in International Relations Theory: The Case of the Idealist-Realist Debate, *European Journal of International Relations* 8(2): 147–186.

Tickner, Arlene B. and Blaney, David L. (eds) 2012: *Thinking International Relations Differently*. London: Routledge.

Tickner, Arlene B. and Wæver, Ole (eds) 2009: *International Relations Scholarship around the World*. London: Routledge.

Wæver, Ole 1996: The Rise and Fall of the Inter-Paradigm-Debate, in Smith, Steve, Booth, Ken and Zalewski, Marysia (eds) *International Theory: Positivism and Beyond*. Cambridge: Cambridge University Press, pp. 149–185.

Wæver, Ole 1998: The Sociology of a Not So International Discipline: American and European Developments in International Relations, *International Organization* 52(4): 687–727.

Wæver, Ole 2013: Still a Discipline After All these Debates, in Dunne, Tim, Kurki, Milja and Smith, Steve (eds) *International Relations Theories: Discipline and Diversity*. 3rd edn. Oxford: Oxford University Press, pp. 306–328.

Waltz, Kenneth N. 1979: *Theory of International Politics*. Reading, MA: Addison-Wesley.

Walzer, Michael 1977: *Just and Unjust Wars*. New York: Basic Books.

Wendt, Alexander 1999: *Social Theory of International Politics*. Cambridge: Cambridge University Press.

Wendt, Alexander 2006: Social Theory as Cartesian Science: An Auto-Critique from a Quantum Perspective, in Guzzini, Stefano and Leander, Anna (eds) *Constructivism and International Relations: Alexander Wendt and His Critics*, London: Routledge, pp. 181–219.

Wendt, Alexander 2010: Flatland: Quantum Mind and the International Hologram, in Albert, Mathias, Cederman, Lars-Erik and Wendt, Alexander (eds) *New Systems Theories of World Politics*. Basingstoke: Palgrave Macmillan, pp. 279–310.

Wendt, Alexander 2014: *Limits of International Relations*. London: Routledge (forthcoming).

Wight, Colin 2006: Agents, Structures and International Relations, in *Politics as Ontology*. Cambridge: Cambridge University Press.

Wight, Colin 2013: Philosophy of Social Science and International Relations, in Carlsnaes, Walter, Risse, Thomas and Simmons, Beth A. (eds) *Handbook of International Relations*. 2nd edn. Los Angeles: Sage Publications, pp. 29–56.

Wight, Martin 1966: Why Is There No International Theory?, in Butterfield; Herbert and Wight, Martin (eds) *Diplomatic Investigations*. London: Allen & Unwin, pp. 17–34.

Wolf, Reinhard 2011: Respect and Disrespect in International Politics: The Significance of Status Recognition, *International Theory* 3(1): 105–142.

Wolf, Reinhard 2012: Der "emotional turn" in den IB: Plädoyer für eine theoretische Überwindung methodischer Engführung, *Zeitschrift für Außen- und Sicherheitspolitk* 5: 605–624.

Realism

Andreas Jacobs

1 Introduction

If you had asked, as late as the 1970s, what was the most frequently quoted theoretical text on international politics, the answer would inevitably have been Hans J. Morgenthau's *Politics Among Nations*, first published in 1948. By now Morgenthau's classic has been eclipsed by other theoretical contributions. Yet *Politics Among Nations* has lost none of its importance as one of the central planks of *realism*, which has long been regarded as one of the foundation stones of International Relations theory. Most subsequent attempts at theory building either expanded on Morgenthau's realism or – rather more often – were formulated in contradistinction to it. Serious criticisms were made of early realist theory building in general and Morgenthau's realism in particular. So it is not surprising that, since the late 1970s at the latest, realism seems to have been relegated to the status of respected and carefully preserved exhibit in the "museum of IR theory". But this impression is misleading. The increasing *postrealist* interest in Morgenthau and the other realists is clear evidence that the legacy of Morgenthau's realism for IR amounts to more than certain basic questions and intellectual stimuli, along with the demand that we see the world as it really is.

Morgenthau saw his theoretical reflections in *Politics Among Nations* only as laying the ground for a theory, while the exponents of realism did not subsequently develop any unified, internally coherent theory of international politics. There is therefore some confusion about what the term *realism* actually means within International Relations theory. This has much to do with the fact that the ideas about the nature and understanding of international relations formulated by Morgenthau and the other realists were part of a long tradition of philosophical writings and historical treatises on the coexistence of nations and polities, and these ideas have often undergone subsequent modification and development. So when discussing Morgenthau's ideas and those theorists close to him both temporally and in their worldview, the literature generally refers to the *realist school* or *classical realism* in order to distinguish these ideas from more recent theoretical developments. In what follows, *realism* is used as a collective term for the theoretical approaches developed under this rubric between the 1930s and 1950s to explain international relations. I refer to ideas that go beyond this as *realist thought*.

While the emergence of realism in the 1930s and 1940s was due to specific circumstances and crises, realist thought stands within a long intellectual tradition whose leading historical exponents are generally identified as Thucydides and Niccolò Machiavelli, along with Thomas Hobbes, Friedrich Nietzsche and Max Weber. In the first major historical work in Western history, *The History of the Peloponnesian War*, Thucydides (460–400 BCE) identified the increase in the power of Athens (Book 1.23) as the key reason for the military conflicts between the Greek city-states. Here, for the first time, power was viewed as the key constitutive and regulative factor in politics. Thucydides understood politics, meanwhile, as the eternal conflict between ideal principles and the application of power and force to further one's own interests (Book 5).

Power also played a significant role in Machiavelli's (1469–1527) political thought. But beyond the emphasis on the dimension of power, a number of other ideas set out in his magnum opus, *The Prince*, place him within the intellectual tradition of realist thought (Machiavelli [1532] 2005). The primary example here is his conception of history as a series of causal connections that can be understood and analysed (*The Prince*: Dedication). In addition, Machiavelli works on the assumption that practice gives rise to theory, but not the other way around (ibid.: 6). Inherent in this idea is the later realist method, when reflecting on politics, of eschewing the assumption that actors are pursuing a pre-given order and instead focusing on the actual circumstances of political action. Ultimately, Machiavelli views ethics as a function of politics rather than politics as a function of ethics (ibid.: 15). Morality and ethical sentiments do play an important role in his thinking, but for him they can do so only if based on effective authority (ibid.: 17). Machiavelli's advice to his prince to get to grips with the way things actually are rather than dwelling on ideal scenarios emerges as the guiding analytical principle of the later realism.

So key assumptions inherent in realist thought were already in place. But the emergence of the theory of realism can be understood only within its specific political and historical context. Realism has often been described as a counter-movement to a political world-view that conceived of history as a process of redemptive advance. This latter idea, whose popularity peaked after the First World War, was linked to the increasing spread of American intellectual thought. On an *idealist* foundation, in other words, one indebted to liberalism and pacifism, this world-view worked on the premise that the shortcomings of the international system could be remedied through systematic evaluation of their causes. Confident that human reason would eventually hold sway, exponents of such views believed that institutions such as the League of Nations would ensure that in future the international community would act collectively to sanction any case of state aggression.

In view of events from the 1930s on, and above all after the Second World War, this faith in progress began to crumble. The failure of the League of Nations and the global economic crisis had already made it clear that securing world peace could not be viewed merely as an organizational problem. Existing global problems could not be solved, critics now began to suggest, solely through the development and entrenchment of international organizations. But the rejection of utopian or idealist notions of international politics – now emerging under the banner of realism – went further still. Beyond the claim that idealists had fallen prey to illusions about the social reality of international relations and failed to understand the true nature of political action, realists accused them of downplaying the realities of politics and ignoring its violent aspects. The quintessence of this critique, then, was that idealist approaches to explaining international politics are not just false but also counter-productive (Frei 1993: 198–200).

Because of the United States' secure geographical position, its rise to the status of world power and its self-generated prosperity, key thinkers there had long been in thrall to illusions about the realities and possibilities of international politics. As a result of the experience of the Second World War and incipient Cold War, however, the question of how to limit and contain power became increasingly central to thinking about politics. Realism was thus partly a response to a type of political thought that declares the pursuit of power the ultimate aim of all politics.

But there was another reason for the new prominence of the variable of *power* in explanations of international relations. The post-war era was characterized by the military and economic supremacy of the United States, which increasingly assumed the responsibilities of a world power. At the same time, it became ever clearer that Roosevelt's plans for worldwide cooperation and the democratization of former wartime enemies were being superseded by the policies of confrontation and containment pursued by Truman and Eisenhower towards the Soviet Union. It was against this political background that the – almost exclusively Anglo-Saxon – realists developed their ideas on the pre-eminent role of power in international relations.

In the USA too, thinkers concerned with international relations now began to focus on identifying the key forces within world politics and on the potential for peaceful coexistence under actually existing conditions. So while realism developed in light of the specifically American experience, it stood within an intellectual tradition inspired by the German conception of science and a continental European view of humanity (Meyers 1977: 57). It is no coincidence that many exponents of realist thought are of German origin (John H. Herz, Henry Kissinger, Hans J. Morgenthau, Reinhold Niebuhr, Georg Schwarzenberger, Arnold Wolfers, Kenneth N. Waltz) and therefore familiar with a political milieu in which people thought and acted in terms of power and self-interest.

With the exception of Morgenthau's pre-eminent role, there is no consensus as to who the key exponents of realism are. Generally, the authors mentioned in this connection are those who either examined power as the central motive for action within international politics or who worked on the assumption that power politics is crucially important to international conditions or a country's foreign policies. Alongside Morgenthau (1904–1980), the leading exponent of realism is usually considered to be French political scientist and sociologist Raymond Aron (1904–1983); other important figures are Edward Hallet Carr (1892–1982), Walter Lippmann (1889–1974), Reinhold Niebuhr (1892–1971), Georg Schwarzenberger (1908–1991), Nicholas John Spykman (1893–1968), and Arnold Wolfers (1892–1986); representatives of the younger generation include Stanley H. Hoffmann (b. 1928), American national security adviser and later Secretary of State Henry Kissinger (b. 1923) and Kenneth W. Thompson (1921–2013). A number of politicians are also avowed realists. Alongside Kissinger, the leading figures here are American diplomat George F. Kennan (1904–2005) and security advisor and chief negotiator Paul H. Nitze (1907–2004).

In view of the realist propensity for empirically-based research and political practice, we may distinguish between two basic types of realist writings on international politics. The first comprises theoretical reflections on the functional conditions and principles of international politics or foreign policy (Niebuhr 1932; Schumann [1933] 1958; Spykman 1944; Carr 1951; Schwarzenberger 1955; Morgenthau 1960; Aron 1963; Hoffmann 1969; Thompson 1969), while the second type encompasses empirical studies on the foreign policies of specific states or on the development of particular webs of relations among states (Morgenthau 1951; Kennan 1954; Kissinger 1957; Wolfers 1959; Thompson 1960).

Of the authors mentioned here, two above all had a lasting influence on the theory of realism developed by Morgenthau. This applies first and foremost to Protestant theologian Reinhold Niebuhr. It is from the work of Niebuhr that Morgenthau's realism gets its basic anthropological and sociological assumptions.[1] The second key author is British historian E. H. Carr, who is regarded as the founder of the English School in International Relations theory (see chapter by Christopher Daase in this volume). Shortly before the outbreak of the Second World War, Carr produced a book with the rather misleading title *The Twenty Years' Crisis, 1919–1939*, thus sparking off the renaissance of realism as a field of research. Carr's book was the first to underline the need for a theory that eschews ideals and utopias and recognizes the dimension of power as the central determinant of international politics. At the same time, however, he calls for the recognition of moral values as an essential precondition for limiting the violent consequences of the pursuit of power (Carr 1951: 146–169).

2 The theory of realism according to Hans J. Morgenthau

Hans Joachim Morgenthau was born into a Jewish family in Coburg, northern Bavaria, in 1904. He studied jurisprudence and state science (*Staatswissenschaften*) at a number of German universities before gaining a doctorate at the Institute for International Studies in Geneva; he taught there until 1935, giving him a close-up view of the failure of the League of Nations. After teaching at the University of Madrid for two years, he emigrated to the USA in 1937, becoming a citizen in 1943. He was appointed to a chair in political science at the University of Chicago the same year, where he composed most of his writings on international politics (Morgenthau 1946, 1958, 1960 and 1962; see also Thompson and Myers 1984).[2] In the 1950s and 1960s, his work mainly analysed American foreign policy or the development of international relations generally, anchored in the theoretical framework he had developed (Morgenthau 1951, 1969, 1971). This sometimes prompted sharp criticism of various US administrations, particularly in cases where he believed he could discern idealistic or moralizing elements in US foreign policy that failed to match his concept of a rational foreign policy, in other words, one anchored in power politics and self-interest. But political scientists' interest in Morgenthau centres above all on the theoretical ideas set out in *Politics Among Nations*, which was first published in 1948 and had reached its seventh edition by 2005.

2.1 Realism as a critique of ideological thought

Politics Among Nations was Morgenthau's comprehensive attempt to develop a rational theory of international politics in light of the critique of idealism. We can thus grasp Morgenthau's basic understanding of international politics only by examining his critique of what he called *ideological thought*. As Morgenthau saw it, the main obstacle to understanding the principles of international politics was the ideology that the role of power in politics could be overcome. While Morgenthau concedes that states may have a range of different motives for their actions, power is always the means of achieving national goals. So Morgenthau saw the constitutive function of ideology as lying in the justification of political interests and thus of political action. Typical here, thought Morgenthau, is the tendency to declare one's self-interest desirable for others or even the overriding goal of political action. But there can be no superordinate collective will of this kind because beyond a slender substructure of common ground, based on elementary features of human existence, people live under quite different conditions and cannot develop the same interests (Morgenthau 1960: 263).

The most important challenge for the study of international politics therefore is "to see through these ideological disguises and grasp behind them the actual political forces and phenomena" (ibid.: 96). The way in which politicians present their own belief systems to the world should not, therefore, be taken too seriously. For Morgenthau, rather than declarations of political intention, what counts is political action. In line with this, he identified the confrontation between blocs within the international system towards the end of the 1940s as a continuation of conventional power politics. The Cold War was not a matter of ideologies, but merely of power (Morgenthau 1951: 78–81). But this does not mean that ideologies cannot be vehicles of truths and thus guides to political action. In this case, however, he speaks not of ideology, but of "political philosophy" (Morgenthau 1960: 263).

2.2 The anthropology of realism

Morgenthau sees International Relations theory as a social science. Morgenthau's political science thus focuses on the contradictions of human existence, the gap between norm and reality, between wants and our ability to achieve them and between creativity and powerlessness (Kindermann 1963: 22). He had already devoted himself to these questions in his 1946 book, *Scientific Man vs. Power Politics*, in which he came to the conclusion that the simultaneous creative and destructive potential of human action rests ultimately on human freedom (Morgenthau 1946: 187–201). The strong influence of Reinhold Niebuhr is apparent here. In his most important book, *Moral Man and Immoral Society*, published in 1932, Niebuhr argued that human altruism is transformed into egotism and aggression the moment human beings organize collectively, when they come together in states, for example (Niebuhr 1932: 83). The greater the degree of altruism and self-sacrifice in the individual's efforts to improve the good of the collectivity, the more aggressive and conflict-laden this collective egotism becomes. For Niebuhr, this makes violence within international relations inevitable. Since persons integrated into a collectivity are subject to fewer moral scruples than discrete individuals, the pursuit of power on the national and international level takes on intensified and more brutal forms. This struggle for power can be reined in only if political action is geared towards ethics and morality (ibid.: 231).

Though Morgenthau is closely aligned with Niebuhr in many respects, he takes a different view of the causes of violence. While Niebuhr tends to view the destructive elements of human life as the result of sociation, Morgenthau believes they are biologically rooted, that is, inherent in human nature. Here Morgenthau follows Hobbes (1588–1679) who defined the drive for power as an essential feature of the human being in his 1651 magnum opus, *Leviathan* (Hobbes [1651] 2008). In much the same way as idealism, which makes inferences about the conduct of collectivities in light of individuals' value-oriented action, Morgenthau applies these anthropological premises to the behaviour of states (Morgenthau 1946: 198). Morgenthau's view of international politics thus rests not on the concept of any kind of international community but on the idea of a system of states in which there is no central decision-making or sanctioning authority, a system which, in analogy to Hobbes' conception, is in a state of nature. The main actor in international politics, then, is the power-seeking sovereign nation state, which attempts to realize its interests against those of other states.

2.3 International politics in realist perspectives

With this view of humankind as its point of departure, Morgenthau's realism is based on three crucial assumptions. First, that politics is in principle amenable to scientific explanation, second, that the categories of power and interests are of central importance to political life, and, third, that morality must play a pre-eminent role in achieving a more peaceful and just world (Morgenthau 1960: 4–15).

The objectivity of politics

Morgenthau's first methodological premise is that all political dynamics rest on fundamental, unchanging elements anchored in human nature, from which we may derive the value-free and universally valid concepts fundamental to political science. In order to develop a political theory that might provide us with a toolkit for analysing political processes, we must filter out the *constants* from the complex whirlwind of political events. Morgenthau puts this as follows:

> Political Realism believes that politics, like society in general, is governed by objective laws that have their roots in human nature. In order to improve society it is first necessary to understand the laws by which society lives . . . For realism, theory consists in ascertaining facts and giving them meaning through reason.
>
> (Morgenthau 1960: 4ff.)

Politics is thus governed by its own laws in the same way as economics, the dispensation of justice or morality. Morgenthau expresses this by making the following oft-cited comparison:

> The economist asks: "How does this policy affect the wealth of society, or a segment of it?" The lawyer asks: "Is this policy in accord with the rule of law?" The moralist asks: "Is this policy in accord with moral principles?" And the political realist asks: "How does this policy affect the power of the nation?"
>
> (ibid.: 11ff.)

Power and interests in international politics

Realists take their lead from the concept of interests, which is understood in light of power. This close linkage of power and interests in Morgenthau's political thinking has often been criticized and misunderstood and thus requires clarification. As Morgenthau sees it, power is not only constitutive of human behaviour, but also renders it understandable and explicable. Because power is the basis of all political action, understanding power is also the key to understanding international politics. So like all politics, international politics is a struggle for power, intended to maintain, increase or demonstrate it (Morgenthau 1960: 27, 38). What is problematic here is that Morgenthau provides no unambiguous definition of power. Power may comprise

> [anything] that establishes and maintains the control of man over man. Thus power covers all social relationships which serve that end, from physical violence to the most subtle psychological ties by which one mind controls another. Power covers the domination of man by man.
>
> (ibid.: 9)

By bringing into play the concept of *domination* at this crucial point, Morgenthau avoids defining exactly what power is. His concept of power therefore remains rather intangible and – as we shall see – open to criticism.

There is, however, a reason for the vagueness of the concept of power in Morgenthau's work. Morgenthau presents the struggle for power as a spatio-temporal universal and views it as an incontrovertible experiential fact requiring no further justification (ibid.: 32). At the same time, because of the self-evident nature of the drive for power, or of the resulting struggle for power, attempts to measure the capacity for power precisely are quite alien to him. For him power is a category that eludes any kind of quantifying evaluation because it becomes manifest as a psychological relationship between power-wielder and power subject, in other words, it is highly dependent on perception (Kindermann 1963: 26). But power's pre-eminent role does not mean that power relations determine all political action. The conception of politics as a matter of power instead serves as a connecting link between political events and our attempts to gain analytical purchase on these events. So the concept of power is primarily a category facilitative of understanding; it "helps orient the observer amid the maze of empirical phenomena and establishes a key criterion of rational order within this labyrinth" (Gebhardt 1991: 92).

In line with this, the state's paramount foreign policy interest lies in accumulating and maintaining power. Specific interests may change and take on differing forms, but in the final analysis they always serve power. So power is at once the means of realizing interests and the object of interests, and it may even become an end in itself (Morgenthau 1946: 101). It will be clear by now that Morgenthau no more clearly delimits or defines the concept of interest than he does that of power. According to Kindermann, however, in other places, Morgenthau distinguished between an objective and subjective concept of foreign policy interest. Subjective interest, Kindermann tells us, refers to the formation of foreign policy on the basis of specific perceptions, and in light of certain conceptions of the meaning and goals of foreign policy. The objective version of the term, meanwhile, refers to the actions a state might take in order best to meet its existential needs (security, power and welfare) (Kindermann 1963: 27).

Despite this attempt to flesh out Morgenthau's concepts of power and interest, we are left with the impression of a circular argument. If there is a way out of this, it is to be found in his methodological ideas. While for Morgenthau power represents the key means of understanding political action, he sees interest as more of an analytical category. This makes the study of foreign policy interests of substantial practical importance. Determining one's foreign policy interests, he believes, is necessary to formulating political standards and coordinating specific domestic interests. Comparison of a given state's interests with those of other states provides us with an overall picture of the web of interests in which a state finds itself. Morgenthau's emphasis on the national interest does not equate with approval of a ruthless and exclusively self-centred foreign policy. In his view, the process of defining the national interest should always take account of the interests of other states. Only in this way can a state get a clear sense of the scope and limits of its foreign policy and thus of the potential for realizing its interests (Morgenthau 1951; 1958: 54–87).[3]

The taming of power through morality

Realism seeks not just to understand and explain but also to provide specific recommendations on political action. This makes it a *normative theory* in the broad sense of the term. Beyond the purely analytical assessment of political realities, normative theories impart political goals that are informed by values.

> There can be no political morality without prudence; that is, without consideration of the political consequences of seemingly moral action. Realism, then, considers prudence – the weighing of the consequences of alternative political actions – to be the supreme virtue in politics. Ethics in the abstract judges action by its conformity with the moral law; political ethics judges action by its political consequences.
>
> (Morgenthau 1960: 10)

The targets of the realist critique of policy and research, then, are not moralists but the complacent exponents of an "ethics of ultimate ends" (*Gesinnungsethik*) who think they can shape the global order in line with their normative conceptions or believe they have the moral right to do so. Against this background, realism aims not just to lay bare the preeminent role of power in politics but also to point up the potential for curbing power.

Morgenthau had already tried to establish how the destructiveness of power politics might be held in check in *Scientific Man vs. Power Politics* (Morgenthau 1946: 9ff.). He even devotes around two-thirds of *Politics Among Nations* to this issue. While he regards it as pointless to act counter to the principles of international politics, he explicitly rejects the idea that we should capitulate to an all-pervasive power politics. He accuses his London colleague and forerunner E. H. Carr of doing just that, but draws methodologically on *The Twenty Years' Crisis* as he attempts to find ways out of the destructiveness of power politics. In much the same way as Carr, in *Politics Among Nations* Morgenthau discusses various ways of curtailing power. As he contemplates international law and its pacific effects, international norms, ideologies, institutions and the principle of collective security, he comes (to simplify somewhat) to a similar conclusion. Ultimately, however positively Morgenthau may view them in some cases, he believes that attempts to limit state sovereignty can never secure world peace over the long term because they are incapable of overcoming nation states' pursuit of power (Morgenthau 1960: 539).

In this connection it is important to point out that Morgenthau does not see the limitation of power through countervailing power, in other words through what is called the *balance of power*, as a functional solution. He regards the idea that we can identify a self-regulating process of this kind on the international level as outmoded and beholden to a mechanistic world-view. According to Morgenthau, history, especially that of the nineteenth and twentieth centuries, has shown that thinking in terms of a balance of power has done little to help achieve stability and order in the international system.

> Failure to fulfil its function for individual states and failure to fulfil it for the state system as a whole by any means other than actual or potential warfare points up the three main weaknesses of the balance of power as the guiding principle of international politics: its uncertainty, its unreality, and its inadequacy.
>
> (ibid.: 205)

Morgenthau derives this critique of the notion of a balance of power not from any defect in the principle itself, but from his concept of power. We cannot accurately measure or compare power, so any attempt to establish a stable international balance of power is doomed to failure (ibid.: 167, 205). It is crucial to underline Morgenthau's scepticism about the pacific effect of a balance of power because otherwise this notion is one of the fixed elements of realist thought.

For Morgenthau, what really constrains power is not a balance of power, but morality. So he also rejects the idea that politicians and statesmen are guided solely by the drive for power. In fact they have often shied away from fully exploiting every opportunity to augment their power, through genocide, for instance, for reasons of morality (ibid.: 237f). Time and again Morgenthau qualified the principle of power politics and paid attention to the role of morality.

> Man is an animal longing for power, but he is also a creature with a moral purpose, and while man cannot be governed by abstract moral principles alone, he cannot be governed by power alone either.
>
> (Morgenthau 1962: 130)

He therefore calls for a responsible approach to power; in Max Weber's terminology, he counters the idealist ethics of ultimate ends with a realist ethics of responsibility (Menzel 2001: 80).

This ethics of responsibility is embodied in the method of "peace through accommodation", which is achieved through diplomacy (Morgenthau 1960: 539). In a responsible, in other words, morally informed diplomacy, in the concept of *statesmanship*, Morgenthau sees the only effective way of preserving peace and stability in international politics. He undergirds this call for a prudent diplomacy that privileges balance with a set of rules of diplomatic conduct, all of which ultimately boil down to an emphasis on the moral and intellectual capacities of the diplomat (ibid.: 560–568). This emphasis on morality shows that realism cannot be equated with political pessimism. Instead Morgenthau calls for a permanent diplomatic struggle to better realize freedom and justice, while being well aware that this struggle will never end. For him, understanding the true laws of political motion is the only basis on which we might begin to bring reality into line with what "ought" to be or what we think desirable (ibid.: 15f, cf. the up-to-date survey by Donnelly 2008).

The different forms taken by realism and its further development

The fact that *Politics Among Nations* remained captive in many respects to a pre-theoretical, rather unsystematic approach allowed others to refine and develop it in a vast range of different ways, drawing on specific dimensions of realist thought. But while many of these approaches went beyond realism as developed by Morgenthau in one way or another, they showed little aspiration to emulate *Politics Among Nations* in attempting to provide the foundation for a theory of international politics. The exceptions here are the various comprehensive attempts at realist theory building made chiefly since the 1970s under the banner of *neorealism* (see the chapter by Niklas Schörnig in this volume). In what follows I highlight the most important examples of the refinement and further development of realism.

Morgenthau's colleague Robert E. Osgood has tried to make a clearer distinction between the concepts of realism and idealism and to explain the central role of the nation state in international relations (Osgood 1975). The aspect of perception in the evaluation of foreign policy interests underlined by Morgenthau was examined in depth by Harold and Margaret Sprout and in the 1970s by Robert Jervis (Sprout and Sprout 1956; Jervis 1976). In his reflections on the role of power in international relations, Inis J. Claude has grappled with Morgenthau's conception of the balance of power, highlighting a number of inconsistencies and ambiguities (Claude 1962: 25–37). Along with many other elements of Morgenthau's theory, Gottfried-Karl Kindermann has analysed Morgenthau's concept of power in depth and developed it further. Power, Kindermann tells us, must be understood as a relative state of affairs within a social relationship, making the concept of power rather more complex analytically than it seems in Morgenthau's work (Kindermann 1986: 64). It would be easy to go on listing modifications to Morgenthau's realism as practically every element in his theory has been questioned, rejected or developed further. But while realist thought in International Relations has generated a plethora of subdivisions that defies easy summary, we shall now take an in-depth look at one of them.

Düsseldorf-born American political scientist John H. Herz has attempted to produce a synthesis of realist and idealist suppositions. His ideas rest on the observation that anarchy in the international system is mitigated and tempered to some extent by such things as international law, while the struggle for power does not always take the most extreme forms (Herz 1950: 158). But Herz's significance to realism was based less on his elaboration of what he called *realist liberalism* than on his suppositions about the structure of the international system and the consequences of this structure for the security of states. In 1950, he published an essay entitled "Idealist Internationalism and the Security Dilemma", which is still well worth reading. Here, with as yet unsurpassed clarity, he articulated a fact that is now one of the staples of realist thought and which ensured that Herz, contrary to his own views, is usually considered a realist. I am referring to the so-called *security dilemma*. This describes:

> a fundamental social constellation, one where a plurality of otherwise interconnected groups constitute ultimate units of political life . . . Groups or individuals living in such a constellation must be, and usually are, concerned about their security from being attacked, subjected, dominated, or annihilated by other groups and individuals. Striving to attain security from such attack, they are driven to acquire more and more power in order to escape the impact of the power of others. This, in turn renders the others more insecure and compels them to prepare for the worst.
>
> (Herz 1950: 157)

Herz thus starts from the premise that disputes and military conflicts are primarily a result of the anarchic structure of the international system. Unlike Morgenthau, then, Herz identifies the problem of war and peace not as an anthropological but as a social problem. On this view, conflicts result not from the innate human drive for power but from the structure of the international system. So the instability of international relations ultimately rests on the lack of a central authority that might establish order and impose sanctions. This was a view subsequently characteristic of *neorealists*.

Criticisms of Morgenthau by other realists had long focused on specific aspects of his thinking. From the late 1960s, however, they began to address more fundamental issues. Realism was a theory based on empirical observations, and it emerged against a specific historical background. As a result of the period of global political détente that began in the 1960s, processes of decolonization in many parts of the world and the increasing economic power of Western Europe and some East Asian states, attention now turned to developmental trends within the international system that realist approaches no longer seemed able to explain. Increasingly, Morgenthau's *Politics Among Nations* was no longer seen as a jumping-off point for realist theory building or as providing tools for the analysis of international politics, but merely as a classical, founding text within International Relations theory, of mainly historical significance.

Only in the mid-1990s did Morgenthau begin to attract renewed interest. As theoretical models within International Relations have become more differentiated, *postrealist, defensive* and *offensive realists* and *neoclassical realists* have increasingly found inspiration in Morgenthau's ideas (Wohlforth 2008: 136–141; for an overview of the realist research programme, see, for example, Schweller 2003; Lobell *et al.* 2009). But this new interest in the founding father of political realism generally relates only to the basic suppositions and specific elements of *classical* realism, which are deployed to advance a given thinker's (realist) theory building.

> Although Morgenthau is regularly identified as the father of modern realism . . . there have been few systematic attempts to unpack the theory of international politics that is embedded in his central text – *Politics Among Nations*. The more prevalent tendency has been for analysts to ransack his writings looking for quotations that confirm their particular take on his approach to international Politics.
>
> (Little 2006)

3 Criticisms of realism

In view of the heterogeneity of realist thought it is hardly surprising that most of the criticisms of Morgenthau came from the realist camp itself. It therefore makes little sense to distinguish between realist and non-realist criticism. The many-layered critique of Morgenthau may be summarized as follows.

3.1 View of human nature

First, critics assail the cavalier way in which Morgenthau adopts centuries-old anthropological ideas of a biologically anchored drive for power. His generalizations about human nature, they underline, have been called into question by recent findings in sociobiology (Siedschlag 1997: 64). His assumption that individuals' pursuit of power can be applied to the state is also contested. Here, some have suggested, Morgenthau brings ideology in through the back door. On this view his theory is built on a specific, ideological conception of humankind not amenable to scientific justification because it rests on mere assumptions about the nature of human action (Hoffmann 1969: 196ff.). In line with this, almost all recent realist theory building follows Niebuhr and Herz in conceiving of the causes of violence in international politics in sociological or structural terms (Masala 2005).

3.2 The concept of power

But it is Morgenthau's concept of power that has attracted the most sustained criticism. Though Morgenthau is considered *the* theorist of power, his conception of power remains peculiarly amorphous and, for many, of limited analytical value (Hoffmann 1969: 192). While the criticism that Morgenthau's concept of power lacks clear definition seems justified, the claim that he and the other realists produced an apologia for power politics is quite wrong. In fact, Morgenthau vehemently rejected those ideas known collectively as *Realpolitik* that had been developed since the mid-nineteenth century, particularly within German political thought. The conceptual proximity of *realism* and *Realpolitik* and the close attention paid by both to the phenomenon of power should not obscure the fact that Morgenthau always rejected the idea of power as an end in itself. While it may be true that Morgenthau's vague concept of power invited the criticism that he was endorsing the ruthless enforcement of national interests using all available means, his writings do not provide the foundations for a naturalistic and biological ethics of force. In fact, many realists warn explicitly of the dangers of deriving from insights into the pre-eminent role of power a kind of *amoral ethics of power* (Spykman 1944: 7; Morgenthau 1958: 357; Thompson 1960: 29).

3.3 Theoretical conception and methods

Exponents of realism have frequently conceded that rather than a cohesive theoretical edifice, realism merely provides points of departure for the development of a theory (Hoffmann 1969: 185; Morgenthau 1969: 77; Thompson 1969: 62). Of more importance is the criticism made chiefly by Kenneth N. Waltz that Morgenthau, along with most other realists of his time, had developed at most a theory of foreign policy rather than a theory of international politics (Waltz 1990: 26). The roots of this fundamental criticism of realism lie in realists' tendency to look at international politics from the perspective of the individual. For Morgenthau, the state or nation is not an empirical object.

> Therefore, when we speak in empirical terms of the power or of the foreign policy of a certain nation, we can only mean the power or the foreign policy of certain individuals who belong to the same nation.
>
> (Morgenthau 1960: 101)

On this basis, realism merely derives assumptions about how states behave towards the external world, not about the functional conditions of politics *between* states. According to Waltz, however, a theory of international politics cannot proceed solely in light of the interacting units, but must focus primarily on the overall framework arising from these interactions (Waltz 1990: 33).

Critics also bemoaned the neglect of key explanatory variables. Stanley Hoffmann, to mention just one of many, attacks Morgenthau for disregarding the relationship between domestic and foreign policy, and the importance of international norms of conduct. The reduction of international politics to the explanatory variable of power, Hoffmann believes, leads to a simplistic, schematic view of politics (Hoffmann 1969: 192f). Finally, the dearth of epistemological and methodological reflection in Morgenthau's arguments also attracted criticism. *Politics Among Nations*, according above all to Robert O. Keohane, lacks both a systematic approach and a comprehensible argumentational structure. On this view, Morgenthau merely articulated commonly known facts about international politics without identifying the causal relationships that might help us analyze and understand them. For Keohane, rather than a well-founded contribution to theory building, much of the book amounts to a commentary on political and historical realities, albeit one of high calibre (Keohane 1986: 7).

The criticisms of the 1970s and 1980s have given way in recent years to new academic interest in the founding father of the theory of international relations. It would probably be going too far to say that Morgenthau has become something of a cult author, but *postrealists* have undoubtedly shown increasing interest in Morgenthau and the other realists since the late 1990s (Rose 1998; Rohde 2004; Hacke *et al.* 2005; Little 2007; Brooks and Wohlforth 2008; Williams 2004, 2007; Bell 2009; Scheuerman 2009). The new attention being paid to Morgenthau is by no means just a matter of historical interest. Many of Morgenthau's ideas and reflections are regarded by theorists (who see themselves as *realists* in the broadest sense) as pertinent to contemporary theory building. At least two aspects should be mentioned here.

The first is the tense relationship between egotism and idealism, or between self-interest and morality, as emphasized by the early realists. The debate on the legitimacy of so-called *humanitarian intervention* shows that questions of morality and ethics are at least as important to the international politics of the present as they were at the time of Carr, Niebuhr and Morgenthau. The broad neglect of this aspect in recent approaches to theory building seems all the more problematic in light of this. But another fact points to the contemporary relevance of realism as well. For Morgenthau, Carr and Niebuhr, the contemplation of politics was anything but a matter of mere theoretical argument or intellectual games. They derived their insights directly from empirical and personal experience and observation and wanted these insights to have an impact on politics. Morgenthau especially had little time for those among his political scientist colleagues who wished to flee from their political responsibility into pure theory building. The contemporary theoretical debate in political science seems largely to have lost this closeness to its object.

4 Notes

1 See Section 2.2 of this chapter.
2 On Morgenthau's intellectual development, see the in-depth biographies by Frei (1993) and Rohde (2004).
3 This idea places Morgenthau close to the German theory of "*Staatsräsonlehre*" or *raison d'état* (Meinecke 1984). See also Frei (1993: 129,159–162). It also entails points of contact with later theoretical ideas on the formation of states' foreign policy interests and the precepts governing their actions. See, for example, Link (1987).

5 Bibliography and recommended reading

5.1 Primary texts

Carr, Edward Hallett 1951: *The Twenty Years' Crisis 1919–1939: An Introduction to the Study of International Relations*. Reprint of the 2nd edn. of 1946. London: Macmillan.

Herz, John H. 1950: Idealist Internationalism and the Security Dilemma, *World Politics*, 2 (January): 157–180.

Morgenthau, Hans J. 1960: *Politics Among Nations*. 3rd edn. New York: Knopf.

Niebuhr, Reinhold 1932: *Moral Man and Immoral Society: Study in Ethics and Politics*. New York: Charles Scribner's Sons.

5.2 Secondary texts

Frei, Christoph 1993: *Hans J. Morgenthau. Eine intellektuelle Biographie*. Bern: Haupt.

Hacke, Christian, Kindermann, Gottfried-Karl and Schellhorn, Kai M. (eds) 2005: The Heritage, Challenge, and Future of Realism, in *Memoriam Hans J. Morgenthau (1904–1980)*. Göttingen: V&R unipress.

Kindermann, Gottfried-Karl 1963: Hans J. Morgenthau und die theoretischen Grundlagen des politischen Realismus – Einleitung, in Morgenthau, Hans J.: *Macht und Frieden. Grundlegung einer Theorie der internationalen Politik*. Gütersloh: Bertelsmann, pp. 19–47.

Rohde, Christoph 2004: *Hans J. Morgenthau und der weltpolitische Realismus*. Wiesbaden: VS-Verlag.

Scheuerman, William E. 2009: *Morgenthau*. Hoboken, NJ: John Wiley & Sons.

Williams, Michael C. 2007: *Realism Reconsidered: The Legacy of Hans Morgenthau in International Relations*. Oxford: Oxford University Press.

5.3 Other texts

Aron, Raymond 1963: *Frieden und Krieg – Eine Theorie der Staatenwelt*. Frankfurt a.M.: Fischer.

Bell, Duncan (ed.) 2009: *Political Thought and International Relations: Variations on a Realist Theme*. Oxford: Oxford University Press.

Brooks, Stephen G. and Wohlforth, William C. 2008: *World Out of Balance: International Relations Theory and the Challenge of American Primacy*. Princeton, NJ: Princeton University Press.

Claude, Inis L. 1962: *Power and International Relations*. New York: Random House.

Donnelly, Jack 2008: The Ethics of Realism, in Reus-Smit, Christian and Snidal, Duncan (eds) *The Oxford Handbook of International Relations*. Oxford: Oxford University Press, pp. 150–162.

Gebhardt, Jürgen 1991: Macht und Maß: Morgenthau und Kissinger, in Greven, Michael Th. (ed.): *Macht in der Demokratie – Denkanstöße zur Wiederbelebung einer klassischen Frage in der zeitgenössischen Politischen Theorie*. Baden-Baden: Nomos, pp. 87–105.

Herz, John H. 1951: *Political Realism and Political Idealism*. Chicago: University of ChicagoPress.

Hobbes, Thomas [1651] 2008: *Leviathan*. Reprint of the 1996 edn. Oxford: Oxford University Press.

Hoffmann, Stanley H. 1969: International Relations – The Long Road to Theory, in Czempiel, Ernst-Otto (ed.) *Die Lehre von den Internationalen Beziehungen.* Darmstadt: Wissenschaftliche Buchgesellschaft, pp. 187–227.

Jervis, Robert 1976: *Perception and Misperception in International Politics*. Princeton, NJ: Princeton: University Press.

Kennan, George F. 1954: *Realities of American Foreign Policy*. Princeton, NJ: Princeton University Press.

Keohane, Robert O. 1986: Realism, Neorealism and the Study of World Politics, in Keohane, Robert (ed.) *Neorealism and Its Critics*. New York: Columbia University Press, pp. 1–26.

Kindermann, Gottfried-Karl 1986: Internationale Politik in Theorie, Analyse und Praxis, in Kindermann, Gottfried-Karl (ed.) *Grundelemente der Weltpolitik – Eine Einführung*, 3rd expanded edn. Munich: Piper, pp. 59–105.

Kissinger, Henry 1957: *A World Restored: Metternich, Castlereigh and the Problems of Peace.* London: Weidenfeld & Nicolson.

Link, Werner 1987: Die außenpolitische Staatsräson der Bundesrepublik Deutschland. Überlegungen zur innerstaatlichen Struktur und Perzeption des internationalen Bedingungsfeldes, in Funke, Manfred, Jacobson, Hans-Adolf, and Schwarz, Hans-Peter (eds) *Demokratie und Diktatur. Geist und Gestalt politischer Herrschaft in Deutschland und Europa. Festschrift für Karl Dietrich Bracher*. Düsseldorf: Droste, pp. 400–416.

Little, Richard 2006: Hans J. Morgenthau's Conception of the Balance of Power. Paper presented at the annual meeting of the International Studies Association, San Diego, Mar 22, 2006. Available at: http://www.allacademic. com/meta/p100822. index.html (accessed 25 May 2009).

Little, Richard 2007: *The Balance of Power in International Relations: Metaphors, Myths and Models.* Cambridge: Cambridge University Press.

Lobell, Steven E., Ripsman, P., Norrin, M. and Taliaferro, Jeffrey W. (eds) 2009: *Neoclassical Realism, the State, and Foreign Policy*. Cambridge: Cambridge University Press

Machiavelli, Niccolò [1532] 2005: *The Prince*. London: Penguin.

Masala, Carlo 2005: Theory and Practice, in Hacke, Christian, Kindermann, Karl-Gottfried and Schelhorn, Kai (eds) *The Heritage, Challenge, and Future of Realism: In Memoriam Hans Morgenthau (1904–1980)*, Göttingen: V&R Unipress, pp. 87–92.

Meinecke, Friedrich [1924] 1984: *Machiavellism: The Doctrine of Raison d'Etat and its Place in Modern History* [Die Idee der Staatsräson in der neueren Geschichte]. Epping: Bowker.

Menzel, Ulrich 2001: *Zwischen Idealismus und Realismus. Die Lehre von den Internationalen Beziehungen*. Frankfurt a.M.: Suhrkamp.

Meyers, Reinhard 1977: *Die Lehre von den Internationalen Beziehungen. Ein entwicklungsgeschichtlicher Überblick*. Düsseldorf: Droste.

Morgenthau, Hans J. 1946: *Scientific Man vs. Power Politics*. Chicago: University of Chicago Press.

Morgenthau, Hans J. 1951: *In Defense of National Interest: A Critical Examination of American Foreign Policy*. New York: Knopf.

Morgenthau, Hans J. 1958: *Dilemmas of Politics*. Chicago: University of Chicago Press.

Morgenthau, Hans J. 1962: The Commitments of Political Science, in Mmrgenthau, Hans J. (ed.) The *Decline of Democratic Politics*. Chicago: University of Chicago Press.

Morgenthau, Hans J. 1969: *A New Foreign Policy for the United States*. London: Pall Mall Press.

Morgenthau, Hans J. 1971: *Politics in the Twentieth Century*. Revised version of the 1962 edition. Chicago: University of Chicago Press.

Osgood, Robert E. 1975: Idealismus und Realismus in der Außenpolitik, in Haftendorn, Helga (ed.) *Theorie der Internationalen Politik. Gegenstand und Methode der Internationalen Beziehungen*. Hamburg: Hoffmann und Campe, pp. 52–68.

Rose, Gideon 1998: Neoclassical Realism and Theories of Foreign Policy, *World Politics* 51(1): 144–172.

Schumann, Frederik L. [1933] 1958: *International Politics*, 6th edn. New York: McGraw-Hill.

Schwarzenberger, Georg 1955: *Machtpolitik – Eine Studie über die internationale Gesellschaft*. Tübingen: Mohr.

Schweller, Randall L. 2003: The Progressiveness of Neoclassical Realism, in Elman, Colin and Fendius Elman, Miriam (eds) *Progress in International Relations Theory*. Cambridge, MA: MIT Press, pp. 311–347.

Siedschlag, Alexander 1997: *Neorealismus, Neoliberalismus und postinternationale Politik. Beispiel Internationale Sicherheit. Theoretische Bestandsaufnahme und Evaluation*. Opladen: Westdeutscher Verlag.

Sprout, Harold and Sprout, Margaret 1956: *Man-Milieu Relationship Hypothesis in the Context of International Politics*. Princeton, NJ: Princeton University Press.

Spykman, Nicholas J. 1994: *The Geography of Peace*. New York: Harcourt, Brace & Co.

Thompson, Kenneth W. 1960: *Political Realism and the Crisis of World Politics: An American Approach to Foreign Policy*. Princeton, NJ: Princeton University Press.

Thompson, Kenneth W. 1969: Toward a Theory of International Politics, in Czempiel, Ernst-Otto (ed.) *Die Lehre von den Internationalen Beziehungen*. Darmstadt: Wissenschaftliche Buchgesellschaft, pp. 41–62.

Thompson, Kenneth W. and Meyers, Robert G. (eds) 1984: *Truth and Tragedy: A Tribute to Hans Morgenthau*, 2nd edn. New Brunswick, NJ: Transaction Books.

Thucydides [460–400 BCE] 1954: *The History of the Peloponnesian War*. Ed. I. M. Finley, trans. Rex Warner. London: Penguin.

Waltz, Kenneth N. 1990: Realist Thought and Neorealist Theory, *Journal of International Affairs* 44(1): 21–37.

Williams, Michael C. 2004: Why Ideas Matter in IR: Hans Morgenthau, Collective Identity, and the Moral Construction of Power Politics, *International Organization* 58(4): 633–666.

Williams, Michael C. 2005: *The Realist Traditions and the Limits of International Relations*. Cambridge: Cambridge University Press.

Wohlforth, William C. 2008: Realism, in Reus-Smit, Christian and Snidal, Duncan (eds) The *Oxford Handbook of International Relations*. Oxford: Oxford University Press, pp. 131–149.

Wolfers, Arnold (ed.) 1959: *Alliance Policy in the Cold War*. Baltimore, MD: Johns Hopkins University Press.

Neorealism

Niklas Schörnig

1 Introduction

Few theories have shaped that branch of political science known as International Relations (IR) as powerfully as neorealism. However, as even one of its avowed exponents, John Mearsheimer, concedes, this theory paints a "rather grim picture of world politics" (1995: 9). The neorealist view of international relations is marked by the absolute dominance of security interests, states' drive for self-preservation and the refusal to cooperate. As there is no authority outside of states (such as a world government) that lays down rules and norms mandatory for all states and that can if necessary ensure compliance by force, states must live in a condition of permanent insecurity regarding their neighbours' intentions. They must always be prepared for the worst to happen, namely, war. These assumptions clearly place neorealism within the tradition of realist authors such as Hans J. Morgenthau, Edward H. Carr and Henry Kissinger, but it goes beyond them when it comes to theory building (hence *neo*realism). The school was founded by Kenneth Waltz in 1979 in the shape of his book *Theory of International Politics* (henceforth TIP). It is hard to overstate the impact of Waltz's work on the IR community. According to, for example, Ole Wæver, "TIP is undoubtedly the most important book produced in the discipline within the last 60 years, possibly ever (at least referring to the discipline in its modern form)" (2009: 203). In light of his decisive influence, Waltz plays a central role in this chapter.

Contrary to realism, which was strongly influenced by the experience of the inter-war period and the Second World War and which explained wars anthropologically by reference to human nature, Waltz rejects such explanations of international relations:

> While human nature no doubt plays a role in bringing about war, it cannot by itself explain both war and peace, except by the simple statement that man's nature is such that sometimes he fights and sometimes he does not.
>
> (Waltz 1959: 29)

Against the central aim of traditional realists, and Morgenthau in particular, to produce a theory of international politics in the form of a theory of *foreign policy* (see the chapter by Andreas Jacobs in this volume), Waltz aspires to develop a *systemic* theory of international politics. Neorealism thus shifts the analytical focus to the level of the international system. It comes to conclusions about the behaviour of states in light of the structure of the international system; because of this, it is often referred to as *structural realism*. The historical genesis of neorealism is closely bound up with the East–West conflict. When the superpowers finally entered a phase of rapprochement in the 1970s after decades of Cold War, traditional realism increasingly lost its explanatory power. Approaches centred on interdependence or world-systems theory seemed far better suited to an international scene marked by increased cooperation (see chapters by Manuela Spindler and Andreas Nölke in this volume). With the Soviet invasion of Afghanistan, however, the short period of *détente* seemed to have come to an end, while in the view of many, the United States no longer exercised much of a pacific influence on international relations, at least after the revolution in Iran. The economic supremacy of the leading Western power also seemed to be under threat in view of the drastic increase in the price of oil. It was during this period of relative US decline within the world economy that Kenneth Waltz's *Theory of International Politics* was published.

*Neo*realism had two central concerns. First, it sought to explain why the bipolar world of the East–West conflict, a world bristling with arms, had proved astonishingly stable and averse to war, despite successive phases of rapprochement and confrontation. Second, in light of the decline of American hegemony in the 1970s and the economic resurgence of Europe and Japan, as well as the global economic crisis, it tried to explain why the US had begun to lose its pre-eminent status. Waltz was looking for a *general* International Relations theory that could explain *both war and periods of peace* in international politics in a systematic fashion.

In addition to the real historical context of the East–West conflict, the theoretical debate between so-called traditionalists and scientismists on the correct scientific *method* – carried on with such vehemence in the 1960s and 1970s – exercised a particularly profound influence on neorealist theory building. Methodological traditionalists, among them the leading realists, generally proceed inductively, producing statements of a general character on the basis of specific empirical observations. Scientismists, meanwhile, gear their research towards the natural sciences or economic theory and attempt to apply the conception of science found in these fields, namely, the deductive-nomological model, to International Relations.[1] For Waltz, clearly aligned with the scientismists in this debate, the focus is on the *deductive* discovery and explanation of *general patterns* of international relations on the basis of a small number of key assumptions. Inspired by economic theories, he applies this approach to the international system. Its *structure*, Waltz tells us, forces states to concentrate on ensuring security and power, but at the same time the system generates webs of power on the international level that prevent armed conflicts. In Waltz's writings, then, the structure of the international system takes on the central role formerly played by power and the pursuit of power in realist analysis. From this perspective, neorealism improves on traditional realism in a dual sense, both in its choice of analytical category and its epistemological approach. So, for Waltz, neorealism was a tremendous scientific advance on the writings of traditional realists.

With the end of the East–West conflict, neorealism initially seemed to be facing a crisis, having failed (along with other IR theories) to predict this development. On September 11 2001, however, neorealist theory received an unexpected boost. Problems of national security and the wars in Afghanistan and Iraq have been central to international politics ever since – though the state-centredness of neorealism initially appeared ill suited to comprehending the "new" threats and security policy challenges. But, as Christopher Layne argues: "There is little reason to believe that postmodern warfare will replace great-power rivalries and security competitions as the most salient phenomenon of international politics" (2004: 106). Given the current tension between nation states in, for example, the Middle East or Asia, it seems obvious that theories which focus on states as the key actors in international politics will continue to be significant into the future, at least in the security realm.

Finally, despite all the criticisms levelled against it, another key reason why neorealism matters is the ongoing role of the (neo)realist world-view in shaping policy in many foreign and defence ministries (Gyngell and Wesley 2003). So in order to understand certain foreign policy decisions, one has to understand how neorealists perceive the world.

2 The neorealism of Kenneth N. Waltz

The core question for neorealism is whether, and if so why, despite differing political systems and different ideologies, states tend to behave in much the same way towards the external world, and why powerful states especially must always expect challenges to their pre-eminence. At the same time this theory attempts to explain why more wars occur during certain periods of history, while others are more peaceful despite great tensions. The theory concentrates solely on "high politics" (in other words the "classical" politics of security) while leaving "low politics" (social and economic issues) out of the account.

The leading and most influential exponent of neorealism continues to be Kenneth N. Waltz. In his book *Theory of International Politics*, Waltz aims to formulate a comprehensive theory of international relations. Because of its highly abstract nature, however, many readers of TIP struggle to reconcile their everyday experience of politics with Waltz's theoretical suppositions and conclusions. To avoid misunderstandings, before presenting the theory itself it is helpful to clarify why Waltz believes it necessary to produce a new IR theory, the aspirations he associates with this theory, and the conception of theory that undergirds his neorealist thinking.

2.1 Epistemological foundations

In his 1959 book, *Man, the State and War*, Kenneth Waltz already distinguishes between three levels of analysis he believes help us explain international politics, and these he calls "images of the world" or "levels of analysis". The "first image of the world" is the *level of the individual* and is based on the assumption of fixed anthropological predispositions that determine the behaviour of political decision-makers. Generally, realists draw on this first level of analysis by attributing to states anthropological traits by analogy to the human individual. A state's *political system* makes up the second level of analysis. Liberal theorists, for example, operate on this level when they examine whether democracies behave in a different way towards the external world than non-democracies (see also the chapter by Andreas Hasenclever in this volume). Finally, Waltz identifies the third level as that of the international system.

As Waltz sees it, most International Relations theories suffer from a serious handicap: their analyses of international politics are limited to the first or second image of the world, and on this basis they make inferences about how the specific foreign policies of a *particular* state have come about. The whole – international politics – is then no more than the sum of its parts, namely states' foreign policies. Waltz calls theories that proceed in this way "reductionist" (Waltz 1979: 18), and for him this applies both to liberal approaches and traditional realism. While it is true that these approaches collect a wealth of empirical data, their power to deduce *general theoretical* statements (in the sense of regularities) about overall conditions within the international system based on this data is limited. Further, Waltz argues, as a result of the tendency to remain analytically on the subsystemic first or second level, these approaches succumb to the temptation to add new variables to a theory *ad hoc* if they have failed to come up with a satisfactory explanation on the basis of those variables so far considered. In sum, Waltz concludes that "[i]t is not possible to understand world politics simply by looking inside of states . . . from simple description no valid generalizations can logically be drawn" (1979: 65). Waltz therefore heads in the exact opposite direction.

According to Waltz, only simplification or "elegance" (ibid.: 69) allows us to conceive of the core and definitive elements of international processes in the abstract without irrelevant factors distorting things. The key term that crops up again and again in this context is theoretical *parsimony*: the smaller the number of variables that must be alluded to in order to explain particular behaviours, the greater a theory's general explanatory power is thought to be.

Waltz's conception of theory thus takes its lead from economics, which he views as a role model for the theory of international politics. According to Waltz, the decisive breakthrough in achieving an economic theory generally recognized as valid was the abstract – and admittedly unrealistic – separation of the economic sphere from other social and political issues (Waltz 1990: 22). Inspired by this, he sees the necessity of producing a theory of international politics that focuses on the *sphere of international politics* in an analogously exclusive fashion, without factoring in economic or social factors. Only in this way it is possible to explain the fundamental realities of international politics. But this inevitably involves a shift of analytical perspective. Waltz focuses on the level of the *international system*, the third image of the world. Just as the market determines the behaviour of firms, by forcing them to sell their product at the normal market price for example, Waltz sees forces at work in the international system that determine the behaviour of states from the outside, forces that states are unable to evade for any length of time. We shall now take a look at these forces.

2.2 The international system: actors and structures

Every International Relations theory whose analytical focus lies on the level of the international system must begin by defining its concept of system. For Waltz, the international system consists of two basic elements: the *actors* or *units* of the system, namely states, and the *structure* of the system. From a neorealist perspective, these two elements must be examined separately.[2]

In the line with the "ban on reductionism", here states are understood as *homogeneous* or *uniform* actors whose "inner life" is of no relevance to formulating a neorealist theory. From a neorealist perspective, the internal organization of states – such as the specific political system – can be disregarded; it represents something of a "black box" that neorealism leaves unopened. So it is irrelevant to the explanation of international politics whether a state is a liberal democracy or whether it is ruled by an autocratic, monarchical or dictatorial regime. The key distinguishing features of states are consciously disregarded. This theory assumes that all states are essentially identical ("like units" or "unitary actors", see Waltz 1996: 54). In light of this assumption, neorealism inevitably exposes itself to the criticism that it neglects crucial aspects of political processes with important influences on the international level. Waltz responds by conceding that to explain some things, such as a specific foreign policy, it is indeed necessary to look at a state's "inner life". But, he explains, his goal is not to develop a theory of foreign policy. It is instead to identify general trends and pressures (Waltz refers to "systemic effects") of relevance to *all* states. Neorealists who take their lead from Waltz thus work with at least three core assumptions:

1 Although the specific interests of individual states are not taken into account (they are in the "black box"), neorealists do assume the existence of at least one central need,

which is the top priority for any state: *survival*. This refers to states' efforts to maintain their political and geographical integrity.

2 States try to realize their core preferences rationally, in other words their decisions are based on the criterion of means–ends rationality.[3] But uncertainty prevails regarding other states' intentions. Their potential aggression and desire for expansion are ever-present threats that must be taken into account.

3 Finally, while the first two assumptions apply to all states, there is one criterion in light of which we might distinguish between them: the extent of their "capabilities" (Waltz 1979: 195), which give them different degrees of "power". How precisely capabilities and power are to be measured is not explained. They remain abstract concepts, hanging in the air (ibid.: 129ff). Waltz does at least imply that determining the power of a state is not a simple matter of counting up its weapons systems and soldiers. Economic and even social factors are also components of state power. In a sense, power is the "unit of account" by means of which states compare themselves with others, just as monetary evaluation makes it possible to distinguish between different goods (Waltz 1986: 333).

It may seem surprising that so far only states have been mentioned as relevant actors within the international system. Neorealists do not, of course, dispute that in reality actors such as transnational corporations, NGOs and international organizations have a certain importance as well. But from the theoretical perspective of neorealism, such actors seem unworthy of attention, as they have no influence on those processes that neorealists consider the key determinants of international politics. In other words: "Realism is designed to understand relations and interactions between states" (Glaser 2003: 407).

While reductionist theories see structure as arising from interactions between states and thus as dependent on these interactions, for Waltz, structure is defined independently of actors, their interests and interactions. From a neorealist perspective, the structure of the international system has an autonomous causal influence on actors and ensures that they behave in basically similar ways in specific situations ("like units"). But if we wish to determine just what is meant by the structure of the international system, we are faced with the problem that this structure cannot be directly observed as such. So we have to make an abstract model of it. According to Waltz's definition, there are three elements to the political structure of the international system: (1) the ordering principle; (2) the functional specifications or characteristics of actors; and (3) the distribution of resources or power among actors.

1 The first structural feature of the international system is its ordering principle. For Waltz, there are two basic ways in which actors can be organized (or ordered) within a system: hierarchically or anarchically (Waltz 1979: 114ff). As with national political systems, a hierarchical structure is distinguished by the presence of a superordinate authority with sanctioning power (a monopoly on violence) that guarantees the safety of the individual units. Conversely, *anarchy* – and this differs from the everyday use of the term – refers to the *absence* of such an authority: under these conditions, each actor is left to its own devices. All neorealists work on the premise that the international system is characterized by anarchy – understood as the absence of a "world government" or superordinate authority. This assumption of anarchy, as we will see, has far-reaching consequences for theory building.

2 The second structural feature that Waltz takes into consideration is the functional differentiation of the units or *character of the units*. Functional differentiation is present if there is a "division of labour" between states, in other words, if different states fulfil

different functions – by analogy to the division of labour in a society. In assessing the extent to which a division of labour between states within the international system is possible, the system's ordering principle plays a crucial role. For Waltz, the assumption of anarchy means that states will be unwilling to risk functional differentiation, in other words, an international division of labour. Anarchy compels each state to focus on its core preference – maintaining its sovereignty, i.e. its own survival – without relying on external help. "The international imperative is: 'take care of yourself'" (Waltz 1979: 107). It is because of this that the system described by neorealists is also referred to as a "self-help system".

3 The third element that characterizes the structure of the international system is the power relation between the individual states (*distribution of capabilities*). While the power of each individual state is an attribute of a given unit, Waltz sees the distribution of power within the international system as a feature of the system's structure (see ibid.: 80, 98). Power may be distributed in three possible ways. The international system may be structured on a unipolar (there exists a particularly powerful state, the hegemon), bipolar (there exist two particularly powerful states, as, for example, during the East–West conflict), or multipolar (there are more than two particularly powerful states) basis.

Now that we've clarified the key assumptions underpinning neorealist theory building, the next section sets out the key political processes within the international system that Kenneth Waltz derives from these assumptions.

2.3 International politics from a neorealist perspective

How does the structure of the international system affect actors? Or to put it in concrete terms, how do states act under conditions of anarchy? The point of departure here is as follows. States that wish to survive in an anarchically structured environment are forced to do everything they can to maximize their security. They are secure, proponents of this argument continue, only when there is a balance of power within the international system, as potentially aggressive states are deterred by the prospect of defeat. In line with this, it is crucial to nip power *im*balances in the bud, because state *x* may become more powerful than state *y*, thus threatening the latter's survival. Neorealists refer to such processes as *balancing*. The key imperative of states within the international system, then, may be summed up as follows: If you want to survive, even out power imbalances. This is how the structure of the international system impinges on the conduct of states, exercising a particular kind of causal effect on them. In the neorealist explanatory model, this structure has the status of an *independent variable*. However, the status of structure as a cause has to be qualified, because as Waltz argues: "Structures are causes but they are not causes in the sense meant by saying that A causes X and B causes Y" (1979: 74). This suggests that Waltz's neorealism does not paint a full picture of why things happens on the international level – and that Waltz is aware of the fact "that structure is not the only cause in play and that the presence of unit-level factors precludes structural determinism" (Humphreys 2012: 400). This rather soft understanding of the causal effect of structure becomes clearer when looking at how actors might react to structural pressure.

For Waltz, the international system exhibits a fundamental proclivity for equilibrium. But this does not mean that states' behaviour is determined, that they *must* always pursue a policy of balancing:

> States' actions are not determined by structure. Rather . . . structures shape and shove . . . . Because states coexist in a self-help system, they are free to do any fool thing they care to, but they are likely to be rewarded for behavior that is responsive to structural pressures and punished for behavior that is not.
>
> (Waltz 1997: 915)

So a balance of power or the tendency for one is not inevitable, but highly probable:

> A self-help system is one in which those who do not help themselves . . . will fail to prosper, will lay themselves open to dangers, will suffer. Fear of such unwanted consequences stimulates states to behave in ways that tend toward the creation of balances of power.
>
> (Waltz 1979: 118)

It follows from these observations that it is particularly important for a state that wants to survive and that acts rationally to constantly compare its capabilities with those of other actors and determine its position within the international system. In essence, a state may compensate for power shifts in another state's favour either by *upgrading its military forces* or *forming alliances*. If a particularly powerful actor makes use of its capabilities in order to improve its position within the international system, it is unlikely that other states will enter into competition with this state unilaterally (e.g. by enhancing their military forces); instead, they will attempt, through the formation of an *alliance*, to re-establish the power balance. If we assume in addition that most states do not have the option of achieving security vis-à-vis more powerful states through military enhancements because they lack the requisite resources, then the need for a balance of power would suggest that states will always band together with the weaker party in order to compensate for the other side's strength.

But when is the international system inclined towards war and when may we expect peaceful periods in world history? This is the second question posed earlier and in what follows Waltz's answers are discussed in detail. Central here are the different power configurations that the international system may exhibit: unipolarity, bipolarity or multipolarity. Waltz works on the assumption that *bipolar systems* featuring two particularly powerful states are least inclined towards war on the international level or are particularly likely to be stable over the long term because bipolar power relations are fundamentally clear and comprehensible. So it is unlikely that a given state will misjudge the power of other states and it is easy to take countermeasures (such as building up one's own military forces) when the opponent changes the status quo. In this case, bringing about a balance of power that impedes war is fairly straightforward (Waltz 1979: 161ff). One empirical example is the Cold War. But Waltz considered another argument relevant to the long phase of bipolarity during the Cold War: the stabilizing effect of nuclear weapons (Waltz 1988: 624). Their huge destructive power and the second strike capability of both superpowers generated a balance of power in which starting a war would have benefited neither of the two actors.[4] *Multipolar systems*, meanwhile, entail far greater problems, as each state inevitably feels threatened by a large number of other states, whose capabilities it can assess only very imprecisely and whose intentions are unclear. Alliances tend to be rather unstable as states have many opportunities to ally. In line with this, it is much more likely that actors, wrongly believing that they can win a war, will attack other states. In sum: "Miscalculation by some or all great powers is a source of danger in a multipolar world; . . . it is . . . likely to permit an unfolding of events that finally threatens the status quo and brings the powers to war"

(Waltz 1988: 623). In a *unipolar system*, meanwhile, a hegemon represents a palpable threat to all other states. As Waltz writes: "The possession of great power has often tempted nations to the unnecessary and foolish employment of force" (Waltz 1979: 201). But even if the hegemon is a benign one, other states cannot be sure whether this good-will will persist in the future. In line with the imperative for balance, other states will therefore forge alliances to compensate for this. This can never be in the interest of the hegemon, so the number of potential disputes and the probability of military conflicts increase.

Is international cooperation possible under these conditions? I mentioned earlier that within the context of a balancing process, states are quite capable of forming alliances. As neorealists see it, this is about as far as voluntary cooperation on the international level can go. States will not enter into more extensive cooperation with the aim of increasing overall prosperity because of the risk of potential dependencies. States must always work on the assumption that potential partners in cooperation will renege on agreements if they can benefit from doing so, by secretly violating the terms of disarmament treaties, for example. Some writers therefore speak of a problem of defection with which states find themselves confronted and which is especially virulent in the security field. For neorealists, the pursuit of security within a self-help system makes dependency and the risk of defection unacceptable. So international institutions and regimes are thought not to play any special role, because they are unable to solve these basic problems in any comprehensive way (see also the critical section in the chapter by Bernhard Zangl in this volume). For neorealists the only conceivable form of international cooperation that goes beyond alliance formation is *hegemonically induced cooperation*. Here the hegemon forces other states to embrace functional differentiation in order to enhance their common welfare. To sweeten things, the hegemon takes over a large portion of the costs and protective functions for cooperating states, thus offering them incentives to engage in cooperation (we might interpret the role of the US in the establishment of the post-war global economic order, with its core institutions of GATT, the International Monetary Fund and the World Bank, in this way). But this form of "cooperation" is basically based on fear rather than free will.

Do states have any room for manoeuvre at all to shape the international system? Here Waltz makes a fundamental distinction between a *change in* and a *change of* or *transformation of* the system (Waltz 1986: 342; Waltz 2000: 6).[5] When states influence the distribution of capabilities, we are dealing with a change *in* the international system. Through a unilateral military build-up, disarmament or a war it is possible for actors, at least over the short term, to make an impact on this structural attribute – before the balancing process works to correct this. This possibility of change must be distinguished from the *transformation of* the system. The latter occurs only if the attribute of anarchy is overcome, for example, through the construction of a world government or if the world is ruled by an overwhelmingly powerful state. Waltz considers this possibility so improbable, however, that he declares the anarchy of the international system and the resulting self-help character of this system *timeless* constants. While changes, such as transitions from bipolarity to multipolarity, are possible in principle, a transformation of the international system is extremely unlikely. We should not rule out the possibility of overcoming anarchy, though this places clear limits on the shelf-life of neorealism: "If the anarchy of international politics were to give way to a world hierarchy, a theory of international politics [in other words, Waltzian neorealism] would become a theory of the past" (Waltz 1986: 340).

Overall, neorealism paints a highly pessimistic picture of international relations. The pressure emanating from the international system forces states to concentrate on ensuring their own security. Power imbalances must be evened out immediately and international cooperation can be achieved only with great difficulty.

3 Differentiation within neorealism and further developments

In debates in International Relations the term neorealism is primarily associated with the works of Waltz. Nonetheless, a very broad range of authors see themselves as neorealists. It is quite possible to view "*neo*realism" as a collective term covering all those studies that are rooted in classical political realism and share its pessimistic world-view but that expand on it in significant ways. It is interesting to note that while TIP caused intense debate within the IR community at large when it was published (see below), more recent debates have been largely amongst realists themselves, either "pinning down in more detail the mechanics of the core theory . . . or adding unit-level variables to make it a theory of foreign policy" (Wæver 2009: 202).

I now highlight some of the more significant studies and themes that seek to address the central propositions found within the TIP, have a critical take on them or develop them further.[6]

3.1 Processing Waltz: responses to TIP within realism

While intra-realist debates after TIP threw up a whole range of objections to Waltz's neorealism, I want to take a closer look at just two fundamental issues.

1 Do states really tend towards behaviour that leads to a balance of power, as Waltz suggests, or is this state of affairs exceptional?
2 Are states really interested in maximizing *security*, or are they more concerned with maximizing their power?

Waltz's balancing hypothesis, according to which weak states form alliances vis-à-vis strong states, soon prompted exhaustive empirical investigations. Stephen Walt, for example, carried out an extensive study of the alliance-forming behaviour of states (Walt 1985). His conclusion is that balancing is indeed a commonly observable empirical phenomenon, but for reasons other than those mentioned by Waltz. Rather than always responding to objective capabilities as they pursue balance, what counts for states is instead the perceived threat. What Walt has done here is to reformulate neorealism as balance-of-threat theory: "Balance-of-*power* theory predicts that states will ally against the *strongest* state in the system, but balance-of-threat theory predicts they will tend to ally against the most *threatening*" (Walt 1997: 933; original emphasis). While at first sight this idea seems fairly plausible, it has been criticized for leaving the systemic level to focus on subsystemic or psychological factors by introducing the category of "threat" (Legro and Moravcsik 1999: 36ff).

In contrast to this reformulation of the balance-of-power hypothesis, it has often been subject to more fundamental critique. Against Walt, Randall Schweller (1994), for example, argues that balancing behaviour can be observed empirically far less often that assumed by Waltz and Walt (a view shared by historian Paul Schroeder (1994) or, more recently, by Wohlforth *et al.* (2007)).[7] Schweller argues that under certain circumstances it makes more sense for weaker states to band together voluntarily with strong ones, even without hegemonic pressure. This conduct is referred to as *bandwagoning*. States are particularly inclined towards bandwagoning if they can gain something from it (Schweller 1994: 74). He calls this approach the "theory of balance-of-interest" (ibid.: 99).

Schweller (2006) also argues that what we often observe empirically is "underbalancing". What he means by this is that despite a clearly recognizable threat, states forego a commensurate unilateral military build-up. Here again, Schweller believes that intra-state factors are responsible (such as the degree of elite consensus and elite cohesion, social cohesion or the stability of the government; see Schweller (2006: 11ff). In so doing, he too lays himself open to the criticism that he has shifted key elements of his ideas to the subsystemic level (Legro and Moravcsik 1999: 30). However, as Schweller – unlike Walt – sees himself located within the tradition of classical realism (hence "*neo*classical realism"), this criticism is less applicable to him.[8]

Finally, the unipolar distribution of power in the international system since the end of the East–West conflict has led to a debate over whether balancing must always occur on the level of military capabilities or whether countervailing power can be achieved in other ways. In a debate carried on chiefly within the pages of the journal, *International Security*,[9] some authors have come to the conclusion that possible challengers to the US, above all the People's Republic of China, which are not (yet) in a position to confront America directly, are instead concentrating their efforts systematically on "soft" factors in order to curb the influence of the US and its capacity to wield power. On this view, so-called "soft balancing" banks on the effect of "international institutions, economic statecraft, and diplomatic arrangements" (Pape 2005: 10) in order to undermine or at least limit aggressive unilateral actions by the US, such as the Gulf War of 2003. Critics, however, question the concept's explanatory power and see neither evidence of the systematic use of soft power against the US nor any relevant constraint on America's room for manoeuvre as a result of "soft balancing" (see Brooks and Wohlforth 2005: 75). Instead, these critics contend that it is the US's own "soft power" that helps it attain exceptional influence within international relations (Nye 2004).

The debate over the extent to which and in what way balancing is in fact empirically observable has far-reaching consequences – depending on whether one is among the critics or proponents of neorealism. This is because balancing is the only key hypothesis amenable to empirical testing (Schroeder 1994). If we assume with Waltz that neorealism is capable only of making statements of probability, and also that balancing is a process that may potentially last for decades, then we minimize the theory's capacity for prediction and immunize it against any strict test – according to critics (such as Guzzini 1998: 130ff). Hence Schweller's view that: "[E]ven system theories must investigate historical cases of state behavior and foreign policy to see if actors spoke and acted in the manner predicted by the explanation" (2003: 322). Neorealists such as Waltz (1996, 1997) and Eilstrup-Sangiovanni (2009), however, are quite unimpressed even by comprehensive "tests" and conflicting empirical observations, as, according to them, the analysis of specific historical cases falls under the rubric of foreign policy research rather than International Relations (Masala 2005: 99). However, this view runs counter to Waltz's own meta-theoretical claim as he states: "The trick, obviously, is to link theoretical concepts with a few variables in order to contrive explanations from which hypotheses can be inferred and *tested*" (Waltz 1979: 17, my emphasis).

A second point of debate within the neorealist camp was whether states go all out to enhance their power or pursue power only to the extent necessary to guarantee their own security and autonomy. Attempts to answer this question led to a – by now widely uncontested – division of neorealists into "defensive" and "offensive" camps. This bifurcation is described by Stephen Walt as the "most interesting conceptual development within the realist paradigm" (1998: 37). Waltz himself is considered a member of the defensive camp. For him, it is security rather than power that is states' top priority. John Mearsheimer, meanwhile, is viewed as one of the most dedicated offensive neorealists, having taken this approach further theoretically than anyone else. His focus is on great powers.

> "Offensive" realists, such as Mearsheimer . . ., argue that great powers seek to maximize security by maximizing their relative power, while "defensive" realists . . . argue that great powers are generally more secure when they refrain from power maximization and seek to defend the status quo.
>
> (Walt 1997: 932ff)

Though at first sight this assumption recalls classical realists such as Morgenthau, Mearsheimer does not see anthropological factors as relevant, instead deriving the pursuit of power maximization as a survival strategy from systemic factors (Mearsheimer 2001: 29). According to Mearsheimer, because of the prevailing uncertainty about other states' behaviour, states pursue power until such time as they have attained hegemonic status – or fail to do so. As soon as a state attains hegemonic status, it ceases to pursue power, as the self-help imperative is no longer relevant (ibid.: 35). As early as 1991, coming from a defensive realist angle, Snyder (1991: 6) claimed that the pursuit of security through expansion would fail because of the inevitable formation of countervailing power and exponentially increasing costs. Waltz, however, has pointed out that the question of whether states pursue security or power has no effect on the logic of his theory: "[A] balance of power system works whether we find states seeking only the minimum of power needed for security or whether some of them strive for domination" (Waltz 1986: 334).[10] Essentially, offensive and defensive realism have more in common than attempts to cleanly separate them would imply. Taliaferro (2000/2001: 130), however, represents a dissenting view in this regard. He argues that the distinction between offensive and defensive realism is extremely important, not least in view of the very different policy recommendations to which they give rise.

3.2 Alternatives to Waltz in times of upheaval? The political economic theory of Robert Gilpin and "power transition theory"

With just a few exceptions, neorealists accept the thesis that American supremacy, which has persisted since the end of the Cold War, is a temporary phenomenon because eventually a countervailing power will emerge. From Waltz's perspective, the formation of such a countervailing power – ideally a return to a bipolar world – would be a welcome development, as this configuration of power has proved particularly stable. Other authors, however, also located broadly within the (neo)realist camp, dispute this "beneficent" effect of a balance of power. Robert Gilpin's theory of political economy and so-called *power transition theory* (PTT) come to some particularly disquieting conclusions.

In his magnum opus, *War and Change in World Politics*, Robert Gilpin also adopts an approach inspired by economic theory, but rather than trying to explain consistencies and stability, his analytical focus is on "dynamics". The questions he asks are therefore different as well: "How and under what circumstances does change take place at the level of international relations? What are the roles of political, economic, and technological developments in producing change in international systems?" (Gilpin 1981: 2). In attempting to answer these questions, Gilpin first appears to share key neorealist assumptions: "International relations continue to be a recurring struggle for wealth and power among independent actors in a state of anarchy" (ibid.: 7). Gilpin, however, does not focus on the international system and how it influences states (top-down). Instead he assumes the existence of individual actors with specific interests and preferences (bottom-up), though in analogy to Waltz, these actors operate within the anarchical environment of the international system.

While Gilpin determines the degree of constraint on state action within the anarchical international milieu partly by considering the material distribution of power, he also takes account of factors such as "prestige" or "authority" (ibid.: 26–39). Alongside the drive to survive, Gilpin analyses other (sub)state interests. States may, for example, have an interest in making the international system conform to their desires, though this entails certain costs. So the system is stable only if "no state believes it profitable to attempt to change the system" (ibid.: 10). Gilpin regards this as unlikely, however: in the course of history, he discerns an unending cyclical change in the international system in which new states are forever emerging as hegemonic. But this hegemony can only ever be maintained for a certain period, namely, until new challengers oust the hegemon. On this view, then, the international system is characterized by "the cycle of hegemony" (ibid.: 220). This conclusion applies even in the nuclear age (Gilpin 1988: 34ff).

Gilpin identifies three key reasons why a hegemon's dominance inevitably comes to an end. First, "Turgot's law of diminishing returns" also applies to states' production of capabilities. A state's power initially grows very quickly, but then ever more slowly,[11] so that eventually potential power rivals can catch up with the hegemon. Second, hegemons tend to consume proportionately more than they invest, which, according to economists, hampers growth. Third, it is impossible for the hegemon to preserve its initial technological edge over the long term as it cannot prevent the dissemination of knowledge. All three aspects enable up-and-coming states, after an initial delay, to "catch up" with the hegemon and to challenge its supremacy, which might ultimately lead to wars: as soon as the existing order of the international system is no longer compatible with the prevailing distribution of power, processes of adaptation, including armed conflict, inevitably ensue.

Much like Gilpin, A.F.K. Organski and Jacek Kugler scrutinize the preconditions for major wars in the context of power transitions. In their magnum opus, *The War Ledger* (1980), they put forward the hypothesis that sooner or later every hegemon will find itself confronted with a challenger. For them, this throws up the question of whether a politics of power balancing can guarantee peace over the long term – a question that Organski had already answered in the negative in the 1950s, against the prevailing balance-of-power mainstream. Organski and Kugler, whose approach has come to be known as *power transition theory* (PTT), come to the conclusion – a surprising, indeed antithetical one for neorealists – that it is in fact periods of relatively balanced power relations between two rival states that entail a particularly great risk of armed conflict. The focus of interest here, as with the work of Gilpin, is on the path towards balance, rather than balance itself. The co-authors too argue that the challenger can increase its power more quickly than the hitherto dominant state because of its higher economic growth, such that the two states' power curves will inevitably cross over. PTT takes no account of the alliance as an external means of enhancing power as it assumes that it is too inflexible an instrument and that states rely primarily on their own power resources. If the challenger wins the contest with the formerly most powerful state, a power transition will occur.

As exponents of PTT see it, however, power transitions do not necessarily lead to wars. This depends instead on whether the challenger accepts the norms and rules of the international system laid down by the formerly dominant state or wants to change them, in other words, whether it behaves in "revisionist" fashion (Organski and Kugler 1980: 23). In the first case a peaceful power transition is possible, while, in the second, war is significantly more probable, and, according to these authors, this war will be started by the new most powerful state *after* the power transition (ibid.: 206).[12] So it is not just the configuration of power in the international system that determines the probability of war, but also whether the challenger is willing to accept the prevailing normative order (whether it is "satisfied") or not (and must therefore be considered "dissatisfied"). On the question of how we might determine whether a given challenger is "satisfied" or not, however, Organski and Kugler remain very vague, and there is an ongoing debate regarding exactly how we might identify different types of states.[13]

All in all, Gilpin's political economic theory and the PTT approach are very similar in their assumptions and their view of international relations. Both approaches see the international order as far more strongly influenced by powerful states than does neorealism with its notion of alliance formation as a means of power balancing. They also refer to the destabilizing effect of power balances, working on the assumption that the probability of war increases in phases of the equal distribution of power. At first sight, then, they seem better equipped to provide predictions and guides to coping with the challenges of contemporary international politics, such as the rise of the People's Republic of China and India. Given that TIP (1979), *The War Ledger* (1980) and *War and Change* (1981) were published at almost the same point in time, it is legitimate to ask "[w]here would the scholarly field of international relations (IR) be today if Robert Gilpin had become the standard bearer for realism instead of Kenneth Waltz?" (Wohlforth 2011: 499) or, one might add, Organski and Kugler. Introducing the (subsystemic) categories of "prestige" or "satisfaction with the prevailing normative order", however, compels these approaches to open the black box of the state. This brings Waltz's dictum back into play: "With both system-level and unit-level forces in play, how can one construct a theory of international politics without simultaneously constructing a theory of foreign policy?" (Waltz 1988: 42).

3.3 Neorealism: not an exclusively American IR theory

It is fair to say that while neorealism is one of the most important IR theories world-wide, its reception and relevance in the academic communities of different countries have been rather mixed. In Germany, for example, neorealism has always had and still has the status of the unloved relative you somehow have to get along with. While it is taught in almost all introductory seminars, only very few scholars publicly subscribe to the theory. But at least some attempts have been made and continue to be made to augment and apply neorealist theory there.

The *Munich School* founded by Gottfried-Karl Kindermann, for example, claims to be *neo*realist in character. As the title of an essay by Reinhard Meier-Walser declares: "Neorealism is more than just Waltz" (Meier-Walser 1994; my translation). This particular approach is characterized by a focus on practical analytical value and a synopsis of systemic and subsystemic factors (e.g. Meier-Walser 1994: 115). Overall, though, the Munich neorealists take their lead much more from Morgenthau, and thus realism, than from Waltz.[14]

Meanwhile, among German scholars, Werner Link (1980) is closer to Waltzian neorealism. On the basis of studies by David Singer, and taking the East–West conflict as an example, he seeks to demonstrate how different ways of dealing with conflict can be explained in light of a given web of power relations or changes in this web. Link thus concludes that the best time to achieve improved relations between the superpowers was during periods when a balance of power had removed the threat to their economic and political survival (Link 1980: 224ff.).

Currently the best-known German neorealist is Carlo Masala, whose theoretical stance is very close to the original Waltzian thinking. He is the author of the most comprehensive volume on Waltz in German (Masala 2005) and a defender of "pure" neorealism (e.g. Masala 2012).

4 Criticisms from outside neorealism

Since the publication of TIP in 1979, there has been a virtually ceaseless flow of criticism from the exponents of other schools – not least because neorealism has seemed an increasingly fissiparous and inconsistent theoretical edifice. In addition, this theory has exhibited glaring explanatory weaknesses with respect to crucial international developments such as increasing European integration[15] or the end of the East–West conflict. This is because it has such a poor grasp, or no grasp at all, of dynamic developments whose causes are to be found on the subsystemic level (see, for example, Schweller and Wohlforth 2000; Waltz 2000). As we have seen, some avowed (neo)realists (such as Walt) make the same point. Most neorealists, however, view the inclusion of subsystemic factors as a concession to a complex reality, without questioning neorealism and its basic pessimism in any fundamental way.

In the following section we turn our attention to two fundamental debates. The first is that between neorealists and neoinstitutionalists in the 1980s (the so-called "neo-neo debate"),[16] the second, the constructionist critique of the neorealist conception of anarchy, which goes back to Alexander Wendt. Both these debates proved especially relevant to the development of International Relations theories as they helped theorists break out of the dominant, pessimistic world-view of neorealism without lapsing into idealist arguments.

Not long after the publication of TIP, neorealism seemed to be confronted with its first crisis. Many observers believed that the US's international pre-eminence had diminished substantially over the course of the early 1980s. Generally, they saw the reasons for this as lying in the economic crises of the 1970s (above all, the oil crises) and the growing economic strength of Europe and Japan. Yet the US's economic weakness seemed to have no effect on the degree of international cooperation, in the GATT or the IMF, for instance, which conflicted with the neorealist hypothesis of hegemonically induced cooperation. Finally, in 1984, against neorealist doctrine, Robert O. Keohane asked whether international cooperation was possible *After Hegemony*.[17]

In an attempt to answer this question, those authors referred to as "neoinstitutionalists" or "neoliberal institutionalists" drew on a wide range of neorealist assumptions. On the basis of these assumptions and with the aid of rational choice theory, particularly game theory, they made systematic studies of opportunities for cooperation in order to refute neorealist pessimism not just empirically but also theoretically. Neoinstitutionalists such as Robert O. Keohane (1984) and Robert Axelrod (1984) believed they could show that cooperation is possible in principle even on the premise of international anarchy and that it facilitates *positive absolute utility* for all cooperating states. They were also convinced that the problem of defection (see above) could be tackled by an appropriate international framework (see also the chapter by Bernhard Zangl in this volume).[18] In the neorealist camp, Joseph Grieco countered this view in 1988 with an argument that was already present in the work of Waltz but that had subsequently been largely overlooked, namely, that relating to "relative gains" (see Waltz 1979: 105; Grieco 1988: 499ff). Because of anarchy and the drive for self-preservation, what matters is not whether states make *absolute* gains through cooperation, but rather how the common gains from cooperation are distributed among those cooperating. Neorealist logic assumes that states always consider to what extent absolute shared gains from cooperation change the existing power balance between them. Even if two states gain from cooperation, one might gain more and thereby achieve a so-called *relative* gain in contrast to the other state, changing the power structure to the former's advantage, thereby destabilizing the international system.[19] By thinking in this way, it is possible to transform every positive sum game (absolute gain for all states involved in cooperation; no one is left worse off) into a zero sum game (that is, any gain by one state necessarily means a corresponding loss by another such that the gains of all those involved add up to zero). This logic also applies to cooperation between states enjoying friendly relations, such that the probability of cooperation even between allies and partners is extremely limited if cooperation changes the power structure between the states: "There is even the danger, however remote, that today's ally will become tomorrow's enemy" (Grieco 1988: 47). Although the argument concerning relative gains as a factor hampering cooperation is logical as far as it goes, game theoretical analyses have shown that the significance of relative gains falls as the number of cooperating actors increases (see Snidal 1991). Waltz and Grieco also fail to take account of the fact that every absolute gain also constitutes a relative gain vis-à-vis states not involved in the cooperation, such that we can estimate the net gain accruing to a state through cooperation only with great difficulty.

Probably the most substantial criticism of Waltzian neorealism was formulated in 1992 by Alexander Wendt in his provocative article "Anarchy is What States Make of It: The Social Construction of Power Politics", with which he ushered in a wave of constructionist criticism (see also the chapter by Cornelia Ulbert in this volume). For Wendt, it is not logically necessary to assume that international anarchy will automatically give rise to a self-help system featuring an irresistible impulse to engage in power politics (Wendt 1992: 394). Here, the constructionist conception of "structure" diverges markedly from that of neorealism. From a neorealist perspective, structure – and especially the element of anarchy – is an exogenous given, such that in principle states have no prospect of affecting the structure of the international system. From a constructionist perspective, on the other hand, structure is always a *social* element, which is crucially *moulded*, and endowed with meaning, by *interactional processes* between states but which in turn has a constitutive effect on actors. For Wendt, there is a mutually constitutive web of relations between actors and structure (the "agent–structure problem"). "Wendt's key assertion is that the culture in which states find themselves at any point in time depends on the discursive social practices that reproduce or transform each actor's view of self and other" (Copeland 2000: 195). From a constructionist perspective, states' conception of the international system, but also of themselves, is the result of a long-term process of repeated interaction between actors, a process whose outcome is *not determined in advance*. To bring out the nature of this relationship, Wendt devises a hypothetical situation in which two actors, ego and alter, meet without background knowledge of one another under conditions of anarchy (Wendt 1992: 404). Wendt shows that in such a situation how relations between the two will develop is not predetermined – if we forego the assumption that each actor will orient itself towards the worst possible case, namely, its own immediate annihilation, should it behave in an accommodating way. In this case, then, anarchy has *no* necessary influence on how actors deal with one another. But if states behave in an egotistical way right from the outset, subsequently putting their faith in military might in order to secure their survival, as assumed in realist and neorealist theory, it becomes ever more difficult for them to extract themselves from this "Hobbesian culture" (Wendt 1999: 259ff) of anarchy. From a constructionist perspective, however, it is always possible to reverse this process and move away from a self-help system – even without being dependent on a hegemon that establishes a hierarchical structure through the threat of violence. As an empirical example, one might look at the relations between France and Germany. While over centuries their relations were highly bellicose, today a war seems virtually impossible. So states are not completely at the mercy of the structural forces identified by Waltz. With this fundamental critique, Wendt's article ushered in the "constructionist turn" in International Relations.

To conclude, it is fair to say that the internal and external debates carried on in the wake of TIP were not without consequence for the development of neorealist theory. Neorealists have increasingly incorporated subsystemic factors or constructionist elements into their analyses, and have rapidly distanced themselves from the parsimony of Waltzian neorealism in its original form. Today, almost all those who describe themselves as neorealists include elements in their work that contradict the basic assumptions of Waltzian theory. This neglect of *systemic* factors in contemporary neorealism ultimately prompted Jeffrey W. Legro and Andrew Moravcsik to ask the provocative question "[i]s anybody still a [neo-]realist?" (see Legro and Moravcsik 1999). "Avowed" exponents of this approach have yet to come up with a satisfactory answer to this very legitimate question.

5 Notes

1 Waltz does not explicitly subscribe to the deductive-nomological (or "covering-law") model but offers a "checklist" restating core assumptions of this approach (Waltz 1979: 13). See also Onuf (2011: 103, fn. 7). There is, however, a tension between Waltz's metatheoretical rhetoric and development of his theory and his own application of the theory to real-world problems in later chapters of TIP. See the very instructive article by Humphreys (2012).

2 Waltz's concept of system thus differs from that of other systemic perspectives, such as, for example, world-system theory. See Ruggie (1983: 262ff) and the chapter by Andreas Nölke in this volume.

3 The assumption that states are rational is not present in explicit form in TIP. In later essays, however, Waltz concedes that he *implicitly* works on this premise. See, for example, Waltz (1986: 330). There is still debate, however, over how rational states actually are according to Waltzian neorealism and how the assumption of rationality is consistent with the Waltzian notion that states are free to act in contradiction to what rationality dictates. See, for example, the critique by Mearsheimer (2009).

4 Based on this reasoning, Waltz argued for deliberate proliferation of nuclear weapons (Waltz 1981) – a stance that has stirred much controversy ever since.

5 Waltz has, however, been inconsistent with his terminology over the years. In TIP, for example, he speaks of the Second World War as a "system-transforming" war (Waltz 1979: 199), while later works refer to transformation as a fundamental change rendering international politics obsolete (Waltz 2000: 6).

6 For a comprehensive survey of the development of the realist paradigm in International Relations and International Political Economy, see Guzzini (1998).

7 For a response to this criticism, see, for example, Eilstrup-Sangiovanni (2009).

8 On realism in general and "neoclassical realism" in particular, see the chapter by Andreas Jacobs in this volume, and Lobell *et al.* (2009).

9 See especially the summer 2005 issue (30:1), in which both cited texts appear, and the winter 2005/06 issue (30: 3), particularly the "Correspondence" section.

10 For an overview of different realist approaches to the concept of a "balance of power" see Little (2007).

11 This law, originally formulated in 1768 with agriculture in mind, states that the output of a production process initially increases *dis*proportionately to the deployment of means, but once a certain level of production has been reached, it increases under-proportionately before finally reaching a maximum. Gilpin references Turgot implicitly rather than explicitly concept of curves. See, for example, Figure 3 in Gilpin (1981: 79).

12 There has been some debate within the PTT camp about the timing of a potential war as it seems equally plausible to assume that the hegemon will start a war to prevent the challenger from overtaking him in the first place. See, for example, the model by Alsharabati and Kugler (2008).
13 See, for example, Tammen (2008).
14 For a discussion of how Waltzian neorealism and the Munich approach differ and overlap, see Meier-Walser (1994: 122ff).
15 Initially, neorealists simply declared the EC or EU a unitary actor; see Grieco (1990).
16 The key essays in this debate have been brought together by Baldwin (1993).
17 To quote the title of his book. See Keohane (1984).
18 An example of absolute gains by two states through cooperation: state *a* gains 50 "units of power" through cooperation, state *b* 100. This means that both benefit vis-à-vis the initial situation, as the "power" of each has now increased in *absolute* terms.
19 An element of imprecision creeps into the accounts of the problem of relative gains in the work of both Kenneth Waltz and Joseph Grieco at this point. They argue that relative gains are avoided by equal distribution of the benefits of cooperation. But this statement applies only to the *special case* of an identical starting point. Let's assume that two actors, *a* and *b*, possess 100 and 50 power units respectively prior to cooperation. If both now gain 50 units each through cooperation, the power ratio shifts from 100:50 to 150:100, or from 2:1 to 3:2. Actor *a* has suffered a relative loss of power *despite* absolutely equal distribution of the benefits of cooperation. See, for example, Schweller (1996: 109ff). The only solution in this case is for the distribution of the collective gain to exactly match the *ex-ante* power structure, i.e. actor *a* receives 66.6 and actor *b* 33.3 units (*ex-post*: 166.6:83.3 = 2:1). This example shows that certain distributions even permit a relative loss *despite* getting more than the other (e.g. *a* receives 60 and *b* 40 which changes the power-relation in *b*'s favour, i.e. 1.78:1). It is interesting to note that this logic resembles Aristotle's concept of distributive justice, which is thought to stabilize society.

6 Bibliography and recommended reading check

6.1 Primary texts

Gilpin, Robert 1981: *War and Change in World Politics*. Cambridge: Cambridge University Press.
Mearsheimer, John 2001: *The Tragedy of Great Power Politics*. New York: Norton.
Organski, A.F.K. and Kugler, Jacek 1980: *The War Ledger*. Chicago: University of Chicago Press.
Waltz, Kenneth N. 1979: *Theory of International Politics*. Reading, MA: Addison-Wesley.
Waltz, Kenneth N. 1986: Reflections on Theory of International Politics: A Response to My Critics, in: Keohane, Robert (ed.) *Neorealism and Its Critics*. New York: Columbia University Press, pp. 322–345.
Waltz, Kenneth N. 2008: *Realism and International Politics*. New York: Routledge (a comprehensive collection of Waltz's major articles).

6.2 Secondary texts

Grieco, Joseph M. 1988: Anarchy and the Limits of Cooperation: A Realist Critique of the Newest Liberal Institutionalism, *International Organization* 42(3): 485–508.
Humphreys, Adam R. C. 2012: Another Waltz? Methodological Rhetoric and Practice in Theory of International Politics, *International Relations* 26(4): 389–408.
Legro, Jeffrey W. and Moravcsik, Andrew 1999: Is Anybody Still a Realist?, *International Security* 24(2): 5–55.
Little, Richard 2007: The Balance of Power in International Relations, in *Metaphors, Myth and Models*. Cambridge: Cambridge University Press.
Nye, Joseph S. 2004: *Power in the Global Information Age: From Realism to Globalization*. London: Routledge.

Schweller, Randall L. 1996: Neorealism's Status-Quo Bias: What Security Dilemma?, *Security Studies* 5(3): 90–121.

Schweller, Randall L. 2006: *Unanswered Threats: Political Constraints on the Balance of Power*. Princeton, NJ: Princeton University Press.

Wendt, Alexander 1992: Anarchy Is What States Make of It: The Social Construction of Power Politics, *International Organization* 46(2): 391–425.

Wendt, Alexander 1999: *Social Theory of International Politics*. Cambridge: Cambridge University Press.

6.3 Other texts

Alsharabati, Carole and Kugler, Jacek 2008: War Initiation in a Changing World, *International Interactions* 34(4): 358–381.

Axelrod, Robert 1984: *The Evolution of Cooperation*. New York: Basic Books.

Baldwin, David A. (ed.) 1993: *Neorealism and Neoliberalism: The Contemporary Debate*. New York: Columbia University Press.

Brooks, Stephen G. and Wohlforth, William C. 2005: Hard Times for Soft Balancing, *International Security* 30(1): 72–108.

Copeland, Dale C. 2000: The Constructivist Challenge to Structural Realism: A Review Essay, *International Security* 25(2): 187–212.

Eilstrup-Sangiovanni, Mette 2009: The End of Balance-of-Power Theory? A Comment on Wohlforth et al.'s. "Testing Balance-of-Power Theory in World History", *European Journal of International Relations* 15(2): 347–380.

Gilpin, Robert 1988: The Theory of Hegemonic War, in Rotberg, Robert and Rabb, Theodore (eds) *The Origins and Prevention of Major Wars*. Cambridge: Cambridge University Press, pp. 15–37.

Glaser, Charles L. 2003: Structural Realism in a More Complex World, *Review of International Studies* 29(3): 403–414.

Goldstein, Judith L., Kahler, Miles, Keohane, Robert O., and Slaughter, Anne-Marie (eds) 2001: *Legalization and World Politics*. Cambridge, MA: MIT Press.

Grieco, Joseph 1990: *Cooperation Among Nations: Europe, America, and Non-tariff Barriers to Trade*. Ithaca, NY: Cornell University Press.

Guzzini, Stefano 1998: *Realism in International Relations and International Political Economy: The Continuing Story of a Death Foretold*. London: Routledge.

Gyngell, Allan and Wesley, Michael 2003: *Making Australian Foreign Policy*. Cambridge: Cambridge University Press.

Hawkins, Darren G., Lake, David A., Nielson, Daniel L. and Tierney, Michael J. (eds) 2006: *Delegation and Agency in International Organizations*. Cambridge: Cambridge University Press.

Keohane, Robert 1984: *After Hegemony: Cooperation and Discord in the World Political Economy*. Princeton, NJ: Princeton University Press.

Koremenos, Barbara, Lipson, Charles and Snidal, Duncan (eds) 2004: *The Rational Design of International Institutions*. Cambridge: Cambridge University Press.

Layne, Christopher 2004: The War on Terrorism and the Balance of Power: The Paradoxes of American Hegemony, in Paul, T. V., Wirtz, James J. and Fortmann, Michel (eds) *Balance of Power: Theory and Practice in the 21st Century*, Stanford, CA: Stanford University Press, 103–126.

Link, Werner 1980: *Der Ost-West-Konflikt. Die Organisation der internationalen Beziehungen im 20. Jahrhundert*. Stuttgart: Kohlhammer. [An English version was published under the title "East/West Conflict: The Organization of International Relations in the 20th Century" by Berg in 1986].

Lobell, Steven E., Ripsman, Norrin M. and Taliaferro, Jeffrey W. (eds) 2009: *Neoclassical Realism, the State, and Foreign Policy*. Cambridge: Cambridge University Press.

Masala, Carlo 2005: *Kenneth N. Waltz: Einführung in seine Theorie und Auseinandersetzung mit seinen Kritikern*. Baden-Baden: Nomos.

Masala, Carlo 2012: Extended Deterrence in the Middle East: A Fuzzy Concept that Might Work?, *Strategic Assessment* 14(4): 115–122.

Mearsheimer, John 1995: The False Promise of International Institutions, *International Security* 19(3): 5–49.

Mearsheimer, John 2009: Reckless States and Realism, *International Relations* 23(2): 241–256.

Meier-Walser, Reinhard 1994: Neorealismus ist mehr als Waltz. Der Synoptische Realismus des Münchner Ansatzes, *Zeitschrift für Internationale Beziehungen* 1(1): 115–126.

Morgenthau, Hans 1963: *Macht und Frieden*. Gütersloh: Bertelsmann.

Onuf, Nicholas 2011: Structure? What Structure?, in Booth, Kenneth (ed.) *Realism and World Politics*. New York: Routledge, 89–106.

Pape, Robert A. 2005: Soft Balancing Against the United States, *International Security* 30(1): 7–45.

Ruggie, John G. 1983: Continuity and Transformation in the World Polity: Toward a Neorealist Synthesis, *World Politics* 25(2): 261–285.

Schroeder, Paul 1994: Historical Reality vs. Neorealist Theory, *International Security* 19(1): 108–148.

Schweller, Randall L. 1994: Bandwagoning for Profit: Bringing the Revisionist State Back In, *International Security* 19(1): 72–107.

—— 2003: The Progressiveness of Neoclassical Realism, in Elman, Colin and Fendius Elman, Miriam (eds) *Progress in International Relations Theory*. Cambridge, MA: MIT Press, 311–347.

Schweller, Randall L. and Wohlforth, William C. 2000: Power Test: Evaluating Realism in Response to the End of the Cold War, *Security Studies* 9(3): 60–107.

Snidal, Duncan 1991: Relative Gains and the Pattern of International Cooperation, *American Political Science Review* 85(3): 701–726.

Snyder, Jack 1991: *Myth of Empire: Domestic Politics and International Ambition*. Ithaca, NY: Cornell University Press.

Taliaferro, Jeffrey W. 2000/2001: Security Seeking under Anarchy, *International Security* 25(3): 128–161.

Tammen, Ronald L. 2008: The Organski Legacy: A Fifty-Year Research Program, *International Interactions* 34(4): 314–332.

Wæver, Ole 2009: Walt's Theory of Theory, *International Relations* 23(3): 201–222.

Walt, Stephen 1985: Alliance Formation and the Balance of World Power, *International Security* 9(4): 3–43.

Walt, Stephen 1997: The Progressive Power of Realism, *American Political Science Review* 91(4): 931–935.

—— 1998: International Relations: One World, Many Theories, *Foreign Policy*, 110: 29–47.

Waltz, Kenneth N. 1959: *Man, the State and War*. New York: Columbia University Press.

—— 1981: The Spread of Nuclear Weapons: More May Be Better. Adelphi Paper 171, International Institute for Strategic Studies, London.

—— 1988: The Origins of War in Neorealist Theory, in Rotberg, Robert and Rabb, Theodor (eds) *The Origins and Prevention of Major Wars*. Cambridge: Cambridge University Press, pp. 39–52.

—— 1990: Realist Thought and Neorealist Theory, *Journal of International Affairs* 44(1): 21–38.

—— 1996: International Politics Is Not Foreign Policy, *Security Studies* 6(1): 54–57.

—— 1997: Evaluating Theories, *American Political Science Review* 91(4): 913–917.

—— 2000: Structural Realism after the Cold War, *International Security* 25(1): 5–41.

Wohlforth, William 2011: Gilpinian Realism and International Relations, *International Relations*, 25(4): 499–511.

Wohlforth, William C., Little, Richard, Kaufman, Stuart J. *et al.* 2007: Testing Balance-of-Power Theory in World History, *European Journal of International Relations* 13(2): 155–185.

Interdependence

Manuela Spindler

1 Introduction

The global financial and sovereign debt crisis and the Euro crisis have been a painful reminder of something that none of us can be entirely unaware of, namely that we live in a world of *mutual dependencies* in which events and decisions in one state inevitably have consequences for the politics and economics of others. As a rule, however, it is usually the crises that highlight the extent of global dependencies and, often, that render them tangible for individuals: processes of economic contraction threaten current levels of material prosperity, while unemployment is on the rise across the globe. What began in the USA in 2007 as the "US property market crisis" shook the system of finance and capital to an almost unimaginable degree, subsequently destabilizing national economies, and even states, across the world. Looking back to the 1990s, the Asian financial, currency and economic crisis ("Asian Crisis") of 1997/1998, originating in Thailand, is still fresh in our minds. When the crisis spread like wildfire beyond East and Southeast Asia to the European, North American and Latin American economies, commentators referred to "contagion". The same goes for the Argentina crisis, whose "contagion effect" was felt well beyond South America into the mid-2000s. More generally, the effects and risks of climate change and threats to global security are further examples of mutual dependencies in an increasingly integrated and networked world.

In the sphere of international politics and economics, the term usually applied to the kind of interrelationships described above is "interdependence". But the phenomenon referred to as interdependence, and reflections on the causes and consequences of mutual dependencies, are not new. They have long formed part of economic writings informed by classical economic theory, which focus on international dependencies in the field of global trade and currency policies and discuss the mutual gains and losses arising from international integration. The intellectual roots of these writings lie in the work of the classical figures of free trade theory and political liberalism such as Adam Smith, David Ricardo and John Stuart Mill (for a detailed account, see Zacher and Matthew 1995). In contrast to economic and political liberalism, however, there is a tradition of thought moulded by realism that discusses not "gains" but rather the dangers and risks of mutual dependencies, particularly in the form of international conflicts – the writings of Niccolò Machiavelli being an early example.

In twentieth-century political science, reflections on interdependence began with idealism, the key figures here being the Britons Norman Angell (1910) and Ramsay Muir ([1933] 1971) and the French syndicalist Francis Delaisi ([1925] 1971) (for a detailed account, see de Wilde 1991). In probably his best-known work, *The Great Illusion*, Angell asserts that national prosperity cannot be achieved through military force. For him, the prosperity of all nations depends instead on economic contacts, that is, the interdependence of markets and the financial sector. The citizens of other nations must have adequate buying power, and these nations in turn must be in a position to sell their products. Traditional military conquests, so the argument goes, cannot therefore be in a state's interest (Angell 1910; see also de Wilde 1991: Chapter 3). This postulate of a connection between interdependence, particularly in the field of trade relations, and peaceful international relations ("trade–peace linkage"), and the opposing thesis of a connection between interdependence and increased conflict continue to be discussed and subjected to empirical verification (see Section 3). What is apparent here is the ambivalent character of mutual dependencies in international politics – one of the great challenges for a theory of interdependence in International Relations.

Despite the existence of intellectual forerunners, the term "interdependence" entered into the theory building of the political science subdiscipline of International Relations (IR) only at a very late stage.[1] In the 1960s, the concept of global interdependence first arose in connection with the East–West conflict, the idea here being that interdependence was a cornerstone of world peace. The background to this was the development of intercontinental missiles and thus the tremendous shortening of the "distance" between states, with the consequence that "neither state can effectively move toward isolation or increase its own autonomy so far as security is concerned" (Morse 1972: 138–139). This *security-related or military-strategic interdependence* was thus the hallmark of a global relationship generated by the conflict between two mutually exclusive conceptions of world politics – and the existence of nuclear weapons as the (threatened) means of resolving this conflict (see also Kuhn 1962).

But it was the work on interdependence that appeared in the late 1960s and above all in the 1970s – written against the background of crisis symptoms in the world economy and conflicts between the Western industrialized countries – that was most significant, exercising a formative influence on the theoretical development of IR. The two most serious economic "shocks" were the collapse of the Bretton Woods monetary system (informed by the principle of fixed exchange rates on the basis of agreed gold parities) when the US administration abolished gold–dollar convertibility in August 1971 and, above all, the first oil crisis. The background to the first oil crisis of 1973 (a second followed in 1979) was the oil embargo imposed by OPEC in retaliation for the USA's and other industrialized countries' support for Israel in the context of the Arab–Israeli conflict (the Yom Kippur War). Oil prices increased dramatically, causing stagflation in the Western industrialized states and conflicts among them over the "best" economic policies to tackle recession and inflation. Until then, the Western welfare states, with their extensive powers, had used very different economic policies to achieve general economic growth. The result was *individual* – and thus unpredictable – national responses to the crisis symptoms, which led to conflicts.[2] The background to the conflicts of the 1970s was the decline of American hegemony as a result of the Vietnam War and the growing economic strength of Europe and Japan. These tensions were heightened by political crises in the leading Western industrialized nations that diminished their governments' credibility and ability to take effective action.[3] In late 1974, new heads of state or government were in office in all four leading Western industrialized countries (the USA, Japan, West Germany and France), and they sought to address the crisis symptoms through global economic coordination. In 1975, for example, the "World Economic Summit" – now the G7/G8 – was established.[4] Still regarded by voters as responsible for the costs associated with adaptation and stabilization, there was a change in the political rhetoric deployed by *individual* Western governments. Their aim was to convey to the general population the *world-wide* interconnections and dependencies affecting efforts to tackle the crisis, and the resulting necessity for international coordination. In other words, they sought to explain that the causes and costs of adaptation were "international" or determined by the "world economy", making it easier to implement economic policies with painful implications for many citizens. The term "interdependence" appeared with increasing frequency in political speeches, especially those of American politicians. This underlines the general decline in governments' ability to shape events and the necessity for multilateral cooperation (in other words the end of "Atlantic" or unilateral control by the USA) in order to solve the problems arising from interdependence (see de Wilde 1991: 44–45). In the 1970s, against the background of the economic crises, and reinforced by East–West détente (the Commission on Security and Cooperation in Europe, arms control), problems were thus *politicized* beyond military security: issues such as how to maintain prosperity, resource availability, and environmental destruction suddenly stood centre stage (for more detail, see Morse 1970, 1972; Cooper 1972). The problem of how to deal politically with the effects of mutual dependencies became a core problem of international politics, and it has posed an increasing challenge to the state's ability to control and shape events ever since. Against this background, a number of economists and political scientists began to cast doubt on the explanatory power of the prevailing realist paradigm, which assumes the pre-eminence of "high politics" (security) and the crucial importance of military power as a political instrument (see the chapters by Andreas Jacobs and Niklas Schörnig in this volume). A number of authors began to make connections between the work of economists and political scientists, moving issues of international political economy (IPE) centre stage (Morse 1969: 319–320; Strange 1970; see also the chapter by Hans-Jürgen Bieling in this volume). The most important impulses came from a book by American economist Richard Cooper, *The Economics of Interdependence* (1968), a series of essays by Edward Morse (above all "The Politics of Interdependence", 1969), and the work of Robert O. Keohane and Joseph Nye on transnational relations (Nye and Keohane 1970a, 1970b).[5] Another key influence was the *integration theory* of the 1950s and 1960s (neofunctionalism), which claimed that the attitudes of political decision-makers had changed as a result of intensifying transnational and transgovernmental contacts, and which examined how regional institutions could drive this process forward (see Keohane and Nye 1975: 394–401; Nau 1979 and the chapter by Thomas Conzelmann in this volume).

The writings of Keohane and Nye are the crucial, landmark studies that provided an initial political science take on interdependence, particularly their 1977 book *Power and Interdependence: World Politics in Transition* (henceforth PaI). The basic insight of PaI is that there has been a shift or change in the structures of the international system. States have lost much of their ability to take effective action and control events. Mutual dependencies thus have major consequences for the achievement of national economic and political goals. PaI examines the potential for nation states to take effective political action under these conditions: in other words, it tries to identify the political instruments most appropriate to dealing with this change. It does this on two levels: (1) the level of foreign policy (how to optimize foreign policy action), and (2) the level of international politics (the potential to shape events through international cooperation). In what follows, the writings of Keohane and Nye will stand centre stage, as they have had a profound influence on theoretical trends in IR up to the present day.[6]

But "interdependence" is not really a theory; it is an analytical concept (reference is also often made to "interdependence analysis") that occupies a key position in subsequent theory building in IR (the key terms here being regime theory and neoliberal institutionalism; see also the chapter by Bernhard Zangl in this volume). Getting to grips with the concept of interdependence is not just a matter of theoretical interest. The concept of "interdependence" or interdependence analysis leads on to the idea that governments should be pursuing a global "politics of interdependence" through international cooperation and political coordination and this idea is undergirded theoretically and conceptually in PaI. As evident in current efforts to cope with the global and European financial crisis, this idea continues to be of great political relevance.

2 Interdependence as a concept within political scientific analysis: Robert O. Keohane and Joseph S. Nye

2.1 Is interdependence measurable? Interdependence and interconnectedness

A glance at the debate of the 1970s shows that sharply contradictory answers have been given to the question of whether or not the present extent and intensity of international integration are greater than that of previous eras (see Deutsch and Eckstein 1961; Deutsch *et al.* 1967; Waltz 1970; Katzenstein 1975). Proponents of the thesis of decreasing interdependence, such as Deutsch, point out that foreign trade as a proportion of gross national product decreases in the later stages of a country's industrial development. He identifies a high point in 1913, after which he claims that interdependence diminished as industrialization intensified (see also Rosecrance and Stein 1973: 5–6). For others, meanwhile, interdependence intensified between 1950 and 1958 but has decreased since (Rosecrance *et al.* 1977: 442). For authors such as Morse (1972), Cooper (1968) and Keohane and Nye, on the other hand, interdependence has been growing continuously since 1945. How are we to explain these differing assessments, which are exemplary of wider trends? First, this is fundamentally a matter of the methods of identifying interdependence, which have been highly contested. Examples of methods include the "export percentage model", which measures exports from country *a* to country *b* as a percentage of country *b*'s total imports, and the "chooser–chosen GNP model", which records the ratio of a country's international transactions to its gross national product. This type of analysis is a reflection of the research of the 1950s and 1960s, which was strongly geared towards quantitative methods. Correlations – in other words the concurrent occurrence of variables and changes in their values – were often viewed as indicators of fundamental patterns of interdependence, when, for example, authors identified a relationship between changes in trade flows and in two types of economic variables – prices and wages. Here, high correlation values were seen as evidence of a high degree of interdependence, while low values supposedly pointed to negligible levels of interdependence – with the result that interdependence fluctuated greatly over the twentieth century as a correlation between variables (on the different methods of measuring interdependence, see Tollison and Willett 1973; Tetrault 1980, 1981; Rosecrance and Gutowitz 1981).[7]

Second, however, these differing findings are connected with the question of *what* is in fact being measured, or what understanding of interdependence underpins the measuring. The remarks above suggest that transactions were often equated with interdependence. It makes more sense, however, to regard the question of whether transactions have increased or decreased as distinct from the issue of increasing or decreasing interdependence (see Katzenstein 1975; also Jones 1995: 91ff.). What is being measured is in fact "interconnectedness" – a concept introduced to the debate on interdependence by Inkeles (1975: 469–470): "Interconnectedness refers to the volume or frequency of communication, interaction, or exchange between two sociocultural systems. It is most often expressed in the exchange of goods and services, i.e., in trade . . ."

Interdependence as conceived by authors such as Morse, Cooper, Keohane and Nye, meanwhile, underlines the *political significance* of empirical interactions (in other words, of interconnectedness) – and thus an aspect that cannot be measured directly. Here, interdependence is *not* dependent on the extent and intensity of transactions: "Thus, *politically* significant interdependence is much higher today than it was during the nineteenth century" (Rosecrance and Stein 1973: 12; my emphasis). I scrutinize this idea in more depth in what follows.

2.2 Political interdependence as conceived by Keohane and Nye

Keohane and Nye introduced the difference between interconnectedness and interdependence through the *criterion of costs*. Only in those cases where interactions impose mutual costs are we dealing with interdependence – though these costs are not necessarily distributed symmetrically among the actors involved in the interrelationship. In cases where interactions impose no significant costs, all we are seeing is mutual interconnectedness (Keohane and Nye 1977: 9). This distinction between interconnectedness and interdependence via the criterion of costs is central to the understanding of the *politics of interdependence* in the work of Keohane and Nye, and we will be looking at this in detail later on (see Section 2.4). What I want to underline at this point is that for Keohane and Nye interdependence is in principle always costly, as it curbs the autonomy of individual states and requires them to adapt. Here, however, the authors introduce a further gradation by distinguishing between two forms of interdependence: *interdependence sensitivity* and *interdependence vulnerability*.

"Sensitivity involves degrees of responsiveness within a policy framework – how quickly do changes in one country bring costly changes in another, and how great are the costly effects?" (Keohane and Nye 1977: 12). So here the authors are referring to costs that arise if there is *no* political counter-reaction by a state affected by changes in another state, that is, if policies remain unchanged. "Vulnerability can be defined as an actor's liability to suffer costs imposed by external events even after policies have been altered" (ibid.: 13). The vulnerability dimension of interdependence thus relates to the costs that must be borne even if political countermeasures are implemented – in other words, if effective adaptations to a changed environment must be made over a given period of time.

The vulnerability dimension of interdependence also has to do with the *relative* availability and cost-intensity of alternative political measures for actors (ibid.: 13). In comparison to interdependence sensitivity, it is the more important dimension of interdependence and has a crucial importance in the work of Keohane and Nye: "Vulnerability interdependence is particularly relevant to analysis of the *structure* of relations" (Keohane and Nye 1975: 370; original emphasis). Again, we will be looking at this idea in more detail later on (see Section 2.4).

Keohane and Nye do not use the concept of interdependence in a teleological sense but as a way of describing how things are at a given time: "Interdependence has normally been defined simply as a condition" (ibid.: 366). Shedding light on a state's potential for action under these "conditions" is what PaI is all about. Keohane and Nye attempt to do this by adopting a critical distance from the realist explanatory model, and they seek to provide explanations on the analytical level of the international system (rather than the level of the state) (Keohane and Nye 1977: viii, 223).

2.3 Realism and "complex interdependence": two ideal types

The appearance of PaI would have caused less consternation if Keohane and Nye had not used a *dual* concept of interdependence: the concept of interdependence as introduced here under Section 2.2 is not identical with "complex interdependence" (for a retrospective survey, see also Keohane and Nye 1987: 730). In PaI, the authors construe complex interdependence as an anti-realist "ideal type" of international system by simply reversing the basic assumptions of realism. The construction of this ideal type must therefore be understood fundamentally as part of the critique of the realist explanatory model that the authors wished to pursue through PaI, a critique whose core arguments I examine in what follows.

According to Keohane and Nye, realist explanatory models of international politics are essentially based on three assumptions (1977: 23–24): (1) states are understood as self-contained units and as the only important or dominant actors in world politics; (2) power is the most efficacious instrument of politics; the exercise or threat of force is the most effective means of exercising power; (3) and there is a clear hierarchy of goals in international politics: issues of military security (high politics) hold sway over goals relating to the economic sphere or social issues (low politics).

If we "reverse" these three basic assumptions, then, for Keohane and Nye we have the ideal type of complex interdependence (ibid.: 24–37):

1. States are not self-contained units and they are not the only actors in world politics. Alongside classical international relations, transnational relations also play an important role, that is, alongside states there exist other influential actors such as multinational companies, banks and groups of scientific experts ("multiple channels of contact").
2. Within interrelationships characterized by complex interdependence, military power is only of secondary importance as an instrument of politics.
3. Goals within international politics are not ordered in line with a pre-given hierarchy: military security is no more *a priori* superordinate than goals relating to the sphere of welfare. Instead there exists a plethora of different "issue areas".

As an ideal type, complex interdependence does *not* reflect political reality; it is a stopgap analytical heuristic, or as the authors put it, the outcome of a "thought experiment" (Keohane and Nye 1987: 737). For Keohane and Nye, "real situations" in international politics generally fall somewhere *between* the two extremes. So complex interdependence is sometimes closer to reality than the realist model: if this is the case, then for these authors "traditional" – in other words, realist – explanations are no longer applicable. According to them, having assessed the extent to which a given situation is characterized either by realist assumptions or complex interdependence, the researcher must decide *which* explanatory model she wishes to apply (Keohane and Nye 1977: 24).

Nonetheless, in PaI, Keohane and Nye conclude that "the conditions of complex interdependence increasingly characterize world politics *in some important issue areas* and *among some countries*" (ibid.: 223; my emphasis). They discern something like complex interdependence *in the relations among the Western industrialized states* (the OECD countries) and especially in the *issue areas of global economic and ecological interdependence* (ibid.: 225–226).

Alongside a focus limited to the Western industrialized states, the distinction between issue areas of world politics such as security, economy and environment takes on a crucial importance. Keohane and Nye assume the validity and applicability of both explanatory models (realism and complex interdependence) in understanding specific issue areas. Under conditions of complex interdependence, however, international politics is fundamentally characterized by *different political processes* than on realist assumptions.

Here, "political processes" is the answer to the question of how a state's power resources are "translated" into power, meaning control over political outcomes. In the realist explanatory model, a state's overall power advantage directly determines the outcomes of international politics. Under conditions of complex interdependence, meanwhile, Keohane and Nye conclude that there is a discontinuity between the overall distribution of power and political outcomes in specific situations of negotiation. The more closely a situation or structure approximates to complex interdependence, the less a state's overall power structure can be "translated" into political results within specific issue areas; this is because *interdependence "works" as an intervening variable* between power resources, on the one hand, and power as the control over political outcomes, on the other (see Keohane and Nye 1977: 29–37):

1 Under these conditions, it is more difficult for militarily strong states to use their general dominance to exercise control in political fields in which they do not occupy a superior position. So the distribution of power and the degree of vulnerability *in specific issue areas* become an important part of the analysis of political processes.
2 The potential for agenda-setting in international politics changes. Increased interdependence leads to a situation in which groups within a state or transnational actors have the ability to politicize certain problems that were previously regarded as domestic in character; these now become components of an international agenda.
3 Under these conditions, international organizations take on a new and significant role within international politics. International organizations exercise influence on the setting of agendas, stimulate the formation of coalitions and function as arenas for articulation of the interests of generally weaker states.[8]

2.4 The politics of interdependence

Power and interdependence

In PaI, Keohane and Nye are centrally concerned with the question of how power can be exercised by states under conditions of interdependence (hence the title, *Power and Interdependence*). They introduce interdependence – which approximates to complex interdependence to a greater or lesser extent – as an intervening variable. This variable "operates" between power, as the independent variable, and the outcomes of the political process as the dependent variable. As a "condition", this variable changes the context and structure of international negotiations. The problem for politics arises from the fact that interdependence is always "costly": it limits states' capacity for autonomous political action. With respect to monetary and currency policy, tax policy, the regulation of businesses and the implementation of redistributive programmes, states can no longer act autonomously.

Interdependence thus requires states to adapt to changed circumstances.[9] In other words, because of its *cost effect*, interdependence generates a classical *problem of political strategy*. Attempts to evade or pass on to others the costs of adaptation are part and parcel of interdependence. So the interests of individual states consist in distribution of the costs and benefits resulting from international exchange to their advantage. PaI is based on the assumption of rational actors acting egoistically in light of their own self-interest and cost-benefit calculations. As a consequence of interdependence, these actors must now operate under changed circumstances, because interdependence imposes restrictions on the realization of their selfish self-interest. Pal thus occupies the fraught conceptual space between the state-centred perspective of realism and the understanding that there now exists a world economy that eludes the control of individual states, a world economy that therefore requires new forms of political organization. Under these conditions, the potential for power and thus the potential to take effective action arise from the fact that specific political fields are generally characterized by *asymmetric interdependence*. In other words, states are vulnerable to differing degrees in the various issue areas, so the costs of adaptation are not distributed equally among the actors involved in an interrelationship. Interdependence vulnerability thus entails a strategic dimension: states in positions of relative invulnerability (*relative*, that is, to the other actors involved in the interrelationship) have the potential to manipulate the international system in order to realize their self-interest. They will attempt to use asymmetric interdependence as a source of power and to influence international organizations to their advantage. For Keohane and Nye, this problem exists on two levels:

1 "From the *foreign policy standpoint*, the problem facing individual governments is how to benefit from international exchange while maintaining as much autonomy as possible".
2 "From the *perspective of the international system*, the problem is how to generate and maintain a mutual beneficial pattern of cooperation in the face of competing efforts by governments (and nongovernmental actors) to manipulate the system for their own benefit" (Keohane and Nye 1987: 730; my emphasis).

By this point, Pal's politically motivated epistemological interest is clearly apparent: Keohane and Nye are explicitly concerned to use their research to help *optimize American foreign policy* in view of the "autonomy illusion" apparent at least since the early 1970s. This they seek to do by providing an alternative form of academic policy advice to replace the formerly dominant realist model (Keohane and Nye 1975: 359, 1977: vii–viii, 242).

Keohane and Nye begin by stating that "[u]nilateral leadership under the conditions of complex interdependence is . . . unlikely to be effective" (1977: 232) and consider the potential of a neoisolationist strategy.[10] In view of the costs, however, they reject this strategy, pointing out that there is another way of reducing one's interdependence vulnerability: "Reducing one's vulnerability to external events can be part of a neoisolationist strategy; but it can also be one element in a *strategy of policy coordination and international leadership*" (ibid.: 239; my emphasis). Keohane and Nye distinguish between three basic "types" of "international leadership" – hegemony, unilateralism and multilateralism – and in light of the loss of American hegemony and the infeasibility of unilateralism under conditions of interdependence, their scholarly recommendation is that the best way to respond to interdependence is with a policy of multilateralism: "[multilateralism] is based on action to induce other states to help stabilize an international regime" (ibid.: 231).

What these authors recommend, then, is that the USA should play an active and leading role in efforts to achieve international policy coordination. This is based on the conviction that international cooperation, and its "embedding" through the formation and stabilization of international organizations and regimes, are a strategy well suited to processing the conflicts arising from interdependence in a cooperative way, one that benefits all parties involved. Keohane, in particular, developed this idea over the course of the 1980s in the shape of regime theory, which is described elsewhere in this volume (see the chapter by Bernhard Zangl). For systematic reasons, however, I shall briefly outline the basic idea below.

Interdependence, cooperation and international institutions

For Keohane and Nye, interrelationships characterized by interdependence, particularly in the fields of economy and ecology, in principle entail the *potential for common gains* through international cooperation (Keohane and Nye 1977: 32). This results from the fact that the realization of individual states' goals depends on decisions made by all states involved in an interdependent relationship (the "collective action problem"). If goals are pursued unilaterally, the production or distribution of a desired good (such as economic prosperity, security or environmental protection) remains suboptimal for all states – an unsatisfactory outcome for everyone. Under certain conditions, therefore, Keohane and Nye believe that interdependence leads to a situation in which cooperation is in the interest of rationally acting "egoists" (Keohane 1984: 8). Here, interdependence is two things: the condition of possibility for cooperation, and the cause of the need for cooperation. Understanding this relational structure is the prerequisite for cooperative behaviour, though the existence of interdependent relationships by no means "automatically" brings cooperation in its wake; it is always linked with certain conditions (for more detail, see the chapter by Bernhard Zangl in this volume).

To sum up, through PaI, Keohane and Nye provided a political scientific foundation for the efforts by Western industrialized states, under the leadership of the USA, to achieve policy coordination through multilateral international institutions in the 1970s and 1980s.

3 Internal theoretical differentiation and further developments

Keohane and Nye understood interdependence as a "condition" – one they introduced as an intervening variable to modify the realist explanatory model of international politics. This idea must be distinguished from conceptions that view interdependence in a teleological or even normative sense and that envisage a transformation of the international system on the basis of basically idealist notions, or that regard such a transformation as desirable (see the classical contributions by Angell (1910), Muir (1933) and Morse (1976), mentioned in the Introduction). As conceptualized by Keohane and Nye, the analysis of interdependence had far-reaching implications for theoretical development in International Relations, because those theoretical "paths" that led to the highly influential *regime theory*, and to *neoliberal institutionalism* were already inherent in such analysis (see the chapter by Bernhard Zangl in this volume). I therefore pay particular attention to these further developments, as well as some other cases of theoretical differentiation, in what follows.

It was primarily ideas about the potential for exercising power within interdependent relationships, that is, the problem of the potential for action and control arising from asymmetric interdependence, along with reflections on international regimes, that had been developed most comprehensively in PaI. In the main, it was these ideas that later regime theorists built on. Interdependence changes the structure and context of international interaction and the analysis of interdependence requires a concept of international negotiations. In light of these two crucial points – that international agendas can be manipulated and that international organizations can modify and regulate the effects of interdependence – it is no surprise that political scientists linked the concept of interdependence with *theories of international negotiations and cooperation*, and developed the *game theoretical variant of regime theory*, particularly studies on *issue linkage* (see, for example, Stein 1980; Haas 1980; Sebenius 1984; Oye 1986) and on the increasing importance of collective goods (see, for example, Benjamin 1980; Ostrom 1990). Through their "preliminary work" in regime theory in the 1970s in PaI, Keohane and Nye made a fundamental contribution to the renaissance in the study of international institutions and thus helped found *neoliberal institutionalism* in IR (see the chapter by Bernhard Zangl in this volume). The "core elements" of the neoliberal-institutionalist research programme, which Keohane and Nye, and Keohane in particular, had already developed by the 1970s and 1980s, include: (1) a new focus on non-state actors, especially international institutions; (2) the nuanced consideration of forms of power beyond military power and threats; (3) theoretical reflection on an international system that is *both* anarchical *and* interdependent; and (4) investigation of conflict and cooperation within international relations, particularly the preconditions for institutionalized cooperation between states and the possibilities and forms of *global governance* (see Milner 2009). Many authors have made reference to these "core elements", developing them further and extending them to new research fields.[11] In theoretical and conceptual terms, the studies produced by Keohane and Nye and particularly by Keohane exercised a huge influence on subsequent generations of IR scholars and led to the establishment of a complex neoliberal research programme. This programme was not of purely theoretical import; given these authors' call for multilateralism and international institutions, it was also of great practical political relevance.

Keohane's recent writings bear witness to the remarkable adaptability of this theoretical and conceptual apparatus to contemporary processes of change in international politics. Concepts such as "globalization", "globalism" and "governance" have become central to it. In PaI itself, Keohane and Nye asked how states can exercise power under conditions of interdependence (see Section 2.4), and this *leitmotif* is also evident in recent works: the core problem is the exercise of power and the potential for political control beyond the state (governance) under conditions of globalization (see, for example, the collection of essays in Keohane (2002) *Power and Governance in a Partially Globalized World*).[12]

But the conceptualization of interdependence was not just the jumping-off point for further developments in theories of cooperation and institutions, but also for studies on the relationship between mutual dependence and international conflicts – as well as examination of the increased potential for conflict and violence within the international system as a result of mutual dependencies more generally. Such reflections were a key source of stimulus for empirical studies of the old liberal thesis that international trade relations have a pacifying effect (*pax mercatoria*). At issue here are the causalities involved in the relationship between economic interdependence and conflictual political relations between states (see, for example, Gasiorowski and Polachek 1982; Mansfield 1994; Barbieri 1996, 2002; Copeland 1996; Crescenzi 2005; see also the contributions in Mansfield and Pollins 2003). Empirical studies lend support to the liberal assumption of a fundamental "trade–peace linkage" within international relations and its "extended effect" of pacifying the international system (see, for example, Maoz 2009: 234). The nature of this relationship requires further clarification, however, in that it cannot be shown to apply to all states equally. The robustness of the findings fluctuates depending on the type of political system (Gelpi and Grieco 2008). Analyses of interdependence show a particularly strong relationship between interdependence and peace in the relations between *democracies*: "Trade among democratic states may shift the decision to use military force from the category of 'very unlikely' to the category of 'virtually unthinkable' " (ibid.: 30). Economic interdependence is thus an important part of the theoretical explanation of interdemocratic peace, albeit secondary to the factor of "democracy" (see also the chapter by Andreas Hasenclever in this volume).

This also applies to studies of *international institutions' contribution to peace*. The underlying thesis here is that international relations are being increasingly "civilized" through the work of international institutions. Some authors have postulated that there is a connection between interdependence (and the need for cooperation to which it gives rise) and the decline in military force as a means of dealing with conflict within the international system (see, for example, Efinger *et al.* 1990: 279; de Wilde 1991). But the conclusion that international institutions have tended to reduce violence within international relations requires qualification: it is chiefly relations between the Western industrialized states that have been "civilized". This finding applies to that group of states whose relations Keohane and Nye described in PaI as characterized by increasingly complex interdependence, and whose relations – following the logic of PaI – unsurprisingly entail a particularly high degree of regulation through a plethora of institutions. Again, this touches on recent research on the so-called "democratic peace" (or "OECD peace"); such research attempts to explain the relationships between states' internal democratic character, their external incorporation into international institutions and the finding that their relations are free of violence as a means of conflict resolution (see especially Russett and Oneal 2001; for an in-depth treatment, see the chapter by Andreas Hasenclever in this volume). In this connection, it is regrettable that the concept of "complex interdependence" was underdeveloped and undervalued in PaI.

The neglect of "complex interdependence" has had another regrettable result. Keohane and Nye missed the opportunity to produce an adequate theory of the role of transnational actors such as multinational companies and other social actors operating across borders. Fundamentally, this is a *problem of the analytical level* of PaI. In their explanations, Keohane and Nye remain on the level of the international system and espouse a state-centred perspective which, like realism, regards states as the dominant actors and as self-contained units. So it is inherent in the logic of this systemic perspective that it remains focused on international institutions (or organizations) as the only theoretically relevant non-state actors (see also Milner 2009). Keohane and Nye thus fail to consider how states are differentiated internally, despite the fact that they consider transnational relations, and thus the actions taken by social actors, as crucial to the character of international interdependence; in other words, the very conceptualization of "complex interdependence" in fact does away with the strict division between the internal sphere of a state and the systemic dimension. The focus on the systemic level cannot explain how state interests come about, for example, through the influence of social actors, transgovernmental networks and policy communities; conversely, neither can it bring out the implications of an international politics of interdependence for the internal life of states. Studies of interdependence have only managed to produce empirically fruitful findings when they have departed from the systemic level and examined the mutual dependency of a limited number of states in specific political fields, taking account of the interplay of domestic, transnational and international processes (Kohler-Koch 1994: 224). Other authors have highlighted this problem and extended the analytical focus to the level of the state (see, for example, Gourevitch 1978; Katzenstein 1978, 1985; see also the contributions in Milner and Moravcsik 2009). This reveals the general impossibility of developing the concept of interdependence further without moving away from the systemic level. In this context, I should mention that when it comes to the issue of levels of analysis, Keohane and Nye clearly "lost sight" of some of their own key insights, which were still of central importance in their studies on transnational relations or the "world politics paradigm" written before PaI. As late as 1970, they still aimed "to transcend the 'level-of analysis problem' both by broadening the conception of actors to include transnational actors and by conceptually breaking down the 'hard shell' of the nation-state" (Nye and Keohane 1970b: 380).

Through their studies produced in the 1970s, Keohane and Nye ultimately made an important contribution to the development of International Political Economy (IPE) as a new academic discipline (see also the chapter by Hans-Jürgen Bieling in this volume, and Moravcsik 2009). At the same time, they have been criticized for focusing so strongly on economic interdependence that they have neglected aspects of strategic and institutional interdependence. Maoz (2009, 2011) attempts to remedy a number of deficiencies found in the original concept of interdependence by developing a multidimensional model of interdependence anchored in a social network approach. His model cross-cuts analytical levels, integrates aspects of economic, strategic and institutional interdependence and attempts to capture how these aspects impact on the tendency for conflict between states and how they affect the level of the international system as a whole. Most importantly, Maoz's work is rooted in a different ontological perspective on international politics compared to that of Keohane and Nye: a focus on *social processes* instead of on states in an interstate system is key to his network approach. Processes are understood "as *emergent structures* of a system of relationships among people, groups, institutions, and nations" (Maoz 2011: 6, my emphasis). Interdependence is thus fundamentally rooted in social processes that may be studied through network analysis.

4 Critical observations on the concept of interdependence

There are other reasons to problematize the concept of "complex interdependence" that cannot be addressed through "further development". Keohane and Nye leave themselves open to the criticism that their conceptualization is *tautological*. In terms of the implications of interdependence for state action, they argue that a high degree of mutual dependence leads to a changed view of foreign policy goals and to a shift in the choice of political means. They mention the new importance of welfare as opposed to security goals, the now secondary significance of military force as an instrument of policy and the increasing importance of individual political fields (see Section 2.3). Yet these very changes are already taken as givens in their characterization of the international system. In other words, in the work of Keohane and Nye, the goals and instruments of state policies appear as *both* characteristics and consequences of complex interdependence, as they themselves later admit:

> Since we define complex interdependence in terms of the goals and instruments of state policy, any general arguments about how goals and instruments are affected by the degree to which a situation approximates complex interdependence or realism will be tautological.
>
> (Keohane and Nye 1987: 738)

It was impossible to develop an internally consistent and methodologically viable alternative to realism on this basis. Keohane and Nye themselves aptly summarize the results of their work:

> Ironically . . . the result of our synthetic analysis in *Power and Interdependence*, and of subsequent work such as Keohane's *After Hegemony*, has been to broaden neorealism and provide it with new concepts rather than to articulate a coherent alternative theoretical framework for the study of world politics.
>
> (ibid.: 733)

For *(neo-)realists*, the problem with PaI is not just its inability to provide an alternative, but its failure to deliver any well-founded critique of realism. For such critics, this was due in significant part to the highly simplified "straw man" version of realism evoked by Keohane and Nye (see, for example, Michalak 1979: 145–150; Holsti 1978: 525). Kenneth Waltz, the leading exponent of neorealism, has tackled the problem of interdependence in depth. On the international level, he describes interdependence as a "myth" (Waltz 1970; also Mearsheimer 2001). His explanatory model sees international order as produced through interaction between functionally equal units (states), which are concerned chiefly with their own security within the self-help system and which differ solely in terms of their "capabilities" (see the chapter by Niklas Schörnig in this volume). For Waltz, however, interdependence can exist only if there is a division of labour or specialization among the units. Following the logic of the neorealist explanatory model, then, there can be very little interdependence within the international system. Fundamentally, Waltz views interdependence as a relationship whose termination would be costly. For him, then, states' unequal capabilities are further evidence of the negligible degree of interdependence. The most powerful states within the system can very rapidly achieve economic autarky and thus independence: "high inequality among like units *is* low interdependence" (Waltz 1970: 207; original emphasis). The economic policies of the powerful states do have significant effects on other states, but this applies only marginally in reverse. For Waltz, then, there is no politically significant interdependence, but rather an unequal distribution of independence and dependence within international relations (ibid.: 214). For him, the "myth" of interdependence masks the power relations existing within the international system.

As set out below, a whole series of criticisms assail *the lack of a "theory of interdependence*" (Kohler-Koch 1990: 119; Zürn 2002: 235).

How does interdependence come about? It may seem surprising that this question has not appeared before in this section on criticisms, but Keohane and Nye are quite unable to answer it. The question of the driving forces and underlying causes of interdependence (as well as globalization) is closely bound up with the wider debate on modernity. What we often find here are vague references to the impersonal "forces of modernization". From this perspective, interdependence is the result of a process driven by technology, economy and communication media (see also Morse 1970). Contrasting with this are perspectives that identify the key sources of intensifying interdependence as goal-directed, instrumental action taken by human actors (rather than impersonal "forces" or "processes") – and thus political decisions informed by actors' political and economic interests.

From the perspective adopted by Keohane and Nye, mutual dependencies are a "given" brought about by "forces of modernization" in a way that remains unexplained (Keohane and Nye 1977: 227–228). What matters is merely to explain how it is possible, under these conditions, to maintain the potential for political control or come up with new forms of political control. The concept of interdependence developed by Keohane and Nye in the 1970s *begins* with an ahistorical perspective (see also de Wilde 1991). So reflection on the causes and driving forces of interdependence plays no part in their work, and this leaves it open to criticism. This applies primarily to their neglect of the role of the state and, closely bound up with this, the question of the extent to which interdependence can be shaped through political action – as well as the charge that their perspective is mere ideology.

Edward Morse (1972: 135ff.) refers to the fundamental interplay between "forces of modernization" and the *political will* to intensify international exchange, such as efforts by the industrialized states to lower and dismantle barriers to economic exchange. In the sphere of trade, this occurs through multilateral negotiating rounds within the framework of the

General Agreement on Tariffs and Trade (GATT)/World Trade Organization (WTO), as well as through agreements establishing free trade areas, customs unions and common markets. Here, interdependence becomes largely a function of two crucial characteristics of modernity: the nation state system and industrial capitalism. Fundamentally, this perspective relates to the political decisions that create the political-legal framework within which the "forces of modernization" can take effect – and thus to the role of the state in a process driven by technology and economics (see Jones 1995: 48). Keohane and Nye do not even begin to consider the role of the state in this process; in their theory, international interdependence remains "external" to the state (Strange 1994: 20–21).

I shall briefly illustrate this interplay between political decisions and the "forces of modernization" by considering the rise of multinational companies and the integration of financial and capital markets. As Gilpin states:

> From this perspective the multinational corporation exists as a transnational actor today because it is consistent with the political interest of the world's dominant power, the United States. This argument does not deny the analyses of economists who argue that the multinational corporation is a response to contemporary technological and economic developments. The argument is rather that these economic and technological factors have been able to exercise their profound effects because the United States – sometimes with the cooperation of other states and sometimes over their opposition – has *created the necessary political framework.*
>
> (1970: 54; my emphasis)

With reference to the sphere of financial and capital markets, Susan Strange points out that even in these cases technological developments – such as new information and communication technologies – do not take effect automatically or immediately (see Strange 1994: 133ff.). What was first required were political decisions or non-decisions taken by the governments of leading Western industrialized states in the past; these made the global integration of financial and capital markets possible in the first place (see Strange 1986; also Walter 1991; Helleiner 1994).[13] Here the "realities" of interdependence within the international political economy are viewed as consequences of contemporary policies as well as past political decisions. This entails a change in the role of the state as such. To comprehend this change requires a "theory of the state" (according to authors such as Cerny 1997). This is a demand that interdependence analysis is unable to meet, simply because of its systemic focus, and it remained unaddressed as such analysis underwent further development (see Section 3). The academic discourse on the changed role of the state is now central to the debate on globalization and governance carried on since the 1990s. This debate impressively illustrates the large number of problems common to interdependence analysis and studies on globalization with respect to the state's diminishing capacity to take effective action and shape events (for a detailed analysis, see Jones 1995 and Zürn 2002; also Keohane and Nye 2001: Chapter 10; see also Section 3). The growing capacity of transnational economic actors to take effective action and shape events (in comparison with the state) has been discussed under the heading of the "retreat of the state" (Strange 1996). Here, "retreat" primarily means a change in the role or functioning of the state; Cerny (1997), for example, sees a transition from the (interventionist) "welfare state" to the "competition state". The "competition state" (also known as the neoliberal state), which privileges deregulation and privatization, is one that increasingly makes room for the free play of market forces, and thus "creates" interdependence. Much the same applies to the role of international institutions, which Keohane and Nye discuss merely as a means of "managing" interdependence and thus as the "results" of the cooperative impulses engendered by mutual dependencies. But these institutions in turn become factors – if not in fact actors in the case of international organizations – that help intensify interdependence (as occurred in the field of global trade through the GATT, established after the Second World War, or the policies of the IMF). Such bodies create a kind of "institutional interdependence" and thus another form of *interdependence of political origin* (Cooper 1972: 163; also Morse 1969: 322).

Keohane and Nye theoretically adumbrate a "problem-solving strategy", one based on a policy of interdependence geared towards international cooperation in specific issue areas. But this concept distorts the question of political actors' capacity to shape events in a more far-reaching sense that transcends political fields, namely with respect to the *politics of global order*, and this blinds us to existing relations of power and domination within the international system (see, for example, Cox 1981). In concrete terms, this relates to the role of the USA as the dominant economic and military force behind the construction of a new political and economic framework for the relations between states following the Second World War – and the transformation of this framework since the 1970s and 1980s. For critical approaches within International Relations – such as neo-Gramscian perspectives – the dominant role of the USA is apparent in its influence on international institutions, over which it is claimed to have erected a global "superstructure of control" (van der Pijl 1989: 161; see also the chapter by Andreas Bieler and Adam D. Morton in this volume). References to interdependence – and here neorealist critics and critical perspectives converge – are thus suspected of being mere ideology: "The word 'interdependence' subtly obscures the inequalities of national capability, pleasingly points to a reciprocal dependence, and strongly suggests that all states are playing the same game" (Waltz 1970: 220).

We may understand the politics of interdependence as the politics of global order, and not just as a matter of the "management" of specific issue areas in the relations between the Western industrialized states under conditions of complex interdependence. On this premise it is reasonable to examine the consequences of the politics of interdependence for the overall structure of the international system. This includes the distribution of power and influence and prospects for participation, the distribution of gains and losses, and above all the way in which conflict and violence in the international system may be *brought about by* the politics of interdependence. Here, researchers in the *dependencia* school refer not to interdependence but to *dependence* as a form of international interdependence. Dependence is essentially exploitative and structurally disadvantageous for dependent states, chiefly those of the South (see, for example, Holsti 1978: 517; see also the chapters by Andreas Nölke and Michael Heinrich in this volume).

So far, research on interdependence – along with its further developments within the framework of regime theory and neoliberal institutionalism – has been generally ignorant of these issues. Against this background, Keohane and Nye's (e.g. 2001: 235–248) notion that interdependence analysis can provide a scientifically grounded source of guidance for political strategy in a globalized world seems very much open to question and in need of critical scrutiny. It stands to reason that the dramatically changing power-political parameters of the contemporary international system, particularly as a result of the growing global political and economic significance of China and India, or the "rise" of Asia as a world region, will change the parameters of any "politics of interdependence" that puts its faith in institutionalized global cooperation. The failure of the most recent global negotiations on climate change held in Copenhagen (2009), Cancún (2010), Durban (2011) and Doha (2012) is impressive testimony to this. And given the failure of the WTO's Doha Round, the urgent need to reform the World Bank and the IMF laid bare by the financial crisis, and the UN's inability to resolve conflicts in Darfur or more recently in Syria, commentators increasingly refer to a crisis of multilateral institutions. It is becoming clear that if we want to get to grips with cooperative behaviour by states and successful management of international politics by institutions, we will require different rationales and arguments than those provided by state-centric, rational institutionalist approaches with their cost-benefit analyses and recommendations for a different power-political politics of interdependence.

5 Notes

1 Osiander (1996) points to the fundamental connection between the increasing interdependence of states and the development of the (Western) theory of International Relations. On this view, international interdependence is quite simply a prerequisite for the emergence of International Relations theories, as the need for intensive theoretical reflection on international relations only arises when people experience international dependencies as socially and politically significant (whether this involves welfare gains through trade, or the awareness of military threats to security). This required the historical development of the nation state and its ongoing international integration within the modern European state system (the Westphalian system).

2 Contemporary efforts to deal politically with the world financial and sovereign debt crisis as well as European political efforts to contain the Euro crisis are also characterized by severe conflicts over the "best" coordination mechanisms and forms of cooperation (e.g. with respect to the need for global economic governance and how best to deal with the threats to the European currency arising from the looming sovereign default in Greece and potentially in other European states as well), the type and extent of measures to regulate banking and finance market reform, and different approaches in different nations (e.g. in the adoption of austerity policies or other measures). Only recently has disunity on the question of how best to move away from debt-financed economic policies and how to avoid "currency wars" led to discord in the run-up to the G20 Summit held in Moscow in February 2013 and the G7 Summit in Aylesbury in May 2013. Inter-European relationships have also suffered in connection with the search for European solutions to the crisis.

3 Such as the 1973 "Watergate scandal" in the USA and the 1974 "Guillaume affair" in West Germany.

4 Efforts to address the crisis through global economic coordination are now being pursued not only in the G7/G8 but also within the framework of the G20.

5 Nye and Keohane conclude that transnational relations – that is, the sum total of cross-border contacts, coalitions and interactions by actors such as multinational companies, trade unions and expert networks – are increasingly diminishing the power of national governments (Nye and Keohane 1970a: xi).

6 Readers looking for an introduction to the debate on interdependence in the 1970s and 1980s are advised to take a look at the journals *Foreign Policy, Foreign Affairs, International Organization* and *World Politics* (whose foci correspond to the levels identified above); it was within their pages that the debate was mostly carried on.

7 Critics of such methods point out that the data is mostly obtained on the basis of individual states or states in bilateral relationships (see Tetrault 1980, 1981; for a contemporary critique of the measurement of the dyadic effects of interdependence, see Gelpi and Grieco 2008: 18; Maoz 2009: 224) and that these methods fail to record qualitative changes in international transactions (such as the 'replacement' of trade flows as the most important type of international exchange by international capital flows; all that is measured in this case is a decline in trade flows. See Morse 1969: 318).

8 Keohane and Nye come to these conclusions by means of case studies carried out with the help of four structural models. The case studies relate to the issue areas of international maritime and monetary policy, and bilateral relations between the USA and Canada and Australia respectively. I am unable to delve further into these studies here. See Keohane and Nye (1977: Chapters 3 and 4–7).

9 "Autonomy" means governments' capacity to formulate and realize national economic goals that diverge from those of other states. Conceptually, national autonomy differs from "economic autarky" and "political sovereignty". See Cooper (1968: 4–5).

10 In order to reduce vulnerability with respect to oil over the short term, they consider the potential of import restrictions, diversification of supply sources, the establishment of an oil reserve and plans for rationing in the case of shortages; over the long term, they call for investment in research on alternative energy sources. See Keohane and Nye (1977: 239).

11 Milner (2009) provides a good overview of neoliberal institutionalism. Important studies in the context of the neoliberal-institutionalist research programme that build on the core ideas of Keohane and Nye and Keohane include *Legalization and World Politics* (Goldstein *et al.* 2001), *The Rational Design of International Institutions* (Koremos *et al.* 2003) and *Delegation and Agency in International Organizations* (Hawkins *et al.* 2006); cf. Milner (2009: 3).

12 Keohane himself summarizes the further theoretical development of his programme "from interdependence and institutions to globalization and governance" (Keohane 2002: 1) in terms of four developmental stages and trends: (1) "from interdependence to institutional theory"; (2) "from institutions to law"; (3) "from interdependence to globalism" (the concept of "thick globalism"); and (4) "from institutions to governance" (Keohane 2002: 1–24). See also the Festschrift for Keohane edited by Milner and Moravcsik (2009).

13 The failure of the state to regulate financial markets is one of the key causal complexes being discussed in connection with the contemporary global and European financial crisis.

6 Bibliography and recommended reading

6.1 *Primary texts*

Cooper, Richard N. 1968: *The Economics of Interdependence: Economic Policy in the Atlantic Community*. New York: McGraw-Hill.

Keohane, Robert O. 2002: *Power and Governance in a Partially Globalized World*. New York: Routledge.

Keohane, Robert O. and Nye, Joseph S. 2001: *Power and Interdependence*, 3rd edn. New York: Longman [includes the original text from 1977, the chapter "Second Thoughts on Theory and Policy" added in 1989 and the chapter "Globalism and the Information Age" added in 2001].

Morse, Edward L. 1976: *Modernization and the Transformation of International Relations*. New York: The Free Press.

6.2 *Secondary texts*

de Wilde, Jaap 1991: *Saved from Oblivion: Interdependence Theory in the First Half of the 20th Century. A Study on the Causality between War and Complex Interdependence*. Aldershot: Dartmouth.

Jones, Barry R. J. 1995: *Globalisation and Interdependence in the International Political Economy: Rhetoric and Reality*. London: Pinter Publishers.

Milner, Helen and Moravcsik, Andrew (eds) 2009: *Power, Interdependence, and Non-State Actors in World Politics*. Princeton, NJ: Princeton University Press.

Zürn, Michael 2002: From Interdependence to Globalization, in Carlsnaes, Walter, Risse, Thomas and Simmons, Beth A. (eds) *Handbook of International Relations*. London: Sage, pp. 235–254.

6.3 *Other texts*

Angell, Norman 1910: *The Great Illusion: A Study of the Relation of Military Power to National Advantage*. London: Heinemann.

Barbieri, Katherine 1996: Economic Interdependence: A Path to Peace or a Source of Conflict?, *Journal of Peace Research* 33: 29–49.

Barbieri, Katherine 2002: *The Liberal Illusion: Does Trade Promote Peace?* Ann Arbor, MI: University of Michigan Press.

Benjamin, Roger 1980: *The Limits of Politics: Collective Goods and Political Change in Postindustrial Societies*. Chicago: University of Chicago Press.

Cerny, Philip G. 1997: Paradoxes of the Competition State: The Dynamics of Political Globalization, *Government and Opposition* 32(2): 251–274.

Cooper, Richard N. 1972: Economic Interdependence and Foreign Policy in the Seventies, *World Politics* 24(2): 159–181.

Copeland, Dale C. 1996: Economic Interdependence and War: A Theory of Trade Expectations, *International Security* 20: 5–41.

Cox, Robert 1981: Social Forces, States and World Orders: Beyond International Relations Theory, *Millennium* 10(2); 126–155.

Crescenzi, Mark J. C. 2005: *Economic Interdependence and Conflict in World Politics*. Lanham, MD: Lexington.

Delaisi, Francis 1971 [1925]: *Political Myths and Economic Realities*. Washington, DC: Kennikat Press.

Deutsch, Karl and Eckstein, Alexander 1961: National Industrialization and the Declining Share of the International Economic Sector: 1850–1959, *World Politics* 13(2): 267–299.

Deutsch, Karl *et al.* 1967: *France, Germany and the Western Alliance: A Study of Elite Attitudes on European Integration and World Politics*. New York: Scribner.

Efinger, Manfred, Rittberger, Volker, Wolf, Klaus Dieter, and Zürn, Michael 1990: Internationale Regime und internationale Politik, in Rittberger, Volker (ed.) *Theorien der Internationalen Beziehungen*. PVS-Sonderheft 21. Opladen: Westdeutscher Verlag, pp. 263–285.

Gasiorowski, Mark and Polachek, Solomon W. 1982: Conflict and Interdependence: East–West Trade Linkages in the Era of Detente, *Journal of Conflict Resolution* 26: 709–729.

Gelpi, Christopher F. and Grieco, Joseph M. 2008: Democracy, Interdependence, and the Sources of the Liberal Peace, *Journal of Peace Research* 45(1): 17–36.

Gilpin, Robert 1970: *The Politics of Transnational Economic Relations*, in Keohane, Robert O. and Nye, Joseph S. (eds) *Transnational Relations and World Politics*. Cambridge, MA: Harvard University Press, pp. 48–69.

Gourevitch, Peter 1978: The Second Image Reversed. The International Sources of Domestic Politics, *International Organization* 32(4): 881–912.

Haas, Ernst B. 1980: Why Collaborate? Issue Linkage and International Regimes, *World Politics* 32(3): 357–405.

Hasenclever, Andreas 2002: The Democratic Peace Meets International Institutions, *Zeitschrift für Internationale Beziehungen* 9(1): 75–111.

Helleiner, Eric 1994: *States and the Reemergence of Global Finance: From Bretton Woods to the 1990s*. Ithaca, NY: Cornell University Press.

Holsti, Kalevi J. 1978: A New International Politics? Diplomacy in Complex Interdependence, *International Organization* 32(2): 513–530.

Holsti, Kalevi J. 1991: *Peace and War: Armed Conflicts and International Order, 1648–1989*. Cambridge: Cambridge University Press.

Inkeles, Alex 1975: The Emerging Social Structure of the World, *World Politics* 27(4): 467–495.

Katzenstein, Peter J. 1975: International Interdependence: Some Long-Term Trends and Recent Changes, *International Organization* 29(4): 1021–1034.

Katzenstein, Peter J. (ed.) 1978: *Between Power and Plenty: Foreign Economic Policies of Advanced Industrialized States*. Madison, WI: University of Wisconsin Press.

Katzenstein, Peter J. 1985: *Small States in World Markets*. Ithaca, NY: Cornell University Press.

Keohane, Robert O. 1984: *After Hegemony: Cooperation and Discord in the World Political Economy*. Princeton, NJ: Princeton University Press.

Keohane, Robert O. 2002: *Power and Governance in a Partially Globalized World*. London: Routledge.

Keohane, Robert O. and Nye, Joseph S. 1975: International Interdependence and Integration, in Greenstein, Fred I. and Polsby, Nelson W. (eds) *International Politics: Handbook of Political Science*, Vol. 8. Reading, MA: Addison-Wesley, pp. 363–414.

Keohane, Robert O. and Nye, Joseph S. 1977: Power and Interdependence, in *World Politics in Transition*. Boston: Little, Brown and Co.

Keohane, Robert O. and Nye, Joseph S. 1987: Power and Interdependence Revisited, *International Organization* 41(4): 725–753.

Kohler-Koch, Beate 1990: Interdependenz, in Rittberger, Volker (ed.) *Theorien der Internationalen Beziehungen*. PVS-Sonderheft 21. Opladen: Westdeutscher Verlag, pp. 110–129.

Kohler-Koch, Beate 1994: Interdependenz-Analyse, in Boeckh, Andreas (ed.) *Internationale Beziehungen. Lexikon der Politik*, Vol. 6. Munich: C.H. Beck, pp. 221–225.

Kuhn, Hans W. 1962: Begriff und Problem der weltpolitischen Interdependenz, in Oberndörfer, Dieter (ed.) *Wissenschaftliche Politik. Eine Einführung in Grundfragen ihrer Tradition und Theorie*. Freiburg: Rombach, pp. 237–250.

Mansfield, Edward D. 1994: *Power, Trade, and War*. Princeton, NJ: Princeton University Press.

Mansfield, Edward D. and Pollins, Brian M. (eds) 2003: *Economic Interdependence and International Conflict: New Perspectives on an Enduring Debate*. Ann Arbor, MI: The University of Michigan Press.

Maoz, Zeev 2009: The Effects of Strategic and Economic Interdependence on International Conflict across Levels of Analysis, *American Journal of Political Science* 53(1): 223–240.

Maoz, Zeev 2011: *Networks of Nations: The Evolution, Structure, and Impact of Networks, 1816–2001*. Cambridge: Cambridge University Press.

Mearsheimer, John 2001: *The Tragedy of Great Power Politics*. New York: Norton.

Michalak, Stanley J. 1979: Theoretical Perspectives for Understanding International Interdependence, *World Politics* 32(1): 136–150.

Milner, Helen 2009: Power, Interdependence, and Non-State Actors in World Politics: Research Frontiers, in Milner, Helen and Moravcsik, Andrew (eds) *Power, Interdependence, and Non-State Actors in World Politics*. Princeton, NJ: Princeton University Press, pp. 3–30.

Milner, Helen and Moravcsik, Andrew (eds) 2009 *Power, Interdependence, and Non-State Actors in World Politics*. Princeton, NJ: Princeton University Press.

Moravcsik, Andrew 2009: Robert Keohane: Political Theorist, in Milner, Helen and Moravcsik, Andrew (eds) *Power, Interdependence, and Non-State Actors in World Politics*. Princeton, NJ: Princeton University Press, pp. 243–263.

Morse, Edward L. 1969: The Politics of Interdependence, *International Organization* 23(2): 311–326.

Morse, Edward L. 1970: Transnational Economic Processes, in Keohane, Robert O. and Nye, Joseph S. (eds) *Transnational Relations and World Politics*. Cambridge, MA: Harvard University Press, pp. 23–47.

Morse, Edward L. 1972: Crisis Diplomacy, Interdependence, and the Politics of International Economic Relations, *World Politics* 24(Suppl.): 123–150

Muir, Ramsay [1933] 1971: *The Interdependent World and Its Problems*. Washington, DC: Kennikat Press.

Nau, Henry R. 1979: From Integration to Interdependence: Gains, Losses, and Continuing Gaps, *International Organization* 33(1): 119–147.

Nye, Joseph S. and Keohane, Robert O. 1970a: Transnational Relations and World Politics: An Introduction, in Keohane, Robert O. and Nye, Joseph S. (eds) *Transnational Relations and World Politics*. Cambridge, MA: Harvard University Press, pp. ix–xxi.

Nye, Joseph S. and Keohane, Robert O. 1970b: Transnational Relations and World Politics: A Conclusion, in Keohane, Robert O. and Nye, Joseph S. (eds) *Transnational Relations and World Politics*. Cambridge, MA: Harvard University Press, pp. 371–398.

Osiander, Andreas 1996: The Interdependence of States and the Theory of Interstate Relations. An Enquiry into the History of Political Thought, *Law and the State* 53/54, 42–68.

Ostrom, Elinor 1990: *Governing the Commons: The Evolution of Institutions for Collective Action*. Cambridge: Cambridge University.

Oye, Kenneth A. (ed.) 1986: *Co-operation under Anarchy*. Princeton, NJ: Princeton University Press.

Rosecrance, Richard *et al.* 1977: Whither Interdependence?, *International Organization* 31(3): 425–455.

Rosecrance, Richard and Gutowitz, William 1981: Measuring Interdependence. A Rejoinder, *International Organization* 35(3): 553–556.

Rosecrance, Richard and Stein, Arthur 1973: Interdependence: Myth or Reality? *World Politics* 26(1): 1–27.

Russett, Bruce M. and Oneal, John R. 2001: *Triangulating Peace: Democracy, Interdependence, and International Organizations*. New York: Norton.

Sebenius, James 1984: *Negotiating the Law of the Sea*. Cambridge, MA: Cambridge University Press.

Stein, Arthur A. 1980: The Politics of Linkage, *World Politics* 33(1): 62–81.

Strange, Susan 1970: International Economics and International Relations: A Case of Mutual Neglect, *International Affairs* 46(2): 304–315.

Strange, Susan 1986: *Casino Capitalism*. Manchester: Manchester University Press.

Strange, Susan 1994: *States and Markets*, 2nd edn. London: Pinter.

Strange, Susan 1996: *The Retreat of the State: The Diffusion of Power in the World Economy*. Cambridge: Cambridge University Press.

Tetrault, Mary A. 1980: Measuring Interdependence, *International Organization* 34(3): 429–443.

Tetrault, Mary A. 1981: Measuring Interdependence: A Response, *International Organization* 35(3): 557–560.

Tollison, Robert D. and Willet, Thomas D. 1973: International Integration and the Interdependence of Economic Variables, *International Organization* 27(2): 255–271.

van der Pijl, Kees 1989: Neoliberalism versus Planned Interdependence. Concepts of Control and the Struggle for Hegemony, in Rosenau, James N. and Tromp, Hylke (eds) *Interdependence and Conflict in World Politics*. Aldershot: Avebury, pp. 147–173.

Walter, Andrew 1991: *World Power and World Money: The Role of Hegemony and International Monetary Order*. New York: Harvester Wheatsheaf.

Waltz, Kenneth N. 1970: The Myth of National Interdependence, in Kindleberger, Charles P. (ed.) *The International Corporation*. Cambridge, MA: MIT Press, pp. 205–223.

Zacher, Mark W. and Matthew, Richard A. 1995: Liberal International Theory: Common Threads, Divergent Strands, in Kegley, Charles W. (ed.) *Controversies in International Relations Theory: Realism and the Neoliberal Challenge*. New York: St. Martin's Press, pp. 107–150.

Zürn, Michael 2002: From Interdependence to Globalization, in Carlsnaes, Walter, Risse, Thomas and Simmons, Beth A. (eds) *Handbook of International Relations*. London: Sage, pp. 235–254.

Regime theory

Bernhard Zangl

1 Introduction

Regime theory emerged in the late 1970s and early 1980s through a process of critical reflection on neorealist theories, which dominated International Relations at the time. As an approach that highlights the relevance of institutions in international relations, regime theory comes under the rubric of so-called neo-institutionalism and must be distinguished from the neorealist and liberal schools. Like neorealism, it assumes: (1) that states are the most important actors in international politics; (2) that they operate within the anarchical structures of the international system; and (3) that they rationally pursue their selfishly defined interests. Regime theory, however, comes to conclusions that are quite different from those of the neorealist school and tends to support ideas that are associated with the liberal school in International Relations (Grieco 1988):

1 On the above-mentioned premises, neorealists who support theories of hegemonic stability underline that enduring international cooperation is possible only if a hegemonic power is prepared to enforce such cooperation vis-à-vis other states. Regime theory, meanwhile, underlines that international cooperation is possible beyond hegemonic power structures, if – in light of cross-border complex interdependencies – cooperation lies in the common interest of all states concerned.
2 On the above premises, neorealism also concludes that international institutions are at most an instrument of hegemonic powers. By contrast, regime theory underlines that, beyond hegemonic power structures, international institutions are important because as an instrument they can help the community of states to solve problems of cooperation – resulting from their complex interdependencies – if cooperation is compatible with their interests.

Regime theory, however, did not emerge solely from the academic debate on the prospects for international cooperation implied by those assumptions identified above that are shared both by neorealists and neoinstitutionalists. The origins of regime theory also lie in the basically empirical debate on the alleged decline of US hegemonic power since the 1970s. Because of this decline neorealism expected that existing international institutions such as the General Agreement on Tariffs and Trade (GATT) and the International Monetary Fund (IMF) would become ineffective in the 1970s and 1980s, and that it would be impossible to maintain the corresponding cooperation in international trade and monetary relations. In fact, cooperation through these institutions did appear to diminish: the GATT, which had contributed to the gradual liberalization of trade relations since 1947, found itself faced with a new protectionism, while the IMF had to abandon the fixed exchange rates agreed in 1944 and adopt flexible ones.

Yet despite the upheavals, these institutions not only continued to exist in the 1970s and 1980s, but also managed to maintain international cooperation. Contrary to neorealist expectations, trade relations were not hampered by competitive protectionism and currencies remained freely convertible (Keohane 1984). Despite declining US power, it proved possible to maintain a basically liberal world economic order in which economic integration actually increased. Furthermore, a large number of new international institutions were founded in the 1970s and 1980s. In the context of the East–West conflict, international institutions emerged such as the Conference on Security and Cooperation in Europe (CSCE), the Treaty on the Non-Proliferation of Nuclear Weapons (NPT) and a number of other arms control regimes (SALT, ABMT); these engendered cooperative relations despite the fact that neither the US nor the USSR held a hegemonic position (Rittberger 1990).

It is these new institutionalized agreements that have shaped the particular view of international institutions characteristic of regime theory. Up to the 1970s, in the framework of traditional institutionalism, international institutions, especially international organizations, had been studied mainly in terms of their formal competencies. Within the framework of neo-institutionalism, researchers were now more concerned with analysing the consequences of a number of widely understood institutions – not just organizations (Martin and Simmons 1998). Regime researchers concentrated on specific institutions – on so-called *international regimes* such as the international trade and the international currency regime or the various arms control, environmental or human rights regimes. As opposed to international organizations, international regimes are not actors. Thus, the UN is an international organization, not an international regime. And as opposed to fundamental principles of international order, international regimes are concerned with specific issue areas of international politics. The fundamental principle of state sovereignty should not therefore be confused with an international regime. International regimes, then, are issue area-specific international institutions that cannot operate as independent actors (Keohane 1989). Regimes are defined as area-specific substantive and procedural principles, norms and rules that are agreed by states and regarded as valid.[1] Here, principles are understood as general behavioural standards; norms, on the other hand, are specific behavioural prescriptions, while rules express verifiable behavioural prescriptions that demand specific behaviours from their addressees or that prohibit them from behaving in certain ways.

As a new approach, regime theory first emerged in the 1970s in North America. Its key focus was the field of international political economy. American regime theorists were concerned with understanding international economic cooperation and thus international regimes backing international economic relations. In the 1980s, in addition to Robert O. Keohane (1984, 1989), on whom this chapter will chiefly focus, the outstanding scholars on the subject were Stephen D. Krasner (1983), Kenneth Oye (1986) and John G. Ruggie (see his 1998 essay collection). It was not until the 1980s, however, that regime theory became established in Western Europe. In view of the particular security threats of the Cold War, German researchers especially concentrated less on international economic relations than on international security. For instance, scholars such as Volker Rittberger and Michael Zürn (1990) always viewed regimes partly as instruments for stabilizing international security.

2 The regime theory of Robert O. Keohane

Through his collaborative work with Joseph Nye, *Power and Interdependence* (1977), Robert O. Keohane had already exercised an enduring influence on the analysis of complex interdependencies. With *After Hegemony* (1984), he also had a crucial impact on regime theory.[2] Since the 1970s, he has been extremely influential both within International Relations and International Political Economy. Over the course of an outstanding academic career he has taught at Stanford, Brandeis, Harvard and Duke. Since 2005, he has been professor of International Affairs at Princeton. *After Hegemony* – surely his most influential work alongside *Power and Interdependence* – is well suited to introducing regime theory.

2.1 International regimes and international cooperation

In *After Hegemony*, Keohane tries to demonstrate that enduring international cooperation is possible, despite the above-mentioned "nasty" premises about international politics (Keohane 1984: 4). At the same time, however, he underlines that because of these premises, international cooperation must be considered precarious even if states have a shared interest in international cooperation as a result of cross-border complex interdependencies.

Keohane draws out how difficult it is to achieve international cooperation despite shared interests by referring to the interest constellation of the so-called prisoner's dilemma (ibid.: 67–69).[3] With regard to international politics, this constellation of interests can be illustrated well by the example of the arms race between the US and the USSR during the Cold War. Each superpower had an interest in gaining a security advantage over the other through military expenditure while at the same time each side did all it could to prevent the other from gaining a security advantage. In line with these interests, each continuously enhanced its military capacity, so neither superpower could improve its own security. Because of the welfare losses both states suffered as a result of high military expenditures, arms control agreements would have been in the interest of both.[4] Yet it proved extremely difficult to achieve arms control agreements that would have advanced these shared interests, because both superpowers had an incentive to secretly renege on such agreements in order to gain a security advantage, while at the same time fearing that the other might gain a security advantage by secretly violating the agreement. In terms of game theory the constellation may be depicted as shown in Table 1.[5]

In such constellations of interest, international cooperation among rational actors – i.e. joint arms control policies of the US and the USSR – seem impossible *at first sight*.[6] Regardless of whether one superpower believes that the other superpower will stick to the arms control agreement, it will benefit from secretly continuing to build up its arms in violation of the agreement.[7] If one superpower assumes that its competitor is continuing to develop its arms secretly, it can at least avoid a security disadvantage by building up its own arms. If, on the other hand, it assumes that its competitor is in fact reducing its arms, then it can gain a security advantage by building up its own arms. No matter what arms policy one imputes to the other, for both superpowers it is always rational to build up their own arms – and thus to eschew international cooperation.

Keohane, however, argues that the problem of cooperation looks different if we consider the fact that these states *repeatedly* find themselves in the same constellation of interests

Table 1 The prisoner's dilemma as exemplified by the arms race

USSR *US*	*Limit arms*	*Build more arms*
Limit arms	3 / 3	1 / 4
Build more arms	4 / 1	2 / 2

(Keohane 1984: 75–78; Oye 1986). Because the superpowers know that they must continually decide which arms policy to pursue, arms control measures appear in a very different light than in the case of one single decision on arms that will not be followed by any subsequent such decisions. Here, joint arms control is possible because both the US and the USSR must factor in the other's future responses when making decisions about arms. In other words, they know that any steps they may take today in contravening arms control agreements may quickly prompt corresponding measures by the other side, such that efforts to control arms will come to nothing. As a result of this *shadow of the future* (Axelrod 1987), then, both superpowers can deter each other from reneging on joint arms control agreements.

Therefore, Keohane argues that despite the "nasty" premises about international politics, in constellations of interest such as the prisoner's dilemma, international cooperation is at least possible in principle if both the states involved repeatedly find themselves in the given constellation of interests. According to Keohane, however, international cooperation is likely only if it is secured through international regimes (Keohane 1984: 78–84). So in *After Hegemony*, Keohane, like most regime theorists, tackles two questions: (1) What are the effects of international regimes?; and (2) Under what circumstances will the formation of international regimes be successful? I shall first consider the effects of international regimes, before taking a closer look at their formation. Only if one is able to convincingly argue that international regimes are effective, does it then make sense to analyze how they emerge.

2.2 Regime effects

According to Keohane, international regimes are instruments that can help states to realize their common interest in international cooperation. So the effect of international regimes does not consist in changing the interests of the states involved – and thus their preference order – in order to facilitate international cooperation. Instead the effect of international regimes is merely to help states realize their pre-existing common interests by means of international cooperation. International regimes, then, function as catalysts for cooperation that leave the interests of states untouched.

In his regime theory, however, Keohane is not satisfied with confirming that international regimes have an effect, but also identifies several pathways through which they facilitate international cooperation. In his view, the main effect of international regimes is to reduce the *transaction costs* associated with international cooperation. They reduce the costs associated with negotiating, monitoring, and enforcing cooperative agreements. Four pathways through which regimes can reduce transaction costs are of particular relevance (Keohane 1984: 89–109):

1 International regimes reduce transaction costs by providing a framework for negotiations within which states can more easily achieve specific cooperation agreements (ibid.: 89–90). As opposed to negotiations outside of international regimes, there is no need for states to engage in time-consuming preliminary negotiations in order to agree on the objectives, partners, and procedures of their negotiations. Such things are usually already determined by the regime. The international trade regime of the GATT or the WTO, for example, not only stipulates who will be negotiating with whom and how negotiations will take place, but also what the negotiations will be about. As a result, the structure of the negotiations is set in advance to such an extent that it is considerably easier to reach agreement on specific issues such as customs tariffs within the negotiations themselves.

2 International regimes also lower the transaction costs associated with monitoring states' compliance with cooperative agreements. By providing joint monitoring mechanisms, they reduce the costs generated if states have to separately monitor each other's compliance with these agreements (ibid.: 97–100). Within the international nuclear non-proliferation regime, for example, the International Atomic Energy Agency (IAEA) is tasked with monitoring whether non-nuclear weapon states comply with their commitments under the Nuclear Non-proliferation Treaty. This reduces states' incentives to secretly produce nuclear weapons because they must expect to be discovered, thus enabling other states to react, while at the same time reducing state fears that others might secretly develop nuclear weapons, thus putting their own security at risk. The monitoring mechanisms of international regimes thus help stabilize international cooperation (ibid.: 92–93).
3 International regimes also reduce the transaction costs of enforcing international cooperative agreements. By linking together a number of specific cooperative agreements within a given issue area, international regimes facilitate the enforcement of each of these cooperative agreements (ibid.: 89–91). In the context of a regime, states have to be aware that violating a specific agreement is likely to have an impact on their partners' cooperation beyond the specific cooperative agreement at stake; it may affect their partners' cooperation within the entire issue area covered by the respective regime. This will reduce not only the incentive to renege on any cooperative agreement within the respective regime, but also the fear that others might renege on cooperation. Within the GATT/WTO regime, for instance, states may refrain from violating specific rules concerning agricultural trade because they fear the consequences this may have for the motor vehicle trade with their GATT/WTO partners.
4 In addition, international regimes reduce the transaction costs associated with enforcing cooperation agreements simply by defining cooperation. As international regimes usually set out what international cooperation entails, it becomes more costly for states to renege on international cooperation. The states in question damage their reputation as trustworthy partners and in future it will be more difficult for them to successfully negotiate cooperative agreements (ibid.: 103–105). Their partners are unlikely to trust their promises of cooperation and might thus require additional safeguards. A state that repeatedly violates international environmental agreements, for example, will struggle to be considered a reliable partner in future negotiations on related environmental issues. In order to avoid these reputation costs, states are often prepared to comply with cooperative agreements even when they face strong non-compliance incentives.

2.3 Regime formation

In Keohane's rational theory, the positive effect of international regimes on international cooperation explains why states establish new international regimes or maintain existing ones. The effect of international regimes anticipated by states, namely an improved capacity to realize common interests by means of international cooperation, explains why states form international regimes. On this view, the US and the USSR established a number of arms control regimes because they could realistically assume that these would help them to realize their common interest in arms control.

For Keohane, however, not every shared interest in international cooperation results in the formation of international regimes. Instead, even when the states involved have a shared interest in international cooperation, regime formation depends on a wide range of conditions – particularly the relationship between the costs and benefits of regime formation. The less it costs to form and maintain regimes, and the greater the benefit associated with the regime, the more likely regime formation is. Meanwhile, the higher the costs of regime formation are estimated to be, and the smaller the benefit that can be gleaned from a regime, the less likely regime formation becomes.

According to Keohane, this cost-benefit ratio is influenced among other things by the *degree of interdependence* in a given issue area (Keohane 1984: 79; Oye 1986). In particular, the degree of interdependence determines the benefit that will accrue to the states involved in a regime. The greater the degree of interdependence, the more they can benefit from international cooperation. It is far more important for states with extensive trade relations to stabilize these by means of an international trade regime than it is for states with negligible trade relations. In other words, the greater the degree of interdependence, the more the costs associated with regime formation and regime maintenance will be offset by the benefit of the regime. So the formation of international regimes is more likely to occur in the case of high levels of interdependence than in the case of low levels of interdependence (for a detailed account of interdependence, see the extensive chapter by Manuela Spindler in this volume).

According to Keohane, however, the cost-benefit ratio is also determined by the *number of states* within a given issue area (Keohane 1984: 78–79; Oye 1986). In particular, the number of states influences the costs of regime formation. The greater the number of states involved in a regime, the more difficult it is to enforce cooperation in a decentralized fashion. While it is usually relatively easy to implement reciprocal monitoring of compliance with cooperative agreements among a small number of states, it is hard to do so effectively among a large number, because, among other things, violations are far more difficult to identify. In the case of a large number of states, therefore, cooperation is only likely to succeed if effective monitoring mechanisms are part of the international regime. Such mechanisms, however, generate additional costs that may cancel out the benefit associated with the regime. So regime formation by a large number of states is hampered simply because of this monitoring problem. Additionally, when a large number of states are cooperating, there is a tendency for them to pass the costs associated with the sanctioning of states that violate the norms and rules of the regime on to other states. But if all states try to pass on sanctioning costs to the other states, then violations of cooperative agreements go unpunished. So with a large number of states, international cooperation often depends on states agreeing on a regime with a stringent sanctioning mechanism. Again, this gives rise to additional costs that may prevent regime formation in the first place (Axelrod and Keohane 1986: 234–237).

Keohane also emphasizes that the *distribution of power* within the issue area concerned may influence the formation of international regimes (Keohane 1984: 31–46). While Keohane regards a hegemonic distribution of power neither as necessary nor sufficient to regime formation, he considers such a power distribution as conducive to the formation (and maintenance) of regimes. After all, the cost-benefit calculations associated with regime formation look very different to a hegemonic power such as the United States than to less powerful states. While the benefits of cooperation for less powerful states are usually not so high that they entirely offset the costs of regime formation, for powerful states that occupy a hegemonic position within an issue area, the benefits of cooperation may be so high that it is profitable for them to bear the costs of regime formation alone. For example, in the 1950s and 1960s, the benefits to the United States of the GATT regime were so enormous that it was able to meet the costs of regime formation (and maintenance) alone. The United States' willingness to meet these costs altered the cost-benefit ratio for the other states, allowing regime formation to occur relatively smoothly.

In sum, Keohane has produced a comprehensive, rational (or "interest-based") theory of international regimes. By referring to the effect of international regimes on the transaction costs of international cooperation, this theory explains why international regimes may foster international cooperation. This in turn explains why states construct and maintain international regimes. But the most persuasive aspect of his theory is probably that it shows that it is possible to explain international cooperation based on pessimistic neorealist premises without having to rely on idealistic premises about international politics. Keohane demonstrates that international cooperation can succeed not just when the international political weather is calm, but also during stormy periods.

3 Further developments in regime theory

In the 1980s, Keohane's version of regime theory sparked off a number of theoretically productive debates on the formation and impact of international regimes within the discipline of International Relations. These debates are based on various approaches to regimes – which must be distinguished from Keohane's approach mentioned above. I will now provide a brief overview of the most important of these: (1) the theory of hegemonic stability; (2) the situational structure approach; (3) the two-level approach; (4) the problem structure approach; and (5) approaches centred on epistemic communities.

1 Keohane distances his regime theory from the *neorealist theory of hegemonic stability*. Yet the theory of hegemonic stability may itself be understood as a form of regime theory. Ultimately, it states that the formation as well as the survival of international regimes depends on the international power structures within a given issue area of international politics (Kindleberger 1976; Krasner 1976). From this perspective, international regimes come about only if a hegemonic power exists that is able and willing to establish and to enforce the relevant regime norms. This theory also states that international regimes can be maintained only as long as the hegemon is able to defend its superior power position. If it loses its position as a hegemon, then the international regimes it had brought about will fall apart. While the theory of hegemonic stability ascribes no independent effect to international regimes, it can still claim to analyse the formation of international regimes.

2 The *situation structure* – or *game theory* – *approach* refined Keohane's regime theory. It abandons the focus on the prisoner's dilemma as *the* (only) constellation of interests that can give rise to international regimes. Instead it emphasizes that the formation of international regimes is possible in a variety of constellations featuring both a common interest in cooperation and an individual interest in self-help (Stein 1983; Snidal 1986; Zürn 1992). Based on game theory, this approach distinguishes between several of these so-called mixed-motive constellations, which permit the formation of international regimes with varying degrees of probability. In particular, it distinguishes between constellations of interests that correspond to a coordination game and those that resemble a dilemma game. Dilemma games differ from coordination games in that all the states involved have an incentive to renege on existing cooperation agreements and all of them are inevitably afraid that their cooperation will prompt other states to deceive them. In coordination games, by contrast, the states involved have no incentive to renege on

cooperation agreements that have already been reached and consequently these states have little reason to fear that their partners will "cheat". Here, however, regime formation is typically impeded because states prefer different cooperative agreements. Despite this, the situation structure approach regards the formation of international regimes in cooperation games as more probable than in dilemma games.

3 The so-called *two-level approach* attempts to go even further in refining Keohane's regime theory. This approach not only distinguishes between several constellations of interests among states, but also between various constellations of interests *within states* in order to assess more precisely the likelihood that international regimes will be formed (Moravcsik 1993; Zangl 1994, 1999; see also the chapter by Siegfried Schieder in this volume). The basic idea here is that in every issue area of international politics, the formation of international regimes is determined by the interplay between the constellation of interests *among* states and *within* states. On this view, the stateswomen and statesmen involved in establishing regimes must carry out simultaneous moves on both the national and international level. That is, when forming regimes they must negotiate not just externally with other states on the basis of their interests but at the same time internally in order to ensure that the planned regime is compatible with key domestic interests. So, according to the two-level approach, the probability of regime formation depends not just on the compatibility of interests among the states involved, but also on the absence of any interests within the society of the states involved that are fundamentally opposed to the regime.

4 Relative to Keohane's regime theory, the *problem structure approach* entails a shift of emphasis. This approach emphasizes that international regimes are established above all in order to deal with conflicts. Here, a conflict does not mean a specific behaviour through which states harm one another. Instead the term conflict is conceptualized as referring to incompatible positions – or only partially compatible interests. On this view, states form international regimes so that they can deal with conflicts cooperatively to their mutual advantage. Here, then, regimes are instruments for the cooperative processing of conflicts. The basic idea of the problem structure approach is that the probability of regime formation varies depending on the prevailing object of conflict within a given issue area of international politics (Rittberger and Zürn 1990). In the case of value conflicts – conflicts in which states cannot even identify common goals with respect to a particular object of conflict – regime formation is regarded as particularly unlikely. In the case of conflicts over means, meanwhile, regime formation is regarded as more likely because, with respect to a given object of conflict, it is only the means of *reaching* goals that are contested, not the goals themselves. In conflicts of interest, the probability of regime formation depends on how a given object of conflict is evaluated. If it is evaluated relative to the proportion of the object of conflict accounted for by other states (as is often the case in an arms race), then the probability is about as negligible as in the case of value conflicts; if it is evaluated in absolute terms, meanwhile, in the sense that each state is concerned only to obtain as large a portion of the object of conflict as possible (but is unconcerned with how much of it others may get, as is often the case with environmental goods such as clean air), then the probability of regime formation is regarded as particularly high – even higher than in the case of conflicts over means.

5 Approaches concerned with *epistemic communities* differ markedly from Keohane's regime theory. From this perspective, the formation of international regimes depends primarily on the "distribution of knowledge" within the issue area under consideration.

> If there is a consensus of knowledge about the causes of particular problems and the effects of possible solutions, then there is a great probability that attempts to form an international regime will succeed. If, on the other hand, knowledge about the cause–effect relations within an issue area of international politics is not consensual, then regime formation is regarded as quite improbable. The development of international regimes thus depends on the existence of so-called epistemic communities. Epistemic communities are composed of experts who share consensual knowledge about the cause–effect relations within a particular issue area (Haas 1989, 1990, 1992). Their importance to the development of international regimes is regarded as especially noteworthy in issue areas in which it is very difficult to assess the causes of problems and the effects of possible solutions due to a high degree of complexity.

4 Criticisms of regime theory

Regime theory has attracted criticism from two very different camps. Beginning in the late 1980s, regime theory was increasingly criticized by neorealists, and from the early 1990s on it drew criticism from the emerging social constructivist camp. Grieco is a particularly trenchant exponent of the *neorealist critique* (1988, 1990; see also Mearsheimer 1994/95). Grieco asserts that regime theory has failed to show convincingly that we can make functionalist or institutionalist statements about international cooperation on the basis of realist or neorealist premises about international politics. In particular, regime theory has failed to grasp the significance of anarchical structures in international politics. Grieco argues that the anarchical structures within international politics give rise to two key obstacles to cooperation, but regime theory pays sufficient attention to just one of them. For regime theorists, according to Grieco, the main reason why anarchical structures are an obstacle to cooperation is that cooperative agreements cannot be centrally enforced, which gives rise to a problem of trust. What regime theory overlooks, however, is that within anarchical structures the *problem of distribution* represents a more profound obstacle to cooperation (Krasner 1991 makes the same point). Regime theory underestimates the problem of distribution because it works on the assumption that, within the anarchical structures of international politics, states behave selfishly, that is, they attempt to increase their absolute gains from cooperation, regardless of the gains of other states. According to Grieco, however, the anarchical structures force states to act "begrudgingly", that is, to prevent other states from making relative gains from cooperation. Because each state must act to protect its own security within the anarchical structures, states cannot afford to pay attention solely to absolute gains from cooperation. States cannot just ask: "Will both of us gain?" Instead they must ensure that they are doing everything possible to prevent relative cooperation gains by other states. The question they must ask is: "Who will gain more?", because given the problem of security within anarchical structures, the cooperating partner of today may be your enemy in war tomorrow. To allow one's partner to make relative gains from cooperation in order to achieve absolute cooperation gains may therefore represent a serious risk to security. Because states must pay attention not just to absolute gains but also to relative gains from cooperation, lasting cooperation supported by international regimes is on the whole highly improbable. Ultimately, international regimes can succeed only if the gains from cooperation can be distributed equally among the states involved.[8]

Social constructivists' key criticism of regime theory is that it treats the interests and identities of states as given.[9] On this view, states encounter one another with their pre-existing interests and identities in order to enter into cooperative relations with one another – supported by international regimes. The international regimes themselves are merely deployed instrumentally by states in order to realize their interests. But as Hurrell (1993) and Wendt (1992, 1999) have suggested, regime theory overlooks the fact that international regimes not only reflect the interests of states, but can also contribute to shaping and changing the interests of states. Like social institutions generally, from this perspective, international regimes are not just deployed instrumentally by states with pre-existing interests in order to better realize these interests. Like every social institution, regimes are *constitutive* of the interests of the states involved. One of the key reasons why regime theory overlooks this constitutive institutional impact is that it assumes that states always pursue their own interests through rational action. But, as Müller (1993, 1994) and Risse (2000) among others have argued, alongside rational action in accordance with a given state's interests, argument-based modes of behaviour – more strongly influenced by regime norms – also play a significant role. The idea here is that states do not always try merely to enforce their interests rationally. Instead they are often open to discovering, together with other states and with reference to rational argument, what interests they *ought* to be pursuing on the basis of the norms anchored in international regimes. States, then, do not always act on the basis of existing interests; instead, within international regimes their interests themselves become the object of action.[10] Because it leaves these modes of action out of account, regime theory significantly underestimates the impact of international regimes.

Regime theorists have addressed both the neorealist and social constructivist critique at length. For the most part, they have rejected neorealist criticisms. An orientation towards relative gains, they assert, is a hindrance to international cooperation only in bilateral contexts, not in multilateral ones. Each state must ask itself whether it will be weakened not just in absolute terms but also in relative terms by refusing to cooperate with those states that have entered into cooperative relations with one another. On this view, in order to prevent these relative gains by other states, a given state may feel compelled to take part in cooperation even if certain states will achieve relatively larger gains from cooperation (Snidal 1993). The social constructivists' critique, however, has changed regime theory. Over the course of the 1990s, regime theory gradually ceased to assume that states act exclusively based on pre-existing interests. In line with this, contemporary regime theory works on the assumption that international regimes are not only deployed by states instrumentally in order to better realize their pre-existing interests, but that international regimes may be constitutive of state interests. In recent regime research, for example, it is largely accepted that the interests of states may change as a result of argumentative action – of the kind fostered by international regimes (Zangl and Zürn 1996, 1999). So regime theory is no longer restricted to the rationalist approach inspired by Keohane, but now includes a variant of a more constructivist character.

Furthermore, in the late 1990s, institutionalism, of which regime theory forms part, shifted away from an exclusive focus on international regimes and began to pay more attention to other international institutions. Increasingly, scholars are examining the design of international institutions. The underlying supposition here is that the effectiveness of international institutions depends – among other things – on their institutional design. So researchers are particularly keen to investigate what differences in the design of international institutions explain differences in their efficacy while at the same time also investigating the causes of differences in design (Koremenos *et al.* 2001). Ultimately, this research on the design of international institutions intersects with research on global governance, though the latter moves beyond the focus on international institutions, which remains constitutive of regime theory, to examine such things as private regimes (Cutler *et al.* 1999).

5 Notes

1 On the debate on the definition of international regimes, see Hasenclever *et al.* (1997: 8–22).
2 See also Keohane (1983, 1989) and Axelrod and Keohane (1986). For an excellent survey of Keohane's theory, see Hasenclever *et al.* (1997: 27–44).
3 The origins of this term lie in its reference to the story of two prisoners which is meant to illustrate a particular constellation of interests. They jointly committed a crime, but there is insufficient evidence to convict them. The public prosecutor therefore offers each of them the opportunity to testify as a state witness. As a result, each is now faced with a difficult decision. He must decide whether to confess, thus betraying his accomplice in order to gain his freedom, or lie in the hope that his accomplice will lie as well. If both lie, it will be advantageous for both of them. But because there is an incentive for each to confess in order to gain immediate freedom and also because each is bound to fear that the other will betray him by confessing, there is a risk that both will confess, thus harming one another.
4 If both superpowers practise arms control, they achieve a so-called Pareto optimum. A Pareto optimum refers to an outcome that does not allow for any joint improvements; any other outcome leaves at least one actor worse off.
5 The game theoretical payoff matrix provides a formalized representation of this constellation of interests. The payoff matrix reveals that the US and the USSR each have two possible courses of action (to make cuts in their arms or expand them) that may lead – in combination – to four possible outcomes. As they allow them to realize their interests to varying degrees, both superpowers assign diverging preferences to these outcomes. In the matrix, a payoff of '4' indicates the most preferred outcome while the payoff of '1' indicates the least desired outcome. For the US to limit arms while the USSR continues to build more arms is thus the outcome least desired by the United States but most desired by the USSR. For an introduction to game theory, see Morrow (1994).
6 In terms of game theory, the arms race between the superpowers represents a so-called Nash equilibrium. A Nash equilibrium represents the result of an action that none of the actors involved can forgo without damaging himself.
7 In the language of game theory, both superpowers can pursue a dominant strategy.
8 On the relevant debates, see, for example, Powell (1991), Snidal (1993), Baldwin (1993) and Keohane and Martin (1995). For a rather different neorealist critique of regime theory, see Krasner (1991, 1993). He asserts that regime theory fails to shed sufficient light on the distribution of power among states.
9 On social constructivist criticisms, see, for example, Hurrell (1993), Müller (1994), Wendt (1992, 1999) and Risse (2000).
10 On the associated debate on what might constitute an adequate concept of social action, see, for example, Müller (1994), Keck (1995), Risse-Kappen (1995), Zangl and Zürn (1996), Schimmelfennig (1997), and Risse (2000).

6 Bibliography and recommended reading

6.1 Primary texts

Keohane, Robert O. 1984: *After Hegemony: Cooperation and Discord in the World Political Economy*. Princeton, NJ: Princeton University Press.

Keohane, Robert O. (ed.) 1989: *International Institutions and State Power: Essays in International Relations Theory*. Boulder, CO: Westview Press.

Rittberger, Volker (ed.) 1990: *International Regimes in East-West Politics*. London: Pinter.

Rittberger, Volker (ed.) 1993: *Regime Theory and International Relations*. Oxford: Oxford University Press.

Zürn, Michael 1992: *Interessen und Institutionen in der internationalen Politik. Grundlegung und Anwendungen des situationsstrukturellen Ansatzes*. Opladen: Leske + Budrich.

6.2 Secondary texts

Hasenclever, Andreas, Mayer, Peter and Rittberger, Volker 1997: *Theories of International Regimes*. Cambridge: Cambridge University Press.

Hasenclever, Andreas, Mayer, Peter and Rittberger, Volker 1996: Interests, Power, Knowledge: The Study of International Regimes, *Mershon International Studies Review* 40(2): 177–228.

Levy, Marc A., Young, Oran R., and Zürn, Michael 1996: The Study of International Regimes, *European Journal of International Relations* 1(3): 267–330.

6.3 Other texts

Adler, Emanuel and Haas, Peter M. 1992: Epistemic Communities, World Order, and the Creation of a Reflective Research Program, *International Organization* 46(1): 367–390.

Axelrod, Robert 1987: Die Evolution der Kooperation. Munich: Oldenbourg.

Axelrod, Robert and Keohane, Robert O. 1986: Achieving Cooperation under Anarchy. Strategies and Institutions, in Oye, Kenneth (ed.) *Cooperation under Anarchy*. Princeton, NJ: Princeton University Press, pp. 226–254.

Baldwin, David A. 1993: Neoliberalism, Neorealism, and World Politics, in Baldwin, David A. (ed.) *Neorealism and Neoliberalism: The Contemporary Debate*. New York: Columbia University Press, pp. 3–25.

Cutler, Claire, Haufler, Virginia and Porter, Tony 1999: *Private Authority and International Affairs*. New York, State University of New York Press, pp. 3–28.

Efinger, Manfred, Rittberger, Volker, Wolf, Klaus-Dieter and Zürn, Michael 1990: Internationale Regime und internationale Politik, in Rittberger, Volker (ed.) *Theorien der Internationalen Beziehungen. Bestandsaufnahme und Forschungsperspektiven*. PVS-Sonderheft 21. Opladen: Westdeutscher Verlag, pp. 263–285.

Grieco, Joseph M. 1988: Anarchy and the Limits of Cooperation. A Realist Critique of the Newest Liberal Institutionalism, *International Organization* 42(3): 485–507.

Grieco, Joseph M. 1990: *Cooperation among Nations: Europe, America, and Non-Tariff Barriers to Trade*. Ithaca, NY: Cornell University Press.

Haas, Peter M. 1989: Do Regimes Matter? Epistemic Communities and Mediterranean Pollution Control, *International Organization* 43(2): 377–403.

Haas, Peter M. 1990: *Saving the Mediterranean: The Politics of International Environmental Cooperation*. New York: Columbia University Press.

Haas, Peter M. 1992: Banning Chlorofluorocarabons: Epistemic Community Efforts to Protect Stratospheric Ozone, *International Organization* 46(1): 187–224.

Haggard, Stephen and Simmons, Beth A. 1987: Theories of International Regimes, *International Organization* 41(3): 491–517.

Hurrell, Andrew 1993: International Society and the Study of Regimes, in Rittberger, Volker (ed.) *Regime Theory and International Relations*. Oxford: Oxford University Press, pp. 49–72.

Keck, Otto 1995: Rationales kommunikatives Handeln in den internationalen Beziehungen. Ist eine Verbindung von Rational-Choice-Theorie und Habermas' Theorie des kommunikativen Handelns möglich?, *Zeitschrift für Internationale Beziehungen* 2(1): 5–48.

Keohane, Robert O. and Martin, Lisa L. 1995: The Promise of Institutionalist Theory, *International Security* 20(1): 39–51.

Keohane, Robert O. and Nye, Joseph S. 1977: *Power and Interdependence: World Politics in Transition*, Boston: Little, Brown and Co.

Kindleberger, Charles P. 1976: Systems of International Economic Organization, in Calleo, David P. and Cleveland, Harold B. van (eds) *Money and the Coming World Order*. New York: New York University Press, pp. 15–39.

Koremenos, Barbara, Lipson, Charles and Snidal, Duncan 2001: The Rational Design of International Institutions, *International Organization* 55(4): 761–799.

Krasner, Stephen D. 1976: State Power and the Structure of International Trade, *World Politics* 28(3): 317–347.

Krasner, Stephen D. 1983: Structural Causes and Regime Consequences: Regimes as Intervening Variables, in Krasner, Stephen D. (ed.) *International Regimes*. Ithaca, NY: Cornell University Press, pp.1–21.

Krasner, Stephen D. 1991: Global Communications and National Power: Life on the Pareto Frontier, *World Politics* 43(3): 336–366.

Krasner, Stephen D. 1993: Sovereignty, Regimes, and Human Rights, in Rittberger, Volker (ed.), *Regime Theory and International Relations*. Oxford: Oxford University Press, pp. 139–167.

Martin, Lisa and Simmons, Beth A. 1998: Theories and Empirical Studies of International Institutions, *International Organization* 52(4): 729–757.

Mearsheimer, John D. 1994/1995: The False Promise of International Institutions, *International Security* 19(3): 5–49.

Moravcsik, Andrew 1993: Integrating International and Domestic Theories of International Bargaining, in Evans, Peter B., Jacobson, Harold K. and Putnam, Robert D. (eds) *Double-edged Diplomacy: International Bargaining and Domestic Politics*. Berkeley, CA: University of California Press, pp. 3–42.

Morrow, James D. 1994: *Game Theory for Political Science*. Princeton, NJ: Princeton University Press.

Müller, Harald 1993: The Internalization of Principles, Norms, and Rules by Governments: The Case of Security Regimes, in Rittberger, Volker (ed.) *Regime Theory and International Relations*. Oxford: Oxford University Press, pp. 361–388.

Müller, Harald 1994: Internationale Beziehungen als kommunikatives Handeln. Zur Kritik der utilitaristischen Handlungstheorien, *Zeitschrift für Internationale Beziehungen* 1(1): 15–44.

Oye, Kenneth A. 1986: Explaining Cooperation under Anarchy: Hypotheses and Strategies, in Oye, Kenneth A. (ed.) *Cooperation under Anarchy*. Princeton, NJ: Princeton University Press, pp. 1–25.

Powell, Robert 1991: Absolute and Relative Gains in International Relations Theory, *American Political Science Review* 85(4): 1303–1320.

Risse, Thomas 2000: "Let's Argue!". Communicative Action in World Politics, *International Organization* 54(1): 1–40.

Risse-Kappen, Thomas 1995: Reden ist nicht billig. Zur Debatte um Kommunikation und Rationalität, *Zeitschrift für Internationale Beziehungen* 2(1): 171–184.

Rittberger, Volker and Zürn, Michael 1990: Towards Regulated Anarchy in East–West-Relations: Causes and Consequences of East–West Regimes, in Rittberger, Volker (ed.) *International Regimes in East–West Politics*. London: Pinter, pp. 9–63.

Ruggie, John Gerard 1998: *Constructing the World Polity: Essays on International Institutionalization*. London: Routledge.

Schimmelfennig, Frank 1997: Rhetorisches Handeln in der internationalen Politik, *Zeitschrift für Internationale Beziehungen* 4(2): 219–254.

Snidal, Duncan 1986: The Game Theory of International Politics, in Oye, Kenneth (ed.) *Cooperation under Anarchy*. Princeton, NJ: Princeton University Press, pp. 25–57.

Snidal, Duncan 1993: The Relative-Gains Problem for International Cooperation. Response, *American Political Science Review* 87(3): 738–742.

Stein, Arthur A. 1983: Coordination and Collaboration: Regimes in an Anarchic World, in Krasner, Stephen D. (ed.) *International Regimes*. Ithaca, NY: Cornell University Press, pp. 115–140.

Taylor, Michael 1987: *The Possibility of Cooperation*. Cambridge: Cambridge University Press.

Wendt, Alexander 1992: Anarchy Is What States Make of It: The Social Construction of Power Politics, *International Organization* 46(2): 391–425.

Wendt, Alexander 1999: *Social Theory of International Politics*. Cambridge, MA: Cambridge University Press.

Zangl, Bernhard 1994: Politik auf zwei Ebenen. Hypothesen zur Bildung internationaler Regime, *Zeitschrift für Internationale Beziehungen* 1(2): 279–312.

Zangl, Bernhard 1999: *Interessen auf zwei Ebenen. Internationale Regime in der Agrarhandels-, Währungs- und Walfangpolitik*. Baden-Baden: Nomos.

Zangl, Bernhard and Zürn, Michael 1996: Argumentatives Handeln bei internationalen Verhandlungen. Moderate Anmerkungen zur post-realistischen Debatte, *Zeitschrift für Internationale Beziehungen* 3(2): 341–366.

Zangl, Bernhard and Zürn, Michael 1999: Interessen in der internationalen Politik. Der akteurszentrierte Institutionalismus, *Zeitschrift für Politikwissenschaft* 99(3): 923–950.

Neofunctionalism

Thomas Conzelmann

1 Introduction

Within the discipline of International Relations, (neo)functionalist approaches fall under liberal and idealist strands of theorizing. Functionalism and its neofunctionalist successor belong to the liberal school of International Relations because they identify societal interests and the satisfaction of societal needs as the key driving force of politics and at the same time as their normative lodestone. (Neo)functionalism can be called idealist because the relevant authors work on the assumption that aggressive and selfish behaviour among states can be overcome, and are centrally concerned with identifying how we might move towards a more peaceful world.[1]

The historical background to functionalist and neofunctionalist approaches is the experience of two world wars and the failure of the League of Nations in the interwar period.[2] In light of these experiences, functionalist authors came to the conclusion that peace through international cooperation cannot be imposed "from above" by means of states' political decisions, but must instead emerge "from below" through cross-border cooperation in specific issue areas. Rather than strengthening international authority and incorporating states into an overarching political framework, the key aim was to weaken and ultimately overcome state borders. This was to be achieved through a gradually expanding, "non-political" and expert-driven form of cooperation that would have to be strictly geared towards resolving specific issues of common interest.

Functionalist concepts attracted a great deal of attention in post-war Europe. This is due, first, to the supposed affinity of the initial steps towards European integration with functionalist thought (an unsustainable idea if we go beyond surface appearances).[3] Second, it was chiefly against the background of the (Western) European integration process that functionalism's "neofunctionalist" successor emerged. The key "reference theorist" for neofunctionalism is German-American political scientist Ernst B. Haas, who was born in Frankfurt in 1924 and died in Berkeley in 2003 (Haas 1961, 1964, 1968, 1970, 1975, 2001, 2004).[4] His contributions remain a key reference point for political scientists working on theories of European integration (Rosamond 2005; Ruggie *et al.* 2005).[5] This is partly because neofunctionalism and its later "supranationalist" development constitute the most important theoretical counterpart of intergovernmentalism[6] in EU scholarship.

This chapter focuses on neofunctionalism as a theory of integration and shows how it was developed further as theorists strove to come to terms with the process of regional integration in Europe and elsewhere. In order to flesh out the new and original aspects of "neo"-functionalism, I begin by examining, with due brevity, the foundation on which Haas built, namely the functionalism (Section 2.1) formulated, above all, by David Mitrany

(1933, [1943] 1966). In the subsequent sections I discuss the main building blocks of the neofunctionalist concept (Section 2.2), its later refinement (Section 2.3) and the way some neofunctionalist tenets are carried on by a new generation of integration theorists (Section 3). The chapter concludes with a discussion of criticisms of neofunctionalism and regional integration theory more generally (Section 4).

2 Ernst B. Haas's neofunctionalist theory of regional integration

2.1 Point of departure: the functionalism of David Mitrany

Though the functionalist debate was already multifaceted in the first half of the twentieth century, David Mitrany is considered to be the preeminent theorist of functionalism.[7] Mitrany's core argument was that, in a territorially fragmented world, common problems of interdependence[8] can be resolved only to a limited degree. Moreover, he portrayed the nation state system as associated with a competitive international order that required peoples to seal themselves off from one another. His alternative vision was one of "non-political" cross-border cooperation in areas of common interest, such as the international postal system or the common use of waterways. Rather than politicians and diplomats, experts and administrative specialists from different states should work together in task-specific (or "functional") agencies. For Mitrany, the objective was not just to establish a different form of international cooperation but also to concentrate on issues genuinely relevant to the general population such as combating hunger, disease and illiteracy. Issues of national security and military enhancement, conversely, had to take a back seat. The essence of this proposal is expressed in the play on words in the title of Mitrany's famous (1943) essay, *A Working Peace System*. Here, "working" does not just mean "functioning" but also "based on (cooperative) work". Mitrany contrasts this idea with a peace based on dissociation, deterrence and the weak support provided by international law ("protected peace"):

> The task that is facing us is how to build up the reality of a common interest in peace. But with a revolutionary element . . . that also demands a new sense of peace: not a peace that would keep the nations quietly apart but a peace that would bring them actively together, not the old static and strategic view but a social view of peace. Or one might say that we must put our faith not in a protected peace but in a working peace; it would indeed be nothing more nor less than the idea and aspiration of social security taken in its widest range.
>
> (Mitrany [1943] 1966: 92)

The incentive for national actors to engage in such cross-border cooperation comes from the recognition of mutual dependence. The welfare gains made possible by technological progress can only be achieved through task-specific cooperation across borders. Such initially limited technocratic cooperation is considered important to advancing peace because it is the seed of more extensive cooperation: the functional connections between the different spheres of regulation, the better satisfaction of societal needs, and learning processes based on everyday cooperation create the foundation for widening cooperation to other tasks. This process is expected to relativize and ultimately overcome the international system anchored in the territorial state and thus to contribute to the emergence of peace. Mitrany explains:

> The only sound sense of peaceful change is . . . to make changes of frontiers unnecessary by making frontiers meaningless through the continuous development of common activities and interests across them. . . . The functional approach may be justifiably expected to . . . help the expansion of such positive and constructive common work, of common habits and interests, making frontier lines meaningless by overlaying them with a *natural growth* of common activities and common administrative agencies.
>
> (ibid.: 62–63; original emphasis)

A further key point for Mitrany was that the institutional form of cooperation must be oriented towards the specific requirements of a given field. He therefore came out against all forms of territorially – rather than functionally – defined cooperation. Regional forms of cooperation such as the later European Economic Community could not meet the fluctuating requirements of functional cooperation (Mitrany 1965; see also Mitrany 1966: 44–46, Rosamond 2000: 36–38). Moreover, Mitrany saw a danger of creating new rivalries through cooperation between fixed groups of states.[9] How the required international agencies should be organized and who could become a member should be determined solely in light of the specific tasks they deal with (Mitrany 1966: 72–73). "Form follows function" – it was by espousing this guiding principle, also found within contemporary theories of architecture and design, that functionalism rose to prominence.

Authors more influenced by conflict theory have been critical of Mitrany's conception, particularly the assumption of the possibility of technical and issue-related cooperation at the expense of "political" task performance. Further, critics assert, it is unclear how exactly individual actors' experience of cooperation might translate into the – ultimately political – decision to engage in further cooperation.[10]

2.2 *Neofunctionalism*

From functionalism to neofunctionalism

Three aspects of neofunctionalism are "new" when compared with Mitrany's conception. First, the functionalist hope that a more peaceful international order might be achieved through functional community building was complemented by the detailed study of concrete empirical cases. While Haas's work is certainly characterized by a normative interest in how to preserve peace, his main concern is to analyse real-world integration processes in an intersubjectively comprehensible way. Looking at the first steps of economic and political integration in Western Europe, Haas wanted to understand

> how and why states cease to be wholly sovereign, how and why they voluntarily mingle, merge and mix with their neighbors so as to lose the factual attributes of sovereignty while acquiring new techniques for resolving conflict between themselves.
>
> (Haas 1970: 610)

Second, like Mitrany before him, Haas thus expected that the existing system of nation states would gradually be superseded by a new political order. But unlike his predecessor, Haas endeavoured to develop a typology of real-world stages of economic and political integration and ask how and why integration processes move from one stage to the next. In the terms developed in *The Uniting of Europe*, Haas examined under what conditions "technical cooperation" would lead to "political cooperation" and ultimately to a "political community".

A third difference from classical functionalism is that Haas developed a detailed theoretical model to explain successful integration. While Haas built on Mitrany's idea that functional necessities and support for further integration from societal groups would be important driving factors, he added the action strategies of pro-integration elites and the activities of supranational bodies as further explanatory factors. Haas considered supranational bodies such as the High Authorities of the European Coal and Steel Community (ECSC), founded in 1951, and the European Economic Community (EEC), established in 1957, as significant forces in integration processes. They were deemed important because they could safeguard integrational achievements and give their own impetus to collaboration among member states, thus facilitating further steps towards integration. In this way, functionalist thought became undergirded by pluralist and institutionalist elements. At the same time, neofunctionalism dropped the idea that it is necessary to sideline "political" task performance as claimed in Mitrany's functionalism. Integration is not just a technocratic optimization strategy but inevitably has a political character (Haas 1964: 23). In this context especially it is evident how closely neofunctionalist concepts drew on the real-world development of European integration (Haas 1968; see also Rosamond 2000: 51–54).

Because of these key differences, neofunctionalism is more than just a refinement of the original body of functionalist thought. It constitutes a social scientific approach to the analysis and explanation of interstate integration rather than (as in Mitrany's functionalism) a normatively grounded attempt to map out routes to international peace beyond the categories of the nation state. Haas takes contemporary forms of international cooperation as his starting point and seeks to provide a general explanation of the processes involved. In doing so, he does not follow a strictly "functional" approach but instead blends functional, structural and intentional explanations. Neofunctionalism can still be considered "functionalist", however, in the sense that it too consciously turns away from federal integration strategies and privileges a type of cooperation that begins in limited sectors and gradually gains traction within the political sphere. Against this background it is particularly interesting to discuss the key elements of Haas's model, which are inspired by classical functionalism but that Haas uses as classificatory concepts or as explanatory variables. These are, first, "technical cooperation", "political cooperation", and "political community" as stages that are gone through in integration processes, and, second, the dynamic element of "spill-over" which drives progress from one stage to the next.

Integration towards a political community

To understand the neofunctionalist concept of integration it is important to distinguish between integration as a process and integration as a state of affairs. Both meanings are mixed together in everyday usage, but neofunctionalists use the term "integration" solely for the *process*, while concepts such as "political cooperation" and "political community" denote different *stages* of integration. In this vein, Haas defines "political integration" as:

> the process whereby political actors in several distinct national settings are persuaded to shift their loyalties, expectations, and political activities toward a new centre, whose institutions possess or demand jurisdiction over the pre-existing national states. The end result of a process of political integration is a new political community, superimposed over the pre-existing ones.
>
> (Haas 1968: 16)

Haas thus views the development of a political community as a final state of affairs, with a number of intermediary stages typically being gone through to reach it. Drawing once again on the specific experiences of European integration (Haas 1964, 1968) and the International Labour Organization (Haas 1964), Haas saw "technical cooperation" within a limited economic sector as sparking off cooperation. The next stage typically involves the expansion of cooperation to other economic sectors. Subsequent stages include "political cooperation" and ultimately the formation of a "political community" overarching the nation states. Haas derived this sequence of integrative steps from the development of the international organizations he researched, which naturally raised the question of which factors drive the process from one step to the next. Haas provided the answer with the concept of "spill-over", to which we now turn.

"Spill-over" as dynamic element

"Spill-over" is a key component of the neofunctionalist approach. The basic idea is that the functional connectedness of different sectors, the tendency for elites' action strategies to become gradually geared towards the supranational level, and the political entrepreneurship of supranational bureaucracies cause integration to "spill over" into neighbouring fields. As originally formulated by Haas, however, this concept is quite unclear. In part "spill-over" is code for integrative achievements, but it is also used as an explanatory mechanism; furthermore, it refers to different dimensions of the integration process. This weak spot is addressed by later neofunctionalist authors (Schmitter 1969: 162–163; Nye 1971: 65; Tranholm-Mikkelsen 1991: 4–6) in different ways. Schmitter (1969, 1970) views "spill-over" as a synonym of successful integration (in other words as a *dependent* variable) and distinguishes it from other less successful outcomes (one of which he interestingly calls "spill back"). These outcomes are distinguished by different combinations of deepening of cooperation within a sector (level of commitment) and the expansion of cooperation into problem areas not hitherto tackled (scope of commitment). Tranholm-Mikkelsen meanwhile – like Nye before him – defines "spill-over" as an *explanatory* factor in integration. In what follows I take this second approach as my basis, and, like Tranholm-Mikkelsen (1991), I distinguish between "functional", "political" and "cultivated" spill-over.[11]

- *Functional spill-over*. This form of spill-over is based on the observation that cooperation usually begins in a limited economic sector, such as coal and steel in the ECSC. Haas explains this by arguing that economic cooperation offers the best opportunities for mutually beneficial cooperation and little reason for political dispute.[12] At the same time, the economic field provides the greatest opportunity for cooperation to expand into other spheres. In this context, Haas refers on a number of occasions to the "expansive logic of sectoral integration". What he means by this, first, is that the individual sectors of national economies are so profoundly intertwined with one another that integration in one economic sector invariably generates integrative tendencies in other sectors. Second, because of the close interconnection between politics and economics in the developed industrialized societies, there is a high probability that economic cooperation will sooner or later generate a need for political cooperation: political integration thus follows on the heels of economic integration (Haas 1968: 311–313). Crucially this "logic" works even in the absence of any political initiatives geared towards integration. Haas explains:

> Sector integration . . . begets its own impetus toward extension to the entire economy even in the absence of specific group demands and their attendant ideologies. Thus, ECSC civil servants speaking for national governments have constantly found it necessary to "harmonize" their separate policies in order to make it possible for the integrated sectors to function, without necessarily implying any ideological commitment to the European idea.
>
> (Haas 1968: 297)

- *Political spill-over*. This form of spill-over is a new idea put forward by Haas. He argues that supranational integration triggers a learning process[13] through which the action strategies of societal groups such as associations, trade unions and parties become more directed to the supranational level. Political loyalty and expectations of political and economic benefit are shifted "upwards". At the same time, groups formerly organized on the national level become integrated with their counterparts in other states. They do this to influence how the supranational bodies exercise their powers, promote shared interests, and secure resources. As national governments are dependent on the support of societal groups, it is likely that national governments will follow suit and will accept the abandonment of sovereignty in favour of increased supranational integration.[14] The growing powers of the supranational bodies and the rational calculation of utility both by societal groups and by the governmental actors dependent on them thus create an increasing momentum towards integration.
- *Cultivated spill-over*. Here spill-over is based on the activities of supranational bodies such as the High Authorities (later called "Commissions") of the ECSC and the EEC. These bodies have a number of strategies at their disposal to foster political and economic integration, such as the transnational organization of societal groups, mediation between states and the putting together of package deals. Neofunctionalist authors argue that by offering organizational support and a say in decisions, supranational bodies stimulate or reinforce the process of cross-border integration among societal groups and, at the same time, foster the reorientation of the latter's loyalties and expectations. Second, neofunctionalists see supranational institutions and bodies as playing an important role in the negotiation of compromises. International negotiations are often hampered by the difficulties of discovering possible bargaining solutions (e.g. Nye 1970: 806–807). By putting forward compromise proposals, the EEC Commission can provide crucial support in this regard. The spill-over dynamic here rests on the Commission's systematic privileging of supranational solutions as it carries out its role as mediator. Schmitter (1969: 162) refers in this context to the "creative talents of political elites, especially the administrators of regional institutions, who seize upon frustrations and crisis in order to redefine and expand central organizational tasks". Taken together with the reorientation of societal actors' political loyalty and political activity towards the supranational level, the most likely outcome is "upgrading the common interests", a scenario in which "the parties [have] succeeded in redefining their conflict so as to work out a solution at a higher level, which almost invariably implies the expansion of the mandate or task of an international . . . governmental agency" (Haas 1961: 368).

For neofunctionalists, then, it is not just the functional interconnections between individual economic sectors that are crucial to the mechanism of spill-over. The altered expectations of societal groups and the activities of supranational bureaucracies also play an important role. Crucially, these three factors are considered mutually reinforcing, so that a certain self-propelling logic sets in; initially limited steps towards cooperation beget initiatives in adjacent areas, loyalties shift, and conflict is now quite likely to be resolved by an "upgrading of the common interest", not least because of the activities of supranational bodies. What we can expect, then, is an integration process that, while not conflict-free, is very likely to continue and expand once the first integrative steps have been taken. It is above all this element of "automaticity" (Schmitter 1969: 164) that was criticized in later debates and ultimately abandoned by neofunctionalist authors.

2.3 The refinement and "obsolescence" of the original concept

Haas developed his ideas chiefly with reference to the European Communities, thus inviting two types of criticism. The first was that neofunctionalism paid insufficient attention to the favourable conditions that fostered the process of integration in Western Europe. For critics, these include the pluralism of Western European societies, their common cultural and historical roots and the relatively high level of economic development. These favourable conditions, they claimed, do not apply to the same degree in other parts of the world. Because of this, neofunctionalism cannot live up to its analytical and normative aspiration to function as a *general* theory of regional integration (Hansen 1969; Nye 1970).

Second, critics claimed that the actual development of the European Communities could not be grasped through the theoretical lenses of neofunctionalism. This criticism was prompted by the so-called "Empty Chair Crisis" of 1965/66,[15] which seemed to lay bare the ongoing significance of national definitions of interests as factors inhibiting further integration. It was argued that neofunctionalism had underestimated the role which nation states continued to play in terms of commanding public loyalty and exercising political power, including within supranational institutions (e.g. Hoffmann 1966). Further, critics claimed, neofunctionalism failed to grasp the crucial difference between the routine regulation of fields of little relevance to sovereignty such as customs duties and agricultural policies and the integration of core aspects of member state sovereignty such as tax and financial policies or foreign policy.[16]

Both these criticisms boiled down to the idea that neofunctionalism is too optimistic in its assessment of the probability of integration and pays too little attention to conditions restraining the process. Neofunctionalists responded to these criticisms by conceptualizing the outcome of the integration process in a more open way. Haas conceded that statesmen prone to "dramatic" action such as de Gaulle and persistent anti-integrative attitudes among elites may hamper processes of integration.[17] At the same time, neofunctionalist scholars Schmitter and Lindberg and Scheingold began to place greater emphasis on the contingencies of integration. The expectation of a constantly expanding integration process gave way to the idea that interaction among strategically acting agents may lead to a variety of results – including "spill-back" or "retrenchment", in which the scope and depth of cooperation would diminish rather than increase (Lindberg and Scheingold 1970; Schmitter 1970; see also Schmitter 2004).

By the early 1960s, Haas had already examined the applicability of the neofunctionalist concept of integration to other parts of the world (Mattli 2005). In a 1961 contribution, he identified several conditions for successful integration that applied with particular force in the case of Europe, namely, a pluralist system of interest mediation structured around similar conflicts, highly developed national economies, extensive political and ideological agreement among participating governments and the existence of relatively strong supranational institutions (Haas 1961: 374–378). In 1964, Haas, in collaboration with Philippe Schmitter, further refined this set of variables. The authors examined general background variables (such as the extent of societal pluralism), processual variables (such as governments' capacity to respond to the disappointments and crises of the integration process), and the degree of regional integration achieved within the framework of economic cooperation. To the extent that these variables were unfavourable, economic cooperation was not expected to spill over into political cooperation (Haas and Schmitter 1964). Further refinements, particularly with respect to the perceived distributive justice of regional integration, were later undertaken by Nye (1970). These reflections relativized the notion of an integration process unfolding almost "automatically" once the first few steps have been taken – but not the assumption of an ideal typical sequence, set out above, of stages of economic and political integration. Haas and Schmitter also left open the question of whether there might be functional equivalents in other parts of the world of the favourable Western European conditions for integration.

In parallel to the efforts of Lindberg, Scheingold, Nye and Schmitter (Lindberg and Scheingold 1970; Lindberg 1971; Nye 1970, 1971; and Schmitter 1969, 1970) to refine and augment neofunctionalist analysis, Ernst Haas increasingly withdrew from the debate. In a 1970 article he declared regional theories of integration such as neofunctionalism to be "pre-theories" that provide a series of empirical generalizations but that suffer from a conceptual and definitional vagueness that makes it difficult to ascertain whether the hypotheses put forward actually hold (Haas 1970). Some years later, Haas had become highly critical of regional integration theory on empirical grounds as well (Haas 1975, 1976). He declared that "theories of regional integration are becoming obsolescent because . . . core assumptions on which these theories have been based are becoming less and less relevant to the behavior patterns actually displayed by governments active in regional organizations" (1976: 173). While the predictions of regional integration theory might still hold under certain circumstances, Haas doubted that attempts to further refine them would be "a good investment of our time and ingenuity. Integration theories, I believe, are becoming obsolete because they are not designed to address the most pressing and important problems on the global agenda of policy and research" (ibid.: 179).

Haas subsequently concentrated on the analysis of international regimes and the transformation of inter-state politics in international organizations (Haas 1980, 1982, 1990; see also Ruggie *et al.* 2005). Here, Haas and other authors again deployed functionalist approaches that trace the emergence or continued existence of cooperation to the necessity to address shared problems. In connection with the decline in the United States' hegemony in the 1960s and 1970s, for example, they asked how we might explain the continued existence or further development of international regimes and organizations in this changed situation. One answer, given by Robert O. Keohane in his landmark book *After Hegemony*, is: by reference to the functional achievements of existing regimes or actors' expectations of the services such regimes can perform (Keohane 1984; see also the chapter by Bernhard Zangl in this volume). The processes of learning and of organizational change within international organizations, discussed by Haas, also stimulated the later constructivist debate within International Relations (Haas 1990; Risse 2005; see also the chapter by Cornelia Ulbert in this volume).

3 Metamorphoses of neofunctionalist integration theory

The period from the mid-1970s to the mid-1980s is sometimes referred to as the "dark ages" of both European integration and integration theory. Following the establishment of the customs union ahead of schedule, the member states of the European Economic Community increasingly began to obstruct market integration and protect domestic producers through non-tariff measures. The ambitious project of creating a European Monetary Union collapsed amid the economic turmoil of the early 1970s and steps towards a Community foreign policy were possible only in terms of declaratory politics. The EEC, moreover, was burdened with protracted disputes over the size of the British contribution to the Community budget. The project of European integration had lost some of its original fascination and appeared to be lapsing into the familiar models of old-style intergovernmental politics. As a result, and in connection with Haas's statements on the obsolescence of integration theory, the theoretical debate began to subside and with it the attention paid to Haas's neofunctionalist work.[18]

While it would be untrue to say that this period of European development was one of political and theoretical stagnation (Caporaso and Keeler 1995: 36–42), it was not until the mid-1980s that the theoretical debate began to intensify again. An important step towards integration was taken in 1986/1987 with the signing of the Single European Act (SEA) and its core project of "completing" the Common Market by 31 December 1992. By increasing the use of majority decisions in the Council of Ministers and upgrading the role of the European Parliament, the SEA reinforced the supranational character of the EEC. At the same time, the EEC was given new powers in a number of policy fields that had previously been dealt with outside of the EEC Treaty. The question of which factors might explain the member states' newfound desire for integration soon moved to the centre of theoretical debate (Faber 2005). Key triggers in this regard were two opposing interpretations of the SEA: first, the supranationally oriented approach of Wayne Sandholtz and John Zysman (1989), often referred to as "neofunctionalist", and, second, an intergovernmental critique of the work of Sandholtz and Zysman by Andrew Moravcsik (1991).[19]

The striking conjunction of the "revival" of the integration process and the appointment of a new Commission under Jacques Delors in 1985 is the starting point of the analysis put forward by Sandholtz and Zysman. Their central argument is that the Commission, in collaboration with a supportive group of economic associations and transnational companies, managed to unite the elites of key member states behind the idea of a common European market.[20] Concentrating on the Commission's initiatives in the preparation of the SEA and the ingenuity of Delors in uniting leaders behind the 1992 programme, Sandholtz and Zysman clearly drew on the concept of cultivated spill-over. Other authors went even further than Sandholtz and Zysman and argued that the process also showed elements of functional and political spill-over (Taylor 1989: 23–24; Tranholm-Mikkelsen 1991). One should note, though, that such references to neofunctionalist concepts are made in a quite eclectic manner. For example, Sandholtz and Zysman do not couch their arguments wholly in neofunctionalist terms, but instead integrate spill-over ideas into a complex explanatory model in which global economic competition and domestic politics also play a major role. Moreover, there is no intention here to contribute to a general theory of regional integration; indeed, Sandholtz and Zysman are quite critical of the analytical aspirations and explanatory accuracy of neofunctionalism (1989: 97–99).[21] In this sense, prevailing analytical and theoretical ambitions are noticeably more limited than during the heyday of the neofunctionalist debate in the 1960s and early 1970s.

These attributes of the debate in the late 1980s – a focus on the actual development of the European Community, the tendency to forgo predictive or prescriptive statements and the combining of neofunctionalist ideas with concepts from other schools of thought – are also characteristic of some contributions of the 1990s that draw explicitly or implicitly on neofunctionalism. Examples here are studies by Corbey (1995), Stone Sweet and Sandholtz (1997) and Burley and Mattli (1993), which are either located within the tradition of neofunctionalism or self-consciously aspire to reformulate or supplement neofunctionalism. One argument advanced by all these authors is that by the 1990s the integration process had placed major restrictions on governments' autonomy of action. This, it is argued, is either because a unilateral approach not agreed with other member states has negative consequences and leads to a loss of efficacy over the long term that can only be compensated for by further integration (Corbey 1995), or because member states are gradually losing control of the agenda of European politics as a result of initiatives by societal actors and supranational bodies (Stone Sweet and Sandholtz 1997).[22] For Burley and Mattli (1993), it is above all the European Court of Justice that is providing important stimuli for integration because of its monopoly on the binding interpretation of European law and its fundamentally pro-integration stance. On this view, the Court has managed to gradually extend the scope of European law and also its own role beyond the limits laid down by the member states in the European treaties. In much the same way as economic integration, these authors argue, the "legal integration" of the Community has occurred through a process that is driven by supranational actors and is largely sealed off from control by the member states. In a process that recalls functional "spill-over", the Court has brought an increasing number of fields under the remit of supranational law.[23]

4 Criticisms and future prospects

As the leading exponent of neofunctionalism, Ernst B. Haas developed his ideas chiefly with reference to the process of integration in (Western) Europe. It is not hard to see the appeal of the European integration process for the purposes of political scientific analysis and theory building. "It is one of the very few current situations in which the decomposition of old nations can be systematically analysed within the framework of the evolution of a larger polity," wrote Haas in the Foreword to *The Uniting of Europe* in 1958.[24] But this predominant focus on European integration is at once the strength and weakness of neofunctionalist theory building. It is a strength because, by looking at the European institutions, the relevant scholars could clearly theorize certain causal interrelationships and stages of community formation. Haas and other neofunctionalists thus developed a compelling analytical model that engendered a tremendously productive theoretical discussion, especially during the first decades of European integration. This would not have been possible if the object of study had been a less successful integration process. But the focus on the European process is also a weakness because neofunctionalism never really managed to free itself from its empirical point of departure in Western Europe and develop a general theory of regional integration. The very particular preconditions under which processes of "spill-over" and community formation were likely to occur entered into the debate only very gradually. Theoretical progress was also inhibited by the rather different trajectories of integration in other world regions. The more neofunctionalism sought to incorporate additional variables into its theoretical framework to accommodate the experiences of other regional integration processes, the more conceptually unclear and theoretically inelegant it became (Haas 1970; Mattli 2005). After the ebbing away of the original neofunctionalist debate in the 1970s, there was also no revival of neofunctionalism within the field of "comparative regionalism".[25] These developments are symptomatic of the process of moving away from "grand theories" to "middle range theories" (Merton 1968: 39–72), a process that has also been occurring in other branches of International Relations and political science.

Both with respect to the general analysis of regional integration processes and with respect to European integration, the great theoretical adversary of neofunctionalism is (liberal) intergovernmentalism (see the chapter by Siegfried Schieder in this volume). The core argument put forward by Hoffmann, Moravcsik and other authors is that neofunctionalism dramatically underestimates member states' potentially curtailing influence on integration processes and has an unrealistic view of how their interests are formed. Intergovernmentalists argue that states are exposed to conflicting domestic political interests that are unlikely to be transformed during the process of European integration, and that states benefit from integration processes to varying degrees. This results in a heterogeneity of interests that is not moderated by interdependence or any gradual reorientation of loyalties to the supranational level. Consequently, the compromises that can be achieved in intergovernmental negotiations generally amount to the lowest common denominator of the conflicting national interests. With respect to the Commission, the relevant authors argue that in a number of cases it had correctly anticipated governments' interests and therefore could put forward proposals that were likely to achieve consensus. But beyond this, the Commission did not exercise any more extensive influence.[26] To the extent that integration has been successfully advanced – through the single market, for example – this was because it was in the economic interests of the member states and involved very little loss of sovereignty (Moravcsik 2005: 358–363).

One explanation of these rather different accounts of the same processes is that intergovernmentalists and neofunctionalists tend to focus on different aspects of integration. While intergovernmentalists predominantly study isolated episodes of high-level treaty negotiations, neofunctionalism tended to foreground the everyday formation of policies and the gradual reorientation of action logics between these highly visible moments of intergovernmental bargaining. Therefore, "to a considerable extent, neofunctionalists and intergovernmentalists talked past each other" (Hooghe and Marks 2008: 4). Not least in connection with this finding, the debate between neofunctionalists and intergovernmentalists has increasingly come to be viewed as unproductive. Recent debates in EU studies are no longer primarily concerned with what forces advance or impede the integration process. Instead their central aim is to bring out the characteristic features of the *existing* system of governance at the European level. This new focus has also been triggered by the greater attention that scholars working in the traditions of institutionalism, policy analysis or political philosophy nowadays pay to the EU. Their key research interests are to understand institutional formation and regulatory politics in the EU, the effects EU policies have on the everyday life of the European citizen, or the quality of democracy and participation in the EU (Pollack 2005; Kohler-Koch and Rittberger 2006; Rosamond 2010). In addressing such questions, contemporary integration scholars make hardly any use of the original concepts of neofunctionalism. Neither the concept of "spill-over" nor the expectation that the integration process will eventually lead to the establishment of a new "political community" at the supranational level play a significant role in the theoretical discussion any longer. However, some elements of the neofunctionalist approach linger on, such as the notion that international power politics can be overcome, and that once steps towards integration have been taken, they entail path dependencies and ratchet effects that place limits on member states' capacity to control the integration process. Moreover, many contemporary theorists of the EU emphasize the importance of supranational actors in advancing integration as well as the power of the EU to "Europeanize" member state policies and institutions and the identities and interests of policy-makers and the electorate. Certain tenets of the neofunctionalist argument have thus been fused with elements of institutionalist and constructivist theories within International Relations to form a new approach, sometimes referred to as "supranationalism" (Rittberger and Schimmelfennig 2005).

In summary, the question of what shape the EU will eventually take has clearly been put on the backburner over the past two decades. This seems to be a legitimate move, given that, despite the many changes to the EU Treaties during the 1990s and 2000s, a basically stable political system has become established at the European level. After the abortive attempt to install a EU Constitution, the 2009 Lisbon Treaty cautiously develops the existing institutional structure without ringing in a new age of European integration. And even if the Constitutional Treaty had not been rejected in two referenda in France and the Netherlands, its entry into force would not have fundamentally changed the EU system. Nonetheless, the EU system is still developing, and the fact that it is relatively stable today may not be a good predictor of the future. The failed referenda on the Constitutional Treaty, the wave of Euroscepticism in the UK and beyond, and the difficulties involved in managing the current sovereign debt crisis in many Euro states show that the direction of future development is as yet unclear. Classical integration theories such as neofunctionalism and intergovernmentalism have concentrated chiefly on *successful* moves towards integration. By definition, integration theory regards "deepening, expansion and reform projects . . . as more worthy of investigation than crises and regressive developments" (Faber and Wessels 2005: 355, my translation). At the same time, classical integration theory has either largely neglected the possible politicization of integration processes (intergovernmentalism) or has discussed it as a factor that would clearly work in favour of further integration (Schmitter 1969: 165–166). Yet it is politicization, crises and setbacks that seem more prominent, at least at the moment, within the EU political system. Present integration theory seems ill-equipped to analyse such developments. For these reasons it may well be the case that the age of "postfunctionalist" integration theory is now upon us (Hooghe and Marks 2008; see also Börzel 2005).[27]

5 Notes

1 For a detailed account of how neofunctionalism fits into the liberal school of IR, see Viotti and Kauppi (2010: 125–129). On the place of neofunctionalism within theories of integration, which have been developed chiefly with reference to the European Community (EC), see Rosamond (2000), Faber (2005) and Niemann and Schmitter (2009).

2 The League of Nations, founded as an international response to the events of the First World War, aimed to preserve international peace and establish a collective system of international security. The League did help resolve a number of conflicts, but ultimately proved powerless in the face of the aggressive and expansionist policies of Japan, Italy and Germany from the early 1930s on (Stiles 2010: Chapter 2).

3 This affinity consists above all in the expectation, expressed in the so-called Schuman Plan of 1950 and in the preamble to the founding treaty of the European Coal and Steel Community (ECSC), that the initially limited steps towards integration would soon be followed by further steps as a result of the "de facto solidarity" and the "fusion of interests" that had been created. The ECSC and the European Community (EC), however, were contrary to one of the central credos of functionalist thought in that their static (though expanding) membership reproduced the old territorial logic of the nation state on a supranational level. They thus did *not* gear the territorial scope of cooperation towards maximum satisfaction of societal needs. See Section 2.1.

4 Haas's key work, *The Uniting of Europe*, was first published in 1958. In what follows I refer exclusively to the second edition of 1968, which includes a highly instructive critical examination of neofunctionalism as originally conceived by Haas. *The Uniting of Europe* was newly published in 2004, featuring a new foreword by Haas, examining the reception of his work over time (Haas 2004).

5 See also the special issue of the *Journal of European Public Policy*, "The Disparity of European Integration: Revisiting Neofunctionalism in Honour of Ernst Haas" (12(2), 2005).

6 See the chapter by Siegfried Schieder in this volume.

7 Other important functionalists are George D. H. Cole and Pittman Porter. On the historical background, see Rosamond (2000: 31–32).

8 In other words, mutual dependence. Mitrany was already using the term interdependence in 1933, about 40 years before it became central to theoretical debates within International Relations. See the chapter by Manuela Spindler in this volume.

9 According to Mitrany:

> There is little promise of peace in the mere change from the rivalry of powers and alliances to the rivalry of whole continents . . . Continental unions would have a more real chance than individual states to practice the autarky that makes for division.
>
> (1966: 45)

10 Senghaas-Knobloch comes to the conclusion that Mitrany's conception

> has an inadequate grasp of the character of political action . . . The new political style is passed off as apolitical. The factual problems that this political style is supposed to resolve, however, only provide a weak foundation because such problems can be understood to require merely technical solutions only if their origins can also be viewed as independent of political action and particular interests.
>
> (1969: 25; my translation)

See also Haas's critical examination of some of Mitrany's basic functionalist assumptions (1964: 47–50).

11 The terms "functional", "political" and "cultivated" spill-over build on the ideas of Haas (1961, 1968: 287–313) and Nye (1971: 64–75), though neither of them introduces these terms systematically in his work.

12 The background here is the classical international political economy argument that economic exchange between nation states leads to increased prosperity for all involved. This idea achieved almost universal acceptance in post-war Europe (see Herbst 1986; in the context of the emergence of the ECSC as the first European Community, and Kohler-Koch *et al.* 2004: Chapter 3). Neofunctionalist scholars Lindberg and Scheingold (1970) used the term "permissive consensus" to refer to the low level of controversy over economic integration among the general population. They saw this consensus as a condition facilitative of successful integration.

13 For Haas, the concept of learning is crucial but he fails to specify the theoretical background in his earlier writings. Later on, Haas began to discuss an instrumental form of learning in which elites discover that their interests can be better pursued through a new approach involving supranational cooperation, and a reflexive variant of "social learning" in which interests and loyalties are redefined as a consequence of experiences of cooperation. See Haas (1964: 48–50; 1970: 642–644). On the obvious points of contact with constructivist theories in International Relations, see Haas (2001, 2004) and Risse (2005). See also the chapter by Cornelia Ulbert in this volume.

14 The anchoring of this argument in pluralist thought is especially evident in this respect, as is also acknowledged by Haas (1970: 628); see also Rosamond (2000: 55–58).

15 Then French President de Gaulle withdrew the French ministers from the meetings of the Council of Ministers in protest at certain supranational tendencies of the EEC (in particular, changes to the financing of the Common Agricultural Policy and the transition to more frequent application of majority voting in the Council). The French chair being 'empty', the EEC was rendered *de facto* incapable of reaching decisions. The crisis was brought to an end by the Luxembourg Compromise of 1966. This conceded to the member states the right to demand unanimous voting in matters of vital national interest even if, according to the Treaty, a majority would suffice. See Dinan (2010: 36–39).

16 In the relevant literature, this discussion is often taken up with reference to the distinction introduced by Hoffmann (1966) between "low politics" and "high politics". For Haas's critical reflection on this argument, see Haas (1970: 621, 629–630).

17 See Haas's Introduction, mentioned earlier, in the second (1968) edition of *The Uniting of Europe*, and Haas (1970: 627–628).

18 From 1973 to 1975, *The Uniting of Europe* was mentioned in the *Social Science Citation Index* an average of 550 times a year. This fell to around 270 from 1976 to 1978 and around or below 200 over the course of the early 1980s. Between 1987 and 1990 the figure doubled again (Caporaso and Keeler 1995: 38).

19 Moravcsik's argument is briefly outlined in Section 4. For an in-depth discussion, see Siegfried Schieder's chapter in this volume.
20 For these authors, one of the important forums in this regard was the so-called European Round Table of Industrialists (ERT), which brought together major European firms for a casual round of talks beginning in the early 1980s. See Green Cowles (1995). For a comparative analysis of the significance of economic elites and of the ERT in processes of regional integration, see Spindler (2003).
21 Regarding the latter point, the two key criticisms are that neofunctionalism is unable to explain the "stop–go nature" of the European integration process and the specific timing of the various moves towards integration, and that it neglects the "national option", in other words, member states' still undiminished capacity to retreat to national solutions.
22 According to Stone Sweet and Sandholtz,

> Thus, we view intergovernmental bargaining and decision-making as embedded in processes that are provoked and sustained by the expansion of transnational society, the pro-integrative activities of supranational organizations, and the growing density of supranational rules . . . These processes gradually, but inevitably, reduce the capacity of the member states to control outcomes . . . As integration proceeds, member state governments become less and less proactive, and more and more reactive to changes in the supranational environment to which they belong.
>
> (Stone Sweet and Sandholtz 1997: 299–301)

23 See also Weiler (1991) and Alter (1998). Garrett (1992) and Schmitter (2004: 72–73) provide a critique of the argument made by Burley and Mattli.
24 Quote from the second edition (1968: xxxi).
25 See, for example, Mattli (1999) or Hettne (2001). A theory-oriented introduction is provided by Sbragia (2008) and Börzel (2012).
26 With regard to the SEA and the single market project, Moravcsik argues that "supranational political entrepreneurs played a significant if secondary role in assembling a particular package of concrete single market proposals and mobilizing transnational interests". Yet, Moravcsik concludes, "the substance of the SEA, as intergovernmental theory predicts, reflected above all the national priorities of the most recalcitrant countries" (1998: 372–373).
27 The argument put forward by Hooghe and Marks is that since the early 1990s European integration has become increasingly politicized and that therefore the EU's institutional development can neither be interpreted as an effective answer to the "functional" problems of economic interdependence, nor as the outcome of elite-based intergovernmental bargains. Rather, the preferences of citizens and the fear of electoral defeat have become decisive to the future shape of integration, which includes the possibility of "downward pressure on the level and scope of integration" (2008: 21). The core problem of the "post-functionalist" age is thus not the elite-driven realization of welfare gains, but the need to ensure that the general population continues to accept the EU's institutions and policies and any possible changes to the EU system. Rather than a "permissive consensus", a "constraining dissensus" is determining the course of the integration process today. See also above, note 12.

6 Bibliography and recommended reading

6.1 Primary texts

Haas, Ernst B. 1964: *Beyond the Nation-State: Functionalism and International Organization.* Stanford, CA: Stanford University Press.

Haas, Ernst B. 1968: *The Uniting of Europe*, 2nd edn. Stanford, CA: Stanford University Press.

Haas, Ernst B. 1970: The Study of Regional Integration: Reflections on the Joy and Anguish of Pretheorizing, *International Organization* 24(4): 607–646.

Mitrany, David [1943] 1966: A Working Peace System: An Argument for the Functional Development of International Organization, in Mitrany, David, *A Working Peace System.* Chicago: Quadrangle Books, pp. 25–99.

Sandholtz, Wayne and Zysman, John 1989: 1992 – Recasting the European Bargain, *World Politics* 42(1): 95–128.

Schmitter, Philippe C. 2004: Neo-Neofunctionalism, in Diez, Thomas and Wiener, Antje (eds) *European Integration Theory*. Oxford: Oxford University Press, pp. 45–74.

6.2 Secondary texts

Mattli, Walter 2005: Ernst Haas's Evolving Thinking on Comparative Regional Integration: of Virtues and Infelicities, *Journal of European Public Policy* 12(2): 327–348.

Niemann, Arne and Schmitter, Philippe C. 2009: Neofunctionalism, in Wiener, Antje and Diez, Thomas (eds) *European Integration Theory*, 2nd edn. Oxford: Oxford University Press, pp. 45–66.

Rosamond, Ben 2005: The Uniting of Europe and the Foundation of EU Studies: Revisiting the Neofunctionalism of Ernst B. Haas, *Journal of European Public Policy* 12(2): 237–254.

6.3 Other texts

Alter, Karen 1998: Who Are the "Masters of the Treaty"? European Governments and the European Court of Justice, *International Organization* 52(1): 121–147.

Börzel, Tanja A. 2005: Europäische Integrationstheorie – nicht obsolet, aber reformbedürftig, *Zeitschrift für Internationale Beziehungen* 11(2): 345–351.

Börzel, Tanja A. 2012: Comparative Regionalism: European Integration and Beyond, in Carlsnaes, Walter, Risse, Thomas and Simmons, Beth A. (eds) *Handbook of International Relations*, 2nd edn. London: Sage Publications, pp. 503–530.

Burley, Ann-Marie and Mattli, Walter 1993: Europe Before the Court: A Political Theory of Legal Integration, *International Organization* 47(1): 41–76.

Caporaso, James A. and Keeler, John T. S. 1995: The European Community and Regional Integration Theory, in Rhodes, Carolyn and Mazey, Sonia (eds) *The State of the European Community: Building a European Polity*? Boulder, CO: Lynne Rienner, pp. 29–62.

Corbey, Dorette 1995: Dialectical Functionalism: Stagnation as a Booster of European Integration, *International Organization* 49(2): 253–284.

Dinan, Desmond 2010: *Ever Closer Union: An Introduction to European Integration*. 4th edn. Basingstoke: Palgrave Macmillan.

Faber, Anne 2005: *Europäische Integration und politikwissenschaftliche Theoriebildung: Neofunktionalismus und Intergouvernementalismus in der Analyse*. Wiesbaden: VS Verlag.

Faber, Anne and Wessels, Wolfgang 2005: Die Verfassungskrise der EU als Krise "der" Integrationstheorie? Plädoyer für eine Neufokussierung der theoretischen Debatte, *Zeitschrift für Internationale Beziehungen* 12(2): 353–359.

Garrett, Geoffrey 1992: International Cooperation and Institutional Choice: The European Community's Internal Market, *International Organization* 46(2): 533–560.

Green Cowles, Maria 1995: Setting the Agenda for a New Europe: The ERT and EC 1992, *Journal of Common Market Studies* 33(4): 501–526.

Haas, Ernst B. 1961: International Integration. The European and the Universal Process, *International Organization* 15(3): 366–392.

Haas, Ernst B. 1975: *The Obsolescence of Regional Integration Theory*. Berkeley, CA: University of California Press.

Haas, Ernst B. 1976: Turbulent Fields and the Theory of Regional Integration, *International Organization* 30(2): 173–212.

Haas, Ernst B. 1980: Why Collaborate? Issue-linkage and International Regimes, *World Politics* 32(3): 357–405.

Haas Ernst B. 1982: Words Can Hurt You, Or: Who Said What to Whom about International Regimes?, *International Organization* 36(2): 207–243.

Haas, Ernst B. 1990: *When Knowledge is Power: Three Models of Change in International Organizations*. Berkeley, CA: University of California Press.

Haas, Ernst B. 2001: Does Constructivism Subsume Functionalism?, in Christiansen, Thomas, Jørgensen, Knud E. and Wiener, Antje (eds) *The Social Construction of Europe*. London: Sage, pp. 22–31.

Haas, Ernst B. 2004: Introduction: Institutionalism or Constructivism?, in Haas, Ernst B. (ed.) *The Uniting of Europe: Politics, Social and Economic Forces, 1950–1957*, 3rd edn. Notre Dame, IN: University of Notre Dame Press, pp. xiii–lvi.

Haas, Ernst B. and Schmitter, Philippe C. 1964: Economics and Differential Patterns of Political Integration: Projections about Unity in Latin America, *International Organization* 18(4): 705–737.

Hansen, Roger D. 1969: Regional Integration. Reflections on a Decade of Theoretical Efforts, *World Politics* 21(2): 242–271.

Herbst, Ludolf 1986: Die zeitgenössische Integrationstheorie und die Anfänge der europäischen Einigung 1947–1950, *Vierteljahreshefte für Zeitgeschichte* 34(2): 161–205.

Hettne, Björn 2001: *Comparing Regionalisms: Implications for Global Development*. Basingstoke: Palgrave.

Hoffmann, Stanley 1966: Obstinate or Obsolete? The Fate of the Nation State and the Case of Western Europe, *Daedalus* 95(3): 862–915.

Hooghe, Liesbet and Marks, Gary 2008: A Postfunctionalist Theory of European Integration: From Permissive Consensus to Constraining Dissensus, *British Journal of Political Science* 39(1): 1–23.

Keohane, Robert O. 1984: *After Hegemony: Cooperation and Discord in the World Political Economy*. Princeton, NJ: Princeton University Press.

Kohler-Koch, Beate, Conzelmann, Thomas and Knodt, Michèle 2004: *Europäische Integration – Europäisches Regieren*. Wiesbaden: VS Verlag.

Kohler-Koch, Beate and Rittberger, Berthold 2006: Review Article: The Governance Turn in EU Studies, *Journal of Common Market Studies* 44(Annual Review): 27–49.

Lindberg, Leon N. 1971: *The Political Dynamics of European Economic Integration*, 2nd edn. Stanford, CA: Stanford University Press.

Lindberg, Leon N. and Scheingold, Stuart A. 1970: *Europe's Would-Be Polity*. Englewood Cliffs, NJ: Prentice-Hall.

Mattli, Walter 1999: *The Logic of Regional Integration: Europe and Beyond*. Cambridge: Cambridge University Press.

Merton, Robert K. 1968: *Social Theory and Social Structure*. New York: Free Press.

Mitrany, David 1933: *The Progress of International Government*. London: Allen & Unwin.

Mitrany, David 1965: The Prospect of Integration: Federal or Functional, *Journal of Common Market Studies* 4(2): 119–149.

Moravcsik, Andrew 1991: Negotiating the European Single Act: National Interests and Conventional Statecraft in the European Community, *International Organization* 45(1): 19–56.

Moravcsik, Andrew 1998: *The Choice for Europe: Social Purpose and State Power from Messina to Maastricht*. Ithaca, NY: Cornell University Press.

Moravcsik, Andrew 2005: The European Constitutional Compromise and the Neofunctionalist Legacy, *Journal of European Public Policy* 12(2): 349–386.

Nye, Joseph. S. 1970: Comparing Common Markets: A Revised Neo-Functionalist Model, *International Organization* 24(4): 796–835.

Nye, Joseph S. 1971: *Peace in Parts: Integration and Conflict in Regional Organization*. Boston: Little, Brown and Company.

Pollack, Mark A. 2005: Theorizing the European Union: International Organization, Domestic Polity, or Experiment in New Governance?, *Annual Review of Political Science* 8: 357–398.

Risse, Thomas 2005: Neofunctionalism, European Identity, and the Puzzles of European Integration, *Journal of European Public Policy* 12(2): 291–309.

Rittberger, Berthold and Schimmelfennig, Frank 2005: Integrationstheorien: Entstehung und Entwicklung der EU, in Holzinger, Katharina *et al.*: *Die Europäische Union. Theorien und Analysekonzepte*. Paderborn: Schöningh, pp. 19–80.

Rosamond, Ben 2000: *Theories of European Integration*. Houndmills: Macmillan.

Rosamond, Ben 2010: New Theories of European Integration, in Cini, Michelle and Pérez-Solórzano Borragán, Nieves (eds) *European Union Politics*, 3rd edn. Oxford: Oxford University Press, pp. 104–122.

Ruggie John G. *et al.* 2005: Transformations in World Politics: The Intellectual Contributions of Ernst B. Haas, *Annual Review of Political Science* 8: 271–296.

Sbragia, Alberta 2008: Review Article: Comparative Regionalism: What Might It Be?, *Journal of Common Market Studies* 46(Annual Review): 29–49.

Schmitter, Philippe C. 1969: Three Neo-Functionalist Hypotheses about International Integration, *International Organization* 23(1): 161–166.

Schmitter, Philippe C. 1970: A Revised Theory of Regional Integration, *International Organization* 24(4): 836–868.

Senghaas-Knobloch, Eva 1969: *Frieden durch Integration und Assoziation. Literaturbericht und Problemstudien*. Stuttgart: Ernst Klett Verlag.

Spindler, Manuela 2003: Toward the Competition Region: Global Business Actors and the Future of New Regionalism, in Hülsemeyer, Axel (ed.) *Globalization in the Twenty-First Century: Convergence or Divergence*? Basingstoke: Palgrave Macmillan, pp. 119–133.

Stiles, Kendall W. 2010: *Case Histories in International Politics*, 6th edn. New York: Longman.

Stone Sweet, Alec and Sandholtz, Wayne 1997: European Integration and Supranational Governance, *Journal of European Public Policy* 4(3): 297–317.

Taylor, Paul 1989: The New Dynamics of EC Integration in the 1980's, in Lodge, Juliet (ed.) *The European Community and the Challenge of the Future*. London: Pinter, pp. 3–28.

Tranholm-Mikkelsen, Jeppe 1991: Neo-Functionalism: Obstinate or Obsolete? A Reappraisal in the Light of the New Dynamics of the EC, *Millennium* 20(1): 1–22.

Viotti, Paul R. and Kauppi, Mark V. 2010: *International Relations Theory*, 4th edn. New York: Longman.

Weiler, Joseph H.H. 1991: The Transformation of Europe, *Yale Law Journal* 100: 2403–2483.

New liberalism

Siegfried Schieder

1 Introduction

By the 1990s at the latest, a renaissance of liberalism had occurred within the theories of International Relations (IR).[1] The new vigour of the liberal approaches that developed in the context of East–West détente and the rise of peace research in the 1970s (see Czempiel 1972) is closely bound up with the end of the Cold War and the collapse of the Communist regimes in Central and Eastern Europe. Like no other series of events, the global political upheaval of 1989/90 allowed us to see into the social depths of international politics and confirmed the validity of liberal analyses of international politics (Doyle 1994). In empirical terms, the optimistic vision of a democratic global order – still cherished by many in the early 1990s – collided with countervailing trends: ethno-national conflicts, regional power struggles and the fight against international terrorism. This prompted a number of observers to refer retrospectively to a "liberal moment" (Latham 1997) with respect to the 1990s. From a historical perspective, however, despite the wars in Iraq and Afghanistan, it is beyond dispute that the global political caesura of 1989/90 advanced the domestication and sociation of foreign policy and international politics, allowing us a clearer view of the true, determinative subject of international politics: society.[2]

But the renaissance of liberal approaches, which long traded under the names of "moralism", "idealism" or "utopianism" and seemed discredited due to their optimistic faith in progress (Moravcsik 1997: 514) is by no means merely a reflection of real-world historical developments. It is linked above all with a growing dissatisfaction with systemic approaches (see Sterling-Folker 1997).[3] Realism's inability to predict the end of the East–West conflict is an example of this (see the chapter by Niklas Schörnig in this volume). Researchers were increasingly dubious about the fundamental realist assumption that states determine international relations. Key exponents of liberalism such as Ernst-Otto Czempiel, Bruce Russett, Michael Doyle, Robert D. Putnam, Thomas Risse and, not least, Andrew Moravcsik take the view that state action derives from societal structures and interests. As they see it, we must move away from the idea of states as coherent and central actors in the international order and replace it with a historically contingent and dynamic view of world politics (Zacher and Matthew 1995: 118).

Despite these commonalities, the notion of "liberal theories" of international relations is anything but uncontested. We need only look at the range of terms used in the literature to see this: "second image approach" (Waltz 1959; Gourevitch 1978, 2002), "domestic theories of international politics" (Putnam 1988), "theories of 'state–society relations' " (Moravcsik 1993a: 6) or simply "pluralism" (Viotti and Kauppi 2009) – to name but a few. Ultimately, the emphasis on the term "liberal" has taken hold because it was originally thinkers in the tradition of the European Enlightenment and liberal political theory who thought it possible for international politics to become civilized and for society to progress (Zacher and Matthew 1995: 111–117). If we take parsimony (with respect to basic theoretical assumptions) and distinctiveness (when comparing these basic assumptions with competing theoretical paradigms) as broadly accepted positivist criteria for persuasive theory building, however, then the old liberalism in IR was long deficient.[4] This has to do, first, with the fact that theorists sharing the same basically liberal stance generated relatively isolated and unsystematic theoretical building blocks. Liberals such as Adam Smith, Immanuel Kant, John Stuart Mill, Giuseppe Mazzini, John Hobson and Woodrow Wilson, made important inferences in light of their philosophical and political assumptions about the connection between the internal character of the state and its behaviour in the world; and liberal theory within IR explicitly built on these inferences (see Richardson 2001). But they did not manage to bring their insights together to create a coherent theoretical edifice that might have served as the foundation for a cumulative intellectual programme (see Lakatos 1970).[5] To an even greater extent than realism, because of its rich historical legacy liberalism was long a rather shapeless entity (see Doyle 1986: 1152; Moravcsik 1997: 514–515; Zacher and Matthew 1995: 107). We can identify a number of different strands of liberalism in line with how key influences on states' foreign policies are conceptualized: *republican liberalism* (democratic states behave more peacefully and cooperatively towards the rest of the world than nondemocratic states), *pluralist liberalism* (a balanced distribution of power and negligible struggles over distribution between social groups promote cooperative conduct towards the rest of the world), *sociological liberalism* (transnational relations promote cooperative behaviour by states) and *free-trade liberalism* (open trade relations and interdependence promote cooperation)[6] – to mention just the most important (Zacher and Matthew 1995: 120–137; Burchill 2009: 57–85).

In addition to its amorphousness, the liberal school was also burdened by a prescriptive view of action. Liberal theory in the tradition of idealism was not content to describe the phenomena of international politics but always attempted to identify ways of changing existing relations of power and domination within societies. This liberalism, then, was always partly concerned to produce social analysis and criticism (Krell 2009: 175–225). The very ambivalence of empirical description and political ideology prevented the development of an analytical approach to the description and explanation of international relations on the basis of key liberal assumptions. We have political scientist Andrew Moravcsik, currently teaching at the Woodrow Wilson School of Princeton University, to thank for remedying this shortcoming by formulating a "liberal international relations theory in a nonideological and non-utopian form appropriate to empirical social science", thus advancing the systematization of liberal theory (Moravcsik 1997: 513). Moravcsik both narrows and expands the liberal theoretical tradition. He narrows it by reducing liberalism to "a minimalist classical liberalism" (Long 1995: 499). At the same time he expands the liberal tradition by presenting a more open and less teleological perspective on progress. The present volume aims to examine IR theory scientifically. Moravcsik has probably done more than anyone else to consistently develop a verifiable liberal theory in IR (see Moravcsik 1991, 1992, 1997, 2003b, 2008) as well as formulating and testing his own approach to (regional) European integration on the basis of this theory in the shape of liberal intergovernmentalism (Moravcsik 1993b, 1988; Moravcsik and Schimmelfennig 2009). He therefore serves as my reference theorist in the discussion of new liberalism that follows.

2 The "positive turn" in the liberal theory of International Relations: Andrew Moravcsik

The roots of liberal theory in IR are to be found in the neofunctionalism of Ernst B. Haas, the bureaucracy model of Graham T. Allison, the transnationalism of Joseph S. Nye and Robert O. Keohane and early studies by James N. Rosenau (see Katzenstein *et al.* 1998: 658ff.). All of them work with a pluralist, "bottom-up" conception of politics. European scholars of foreign policy such as Czempiel (1979, 1981), and studies on the mutual influence exercised by states, societal structures and social actors on foreign policy behaviour (e.g. Katzenstein 1976) drew on this theoretical tradition, which was also taken up by younger authors such as Evangelista (1995), Risse-Kappen (1991, 1995a) and recently Narizny (2003a, 2003b, 2007) (for an overview, see Dunn 2010). Since the 1990s, Moravcsik has been primarily responsible for putting liberalism back on the agenda of International Relations.[7]

Based on a positivist conception of knowledge and through critical reflection on systemic approaches, Moravcsik developed a liberal theory fundamentally different from neorealism and institutionalism: "For liberals, the configuration of state preferences matters most in world politics – not, as realists argue, the configuration of capabilities and not, as institutionalists . . . maintain, the configuration of information and institutions" (Moravcsik 1997: 513, see also 2003b: 170; 2008: 234). Through his preference-oriented liberal theory, Moravcsik self-consciously lays claim to the status of a verifiable general theory akin to the other prominent theoretical schools of IR. As he succinctly puts it: "Liberal international theory is a paradigmatic alternative theoretically distinct, empirically coequal, and in certain respects analytically more fundamental, than existing paradigms such as realism, institutionalism, or constructivism" (Moravcsik 2008: 235).

Moravcsik's liberal theory stands in the tradition of methodological individualism, as it is essentially interested in the action of social individuals (Moravcsik 1992: 4–6). It is true that individuals generally come together to form action-capable social groups such as parties, trade unions, religious or ethnic groups and even states. But the action of groups can always be traced back to the acts of individuals. The corresponding conception of the human being here is that of "homo economicus", a rational utility maximizer. Moravcsik, however, has a qualified notion of rationality, namely that of "bounded rationality" (Moravcsik 1998: 21–23). It is true that the aggregate of interests represented by the state is not necessarily the same over long periods of time, just as it is not always geared towards material utility. Nonetheless, Moravcsik works on the assumption that every government tries to realize, as rationally and efficiently as possible, "state preferences" (in contrast to "state strategies" or "policy positions"), which develop in liberal fashion via processes of negotiation within states and in the transnational sphere.[8] The state-internal and transnational social action context, in which state action is embedded, varies substantially both in spatial and temporal terms. "The resulting globalization-induced variation in social demands and state preferences is a fundamental cause of state behavior in world politics. This is the central insight of liberal international relations theory", Moravcsik tells us (2008: 234).

2.1 Actors, representation, preferences: three basic assumptions of the new liberalism

Moravcsik develops his three core assumptions on the fundamental premise of every liberal theory that state action is substantially moulded by the relations between states and their state-internal and transnational social environments (Moravcsik 1997: 516–521; 2003b: 161–167; 2008: 236–239).

1 *The precedence of the social actor and society over the state.* While neorealists and neoinstitutionalists regard states as the key actors in international politics, Moravcsik privileges autonomous, action-capable individuals and social groups, which – in line with their various preferences – realize their material and values-based interests within the state but also within the transnational web of relations (Moravcsik 1997: 516; 2008: 236).[9] Social groups and individuals are expected to act in a rational and risk-averse manner and to compete for influence on governmental decisions. For Moravcsik, the state is not a fixed variable but always the outcome of very specific social relations. "Society is analytically prior to the state, and domestic state-society relations constitute the central issues of politics" (Moravcsik 1992: 7).

In contrast to systemic IR theories, which privilege states' exogenous interests and preferences, for liberals such as Moravcsik, both the functional differentiation and definition of the interests of societal and transnational actors are of central theoretical significance. According to Moravcsik (2008: 236), as a result of globalization, social individuals and groups make differing demands of the international political sphere. Liberals reject the idea that there is a harmony of interests within society; for them, society is characterized by ceaseless competition between both individual and group interests (Moravcsik 1997: 517; 2003b: 162). The probability of conflicts within society is high whenever divergent values about life together in society, conflicts over scarce resources or unequal access to the political realm exist within a state (Moravcsik 1997: 517). Conflicts are more likely to arise in cases where there is inequality with respect to social influence because certain social groups have the ability to pass on costs to the rest of society. Where social power is fairly distributed, meanwhile, costs and benefits can be more easily internalized, through legitimized political institutions for example. How competition within society ultimately unfolds and which societal interests and values shape official government policies via the state-internal process of negotiation depend above all on the political system and the relations of power between the competing social actors (Milner 1998: 767–779; see Moravcsik 2003b: 163).

2 *Representation within society and the formation of state preferences.* Competition between social actors is determined by state-internal structures and institutions tasked with mediating between the interests of state and society (Moravcsik 1997: 518). States (or other political institutions) represent one part of society and are thus a "transmission belt" for dominant societal preferences, which spill over into a state's foreign policy. In contrast to realist and institutionalist approaches, however, the state is not viewed as a coherent actor, but as "a representative institution constantly subject to capture and recapture, construction and reconstruction by coalitions of social actors" (Moravcsik 1997: 518). Pluralist liberal theorists assume neither that all individuals and groups have the same influence on governments nor that state institutions are irrelevant. Quite the opposite: every government represents certain groups and individuals more or less comprehensively than others – from Stalinist-style dictatorships to broad forms of democratic participation. It is the specific character of representative institutions – and for Moravcsik, state-internal representation cannot be reduced to the formal characteristics of state bodies, so it includes informal institutions – that is the decisive factor determining which social groups influence the "national interest" (Moravcsik 2003b: 164).

The assumption that a state's behaviour is the expression of the aggregate of social actors' preferences, which are realized through a complex process of interest mediation and decision-making, has important implications for how states behave within the world. From a liberal perspective, governments do not automatically seek to maximize security and power, because social actors do not generally strive to uphold any *raison d'état*. Instead their basic motive is obtaining welfare gains. This, however, does not exclude the possibility that power politics, in the sense of the maximization of state autonomy and influence, may lie in the interest of influential social groups and that they may successfully pursue such power politics (Freund and Rittberger 2001: 77). Snyder (1991), for example, has elaborated the central role of elites in mobilizing the population to achieve imperialist goals; in articles on party conduct with respect to rearmament and the political economy of security strategies, Narizny (2003a, 2003b) has shown that

> a nation's grand strategy rarely serves the best interests of all its citizens. Instead, every strategic choice benefits some domestic groups at the expense of others . . . As a result, the overarching goals and guiding principles of grand strategy, as formulated at the highest levels of government, derive from domestic coalitional interests.
>
> (Narizny 2007: 3)

So in contrast to the goal of action always postulated by realists, namely "national interest", because of state-internal party competition, "national security may not be present to the necessary and possible extent; a problem unknown to realism in this form" (Hasenclever 2001: 88).

3 *International environment and the interdependent ordering of preferences.* Exponents of liberal IR theory do not doubt that the international environment provides important stimuli for action. But they turn the realist perspective on its head by regarding action options within the international environment as a function of the state-internal and society-internal process of preference formation. For pluralist liberals, patterns of action within international politics do not arise from the international distribution of power or international institutions. Instead, "what states want is the primary determinant of what they do" (Moravcsik 1997: 521).

The theoretical connection between state preferences and states' behaviour towards the rest of the world is established through the concept of so-called "policy interdependence" (Moravcsik 1997: 520; 2003b: 165–166). Moravcsik understands this to mean

> [the] distribution and interaction of preferences – that is, the extent to which the pursuit of state preferences necessarily imposes costs and benefits upon other states, independent of the "transaction costs" imposed by the specific strategic means chosen to obtain them.
>
> (Moravcsik 2008: 239)

While realist approaches presuppose conflictual relations between states, Moravcsik argues that the ordering of interdependent preferences imposes very specific restrictions on how states behave towards the rest of the world. States' willingness to spread their resources or, alternatively, to make concessions in negotiations, is thus primarily a function of state preference formation rather than being determined by an independent portfolio of political power. States are "rarely prepared to mortgage their entire economy or military capabilities in pursuit of any single foreign-policy goal. Few wars are total, few peaces Carthaginian" (ibid.: 239–240).

Moravcsik distinguishes between three kinds of the distribution of interdependent preferences. If the specific preferences of different states are compatible, or if they converge, this produces strong incentives for negotiations and international cooperation. Divergent state preferences, meanwhile, bring about tensions and conflicts between states. This leads to zero-sum constellations that leave little space for mutual cooperation because the dominant social groups within a country attempt to realize their preferences through state policies, and these policies inevitably mean costs for other important social groups in other countries. In the case of complementary national preferences, meanwhile, there are sufficient incentives for international negotiations, concessions and forms of international policy coordination (Moravcsik 1992: 10–11; 2008: 239–240).

2.2 Three theoretical variants: ideational, commercial and republican liberalism

From his three core assumptions about the nature of actors and the demands they make of international politics, the nature of states and of the international system, Moravcsik derives three specific theoretical variants: *ideational, commercial and republican liberalism* (Moravcsik 1997: 524–533; 2003b: 167–176; 2008: 240–246). Each of them emphasizes different influencing factors and causal mechanisms lying between national preference formation and state behaviour: identity, interest and institutions.

1 *Ideational liberalism.* The first source of state preference formation comprises state-internal conceptions of social order and social identities. With reference to liberals such as Mill, Mazzini, Wilson and Keynes, Moravcsik assumes that foreign policy preferences are determined by social identities and values regarded as legitimate within the state. Social identity includes

> [a] set of preferences shared by individuals concerning the proper scope and nature of public goods provision, which in turn specifies the nature of legitimate domestic order by stipulating which social actors belong to the polity and what is owed them.
>
> (Moravcsik 1997: 525)

Liberals highlight national identity, political ideology and the regulation of socioeconomic welfare as the key sources of legitimacy of state-internal social orders (Moravcsik 1997: 525; 2003b: 168–171).[10] Depending on how highly developed these political, social and socioeconomic identities are within a state, we may derive various hypotheses about how states will behave towards other states. Converging state-internal preferences regarding ideational interests foster cooperation with other states, while divergent ideational foreign policy preferences lead to international tensions and conflicts. With reference to a number of examples from European and international politics, Moravcsik tries to show empirically that

> substantial prior convergence of underlying values is a necessary prerequisite for cooperation in regulatory issue areas like environmental and consumer protection, . . . social policies, immigration, and foreign policies, as well as for significant surrenders of sovereign decision making to supranational courts and bureaucracies.
>
> (Moravcsik 1997: 528)

2 *Commercial liberalism.* A second source of liberal preference formation within the state is economic in nature. Commercial liberalism explains the individual and collective conduct of states by examining the market incentives with which domestic and transnational economic actors such as corporations find themselves confronted. How states behave towards the rest of the world is dependent on the gains and losses of social actors as a result of transnational economic exchange relations (Moravcsik 1997: 524; 2003b: 171; 2008: 242–244). The more producers and consumers benefit from the international division of labour, the more they will work to achieve open markets and stable economic relations and reject protectionism, which endangers their advantageous trade relations. Conversely:

> The more costly the adjustment imposed by the proposed economic exchanges, the more opposition is likely to arise. The resulting commercial liberal explanation of "relative gains-seeking" in foreign economic policy is quite distinct from that of realism, which emphasizes security externalities and relative (hegemonic) power, or that of institutionalism, which stresses informational and institutional constraints on optimal interstate collective action . . . Liberal IR theory . . . employs market structure as a variable to explain both openness and closure.
>
> (Moravcsik 2003b: 171f; see also Keohane and Milner 1996)

Commercial liberalism has important implications for security policy. Governments are aware of the fact that wars, sanctions and other coercive military policies are far more costly than the transnational exchange of goods and services. Consequently, there is a strong economic incentive within society for states to behave cooperatively towards other states and forgo aggressive self-help strategies.

3 *Republican liberalism.* While ideational and commercial liberalism view preference formation as the outcome of specific patterns of social identities and economic interests, republican liberalism foregrounds the procedures of state-internal representation. The aim here is to explain which social groups are able to incorporate their interests into the process of foreign policy preference formation. The relevant authors thus examine the ways in which social interests are aggregated through political institutions. Moravcsik refers to the way in which certain groups "capture" the state (Moravcsik 1997: 530–533; 2003b: 173–174; 2008: 244–246).

Generally speaking, the more a social group is represented within the key decision-making bodies, and the more effectively these can be sealed off from other influences, the greater its political influence will be (Moravcsik 1997: 530; 2003b: 174–175). A more nuanced perspective on the mechanisms of aggregation of social preferences emerges if we examine the influence of particularist interests ("rent-seeking"). If political influence in society is exercised by a small number of groups with specific interests, liberals generally expect a confrontational rather than cooperative foreign policy. Confrontation and state expansionism rarely involve net benefits for society as a whole. The opposite is more likely to apply. So if political influence within society is distributed equally, there is a greater tendency for states to embrace cooperation in order to avoid conflicts. If influence is concentrated in a small number of groups, meanwhile, these have greater opportunities to shape and enforce expansionist or confrontational policies in such a way that the material and ideational benefits accrue mainly to them. The risks and costs, meanwhile, are disproportionately borne by the under-represented rest of society.[11] But because most individuals and social groups tend to behave in a risk-averse manner, in cases of broad political representation there will be a lack of support for a conflictual and cost-intensive foreign policy. Moravcsik comes to the conclusion that aggressive behaviour towards other states is most likely to occur in authoritarian regimes and dictatorships because here it is relatively simple for privileged individuals to pass the consequences of international conflicts and wars on to the rest of society. Democratic states, meanwhile, are far less likely to engage in conflictual conduct as influence on political decisions lies in the hands of a broad group of decision-makers and these must ultimately bear the costs as taxpayers. Moravcsik puts the fact that democratic states sometimes wage wars against authoritarian regimes down to the willingness of political decision-makers to take risks or to rent-seek. "There is substantial historical evidence that the aggressors who have provoked modern great power wars tend either to be extremely risk-acceptant individuals, or individuals well able to insulate themselves from the costs of war, or both" (Moravcsik 2003b: 175).

2.3 How progressive and effective is Moravcsik's research paradigm?

With his new liberalism, Moravcsik claims to have developed a "systemic theory" (Moravcsik 2008: 246), thus establishing its superiority in the context of possible theoretical syntheses with realism or institutionalism.[12] He explicitly extends the explanatory reach of his liberal research programme to the systemic level, that is, to interaction *between* states. Here his ambitions go well beyond those of the liberal IR theory founded in Germany by Czempiel and deployed in numerous studies on liberal German and US foreign policy since the 1990s (see, for example, Medick-Krakau 1999; Ikenberry 2007). Building on David Easton's system theory, Czempiel soon developed a complex model for the liberal explanation of the connections between action within the political system, social environments and international environment, for which he coined the term "asymmetric, fragmentary grid" (Czempiel 1981). In his book *Friedensstrategien* ("Peace strategies"), with reference to this model, he attempts to bring out the effect of structures of domination and systemic structures on actors' internationalizing politics (Czempiel 1986). He has frequently pointed out, however, that (as yet) political science lacks the theoretical tools to adequately depict interactions *between* interdependent states (ibid.: 362). It is this shortcoming of liberal theory building that Moravcsik has remedied in his liberal theory of *international* relations.

If the new liberalism wishes to be taken seriously as a "systemic theory", it must be applicable to *all* states, regardless of whether they are totalitarian, authoritarian or democratic. In contrast to the theory of inter-democratic relations, preference-oriented liberal theory in IR is not tied to the presence of historically contingent state forms. Particularly when it comes to explaining conflict and cooperation, the growth of an international legal framework and, not least, the "democratic peace", the liberal research programme has proved its value empirically (see Moravcsik 2000; Wolf 2002; Narizny 2007; see also the chapter by Andreas Hasenclever in this volume and the literature on the "democratic peace" cited there). Particularly in comparison to the realist research programme, its liberal counterpart emerges as more progressive: realism was unable to remedy existing shortcomings and anomalies (Legro and Moravcsik 1999; for a critical evaluation of the liberal research programme, see Rathbun 2010). At present, the real challenge to liberal theory is not so much the realist as the constructivist research paradigm. The extent to which the new liberalism can assert itself against the background of the "constructivist countermovement" ultimately depends on its empirical explanatory power. In the shape of liberal intergovernmentalism, Moravcsik himself has made an exemplary contribution in this regard that underlines the openness of the liberal research programme to theoretical syntheses.[13]

2.4 Empirical application and criticisms: liberal intergovernmentalism

In the late 1980s, based on his study of the dynamics of European integration, Moravcsik began to develop liberal intergovernmentalism (LI), according to which the deepening and expansion of the European integration process can be explained as a result of the convergence of member states' national preferences (Moravcsik 1991, 1993b, 1998; Moravcsik and Vachudova 2003; Moravcsik and Schimmelfennig 2009). He first adopts the premises of "classical" or realist intergovernmentalism (Hoffmann 1966, 1982), which explains the dynamics of the integration process as an outcome of international negotiations. At the same time, however, Moravcsik goes beyond neorealist integration theory by introducing to this approach a "principal-agent" model of domestic political decision-making processes in order to explain the liberal development of state preferences (Moravcsik 1993b: 474).[14] Finally, in *The Choice for Europe* (Moravcsik 1998), which provides the clearest theoretical explanation of LI, Moravcsik proposes a three-stage model to explain European integration. Here, very much in line with the kind of theoretical synthesis he has propagated, each of the three stages is associated with a middle-range theory (for an overview, see Rittberger and Schimmelfennig 2005: 23–31).

In the first stage, with the help of the liberal theory of preference formation, Moravcsik asks how governments' preferences take shape (Moravcsik 1993a: 481; Moravcsik and Schimmelfennig 2009: 69–70). In order to identify the dominant social actors, Moravcsik draws on the theory of the logic of collective action put forward by Olson (1965). On this view, whether social groups gain access to government decisions does not depend on a high degree of representation or large organizations' special capacity to achieve mobilization. Instead, the smaller the group, the greater the degree of mobilization. It is above all clearly defined groups who have a lot to gain and to lose who exercise the greatest influence on government action. If the government has to weigh up the interests of small and well-organized groups (such as producers or lobbying groups) and the more general, often rather "latent" interests of diffuse groups (such as taxpayers or consumers), it will usually prioritize the former (Steinhilber 2005: 178–180).

At the second stage, preferences are realized through international negotiations. This is explained through a theory of negotiation or bargaining within international cooperation (see Putnam 1988; Moravcsik 1993a). Here the realist element of LI comes into play. Once the national process of preference formation with respect to a specific issue is completed, the preferences of the social group are assumed to be stable until the conclusion of the negotiations. If the demand for international cooperation defines national preference formation, it is international negotiations that determine the capacity for coordination. A number of assumptions are associated with the introduction of the negotiation theory of international cooperation (Moravcsik 1998: 60ff.): joint decisions by governments are made at the negotiating table on a voluntary basis, without the threat of force. Further, the governments have a wide range of knowledge about the implications of the various policy options and plenty of information about their negotiating partners' preferences and the room for manoeuvre within the negotiations. States are not dependent on international or supranational institutions in order to negotiate effectively (Moravcsik 1998: 7). Ultimately, the outcome of negotiations depends on governments' relative negotiating power and the potential for different issues to be linked together. Moravcsik (ibid.: 62) puts this down to the intensity of state-internal preferences.

Finally, the third stage is centred on the choice of European institutions. Here Moravcsik draws on a functional theory of international institutions (see Pollack 2003; Franchino 2007).

He argues that nation states pool or delegate sovereignty and enter into institutional arrangements at the EU level only in order to credibly commit to cooperation (Moravcsik and Nicolaïdis 1999). European institutions, however, can help improve the conditions for cooperation by reducing transaction costs and may contribute to the resolution of so-called "second-order" problems of international cooperation (monitoring of compliance by the EU Commission, legal sanctions imposed by the ECJ or the distribution of gains from cooperation) (Wolf and Zangl 1996). The transfer of national authority or the creation of new loyalties on the European level, meanwhile, recedes into the background (see the chapter by Thomas Conzelmann in this volume).[15]

It is in *The Choice for Europe* that Moravcsik has gone furthest in applying his LI empirically (Moravcsik 1998).[16] The aim of Moravcsik's historical analysis is to "explain why sovereign governments in Europe have chosen repeatedly to coordinate their core economic policies and surrender sovereign prerogatives within an international institution" (ibid.: 1). To this end, he examines the key treaty negotiations during the founding era of what would later be the EU (Messina 1955) up to the Treaty of Maastricht of 1992. According to Moravcsik, none of the typically mentioned motives for integration were central to the decisions made with respect to these treaties. Technocratic incentives as envisaged by neofunctionalists, the geopolitical considerations so beloved of realists, European idealism or attempts to save the European welfare state (Milward 2000) – none had much impact on these decisions. Instead, the milestones of European integration arose from the rational calculations of governments. The convergence of three factors was crucial here: "patterns of commercial exchange, the relative bargaining power of national governments, and the incentives to enhance the credibility of interstate commitments". Most fundamental of these was commercial interest. "When such interests converged, integration advanced" (Moravcsik 1998: 3). Moravcsik ascribes no crucial influence on the outcome of negotiations to European institutions, and is particularly dismissive of their leading officials (ibid.: 479–485).

While the LI has clear explanatory advantages over the teleologically fixed federalist and neofunctionalist theories of integration, Moravcsik has been criticized from a number of angles.[17] I can mention only the most important criticisms here.

1. Moravcsik focuses his attention on the major historical treaty negotiations, thus overlooking important aspects of the everyday reality of EU integration. The various processes of communication and decision-making by the Commission, Council and Parliament are linked with one another in such a complicated way that the unintended consequences of so-called day-to-day politics for the integration process are not immediately apparent (see, for example, Wincott 1995; Tsebelis and Garrett 2000).
2. Mainly from an institutionalist perspective, critics have suggested that Moravcsik underestimates the dynamics and self-interest of European institutions, which are far more than member state-controlled instruments for reducing transaction costs and supervising decisions (Gehring 2002; Sandholtz and Stone Sweet 2004; Rittberger and Schimmelfennig 2005: 78–80).
3. The LI fails to recognize the logic of functional "spill-over" effects, which were significant determinants of the "rationality" of national governments during the transition from the customs union to the single market and from the single market to economic and monetary union (see the chapter by Thomas Conzelmann in this volume).
4. Moravcsik traces the process of European integration primarily back to material economic interests within societies, thus failing to take account of effects produced by socialization and European learning processes (see Risse 2009).

5 Finally, Moravcsik's assessment of the problem of legitimacy within the EU is flawed: he sees the democratic deficit in a crude and one-sided way as a fundamental source of the success of integration (see, for example, Føllesdal and Hix 2006). Yet it is only since Maastricht, critics argue, that the democratic deficit has become a key challenge to European integration.[18]

3 Internal theoretical differentiation

Moravcsik's efforts to bring order to the analytical confusion of liberal theories and to relate them to one another in a systematic way undoubtedly led to greater integration in liberal theory building in IR in the 1990s. Nonetheless, a broad spectrum of complementary liberal approaches continues to exist. In addition to Moravcsik's preference-oriented liberal theory, it was above all the so-called two-level approaches that became established in the 1990s.[19] The key impulse for the integration of the international and national levels came from Robert Putnam (1988) (see also Evans *et al.* 1993). He and associated theorists responded, first, to the shortcomings of explanations structured around the *domestic* dimension (Freund and Rittberger 2001), and, second, to the need for international policy coordination, which had become increasingly pressing since the 1970s. With his metaphor of the "two-level" game, Putnam assumes that the governments of states play at two tables at the same time: with the international negotiators of other states and with domestic political actors and interest groups. Political decisions can be made and implemented only if they are accepted and implemented both on the international level and in all relevant national decision-making arenas (Putnam 1988: 433–441).

Analyses of domestic political constellations have shown that not all the relevant interest groups have the same influence. First, the organizational capacity and size of interest groups have a decisive influence on their political efficacy. Empirical studies on US trade policy have shown that small and well-organized groups have a greater than average ability to promote their interests through national processes of negotiation (see, for example, Destler 2005). Second, the formal institutions of the political system and the organization of parties have an impact on the constellation of veto players,[20] whose agreement is necessary for transnational policy coordination. On the basis of the domestic constellation of political actors, Bernhard Zangl has suggested that there is a connection between the game structure on the international level and the interplay of state actors and social actors within the framework of international negotiations, thus building a bridge between neoinstitutionalism, liberalism and social constructivism (Wolf and Zangl 1996; Zangl 1999: 91–114).

As helpful as the two-level metaphor has proved to be in the practical analysis of international politics, when it comes to the development of governments' preferences – as Gourevitch has correctly noted – the model as a whole has remained theoretically deficient:

> We do not have very good theories to handle what happens when both are in play, when each influences the other, when the domestic politics of one country interact with the domestic politics of other, an interaction which itself helps define a system that reverberates back on the parts. We have good metaphors, but not clear research programs.
> (Gourevitch 2002: 321)

While Putnam's main conclusion is that, as the nation's chief negotiator, the executive strives to "get its hands tied" domestically in order to strengthen its position within international negotiations, in his political resource approach Moravcsik turns this conclusion on its head. According to Moravcsik, social groups' capacity to control the executive with respect to foreign policy depends on whether, by procedural means, they can control the political agenda (initiative) and influence the decision-making process (institutions), whether they have enough information about the executive's action options and whether they can convince other state-internal groups of the value of their political objectives (ideas) (Moravcsik 1994: 4). So the relations of power between executive and social groups are crucially important. International cooperation, however, gives governments greater room for manoeuvre vis-à-vis domestic political and societal actors because they have the upper hand with respect to foreign policy (Moravcsik 1994: 43). Further, however, the executive can also manipulate the influence of societal groups by changing formal or informal ratification procedures or the domestic balance of power through compensatory funding, increased party discipline or the selective mobilization of political groups (Moravcsik 1993a: 24–27).

Moravcsik's main argument is that national executives can deploy the logic of the two-level game to realize domestic political goals as well. Governments instrumentalize international cooperation in order to deny social groups control over critical power resources (initiative, institutions, information and ideas) so that they are no longer in a position to exercise a positive or negative influence on government policy. For Moravcsik, this explains states' rational motivation for engaging in international processes of cooperation and integration despite the associated loss of sovereignty (Moravcsik 1994: 1). In *Die Neue Staatsräson* ("The new *raison d'état*"), Klaus Dieter Wolf (2000) has expressed similar views. With the help of two-level analysis, he shows that, during periods of globalization, states may quite consciously deploy international cooperation and make commitments that limit their power in order to regain their autonomy vis-à-vis their societies, though at the price of undermining the democratic legitimacy of policies. Along with other authors, meanwhile, Moravcsik has asserted that state integration into multilateral organizations (MLOs)

> can enhance the quality of national democratic processes, even in well-functioning democracies . . . by restricting the power of special interest factions, protecting individual rights, and improving the quality of democratic deliberation, while also increasing capacities to achieve important public purposes.
>
> (Keohane *et al.* 2009: 2)[21]

Helen Milner (1997, 1999) has developed a theory akin to preference-oriented liberalism that draws on the "two-level game".[22] In *Interests, Institutions, and Information*, with reference to key international negotiations on the establishment of post-war international economic institutions, she investigates the conditions under which states cooperate in particular political fields. International cooperation depends less on relative gains from cooperation than on the "domestic distributional consequences of cooperative endeavors" (Milner 1997: 9; see also Keohane and Milner 1986). Cooperation creates winners and losers within a country, which in turn means that some will support cooperation while others will oppose it. It is domestic political competition and the struggle between these groups that create the conditions of possibility for international cooperation, which Milner traces back to three key domestic political factors: "the structures of domestic preferences, the nature of domestic political institutions, and the distribution of information internally" (Milner 1997: 234). Milner's liberal theory is in some respects more detailed than its predecessors, but loses much of its acuity as soon as it is applied to anything other than the economic relations between (liberal) democracies (Wolf 2002). While she argues that the interests of societal actors are determined by material expectations, Moravcsik does not rule out the possibility that social groups with ideational interests and values may "capture" the state (Moravcsik 2008: 240–242).

4 External criticisms

Moravcsik's paradigmatic renewal of the liberal theoretical tradition prompted a number of different reactions. There is no space here to examine all the criticisms, so I shall limit myself to three crucial ones. First, exponents of traditional systemic approaches perceived preference-oriented liberalism as a particular challenge. Second, constructivists rejected Moravcsik's rationalistic ontology and rigorous methodological conception. Third, and finally, a number of authors made criticisms from a normative or ideological standpoint.

1 Exponents of systemic theories criticized the liberal theory of IR for being "too complex" to provide a "systemic" analysis of international politics, as it always cites different state-internal factors to explain states' behaviour towards the rest of the world. Keohane therefore suggested turning to domestic political factors to explain anomalies only if a state's behaviour in the world cannot be explained with reference to systemic factors (Keohane, quoted in Moravcsik 1993a: 9; see also Schweller 2006). Further, neoinstitutionalists claimed that while institutions within national political systems influence the interaction between the different groups within a state, institutions within the international system have little impact on the interaction between different states. For rationalist institutionalists, Moravcsik's fundamentally different assessment of structures on the subsystemic and systemic levels is quite implausible (Zangl 1999: 55; see also Keohane 1994). Other critics asserted that every conception of the state as the mere mirror of powerful economic or civil society interests is inadequate (Freund and Rittberger 2001). Instead, as in the bureaucracy model (Allison and Zelikow 1999), we must also take account of actors and their preferences within the state apparatus as part of the political-administrative system.
2 Social constructivists put forward a rather more fundamental critique of new liberalism.[23] While Moravcsik argues that institutions within national political systems mould the identities of states and their processes of preference formation, he suggests that institutions within the international system have little impact on the identities of states. A number of studies, however, have shown how important international institutions are in the formation of identities. The process of European integration, for example, not only entails the redistribution of state-internal power resources as goal-oriented actors seek to maximize their utility and exchange fixed preferences through strategic interactions; it also involves the development of new community norms and the formation of identities. EU membership "matters", in other words, actors' rationality is always context-dependent and socially constructed. Norms, ideas and identities facilitate appropriate social action by providing shared meanings and expectations (on the basic issues at stake here, see Wendt 1999). On this view, then, institutions are not determined exclusively by actors but in fact help constitute actors' preferences and thus have an impact on the identities of individual member states. Because Moravcsik ignores the ways in which social actors and social structures are mutually constituted and the socializing effect of international institutions, he ultimately fails to grasp the fundamental driving forces of European integration.

> A significant amount of evidence suggests that, as a process, European integration has a *transformative* impact on the European state system and its constituent units. European integration itself has changed over the years, and it is reasonable to assume that in the process agents' identity and subsequently their interests and behaviour have equally changed. While this aspect of change can be theorized within constructivist perspectives, it will remain largely invisible in approaches that neglect processes of identity formation and/or assume interests to be given exogenously.
>
> (Christiansen *et al.* 1999: 529, original emphasis)

Moravcsik has responded to constructivist criticism by discerning a "characteristic unwillingness of constructivists to place their claims at any real risk of empirical disconfirmation". "*Hardly a single claim . . . is formulated or tested in such a way that it could, even in principle, be declared empirically invalid*" (Moravcsik 1999b: 670, original emphasis).[24] First, according to Moravcsik, constructivists have failed to develop distinctive hypotheses and subject them to wide-ranging empirical tests. Second, they lack suitable methods to test their hypotheses against alternative middle-range theories (Moravcsik 1999b: 670).[25] For their part, constructivists have retorted that Moravcsik privileges rationalistic explanations *per se*, attempting to impose hegemonic control on theoretical discourse by demanding higher empirical and methodological standards for constructivist approaches than for his own (Risse and Wiener 1999: 777–781; see also Risse 2009 and Diez 1999). Yet, of all things, it is research on Europe that has now shown that "most empirical work from a constructivist perspective does engage alternative explanations and demonstrates its claims against competing hypotheses. Thus, social constructivist research on the EU has quickly entered the realm of 'normal social science' " (Risse 2009: 158). Post-modern authors have gone even further in their criticisms, rejecting Moravcsik's liberal research programme with its devotion to hypothesis-testing and falsification (see, for example, Diez 1999).

3 Finally, Moravcsik's new liberalism has been criticized from a normative perspective. David Long has argued that

> [E]ach of Moravcsik's propositions involves a significant narrowing . . . of liberal political thought. On the one hand, there is a reduction to a minimalist classical liberalism. On the other, there is a bad positivism that dispenses with liberal philosophy. . . . The result is a distortion of liberalism and a misnaming of a theory of international relations.
>
> (Long 1995: 499)

Christian Reus-Smit has also highlighted the fact that Moravcsik's reformulation of liberal theory undermines its political character:

> The ideational and material preferences of individuals, which are the bedrock of his liberal understanding of the world, are forged in a pre-political realm, and thus fall outside of the explanatory purview of his theory. It is only when we come to the secondary tier of preferences – the state preferences derived from ascendant individual or group preferences – that his theory comes close to taking preferences seriously.
>
> (Reus-Smit 2001: 584)

> On this view, by neglecting the genuinely political and working with a "thin" conception of preferences, Moravcsik removes normative reflection from the sphere of serious social scientific research (ibid.: 574).

This non-political conception of liberal theory, which takes no account of the social character of international and European politics, has also been criticized from a Marxist perspective. The relevant authors here suggest that Moravcsik simply assumes the continuance of the existing international order in an ahistorical manner. He does take account of the pluralistic competition of interests within nation states, "but he fails to consider the fundamental mechanisms of power and domination and the relative political strength of different forces" (Steinhilber 2005: 188). In a number of places, Moravcsik himself points out the parallels between liberal and Marxist theory and considers the non-teleological assumptions of Marxism – "the centrality of domestic economic interests, the importance of transnational interdependence, the state as a representative of dominant social forces" – as entirely compatible with the premises of his reformulated liberalism (Moravcsik 1997: 522). He rejects the normative perspective of Marxism and its ideological critique, however, as incompatible with a positive liberal theory of IR.

Against Moravcsik's aspiration to produce a nonideological liberal theory of international relations, meanwhile, Beate Jahn describes Moravcsik's new liberalism as "deeply ideological" (Jahn 2009: 409). In an article entitled "Liberal Internationalism: from Ideology to Empirical Theory – and Back Again" in the journal *International Theory*, she not only criticizes the normative assumptions inherent in Moravcsik's empirical research programme, but casts doubt on new liberalism's claim to be a distinct theory of international relations.[26] Ultimately, for Jahn, liberal theory has undesirable political implications because it helps further the spread of the liberal narrative in a nonliberal world. Referencing Richard Wagner's *Mastersingers of Nuremberg*, Moravcsik responded with an article characteristically entitled "Wahn, Wahn, Überall Wahn" (Moravcsik 2010a – "Folly, folly, everywhere folly"). Moravcsik not only accuses Jahn of intellectual dishonesty and misrepresentation but also firmly rejects the criticism that every attempt to formulate a generalizable theory in the social sciences is inherently ideological. Jahn (2010) responded with equal vehemence in an article entitled "Universal Languages?", prompting Moravcsik (2010b: 172) to respond:

> She [Beate Jahn] has spent dozens of pages tilting at paradigmatic windmills rather than doing the hard empirical and mid-range work required to establish her argument vis-à-vis those of other scholars who have invested in the topic. This isolates her work intellectually.

This recent debate between Moravcsik and his critics recalls earlier ones over the assumed methodological unity of the sciences. It is interesting and instructive in the sense that liberal theoretical approaches within International Relations would do well to reflect on the normative as well as positive dimensions of their subject. Clearly, as scientists, we must not confuse the two. But we cannot hope to avoid normative issues by focusing exclusively on the positive aspects of political topics. Recent introductions to the theories and subject matter of International Relations take it for granted that empirical and normative issues must both be taken into account and that it is therefore worthwhile rendering explicit the implicit normative content of the new liberalism (Simpson 2008).

5 Notes

1 On the renaissance of the liberal theoretical perspective, see, for example, the review articles by Zacher and Matthew (1995), Gourevitch (2002) and Schultz (2013); for an overview of liberalism as a tradition of political theory, see Richardson (2001).

2 "Sociation" means the increasing participation of social interest groups in the foreign policy decision-making process (Czempiel 1994; see the early contribution by Krippendorff 1963). Because these are predominately transnational in character, foreign policy changes as well (on the essentials, see Risse-Kappen 1995b). "Domestication", meanwhile, refers to a process in which domestic political actors attempt to tie democracies' foreign policy behaviour to particular internal norms (see Harnisch and Schieder 2006; Harnisch 2009).

3 The core ideas of liberalism are already inherent in idealism as one of the two "primordial theories" of IR.

4 On the positivist orthodoxy, see King *et al.* (1994).

5 A scientific research programme should offer a guide to research, both in positive and negative terms. Drawing on theorist of science Imre Lakatos, Moravcsik (2003b) sees a scientific research programme as entailing a "hard core" surrounded by a "protective belt" of auxiliary hypotheses. The "hard core" consists of a research group's basic beliefs; they regard this core as indispensable and non-falsifiable. Around this core a fringe of auxiliary hypotheses takes shape that – in contrast to the core – can be tested against experience and may potentially be falsified.

6 Keohane (1990) has also referred to *regulatory liberalism*. But this is a foreign body within liberalism as it explains enduring progress and peace not primarily in "liberal" but in institutionalist terms.

7 His first attempt to establish a liberal theory came in 1992 (Moravcsik 1992). In the oft-cited essay "Taking Preferences Seriously" (Moravcsik 1997), he set out his ideas in more detail. For an assessment of his liberal research programme, see Moravcsik (2003b, 2008).

8 It is important to distinguish between interests, preferences and strategies. Interests represent the basic goals of actors. They are relatively stable and change little over time. "State preferences", meanwhile, are seen as the comparative evaluation of different action alternatives. In contrast to strategies and tactics, preferences are formed regardless of the international environment or the interests of other states (Moravcsik 1993b: 519; Frieden 1999). In Moravcsik's words (2010a: 116):

> State preferences . . . comprise a set of fundamental interests defined across "states of the world". Preferences are thus *by definition* causally independent of and analytically prior to specific interstate political interactions, including external threats, incentives, manipulation of information, or other tactics – at least in the short term. By contrast, strategies and tactics are policy options defined across intermediate political aims, as when governments declare an "interest" in "maintaining the balance of power", "containing" or "appeasing" an adversary, exercising "global leadership", or "maintaining imperial control".
>
> (original emphasis)

9 Moravcsik (2003b: 162) views the idea that social groups develop preferences on the basis of material interests and ideas as far less controversial than the literature might lead us to expect:

> Neither the assumption that individuals pursue their preferences instrumentally, nor the assumption that the formation of such preferences is exogenous to interstate politics, implies that individual preferences are atomistic. Cultural or sociological arguments that privilege collective social beliefs, either domestic or transnational, as sources of such social preferences, are not excluded. Some metatheoretical discussions between "constructivists" and "rationalists" obscure this potential complementary between rationalist and cultural explanations.

10 There are countless affinities here between ideational liberalism and constructivist studies, which also underline the significance of social, legitimate orders, collective identities and the social origins of socialization processes (Moravcsik 2008: 214). See the chapter by Cornelia Ulbert in this volume.

11 A number of studies have shown that under conditions of oligarchy or imperialist state structures, privileged groups see little reason to accept any curtailment of their objectives. Dominant groups

are far more likely to attempt to amalgamate their confrontational objectives to produce a basically antagonistic programme ("log-rolling coalitions"), not least because risks and costs can be passed on if there is no decision-making body superordinate to these elites and accepted by all of them (see Moravcsik 1997: 532; 2003b: 175). On the liberal theory of war, which is inspired by republican thought, see, for example, Snyder (1991), Wolf (2002), Narizny (2007) and the chapter by Andreas Hasenclever in this volume.

12 According to Moravcsik, for a liberal theory to be of use to empirical studies, four criteria must be met. First, it must be simple and generate a broad spectrum of previously unconnected hypotheses about phenomena that cannot be explained by available theories; second, it must clearly define its own conceptual boundaries; third, it must highlight anomalies and methodological weaknesses in available theories and empirical studies; and, fourth, it must demonstrate how it can be rigorously combined with other theories in order to produce coherent multicausal explanations (Moravcsik 1997: 533). Moravcsik has critically examined the liberal theory of IR with reference to three key criteria identified by Lakatos for evaluating scientific research programmes – "strict temporal novelty", "the heuristic definition of novelty" and "background theory novelty" – and shown that liberal IR theory may be considered an innovative research paradigm (Moravcsik 2003b: 160ff., 177–196). While Lakatos's scientific standards play into the hands of liberal theory, Moravcsik has qualified their significance to IR and called instead for theoretical synthesis (Moravcsik 2003a):

> Yet Lakatos's focus on the scope of theories might encourage scholars to advance "universal" and mono-causal claims when it is inappropriate to do so. More appropriate may be a clear specification of proper empirical limits or more subtle theoretical syntheses. Overall, a more pragmatic "problem-solving" approach based on Larry Laudan's philosophy of science seems more appropriate than one based on strict Lakatosian criteria.
>
> (Moravcsik 2003b: 196, 204)

13 Moravcsik (2008: 246) has repeatedly highlighted three key implications of liberal theory building: "its unique empirical predictions, its status as systemic theory, and its openness to multitheoretical synthesis".

14 According to this economic model, societal "principals" delegate or limit the power of the "governmental agent". They can do so because in democracies governments ultimately depend on the support of a broad "coalition" of voters, parties, interest groups and bureaucracies.

15 In contrast to neofunctionalism or supranationalism, LI concedes to supranational authorities such as the EU Commission at most the role of an agent within international negotiations (Moravcsik 1991, 1999a).

16 See also the symposium "The Choice for Europe: Social Purpose and State Power from Messina to Maastricht" in *Journal of European Public Policy* (Wallace *et al.* 1999) with a reply from Moravcsik. *The Choice for Europe* has been translated into a number of languages.

17 Since the 1990s, the theoretical debate between LI and neofunctionalism has been largely played out in three journals: *International Organization, Journal of Common Market Studies* and *Journal of European Public Policy.*

18 In the past few years, the key disputes have been over whether and if so to what extent the EU suffers from a "democratic deficit". In a number of contributions, Moravcsik has consistently denied this (e.g. Moravcsik 2002, 2006, 2008).

19 One important liberal current is the theory of the "democratic peace". See the chapter by Andreas Hasenclever in this volume.

20 Veto players are those individuals and collective actors whose consent is necessary to achieve a change in a given political field. For a detailed account, see Tsebelis (2002).

21 A controversy over this argument and in subsequent criticism (Gartzke and Naoi 2011) and response (Keohane *et al.* 2011) exists about the 'right' conception of democracy, the decision-making process of MLOs and the distributional effects of MLOs. Whereas Gartze and Naoi (2011: 589) argued that the influence of multilateral organization "can be detrimental to democracies not because MLOs are distant, elitist, and technocratic but precisely because MLOs are highly political", Keohane, Macedo and Moravcsik (2011: 599) insisted on their position and rejected the conventional wisdom that "MLOs are necessarily democracy-degrading simply because they are not directly participatory." According to Keohane *et al.* (ibid.: 600), Gartze and Naoi "misstate . . . how multilateralism affects democracy; fail to engage with our multidimensional conception of democracy; overlook the distinction . . . between interest groups that support the general interest

and those that do not; and overgeneralize from existing research". In one respect, however, Keohane, Macedo and Moravcsik (ibid.: 603) agree with their critics – namely, that MLOs can have "distributional impacts, making them likely subjects of special interest pressure or influence".

22 On this liberal school of theory, which is chiefly concerned with the state-internal preconditions for international trade agreements, see Mansfield *et al.* (2007).

23 See the 1999 special issue of the *Journal of European Public Policy*, "The Social Construction of Europe", edited by Thomas Christiansen, Knut E. Jørgensen and Antje Wiener, with articles by, among others, Jeffrey T. Checkel, Thomas Diez and Thomas Risse. In 2001, these articles were published in book form.

24 Moravcsik (1999b: 669) gave his critique the provocative title, "Is Something Rotten in the State of Denmark? Constructivism and European Integration", alluding to the "Copenhagen School", from which "the force of continental constructivist theories" seems to radiate. See also the dispute between Checkel and Moravcsik (2001).

25 Moravcsik rejects the allegation that rationalist explanatory approaches assume that actors are devoid of ideas.

> Collective ideas are like air; it is essentially impossible for humans to function as social beings without them. In this (trivial) sense there is little point in debating whether "ideas matter." *Existing rationalist theories claim only something far more modest, namely that ideas are causally epiphenomenal to more fundamental underlying influences on state behavior.*
>
> (Moravcsik 1999b: 674, original emphasis)

26 Jahn (2009: 419) asserts that "the liberal paradigm does not fulfil the criterion of distinctness. Moravcsik's general assumptions are shared by a host of other 'approaches'" – an interpretation Moravcsik rejects, claiming that Jahn fails to properly understand his work (Moravcsik 2010a: 115).

6 Bibliography and recommended reading

6.1 Primary texts

Milner, Helen V. 1997: *Interests, Institutions, and Information: Domestic Politics and International Relations*. Princeton, NJ: Princeton University Press.

Moravcsik, Andrew 1997: Taking Preferences Seriously: A Liberal Theory of International Politics, *International Organization* 51(4): 513–553.

Moravcsik, Andrew 1998: *The Choice for Europe: Social Purpose and State Power from Messina to Maastricht*. Ithaca, NY: Cornell University Press.

Moravcsik, Andrew 2008: The New Liberalism, in Reus-Smit, Christian and Snidal, Duncan (eds) *The Oxford Handbook of International Relations*. Oxford: Oxford University Press, pp. 234–254.

Putnam, Robert D. 1988: Diplomacy and Domestic Politics: The Logic of Two-Level Games, *International Organization* 42(3): 427–460.

6.2 Secondary texts

Long, David 1995: The Harvard School of Liberal International Theory: A Case for Closure, *Millennium* 24(3): 489–505.

Moravcsik, Andrew and Schimmelfennig, Frank 2009: Liberal Intergovernmentalism, in Diez, Thomas and Wiener, Antje (eds) *European Integration Theory*, 2nd edn. Oxford: Oxford University Press, pp. 67–87.

Reus-Smit, Christian 2001: The Strange Death of Liberal International Theory, *European Journal of International Law* 12(3): 573–594.

Zacher, Mark W. and Matthew, Richard A. 1995: Liberal International Theory: Common Threads, Divergent Strands, in Kegley, Charles W. Jr. (ed.) *Controversies in International Relations Theory: Realism and the Neoliberal Challenge*. New York: St Martin's Press, pp. 107–149.

6.3 Other texts

Allison, Graham T. and Zelikow, Phillip 1999. *Essence of Decision: Explaining the Cuban Missile Crisis*, 2nd edn. New York: Longman.

Burchill, Scott 2009: Liberalism, in Burchill, Scott, Linklater, Andrew, Devetak, Richard, Donnelly, Jack, Nardin, Terry, Paterson, Matthew, Reus-Smit, Christian and True, Jacqui 2009: *Theories of International Relations*, 5th edn. New York: Palgrave, pp. 57–85.

Checkel, Jeffrey T. and Moravcsik, Andrew 2001: A Constructivist Research Program in EU Studies, *European Union Politics* 2(2): 219–249.

Christiansen, Thomas, Jørgensen, Knut E. and Wiener, Antje 1999: The Social Construction of Europe, *Journal of European Public Policy* 6(4): 528–544.

Czempiel, Ernst-Otto 1972: *Schwerpunkte und Ziele der Friedensforschung*. Munich: Grünewald-Kaiser.

Czempiel, Ernst-Otto 1979: *Amerikanische Außenpolitik. Gesellschaftliche Anforderungen und politische Entscheidungen*. Stuttgart: Kohlhammer.

Czempiel, Ernst-Otto 1981: *Internationale Politik. Ein Konfliktmodell*. Paderborn: Schöningh.

Czempiel, Ernst-Otto 1986: *Friedensstrategien*. Opladen: Westdeutscher Verlag [new edition 1998].

Czempiel, Ernst-Otto 1994: Vergesellschaftete Außenpolitik, *Merkur* 48(1): 1–14.

Destler, I. Mac 2005: *American Trade Politics*, 4th edn. Washington, DC: Peterson Institute for International Economics.

Diez, Thomas 1999: Riding the AM-track Through Europe; or, the Pitfalls of Rationalist Journey Through European Integration, *Millennium* 28(2): 355–369.

Doyle, Michael 1986: Liberalism and World Politics, *American Political Science Review* 80: 1151–1169.

Doyle, Michael W. 1994: Liberalism and the Transition to a Post-Cold War System, in Clesse, Armand, Cooper, Richard and Sakamoto, Yoshikazu (eds) *The International System After the Collapse of the East-West Order*. Dordrecht: Martinus Nijhoff Publishers, pp. 85–105.

Dunne, Tim 2010: Liberalism, in Baylis, John, Smith, Steve and Owens, Patricia (eds) *The Globalization of World Politics: An Introduction to International Relations*. 4th edn. Oxford: Oxford University Press, pp. 108–122.

Evangelista, Matthew 1995: The Paradox of State Strength: Transnational Relations, Domestic Structures, and Security Policy in Russia and the Soviet Union, *International Organization* 49(1): 1–38.

Evans, Peter B. Jacobson, Harold K. and Putnam, Robert D. (eds) 1993: *Double-Edged Diplomacy: International Bargaining and Domestic Politics*. Berkeley, CA: University of California Press.

Føllesdal, Andreas and Hix, Simon 2006: Why There Is a Democratic Deficit in the EU: A Response to Majone and Moravcsik, *Journal of Common Market Studies* 44(3): 533–562.

Franchino, Fabio 2007: *The Powers of the Union: Delegation in the EU*. Cambridge: Cambridge University Press.

Freund, Corinna and Rittberger, Volker 2001: Utilitarian-Liberal Foreign Policy Theory, in Rittberger, Volker (ed.) *German Foreign Policy Since Unification: Theories and Case Studies*. Manchester: Manchester University Press, pp. 68–104.

Frieden, Jeffry 1999: Actors and Preferences in International Relations, in Lake, David A. and Powell, Robert (eds) *Strategic Choice and International Relations*. Princeton, NJ: Princeton University Press.

Gartzke, Erik and Naoi, Megumi Naoi 2011: Multilateralism and Democracy: A Dissent Regarding Keohane, Macedo, and Moravcsik, *International Organization* 65(3): 589–598.

Gehring, Thomas 2002: *Die EU als komplexe internationale Organisation. Wie durch Kommunikation und Entscheidung soziale Ordnung entsteht*. Baden-Baden: Nomos.

Gourevitch, Peter A. 1978: The Second Image Reversed. The International Sources of Domestic Politics, *International Organization* 32(4): 881–912.

Gourevitch, Peter A. 2002: Domestic Politics and International Relations, in Carlsnaes, Walter, Risse, Thomas and Simmons, Beth (eds) *Handbook of International Relations*. London: Sage, pp. 309–328.

Harnisch, Sebastian 2009: German Politics Lecture: The Politics of Domestication: A New Paradigm in German Foreign Policy, *German Politics* 18(4): 455–468.

Harnisch, Sebastian and Schieder, Siegfried 2006: Germany's New European Policy: Weaker, Leaner, Meaner, in Maull, Hanns W. (ed.) *Germany's Uncertain Power: Foreign Policy of the Berlin Republic*. New York: Palgrave, pp. 95–108.

Hasenclever, Andreas 2001: *Die Macht der Moral in der internationalen Politik. Militärische Interventionen westlicher Staaten in Somalia, Ruanda und Bosnien-Herzegowina*. Frankfurt a. M.: Campus.

Hoffmann, Stanley 1966: Obstinate or Obsolete? The Fate of the Nation-State and the Case of Western Europe, *Daedalus* 95: 862–915.

Hoffmann, Stanley 1982: Reflections on the Nation-State in Western Europe Today, *Journal of Common Market Studies* 21(1–2): 21–37.

Ikenberry, John G. 2007: *American Foreign Policy: Theoretical Essays*, 6th edn. New York. W. W. Norton.

Jahn, Beate 2009: Liberal Internationalism: From Ideology to Empirical Theory – and Back Again, *International Theory* 1(3): 409–438.

Jahn, Beate 2010: Universal Languages? A Reply to Moravcsik, *International Theory* 2(1): 140–156.

Katzenstein, Peter J. 1976: International Relations and Domestic Political Structures: Foreign Economic Policies of Advanced Industrial States, *International Organization* 30(1): 1–45.

Katzenstein, Peter J., Keohane, Robert O. and Krasner, Stephen D. 1998: International Organization and the Study of World Politics, *International Organization* 52(4): 645–685.

Keohane, Robert O. 1990: International Liberalism Reconsidered, in: Dunn, John (ed.): *The Economic Limits to Modern Politics*. Cambridge: Cambridge University Press, 165–194.

Keohane, Robert O. 1994: *After Hegemony: Cooperation and Discord in the World Political Economy*. Princeton, NJ: Princeton University Press.

Keohane, Robert O., Macedo, Stephen and Moravcsik, Andrew 2009: Democracy Enhancing Multilateralism, *International Organization* 63(1): 1–31.

Keohane, Robert O., Macedo, Stephen and Moravcsik, Andrew 2011: Constitutional Democracy and World Politics: A Response to Gartzke and Naoi, *International Organization* 65(3): 599–604.

Keohane, Robert O. and Milner, Helen V. (eds) 1996: *Internationalization and Domestic Politics*. Cambridge: Cambridge University Press.

King, Gary, Keohane, Robert O. and Verba, Sidney 1994: *Designing Social Inquiry: Scientific Inference in Qualitative Research*. Princeton, NJ: Princeton University Press.

Krell, Gert 2009: *Weltbilder und Weltordnung. Einführung in die Theorie der internationalen Beziehungen*. 4th revised and updated edn. Baden-Baden: Nomos.

Krippendorff, Ekkehart 1963: Ist Außenpolitik Außenpolitik?, *Politische Vierteljahresschrift* 4(3): 243–266.

Lakatos, Imre 1970: Falsifikation and the Methodology of Scientific Research Programmes, in Lakotos, Imre and Musgrave, Alan (eds) *Criticism and the Growth of Knowledge*. Cambridge: Cambridge University Press, pp. 191–196.

Latham, Robert 1997: *The Liberal Moment: Modernity, Security, and the Making of Postwar International Order*. New York: Columbia University Press.

Legro, Jeffrey W. and Moravcsik, Andrew 1999: Is Anybody Still a Realist?, *International Security* 24(2): 5–55.

Mansfield, Edward D. and Milner, Helen V. 2012 (eds) *Votes, Vetoes, and the Political Economy of International Trade Agreements*. Princeton, NJ: Princeton University Press.

Mansfield, Edward D., Milner, Helen V. and Pevehouse. Jon C. 2007: Vetoing Cooperation: The Impact of Veto Players on International Trade Agreements, *British Journal of Political Science* 37(4): 403–432.

Medick-Krakau, Monika (Ed.) 1999: *Außenpolitischer Wandel in theoretischer und vergleichender Perspektive: Die USA und die Bundesrepublik Deutschland.* Baden-Baden: Nomos.

Milner, Helen V. 1998: Rationalizing Politics: The Emerging Synthesis of International, American and Comparative Politics, *International Organization* 52(4): 759–786.

Milner, Helen V. 1999: The Political Economy of International Trade, *Annual Review of Political Science* 2: 91–114.

Milward, Alan S. 2000: *The European Rescue of the Nation-State.* London: Routledge.

Moravcsik, Andrew 1991: Negotiating the Single European Act. National Interest and Conventional Statecraft in the European Community, *International Organization* 45(1): 651–688.

Moravcsik, Andrew 1992: *Liberalism and International Relation Theory.* Cambridge, MA: Harvard University, CFIA Working Paper 1992.

Moravcsik, Andrew 1993a: Integrating International and Domestic Theories of International Bargaining, in Evans, Peter B. Jacobson, Harold K. and Putnam, Robert D. (eds) *Double-Edged Diplomacy: International Bargaining and Domestic Politics.* Berkeley, CA: University of California Press, pp. 3–42.

Moravcsik, Andrew 1993b: Preferences and Power in the European Community. A Liberal Intergovernmentalist Approach, *Journal of Common Market Studies* 31(4): 473–524.

Moravcsik, Andrew 1994: *Why the European Community Strengthens the State: Domestic Politics and International Cooperation.* Center for European Studies Working Paper No. 52. Cambridge, MA: Harvard University.

Moravcsik, Andrew 1996: Federalism and Peace: A Structural Liberal Perspective, *Zeitschrift für Internationale Beziehungen* 3(1): 123–132.

Moravcsik, Andrew 1999a: A New Statecraft? Supranational Entrepreneurs and International Cooperation, *International Organization* 53(2): 267–306.

Moravcsik, Andrew 1999b: "Is Something Rotten in the State of Denmark?" Constructivism and European Integration, *Journal of European Public Policy* 6(4): 669–681.

Moravcsik, Andrew 2000: The Origins of Human Rights Regimes: Democratic Delegation in Postwar Europe, *International Organization* 54(2): 217–252.

Moravcsik, Andrew 2002: In Defence of the Democratic Deficit: Reassessing Legitimacy in the European Union, *Journal of Common Market Studies* 40(4): 603–624.

Moravcsik, Andrew 2003a: Theory Synthesis in International Relations: Real Not Metaphysical, *International Studies Review* 5(1): 131–136.

Moravcsik, Andrew 2003b: Liberal International Relations Theory. A Scientific Assessment, in Elman, Colin and Elman, Miriam F. (eds) *Progress in International Relations Theory: Appraising the Field.* Cambridge, MA: MIT Press, pp. 159–204.

Moravcsik, Andrew 2006: What Can We Learn from the Collapse of the European Constitutional Project?, *Politische Vierteljahresschrift* 47(2): 219–241.

Moravcsik, Andrew 2008: The Myth of Europe's "Democratic Deficit", *Intereconomics*, November–December: 331–340.

Moravcsik, Andrew 2010a: "Wahn, Wahn, Überall Wahn": A Reply to Jahn's Critique of Liberal Internationalism, *International Theory* 2(1): 113–139.

Moravcsik, Andrew 2010b: Tilting at Windmills: A Final Reply to Jahn, *International Theory* 2(1): 157–173.

Moravcsik, Andrew and Nicolaïdis, Kalypso 1999: Explaining the Treaty of Amsterdam: Interests, Influence, and Institutions, *Journal of Common Market Studies* 37(1): 59–95.

Moravcsik, Andrew and Vachudova, Milada A. 2003: National Interests, Statepower, and EU Enlargement, *East European Politics and Societies* 17(1): 42–57.

Narizny, Kevin 2003a: Both Guns and Butter, or Neither: Class Interests in the Political Economy of Rearmament, *American Political Science Review* 97(2): 203–220.

Narizny, Kevin 2003b: The Political Economy of Alignment: Great Britain's Commitments to Europe, 1905–39, *International Security* 27(4): 184–219.

Narizny, Kevin 2007: *The Political Economy of Grand Strategy*. Ithaca, NY: Cornell University Press.

Olson, Mancur 1965: *The Logic of Collective Action: Public Goods and the Theory of Groups*. Harvard, MA: Harvard University Press.

Pollack, Mark A. 2003: *The Engines of European Integration: Delegation, Agency and Agenda Setting in the EU*. Oxford: Oxford University Press.

Rathbun, Brian C. 2010: Is Anybody Not an (International Relations) Liberal?, *Security Studies* 19(1): 2–25.

Richardson, James L. 2001: *Contending Liberalisms in World Politics: Ideology and Power*. Boulder, CO: Westview Press.

Risse, Thomas 2009: Social Constructivism and European Integration, in Wiener, Antje and Diez, Thomas (eds) *European Integration Theory*. 2nd edn. Oxford: Oxford University Press, pp. 144–161.

Risse, Thomas and Wiener, Antje 1999: "Something Rotten" and the Social Construction of Social Constructivism: A Comment on Comments, *Journal of European Public Policy* 6(5): 775–782.

Risse-Kappen, Thomas 1991: Public Opinion, Domestic Structure, and Foreign Policy in Liberal Democracies, *World Politics* 43: 479–512.

Risse-Kappen, Thomas 1995a: *Cooperation among Democracies: The European Influence on U.S. Foreign Policy*. Princeton, NJ: Princeton University Press.

Risse-Kappen, Thomas (ed.) 1995b: *Bringing Transnational Relations Back In: Non-State Actors, Domestic Structures and International Institutions*. Cambridge: Cambridge University Press.

Rittberger, Berthold and Schimmelfennig, Frank 2005: Integrationstheorien: Entstehung und Entwicklung der EU, in Holzinger, Katharina *et al.*: *Die Europäische Union. Theorien und Analysekonzepte*. Paderborn: Schöningh, pp. 19–80.

Sandholtz, Wayne and Stone Sweet, Alec 2004: *European Integration and Supranational Governance*. Oxford: Oxford University Press.

Schultz, Kenneth 2013: Domestic politics and international relations, in Carlsnaes, Walter, Risse, Thomas and Simmons, Beth (eds) *Handbook of International Relations*. London: SAGE, pp. 478–503.

Schweller, Randall L. 2006: *Unanswered Threats: Political Constraints on the Balance of Power*. Princeton, NJ: Princeton University Press.

Simpson, Gerry 2008: The Ethics of the New Liberalism, in Reus-Smit, Christian and Snidal, Duncan (eds) *The Oxford Handbook of International Relations*, Oxford: Oxford University Press, pp. 255–266.

Snyder, Jack 1991: *Myths of Empire: Domestic Politics and International Ambition*. Ithaca, NY: Cornell University Press.

Steinhilber, Jochen 2005: Liberaler Intergouvernementalismus, in Bieling, Hans-Jürgen and Lerch, Marika (eds) *Theorien der europäischen Integration*. 2nd edn. Wiesbaden: VS Verlag, pp. 169–196.

Sterling-Folker, Jennifer 1997: Realist Environmental, Liberal Process, and Domestic-Level Variables, *International Studies Quarterly* 41: 1–25.

Tsebelis, George 2002: *Veto Players: How Political Institutions Work*. Princeton, NJ: Princeton University Press.

Tsebelis, George and Garrett, Geoffrey 2000: Legislative Politics in the European Union, *European Union Politics* 1(1): 9–36.

Viotti, Paul R. and Kauppi, Mark V. 2009: *International Relations Theory: Realism, Pluralism, Globalism and Beyond*, 4th edn. Englewood Cliffs, NJ: Prentice Hall.

Wallace, Helen, Caporaso, James A., Scharpf, Fritz W. and Moravcsik, Andrew 1999: Review Section Symposium: The Choice for Europe, *Journal of European Public Policy* 6(1): 155–179.

Waltz, Kenneth N. 1959: *Man, the State and War*. New York: Columbia University Press.

Wendt, Alexander 1999: *Social Theory of International Politics*. Cambridge: Cambridge University Press.

Wincott, Daniel 1995: Institutional Interaction and European Integration: Towards an Everyday Critique of Liberal Intergovernmentalism, *Journal of Common Market Studies* 33(4): 597–609.

Wolf, Dieter and Zangl, Bernhard 1996: The European Economic and Monetary Union: Two-level Games and the Formation of International Institutions, *European Journal of International Relations* 2(3): 355–393.

Wolf, Klaus Dieter 2000: *Die Neue Staatsräson. Zwischenstaatliche Kooperation als Demokratieproblem in der Weltwirtschaft*. Baden-Baden: Nomos.

Wolf, Reinhard 2002: How Partners Become Rivals: Testing Neorealist and Liberal Hypotheses, *Security Studies* 12(2): 1–42.

Zangl, Bernhard 1999: *Interessen auf zwei Ebenen. Internationale Regime in der Agrarhandels-, Währungs- und Walfangpolitik*. Baden-Baden: Nomos.

Liberal approaches to the "democratic peace"

Andreas Hasenclever

1 Introduction

In the mid-1980s, statisticians noticed something they had previously overlooked. Originally, they had thought that democracies were just as violent as other states. Clearly, democracies did not hesitate to engage in military conflicts or armed intervention in the internal affairs of other countries. The United States went to war in Vietnam, the UK over the Falkland Islands, France in Sub-Saharan Africa and India against Pakistan, to mention just four examples. Further, for decades Western democracies maintained a policy of nuclear deterrence. They signalled their determination, in case of a Soviet attack, to accept the deaths of huge numbers of innocent civilians rather than submit to a foreign power.

At first sight, this obvious willingness of elected governments to engage in violence seemed to confirm the realist expectation that domestic politics has no significant impact on foreign policy (see the chapter by Andreas Jacobs in this volume). After all, the "normal" behaviour of democracies showed that under conditions of international anarchy all states pursue their national interests as rationally as they can and if needed by military means. For realists, therefore, hopes that the international community would be pacified through the democratization of its members rested on shaky foundations. Arguably, the behaviour of elected governments towards the rest of the world was not especially restrained. They appeared to have a perfect command of the rules of power politics and to play the "great game" of alliance formation and zones of influence with aplomb.

What went unnoticed in realist analysis, however, was that democracies rarely, if at all, wage war on one another. Even at the sub-war level, they are involved in markedly fewer military conflicts against other democracies than statistics would lead us to expect. We have Michael Doyle (1983) to thank for highlighting this remarkably low level of violence in interdemocratic relations. Countless social scientists have since attempted to explain this phenomenon from a liberal perspective. In this regard the term "liberal" refers to all those approaches that attempt to trace the peacefulness of democracies towards other members of the same "species" back to their *domestic political character*.[1] On this view, elected governments are in a position to form international security communities together with other elected governments. In these communities, as envisaged by Karl W. Deutsch (Deutsch *et al.* 1957), wars are a concept of the past. In the view of many liberal analysts, therefore, democracies ought to ensure that their system of rule spreads across the world. That this idea has made it to the upper echelons of politics after the end of the Cold War is evident in a quote from former US President Bill Clinton, who declared in the early 1990s that the democratization of authoritarian systems "serves all of America's strategic interests – from promoting prosperity at home to checking global threats abroad", precisely because "democracies rarely wage war on one another" (quoted in Gowa 1999: 3).

As we shall see, however, the conduct of democracies has resisted easy incorporation into liberal theory building. On the one hand, some evidence could be found that elected governments are in general less prone to use violence in international politics. On the other hand, the dual finding still applies: democracies behave more aggressively towards states with non-democratic political systems than towards other democracies. So, while realists have problems explaining the "(inter-)democratic peace", liberal authors are faced with the puzzle that democracies frequently act like traditional great powers in relation to non-democratic states, and that this is accepted by their populations.

The work of American political scientist Bruce Russett and his German colleague Ernst-Otto Czempiel is central to this chapter (see Section 2).[2] Both authors have had a substantial impact on liberal research on the "democratic peace". Russett tends to analyse the phenomenon from the perspective of pairs of states, so-called dyads, while Czempiel takes the view that democracies are not just more peaceful towards one another but also in general. According to Czempiel, this is due to their inherently peaceful nature.[3] My focus on these two reference theorists should not obscure the fact that many other researchers have done a huge amount of work on the theorem of the "democratic peace" over a period of almost twenty years and I will mention their findings where space allows.[4] After looking at the modern classics on the "democratic peace", I briefly examine three current developments in liberal theory building in Section 3. All of them share the desire to move established research away from its strict focus on domestic politics, and open it up to the special features of inter-democratic relations. But while some argue that democracies develop some sort of common identity preventing them from using force against members of the same tribe, others focus on the ambivalence of liberal culture, which supposedly explains the differing proclivity for violence towards democracies and non-democracies. Finally, some authors emphasize that zones of democratic peace are permeated by international institutions to a particularly high degree, rendering violence dysfunctional in these regions. In the fourth section of this chapter we hear from the critics of liberal approaches to the "democratic peace". Their criticisms make it clear that the theoretical debate on the reasons for the striking lack of violence in interdemocratic relations is far from over.

2 Modern classics of liberal research on the "democratic peace": Bruce Russett and Ernst-Otto Czempiel

There is as yet no satisfactory liberal explanation of the "democratic peace". Nonetheless, research has generated some key arguments that might be considered necessary building blocks of such an explanation. What they have in common is an aspiration to trace the use of violence towards other states back to domestic political interests and power structures (Risse-Kappen 1995a: 24–34; Moravcsik 1997: 516–521). On this view, governments act in social contexts and react to the demands of organized groups within their decision-making milieu. Which of these demands find expression in foreign policy action and in what way depends largely on the political system and political culture. Both Czempiel (1986: 112–131) and Russett and Oneal (2001: 53–58) therefore declare the political system and the political culture to be key contextual factors determining the use of violence towards other states.[5]

A country's *political system* determines who the government is accountable to. Does the stability of its rule depend on broad agreement among the general population or on a relatively small group? A country's *political culture* tells us about the general disposition of a society to use force for the settlement of political conflicts. Is the use of organized coercion by political elites generally regarded as normal and legitimate or reprehensible? The first context gives an indication of the opportunities for political participation for different segments of a society, while the second tells us whether violence is an everyday feature of domestic disputes. According to Russett and Oneal (2001: 55), in both regards we can identify typical characteristics of democracies that make them "doves" within the international system. They appear to be particularly averse to violence, and both authors believe that the effects of this aversion are most visible within interdemocratic relations.

2.1 The political system as a contextual factor in states' behaviour towards other states

Democratic systems are characterized by the checks and balances of the legislative, executive and judicial branches and resist any enduring concentration of political power in the hands of homogeneous elites. To this end, the authority and composition of all three branches of the state are tied directly or indirectly to free, universal and secret elections that take place on a regular basis. Governments striving for re-election must ensure that their policies are compatible with the power relations in the legislative and judicial branches if they wish to avoid image-damaging gridlock or implementation problems. At the same time, it is vital that their decisions meet with general public approval. Elected governments thus face the imperative of dual consonance. They must persuade not only most of the political elite to sign up to their programmes voluntarily but also the majority of their citizens. These same citizens, however, share a deep aversion to war, as already noted by Immanuel Kant in his famous treatise on *Perpetual Peace*:

> If . . . the agreement of the citizens is required to decide whether or not one ought to wage war, then nothing is more natural than that they would consider very carefully whether to enter into such a terrible game, since they would have to resolve to bring the hardships of war upon themselves (which would include: themselves fighting, paying the costs of the war from their own possessions, meagerly repairing the ravages that war leaves behind, and, finally, on top of all such malady, assuming a burden of debt that embitters the peace and will never be repaid [due to imminent, constantly impending wars]).
>
> (Kant [1795] 2006: 75)

In brief, liberals believe that taxpayers loathe wars (Czempiel 1996: 80; Russett and Oneal 2001: 272–273). Accountable governments, therefore, will enter into such a hazardous enterprise only if they can provide very good reasons for doing so. Generally speaking, this means highlighting that the country and its vital interests are threatened by an external enemy.

Autocratic systems, conversely, are characterized by a tendency to systematically exclude the majority of the population from political decision-making. There is thus less need for their governments to take account of citizens' interests (Czempiel 1986: 130; Russett and Oneal 2001: 54). Instead they gear themselves towards the preferences of those social groups that underpin their rule, whether they are major landowners, industrialists, clerics, military leaders, state bureaucrats or a mixture of these groups. The liberal view, then, is that autocratic governments have greater scope for deploying troops because they can pass on the associated costs to the general public and privatize the gains.

Empirical studies do in fact show that democratic governments gain nothing from an aggressive foreign policy (Chiozza and Goemans 2004; Goemans 2008). Their prospects of re-election are not influenced by successful military campaigns. Autocracies, on the other hand, have strong incentives to hold their ground in international crises and to escalate a conflict into war if appropriate. This is because success in a crisis improves autocratic governments' prospects of retaining office, while the risk of losing office after defeat in war is no greater than after defeat in a crisis. The counter-intuitive finding that autocratic governments do in fact run a greater risk of being driven from office and of being severely punished after losing a war than democratic governments is also considered to be a corollary of democracies' accountability to society as a whole (Bueno de Mesquita *et al.* 2003: 264). Elected governments take much greater care to allow conflicts to escalate only if they are very likely to win them or in cases where even a negative outcome will not significantly damage their chances of re-election. As Philip Arena (2008) has shown, the latter applies if the government succeeds in integrating the opposition into its war policy. In line with this, empirical studies by Dan Reiter and Allan C. Stam (2002; Reiter *et al.* 2009) show that democracies select their war aims carefully and therefore have a better than average record of winning them.

2.2 Political culture as a contextual factor in states' behaviour towards other states

According to Czempiel (1986: 112–115) and Russett (1993: 30–38, 90–92), it is not just democracies' political institutions that resist the use of force abroad but also their political culture, which is taken to be characterized by respect for individuals, their lives and their property. On this view, democracies are typically governed by the rule of law, and the resolution of political conflicts is based on party competition, elections and protection for minorities. Accordingly, democrats reject violence as an instrument of political conflict.[6] This fundamental respect for the dignity and rights of the other engenders a basic preference for compromise and integrative conflict resolution. In other words, according to Russett (1993: 31), a culture of "live and let live" has become established in democracies; this culture also leaves its mark on democratic states' international relations because citizens expect their governments to use the minimum of violence possible when pursuing national interests.

For liberal authors, autocracies are dominated by a culture of violence. According to Czempiel (1986: 113–114), this is the only way to explain how a minority can succeed in governing at the expense of the majority. On this view, autocratic systems necessarily go hand-in-hand with an unfair distribution of welfare and lop-sided citizen participation. If this were not the case, they could put their policies to the vote in free elections. Over the long run, however, injustice can only be maintained through organized coercion. This prompts Doyle (1986: 1161) to state that "non-liberal governments are in a state of aggression with their own people". Because culturally moulded behavioural dispositions are indivisible, domestic discord carries over into external discord. Autocratic governments are viewed as notoriously incapable of solving conflicts through peaceful means. In fact they represent a permanent risk to international peace and security. Democracies must therefore be highly vigilant when dealing with autocracies (Russett 1993: 32–33).

Liberal thinkers, then, explain the "democratic peace" in light of elected governments' domestic political decision-making environment. To retain office, officials must strive to mobilize broad and enduring support within the political system and among the general population if they are contemplating military involvement in international conflicts. Otherwise there is a great risk that opposition parties will make capital out of this topic, attacking the government for political incompetence at the next election, if not before.

The opposition is likely to assert that the lives of soldiers and the nation's wealth were put at risk through a conflict that should never have been allowed to escalate into an armed confrontation.[7] For liberal thinkers, therefore, elected governments are particularly cautious when it comes to the use of force abroad. This caution is reflected empirically in the finding that democracies generally begin wars voluntarily only if they rate their chances of success as high and believe that the conflict will not last long (Reiter and Stam 2002; Reiter *et al.* 2009).

For liberals, there is a simple reason why democracies' reluctance to use force in international conflicts is restricted to fellow democracies only (Russett and Oneal 2001: 54f., 90). Since elected governments see no reason to believe that autocratic governments are subject to the same kind of restrictions on violence as they are, their relations approach the famous "state of nature". Deep distrust prevails under these conditions and the impact of the security dilemma is keenly felt (see the remarks by Andreas Jacobs in this volume). This in turn leads democratic governments to believe that they must protect themselves from attempts by belligerent autocracies to exploit their natural restraint. They therefore ensure that they are in a position to respond quickly, forcefully and if need be even pre-emptively to threats to their interests posed by autocratic states. In contrast, the security dilemma is ameliorated in interdemocratic relations because elected governments are aware that interests and culture will make their political opponents cautious (Czempiel 1996: 82; Russett 1993: 31–32). Those in power see that neither they nor other elected governments can make their populations believe that a democracy poses a serious threat to international peace and security. Consequently, citizens would evaluate any escalation of conflict with another democracy as a political failure.

2.3 The contradictory empirical data on the "democratic peace"

At first sight, a whole series of findings backs up the liberal interpretation of the "democratic peace". Democracies almost never go to war against one another and are very rarely involved in violent conflicts with other democracies below the level of war.[8] In fact, empirical studies show that democracies act with greater reserve, militarily speaking, than we would expect on the basis of international averages, even in their relations with states with different systems of rule (see Ray 2000: 300–302; Russett and Oneal 2001: 116). Moreover, an increasing number of authors suggest that we need to think carefully about what we mean by involvement in war. According to Gleditsch and Hegre (1997: 294), democracies have a tendency to form alliances with other democratic countries and to take part in wars waged by other democracies. But their participation is often of merely symbolic significance and in many cases the losses suffered by allies are negligible. Yet in the statistics their engagement shows up as fully-fledged involvement in war. This gives rise to the false impression that democracies are involved in military conflicts more or less as often as other states.

Further, earlier studies failed to take account of the fact that democracies provoke international crises less often than other states – and such crises lay the ground for military conflicts (Rousseau *et al.* 1996). Gleditsch and Hegre (1997: 295–297) point out that the great conflicts of the twentieth century were begun by non-democratic states. They are thinking here of the First World War, the Sino-Japanese War, the Second World War, the Korean War and the Iran–Iraq War. Finally, according to Rummel (1995), the wars started by democracies involved fewer casualties than the international average. The impression of equivalent propensity for violence could arise only if no distinction is made between wars in light of the severity and scale of associated atrocities.

Alongside this direct confirmation of liberal expectations regarding the use of violence by democratic states, there is indirect evidence that supports the key causal mechanisms of the liberal explanatory model in one way or another – in other words, with respect to the material interests of citizens, the political culture of democracies and the political calculations of elected governments. Dixon (1994), for example, notes that, on average, interdemocratic disputes are dealt with more often through negotiation, with the aid of mediation by third parties or through adjudication. The observation that democracies consciously seek and use civil forms of conflict resolution within the international system is matched by the finding that they are involved remarkably often in international institutions and that they are viewed as particularly reliable partners within the international community. There are good reasons why the trade relations between democracies are unusually intensive and the exchange of goods, services and capital is particularly high, underlining the significance of material welfare for democratic governments' prospects of re-election (Russett and Oneal 2001; Lipson 2003).

Despite this evidence, liberal approaches to the "democratic peace" are still faced with empirical inconsistencies and anomalies. We need only think of the imperial policies of France and Great Britain in the nineteenth and twentieth centuries or the bloody colonial wars since 1945. These facts scarcely suggest a specifically democratic culture of restraint or even of national economic rationality. Further, there have been numerous cases in which powerful democracies have launched military assaults on small autocracies, particularly in the southern half of the globe, despite the lack of any serious threat to their vital interests emanating from these countries (Czempiel 1996: 82; Bueno de Mesquita *et al.* 1999: 792). Examples here include the repeated deployment of French troops in Sub-Saharan Africa and the numerous US interventions in Latin America. But if large democracies frequently use massive force against small autocracies, why do they refrain from doing so against small democracies as well?

2.4 A first attempt at resolving the empirical contradictions: the "democratic peace" as a peace of deterrence

In view of these and similar inconsistencies, Bueno de Mesquita and his colleagues (1999, 2003, 2012) have attempted to interpret the "democratic peace" as a "peace of deterrence" between particularly risk-averse states. They also assume that elected governments use violence-based strategies in international conflicts only if they are forced to do so by an external enemy or if they believe they can achieve an easy victory. The latter manifestly applies to most of the small-scale campaigns in countries of the global South. In conflicts with other democracies, in contrast, democracies act with restraint. In such cases, experience suggests poor prospects of a quick military victory. Instead, the statistics show that democracies are formidable opponents, as they win their wars significantly more often than other states (Bueno de Mesquita *et al.* 1999: 791; Russett and Oneal 2001: 66). This is put down to the fact that they mobilize massive resources in a very short time in order to end the conflict to their advantage as quickly as possible. Things get critical for elected governments mainly when conflicts drag on and casualties increase (Russett and Oneal 2001: 67). Because this scenario is likely to apply in cases of interdemocratic wars, elected governments shy away from armed confrontations with fellow democracies.

In asymmetric conflicts between democracies, by contrast, the weaker side tends to back down (Bueno de Mesquita *et al.* 1999: 801). If there is no serious chance of prevailing, an elected government will accept even a bad compromise in order to avoid a risky and bloody armed confrontation. Conversely, as losses on the battlefield are unlikely to hurt an autocratic government more than a defeat in a crisis, they are much more likely to take risks and to escalate conflicts. Consequently, there are numerous examples of autocratic governments entering into war with democracies (ibid.: 794). History shows, however, that they often lose in such cases. So the stakes are high for them, but not as high as for democracies.

The interpretation of the "democratic peace" as a peace of deterrence is attractive intellectually. First, it takes account of democracies' special political system, which makes them more cautious actors than other states. Second, it dovetails with the common interpretation of the "long peace" (John Lewis Gaddis) between East and West during the Cold War, which is also considered a peace of deterrence. Finally, we can explain why democracies have not so far voluntarily entered into wars with formidable opponents. The explanations provided by Bueno de Mesquita and his colleagues, however, cannot solve all the puzzles thrown up by the findings on the "democratic peace". Contrary to expectation, small democracies do not always shy away from serious conflicts with large democracies. During several conflicts over fishing with the UK, Iceland appeared to be quite unimpressed by the British fleet, and got its way despite its opponent's undoubted military superiority (Hellmann and Herboth 2001). Moreover, in his landmark analysis of decision-making conflicts within NATO, Thomas Risse-Kappen (1995a) shows that it was by no means always the militarily superior members that managed to enforce their views. Ultimately, there is little indication in Western Europe and in transatlantic relations that small democracies shy away from making political demands because they fear their powerful neighbours. A stable security community has become established in Western Europe and in transatlantic relations in which the use of military force, even far below the level of war, has become almost unthinkable (ibid.).

2.5 A second attempt at resolving the empirical contradictions: the imperfections of the "democratic peace" as a consequence of imperfect democracies

By looking at the puzzling findings on the "democratic peace", Czempiel (1996: 82) provides a solution that is astonishingly simple at first sight. He suggests that in fact *real* democracies reject violence as a tool of foreign policy and deploy it only for self-defence. Since Kant, this has been the logical corollary of the normative theory of democracy: the citizens of a state cannot favour something that manifestly damages them, and responsive governments must take their population's interests into account. According to Czempiel (1996: 82f.), the observation that governments have often deviated from this ideal, sometimes egregiously, is bound up with the fact that even Western democracies are far from being democracies in the full sense. In fact, analysis of political processes in these countries demonstrates "particularist interest groups' privileged access to the political system's monopoly on violence" (Czempiel 1996: 86). Again and again, small elites manage to capture the state for their limited purposes and involve it in military confrontations while ignoring the legitimate interests of the broader population. For Czempiel, then, in light of the available evidence on Western democracies' behaviour towards other states, it is "only a slight exaggeration to describe them as collective monarchies" (ibid.: 86). The usurpation of the military power of democratic states is reinforced by citizens' lack of interest in foreign affairs. They thus allow the gamblers to have their way.

Czempiel (ibid.: 86–87) explains the fact that the incomplete democratization of democracies has not yet been subjected to serious academic study by pointing to the formalistic conception of democracy that has dominated the research hitherto. Most studies are underpinned by typological criteria that focus on states' constitutional attributes while leaving political processes within a given country out of account. Russett and Oneal (2001: 44), for example, hold a state to be democratic if: (1) the majority of citizens has the right to vote; (2) the government was elected through free and fair elections, in which at least two parties competed to obtain a majority of the votes; and (3) the executive is accountable either directly or to the electorate or parliament. According to Czempiel, these or similar criteria may apply yet fail to prevent the usurpation of foreign policy by small power elites. We must therefore examine in detail and with respect to every democracy the extent to which its international relations are really based on the will of the majority. In many cases, Czempiel tells us, we would find that citizens are very far from having a meaningful role in shaping decisions. Because of this, it is hardly surprising if their interests and values play very little role in foreign policy-making.

In a recent study, Sandra Dieterich, Hartwig Hummel and Stefan Marschall (2009) build on Czempiel's intuition. With respect to 25 European democracies, they examine whether differences in the "parliamentarization" of security policy can explain their propensity for violence. They found that in the Iraq conflict of 2003, democracies with powerful parliaments with regard to security policy behaved in a more war-averse way than those in which the executive clearly dominates security and defence policy.

So along with Dieterich, Hummel and Marschall, Czempiel seeks to explain "lapses" in the "democratic peace" – understood as situations in which, beyond self-defence, a structurally peaceful state uses violence, chiefly against weak autocracies – as a result of the general population's lack of opportunity to shape decisions and the existence of parliaments with little sway over security policy. But this solution also has its drawbacks. It remains unclear why even deficient democracies have so far waged *no* wars against one another or very rarely fall back on other violence-based strategies when dealing with one another. Conversely, it is a strength of the studies criticized by Czempiel that the connection between democracy and peace remains even if the public influence on policy in a given country is minimal (Gleditsch and Hegre 1997: 289–291; Maoz 1997: 180). To put it in statistical terms, the findings on the (inter-)democratic peace are remarkably robust. They hold true even if we use very broad criteria to identify democratic systems, resulting in the inclusion in our samples of states that can scarcely be considered developed democracies.

3 New perspectives on the "democratic peace": factoring in interdemocratic relations

To oversimplify, the central puzzle for liberal approaches to the democratic peace is that elected governments do not infer any security risks for themselves from their fellow democracies' aggressiveness towards smaller autocracies. Evidently, they expect no spill-over effects from behavioural patterns in mixed dyads into democratic peace zones. Violence against autocrats clearly does not inspire insecurities among democrats. Current research suggests three approaches to explaining this remarkable finding and these three explanations might possibly be combined. What they have in common is that they concentrate on the characteristics of interdemocratic relations. There are a number of reasons to believe that democracies behave differently when they encounter other democracies. But these differences in behaviour are not necessarily due exclusively to *actor attributes*, but may also have something to do with the nature of their relations. While exponents of the first approach argue that, given their structural affinities, democracies develop a shared identity that prevents the use of violence against members of their tribe, proponents of the second approach focus on the efficacy of a common political culture, which ensures peace between democracies but whose inherent ambivalence can also explain the use of violence against autocracies. Finally, exponents of the third approach point out that zones of democratic peace are pervaded by international institutions in a particular way, making violence as a tool of politics dysfunctional in these regions.

3.1 The "democratic peace" as a consequence of group formation processes

According to Risse-Kappen (1995b: 502–509, 1996: 366–371), interdemocratic relations are shaped by a high degree of mutual sympathy and regard. Democracies trust one another, and concerns about relative losses from international ventures play only a subordinate role. Thomas Risse puts this special property of interdemocratic relations down to the fact that because of institutional similarities, democracies band together to create an "in-group" that marks itself off from an "out-group", namely, the nondemocratic states.

This demarcation process goes hand-in-hand with a friend–enemy distinction that in turn leads to conflicts within the group being evaluated as unproblematic, while conflicts with the outside world are viewed as high-risk. This differing perception of conflicts depending on the similarity or dissimilarity of the parties gives rise to a certain momentum within interdemocratic relations. Affinity engenders trust and facilitates cooperation. Difference produces distrust and hampers cooperation. The relations between democratic states appear comparatively stable and advantageous, while relations with the rest of the world are perceived as unreliable and problematic. As a result, a democratic security community takes shape that is characterized internally by understanding and solidarity and externally by an emphasis on independence and distance. The members of this community develop a strong group consciousness or "we-feeling". They have a common interest in maintaining their group's coherence and are increasingly prepared to mobilize resources in its defence. Once again, this reinforces internal cohesion and reduces the risk of destructive conflicts between members.

But the explanation of the "democratic peace" through "in-group–out-group" interactions also has its weaknesses. The supposition that similarities between states encourage the formation of groups, for example, is theoretically underdeveloped. In fact, it describes more than it explains. Why, for instance, should it be shared political-institutional features that bring states together rather than religious or cultural commonalities? Further, research on civil wars has shown that similarities, regardless of their character, are often not enough to create trust and solidarity between groups. Finally, the assumption that democracies constitute a collective identity that guides their action on the international level is not well-founded empirically. Generally, the "in-group–out-group" hypothesis has proved its validity only in the context of small groups. So far, attempts to apply it on the level of the nation state have produced no consistent results.

3.2 The ambivalence of liberal culture: analysis of democracies' propensity for violence

In his work, Harald Müller has frequently underlined the so-called "antinomies of the democratic peace" (Müller 2002, 2004, 2008; Müller and Wolff 2006). Antinomy in this context refers to essentially contradictory tendencies inherent in one and the same structure. Applied to democracies, this means that both an imperative to behave cautiously towards the rest of the world as well as the inclination to vigorously spread one's own political system throughout the world are an inherent feature of the democratic political culture. In fact, both imperatives are based on universally recognized human rights. On this view, all men, women and children have a right to live their lives in dignity and peace, and this means that *prima facie* they have an unqualified right to protection from war *and* from state repression.

In the view of many liberals, both goals can generally be achieved through the nonviolent dissemination of democracy as a form of government. But it is also possible to imagine situations in which we might have to decide whether the use of force is permissible, if not imperative. This is the case when we are up against an "unjust enemy" (Immanuel Kant, quoted in Müller 2006: 236). An "unjust enemy" of this kind is not just an international adversary but an actor that infringes citizens' basic rights systematically, enduringly and gravely. In other words, we are talking about a state that is fundamentally unjust from a human rights perspective. Under such conditions, everything depends on how the instrument of war is assessed in light of the aspiration to democratize. Can the state of injustice be ended through armed force, while bearing in mind the principle of proportionality, and a just form of government be established, or does this appear impossible?

As Müller sees it (2004: 507–510; Müller and Wolff 2006: 58–62), the answer to this question is crucially influenced by the dominant political culture in specific democracies. Here he distinguishes between pacifist liberalism and militant liberalism. While in militant liberalism the emphasis lies on the active liberation of people from unjust conditions and military force is viewed as a potential tool for this purpose, exponents of pacifist liberalism put their faith in the irresistible force of modernization. For them, autocratic structures will eventually collapse as society evolves, to be replaced by democracy.

While the liberal culture common to all democracies strictly delegitimizes the use of violence against other democracies, making war highly unlikely to occur, democracies' differing proclivity for the use of force against autocracies is due to the type of liberal culture that prevails in a given state. Democracies with a generally pacifist culture, such as Germany and Japan, tend to act with military restraint. Democracies with a more militant culture, such as the UK, India, Israel and the United States, are significantly more prone to violence. According to Müller, this is bound up with the fact that it is much easier for the governments of these countries to convince their societies that military action against a non-democratic state is appropriate than in democracies with a pacifist culture. So it is the difference in governments' potential to justify armed violence that leads to the marked differences in the conflict-prone behaviour of democracies towards non-democracies. Researchers are currently subjecting this internally coherent argument to strict empirical examination.

3.3 The "democratic peace" as a consequence of interdemocratic institutions

A third attempt to approach the democratic peace in light of the kind of relations prevailing between democracies begins with the observation that nowhere else within the international system do we find a web of organizations and regimes as dense as the one pertaining between democracies (Rittberger 1987: 9f.). We need think only of the European Union, the Council of Europe, NATO and the OECD, whose members consist exclusively or overwhelmingly of elected governments. Democracies thus seem particularly prepared to cooperate with other democracies to solve international problems and to establish institutions for this purpose.[9]

For a long time, liberal researchers paid, at most, marginal attention to the heavy concentration of international institutions between democracies and failed to incorporate the topic into their analyses. The prevailing view was that international institutions are generally of secondary significance in preserving peace (for a more detailed account, see Hasenclever 2002: 82–83). Against this background, we have Russett and Oneal (2001: 157–196) to thank for having shaken things up. With quantitative methods, they were able to show that contrary to the widespread scepticism, there is a connection between states' involvement in institutions and their proneness to violent action against others states: the higher the number of international organizations shared by two states, the less likely war is to break out between them. This correlation, however, is weak, and is eclipsed by the effect of other variables such as the constitution of the interacting states, their membership of the same alliances, the distribution of power within the international system, and the degree of economic integration.

The glaringly weak nature of the statistical findings in the work of Russett and Oneal may be connected with the fact that they make no distinction between different types of international organization. Instead they treat all international regulatory frameworks equally in terms of their possible impact on peace (Russett and Oneal 2001: 170). In one recent study, Pevehouse and Russett (2006) distinguish between international organizations with respect to the composition of their membership. What emerges here is that international organizations with predominantly democratic member states significantly reduce the risk of violent confrontations between members. The authors do not, however, provide us with any plausible explanation for their findings.

I am unable to examine these points in depth here.[10] But there are good reasons to assume that interdemocratic institutions, in contrast to other regulatory frameworks within international politics, are well suited to stabilizing security relations between their members, to promoting cooperation with respect to economy, environment and culture and to enhancing the autonomy of regulated political fields. If this is the case, it would block off three high-risk paths to escalation within international politics. Research on the causes of war (see the contributions in Midlarsky 2000, and Vasquez 2000) has shown that international conflicts entail a particularly high risk of culminating in armed clashes if the parties involved: (1) see their security threatened; (2) rely on unilateral self-help strategies; and (3) if their relations become polarized.[11] Interdemocratic institutions help prevent such outcomes in a sustained way: (1) they reliably organize a common defence policy; (2) they function as effective early warning systems with respect to possible shifts in the balance of power; (3) they increase their members' utility through cooperation while increasing the costs of relying on self-help strategies, and (4) they forge links between problem-solving on the international level and interested domestic actors, who work to ensure that specific issues resolvable through negotiation do not fuse together to form overarching, multi-stranded conflicts.

Finally, paying more attention to the way in which the "democratic peace" – understood as the network of institutions that link democratic states with one another – is organized internationally gives us an opportunity to grasp analytically how shared identities develop, as envisaged by Risse-Kappen (1995b; 1996). By now a number of studies have been published that demonstrate that enduring cooperation within the framework of shared institutions promotes the development of a sense of "we-ness" among participants. They increasingly perceive themselves as a group and begin to take steps to preserve this group. In addition to the concrete benefits of cooperation, then, states stick to shared rules out of respect for the legitimate interests of partner states. This respect translates into a moral obligation to comply with contractual agreements and the associated rights of others. Cooperation thus becomes more robust. The parties involved begin to trust one another and cease to suspect that their good intentions might be exploited at the least provocation. To the extent that democracies have a special capacity for rule-based cooperation because of their political system, they are more likely to develop shared identities – a sense of "we". Such identities strengthen the civilizing impact of the institutions found in the democratic zone, though they cannot replace them.

4 Criticism of liberal interpretations of the "democratic peace"

Exponents of other schools of thought within International Relations have criticized various aspects of liberal interpretations of the "democratic peace" and the associated hope that the world might be made safer through democratization. I shall briefly outline four objections that are particularly prominent in the literature: (1) the assumption that the "democratic peace" is in reality a peace of alliance; (2) the suspicion that the "democratic peace" is primarily a peace of exploitation; (3) the concern that processes of democratization provoke armed conflicts with other countries; and (4) the expectation that democracy as a form of government will dissolve as a result of globalization.

1 Realist authors such as Gowa (1999), Henderson (2002) and Rosato (2003, 2005) are unimpressed by the liberal interpretation of the "democratic peace". For them, the absence of major military confrontations between democracies after 1945 is the consequence of the division of power within the international system. On this view, the democratic states under the leadership of the United States came together to form a defensive alliance against the Soviet Union and its satellite states, and strove to ensure that their military strength was not undermined by internal conflicts. The end of the Cold War, then, is likely to usher in the decline of the "democratic peace".

   So far, however, realist authors' expectations remain unfulfilled. Relations between democracies continue to feature almost no violence and there is no obvious reason to believe that this will change in the foreseeable future. In addition, realist authors have a problem with consistency. Military alliances against a common enemy do not always go hand-in-hand with nonviolent relations between their members. Tensions within the Eastern Bloc, for example, repeatedly led to the deployment of Soviet troops against allies. So the special relations between democracies cannot simply be put down to external threats. Finally, the realist conception fails to clarify why democracies all found themselves on the same side in the Cold War. This also suggests that they formed an orderly group initially because of their internal characteristics, a group whose existence was only secondarily consolidated by a common enemy (Russett and Oneal 2001: 60–61).

2 Proponents of critical approaches within International Relations put forward a very different explanation of the "democratic peace". For Barkawi and Laffey (1999), for example, the lack of armed conflict in the democratic zone results from an alliance of convenience among powerful industrial states in order to better exploit the rest of the world. On this view, the industrialized countries pool their strength to enforce the globalization of capitalist markets and to reap maximum profit from it. In this context, Barkawi and Laffey also criticize the liberal concept of peace. Here peace is equated with the absence of military violence in international relations. By this yardstick, democracies do indeed seem to have been extremely peaceful since the 1980s, if not before. This, however, is only because the many forms of concealed and structural violence used by the global North against the global South are ignored, along with military support for oppressive regimes through military supplies and the deployment of combat advisors. If these are included in the analysis, the democratic zones within the international system seem less like regions of peace than the core of a brutal system of

injustice. The lack of violence between democracies, then, is not necessarily reflected in the level of violence used against other countries and in the many bloody conflicts in the states of the Third World.

An informed debate between the liberal protagonists of the "democratic peace" and their left-wing critics has yet to take place. They would have to clarify, first, whether the origins of armed conflicts in many parts of the world really lie in the more or less violent globalization of Western forms of society and production or whether they are due chiefly to local and regional rivalries. Second, exponents of critical positions would have to identify the causal mechanisms that link the peace between democracies at differing stages of economic development with their non-peaceful behaviour towards states outside of the democratic zones in a way that is both comprehensible and verifiable. Finally, from a neo-Gramscian perspective, Anna Geis and Jonas Wolff (2007) argue that there are inherent limits to the promotion of a liberal world order by means of military control. In fact, any ruthless use of force by Western states has the potential to backfire and compromise the ideological resources that are necessary to maintaining a globalized market regime. The soft democratization of peripheral countries is thus the instrument of choice for Western states precisely because they do not want to waste their military muscle on a lost cause.

3 A third criticism of liberal research relates to its practical recommendation to promote peace by spreading democracy as a form of government. Edward Mansfield and Jack Snyder (2002, 2005, 2009), for example, fear that democratization, particularly that occurring in weak states, increases the risk of war. Either newly elected officeholders will opt to use violence abroad during critical phases of democratic transformation at home in order to divert attention away from domestic conflicts, or the internal conflicts within a society in transition will provoke external powers into military intervention. The hypotheses put forward by Mansfield and Snyder on the link between a country's democratization and its susceptibility to the use of violence abroad, however, remain heavily contested (see Russett and Oneal 2001: 116–122; Zimmermann 2009: 50). Some authors suggest that political instability generally increases the risk of armed conflict with other states. Other studies show that the risk of war as a consequence of democratization is context-dependent. While it is high within a generally autocratic international environment, there is virtually no risk in a democratic environment. Further, continuous processes of transformation appear to be less dangerous than an unstable oscillation between autocracy and democracy. Overall, it is safe to say that the connection between democratization and the proclivity to use violence abroad is far from having been researched in a methodologically reliable way.

4 The fourth and, in our context, final objection to the liberal research programme on the "democratic peace" was put forward by Teusch and Kahl (2001). These authors predict the end of democracy as a form of government. National governments, they suggest, will lose their independence in the wake of globalization and become the playthings of transnational economic interests. Democratic elections will degenerate into "merely formal procedures with no practical consequences" (ibid.: 301), as political power becomes increasingly autocratic in nature. It is likely, then, that the end of traditional democracy will go hand-in-hand with a new era of uncontrolled violence in much of the world. As a result, "the thesis of the 'democratic peace' [can] be considered valid only with respect to a limited historical period" (ibid.: 313).

As yet, the future scenarios outlined by Teusch and Kahl are little more than informed speculation. How the process of globalization will impact on the organization of

> political power across the world is anything but foreseeable. It is not certain that there will be a global renaissance of authoritarian rule. But Teusch and Kahl are right to remind us that the "democratic peace" cannot be taken for granted. Free societies often unleash international forces that undermine citizens' rights to political participation over the long term. So it is no coincidence that observers complain of a massive democratic deficit in the European Union. Its democratic integration manifestly lags behind its economic and political integration. We see similar imbalances between state decision-making powers and citizens' power of control in other international organizations as well, where important political decisions are now being made.

The debate on the liberal interpretation of the "democratic peace" in International Relations continues to fascinate (Hayes 2012; Ungerer 2012). Clearly, however, what was originally a very limited question – "Can the democratic peace be shown to exist in a methodologically uncontroversial way and, if so, how do we explain the absence of armed conflicts between democracies?" – has given rise to an extensive research programme. Its objective is to identify as many features as possible special to the relations between democracies and in their behaviour towards other states, in order to trace them back consistently to internal characteristics. Researchers examine, for example, the unusually intensive economic integration between democracies, their engagement in international institutions and elected governments' proclivity for covert military operations. The more the core liberal assumptions and causal mechanisms prove their validity in a wide variety of research contexts, and the more they shed light on the "dark sides" of the "democratic peace", the more difficult it will be for critics to question the liberal research programme by referring to isolated anomalies and inconsistencies. Two things will be particularly important in this regard (see Müller 2002). Liberal researchers will have to address the concern that peace within the democratic zones goes hand-in-hand with a lack of peace in and towards the rest of the world. They will also have to examine whether democracy as a form of governance is under threat from the play of social and economic forces that it originally unleashed.

5 Notes

1 For an in-depth discussion of the specific attributes of liberal thought within International Relations, see the chapter by Siegfried Schieder in this volume. Two non-liberal attempts to explain the democratic peace are briefly presented and discussed in Section 4.

2 Key publications by these two authors are Czempiel (1986, 1996); Russett (1993, 2009); Russett and Oneal (2001).

3 Russett has now begun to approach Czempiel's position (see Russett and Oneal 2001: 116). This is a clear indication that the long-standing distinction between dyadic and monadic research perspectives was always artificial and is now of significance, at most, in theoretical history terms (see also Mueller 2004).

4 Useful and highly critical surveys on the state of this complex field of research, in which new specialisms and subdivisions are constantly emerging, are provided by Geis and Wagner (2006); Hayes (2012); Ungerer (2012); and Zimmermann (2009).

5 In recent studies, Russett moves away from contrasting political-institutional and political-cultural approaches to the "democratic peace" (Russett and Oneal 2001: 53). Instead he follows Bueno de Mesquita and his colleagues (1999; Bueno de Mesquita and Smith 2012), who integrate both approaches into a model of strategic decision-making by elected governments.

6 Empirical studies show that democracies as a group exhibit an unusually low level of internal violence (Hegre *et al.* 2001). The only other group of states that achieve similarly low figures are highly repressive dictatorships. Here, figuratively speaking, the 'peace of the graveyard' prevails.

7 Arena (2008), for example, shows that democratic governments can expect to be punished for their war policy at the next election if the opposition has consistently criticized the government's policy.
8 The statistical calculations are based on analysis of the incidence of violence in politically relevant dyads per year. Politically relevant dyads are those in which either both states are geographically close or at least one of the two states is a superpower. With a view to the extent of international violence, wars are distinguished from other forms of militarized conflict such as the threat of military force, troop build-ups and small-scale clashes (see Russett and Oneal 2001: 94–96, 100–102).
9 On the analysis of international institutions, see the chapter on regime theory by Bernhard Zangl in this volume.
10 For more detail, see Hasenclever (2002: 87–100), Hasenclever and Weiffen (2006) and Prins and Daxecker (2007). For a critical account of this argument's explanatory power in dyads of non-Western democracies, see Zimmermann (2009).
11 Polarization means that distinct conflicts in a variety of political fields converge to create one overarching "us against them" conflict, rather than being dealt with individually. Such processes are dangerous because the sense of hostility between the two parties increases and mutual trust declines, and because we know that, as a rule, wars are waged over a number of vexed issues rather than one.

6 Bibliography and recommended reading

6.1 Primary texts

Czempiel, Ernst-Otto 1986: *Friedensstrategien. Systemwandel durch Internationale Organisation, Demokratisierung und Wirtschaft*, 2nd edn. Paderborn: Schöningh.

Czempiel, Ernst-Otto 1996: Kants Theorem. Oder: Warum sind die Demokratien (noch immer) nicht friedlich?, *Zeitschrift für Internationale Beziehungen* 3(1): 79–101.

Russett, Bruce M. and Oneal, John R. 2001: *Triangulating Peace: Democracy, Interdependence, and International Organizations*. New York: Norton.

6.2 Secondary texts

Geis, Anna and Wagner, Wolfgang 2006: Vom demokratischen Frieden zur liberalen Friedens- und Konfliktforschung, *Politische Vierteljahresschrift* 47(2): 267–309.

Hayes, Jarrod 2012: The Democratic Peace and the New Evolution of an Old Idea, *European Journal of International Relations* 18(4): 767–791.

Ray, James Lee 2000: Democracy: On the Level(s), Does Democracy Correlate with Peace? in Vasquez, John A. (ed.) *What Do We Know about War?* Lanham, MD: Rowman & Littlefield Publishers, pp. 299–316.

Ungerer, Jameson Lee 2012: Assessing the Progress of the Democratic Peace Research Program, *International Studies Review* 14(1): 1–31.

6.3 Other texts

Arena, Philip 2008: Success Breeds Success? War Outcomes, Domestic Opposition, and Elections, *Conflict Management and Peace Science* 25(1): 136–151.

Barkawi, Tarak and Laffey, Mark 1999: The Imperial Peace: Democracy, Force and Globalization, *European Journal of International Relations* 5(4): 403–434.

Bueno de Mesquita, Bruce *et al.* 1999: An Institutional Explanation of the Democratic Peace, *American Political Science Review* 93(4): 791–807.

Bueno de Mesquita, Bruce, Smith, Alastair, Siverson, Randolph M. and Morrow, James D. 2003: *The Logic of Political Survival*. Cambridge, MA: MIT Press.

Bueno de Mesquita, Bruce and Smith, Alastair 2012: Domestic Explanations of International Relations, *Annual Review of Political Science* 15(1): 161–181.

Chiozza, Giacomo and Goemans, Henrik E. 2004: International Conflict and the Tenure of Leaders: Is War Still Ex Post Inefficient?, *American Journal of Political Science* 48(3): 604–619.

Deutsch, Karl W. *et al.* 1957: *Political Community and the North Atlantic Area: International Organization in the Light of Historical Experience*. Princeton, NJ: Princeton University Press.

Dieterich, Sandra, Hummel, Hartwig and Marschall, Stefan 2009: "Kriegsspielverderber"? Europäische Parlamente und der Irakkrieg 2003, *Zeitschrift für Internationale Beziehungen* 16(1): 5–38.

Dixon, William 1994: Democracy and the Peaceful Settlement of International Conflict, *American Political Science Review* 88(1): 14–32.

Doyle, Michael 1983: Kant, Legal Legacies, and Foreign Affairs: Part 1, *Philosophy and Public Affairs* 12(1): 205–335.

Doyle, Michael 1986: Liberalism and World Politics, *American Political Science Review* 80(4): 1151–1169.

Geis, Anna and Wolff, Jonas 2007: Demokratischer Frieden, Demokratischer Krieg und das Projekt globaler Demokratisierung. Hegemonietheoretische Überlegungen aus neo-gramscianischer Perspektive, in Buckel, Sonja and Fischer-Lescano, Andreas (eds) *Hegemonie gepanzert mit Zwang. Zivilgesellschaft und Politik im Staatsverständnis Antonio Gramscis*. Baden-Baden: Nomos, pp. 181–198.

Gleditsch, Nils Petter and Hegre, Havard 1997: Peace and Democracy: Three Levels of Analysis, *Journal of Conflict Resolution* 41(2): 283–310.

Goemans, Henrik E. 2008: Which Way Out? The Manner and Consequences of Losing Office, *Journal of Conflict Resolution* 562(6): 771–794.

Gowa, Joanne 1999: *Ballots and Bullets: The Elusive Democratic Peace*. Princeton, NJ: Princeton University Press.

Hasenclever, Andreas 2002: The Democratic Peace Meets International Institutions – Überlegungen zur internationalen Organisation des demokratischen Friedens, *Zeitschrift für Internationale Beziehungen* 9(1): 75–111.

Hasenclever, Andreas and Weiffen, Brigitte 2006: International Institutions are the Key. A New Perspective on the Democratic Peace, *Review of International Studies* 32(4): 563–585.

Hegre, Havard *et al.* 2001: Toward a Democratic Civil Peace? Democracy, Political Change, and Civil War, 1816–1992, *American Political Science Review* 95(1): 33–48.

Hellmann, Gunther and Herboth, Benjamin 2001: Democratic Peace and Militarized Interstate Disputes in the Transatlantic Community. Paper presented at the 42nd Annual Convention of the International Studies Association, Chicago.

Henderson, Errol A. 2002: *Democracy and War: The End of an Illusion*. Boulder, CO: Lynne Rienner.

Kahl, Martin and Teusch, Ulrich 1998: Zur Bedeutung interner Verfaßtheit für das auswärtige Verhalten von Staaten, in Masala, Carlo and Roloff, Ralf (eds) *Herausforderungen in der Realpolitik. Beiträge zur Theoriebildung in der Internationalen Politik*. Cologne: SH-Verlag, pp. 227–268.

Kant, Immanuel [1795] 2006: Toward Perpetual Peace. A Philosophical Sketch, in Kant, Immanuel, *Toward Perpetual Peace and Other Writings on Politics, Peace, and History*. New Haven, CT: Yale University Press, pp. 67–109.

Lipson, Charles 2003: *Reliable Partners: How Democracies Have Made a Separate Peace*. Princeton, NJ: Princeton University Press.

Mansfield, Edward D. and Snyder, Jack 2002: Democratic Transitions, Institutional Strength, and War, *International Organization* 56(2): 297–337.

Mansfield, Edward D. and Snyder, Jack 2005: *Electing to Fight: Why Emerging Democracies Go to War*. Cambridge, MA: MIT Press.

Mansfield, Edward D. and Snyder, Jack 2009: Pathways to War in Democratic Transitions, *International Organization* 63(3): 381–390.

Maoz, Zeev 1997: The Controversy over the Democratic Peace, *International Security* 22(1): 162–198.

Midlarsky, Manus I. (ed.) 2000: *Handbook of War Studies II*. Ann Arbor, MI: University of Michigan Press.

Moravcsik, Andrew 1997: Taking Preferences Seriously: A Liberal Theory of International Politics, *International Organization* 51(4): 513–553.

Müller, Harald 2002: Antinomien des demokratischen Friedens, *Politische Vierteljahresschrift* 43(2): 46–81.

Müller, Harald 2004: The Antinomy of Democratic Peace, *International Politics* 41(4): 494–520.

Müller, Harald 2006: Kants Schurkenstaaten: der "ungerechte Feind" und die Selbstermächtigung zum Kriege, in Geis, Anna (ed.) *Den Krieg überdenken. Kriegsbegriffe und Kriegstheorien in der Kontroverse*, Baden-Baden: Nomos, pp. 229–250.

Müller, Harald 2008: Der "demokratische Frieden" und seine außenpolitischen Konsequenzen, *Aus Politik und Zeitgeschichte* B 43/2008: 41–46.

Müller, Harald and Wolff, Jonas 2006: Democratic Peace: Many Data, Little Explanation?, in Geis, Anna, Brock, Lothar and Müller, Harald (eds) *Democratic Wars: Looking at the Dark Side of the Democratic Peace*. Basingstoke: Palgrave, pp. 41–73.

Pevehouse, Jon and Russett, Bruce 2006: Democratic International Governmental Organizations Promote Peace, *International Organization* 60(4): 969–1000.

Prins, Brandon C. and Daxecker, Ursula E. 2007: Committed to Peace: Liberal Institutions and the Termination of Rivalry, *British Journal of Political Science* 38(1); 17–43.

Reiter, Dan and Stam, Allan C. 2002: *Democracies at War*. Princeton, NJ: Princeton University Press.

Reiter, Dan, Stam, Allan C. and Downes, Alexander B. 2009: Correspondence: Another Skirmish in the Battle over Democracies and War, *International Security* 34(2); 194–200.

Risse-Kappen, Thomas 1995a: *Cooperation Among Democracies: The European Influence on U.S. Foreign Policy*. Princeton, NJ: Princeton University Press.

Risse-Kappen, Thomas 1995b: Democratic Peace – Warlike Democracies? A Social Constructivist Interpretation of the Liberal Argument, *European Journal of International Relations* 1(4): 491–517.

Risse-Kappen, Thomas 1996: Collective Identity in a Democratic Community: The Case of NATO, in Katzenstein, Peter J. (ed.) *The Culture of National Security: Norms and Identity in World Politics*. New York: Columbia University Press, pp. 357–399.

Rittberger, Volker 1987: Zur Friedensfähigkeit von Demokratien. Betrachtungen zur politischen Theorie des Friedens, *Aus Politik und Zeitgeschichte* B 44/87: 3–12.

Rosato, Sebastian 2003: The Flawed Logic of Democratic Peace Theory, *American Political Science Review* 97(4): 585–602.

Rosato, Sebastian 2005: Explaining the Democratic Peace, *American Political Science Review* 99(3): 467–472.

Rousseau, David L., Gelpi, Christopher, Reiter, Dan and Huth, Paul K. 1996: Assessing the Dyadic Nature of the Democratic Peace, *American Political Science Review* 90(3): 512–533.

Rummel, Rudolph J. 1995: Democracies ARE Less Warlike Than Other Regimes, *European Journal of International Relations* 1(4): 457–479.

Russett, Bruce 1993: *Grasping the Democratic Peace: Principles for a Post-Cold War World*. Princeton, NJ: Princeton University Press.

Russett, Bruce M. 2009: Democracy, War and Expansion through Historical Lenses, *European Journal of International Relations* 15(1): 9–36.

Teusch, Ulrich and Kahl, Martin 2001: Ein Theorem mit Verfallsdatum? Der "Demokratische Friede" im Kontext der Globalisierung, *Zeitschrift für Internationale Beziehungen* 8(2): 287–320.

Vasquez, John A. (ed.) 2000: *What Do We Know about War?* Lanham, MD: Rowman & Littlefield Publishers.

Zimmermann, Lisbeth 2009: Wann beginnt der (Demokratische) Frieden? Regimewechsel, Instabilitäten, Integration und ihr Einfluss auf den Konflikt zwischen Ecuador und Peru, *Zeitschrift für internationale Beziehungen* 16(1): 39–74.

The English School[1]

Christopher Daase

1 Introduction

Isn't it strange that at a time of globalization and denationalization a theoretical approach that bears the name of a particular nation can still cause a stir?[2] The "English School" has been enjoying an astonishing comeback for more than 20 years. Declared dead and almost forgotten in the 1980s, an increasing number of articles and books on the school or written in its spirit appeared in the 1990s. The English School was officially resurrected in 1999 at the annual conference of the British International Studies Association (BISA) (Buzan 2001); with its own website,[3] it is probably one of the best organized theoretical approaches in the discipline of International Relations.

Despite all this activity, however, there remain serious doubts about whether the English School represents a coherent research programme in the first place and whether it has the theoretical potential vital to the progressive investigation of international relations. In fact, the term "English School" was first used in a polemical critique that called for this chapter of political science research to be closed due to its sterility and empirically unproductive nature (Jones 1981). Yet this very call for the dissolution of the English School roused its group consciousness and contributed to its rebirth.

In the first systematic account of the history of the English School, Tim Dunne identified three criteria that distinguish the school's members from representatives of other theoretical approaches in International Relations (Dunne 1998: 6–11). First, identification with a particular research tradition. From the mid-1960s at the latest, historians Herbert Butterfield and Martin Wight established an institution in which researchers of like mind could discuss their work and exchange ideas, in the shape of the British Committee on the Theory of International Politics. The first publication from this circle, the *Diplomatic Investigations* (Butterfield and Wight 1966), functioned as a kind of manifesto for the group. Older members such as Butterfield and Wight introduced their PhD students into this circle, particularly Adam Watson and Hedley Bull, helping establish an intellectual tradition. Later exponents such as R. J. Vincent explicitly saw themselves as located within this tradition. The second criterion for membership of this school identified by Dunne is a commitment to an interpretive approach. Beginning with Martin Wight's "three traditions" (see Wight 1991) and extending to Hedley Bull's polemic against social scientific approaches in the United States (Bull 1966), the English School is pervaded by a strong aversion to positivist research inspired by the model of the natural sciences. Finally, as the third attribute of members of the English School, Dunne identifies the conviction that the theory of international relations must be a normative theory. Wight's attempts to formulate a clear moral position with respect to international politics (Wight 1977) and Bull's development of the concept of an "international society" (Bull [1977] 1995) point to a common normative project aimed at developing ethical standards for international relations.

Even if we accept these three aspects as the common denominator of the English School, it is hard to decide exactly who is a member and who is not. Dunne includes E. H. Carr, whose book *The Twenty Years' Crisis* was certainly highly influential (Carr [1939] 1962), but who was in no way part of the discussion group around Butterfield and Wight and would have had little time for the school's normative credo (see also the chapter on realism by Andreas Jacobs in this volume). Dunne's exclusion of Charles Manning, whose book *The Nature of International Society* (Manning 1975) had a major impact on Bull, is equally problematic. Because of personal animosities between Manning and Wight, he was not invited to the British Committee, and he tends to be passed over even now because of his defence of the policy of Apartheid in South Africa. All of this would be merely a curious, peripheral aspect of intellectual community-building and scarcely worth talking about but for the fact that the discipline's "revisionist historiography", which Dunne advocates, aims not just to re*discover* but also to re*vive* the English School. In this light, the selective identification of the "real" members of the English School matters, and we begin to understand that what we are seeing here is the "construction" of a theoretical tradition.

If we apply different criteria to membership of the English School, such as a commitment to the notion of the "international community" as a social order or a particular relationship to political practice (Jones 1981; Suganami 1983; Grader 1988), then Hedley Bull is the only author left who ticks all the boxes. A slightly larger core would include Martin Wight, Herbert Butterfield, Hedley Bull, and Adam Watson. The next circle would add R. John Vincent, Charles Manning, Michael Howerd, Allen James, James Mayall and younger scholars such as Richard Little, Barry Buzan, and even younger ones such as Nicholas Wheeler and Tim Dunne. It seems justified to me, therefore, to concentrate on Hedley Bull as I continue this account of the English School; his book *The Anarchical Society: A Study of Order in World Politics* (Bull [1977] 1995) can certainly be viewed as *one*, if not *the* main work of the English School.

2 The English School: Hedley Bull

Hedley Bull is undoubtedly one of the major theorists of his generation. His attempt to develop a theory of international relations that is neither realist nor idealist and to expound a method that is neither historical nor natural scientific, however, has turned him into something of a tragic hero, who has failed to exercise a formative influence on the discipline as a whole because he has been misunderstood. There is still no agreement on how Hedley Bull fits into the development of the theory of international relations. Some make no bones about calling him a realist (Griffiths 1992: 155–167; Halliday 1992: 438; Brown 2001: 424), while others regard him as a pioneer of a critical theory of international politics (Linklater 1990: 14; Wheeler and Dunne 1996: 94). Bull himself must carry some of the blame for this. He repeatedly expounded strong views but was often unable to justify them. And he never missed an opportunity to indulge in polemics, despite failing to stick to his own principles. In some ways, you might say that here too Hedley Bull is paradigmatic of the English School: he embodies all its contradictions.

In what follows I address five aspects of Hedley's Bull's work that clarify his place within the English School, as well as how his work relates to other theories of international relations. First, I show how, on the basis of Wight's division of the history of political thought into three traditions, Hedley Bull opted to take a theoretical middle path, establishing "international society" as the central idea of the English School. Second, building on this, I discuss his conception of the "balance of power", which differs markedly from realist and neorealist conceptions. This makes it necessary, third, to understand Bull's interpretive methodology and, fourth, to elucidate his normative concept of theory. I conclude by briefly examining his relationship to political practice.

2.1 Three theoretical traditions and "international society"

There is a certain irony in the fact that an Australian was to become the standard-bearer of the English School. Hedley Bull completed his Master's degree at the University of Sydney in 1952. He then went to Oxford to study for his PhD and became an assistant to Charles Manning at the London School of Economics (LSE) in 1955. In the late 1950s he worked with Philip Noel-Baker on a project focused on disarmament. But it was Bull's academic mentor at the LSE, Martin Wight, who exercised the greatest intellectual influence on him. Bull returned to Oxford as a professor, where he died in 1985.

Bull took from Wight the division of the history of political thought into three philosophical traditions, the "three Rs": realism, rationalism and revolutionism. For Wight, realism was the anthropologically pessimistic world-view that reduces human beings to their lust for power and regards international politics as a field determined by anarchy, power politics and warfare. Wight applied the term revolutionists to cosmopolitan idealists who believe in the existence of universal values and work to establish a world society. Finally, "rationalists" was Wight's term for those who recognize political realities but believe in human reason and underline the potential for a better world through social institutions. Wight favoured this rationalist tradition, which he referred to as the "broad middle road of European thinking" (Wight 1991: 14).

For Bull, however, these traditions as such were not important. He was interested not so much in intellectual history as in using it to assess the contemporary international situation. In his book, *The Anarchical Society*, he further abstracted Wight's "Rs", reducing them to three competing intellectual traditions, which he referred to paradigmatically as realist or Hobbesian (after Thomas Hobbes, 1588–1679), universalist or Kantian (after Immanuel Kant, 1724–1804), and internationalist or Grotian (after Hugo Grotius, 1583–1645). For Bull, Thomas Hobbes embodied realist thought. Bull simply applied Hobbes's conception of the state of nature to international politics, in which states exist in a permanent state of war. Because there is no central authority, peace can only be a temporary state of affairs. He identified Immanuel Kant, on the other hand, with the universalist tradition, which privileges human individuals rather than states. The aim of this tradition is not to achieve peace between nations, but to create a community of world citizens. Finally, Hugo Grotius represents the internationalist tradition, which takes as given that the international political reality is one of anarchy, but holds to the possibility that the scale of war and conflict can be limited by universal rules and institutions (Bull [1977] 1995: 22–26).

This schematization may strike historians of philosophy as too superficial and Bull received a great deal of criticism for his simplistic analysis. His intention, however, was not to provide a precise interpretation but rather a rough categorization of theoretical currents. Bull emphasized that none of these traditions should be seen as the one true faith. But Bull himself strongly preferred the Grotian perspective (Bull *et al.* 1990). This indecision is partly responsible for the fact that it is so difficult to determine Bull's own position within the theoretical debate. His stance towards realism in particular requires clarification.

The Hobbesian tradition of realism can present international politics as a *system* and explain it on the basis of mere interaction between atomistic units within an empty space:

> A *system of states* (or international system) is formed when two or more states have sufficient contact between them, and have sufficient impact on one another's decisions, to cause them to behave – at least in some measure – as parts of a whole.
>
> (Bull [1977] 1995: 9)

Within the international system, the relations between states are pure conflicts: the interests of one state preclude those of all other states. International politics is a zero-sum game (ibid.: 23). In Bull's view, however, this perspective is one-sided. For him it is equally important, from a Grotian perspective, to see the norms and rules that transform the international system into an international *society*:

> A *society of states*(or international society) exists when a group of states, conscious of certain common interests and common values, form a society in the sense that they conceive themselves to be bound by a common set of rules in their relations with one another, and share in the working of common institutions.
>
> (ibid.: 13)

This distinction between the international system and international society is central to the English School as a whole. In some ways the international system is more fundamental than international society. There can be a system without a society, but no society without a system. In a later essay, Hedley Bull points out that the expansion of Europe in the fifteenth century led to a system of states long before the emergence of a society of European states (Bull 1984b). But if an international system is the precondition for an international society, the question arises as to how we are to describe the transition from one to the other. To put it in a nutshell: How do we know that a society of states is emerging? Bull is not much help here. He argues that an international society is based on the idea of an "international order", defining this order as the "arrangement of social life such that it promotes certain goals or values" (Bull [1977] 1995: 4). For him, order and society seem to be synonymous, and his argument risks becoming tautological.

Essentially, the concept of the "international society" throws up *two* questions, one theoretical and one historical. The theoretical question is: What do we gain by regarding international constellations as "international societies" as opposed to conceptualizing them as "international systems"? This question is independent of the stage of historical development of such constellations, as it would surely be difficult to imagine a *purely* "international society" as a rule-based social organism or a *purely* "international system" completely devoid of social rules. The answer lies in the fact that social norms and rules that mould the behaviour of states can be better described and explained *within* the paradigm of the "international society". But this does not explain how an "international society" comes about *in the first place*. This brings us to the second, historical question. Do "international systems" develop into "international societies" and, if so, how are we to explain this development? The problem here is that the historical evidence for such developments does not constitute a social scientific explanation. So for the time being, the question of how an "international society" is *possible* remains unanswered.

2.2 The balance of power as an example

A more detailed look at the theory of the balance of power is helpful at this point. Bull fully recognizes the value of the realist perspective. There are good reasons why his definition of the international system resembles that of John Herz and Hans Morgenthau (see the chapter on realism by Andreas Jacobs in this volume). However, in light of the definition of the international system as an interaction between power-maximizing states, realists draw conclusions different from those of Bull, in that they assume the existence of an automatic mechanism that stabilizes the balance of power and, when it becomes unbalanced, restores it (Morgenthau 1948; Gilpin 1981). Bull counters this by pointing out that states are by no means always concerned to expand their power. Because of this, there can be no question of a *necessary* tendency to establish a balance of power. At most, a *fortuitous* balance of power may come into being, but it will remain unstable if there is no political will on the part of the states involved (Bull [1977] 1995: 100).

This idea of a *fortuitous balance of power* is strongly reminiscent of the neorealist theory of the balance of power in the work of Kenneth Waltz. Waltz describes the emergence of the balance of power as an unintended consequence of systemic factors: states that must assert themselves within an anarchical self-help system are compelled to form a counter-weight to the strongest state or strongest group of states in order to ensure their survival over the long term. Because the anarchical structure of the international system is insuperable, the balance of power is a necessary result of international politics (Waltz 1979: 102–128; see also the chapter by Niklas Schörnig in this volume). For Bull, meanwhile, the anarchy of the international system is not an eternal structural attribute and states' focus on power and survival is not absolute. For him and other representatives of the English School, the balance of power is a fortuitous rather than necessary outcome of international politics (Little 2000: 406).

So the benefits of looking at international politics from the perspective of the international system are limited. The example of the balance of power shows that for Bull it is not enough to stop at the international system; we must also take account of international society. A balance of power may be intended, and may become an institutional element of international relations. In order to understand this *contrived* balance of power, however, it is necessary to conceive of international politics not in realist terms as a system, but in internationalist terms as a society. Bull defines "international society" as a number of states that are *aware* of shared interests and values and act in accordance with this awareness. On this basis, Bull asserts that a stable balance of power can exist only if a sufficient number of powerful states decide to create and maintain a balance of power. The decision for or against a balance of power is not simply a cost-benefit calculation, let alone something dictated by the anarchical structure of the international system. It is in fact a normative agreement regarding how best to stabilize the society of states. Ultimately, then, a balance of power is based not simply on the capacity to impose constraints on others, but on the willingness to subject *oneself* to constraints (Bull [1977] 1995: 97–121).

The transition from an international system to an international society, then, can be observed when a number of states become aware of shared values and ideas and these come to guide their actions. It is evident here that international systems and international societies are based on completely different ontological preconditions, that is, they require different understandings of social reality and they therefore require different investigative methodologies (Little 2000: 408). For the identification and analysis of international systems, it is sufficient to observe the interaction between states and use positivist methods. International societies, in contrast, presuppose an element of intersubjective agreement among actors and thus require an interpretive method capable of analysing the considerations and motives, the ideas and values of actors. In brief, using the categories provided by Hollis and Smith (Hollis and Smith 1990): we can *explain* international systems, but we must *understand* international societies.

For Bull, then, if we wish to grasp the pattern of the balance of power in international politics, it is not enough to observe the interaction between states in the international system and draw causal conclusions on this basis – as do neorealists such as Waltz. Instead we must analyse the development of the concept of the balance of power and show how conceptual change has found political expression. Here Bull could base himself on the historical groundwork done by his colleagues on the British Committee, Herbert Butterfield and Martin Wight. They had established that the politics of balance in other international systems such as ancient Greece or among the Italian city-states of the Renaissance were quite different than in the international society of seventeenth- and eighteenth-century Europe (Butterfield 1966; Wight 1966). It was the *idea* of a balance of power and the associated notions of sovereignty and legitimacy that turned the balance of power into an institution and helped make the European international system into a European international society.

2.3 Interpretive methodology

The significance of ideational and normative factors to the English School's central theorem – the international society – explains why the British Committee saw the introduction of natural scientific methods limited to empirical observation as such a threat. Ideas and values – all that goes to make an international *system* into an international *society* – are irrelevant in positivist methodology because they cannot be operationalized and therefore cannot be observed. The call for scientific theory building in International Relations of the kind made by Morton Kaplan (Kaplan 1961) was thus anathema to the English School.

Against the background of this fundamental questioning, it is not hard to understand the hostility with which members of the British Committee viewed the methodological innovations of American political science. The same applies to Hedley Bull's vehement polemics against Morton Kaplan, Thomas Schelling, Karl Deutsch, and Kenneth Boulding, those authors, in other words, who ushered in the behaviouralist turn in International Relations. With his infamous 1966 article "International Theory. The Case for a Classical Approach", Hedley Bull became the most vocal opponent of the introduction of game theory, the growth of statistics and the use of other methods learned from the modern natural sciences within International Relations. His key argument was that "the scientific approach is likely to contribute very little to the theory of international relations, and in so far as it is intended to encroach upon and ultimately displace the classical approach, it is positively harmful" (Bull 1966: 366).

Bull accused positivists within political science of making seven crucial mistakes (ibid.: 366–376). First, the focus on issues of methodology was causing scholars to lose sight of the great questions of international politics. Second, the preoccupation with formal models diminishes the capacity to make reasoned judgements. Third, positivists espouse a naïve notion of scientific progress. Fourth, their formal models distort political reality. Fifth, the mania for measuring each and every social phenomenon leads to false conclusions. Sixth, positivists claim to be in sole possession of scientific virtue despite the fact that rigour and precision also form part of the classical tradition, and, seventh, the distancing of philosophy and history results in a loss of self-reflection and the capacity for self-criticism.

This list contains criticisms that must be taken seriously as well as straightforward resentment. The basic thrust of Bull's essay is an aggressive rejection, not underpinned by any substantive reflections in the theory of science, of the application of scientific standards to research on international politics. Bull makes little effort to comprehend his opponents' metatheoretical premises or assess the value of their research. He is equally unsuccessful in justifying his own position. The vigour of his attack on scientism is matched by the weakness of his defence of traditionalism. Again, Bull makes no effort to draw on hermeneutic or phenomenological theories of science in order to undergird his assertion that the investigation of international politics is best served through recourse to philosophy, history and law (ibid.: 361).

Bull's polemic undoubtedly captured the basic mentality of members of the British Committee; and quite rightly this essay is considered the English School's methodological profession of faith. But how this pamphlet could have been stylized as the high point of the second great debate[4] within International Relations must always remain a secret. Why scientism won the debate on points, on the other hand, is plainly apparent.

2.4 Normative theory

There is one sense in which Bull's methodological critique of scientism and his political critique of realism converge, namely in that he accuses both of lacking a normative component, which is central to his own theoretical conception. In an essay on E. H. Carr's influential book *The Twenty Years' Crisis*, Bull develops an alternative to what he calls moral relativism. Realists such as Carr, according to Bull, deny that ethical-moral arguments have any kind of independent significance:

> The idea of an international society – of common interest and common values perceived in common by modern states – is scarcely recognized in the *Twenty Years' Crisis*. In the course of demonstrating how appeals to an overriding international society subserve the special interests of the ruling group of powers, Carr jettisons the idea of international society itself.
>
> (Bull 1969: 638)

On close reading of Carr's book, this assertion may appear overstated, but it shows how important the specifically normative aspect of his concept of an "international society" is to Bull.

Bull counters realists' well-known objection that states obey international law only if it is in their interest to do so anyway by claiming that it is far more revealing to reflect on why states so often consider it opportune to obey international law (Bull [1977] 1995: 140). His answer is that states live in an international society whose legal framework they consider so valuable that they often comply with rules and norms even when this does *not* correspond to their immediate interests.

For Bull, then, there are values within international politics of a more or less objective character, such as "order", and values such as "justice" that have a subjective character. In Bull's conception of international society, the state as such takes on an objective value. The rejection of a universalist conception of justice that grants the individual normative priority over all other social units, and the emphasis on the aspect of international order as an order of states show unmistakably that Bull's internationalist position ascribes to the state an independent value as guarantor of international society. In this sense, Bull's theory is clearly state-centred. And it was just these reflections that led him to reject the concept of "humanitarian intervention" in a multi-authored volume he himself edited in 1984:

> As regards the right of so-called humanitarian intervention . . . there is no present tendency of states to claim, or for the international community to recognize, any such right. The reluctance evident in the international community even to experiment with the conception of a right of humanitarian intervention reflects not only an unwillingness to jeopardise the rules of sovereignty and non-intervention by conceding such a right to individual states, but also the lack of any agreed doctrine as to what human rights are.
>
> (Bull 1984c: 193)

As Nicholas Wheeler and Tim Dunne sum it up, while Bull did have a certain leaning towards universalist notions of justice, his conviction that it is international society that is the ultimate stronghold of international order prevented him from opening his mind to a more extensive "solidaristic politics" (Wheeler and Dunne 1996: 98).

2.5 Theory and practice

Hedley Bull's strong commitment to the normativity of international theory and rejection of value-free research seem to sit uneasily with his great contempt for academic colleagues who saw it as part of their responsibility to intervene actively in politics.

By the late 1950s, Bull had fallen out with Philip Noel-Baker, who advocated comprehensive disarmament in his book *The Arms Race: A Programme for Disarmament* (Noel-Baker 1958). Bull favoured a far less "radical" approach. The arms race should be brought under control within the framework of the institutions of international society, in other words, the balance of power, through the imposition of gradual restrictions on arms (O'Neill and Schwartz 1987). Bull considered Noel-Baker's advocacy of more extensive disarmament unscientific. He was even more critical of Richard Falk, a prominent legal scholar at Princeton University, who spoke in favour of universal moral values such as peace, distributive justice, ecological equilibrium and human rights. Falk, Bull warned, had departed from the path of scientific objectivity and was now producing political propaganda:

> The task of the academic inquirer is not to jump on bandwagons but to stand back and assess, in a disinterested way, the direction in which they are going. Any writer can join a political movement and devote his intellectual talents to supplying the rhetoric, the exaggeration, the denunciation and the slurring of issues which will help to speed it on its way. It does not seem the best use for the talents of the Albert G. Milbank Professor of International Law.
>
> (Bull 1972: 588)

But it was not just peace researchers who fell victim to Bull's invective. He criticized academics who got too involved in politics on the other side of the political spectrum as well. He described Henry Kissinger as "a very unfortunate example of a profession whose business is, after all, with thinking, not with doing" (Bull 1980: 484). Yet Bull himself was not politically abstinent. In the 1960s, he was a member of the British Special Advisory Group on Arms Control. His criticisms appear to be mainly politically motivated in that he criticizes only scholars who are adherents of the realist and universalist traditions but not, like him, the internationalist tradition. Bull appears to have found Grotian political advisors acceptable, but not Kantian and Hobbesian ones.

3 The English School: the second generation

Hedley Bull was neither the first theorist of the English School nor the last. Like no one else, however, he formulated its basic ideas, fleshed them out and espoused them within international discourse with a vigour that made it impossible to ignore them. His desperate struggle to be heard expresses the fate of a small research community at risk of being colonized and ultimately swallowed by an overpowering rival. It is no coincidence that Stanley Hoffmann referred to International Relations as an "American discipline" (Hoffman 1977). But while academic subcultures within International Relations could survive in other European states because of language differences, the British discipline was directly exposed to the "behaviouralist revolution", as the triumph of natural scientific methods in the United States was often called. So it is no surprise that the early adherents of the School on the British Committee on the Theory of International Politics saw themselves as a specifically *national* group of theorists (Holsti 1985) and even today the "English" aspect of the English School may be understood in highly programmatic terms as "non-American" (yet English-speaking) (Dunne 1998).

This does not mean, however, that it is nationalistic in the sense that only English people are members. On the contrary, in the last few years the English School has been internationalized by the addition of Australians, South Africans, Canadians, other Europeans and Asians.[5] But beyond their opposition to mainstream American political science, which they perceive as hegemonic, what unites these researchers is increasingly unclear. References to the English School as an intellectual tradition are becoming less and less credible as the interpretation of this tradition is increasingly contested.

Those engaged in the interpretation and development of the English School deploy two main strategies. First, they emphasize the pluralism of the English School and seek ways of connecting it with mainstream American approaches, especially neorealism and regime theory (Buzan 1993; Buzan and Little 2000; Little 2000). Second, they interpret the English School in a very specific way that makes it the predecessor of critical theory and lends support to universalist positions (Wheeler and Dunne 1996; Dunne 1998; Wheeler 2000). What these strategies have in common is that, inspired by the work of Hedley Bull, they draw on the work of Martin Wight – before going beyond Bull with Wight's help.

3.1 The English School as the analysis of international systems

It makes sense to view the three traditions that Bull uses to make his distinction between "international systems", "international societies" and "world societies" as incompatible and rival paradigms. Richard Little (2000), however, has emphasized that the English School sees it as one of its tasks if not to reconcile these traditions, then at least to accept that each has its own strengths. Wight views these traditions as "three interrelated political conditions which comprise the subject matter of what is called international relations" (Wight 1991: 7).

As Wight sees it, the problem with these three traditions is that each of them emphasizes just *one* aspect of international politics. Realists underline the systemic condition of anarchy, because they consider the lack of a central authority to be a permanent and unchanging condition of international politics. Rationalists, meanwhile, focus on diplomacy and economic relations because they believe that regular contact between actors within international politics can alleviate the consequences of anarchy. Finally, revolutionists concentrate on the question of how states might develop a normative and cultural order capable of overcoming the conditions of anarchy. Little emphasizes that the reduction of the English School to a "rationalist" position in Wight's sense and to the idea of an "international society" in Bull's sense is an oversimplification. In reality, the English School has much more to offer (Little 2000: 398).

An emphasis on the ontological and methodological pluralism of the English School allows us to look for points of contact with other theories of international relations, especially with those of a supposedly "positivist" character. In an earlier book that Little wrote in collaboration with Barry Buzan and Charles Jones, the authors get to grips with the neorealism of Kenneth Waltz in an effort to develop his ideas, along with those of the English School, into an integrative, coherent theory of international relations (Buzan *et al.* 1993). Buzan especially was concerned to show that an international society (of the kind envisaged by the English School) can emerge as a natural product of the logic of anarchy (in the neorealist sense). Buzan distinguishes between two different paths: one that creates a community "organically" through cultural and normative adaptation (in line with the ideas of Tönnies [1887] 2002) and one which, through social and legal agreements, constructs a "rational" society. Buzan explains the emergence of "international societies" (in Hedley Bull's sense), first, with the help of neorealism, which allows us to explain the rational construction of society (of the kind Tönnies had in mind) on the basis of common interests, and, second, with the help of the English School, which allows us to understand the cultural construction of community (in Tönnies' sense) on the basis of shared values (Buzan 1993: 348; see also the chapter on world society and globalization by Ingo Take in this volume).

In their most recent book, Buzan and Little attempt to apply these ideas comparatively to other international systems in order to open up a new perspective on the study of international politics that is "more holistic, more integrated and more historically contextualized" (Buzan and Little 2000: 1). They are quite relaxed about the fact that this takes them ever further away from the traditional ideas of the English School. Their laconic response to a critic who accused them of changing the essence of English School theory (Hall 2001: 941) was that they did not intend to write "an English School book" in the first place (Buzan and Little 2001: 944). They are far more concerned to creatively develop the English School as an "underexploited resource" (Buzan 2001).

3.2 The English School as critical theory

A younger generation of political scientists has something quite different in mind as it attempts to systematically reassess the history of the English School and reinterpret it in a particular way (Dunne 1998; Epp 1998). Tim Dunne candidly admits that he is not concerned with authenticity, with whether his interpretation "does justice" to English School authors. Instead he aims to identify the normative potential of their work and determine "What can we make of it?" (Dunne 1998: 182).

Here Dunne builds on the work of Andrew Linklater, who has proposed an original interpretation of Wight's "three traditions". According to Linklater, we can reinterpret the "three Rs" of realism, rationalism and revolutionism in methodological terms as positivism, hermeneutics and critical theory. Furthermore, Linklater sees a dialectical relationship between them, with the thesis of "positivism" and antithesis "hermeneutics" resulting in the synthesis of "critical theory" (Linklater 1990: Chapter 1; see also the chapter on critical theory by Christoph Humrich in this volume). Through this manoeuvre, which certainly does not match the original intentions of the first generation of the English School, let alone those of Hedley Bull, the English School becomes the pioneer of a critical theory of International Relations.

Nicholas Wheeler and Tim Dunne take much the same approach in an article that seeks to establish a "solidarist" theory of international society and provide a normative rationale for the right to humanitarian intervention. In the English School, "solidarism" means a universalist commitment to global values and contrasts with "pluralism", the notion that norms and values are culture-dependent. Wheeler and Dunne too focus mainly on the writings of the "older" representatives of the English School and seek out intellectual developments which they might consistently extrapolate from and develop in a particular direction. They interpret Bull's dissatisfaction with the moral relativism of realism, for example, as a move away from realist towards pluralist positions which, if it had been pursued consistently, would have resulted in a "solidarist" conception of international politics. Despite Bull's repeated rejection of universalist values, Wheeler and Dunne get to the point where they can claim "Bull was a solidarist" (Wheeler and Dunne 1996: 106). Here Hedley Bull, who came out explicitly against "humanitarian intervention" in 1984 (Bull 1984b), becomes an exponent of universalist values and a pioneer of humanitarian intervention.

More traditionally-minded contemporaries may describe this form of interpretation as simply unserious, but it is very much in line with the logic of revisionist historiography within the discipline of International Relations, which Dunne expounds by arguing that all theory is normative and what matters is to develop the notion of the "international society" in a cosmopolitan-universalist direction (Dunne 1998: 181–190). Nicholas Wheeler shares "the same normative agenda of radicalizing the English School" (Wheeler 2000: xi) and in his book, *Saving Strangers: Humanitarian Intervention in International Society*, he tries to justify the "solidarist" understanding of international society. In his discussion of the normative arguments *for* humanitarian intervention, he draws on the work of three authors, R. J. Vincent, Michael Walzer and Fernando Téson, of which only the first is considered a member of the English School but is an exponent of a "pluralist" position, while the other two do not belong to the English School but take a "solidarist" stance. Because Wheeler wishes to show that the right to humanitarian intervention accords with the logical development of the English School, he simply co-opts Téson as "located in the solidarist wing of the English School" (Wheeler 2000: 39).

Robert Jackson has a quite different evaluation of the problem of intervention. He too claims to develop the classical approach of the English School and to provide answers to present-day normative questions. In contrast to Dunne and Wheeler, however, Jackson accentuates not the solidarist but the pluralist position and thus ascribes greater importance to the norm of sovereignty than to human rights. States, for him, do indeed have a responsibility to ensure international justice whenever possible, but they must not thereby violate other fundamental values of international society:

> International order and stability, international peace and security, are such values. In my view, the stability of international society, especially the unity of the great powers, is more important, indeed far more important, than minority rights and humanitarian protections in Yugoslavia or any other country – if we have to choose between those two sets of values.
>
> (Jackson 2000: 291)

Regardless of whether we consider the arguments for or against humanitarian intervention more valid, it is apparent from the debate between solidarists and pluralists that no unambiguous normative statements can be derived from the English School and the concept of international society. But the English School at least provides the vocabulary and categories that allow us to discuss these and other ethical questions in the first place (Mapel and Nardin 1998). And it is in precisely this respect that the English School is superior to many other theoretical approaches within International Relations.

4 The English School: what future?

Current theoretical tendencies within the English School point in opposite directions. Some key thinkers underline ontological and methodological pluralism and seek dialogue with American mainstream approaches; others highlight normative-critical components, welding them into a paradigm directly opposed to the mainstream. For now representatives of the two currents still contribute to the same multi-authored volumes on the theoretical development of the English School (Roberson 2002; Linklater and Suganami 2006; Little and Williams 2006). But it is becoming increasingly unclear what scholars who see themselves as located within the tradition of the English School actually have in common.

Roy Jones, in any event, asked this question 30 years ago, and announced that it was time to close the chapter known as the "English School" (Jones 1981). Ian Hall has resumed this critique, but radicalizes it by claiming that there is no need to close this chapter because the English School no longer exists "as a cohesive approach to the study of international relations" (Hall 2001: 942). Indeed, it is probably best to refer to the English School not in the sense of a particular theory, and not even as a paradigm, but simply "as a tradition of conversation, marked off from others by its focus on the 'three traditions' as a set, in which people can participate without being committed to particular strictures" (Buzan and Little 2001: 944). This would solve some of the problems with which the English School would find itself faced, were it to continue to expound the illusory idea that it is a coherent research programme within International Relations.

One of these problems is the diversity that could be lost were the English School to be understood more narrowly as a particular theoretical position. This is what Ole Wæver (1999) had in mind when he warned against overemphasizing the parallels between the English School and what is generally referred to as constructivism. There are certain parallels in the emphasis on the *via media* in the English School (a middle way in terms of the history of political thought in the work of Wight and in terms of methodology in the work of Bull), on the one hand, and the search for the epistemological middle ground in the work of constructivists (Adler 1997; Wendt 1999), on the other (see also the chapter on social constructivism by Cornelia Ulbert in this volume). But these similarities are far outweighed by differences. These give rise to differing strengths. The English School is good at researching macrohistorical change and tackling questions of political ethics, while constructivism's strength lies in analysing causal mechanisms and subjecting normative ideas to empirical study. Wæver concludes: "Both the English School and (American mainstream) constructivism are valuable, but it would be a pity to give up one in order to look like the other" (Wæver 1999: 13).

This does not exclude the possibility that both approaches might stimulate one another in a positive way. Hidemi Suganami, for example, suggests that constructivism, which – at least in its mainstream form *à la* Wendt – is highly abstract and nothing less than anti-empirical, might take inspiration from the English School to produce historical analyses, while the English School, which – at least in its classical variant – has made very little effort to generalize its historical findings, might be prompted to engage more consistently in theory building (Suganami 2001). In this way, constructivism and the English School might work in a complementary fashion, one deductively and the other inductively, on the common project of identifying the conditions of "international society". As Martha Finnemore notes, however, members of the English School have some preliminary work to do before engaging in such cooperation. To this day, she tells us, it is quite unclear what theoretical and methodological claims the English School is making in the first place (Finnemore 2001). For Finnemore, when it comes to methodological reflection and theoretical clarity, the English School has more to learn from constructivism than the other way round.

Another problem could be solved if the English School is understood not as a theory but as a "tradition of conversation", namely, the notorious attempts by scholars of other schools to "refute" the English School through empirical falsification. One of the few American authors to take the English School seriously is Stephen Krasner. In his book, *Sovereignty: Organized Hypocrisy*, he discusses a number of theories (neorealism, neoliberalism and the English School) with respect to whether they can explain international politics within the framework of the Westphalian system. He describes how the English School views the "Westphalian system" as an international society that consists of generalized norms of sovereignty and non-intervention. But he comes to the conclusion that

> [E]mpirically, the frequency with which the domestic autonomy of states has been violated suggests that the shared norms and internalized constraints stipulated by the English school do not exist at least with regard to the Westphalian model. Even the rules associated with international legal sovereignty are not taken for granted.
>
> (Krasner 1999: 55f.)

The fact that institutions and rules are disobeyed, however, does not mean that they do not exist. And Krasner's observation fails to address the normative core of the statement that the Westphalian system is an international society founded on institutions.

Finally, a less rigid understanding of the English School might render superfluous the "scholasticism" (Hurrell 2001: 489) concerning what exactly the doctrine of the English School is and which scholars have the right to describe themselves as members. At present, attempts to artificially construct a theoretical tradition have merely resulted in more research being done *on* the English School than *in the spirit of* the English School. As understandable as it is that some scholars have sought to protect their own (national) research tradition against the overwhelming challenge posed by the United States, its isolation and opposition to the mainstream approaches have hindered the theoretical development of the English School. Perhaps a little fresh air would do the English patient a power of good.

5 Notes

1 This chapter has not been revised and the translation reflects the version in the German edition printed in 2010. The editors take responsibility for the addition of relevant titles in the secondary reading section at the end of this chapter.
2 My thanks go to Tina Burns for researching and procuring the relevant literature.
3 The address is http:www.leedsac.uk/polis/englishschool/.
4 The second debate refers to the methodological dispute between traditionalists and behaviouralists in the 1960s. See the contributions in Knorr and Rosenau (1969).
5 A list of members of the second generation of the English School and its sympathizers can be found on the website mentioned in note 3.

6 Bibliography and recommended reading

6.1 Primary texts

Bull, Hedley 1966: International Theory: The Case for a Classical Approach, *World Politics* 18(3): 361–377.

Bull, Hedley [1977] 1995: *The Anarchical Society: A Study of Order in World Politics*, 2nd edn. New York: Macmillan.

Butterfield, Herbert and Wight, Martin (eds) 1966: *Diplomatic Investigations: Essays in the Theory of International Politics*. London: Allen & Unwin.

Wight, Martin 1991: *International Theory: The Three Traditions*. Ed. Gabriele Wight and Brian Porter. Leicester: Leicester University Press.

6.2 Secondary texts

Buzan, Barry 2001: The English School: An Underexploited Resource in IR, *Review of International Studies* 27(3): 471–488.

Dunne, Tim 1998: *Inventing International Society: A History of the English School*. Basingstoke: Macmillan.

Little, Richard 2000: The English School's Contribution to the Study of International Relations, *European Journal of International Relations* 6(3): 395–422.

6.3 Editors' supplement

Adler, Emanuel 2005: Barry Buzan's Use of Constructivism to Reconstruct the English School: Not All the Way Down, *Millennium* 34(1): 171–182.

Ayson, Robert 2012: *Hedley Bull and the Accommodation of Power*. Basingstoke: Palgrave Macmillan.

Bellamy, Alex J. (ed.) 2005: *International Society and its Critics*. Oxford: Oxford University Press.

Buzan Barry 2004: *From International to World Society? English School Theory and the Social Structure of Globalization*. Cambridge: Cambridge University Press.

Buzan, Barry 2010: The English School and International Security, in Dunn Cavelty, Miriam and Mauer, Victor (eds) *The Routledge Companion to Security Studies*. London: Routledge.

Cochran, Molly 2008: The Ethics of the English School, in Reus-Smit, Christian and Snidal, Duncan (eds) *The Oxford Handbook of International Relations*. Oxford: Oxford University Press, pp. 286–297.

Dunne, Tim 2005: System, State and Society: How Does It All Hang Together?, *Millennium* 34(1): 157–170.

Dunne, Tim 2008: The English School, in Reus-Smit, Christian and Snidal, Duncan (eds) *The Oxford Handbook of International Relations*. Oxford: Oxford University Press, pp. 267–285.

Hurrell, Andrew 2007: *On Global Order: Power, Values and the Constitution of International Society*. Oxford: Oxford University Press.

Weinert, Matthew 2011: Reframing the Pluralist-Solidarist Debate, *Millennium* 40(1): 21–41.

6.4 Other texts

Adler, Emanuel 1997: Seizing the Middle Ground: Constructivism in World Politics, *European Journal of International Relations* 3(3): 319–363.

Brown, Chris 2001: World Society and the English School: An "International Society" Perspective on World Society, *European Journal of International Relations* 7(4): 423–441.

Bull, Hedley 1969: The Twenty Year's Crisis Thirty Years On, *International Journal* 42(4): 626–638.

Bull, Hedley 1972: International Law and International Order, *International Organization* 26(2): 583–588.
Bull, Hedley 1980: Kissinger: The Primacy of Geopolitics, *International Affairs* 56(2): 484–487.
Bull, Hedley 1984a: Intervention in the Third World, in Bull, Hedley (ed.) *Intervention in World Politics*. Oxford: Clarendon Press, pp. 135–156.
Bull, Hedley 1984b: The Emergence of a Universal International Society, in Bull, Hedley and Watson, Adam (eds) *The Expansion of International Society*. Oxford: Clarendon Press, pp. 117–126.
Bull, Hedley (ed.) 1984c: *Intervention in World Politics*. Oxford: Clarendon Press.
Bull, Hedley, Kingsbury, Benedikt and Roberts, Allan (eds) 1990: *Hugo Grotius and International Relations*. Oxford: Clarendon Press.
Butterfield, Herbert 1966: The Balance of Power, in Butterfield, Herbert and Wight, Martin (eds) *Diplomatic Investigations*, London: Allen & Unwin, pp. 132–148.
Buzan, Barry 1993: From International System to International Society: Structural Realism and Regime Theory Meet the English School, *International Organization* 47(3): 327–352.
Buzan, Barry, Jones, Charles and Little, Richard 1993: *The Logic of Anarchy: Neorealism to Structural Realism*. New York: Columbia University Press.
Buzan, Barry and Little, Richard 2000: *International Systems in World History: Remaking the Study of International Relations*. Oxford: Oxford University Press.
Buzan, Barry and Little, Richard 2001: The "English Patient" Strikes Back: A Response to Hall's Mis-Diagnosis, *International Affairs* 77(3): 943–946.
Carr, Edward H. [1939] 1962: *The Twenty Year's Crisis, 1919–1939*. London: Macmillan.
Epp, Roger 1998: The English School on the Frontiers of International Society: A Hermeneutic Recollection, *Review of International Studies* Special Issue, 24: 47–63.
Finnemore, Martha 2001: Exporting the English School, *Review of International Studies* 27(3); 509–513.
Gilpin, Robert 1981: *War and Change in World Politics*. Cambridge: Cambridge University Press.
Grader, Sheila 1988: The English School of International Relations: Evidence and Evaluation, *Review of International Studies* 14(1): 29–44.
Griffiths, Martin 1992: *Realism, Idealism and International Politics: A Reinterpretation*. London: Routledge.
Hall, Ian 2001: Still the English Patient? Closures and Inventions in the English School, *International Affairs* 77(3): 931–942.
Halliday, Fred 1992: International Society as Homogeneity, *Millennium* 21(3): 435–461.
Hoffmann, Stanley 1977: An American Social Science: International Relations, *Daedalus* 106(3): 41–60.
Hollis, Martin and Smith, Steve 1990: *Explaining and Understanding International Relations*. Oxford: Clarendon Press.
Holsti, Kal J. 1985: *The Dividing Discipline: Hegemony and Diversity in International Relations Theory*. London: Allen & Unwin.
Hurrell, Andrew 2001: Keeping History, Law and Political Philosophy Firmly within the English School, *Review of International Studies* 27(3): 489–494.
Jackson, Robert H. 2000: *The Global Covenant: Human Conduct in a World of States*. Oxford: Oxford University Press.
Jones, Roy E. 1981: The English School of International Relations: A Case for Closure, *Review of International Studies* 7(1): 1–13.
Kaplan, Morton A. 1961: Problems of Theory Building and Theory Confirmation in International Politics, *World Politics* 14(1): 6–24.
Knorr, Klaus and Rosenau, James N. 1969: *Contending Approaches to International Politics*. Princeton, NJ: Princeton University Press.
Krasner, Stephen D. 1999: *Sovereignty: Organized Hypocrisy*. Princeton, NJ: Princeton University Press.

Linklater, Andrew 1990: *Beyond Realism and Marxism: Critical Theory and International Relations*. London: Macmillan.

Linklater, Andrew and Suganami, Hidemi (eds) 2006: *The English School of International Relations: A Contemporary Reassessment*. Cambridge: Cambridge University Press.

Little, Richard and Williams, John (eds) 2006: *The Anarchical Society in a Globalized World*. Basingstoke: Palgrave.

Manning, Charles 1975: *The Nature of International Society*. London: Macmillan.

Mapel, David R. and Nardin, Terry (eds) 1998: *International Society: Diverse Ethical Perspectives*. Princeton, NJ: Princeton University Press.

Morgenthau, Hans J. 1948: *Politics Among Nations: The Struggle for Power and Peace*. New York: Knopf.

Noel-Baker, Philip 1958: *The Arms Race: A Programme for World Disarmament*. London: Stevens.

O'Neill, Robert and Schwartz, David (eds) 1987: *Hedley Bull on Arms Control*. London: Macmillan.

Roberson, Barbara A. (eds) 2002: *International Society and the Development of International Relations Theory*. London: Pinter.

Suganami, Hidemi 1983: The Structure of Institutionalism: An Anatomy of British Mainstream International Relations, *International Relations* 7(5): 2363–2381.

Suganami, Hidemi 2001: Alexander Wendt and the English School, *Journal of International Relations and Development* 4(4): 403–435.

Tönnies, Ferdinand [1887] 2002: *Community and Society*. Mineola, NY: Dover.

Waltz, Kenneth N. 1979: *Theory of International Politics*. New York: McGraw-Hill.

Wæver, Ole 1999: Does the English School's *Via Media* Equal the Contemporary Constructivist Middle Ground?, paper prepared for the Panel: A Reconsideration of the English School: Close or Reconvene?, the 24th Annual Conference of the British International Studies Association, Manchester. Available at: http://www.ukc.ac.uk/politics/englishschool/weaver99.htm.

Wendt, Alexander 1999: *Social Theory of International Politics*. Cambridge: Cambridge University Press.

Wheeler, Nicholas J. 2000: *Saving Strangers: Humanitarian Intervention in International Society*. Oxford: Oxford University Press.

Wheeler, Nicholas J. and Dunne, Timothy 1996: Hedley Bull's Pluralism of the Intellect and Solidarism of the Will, *International Affairs* 72(1): 91–107.

Wight, Martin 1966: The Balance of Power, in Butterfield, Herbert and Wight, Martin (eds) *Diplomatic Investigation*, London: Allen & Unwin, pp. 149–175.

Wight, Martin 1977: *Systems of States*. Leicester: Leicester University Press.

World society and globalization

Ingo Take

1 Introduction

World society and globalization are terms found in a number of academic disciplines.[1] The resulting diversity of contexts in which these terms are used has hindered attempts to systematize them in a way that might render them analytically valuable to future – interdisciplinary – research.[2] Regardless of differences in usage, however, the common thread is the aspiration to conceptualize *changes* in the world and their *consequences* for politics, economics and society. Here, globalization is regarded as the ways in which social relations are defined through global contexts. On this view, state systems, political culture and identity, as attributes of society, are subject to systemic change imposed by globalization-induced developments. If we regard society as a global system of social relations in which everyone is connected with everyone else through the unifying forces of modern production, markets, and communication, as well as cultural symbols and political institutions, and in which people interact through a multitude of globally, regionally, nationally and locally segmented and differentiated spaces, then we can already refer to the existence of a world society (see Albert 2009). From this perspective we would conceptualize world society as a field of social relations in which a plethora of different interactional contexts have taken shape – some of them already possessing global reach, others on the way to doing so and others again limited to national or local contexts. This casts doubt *from above and below* on the concept of states that holds sway within International Relations as sovereign actors that largely structure the field of international relations alone. Alongside the development of specific global institutions to regulate cross-border economic processes (the WTO, the IMF, the G8, etc.) and political processes (the UN, NATO, etc.), we can also observe an increase in the capacity for collective action by *civil society* and *private economic* actors. Supported by cross-border networks and globe-spanning expectations, values and goals, NGOs, but increasingly businesses as well, strive to respond to specific global crises and seek to influence international politics. Here the "societal world" (*Gesellschaftswelt*) comes into conflict with the "world of states" (*Staatenwelt*), whose traditional forms of political control are increasingly ineffective in light of ever more complex governance requirements. Nation states' diminishing capacity for effective governance contrasts with the increasing political resources of non-state actors focused on specific issues. Social actors question established power structures; at the same time, they are an expression of a functional differentiation that is becoming increasingly important as a principle of global order (Buzan and Albert 2010). Theory building in International Relations is thus faced with the challenge of abandoning its limitation to politics between states and its separation of domestic and foreign policy. This is the aim of concepts of cross-border social interaction that take account of non-state actors as well as states, and that trade under the name of "global governance".[3]

The proliferation of *actors and levels of action* as dimensions of international societization was already considered within the debate on transnationalism towards the end of the 1960s. "Transnational politics" was the basic analytical category with which the discipline of International Relations responded to the diminishing significance of both real-world borders between societal, domestic and international politics and analytical-categorical boundaries, a decline that went hand-in-hand with processes of socioeconomic and political integration (see Risse 2002). "Transnational politics" highlights societal processes emanating from other states that have an impact on a given society and thus indirectly influence state policies. In his book, *World Society* (1972), John Burton describes a number of different functionally definable webs of relationship that link actors, on the various levels of action, with a multitude of other actors, including non-state actors, in a "spider's web model". From this perspective, as most cross-border interactions take place between non-state actors, the territorial principle is no longer appropriate to differentiate and categorize these relations. Instead it is functional systems of relations that are constitutive, and only a world society model can capture these in a comprehensive way. With his spider's web model, Burton takes account of interactional processes occurring below and beyond the level of the state, integrating them into a productive political scientific analysis. Burton's approach thus overcomes the realist school's state-centred approach. In the 1970s, the model of complex interdependence (see the chapter by Manuela Spindler in this volume) was another attempt to produce a persuasive account of the increased complexity of international processes and structures. This model aims to analyze both the generally asymmetric structures of dependency among political actors and systems and the mutual interpenetration of political, social and economic processes. Because these structures of dependency differ from case to case, the model of interdependence allows no generalizable statements. It does, however, provide an analytical framework for the increasingly complex character of international relations by redefining the role of the nation state and eliminating the division between international and domestic politics. The idea hinted at here, that International Relations should abandon its exclusive focus on states, could not hold sway for long against established theories of neorealism and neo-institutionalism (see the chapters by Niklas Schörnig and Bernhard Zangl in this volume).

The end of the East–West conflict intensified the globalization of the economy, as well as the globalization of migration, environment and security, and this bolstered the integration of national economies. Only then did International Relations scholars modify the state-centred perspective previously dominant within the discipline, subsequently placing greater emphasis on interactions between political systems or parts of such systems, non-state actors, social groups and international institutions (Brock and Albert 1995). But the concept of transnationalization and consideration of social actors alone did not provide a framework capable of addressing the globalization-induced challenges and changes of the contemporary era. Because of this, recent concepts of global governance are characterized by more open, multi-layered perspectives that take account of the global networking of social actors and their rooting in communities (Joerges *et al.* 2004; Djelic and Sahlin-Andersson 2006; Graz and Nölke 2008; Take 2012). The relevant authors here see the beginnings of a world society in these global networks, in the form of public–private partnerships or purely private forms of self-regulation and in the development of collective values. The World Society Research Group (*Forschungsgruppe Weltgesellschaft* or FWG in what follows)[4] has developed criteria for conceptualizing world society with which we might systematically analyze the key dimensions of change in international relations. At the same time, their conceptual framework is open to contradictory developments in world politics. I provide a more detailed account of the FWG's concept of world society in Section 2 as a useful means of introducing the topic of world society. The FWG does not have the status of a reference theorist on whose work other theorists have built. Because of the diversity of concepts of globalization and world society, however, there can be no such reference theorist. The justification for grappling with the FWG conceptual framework is that we can use it to analyze central issues in the discipline of International Relations, such as the different dimensions of change in international relations, the resulting governance requirements and the response of actors within world politics to these challenges. In Section 3 I turn to other conceptualizations of world society such as those put forward by constructivists and system theorists. Finally, in Section 4, I discuss criticisms of concepts of world society in general and the FWG in particular.

2 The conceptual framework of the World Society Research Group

Concepts of world society are based on the assumption that the dominance of nation states, the key structuring factor in international relations, has been curtailed by the increasing importance of non-state actors. In addition to the exponents of transnationalism mentioned above, this has been highlighted by representatives of the so-called "English School" with their concept of "international society" (see the chapter by Christopher Daase in this volume). Both reject the realist school's assumption of an anarchical international system based exclusively on self-help. Central to the international system is regular contact between states and the mutual expectations that result from this. Conversely, the hallmark of an international society is that a group of states, conscious of shared interests and values, forms a society – in the sense that these states feel bound to a shared set of rules in their relations with one another and cooperate within shared institutions to enhance the level of political organization within the international system (see Bull 1977: 13). The English School sees the foundations of an international society of states in the recognition of an international law that goes beyond the principle of the formal equality of states and the principle of sovereignty, compliance with this law, and the establishment of international regimes and institutions that enable states to deal with shared problems. The idea is that as it is developed further on the basis of interests and norms, this international society will help moderate the conflictual character of the international system and help create a new and better international order or world order based on universally recognized values. Further, some English School theorists attempted to understand social developments as fostered by more than just the international state system, instead predicting the emergence of a world society based on universalist values and legally enforceable individual rights. While Bull (1977) describes international society as emerging from the international system of states, Buzan expands on this concept by including other social actors. If we take Buzan's approach, international society is a kind of "staging post" on the historical path away from unregulated anarchy towards a world society (see Buzan 1993: 338). While states form the crucial element in a legally constituted society of states, it is individuals that make up the constitutive element of world society (Buzan 2004: 90f).[5] Both are based on shared norms, rules and identities, in one case, on the level of states and, in the other, on the level of individuals. On this view, a notion of the commonweal is a precondition for a world society, a notion that encompasses the common goals and values of a universal society. There is no world society as long as there is no coherent, shared system of values and a shared framework of understanding to which international society can at least begin to make reference. From this perspective, international society has the task of alleviating the negative effects of anarchy and providing a framework in which a world society can develop. From a functionalist perspective, international society is a long-term reaction to the existence of an increasingly dense and interactive system (see Buzan 1993: 334). This increasing governance-related density and interaction in the society of states have consequences for the societies of the countries involved. Regulations, institutions and norms, which make up the foundation of an international society, offer points of contact for individuals or social interest groups to make their interests felt on the international level and exercise an influence on this level. They may also help shape identities. On this view, the development of a society of states is concomitant with the development of universal principles that help establish a world society. In this world society, it is individuals, social actors and the people of the world as a whole that form the focus of global social identities and relations (ibid.: 337). With this concept of world society, Buzan makes the social dimension, neglected by Bull, an element of international relations in the shape of transnational networks. In his work, the concept of international society and the concept of world society are complementary. However, he not only denies that states have the capacity to create a community of states but also that non-state actors can be political actors. In other words, he neglects the interplay between processes of societization and communitization.

The concept of "international society" reflects the historical background of the East–West conflict, but this does not mean that the concept is no longer of any use. It is, however, being challenged by contradictory developments which its theoretical premises leave it unable to explain. First, the resurgence of nationalism and ethnic conflicts has led to sub-international conflicts becoming increasingly important within the international system. Second, an ever greater number of states are seeking to reach cross-border agreements and refer – at least rhetorically – to Western principles and norms, while principles such as sovereignty and non-intervention are diminishing in significance, principles that are among the theoretical premises of the concept of international society (Albert and Brock 2009). The driving force of these developments in international relations is globalization. As early as 1990, James N. Rosenau highlighted that in analysing international politics we must examine qualitative changes in the international system, changes that are generally referred to as globalization and are interpreted as having a major impact on the structure of future cross-border politics. Given that a number of world regions remain more or less excluded from the developments discussed under the banner of globalization, the term *denationalization* seems more apt (Zürn 1992). From a functional perspective, meanwhile, the concept of globalization often seems too narrow. At present, we are seeing the compression of action contexts or societal denationalization in a multitude of fields. Here globalization means an increase in the intensity, scope and speed of cross-border relations of exchange and interaction in the fields of communication and culture, mobility, security, environment, and economy (Beisheim *et al.* 1999). Against the background of this "dissolution of boundaries" (see Brock and Albert 1995), new forms of global governance are taking shape characterized by specific logics of action and resulting path dependencies (Brock 2004).[6] The World Society Research Group sees in these developments three dimensions of change in the international system:(1) the *institutionalization of cross-border relations*, apparent in the increase in global governance arrangements and their increasing legalization; (2) the *differentiation of action levels*, which comprise, alongside state and international governance, transnational (state or international actors and non-state actors) and private (private economic and civil society actors) governance; and (3) the *diffusion of actors* (FWG 1996: 15–16). In addition, the non-simultaneous denationalization of political action contexts, on the one hand, and economic and social contexts, on the other, leads either to political integration in the form of a democratic, complex world government (Zürn 1998), featuring different levels of governance, or to political fragmentation with protectionist tendencies. The concept of the FWG is open to *both* tendencies: "We take the view that the resulting new inter- and transnational conflicts and their fusion are constitutive of the development of world society" (FWG 1996: 12).[7]

2.1 The transformed conditions of governance within international relations

In the contemporary era of accelerated and qualitatively novel global change, states' capacity for action is being eroded in a number of ways – through the demands of various ethnic and other groups, globalization of the economy, the growing influence of social organizations and the spread of global interdependencies, stimulated by financial crises, scarcity of resources, state collapse, transnational terrorism, the spread of weapons of mass destruction and many other global problems. The increase in problems of global scale shows how global dynamics have a direct influence on people's lives. The loss of states' or governments' capacity for action and the weakening of social institutions (political parties, trade unions) go hand-in-hand with an increase in new social forms of collective action – beyond the boundaries of the nation state. These institutionalized forms of collective action have become established as actors in world politics, in the shape of both transnational and purely private regulatory arrangements (Brock 2007: 162–163; Wolf 2008: 226; Take 2012). This implies the elimination of the conventional distinction between domestic and foreign policy and between state and society, as well as demanding new modes of governance (consensus-orientation, argumentation, negotiation and learning rather than subordination and majority decisions). The dimensions of change in international politics identified by the FWG are intended to bring together the different strands of research on influences between and within societies and to establish links with the debate on the institutionalization of cross-border action contexts. This fusion helps illuminate globalization-induced governance requirements and governance capacities, which the FWG approaches through the two key categories of sovereignty and autonomy. As the degree of organization of the international system changes (and as classical spheres of state action within the world are pervaded by social, economic, technological and ecological forces), state sovereignty is becoming less important and the question of how to distribute responsibilities on the various levels of action is now of central importance. The diffusion of autonomy implies a change in the character of statehood in the sense that international, state and non-state political, economic, social, local, national and transnational actors interact to deal collectively with public problems and conflicts (Wolf 2008). This is happening against the background of the development of shared institutions and norms that help overcome the anarchical international system, and through the growth of resources relevant to governance on the part of non-state actors. The FWG models these developments as a whole in ideal typical fashion as dimensions of a world society that "differs from international society in the sense that the international level of action becomes relatively less important while transnational and transgovernmental, as well as local-global relations become more significant and actors within supranational spaces become more differentiated" (Brock 1998: 55; see also: Forschungsgruppe Weltgesellschaft 1996).[8] Here, the boundaries between action levels and between the spheres of the political, economic and social or socio-cultural are increasingly dissolving (Brock and Albert 1995: 276). Alongside cross-border relations between states, we are seeing the emergence of trans-state economic spaces and transnational communities. The latter confront state and economic actors with increased societal claims and demands for participation and aim to influence international politics. The global spread of new communication technologies fosters the awareness of global interdependence and results in demands – articulated with ever increasing vigour – for the enforcement of human rights and globally valid social and environmental standards. Against this background, we can no longer conceptualize foreign policy as the domain of state diplomacy. This proliferation of actors and action levels does not mean the replacement of a state-centred perspective by a society-centred one. The FWG concept instead focuses on the interactions between the different groups of actors involved in cross-border relations.

Having outlined the new requirements for governance resulting from globalization, I now turn to the question of which actors, within the process of international societization, are gaining or losing the capacity to shape events and in what ways. Through cooperation with other states, nation states attempt to expand their room for manoeuvre in the form of horizontal governance. Against this background, numerous international institutions have formed over the years to regulate cross-border problems. Shared norms have also been developed; to a certain extent, these bind states to collectively formulated rules and agreements (Zangl and Zürn 2004). As the FWG sees it, an international society – like the Western society of states during the East–West conflict – that is accompanied by a vigorous process of community building, in other words that is based on common values and notions of order, is particularly resilient. Examples include European integration on a regional level and the charter of the United Nations (particularly the Preamble) and Universal Declaration of Human Rights on a global level. When dealing with non-state actors, nation states essentially have two strategic options. They can decide whether to gear their policies towards the requirements of effective problem-solving and to this end cooperate with social actors, thus benefitting from their resources. But states may also behave strategically and attempt to "get back" room for manoeuvre or autonomy from their societies through reciprocal treaty-based commitments (Wolf 2000). It is not just states but also non-state actors that are conceptualized as units of action that pursue content-related as well as strategic goals in order to secure their own autonomy. The institutionalization of cross-border relations between both state and non-state actors and the differentiation of action levels opens up to civil society and private economic actors a number of ways of influencing political processes. They can get topics onto the political agenda and inject their concerns into international politics. They also have resources at their disposal that enable them to monitor the implementation of decisions reached on the international level and if need be impose sanctions (Take 2000). When NGOs take legal action against states with reference to universal values, thus casting doubt on their legitimacy, they help make international law more responsive (Brozus *et al.* 2003). They also aim to expand the scope of international law to include individuals, deploying the same strategy to enforce individual human rights against state interests (Risse *et al.* 2002). Ultimately, in terms of their rule-setting function, NGOs, businesses and other non-state actors are increasingly competing with or supplementing state or international efforts at governance (Conzelmann and Wolf 2007; Wolf 2008; Take 2012). The number of NGOs increased greatly again in the 1990s; they have an enhanced status in political bodies on all levels of politics and they are more networked internationally than their predecessors. These things point to an intensification of the cross-border societization and communitization of social relations, constitutive elements in the development of a world society. When examining societization, it thus seems appropriate to go beyond the international level. We must also take account of non-state actors as potential agents of societization (and not just of communitization). Over the last few years, non-state actors have managed to gain influence over other states' foreign policies and over international politics by networking intensively with one another across borders. Examples include the demonstrations in Seattle during the 1999 WTO conference, as well as those in Genoa (2001) and Heiligendamm (2007) during the G8 summits. Resistance to the globalization strategies of these international organizations constituted a community of protest that forgoes an institutional structure and proceeds solely by means of ad hoc communication via the internet and mobile phones. Its criticisms are based on a global sense of responsibility. It links political, social, economic and ecological problems and is thus open to far-reaching alliances of social actors, including on the transnational level (Brunnengräber 2005). This throws up the question of whether Seattle was the prelude to a new era of protest or mobilization. For the FWG, the structural elements of a world society may already be taking shape within such protest movements (see FWG 1996: 14).

2.2 Communitization and societization

But the dimensions of change within international relations identified by the FWG not only change the conditions for political governance, but also foster tendencies towards integration and fragmentation. These give rise to new fusions of inter- and transnational conflicts, which the FWG sees as constitutive of the development of world society (FWG 1996: 12; Bonacker and Weller 2006; Take 2006; Weller 2007).[9] In order to capture both tendencies towards integration and fragmentation through its concept of world society, the FWG draws on Ferdinand Tönnies' distinction between communitization and societization. Here communitization refers to a social relation based on a subjective sense of solidarity among those involved, while societization means a social relation based on the rationally motivated balancing or linking of interests. While Buzan (1993) conceptualizes states within international relations as the agents of societization, which foster the development of collective rules and shared institutions and norms, he regards NGOs as agents of communitization in that they generate a sense of solidarity not based on interests or calculations of utility. The FWG criticizes this limiting categorization by pointing out that it leaves non-state actors and multinational companies out of account as well as the societization emerging through the institutionalization of cross-border relations among members of civil society and private economic actors. The FWG, then, refuses to accept the notion that societization occurs only on the international level while communitization occurs only on the transnational level. Instead it highlights:

> processes of communitization that occur within the framework of international relations and that partly advance and secure international societization [such as European integration] and partly respond to this societization and aim to evade it or immunize themselves against it [such as new forms of nationalism].
>
> (FWG 1996: 21)

The probability of particularist processes of communitization increases to the degree that certain groups believe that their identity or interests are being threatened by processes of societization. These disintegrative tendencies, which take the form of community-creating processes within specific groups of states and find expression in new forms of nationalism, are also an expression of the transformation of international relations; according to the FWG, they must be included in any meaningful analysis (see Brock 2004: 90). Community formation within certain groups of states is possible only to a limited degree on the basis of existing interdependencies, while the integrative mechanisms vital to a world society – a conducive social environment and collective and moral foundations – are lacking. Because of this, the FWG works on the assumption that there will continue to be a tense relationship between tendencies towards particularist communitization and universalist societization.[10] "The positive interplay between societization and communitization thus has a negative counterpart" (ibid.: 20). There is empirical evidence of both types of interplay within international relations. Efforts to establish globally accepted norms and collective commitments, in the framework of the major UN conferences of the 1990s, for example, or the establishment of an International Criminal Court, contrast with new forms of nationalism, fundamentalism and the defensive promotion of values as a reaction to processes of societization. On a lower organizational level, we see a growing number of functionally distinct cross-border networks made up of social groups that collectively pursue specific political or social objectives. It is anything but a foregone conclusion that individuals will form global networks in an effort to realize universal values and goals rather than joining smaller groups more concerned with identity politics and the pursuit of a narrowly defined self-interest. We may interpret the diminishing importance of identities based on territorial states in favour of new forms of political and social identity both as the source of novel ethnic and religious conflicts within nation states and beyond national borders,[11] and as prerequisites for the development of a collective identity based on global economic and cultural integration and a sense of global responsibility. On this view, transnational collective identities represent a form of communitization on a transnational level that may contribute both to globalization and to the fragmentation of cross-border relations; on the one hand, they function as connecting links between different national societies but on the other as a challenge to these same societies (Weller 2000; Albert 2002: 80). On a global level, we do in fact see two contradictory developments: an integrative process through which societies are becoming increasingly dependent on one another and a disintegrative process characterized by increasing efforts to achieve autonomy by those parts of society that see their identity or interests as threatened by the above-mentioned developments. For the FWG, the conflictual structures arising from these developments are of particular interest.[12] If the formation of collective identities continues to reflect geographical boundaries, then conflicts are likely to be resolved through recourse to violence. Most societies, however, have undergone a process of pluralization as a result of migration and cultural change. They are no longer held together solely by a national identity but also by a plethora of identities that transcend borders, identities that take a variety of forms in both territorial and functional terms. People see themselves, for example, as Berliners, Germans and Europeans, but may identify themselves as environmentalists, humanities scholars and social democrats as well. When the boundaries of collective identities overlap, the chances are that conflicts will be resolved peacefully (see Weller 2000). These integrative and disintegrative processes increasingly place a question mark over the state's function as a means of social integration and highlight the fact that when we analyze societies, we can no longer identify a single identity as the dominant principle of differentiation. Instead we must always take account of the global networking of social relations.

To sum up: processes of societization always occur through a positive interplay with an – at least rudimentary – process of communitization, but may at the same time engender or encourage particularist processes of communitization that contrast or clash with those of societization. In reality, then, the ideal types of social relations occur as hybrids, with varying emphases on societization and communitization. Because of this, the FWG is centrally concerned with the complex interplay of these processes and between different groups of actors and levels of action. Since, as I have suggested, the interactions mentioned above may have both an integrative and disintegrative impact, it is not immediately obvious what the consequences of the development of a world society will be. In line with this, the FWG refrains from making normative judgements about the contrasting variants of communitization across the globe. The conceptual framework of the FWG also casts doubt on the traditional notion that community and society entail a clear temporal sequence (as reflected in the traditional/modern dichotomy) by allowing for the possibility that societization may trigger processes of communitization. Rather than assuming a linear process, the FWG explicitly considers the possibility that this process may go into reverse. The FWG merely highlights the civilizational achievements concomitant with the development of world society, which "open up opportunities for positive developments such as reducing violence and dealing with problems more effectively" (FWG 1996: 23; see also Weller 2007: 46).

3 Alternative concepts of world society

The concept of world society put forward by the FWG was developed in light of other concepts of world society (such as that of the English School) and transnationalism. The FWG concept claims to present a more complete picture of recent developments in international relations in all their complexity and inconsistency, while also providing the criteria for conceptualizing world society in a way that avoids being "theoretically biased, normative or teleological" (FWG 1996: 5). Here the FWG clearly distinguishes itself from John Meyer's concept of world society which, as we shall see in what follows, is less open to the diverse range of contradictory elements entailed in the development of world society. Finally, I outline the conception of world society found in modern system theory as adapted by Albert, which has received a great deal of attention within the discipline of International Relations, particularly in recent years.

First, Meyer *et al.* (1997) depict a process of global societization that differs from the ideas of the World Society Research Group, one characterized by the global dissemination of uniform cultural patterns, norms and political concepts and objectives (see also Meyer 2005). According to Meyer *et al.*, the cultural patterns, norms and objectives that dominate the world build on Western Christianity and on processes of rationalization and are being developed further primarily through academic discourses. These patterns, norms and objectives determine the perception, structures and actions of social, state and international actors in virtually all fields of society. So while the FWG explains the process of global societization from an actor-centred perspective (Brock 2004: 101), Meyer *et al.* adopt the system perspective of a global process of cultural rationalization; this determines the structures and agendas of the international system as well as the action of the actors operating within it. While the FWG's concept of world society no longer defines the key actors in a globalized politics in territorial terms but functionally with respect to the degree of autonomy of decision-making and action they enjoy and how successfully they carry out certain functions and tasks, Meyer *et al.* see the nation state and the governments that represent it in the wider world not merely as a subset of the aggregate of actors operating on the international level – itself highly differentiated – but as agents and results of globalization. As these authors see it, actors routinely organize and legitimize themselves with reference to universalist models such as that of citizenship, civil rights, socioeconomic development and justice. So for Meyer *et al.*, nation states are culturally constructed and incorporated into a culture whose elements enjoy worldwide recognition.

This world culture is highly dynamic in the sense that the successes and failures of individual states engender learning processes and help diffuse new concepts of problem-solving. The elements of world culture (norms, models, objectives) lay down globally accepted standards and lay claim to global applicability, and are thus constitutive of world society. But since world culture entails a plethora of competing models, which come into conflict if they are implemented in eclectic fashion, their adoption has consequences that are sometimes dysfunctional for the societies applying them. In addition, the processes of diffusion occurring on different levels and through a wide range of actors' coalitions lead to a lack of fit with the practices, requirements and cost structures present in the different nation states. Inconsistencies and contradictions with respect to widely held values (equality versus freedom, growth versus justice, protection of the natural environment versus growth) find expression in disputes over too much or too little freedom, state regulation and nationalism. Such differences, according to Meyer *et al.*, must be included in our analyses given the decentralized, multilevel character of modern politics and in the absence of a world government.

This indicates that if actors are guided by universal values and objectives, this may be more explosive than a segmented world. In the view of Meyer *et al.*, the failure of world society in Bosnia (norm: human rights) and Africa (model: development) and the diminishing sense of responsibility of decision-makers across the world show the strengths of these institutions of world culture rather than their weaknesses. Phenomena such as torture, the dumping of waste and corruption, which until quite recently were paid very little attention or were dismissed as tragic local deviations from the norm, are now acknowledged across the world and face resistance. These days, local deviations from globally accepted norms and goals can be justified only with reference to universal principles. In other words, it is the integrative character of world society that prevails, despite the fact that it also entails disintegrative tendencies. The concept of world society put forward by Meyer *et al.*, then, differs from that of the FWG not just in terms of its system perspective, but also in that it is less cautious than the FWG when it comes to making normative evaluations.

Second, for a number of years, Mathias Albert, one of the original members of the World Society Research Group, has been attempting to exploit Niklas Luhmann's modern system theory in order to analyze international relations. He laments the fact that International Relations scholars tend to analyze the international system and social change in isolation from one another, and asserts that society is conceived primarily as a national society, rather than a world society. We should regard world society as something that contains national societies rather than something that exists alongside them (Albert 2004: 17). Modern system theory includes consideration of international relations by understanding society as a unit differentiated primarily in a functional sense (economic, science and legal systems), parts of which may be differentiated territorially, though even then only secondarily (political system). Because social functional systems are reproduced through communication, now that communication has become disseminated across the globe, we must understand society as world society.[13] It is impossible to conceptualize a social system that encompasses all communication as a unity, let alone an integrated unity. The question, then, is not what holds a society together, but how it is internally differentiated (ibid.: 18).

How might we analyze extreme inequalities as the internal differentiation of a social system? In light of the complexity of communication and the potential to refuse communication, how can communication be maintained and stable social forms emerge? Here, symbolically generalized communication media play a key role (money in the economic system, truth in the science system, power in the political system, etc.), which are the functional equivalent of normatively based social cohesion. They have an influence on the likelihood that communication will be accepted or rejected and thus replace morality, which under the conditions of a functionally differentiated world is no longer capable of playing this role. A theory of society of this kind does not attempt to explain homogeneity within a society, but to explain its cohesion despite a lack of homogeneity (ibid.: 18).

The world society achieves its coherent form not through integration but through its internal (functional) differentiation, thus distinguishing it from stratified or segmented societies. There is no global, regional or local system level, so that world politics encompasses all mutually accessible communications within the political system. In this sense, world politics does not have to be "global". None of the subsystems is responsible for the integration of the society (not even the political system). The functional differentiation of world society leads instead to conflicts between the different functional systems, which observe one another (Albert 2009). These conflicts can be traced back to the different forms of differentiation of the individual functional systems. While the political system is still internally differentiated largely in segmentary or territorial terms (in the form of states), the economic system is mainly differentiated in functional terms, such that these systems are sealed off from one another.[14] Conflicts also arise within functional systems during the transition from one form of internal differentiation to another. The political system is especially susceptible in this respect because it observes its own segmentary differentiation but is at the same time confronted with functionally defined global problems (ibid.). Modern system theory thus features an entirely different concept of societization (essentially as a process of functional differentiation) and communitization (essentially as the reduction of complexity within functional systems) than the approaches described so far. It remains to be seen to what extent modern system theory is capable of providing alternative explanations for the phenomena of international relations.

4 External criticisms

Criticisms of world society concepts revolve around a number of different issues. Critics not only dispute that international relations have changed significantly (neorealist perspective) but also question how realizable (functionalist perspective) and desirable (normative perspective) a world society is. The first question to consider is whether international relations have really changed to such an extent as to justify the use of the concept of world society. Societies have always influenced one another. There have always been transnational relations as well as international relations. It is not just since 1945 that the nation state has come "under pressure", though the Cold War did contribute to its preservation. Even since the Cold War ended, however, the nation state has remained the most important actor in cross-border relations. Since 1989, nationalism has in fact gained new momentum. Multinational constructs such as the Soviet Union and Yugoslavia have broken up and a plethora of small nation states has emerged within which various ethnic groups are struggling for supremacy and erecting new borders. This new nationalism does not possess the integrative character of earlier nation state constructs, within the framework of which different cultures were fused into a totality, and instead privileges an ethnically homogenous nation that excludes other groups. This disintegration is not always motivated solely by ethnicity: religious, social and cultural identities also play a role. Against this background it is unrealistic to imagine that a globally shared system of norms and values will come into being in the near future, and with it institutions that enjoy general recognition and support this system.[15] Such developments would not only have to win through despite the principles of sovereignty and non-intervention but would also imply a new division of the roles, rights and duties of citizens, societies, states, the state system and international institutions. This would have a substantial impact not just on the interests of all states but also on whatever democratic structures they might entail. But because the inertia of the international system and the major powers within it is tremendous, such a change seems unlikely to come any time soon, at least from a neorealist perspective.

Further, it is not just the concept of world society that is subject to dispute within the discipline of International Relations. Critics also question whether a world society is achievable and desirable. Here criticisms of world society tend to divide into essentially two types. From a functionalist perspective, critics argue that the development of a world society is unlikely because of the multiplicity of political, social, cultural and economic differences on a global level. A key question here, then, is how realistic it is to expect the development of a global "community of responsibility" as one of the core elements of an emerging world society (see Kielmansegg 1996; Scharpf 2005). From a normative angle, meanwhile, some have debated whether it is even possible to conceive of a world society in democratic terms. At issue here – assuming functionalist critics are wrong and a world society could come into existence – is whether international or global politics might be governed effectively and democratically (see Habermas 2001; Schmalz-Bruns 2005; Höffe 2007).

I will mention two other criticisms here. Critical perspectives that focus on structures of power and domination within the international system conceive of the state formulation of policy as a dependent function of dominant constellations of social interests; these find expression both within the state and within the international political process and instrumentalize the state. This institutionalized extension of national class structures is based on a vertical international division of labour. From this perspective, world society is characterized not by mutual interdependence but by relations of dependence rooted in the unequal distribution of opportunities to enforce one's views. The international order to which this gives rise reflects the interests of dominant transnational interest groups (especially multinational companies) and is supported by various state and international, economic and political institutions. On this view, the main driving force behind the dynamics of (world) societal development is capital's inherent tendency to create a world market. One of the main criticisms of the World Society Research Group is that it fails to take proper account of the primacy of the economy as the globally dominant ordering principle and power structures anchored in economic performance (see Altvater and Mahnkopf 1996; Wallerstein 2000; Lederer and Müller 2005).

From a different perspective, Jung criticizes the FWG's concept of society as reductionist because it divides society off from politics and economics and creates "a kind of antithesis" to the state by making a distinction between "international" and "inter-society" (Jung 1998: 245). For Jung, then, the FWG deprives itself of the possibility of "grasping the true complexity of change within international relations as an overall social context" (ibid.: 248) while also remaining blind to "issues of social change in the regions of the Third World and the specific regional attributes of such change" (ibid.: 248). Critics have also suggested that the three dimensions of change in international politics identified by the FWG are mainly to be found in the OECD states. On this view, while developing countries do participate in the functional integration of states within international institutions, the social lifeworld dominant within them is characterized by both traditional and modern elements and cannot keep up with this development. Yet a global sense of community can develop only on the basis of a rationalized lifeworld and a conscious sense of solidarity. Such a basis is lacking in the societies of the developing world, which are often driven by internal conflicts. But even in the European Union, where such preconditions pertain more than anywhere else, a sense of

European identity is at best in its infancy. Nor is it meaningful to speak of a differentiation of action levels or growing opportunities for participation by social actors in the sense of a proliferation of actors in the developing countries. As Jung asks,

> [How can] the functional and social integration of modern life that has occurred within the institution of the nation state and thus the rationalization of the lifeworld necessary to the legitimation of an international democratic peace policy be achieved in regions of the world in which the requisite processes of legalization and consciousness-formation have scarcely begun?
>
> (ibid.: 262)

Again, this brings out the analytical value of the FWG's concept, which rejects the idea of a teleological development culminating with world society and instead views processes of fragmentation as an integral part of the emergence of world society. This concept places special emphasis on the conflictual character of societization and communitization, leaving open for now the question of the consequences of world society.

5 Notes

1 An account of the conceptual history of globalization and world society is provided by Tyrell (2005), who includes consideration of the relevant schools of thought.
2 An interesting and original starting point in this regard is suggested by Albert in his study *Zur Politik der Weltgesellschaft* (2002; "On the politics of world society"), which identifies points of contact between system theoretical social theory and theories of International Relations (IR). In another text he emphasizes the potential value to IR of a theory of differentiation (Albert 2009).
3 Conceptions of global governance extend the frame of reference within which theories of IR have operated hitherto by integrating new actors and interactional spaces into theory building. This places the theories of IR, which contain scientifically backed statements about the regularities underpinning the international system, in a new context. This does not mean that these concepts themselves provide statements about regularly occurring interrelationships.
4 The World Society Research Group has existed since 1994 as a shared forum for researchers at the Technische Universität Darmstadt, Goethe University Frankfurt and the University of Bielefeld. The group has generated a number of research projects, all of which are united in their efforts to embed global political change within a wider theoretical framework centred on the state and governance. On the basis of the FWG concept of world society, its members' research foci have, however, become increasingly varied and specialized.
5 Individuals become agents of a world society by interacting across national boundaries as sovereignty-free actors, thus helping supplement international relations between states with relations between individuals, groups and societies (Rosenau 1990: 11).
6 Brock (2004) assumes that the international system, international society and world society are reference systems of politics and science that exist alongside one another and are cited in order to frame actions in accordance with preferences (see, for example, the simultaneous occurrence of nationalism, the development of the first international organizations and the emergence of humanitarian international law). This framing, which is always informed partly by a particular logic of action (self-help, self-discipline, constitutional constraints on freedom of action), gives rise to path dependencies within a given argument or policy. So world society is just as much a frame of reference for state policies (human rights, responsibility to protect, tackling poverty) as for social actors and international organizations.
7 For an analysis of the actors, structures and dynamics of conflicts in world society, see Bonacker and Weller (2006).
8 This entails a transformation of the primary principle of differentiation of global politics. Territorial differentiation has been supplemented by functional differentiation, which offers new jumping-off points for the development of a world society (Albert 2002; Buzan and Albert 2010).

9 A related conception sees conflicts as resulting from the concurrence and overlap of logics of action and forms of global structuring within the international system, international society and world society (Albert and Brock 2009).

10 Albert and Brock highlight another fraught relationship, namely that between international norms that arise within the referential frame of the international system, international society and world society. On this view, what we are dealing with is "the concurrent mutual recognition of the right to self-help, the prohibition of violence and the responsibility to protect of states and of the international community with respect to civil society" (Albert and Brock 2009: 64).

11 Albert (2009) also refers to conflicts between and within functional systems that can be traced back to different forms of system differentiation (mostly segmentary differentiation in the political system versus mostly functional differentiation in the economic system).

12 Among other things, the multi-authored volume *Konflikte in der Weltgesellschaft* (2006; "Conflicts in world society") edited by Bonacker and Weller gets to grips with these new conflictual structures. It uses the world society perspective to understand conflictual constellations as a consequence of the globalization and de-bordering of their structures.

13 For Luhmann, communication is "not simply an act of utterance that 'transfers' information but an independent autopoietic operation that combines three different selections – information, utterance and understanding – into an emergent unity that can serve as the basis for further communication" (Luhmann 1989: 143).

14 According to Albert and Stetter:

> These new forms of conflict and war are hardly surprising simply because the "readjustments" of familiar semantic and structural forms that occur in the process of functionally determined de-bordering not only meet with approval but also provoke *resistance* – and thus conflict.
> (2006: 71)

15 In this connection the reader is referred to the study by Koenig (Koenig 2005). He examines the world societal factors in the changing form of the nation state as articulated in conflicts over the recognition of collective identities. His analysis pays particular attention to how the meaning of human rights has changed over the course of their institutionalization.

6 Bibliography and recommended reading

6.1 Primary texts

Albert, Mathias and Brock, Lothar 2009: Zwischen Handlungslogiken und Strukturwandel: Was ist heute "international"?, in Hummel, Hartwig and Loges, Bastian (eds) *Gestaltungen der Globalisierung: Festschrift für Ulrich Menzel*. Opladen/Farmington Hills: Budrich UniPress Ltd, pp. 51–72.

Albert, Mathias, Brock, Lothar and Wolf, Klaus Dieter (eds) 2000: *Civilizing World Politics: Society and Community Beyond the State*. Oxford: Rowman & Littlefield.

Brock, Lothar 2004: World Society from the Bottom Up, in Albert, Mathias and Hilkermeier, Lena (eds) *Observing International Relations: Niklas Luhmann and World Politics*. London: Routledge, pp.86–103.

Forschungsgruppe Weltgesellschaft 1996: Weltgesellschaft: Identifizierung eines "Phantoms", *Politische Vierteljahresschrift* 37(1): 5–26.

Wolf, Klaus Dieter 2008: Emerging Patterns of Global Governance: The New Interplay between the State, Business and Civil Society, in Scherer, Andreas Georg and Palazzo, Guido (eds) *Handbook of Research on Global Corporate Citizenship*. Cheltenham: Edward Elgar, pp. 225–248.

6.2 Secondary texts

Albert, Mathias 2004: On the Modern Systems Theory of Society and IR: Contacts and Disjunctures Between Different Kinds of Theorizing, in Albert, Mathias and Hilkermeier, Lena (eds) *Observing International Relations: Niklas Luhmann and World Politics*. London: Routledge, pp. 13–29.

Bonacker, Thorsten and Weller, Christoph 2006: Konflikte in der Weltgesellschaft: aktuelle Theorie- und Forschungsperspektiven, in Bonacker, Thorsten and Weller, Christoph (eds) *Konflikte der Weltgesellschaft*. Frankfurt am M.: Campus, pp. 9–48.

Jung, Dietrich 1998: Weltgesellschaft als theoretisches Konzept der Internationalen Beziehungen, *Zeitschrift für Internationale Beziehungen* 5(2): 241–271.

Stichweh, Rudolf 2000: *Die Weltgesellschaft. Soziologische Analysen*. Frankfurt am M.: Suhrkamp.

6.3 Other texts

Albert, Mathias 2002: *Zur Politik der Weltgesellschaft*. Weilerswist: Velbrück.

Albert, Mathias 2009: Modern Systems Theory and World Politics, in Albert, Mathias, Cederman, Lars-Erik and Wendt, Alexander (eds) *New Systems Theories of World Politics*. London: Palgrave.

Albert, Mathias and Stetter, Stephan 2006: Viele Weltgesellschaften, viele Konflikte? Zur Rolle von "Konflikt" in Weltgesellschaftstheorien, in Bonacker, Thorsten and Weller, Christoph (eds) *Konflikte der Weltgesellschaft*. Frankfurt a. M.: Campus, pp. 49–76.

Altvater, Elmar and Mahnkopf, Birgit 1996: *Grenzen der Globalisierung: Ökonomie, Ökologie und Politik in der Weltgesellschaft*. Münster: Westfälisches Dampfboot.

Beisheim, Marianne, Dreher, Sabine, Walter, Gregor, Zangl, Bernhard and Zürn, Michael 1999: *Im Zeitalter der Globalisierung*. Baden-Baden: Nomos.

Brock, Lothar 1998: Staatenwelt, Weltgesellschaft und Demokratie, in Messner, Dirk (ed.) *Die Zukunft des Staates und der Politik. Möglichkeiten und Grenzen politischer Steuerung in der Weltgesellschaft*. Bonn: Dietz, pp. 44–73.

Brock, Lothar 2007: Innerstaatliche Kriege und internationale Gewaltanwendung seit dem Ende des Ost-West-Konflikts: Indiz für die Emergenz oder das Ausbleiben von Weltstaatlichkeit?, in Albert, Mathias and Stichweh, Rudolf (eds) *Weltstaat und Weltstaatlichkeit. Beobachtungen globaler politischer Strukturbildung*. Wiesbaden: VS, pp. 158–183.

Brock, Lothar and Albert, Mathias 1995: Entgrenzung der Staatenwelt. Zur Analyse weltgesellschaftlicher Entwicklungstendenzen, *Zeitschrift für Internationale Beziehungen* 2(2): 259–285.

Brozus, Lars, Take, Ingo and Wolf, Klaus Dieter 2003: *Vergesellschaftung des Regierens? Der Wandel nationaler und internationaler politischer Steuerung unter dem Leitbild der nachhaltigen Entwicklung*. Opladen: Leske + Budrich.

Brunnengräber, Achim 2005: Gipfelstürmer und Straßenkämpfer. NGOs und globale Protestbewegungen in der Weltpolitik, in Brunnengräber, Achim, Klein, Ansgar and Walk, Heike (eds) *NGOs im Prozess der Globalisierung*. Wiesbaden: VS, pp. 328–365.

Bull, Hedley 1977: *The Anarchical Society: A Study of Order in World Politics*. London: Macmillan.

Burton, John 1972: *World Society*. Cambridge: Cambridge University Press.

Buzan, Barry 1993: From International System to International Society: Structural Realism and Regime Theory Meet the English School, *International Organization* 47(3): 325–352.

Buzan, Barry 2004: *From International to World Society? English School Theory and the Social Structure of Globalization*. Cambridge: Cambridge University Press.

Buzan, Barry and Albert, Mathias 2010: Differentiation: A Sociological Approach to International Relations Theory, *European Journal of International Relations* 16(3): 315–337.

Conzelmann, Thomas and Wolf, Klaus Dieter 2007: The Potential and Limits of Governance by Private Codes of Conduct, in: Graz, Jean-Christophe and Nölke, Andreas (eds) 2008: *Transnational Private Governance and its Limits*. London: Routledge, pp. 98–114.

Djelic, Marie-Laure and Sahlin-Andersson, Kerstin (eds) 2006: *Transnational Governance: Institutional Dynamics of Regulation*. Cambridge: Cambridge University Press.

Graz, Jean-Christophe and Nölke, Andreas (eds) 2008: *Transnational Private Governance and its Limits*. London: Routledge.

Habermas, Jürgen [1998] 2001: *The Postnational Constellation: Political Essays*. Cambridge: Polity.

Höffe, Otfried [1999] 2007: *Democracy in an Age of Globalization*. Dordrecht: Springer.

Joerges, Christian, Sand, Inger-Johanne and Teubner, Gunther (eds) 2004: *Transnational Governance and Constitutionalism*. Portland, OR: Hart.

Kielmansegg, Peter, Graf 1996: Integration und Demokratie, in Jachtenfuchs, Markus and Kohler-Koch, Beate (eds) *Europäische Integration*. Wiesbaden: VS, pp. 49–83.

Koenig, Matthias 2005: Weltgesellschaft, Menschenrechte und der Formwandel des Nationalstaats, in Heintz, Bettina, Münch, Richard and Tyrell, Hartmann (eds) *Weltgesellschaft. Theoretische Zugänge und empirische Problemlagen. Sonderheft der Zeitschrift für Soziologie*. Stuttgart: Lucius & Lucius, pp. 374–393.

Lederer, Markus and Müller, Philipp (eds) 2005: *Criticizing Global Governance*. New York: Palgrave.

Luhmann, Niklas [1986] 1989: *Ecological Communication*. Chicago: University of Chicago Press.

Meyer, John W. 2005: *Weltkultur. Wie die westlichen Prinzipien die Welt durchdringen*. Frankfurt am M.: Suhrkamp.

Meyer, John W., Boli, John, Thomas, George M. and Ramirez, Francisco O. 1997: World Society and the Nation-State, *American Journal of Sociology* 103(1): 144–181.

Risse, Thomas 2002: Transnational Actors and World Politics, in Carlsnaes, Walter, Risse, Thomas and Simmons, Beth A. (eds) *Handbook of International Relations*. London: Sage, pp. 255–274.

Risse, Thomas, Jetschke, Anja and Schmitz, Hans Peter 2002: *Die Macht der Menschenrechte. Internationale Normen, kommunikatives Handeln und politischer Wandel in den Ländern des Südens*. Baden-Baden: Nomos.

Rosenau, James N. 1990: *Turbulence in World Politics*. Brighton: Harvester Wheatsheaf.

Scharpf, Fritz W. 2005: Legitimationskonzepte jenseits des Nationalstaats, in Schuppert, Gunnar Folke, Pernice, Ingolf and Haltem, Ulrich (eds) *Europawissenschaft*. Baden-Baden: Nomos, pp. 705–741.

Schmalz-Bruns, Rainer 2005: Demokratie im Prozess der Globalisierung: Zur Demokratieverträglichkeit von Global Governance, in Behrens, Maria (ed.) *Globalisierung als politische Herausforderung*. Wiesbaden: VS, pp. 79–98.

Take, Ingo 2000: The Better Half of World Society, in Albert, Mathias, Brock, Lothar and Wolf, Klaus Dieter (eds) *Civilizing World Politics: Society and Community Beyond the State*. Oxford: Rowman & Littlefield, pp. 199–214.

Take, Ingo 2012: Die Schattenseite der Weltgesellschaft. Die transnationale Vernetzung von Gewaltakteuren als weltgesellschaftliche Herausforderung, in Bonacker, Thorsten and Weller, Christoph (eds) *Konflikte der Weltgesellschaft*. Frankfurt a. M.: Campus, pp. 103–126.

Take, Ingo 2012: Global Governance Put to Test. A Comparative Study of the legitimacy of international, transnational and private forms of governance, in: *Swiss Political Science Review* 18(2), Special Issue, 220–248.

Tyrell, Hartmann 2005: Singular oder Plural – Einleitende Bemerkungen zu Globalisierung und Weltgesellschaft, *Zeitschrift für Soziologie, Sonderheft "Weltgesellschaft"*. Stuttgart: Lucius & Lucius, pp. 1–50.

Wallerstein, Immanuel 2000: *The Essential Wallerstein*. New York: The New Press.

Weller, Christoph 2000: Collective Identities in World Society, in Albert, Mathias, Brock, Lothar and Wolf, Klaus Dieter (eds) *Civilizing World Politics. Society and Community Beyond the State*. Oxford: Rowman & Littlefield, pp. 45–68.

Weller, Christoph 2007: Welchen Frieden sucht die Weltgesellschaft?, *Zeitschrift für Genozidforschung* 1: 36–47.

Wolf, Klaus Dieter 2000: *Die Neue Staatsräson. Zwischenstaatliche Kooperation als Demokratieproblem in der Weltgesellschaft*. Baden-Baden: Nomos.

Zangl, Bernhard and Zürn, Michael (eds) 2004: *Verrechtlichung – Baustein für Global Governance*? Bonn: Dietz.

Zürn, Michael 1992: Jenseits der Staatlichkeit: Über die Folgen der ungleichzeitigen Denationalisierung, *Leviathan* 20: 4, 490–513.

Zürn, Michael 1998: *Regieren jenseits des Nationalstaates*. Frankfurt am M.: Suhrkamp.

The theory of imperialism

Michael Heinrich

1 Introduction

Imperialism means, first, those policies pursued by a state that aim to extend its power and influence beyond its borders, whether directly by expanding its territory, or indirectly by striving to achieve political, economic or military dominance over other states. Second, imperialism refers to a specific historical period that began in about 1880 and over the course of which a number of European states, along with the United States and Japan, sought to incorporate other parts of the world (particularly in Asia, Africa and Latin America) into their spheres of power and use them to advance their own interests, either through conquest or through economic domination. This classical imperialism led to vast colonial empires and their economic exploitation, bloody colonial wars and the division of much of the world among the major capitalist powers. Even before the First World War, this imperialist expansion produced arms races and increasing tensions among the major powers. The liberal conception of "peace through trade" was *de facto* refuted by imperialist policies. Trade interests led to the conquest of foreign countries and in global terms the consequence of capitalist competition was world war. Classical imperialism came to an end in the 1960s with decolonization, though this did not bring an end to the influence and direct intervention of the developed capitalist countries in the so-called Third World. But whether, and if so to what extent, such influence allows us to describe the contemporary foreign policies of specific states or the present-day lattice of international relations as "imperialist" is a matter of some controversy.

Theories of imperialism seek to provide an explanation for the emergence and spread of imperialist policies. Depending on the explanatory factors cited, we can distinguish very roughly between *political* and *economic theories of imperialism*. The former are geared towards aspects of international politics or of the domestic politics of given countries, while the latter focus on problems related to the valorization of capital within the imperialist countries.[1]

In terms of both their theoretical content and historical efficacy, it is the economic theories of imperialism that are most significant. They may be placed under the rubric of the "structuralist" paradigm in the theory of International Relations (Menzel 2001: 182).[2] In this paradigm it is the structures of the world market, the international division of labour and international competitiveness that are considered the crucial material basis for the system of international relations.[3] Lenin's theory of imperialism in particular became politically important: until the end of the Soviet Union, it was part of the official world-view both of the Warsaw Pact states and of the Communist Parties of the West. Because of this, theories of imperialism are often equated with a Marxist conception of international politics. This not only disregards the fact that there are also non-Marxist theories of imperialism (just as structuralism has both Marxist and left-liberal exponents). There is also a question mark over whether Lenin's theory of imperialism is a genuine continuation of the Marxist critique of economics, as repeatedly asserted by exponents of "Marxism-Leninism".

It was not just during the period of classical imperialism that theories of imperialism played an important role. In the 1960s and 1970s, a number of theoretical approaches sought to demonstrate that imperialist structures of dependency continued to exist even after the end of decolonization. Concepts of imperialism moved centre stage once again in the debate on globalization beginning in the mid-1990s, in the sense that globalization was conceptualized not as a force of nature but as a process determined by interests and power relations.

The key theoretical source for Lenin's theory of imperialism was John A. Hobson's book *Imperialism* (London 1902). Hobson was not a Marxist but a left-liberal, socially reformist author. In his text, *Imperialism: The Highest Stage of Capitalism* (Lenin [1917] 1940), Lenin essentially adopted Hobson's conception of the connection between capitalism and imperialism and fit it into a Marxist context. I shall begin by using Hobson as reference author in the following account of theories of imperialism.

2 John A. Hobson's theory of imperialism

John Atkinson Hobson (1858–1940) was an English journalist whose many articles dealt chiefly with economic issues. As an economic "heretic" who refused to go along with the mainstream and sing the praises of the free market, and instead revived the theory of under-consumption, he was rejected by the academic guild and was never made a professor.

The theoretical core of the prestige of the market is "Say's Law". According to this "law", through the income generated over the course of its production, all supply creates an equal quantity of demand.[4] There may therefore be imbalances between supply and demand only within specific economic sectors but not in the economy as a whole. On this view, the capitalist market economy should be free of inherent crises. If crises do occur, they are viewed as the effects of external shocks (natural disasters, wars, flawed economic policy, etc). The theory of under-consumption, however, disputes the validity of Say's Law. In the early nineteenth century it was espoused above all by Malthus, but for the economic mainstream the theory of under-consumption was then refuted by the work of David Ricardo. In *The Physiology of Industry* (1889), which he wrote in collaboration with F. A. Mummery, Hobson breathed new life into the theory of under-consumption and sought to establish that societal "over-saving" reduced consumption, resulting in a trend towards general over-production. John Maynard Keynes, though critical of some of its details, later paid fulsome tribute to Hobson for revising the theory of under-consumption (see Keynes [1936] 1973: 364–371). In terms of economic theory, the theory of under-consumption was the most important underpinning of Hobson's analysis of imperialism.

The historical background to Hobson's theory of imperialism is the phase of imperialist expansion alluded to above that began in around 1884, for which Hobson provided the first comprehensive economic explanation. Hobson did not limit himself, however, to a purely scientific account. His primary aim was to critique imperialist policies. He condemned imperialism as a policy that was detrimental not just to those living in the acquired territories but also to most of the people within the imperialist countries themselves. Hobson's book stood in the tradition of English social reform, with its combination of moral-idealistic and utilitarian motifs. It was intended to enlighten, and to help change the policies he criticized: under-consumption should be tackled through social reforms rather than imperialist expansion.[5]

Hobson wants to explain the drive to expand among the leading capitalist countries so evident during his time. This expansionist drive was backed by a far-reaching consensus among the educated classes. Large colonial possessions seemed indispensable to a prosperous national economy. But Hobson tears to pieces the usual arguments put forward to justify this. With reference to the United Kingdom, he shows convincingly that there is a significant discrepancy between the costs of acquiring and maintaining the colonies, on the one hand, and the benefits of trade gleaned from their possession, on the other. Since most colonies are not particularly important in absorbing emigrants, their utility to the expanding countries is by no means as unambiguous as public opinion would imply. So what we need to explain is why imperialist policies have taken off (in the UK and elsewhere) and why they meet with such broad assent. Hobson answers this question on two levels, one framed in terms of economic sociology and the other economic-structural in character.

2.1 Explaining imperialism in terms of economic sociology

Even if the nation as a whole loses as a result of imperialism, according to Hobson, there are nonetheless certain interest groups that benefit from it: the producers of goods required in the colonies, the associated transportation businesses, the armaments industry, the armed forces, which have an imperialistic orientation on professional grounds, and finally aristocratic groups that see opportunities for social advance through military service and within the colonial bureaucracy. These groups with an interest in imperialism, which Hobson refers to as the "economic parasites of imperialism", use their influence in media, political parties, churches, schools and universities in order to promote ideologies that support imperialism. As Hobson sees it, they benefit from the fact that purely economic interests are blended with other motives extending from a desire for adventure to enthusiasm for national greatness. In this way, an "interested bias towards imperialism" (Hobson [1902] 1988: 51) emerges within military, clerical, academic and bureaucratic circles that is concealed behind supposedly noble intentions such as a desire to spread civilization and Christianity.

By identifying various professional groups and classes that either directly make money out of imperialism or obtain opportunities for social advance through it, Hobson explained imperialism sociologically. But this explanation proves unsatisfactory. It fails to resolve the question of why these circles that have an interest in and profit from imperialism managed to get their way in the late nineteenth century and why they managed to do this in almost every developed capitalist country.

2.2 The economic-structural explanation of imperialism

The answer to these questions is found in another argument put forward by Hobson that is economic-structural in nature. For him, the most important factor leading to imperialist policies is the capital invested in foreign countries. The mounting profits from foreign investments greatly exceed those based on the export of goods. Hobson sees the safeguarding of these profits as the true cause of imperialism.

> To a larger extent every year Great Britain has been becoming a nation living upon tribute from abroad, and the classes who enjoy this tribute have had an ever-increasing incentive to employ the public policy, the public purse, and the public force to extend the field of their private investments, and to safeguard and improve their existing investments.
>
> (Hobson ibid.: 54)

But it is not just businesses that invest abroad that have an interest in imperialist policies, but also the banks and major financiers. Since investors are always dependent on credit, financiers have the same interests as businesses investing abroad. Further, though, financial circles have an additional interest in imperialism since imperialist policies cannot be funded without public borrowing. Hobson argues that imperialism inevitably leads to higher national debt. If the cost of the massive armament programmes and the maintenance of the colonies were met by taxes, then much of the population would oppose them. But banks and financiers can profit without risk through national borrowing. Hobson sees banks and financial circles as the key drivers of imperialist policies (ibid.: 58).

In the shape of capital-exporting businesses and the major banks, Hobson has not just identified two other groups with an interest in imperialist policies. By demonstrating that export is the necessary result of the unbridled development of capitalism, he also seeks to provide a genuinely economic-structural explanation of imperialism. Hobson argues that the era of unrestricted capitalist competition has already led to a significant concentration of capitals. A vast amount of wealth has become concentrated in the hands of a small number of capitalist tycoons, who now have enormous savings at their disposal, leading to ever higher production. Because of this, productive force exceeds effective consumption – the situation that pertains is thus one of under-consumption – and it becomes increasingly difficult to profitably invest capital. Under-consumption leads to the formation of cartels and trusts.[6] This certainly limits production and keeps it profitable but the problem of excess capital is, if anything, made worse: the invested capital remains profitable but these profits can no longer be invested in the same economic sector. This process is repeated successively in almost every branch of industry. Capital can now be invested only if the surplus production is exported or – significantly more effective – if foreign countries serve as investment areas. In the capital surplus and resulting capital exporter, Hobson (ibid.: 71) sees "the economic taproot of imperialism".

2.3 Imperialism and politics

The capital export that leads to imperialism is not an interchangeable, optional strategy adopted by a group of capitalists but a structural feature of an economy that produces a constant capital surplus. According to Hobson, however, this structure is not caused by the capitalist mode of production as such or by technological progress but by the "mal-distribution of consuming power" (Hobson ibid.: 85). But if it is merely the unequal distribution of wealth that generates the capital surplus, then this situation that ultimately leads to imperialism can be changed by political means: namely, through a different mode of distribution.

Hobson sees imperialism not just as a waste of societal resources but also as highly harmful in political terms, both domestically and with respect to other parts of the world. Within the domestic sphere of the imperialist countries, social reforms are hampered by imperialist policies and a tendency takes hold towards militarism and authoritarian forms of government: domestically, imperialist policies require a strong state. Conservative circles are thus receptive to imperialist propaganda, or use it quite deliberately to secure their political power. Imperialism is a danger to the rest of the world since the various empires are in a permanent state of rivalry and undertake major programmes of arms-building. Imperialist policies thus pose a major risk to peace. To overstate things slightly, Hobson's theory of imperialism suggests that it is imperialist expansion itself that produces the security dilemma always presupposed by realist paradigms within the theory of International Relations as the unavoidable and natural condition of the international system (see the chapters by Andreas Jacobs and Niklas Schörnig in this volume).

Given that social reform and imperialism are antagonistic projects, Hobson views the labour and trade union movement as the natural enemy of imperialism. He is quite aware of the fact that those employees that profit from imperialist policies are receptive to imperialist propaganda (ibid.: 105). For him, though, it is above all industrial and financial capitalists who have "mainly engineered this policy" (ibid.: 96). In light of this it is only a "genuine democracy", in which the people truly determine policies, which can break the power of imperialist forces (ibid.: 360). These genuine democracies would eliminate the risk of war always latent under imperialism: enlightened democracies would recognize the commonality of their interests and secure them through amicable policies. Hobson's emphatic vision here, very similar to that of Immanuel Kant in his *Toward Perpetual Peace: A Philosophical Sketch*, expresses the basic idea propagated by the idealist paradigm in the theory of International Relations, though he remains sceptical about the prospects of realizing it. He also sees the possibility that an imperialist alliance,

> a larger alliance of Western States, a European federation of great Powers which, so far from forwarding the cause of world-civilization, might introduce the gigantic peril of a Western parasitism, a group of advanced industrial nations, whose upper classes drew vast tribute from Asia and Africa.
>
> (ibid.: 364)

For Hobson, this is a grouping likely to subject the world to its "parasitic imperialism" (Hobson ibid.: 365).

3 Theories of imperialism in the twentieth and twenty-first centuries

3.1 Classical theories of imperialism

In the shape of Hobson, a representative of the left-liberal bourgeoisie produced an early analysis of imperialism. This was to take a little longer on the (Marxist) left. The first two significant Marxist attempts to get to grips with imperialism, though they were not influenced by Hobson's book, can be found in the work of Rudolf Hilferding and Rosa Luxemburg.[7]

Debates within Marxist social democracy: Rudolf Hilferding and Rosa Luxemburg

Building on Marx's *Capital*, Hilferding analysed money, credit and banks. He coined the term "finance capital": bank capital that is transformed into industrial capital through loans or shares (Hilferding [1910] 1981: 309). He viewed the dominance of finance capital and thus also industry's dependence on the banks as an attribute of the new phase of capitalism that had superseded free trade and competition. Finance capital no longer wished to reduce the state to the liberal night watchman state. Instead,

> [I]t needs the state which can guarantee its domestic market through a protective tariff policy and facilitate the conquest of foreign markets . . . Finally, finance capital needs a

> state which is strong enough to pursue an expansionist policy and the annexation of new colonies.
>
> (Hilferding 1981 [1910]: 334)[8]

While Hilferding derived imperialism from the transformation of capitalist relations, Rosa Luxemburg understood it as a consequence of the functioning of capitalist accumulation. To keep on accumulating, capitalism, she thought, relies on a "non-capitalist milieu": first, in order to obtain cheap labour and raw materials and, second, to realize within this medium the surplus value created within capitalism. This is because this surplus value requires non-capitalist consumers. In much the same way as Hobson, Rosa Luxemburg works on the assumption of a structural under-consumption that determines the export of goods and capital. But the capitalist penetration of the non-capitalist milieu leads to the establishment of capitalist relations in such a way that the same problems arise once again. During the initial stages of its emergence, capitalism could ensure accumulation by penetrating the non-capitalist milieu within a given nation and dissolving all pre-capitalist relations based on a subsistence economy or the simple production of goods. Now, however, it is compelled to turn outwards, and this is the phase of imperialism: "Imperialism is the political expression of the accumulation of capital in its competitive struggle for what remains still open of the non-capitalist environment" (Luxemburg [1913] 1963: 446).

On this view, with the dividing up of the world and the disappearance of free territories, capitalism has reached the end of its developmental options, with the "mere tendency towards imperialism of itself" transforming the final phase of capitalism into a "period of catastrophe" (Luxemburg ibid.: 446).[9]

Lenin's theory of imperialism

The most significant development of Hobson's theory of imperialism was that undertaken by Vladimir I. Lenin (1870–1924). In terms of basic political and theoretical issues, before the First World War, Lenin largely agreed with the kind of Marxism popularized by the Social Democrats, as represented above all by Karl Kautsky. Within the international labour movement, after the death of Friedrich Engels in 1895, Kautsky was regarded as the leading Marxist theorist. A dramatic shift occurred following the outbreak of the First World War, when most of the social democratic parties supported their various governments' war policies and justified the war as a "war of defence". Lenin opposed this policy, which ran counter to every previous resolution expressing a commitment to peace. It was through this conflict that the labour movement split into a social democratic and communist wing.

Lenin's text on imperialism was intended to advance specific political objectives. He sought to show that the war was an imperialist war being fought in order to divide up the world among the major powers, one in which the labour movement could not justify supporting a particular state. At the same time, Lenin tried to explain why not just the leaders but also many members of social democratic parties were prepared to support policies of war. He also wanted to make it clear that it is with imperialism that the decline of capitalism begins, something he regarded as the precondition for proletarian revolution.

The theoretical foundation for his analysis of imperialism was Hilferding's *Finance Capital* and Hobson's book, whose central statements Lenin translated, as it were, into "Marxist" terms. Here Lenin's Marxism was located largely within the schematic framework which, building on the popularizing late works of Friedrich Engels, had become established within the social democratic labour movement. This popular Marxism was often characterized by a crude economism (ideology and politics are reduced to a direct and conscious "translation" of economic interests) and a strong historical determinism (the necessary ascent of capitalism and equally necessary proletarian revolution). Economism and historical determinism are also characteristic of Lenin's theory of imperialism.

Lenin sums up the fundamental attributes of imperialism as follows:

1 The concentration of production and capital developed to such a high stage that it created monopolies which play a decisive role in economic life.
2 The merging of bank capital with industrial capital, and the creation, on the basis of this "finance capital", of a financial oligarchy.
3 The export of capital, which has become extremely important, as distinguished from the export of commodities.
4 The formation of international capitalist monopolies which share the world among themselves.
5 The territorial division of the whole world among the greatest capitalist powers is completed (Lenin [1917] 1940: 194).

The notion, already espoused by Hobson, that competition between individual capitals is replaced by monopolies, is incorporated by Lenin into a deterministic scheme: the "old" capitalism of competition inevitably turns into a "new" capitalism, monopoly capitalism, characterized by the "domination of financial oligarchy" (ibid.: 110). With its interest in capital export, this represents the driving force behind imperialist endeavours. While Hobson seeks to establish the necessity of capital export by means of the theory of under-consumption, in Lenin's work we merely find the assertion that "in a few countries capitalism has become 'over-ripe' " and that because of this capital lacks the potential for profitable activity (ibid.: 140).

In contrast to Hobson, Lenin regards imperialism as an ineluctable historical necessity. For Lenin, imperialism is the "highest" and thus also the last "stage" of capitalism. So contrary to Hobson's work, it cannot be overcome by reforming distributive conditions, but only through the proletarian revolution that will eliminate capitalism as a whole.

It is this economic and historical inevitability of imperialism that Lenin highlights in opposition to Kautsky's notion of a possible "ultra-imperialism", a peaceful, cartel-like balance between the imperialist countries (Kautsky 1914). In contrast, Lenin underlines that the expansionist policies of imperialism cannot be exchanged for a different policy but are instead the necessary consequence of the economic foundation: monopolies require this expansion. But the division of the world among trusts, like its division among the imperialist countries, is not stable because the "disparity between development" of productive forces and of accumulation changes the balance of power. Because the process of dividing up the world has already been largely completed, the only option left is for territories to be divided anew among the imperialist countries. And this can only be done through war (Lenin ibid.: 210).

In Lenin's work, the theory of imperialism is an element in the justification of revolutionary politics. To point up the weakness of imperialism, which makes revolution possible in the first place, Lenin characterizes imperialism as "parasitism", as Hobson had done already, supplementing this characterization with the concept of "decay". But what this decay consists of remains vague. On the one hand, Lenin (ibid.: 212) writes that monopoly "inevitably gives rise to a tendency to stagnation and decay". As monopoly prices become fixed, even temporarily, "the stimulus to technical and, consequently, to all progress, disappears to a certain extent" (ibid.: 212). On the other hand, he emphasizes that monopolies overcome the anarchy of capitalist production and bring it close to the socialist "socialization of production" (ibid.: 54). Finally, he states categorically that: "It would be a mistake to believe that this tendency to decay precludes the possibility of the rapid growth of capitalism" (ibid.: 254).

By "parasitism", Lenin means the "exploitation of an increasing number of small or weak nations by an extremely small group of the richest or most powerful nations" (Lenin ibid.: 254). For Lenin, this parasitism also has an effect on the working class: because of the high monopoly profits, sections of the working class can be "bribed" and turned into supporters of imperialism. In light of these characteristics, at the end of his text Lenin concludes, rather surprisingly, that: "From all that has been said in this book on the economic nature of imperialism, it follows that we must define it as capitalism in transition, or, more precisely, as moribund capitalism" (ibid.: 258).

The notion of a necessary "collapse" of capitalism, of which there is very little indication in Marx's *Capital* but which was widespread in the popular social democratic Marxism of the pre-1914 period, appears here in a new form: imperialism as the crisis-ridden closing stage of capitalism, which is no longer capable of any lasting development but merely generates an endless series of imperialist wars.[10]

For decades, Lenin's theory of imperialism served Communist Parties worldwide as *the* theoretical basis for analysing contemporary capitalism. As an authoritarian state socialism took hold in the Soviet Union in the 1920s, the theoretical discussion in the Communist Parties also degenerated. What emerged was an official "Marxism-Leninism" that combined the old popular social democratic Marxism with Lenin's political pamphlets. This amalgam, reduced to simple formulas and squeezed into countless textbooks, was given the status of incontrovertible truth and served primarily to legitimize the various policies pursued by party leaders or, in the case of the Soviet Union, state leaders. In this context, the theoretical development of the theory of imperialism was very limited.

3.2 The renaissance of structuralist approaches

After the Second World War, global politics was very different, being entirely dominated by the antagonism between East and West. This antagonism, along with the tremendous economic and military superiority of the United States vis-à-vis the other Western countries, reined in the competition between capitalist states. Furthermore, there was a concomitant process of decolonization, which was largely complete by the 1960s. Imperialist expansion having already come to an end with the First World War, the theory of imperialism now seemed to have finally lost its object.

Yet it was at precisely this point, after the debate had been interrupted by fascism, Stalinism and the Cold War, that the renaissance of the structuralist paradigm began. It was impossible to overlook the fact that the now independent colonies often remained economically dependent on the former colonial powers and that even countries such as those of Latin America had very little chance to fundamentally change their subaltern economic position within the capitalist world market. In addition, the Vietnam War in the 1960s demonstrated that the major capitalist powers had by no means ceased to intervene in the "Third World". The old imperialism had seemingly been transformed into neo-imperialism. With the protests against the Vietnam War and the students' movement, a new interest in Marxism and the analysis of neo-imperialism also arose in many Western countries.

Theories of neo-imperialism

In the Eastern Bloc countries, Lenin's theory of imperialism continued to be an official doctrine. Following the Second World War, it was expanded into a theory of "state monopoly capitalism" that was defined as follows in one textbook:

> The essence of state monopoly capitalism lies in combining the power of monopolies with the power of the imperialist state to create a hegemonic mechanism that ensures higher monopoly profits, saves the capitalist order and combats the revolutionary forces of the world.
>
> (Richter 1989: 336)[11]

This theory incorporated the insight, gained during the period of decolonization, that it is not necessary for a country to have the status of a colony for others to exploit their political and economic dominance, and that trade treaties, military pacts, lending, and so on may also serve as a means of imperialist domination. Important changes to Lenin's original approach were, however, generally made quietly and implicitly: both the notion of the impending demise of imperialism and the necessity of constant imperialist wars over the division of the world were tacitly dropped.

In political terms, the theory of imperialism formed the basis for the alliance with the colonized peoples of the Third World that the Soviet Union was soon keen to achieve and with the "national liberation movements" that had arisen in the course of decolonization, movements that took up the struggle against the ruling, Western-capitalist oligarchies. Beyond the Soviet Union, many Western solidarity groups also considered the nationalism of these liberation movements to be "progressive"; after all, it was opposed to the capitalist countries' imperialism.

The discussion of theories of imperialism within the framework of "Western Marxism" – to use the term introduced by Perry Anderson (1976) for Marxist approaches in the Western countries beyond the traditional parties of the labour movement – took a more open and less dogmatic form than in Eastern Europe. This greater openness applies even to the Trotskyist variant of Marxism-Leninism as represented by the likes of Ernest Mandel (1978), who sought to combine Lenin's theory of imperialism with a number of other theoretical developments.

Paul Sweezy's arguments were initially quite close to Lenin's theory of imperialism. He expanded on this theory by emphasizing that "the annexationist urge of imperialist nations is by no means confined to backward, non-industrialized regions" (Sweezy [1942] 1962: 320). He placed particular emphasis on the new role of the state. According to him, the state must now not only establish the preconditions for the successful valorization of capital, but in the age of monopoly capitalism the state is used directly to find new markets for, and valorize, the capitalist "surplus" (Baran and Sweezy 1966), which also represents an alternative to capital export. While the old imperialism was still characterized by competition between rival imperialist powers, neo-imperialism seemed like a common front among the imperialist countries which, under the leadership of the United States, stood opposed to the Third World and the Eastern Bloc. O'Connor (1970: 121) even referred to the "consolidation of an international ruling class constituted on the basis of ownership and control of the multilateral corporations".

Dependency theory and the structural theory of imperialism

While these approaches tended to focus their attention on the developed capitalist countries and elaborate the causes of neo-imperialism, an increasing number of authors examined its consequences for the "Third World". A number of approaches sought to show that its "underdevelopment" was not the result of internal problems but of the "development" of the leading capitalist countries. In a certain sense, then, they re-engaged with the idea to which Hobson and Lenin applied the term "parasitism". A number of authors, basing themselves on the Marxian theory of value, tried to demonstrate the existence of "unequal exchange" between the First and Third World (Emmanuel 1972; Amin and Palloix 1973; Amin 1976).[12] "Dependency theory" (Frank 1971; Sunkel 1972; Cardoso and Faletto 1979), stimulated by investigations of the situation of Latin America, underlined that the underdeveloped countries, assisted by an indigenous "comprador bourgeoisie" were integrated into the world market in a way exclusively geared towards the interests of multinational companies and the economy of the developed countries. On this view, the concentration on raw materials' extraction and agricultural monocultures along with a constant outflow of profits is an obstacle to independent development. It is not "modernization" but "structural underdevelopment" that is the result of the capitalist world market. The theory of "peripheral capitalism" is underpinned by similar ideas (Amin 1974). The "autocentred" development of the industrial countries of the North was contrasted with the "dependent development" of "peripheral capitalism", which is not necessarily distinguished by a lack of accumulation, but by a form of "fragmented" accumulation geared towards the interests of the developed countries (see the contributions in Senghaas 1974; for a critical take, see Elsenhans 1979 and 1991). For dependency theory approaches, direct political domination plays only a subordinate role. In contrast to the Marxist-Leninist tradition, which views the activities of the state, under the influence of monopolies, as responsible for generating dependencies, here it is the structural impact of the world market that brings about an "imperialist" situation. "Direct" violence is less important than the "structural" violence of economic relations.

Building on such ideas, Johann Galtung, who had already introduced the concept of "structural violence" into the social sciences, developed a highly formal "structural theory of imperialism" (Galtung 1972 and 1980). He distinguishes between central nations (developed countries) and peripheral nations (developing countries) and within a given country between the centre (privileged groups) and periphery (underprivileged groups). For Galtung, imperialism does not refer to every instance of the exercise of power by central nations over peripheral nations, but only those forms of the exercise of power in which there is a harmony of interests between the centre of the central nation and the centre of the peripheral nation: the centre of the peripheral nation functions as the "bridgehead" of the centre of the central nation. It serves as a "conveyor belt", transporting value from the periphery to the central nation. The centre of the central nation may allow its own periphery a share in this transfer of value, and with this conception Galtung explicitly builds on Lenin's thesis of the "bribing" of the "workers' aristocracy". As a consequence, the clash of interests between centre and periphery in the central nation is less pronounced than in the peripheral nation and a conflict of interest emerges between the peripheries of the central and peripheral nations (Galtung 1972: 35ff.).

What Galtung has done here is to present within a formal framework what Hobson and Lenin referred to as "parasitism". In addition, he outlines two "mechanisms of imperialism" and thus takes up the theme of "structural underdevelopment" emphasized by dependency theory. He refers to the relationship between actors in centre and periphery as a "vertical relation of interaction": in economic terms, this is not just a matter of exploitation mediated through unequal exchange, but above all of the consequences for the actors themselves. If, for example, quality finished products made in the central nation are exchanged for the raw materials of a peripheral country, this will promote the industrial development of the centre rather than the periphery. A horizontal relation of interaction would not be imperialistic, but this would presuppose production structures on a similarly high level. Galtung refers to the second mechanism as a "feudal interactional structure": the peripheral countries are geared towards the central nation in a one-sided way, such that interaction between the peripheral countries is largely impossible, further reinforcing dependency on the central nation. In sum, the "mechanisms of imperialism" make the periphery structurally dependent on the centre, such that the deployment of direct force becomes superfluous: "it is only an imperfect imperialism that requires weapons; professional imperialism relies more on structural than direct force" (ibid.: 55).

While both classical theories of imperialism and theories of neo-imperialism gave precedence to the economic dimension, Galtung distinguished five different types of imperialism – economic, political, military, cultural and communicative imperialism – and underlined that none of these types is more fundamental than any other. Mediated by the two "mechanisms of imperialism" outlined above, an imperialist relationship may be based on each of these types, and the different types may reinforce one another (ibid.: 55ff.). When the (supposed) "American decline" was widely discussed in the 1970s and 1980s, critics of this thesis based themselves mainly on these aspects of an expanded concept of imperialism (see Russett 1985; Strange 1987).

From "postimperialism" to "empire"

The 1990s brought profound changes in international relations. The collapse of the Soviet Union brought the East–West conflict to an end but it quickly became clear that this was by no means leading to any reduction in international conflicts, as so clearly evident in the second Gulf War (1991), the Kosovo War, armed conflicts in the Soviet successor states and, last but not least, the war against Afghanistan and the occupation of Iraq in 2003. At the same time, the processes summed up under the label of "globalization" pointed to a substantial modification of the economic and political system, particularly with respect to the role and potential influence of the nation state, though it remained a matter of much dispute how far these modifications actually extend (for a comparison of globalization and imperialism, see Kößler 2003).

Some of the key themes of the globalization debate were already addressed at an early stage in unorthodox variants of imperialism theory. Warren (1973 and 1980), building on Marxist studies of India, sought to show that imperialism is by no means a phase of the decline of capitalism but is in fact the precondition for the thoroughgoing capitalist penetration of the world, which also contributes to the modernization of the Third World, contrary to theories of dependency. The post-imperialist approach of Sklar and Becker is informed by similar ideas (Becker *et al.* 1987; Becker and Sklar 1999). They question the notion that capitalist expansion inevitably leads to the imperialist exploitation and underdevelopment of the periphery. For them the key actors are not so much states as multinational companies, whose spread fosters the development of transnational class formations, which, these authors argue, certainly have a shared interest in the capitalist development of the peripheral countries. On this view, then, postimperialism is accompanied by a new "postnational era".

In recent years, the debate on theories of imperialism has been influenced by "postcolonial studies", which is centrally informed by the concept of culture. This field "deconstructs" the usual distinctions between centre/periphery and civilized/uncivilized: these dichotomies, so the argument goes, rather than expressing objective facts, structure the perception of colonized peoples, imperialism and so on, and legitimize subjugatory practices. The critical examination of imperialism undoubtedly took place primarily in the cultural sphere (Said 1993; Darby 1997, 1998), but the postcolonial critique of Eurocentrism has also been discussed by theoreticians of imperialism such as Samir Amin (1989). In his critique of ideology, Amin rejects the concept of globalization to the extent that it conceals the imperialist structure of the world system (Amin 1998). In his late works, André Gunder Frank went a step further and criticized key concepts found in theories of dependency and imperialism such as "development", "capitalism" and "dependency", claiming that they are beholden to a European Western, ethnocentric perspective (Frank 1998: 336f.). The contributions in the multi-authored volume edited by Randeria and Eckert (2009) seek to discuss issues of globalization and imperialism from a non-Western perspective with reference to a wide range of case studies.

In a much-discussed contribution to the debate on theories of imperialism, Antonio Negri and Michael Hardt combine the notion that nation states have lost sovereignty, as asserted within the debate on globalization, with concepts geared towards the analysis of power that go back to Michel Foucault. On this view, the world-system is no longer characterized by rivalry between imperialist powers. Instead we are seeing the development of an all-encompassing "empire". This, however, is not the project of a specific state but rather a globe-spanning network (Hardt and Negri 2000: 11). So exploitation has by no means disappeared; on the contrary, society as a whole has now been subjugated to a "biopolitical order" that regulates life in line with capitalist valorization (ibid.: 319). The state is losing its autonomy, while its functions are being integrated into the command mechanisms of transnational companies. For these authors, there is no longer any definable working class, but merely a "multitude". Power and exploitation are not enforced through the violence of a given ruler, but by means of a structural logic to which everyone in the "society of control" – on both national and international levels – is subject. Power is thus intangible but omnipresent (ibid.: 202). In view of the seemingly endless war against terror declared by the United States and the tendency towards increased competition between the United States and the EU, the ideas of Negri and Hardt appear highly questionable (for a critical examination, see, for example, Brand 2002; Hartmann 2002; ten Brink 2008b: 66ff., 166ff.; Dunn 2004; and the multi-authored volumes edited by Atzert and Müller 2002 and 2004).

The United States' war against Afghanistan and occupation of Iraq following the attacks of 11 September 2001 were a major stimulus to debates on theories of imperialism. An affirmative debate carried on mainly in the United States quite openly emphasized the necessity of an (American) empire to uphold world order, as in the work of Michael Ignatieff (2003). This was the pinnacle of a discussion that had been going on among neoconservatives since the late 1990s (its most famous manifestation being the report published by the "Project for a New American Century", 2000). Within the German debate, Münkler (2007) has been the leading exponent of the idea that the US Empire has beneficial effects: largely disregarding economic structures and interests, this idea is justified with reference to a universal, historical "logic of world domination".

Other authors, building on the theories of imperialism, have analysed the imperialist tendencies of US policies from a critical perspective and have identified a "new imperialism" (for an introduction to recent debates, see Deppe *et al.* 2004). Against the thesis that the nation state has lost significance, Panitch and Gindin (2004) emphasize the state's continuing importance to capitalist development. They underline the ongoing hegemony of the United States, the "prototypical global state" (Panitch 2002: 80), which has largely succeeded in integrating other states and thus comes very close to Kautsky's notion of "ultra-imperialism" (for further discussion, see also *Socialist Register* 2004). While Panitch and

Gindin (2004) assume that US dominance has been constant, Harvey (2005) emphasizes the increasing rivalry, particularly in recent times, between the capitalist centres and the weakness of capitalist development. According to him, this has led to "accumulation by dispossession", supported by imperialist policies, which refers to state-mediated access to resources (oil in the case of the Iraq War), privatizations of benefit to capital and deprivation of the rights of local populations. These, Harvey tells us, reproduce the mechanisms of pre-capitalist "primitive accumulation" based on direct relations of force (Marx [1867] 1976: 893ff.) (see also the contributions in Zeller 2004). The significance of competition between imperialist states is also underlined by Callinicos (2007, 2009) and in the broadly-based study by ten Brink (2008b), with the latter in particular highlighting the fact that there is no universally valid pattern of conflict applicable to this competition between states: the character and course of such competition and the political patterns to which they give rise depend on the "phases of world order", which must be distinguished historically.

4 Criticism of theories of imperialism

In what follows, I present criticisms of fundamental elements of theories of imperialism, particularly the classical economic ones. Here we can make a distinction between "external" criticisms that call into question the fundamental assumptions of the economic-structuralist paradigm and "internal" criticisms that remain within this paradigm but nonetheless identify fundamental deficiencies in theories of imperialism.

As a rule, external critics question the tendency to explain imperialist policies essentially in terms of economics. Joseph Schumpeter criticized the theories of Hobson and Lenin from a universal-historical perspective. By imperialism, Schumpeter means "the state's objectless tendency for a form of violent expansion with no discernible limits" (Schumpeter 1919: 74). He saw the imperialist drive to expand not as due to specific economic interests but to the psychological disposition of ruling aristocratic classes developed over the course of history. The tendency to expand, for Schumpeter, is thus not based on any rational objective, but is instead "objectless" – it is irrational, arising from an instinctive tendency to conquer. Understood in this way, imperialism is not the "highest" stage of capitalism as in the work of Lenin, but rather a historical remnant, an "atavism" (ibid.: 119). Monopolistic practices that might ensnare states in imperialist policies are remnants of pre-capitalist relations. For a fully developed competitive capitalism, violent expansion is a foreign body that will increasingly disappear as capitalism develops further.

David Landes (1961) presented a more nuanced argument. While he was in no doubt about the influence of economic interests, he underlined that these always play a role, not just in the case of imperialist policies. Because of this, they have nothing like the tremendous explanatory relevance that they possess within economic theories of imperialism. Instead, the emergence of imperialism is or was fostered if there is a power imbalance. But Landes does not view power solely as state power but as the totality of political, economic, technological and cultural instruments of power. It is thus not just violent expansion but also the enforcing of "influence" that may be understood as the imperialist exploitation of a power imbalance.

The reawakened interest in Marxism in the 1960s not only gave rise to theories of neo-imperialism that built to a greater or lesser extent on the ideas of Hobson and Lenin. In Western countries, the formerly common identification of Marxism-Leninism with Marxism *per se* was called into question. Judging by the incomplete project of the Marxian critique of political economy, which emphasized the specifically social manifestations of the capitalist economy and resulting fetishization, to which both workers and capitalists are subject, Marxism-Leninism looked like a dogmatic construct[13] that reduced the analysis of capitalism to a sociology of domination and exploitation (in other words, to what capitalism has in common with pre-capitalist societies). While Marx emphasized the impersonal domination of the law of value, which exercises its effect "behind the backs" of actors, Marxism-Leninism underlined the conscious domination of fractions of capital and the political elite associated with them. These differences led to the Marxist critique of the classical theory of imperialism, which I briefly outline in what follows.[14]

Critics attacked the very notion of a change of historical phase, the transition from "competitive capitalism" to "monopoly capitalism". Both Hobson and Lenin assumed that a fundamental shift in economic structure would go hand-in-hand with the increasing size of many businesses and with the fact that in many economic branches a small number of businesses account for much of production: the economy is no longer guided by the anonymously operating "law of value" but by the domination of monopolies; society is now at the mercy of "arbitrariness" (Lenin [1917] 1940: 90). While Marx distinguished capitalism from pre-capitalist formations precisely by stating that the "silent compulsion of economic relations" (Marx [1867]1976: 899) had superseded personal domination within the economy, Lenin sees this personal domination at work again in the shape of the monopolies.[15]

On this premise, it also seems plausible that the monopolies or "financial oligarchies" will enforce their interests directly by using the state. Marx and Engels, meanwhile, conceived of the state as the "ideal" total capitalist: the state must ensure that the general conditions and preconditions for capital valorization are in place; precisely because of this, the state must (at least in principle) be independent of the particular interests of given capitalists. Lenin, on the other hand (and here he was essentially following Hobson, and not Marx and Engels), reduced the state to a mere instrument in the hands of the monopolists and bankers and thus essentially denuded Marxism of any theory of the political.

What was introduced instead was a critique with a moralizing undertone as Lenin, building on Hobson, insisted on the "parasitism" of imperialism. The fact that capitalists exploit the working class of foreign countries and not just their own country is viewed by both Hobson and Lenin as particularly scandalous. This is understandable in the case of Hobson as he is not putting forward a fundamental critique of capitalism but instead wants to correct its malformations through reforms and in this sense must always presuppose the concept of a "healthy" or normally functioning capitalism (in his case, an autonomous national development not dependent on international profit transfers). Within the framework of Lenin's fundamental critique of capitalism, however, it remains unclear why the exploitation of foreign countries should be worse than that of the domestic working class.

The classical theories of imperialism seem highly questionable, particularly with respect to their specific economic underpinning: despite all the tendencies towards concentration, we can neither assume a transition from competitive to monopoly capitalism based on personal domination nor are problems of valorization within the metropolis the main reason for capital export: the largest share of capital export goes not from capitalist metropolises to an imperial periphery but to other metropolises.

The debate on globalization has certainly lent plausibility to the structuralist paradigm in the theory of international relations and many "critiques of globalization" feature argumentational tropes analogous to elements of classical theories of imperialism (see the chapter on Susan Strange by Hans-Jürgen Bieling in this volume with respect to the dominance of the financial markets). At the same time, however, theories of imperialism and neo-imperialism have an undeniably foreshortened concept of politics and the state: the reduction of states' international actions to safeguarding the interests of major companies is fundamentally limited, even if there is clear evidence of such behaviour by governments in many specific instances.[16]

The state in whose territory a capitalist economy exists – even in the absence of influence from specific capitalists – is bound to have an interest in the success of this capitalism since it forms its own economic foundation. But the state does not promote prosperity by enforcing specific capital interests but rather "general" ones, or by making it possible to define such general interests in the first place. It is after all not immediately clear how much welfare state or how much international influence is really necessary to ensure the successful accumulation of total social capital. It is the very "autonomy" of the state, which is denied in the classical theories of imperialism, that makes it possible to ascertain these "general" capital interests within the "public sphere" and within political institutions in the first place, to justify them normatively and, finally, to bring about the greatest possible degree of social consensus. On the international level, then, states are not concerned solely to enforce specific interests, but are always also concerned to provide themselves with action *options* in the first place, whether through "power politics" or through institutional strategies, unilateral or multilateral action – depending on their highly unequal economic, political and military parameters.[17]

5 Notes

1 A good overview of the various theories of imperialism is provided by Mommsen (1981). Still informative are Wehler (1976), Hampe (1976) and Krippendorff (1976). For studies focused on Marxist theories of imperialism, see Brewer (1980), Barone (1985), Nachtwey (2005) and ten Brink (2008b). Wolfe (1997) provides an overview mainly of recent contributions influenced by the Marxist debate as well as "postcolonial studies".

2 See, for example, the chapter by Andreas Nölke in this volume.

3 This structuralist paradigm in the theory of International Relations should not be confused with what is commonly meant by "structuralism": a school of thought originating in France in the 1960s that is influential above all in anthropology, sociology, philosophy, linguistics and literary studies.

4 French economist Jean-Baptiste Say formulated this "law" at the beginning of the nineteenth century, and in modified form it still underpins contemporary neoclassical theory-building.

5 The circumstances that prompted him to write his book are explained in an autobiographical sketch (Hobson 1938). For an introduction to his work, see Schröder (1976).

6 The term cartel is used in cases where legally independent firms limit their competition, for example, through price agreements. A trust, meanwhile, involves a number of firms joining together under unified leadership.

7 On early analyses of imperialism, see Schröder (1973). Paul (1978) provides a critical examination of these analyses in light of their specific reception of Marx.

8 A critical examination of Hilferding's book *Finance Capital* is provided, for example, by Schimkowsky (1974a, 1974b) and Stephan (1974).

9 The theoretical core of Luxemburg's theory of imperialism, which is based on a specific interpretation of Marx, namely the idea that capitalist reproduction always presupposes a non-capitalist milieu, was criticized by Otto Bauer as early as 1913. Rosdolsky (1977) provides an in-depth examination of this problem.

10 See also Lenin's preface to the French edition of his book.

11 For a fundamental Marxist critique, see Wirth (1973).

12 A Marxist critique of the notion of "unequal exchange" is provided by Busch (1973).

13 See Heinrich (2011), Elbe (2008) and Hoff (2009) on the new understanding of Marxism, which is opposed to traditional Marxism and which took hold in (West) Germany and elsewhere from the 1970s on.

14 See, for example, Neusüss (1972: part 1); Jordan (1974); Held and Ebel (1983: 48–65). This criticism that the classical theories of imperialism, despite the Marxist vocabulary, actually break

with Marx's criticism of political economy rather than building on it, is taken up systematically by Milios and Sotiropoulos (2009), who use it to produce a productive analysis of international relations of dependency and domination; see also the further development of their ideas in Sotiropoulos *et al.* (2013).

15 Lenin thus refers not just to the idea that the "yoke of a few monopolists on the rest of the population becomes a hundred times heavier" (Lenin [1917] 1940: 56), but also emphasizes:

> Domination, and violence that is associated with it, such are the relationships that are most typical of the "latest phase of capitalist development"; this is what must inevitably result, and has resulted, from the formation of all-powerful economic monopolies.
>
> (ibid.: 60)

16 This reductive economistic conception of the state is also criticized in the recent contributions to the imperialism debate in Harvey (2005) and above all in Panitch and Gindin (2004).

17 For an introduction to the relationship between state, capital and world market, following the concepts of Marx's *Capital*, see Heinrich (2012), Chapter 11.

6 Bibliography and recommended reading

6.1 Primary texts

Hardt, Michael and Negri, Antonio 2000: *Empire*. Cambridge, MA: Harvard University Press.
Harvey, David 2005: *The New Imperialism*. Oxford: Oxford University Press.
Hobson, John A. [1902] 1988: *Imperialism: A Study*. London: Unwin Hyman.
Lenin, Vladimir I. [1917] 1940: *New Data for V. I. Lenin's Imperialism, the Highest Stage of Capitalism*, ed. Eugen Varga and Lev Abramovich Mendelsohn. New York: International Publishers.
Neusüss, Christel 1972: *Imperialismus und Weltmarktbewegung des Kapitals*. Erlangen: Politladen.
Panitch, Leo and Gindin, Sam 2004: *Global Capitalism and American Empire*. London: Merlin.
Senghaas, Dieter (ed.) 1972: *Imperialismus und strukturelle Gewalt*. Frankfurt a. M.: Suhrkamp.
Senghaas, Dieter (ed.) 1974: *Peripherer Kapitalismus. Analysen über Abhängigkeit und Unterentwicklung*. Frankfurt a. M.: Suhrkamp.

6.2 Secondary texts

Deppe, Frank, Heidbrink, Stephan, Salomon, David, Schmalz, Stefan, Schoppengerd, Stefan and Solty, Ingar 2004: *Der neue Imperialismus*. Heilbronn: Distel.
Milios, John and Sotiropoulos, Dimitris P. 2009: *Rethinking Imperialism: A Study of Capitalist Rule*. New York: Palgrave Macmillan.
Mommsen, Wolfgang J. 1981: *Theories of Imperialism*. London: Weidenfeld & Nicolson
Nachtwey, Oliver 2005: *Weltmarkt und Imperialismus. Zur Entstehungsgeschichte der klassischen marxistischen Imperialismustheorie*. Cologne: Neuer ISP.
ten Brink, Tobias 2008b: *Staatenkonflikte. Zur Analyse von Geopolitik und Imperialismus – Ein Überblick*. Stuttgart: Lucius & Lucius/UTB.
Wolfe, Patrick 1997: History and Imperialism: A Century of Theory, from Marx to Postcolonialism, *American Historical Review* 102(2): 388–420.

6.3 Other texts

Amin, Samir 1974: Zur Theorie von Akkumulation und Entwicklung in der gegenwärtigen Weltgesellschaft, in Senghaas, Dieter (ed.) *Peripherer Kapitalismus. Analysen über Abhängigkeit und Unterentwicklung*. Frankfurt a. M.: Suhrkamp, pp. 71–97.
Amin, Samir 1976: *Unequal Development: An Essay on the Social Formations of Peripheral Capitalism*. Hassocks: Harvester.

Amin, Samir 1989: *Eurocentrism*. New York: Monthly Review Press.

Amin, Samir 1998: Imperialismus und Globalisierung, in Hobsbawm, Eric: *Das Manifest heute. 150 Jahre Kapitalismuskritik*. Hamburg: VSA, pp. 137–149.

Amin, Samir and Palloix, Christian 1973: *Neuere Beiträge zur Imperialismustheorie*. Munich: Trikont Verlag.

Anderson, Perry 1976: *Considerations on Western Marxism*. London: NLB.

Atzert, Thomas and Müller, Jost (eds) 2002: *Kritik der Weltordnung. Globalisierung, Imperialismus, Empire*. Berlin: ID-Verlag.

Atzert, Thomas and Müller, Jost (eds) 2004: *Immaterielle Arbeit und imperiale Souveränität. Analysen und Diskussionen zu "Empire"*. Münster: Westfälisches Dampfboot.

Baran, Paul and Sweezy, Paul 1966: *Monopoly Capital: An Essay on the American Economic and Social Order*. New York: Monthly Review Press.

Barone, Charles E. 1985: *Marxist Thought on Imperialism: Survey and Critique*. New York: Macmillan.

Becker, David G., Frieden, Jeff, Schatz, Sayre P., and Sklar, Richard L. (eds) 1987: *Postimperialism: International Capitalism and Development in the Twentieth Century*. London: Lynne Rienner.

Becker, David G. and Sklar, Richard L. (eds) 1999: *Postimperialism and World Politics*. Westport, CT: Prager.

Brand, Ulrich 2002: Die Revolution der globalisierungsfreundlichen Multitude. "Empire" als voluntaristisches Manifest, *Das Argument* 245: 209–219.

Brewer, Anthony 1980: *Marxist Theories of Imperialism: A Critical Survey*. London: Routledge.

Busch, Klaus 1973: Ungleicher Tausch. Zur Diskussion über internationale Durchschnittsprofitrate, ungleichen Tausch und komparative Kostentheorie anhand der Thesen von Arghiri Emmanuel, *Probleme des Klassenkampfs* 3(3): 47–88.

Callinicos, Alex 2007: Benötigt der Kapitalismus das Staatensystem?, in Kaindl, Christina, Lieber, Christoph, Nachtwey, Oliver, Rilling, Rainer and ten Brink, Tobias (eds) *Kapitalismus reloaded. Kontroversen zu Imperialismus, Empire und Hegemonie*. Hamburg: VSA, pp. 11–32.

Callinicos, Alex 2009: *Imperialism and Global Political Economy*. London: Polity Press.

Cardoso, Fernando and Faletto, Enzo 1979: *Dependency and Development in Latin America*. Berkeley, CA: University of California Press.

Darby, Phillip (ed.) 1997: *At the Edge of International Relations: Postcolonialism, Gender and Dependency*. London: Pinter.

Darby, Phillip 1998: *The Fiction of Imperialism: Reading between International Relations and Postcolonialism*. London: Cassell.

Dunn, Kevin C. 2004: Africa's Ambiguous Relationship to Empire and *Empire*, in Passavant, Paul A. (ed.) *Empire's New Clothes: Reading Hardt and Negri*. London: Routledge, pp. 143–162.

Elbe, Ingo 2008: *Marx im Westen. Die neue Marx-Lektüre in der Bundesrepublik seit 1965*. Berlin: Akademie Verlag.

Elsenhans, Hartmut 1979: Grundlagen der Entwicklung der kapitalistischen Weltwirtschaft, in Senghaas, Dieter (ed.) *Kapitalistische Weltökonomie. Kontroversen über ihren Ursprung und ihre Entwicklungsdynamik*. Frankfurt a. M.: Suhrkamp, pp. 103–148.

Elsenhans, Hartmut 1991: *Development and Underdevelopment: The History, Economics and Politics of North-South Relations*. London: Sage.

Emmanuel, Arghiri 1972: *Unequal Exchange: A Study of the Imperialism of Trade*. London. NLB.

Frank, André Gunder 1971: *Capitalism and Underdevelopment in Latin America*. Harmondsworth: Penguin.

Frank, André Gunder 1998: *ReORIENT: Global Economy in the Asian Age*. Berkeley, CA: University of California Press.

Galtung, Johann 1972: Eine strukturelle Theorie des Imperialismus, in Senghaas, Dieter (ed.) *Imperialismus und strukturelle Gewalt*. Frankfurt a. M.: Suhrkamp, pp. 29–104.

Galtung, Johann 1980: A Structural Theory of Imperialism: Ten Years Later, *Millennium* 9(3): 183–196.

Hampe, Peter 1976: *Die ökonomische Imperialismustheorie. Kritische Untersuchungen*. Munich: C.H. Beck.

Hartmann Detlef 2002: *"Empire". Linkes Ticket für die Reise nach rechts*. Berlin: Assoziation A.

Heinrich, Michael 2011: *Die Wissenschaft vom Wert. Die Marxsche Kritik der politischen Ökonomie zwischen wissenschaftlicher Revolution und klassischer Tradition*, 5th edn. Münster: Westfälisches Dampfboot.

Heinrich, Michael 2012: *An Introduction to the Three Volumes of Karl Marx's Capital*, New York: Monthly Review Press.

Held, Karl and Ebel, Theo 1983: *Krieg und Frieden. Politische Ökonomie des Weltfriedens*. Frankfurt a. M.: Suhrkamp.

Hilferding, Rudolf 1981: *Finance Capital: A Study of the Latest Phase of Capitalist Development*. London: Routledge.

Hobson, John A. 1938: *Confessions of an Economic Heretic*. London: Allen & Unwin.

Hobson, John A. and Mummery, F. A. [1889] 1994: The Physiology of Industry, in Pheby, John (ed.) *J. A. Hobson after Fifty Years: Free Thinker of the Social Sciences*. Basingstoke: Macmillan, pp. 78–99.

Hoff, Jan 2009: *Marx global. Zur Entwicklung des internationalen Marx-Diskurses seit 1965*. Berlin: Akademie Verlag.

Ignatieff, Michael 2003: The Burden, *The New York Times Magazine*, 5.1.2003.

Jordan, Dirk 1974: Der Imperialismus als monopolistischer Kapitalismus. Zur Imperialismus-Analyse Lenins als Basis der Theorie des staatsmonopolistischen Kapitalismus, in Ebbinghaus, Rolf (ed.) *Monopol und Staat. Zur Marx-Rezeption in der Theorie des staatsmonopolistischen Kapitalismus*. Frankfurt a. M.: Suhrkamp, pp. 212–242.

Kautsky, Karl 1914: Der Imperialismus, *Die Neue Zeit* 32: 908–922.

Keynes, John Maynard [1936] 1973: *The General Theory of Employment, Interest and Money (The Collected Writings of John Maynard Keynes*, vol. VII). London: Macmillan.

Kößler, Reinhart 2003: Imperialismus und Globalisierung. Anmerkungen zu zwei Theoriekomplexen, *PROKLA* 133 33(4): 521–544.

Krippendorff, Ekkehart 1976: Imperialismusbegriff und Imperialismustheorien, *Neue Politische Literatur* 21(2): 141–155.

Landes, David S. 1961: Some Thoughts on the Nature of Economic Imperialism, *Journal of Economic History* 21: 496–512.

Luxemburg, Rosa [1913] 1963: *The Accumulation of Capital*. Trans. Agnes Schwarzschild. London: Routledge.

Mandel, Ernest 1978: *Late Capitalism*. London: Verso.

Marx, Karl [1867] 1976: *Capital*, vol. 1, Harmondsworth: Penguin.

Menzel, Ulrich 2001: *Zwischen Idealismus und Realismus. Die Lehre von den Internationalen Beziehungen*. Frankfurt a. M.: Suhrkamp.

Münkler, Herfried 2007: *Empires: The Logic of World Domination from Ancient Rome to the United States*. Cambridge: Polity.

O'Connor, James 1970: The Meaning of Economic Imperialism, in Rhodes, Robert I. (ed.) *Imperialism and Underdevelopment: A Reader*. New York: Monthly Review Press, pp. 101–152.

Panitch, Leo 2002: Neuer Imperialismus – neue Imperialismustheorie, *Z. Zeitschrift marxistische Erneuerung* 13(4): 77–87.

Paul, Hans-Holger 1978: *Marx, Engels und die Imperialismustheorie der II. Internationale*. Hamburg: VSA.

Project for a New American Century 2000: *Rebuilding America's Defenses: Strategy, Forces and Resources for a New Century*. Available at: http://www. newamericancentury. org/publicationsreports.htm (accessed 2 February 2010).

Randeria, Shalini and Eckert, Andreas (eds) 2009: *Vom Imperialismus zum Empire. Nicht-westliche Perspektiven auf Globalisierung*. Frankfurt a. M.: Suhrkamp.

Richter, Horst (ed.) 1989: *Politische Ökonomie des Kapitalismus und Sozialismus. Lehrbuch für das marxistisch-leninistische Grundlagenstudium*, 15th edn. Berlin: Dietz Verlag.

Rosdolsky, Roman 1977: *The Making of Marx's "Capital"*. Trans. Pete Burgess. London: Pluto Press.

Russett, Bruce M. 1985: America's Continuing Strengths: The Mysterious Case of Vanishing Hegemony; or, Is Mark Twain Really Dead? *International Organization* 39(2): 207–231.

Said, Edward W. 1993: *Culture and Imperialism*. New York: Knopf.

Schimkowsky, Reinhard 1974a: Zur Marx-Rezeption bei Hilferding. Die Bestimmungen von Konkurrenz und Monopol im "Finanzkapital", in Ebbinghaus, Rolf (ed.) *Monopol und Staat. Zur Marx-Rezeption in der Theorie des staatsmonopolistischen Kapitalismus*. Frankfurt a. M.: Suhrkamp, pp. 173–211.

Schimkowsky, Reinhard 1974b: Exkurs über Hilferding: Vom Generalkartell zur Konzeption des organisierten Kapitalismus, in Ebbinghaus, Rolf (ed.) *Monopol und Staat. Zur Marx-Rezeption in der Theorie des staatsmonopolistischen Kapitalismus*. Frankfurt a. M.: Suhrkamp, pp. 279–292.

Schröder, Hans Christoph 1973: *Sozialistische Imperialismusdeutung*. Göttingen: Vandenhoeck & Ruprecht.

Schröder, Hans Christoph 1976: Hobsons Imperialismusdeutung, in Wehler, Hans-Ulrich (ed.) *Imperialismus*. Cologne: Kiepenheuer & Witsch.

Schumpeter, Joseph A. [1919] 1953: Zur Soziologie der Imperialismen, in Schumpeter: *Aufsätze zur Soziologie*. Tübingen: Mohr, pp. 72–146.

Socialist Register 2004: *The New Imperial Challenge*. London: Merlin Press.

Sotiropoulos, Dimitris P., Milios, John and Lapatsioras, Spyros 2013: *A Political Economy of Contemporary Capitalism and its Crisis: Demystifying Finance*, London: Routledge.

Stephan, Cora 1974: Geld und Staatstheorie in Hilferdings "Finanzkapital", *Gesellschaft: Beiträge zur Marxschen Theorie* 2: 111–154.

Strange, Susan 1987: The Persistent Myth of Lost Hegemony, *International Organization* 41(4): 551–574.

Sunkel, Osvaldo 1972: Transnationale kapitalistische Integration und nationale Desintegration: Der Fall Lateinamerika, in Senghaas, Dieter (ed.) *Imperialismus und strukturelle Gewalt*. Frankfurt a. M.: Suhrkamp, pp. 258–315.

Sweezy, Paul 1962 [1942]: *The Theory of Capitalist Development: Principles of Marxian Political Economy*. London: Dennis Dobson Limited.

ten Brink, Tobias 2008a: *Geopolitik. Geschichte und Gegenwart kapitalistischer Staatenkonkurrenz*. Münster: Westfälisches Dampfboot.

Warren, Bill 1973: Imperialism and Capitalist Industrialization, *New Left Review* I(81): 3–44.

Warren, Bill 1980: *Imperialism: Pioneer of Capitalism*. London: New Left Books.

Wehler, Hans-Ulrich (ed.) 1976: *Imperialismus*. Cologne: Kiepenheuer & Witsch.

Wirth, Margaret 1973: Zur Kritik der Theorie des staatsmonopolistischen Kapitalismus, *Probleme des Klassenkampfs* 3(3): 17–44.

Zeller, Christian (ed.) 2004: *Die globale Enteignungsökonomie*. Münster: Westfälisches Dampfboot.

World-system theory

Andreas Nölke

1 Introduction

World-system theory is a theory of international relations with Marxian origins. Its core argument is that the world as it is today can be understood only in the context of the development of global capitalism. In light of globalization and financial crises, this is a theory of undiminished relevance. From this theoretical perspective, many aspects of globalization look like modern forms of centuries-old developments, and the same goes for the development of global economic crises. Compared with approaches such as interdependence analysis or neorealism, however, world-system theory offers a rather unusual perspective on international politics. While conventional approaches resemble the kind of reports found in the media, world-system theory offers a perspective that foregrounds deeper, less obvious developments. Further, the point of view favoured by world-system theory is discomfiting for many observers (especially in the Western industrialized countries) because it highlights that one of the key functions of the present world-system is to ensure the well-being of the rich and powerful at the expense of the poor and weak (Hobden and Jones 1997: 125f.).

The Marxian roots of world-system theory are plainly apparent. In contrast to his journalistic writings, however, Marx himself paid little attention to international politics in his theory. The first systematic application of Marxian concepts to international politics was undertaken by theorists of imperialism such as Hobson (though he was no Marxist), Luxemburg and Lenin (see the chapter by Michael Heinrich in this volume). World-system theory picks up mainly on a strand of Marxian theory developed by Lenin (see Shannon 1996: 12f.; Hobden and Jones 1997: 127). Lenin argues that the nature of capitalism has changed since the publication of *Capital* in 1867, with the international context becoming increasingly important. Marx assumed that there was a straightforward antagonism between proletariat and bourgeoisie regardless of geographical realities and no clash of interests between workers in different countries. Lenin, on the other hand, argues that capitalism has generated a hierarchical structure within the world-economy, in which a dominant centre exploits a less-developed periphery. This, however, eliminates the assumption of a simple clash of interests between capital and labour and of a harmony of interests between the workers of different countries. Now the bourgeoisie in the centre can improve the lot of workers in the centre on the basis of exploitation of the periphery, "paying them off" to depart from the international proletarian alliance. This crude account of Lenin's theory of imperialism already sheds light on some of the basic principles of the world-system theory built upon it: no policy, whether national or international, can be understood without taking account of the capitalist world-system. States are not the only relevant actors in international politics, and social classes are the true driving force. Embeddedness in the structure of the capitalist world-system determines the behaviour and interactions of specific classes and states (Hobden and Jones 1997: 127) – in much the same way as structural realists believe that the incorporation of states into the international division of power determines their behaviour (see the contribution by Niklas Schörnig in this volume).

Marxist analyses of international politics were largely out of favour in the first two decades following the Second World War. The long post-war boom and decolonization made the exploitation of the periphery by the capitalist world-system seem less inevitable. The Cold War not only inspired sweeping condemnations of Marxist thinkers as collaborators, but made economic issues seem less relevant than military ones. This changed only in the late 1960s and early 1970s when the collapse of the Bretton Woods system, oil crises and subsequent recessions, on the one hand, and the process of détente on the other brought about a historically more favourable climate for critical analyses of capitalism (Hobden and Jones 1997: 128). A series of Marxian analyses of the effects of global capitalism on North–South relations appeared in this context, often referred to collectively as *dependency theory*. Important preliminary work was done by Raúl Prebisch, first director of the United Nations Economic Commission for Latin America (ECLA), who developed the – theoretically and statistically contested – argument that international exchange relations were getting steadily worse from the perspective of the developing countries. On this view, because of pricing trends within the international economy, the developing countries can import ever fewer processed goods from the industrial countries in exchange for the primary goods they export. Building on these ideas, other authors went on to develop more comprehensive theories of North–South dependencies in polemical but highly popular (André Gunder Frank) and more nuanced variants (Enzo Faletto in collaboration with Henrique Fernando Cardoso, later the president of Brazil). Unlike most of the early theories of imperialism, however, dependency theorists were concerned less with explaining the reasons for capitalist expansion (in Europe) than with the effects of this expansion on the dominated countries (Boeckh 1985: 58). The counterparts of dependency theories were theories of modernization, which made traditional economic, political and social structures – rather than exogenous influences – responsible for the persistent underdevelopment of the South (see Shannon 1996: 2–8).

One important theoretical development in this connection was Immanuel Wallerstein's comprehensive world-system theory and the coherent theoretical edifice associated with it. In contrast to dependency theorists, Wallerstein does not limit himself to analysis of current exchange relations between a limited group of states (and in some cases their colonial predecessors), but instead develops his theory with respect to a broader geographical and temporal framework. Like theorists of imperialism, he explains the causes of capitalist expansion and, like dependency theorists, he also explains its consequences. In addition to Marxian and dependency theories, Wallerstein draws chiefly on the groundwork done by the *Annales* School.[1] Particularly important in this context is the influence on Wallerstein of *Annales* historian Fernand Braudel with his emphasis on long-term historical influences – up to and including the effects of global climate change on the *longue durée* (Hobden and Jones 1997: 128f).[2]

Wallerstein's four-volume history of the modern world-system is central to his work (Wallerstein 1974, 1980, 1989, 2011). Though Wallerstein's theory building remains a work in progress (see Wallerstein 2000), and has by now been supplemented by a broad research programme involving numerous other authors (including Samir Amin, Giovanni Arrighi and André Gunder Frank), this impressive trinity remains one of the intellectual nodes of the world-system theory that I shall be outlining in what follows.

2 The world-system theory of Immanuel Wallerstein

2.1 What is a world-system?

Central to the understanding of Wallerstein's work is the concept of the world-system. Wallerstein works on the assumption that the world-system is the appropriate unit of analysis for the study of the most varied range of social phenomena (Wallerstein 2000: 149) – not just international politics. Here a system is defined through two key attributes (see Hobden and Jones 1997: 130f.). First, a dynamic relationship exists between all the elements of a system. If we wish to understand the behaviour of one element, we have to understand its position within the system as a whole. This assumption may be understood, first of all, in spatial terms. We can analyse the behaviour of a state, for example, only in connection with its position within the international system. Further, a system does not consist of purely political or economic or socio-cultural phenomena. Wallerstein's *holistic perspective* demands the inclusion of the range of interdependencies that pertain between these phenomena. Wallerstein thus advocates a highly transdisciplinary approach – by drawing on sociology (his original disciplinary home), political science, economics, history, and so on – and consistently argues that the social sciences should be "reunified" (Wallerstein *et al.* 1996). The second attribute consists in the fact that a system is more or less self-sufficient, in other words independent of the rest of the world. So if we wish to explain changes in a system, we must focus not on external shocks but on internal system dynamics. The prefix "world" does not mean that every system must necessarily encompass the entire globe, but merely that we are dealing with distinguishable, internally coherent spheres (Hall 2000: 4). Wallerstein regards the Roman Empire, for example, as a world-system, despite that fact that it did not take in the entire world. World-systems, then, are geographically definable spaces, "governed" by a uniform logic. One of the novel aspects of the modern world-system is that it does in fact encompass the entire globe (see Section 2.2).

Wallerstein distinguishes between two basic types of world-system: "world-empires" and "world-economies" (he spends very little time analysing a third type, "mini-systems"). The key difference between these two types lies in the ways in which decisions on resource distribution are made. In a world-empire, the central political system uses its power to redistribute resources from the periphery to the centre, in the form of tribute payments, for example. In a world-economy, meanwhile, there is no single centre of political power but instead a number of competing power centres. The redistribution of resources – from the periphery to the centre – thus occurs not so much by means of political decisions as within the framework of the transnational market mechanism. The modern world-system is an example of a world-economy. This specific world-economy, according to Wallerstein, emerged in Europe in the "long" sixteenth century (c. 1450–1620) before going on to spread around the world. The central dynamic of this specific world-economy is its capitalist character – in the sense of the ceaseless accumulation of capital through a highly developed worldwide division of labour to the benefit of the centre; workers, particularly those on the periphery, are systematically exploited by the underpayment associated with "unequal exchange" (Arghiri Emmanuel; cf. Shannon 1996: 34–36). The individual elements within this world-system do not remain constant, but are permanently changed by the dynamics of capitalist accumulation, regardless of whether we are dealing with economic institutions such as corporate governance or social and political institutions such as states and the organization of budgets (on the latter, see Wallerstein 2000: 234–252). Like other world-systems, the modern capitalist system is temporally limited. It began at a particular point in time and it will eventually come to an end as well – in the not too distant future, Wallerstein suspects (Wallerstein 1979: 66f.).

2.2 The spatial and temporal definition of the modern world-system

The spatial dimension of the modern world-system relates to the various roles played by regions in the global capitalist economy. Here Wallerstein's perspective differs from conventional dependency theoretical centre–periphery models that built on Lenin. In the first instance, Wallerstein too assumes that the production taking place in the centre requires more advanced skills and greater capital investment, while the periphery supplies raw materials and is subject to a ruthless siphoning-off of surplus value. Wallerstein, however, introduces a new category, the intermediate "semiperiphery". This semiperiphery fuses some of the characteristic features of the centre and periphery. Though it is exploited by the centre, at the same time it includes successful companies in certain branches of manufacturing. Within the capitalist world-system, the semiperiphery's key functions include supplying workers, which limits the tendency for the scarcity of labour in the centre to lead to wage increases; it also provides a home for those industries in the centre that are no longer profitable enough, such as the textiles industry. The semiperiphery obeys the core logic of the capitalist world-system, in which the stronger region exploits those weaker than it (Hobden and Jones 1997: 131; see also Section 2.4). In contrast to dependency theorists, however, Wallerstein works on the assumption that a certain mobility is possible between these economic regions (see Shannon 1996: 146–149). What is not possible, he believes, again in contrast to dependency theorists, is for the semiperiphery to be sealed off from the centre. For Wallerstein, capitalism can only be overcome as a whole (Hobden 1998: 144).

But there is more to Wallerstein's analysis of the modern world-system than this fairly static spatial differentiation. We can understand how this system works only if we also factor in its temporal dynamics (see Hobden and Jones 1997: 132–134; Wallerstein 2000: 207–220). Here Wallerstein identifies four types of process within the modern world-system:

1 *Cyclical rhythms* refer to the tendency of the capitalist world-economy to go through regular phases of massive growth and recession, as described, for example, by Russian economist, Nikolai D. Kondratiev (a Kondratiev cycle lasts 40–60 years). The cycles of political hegemony in the centre are also economically determined (see Section 2.4).
2 *Secular trends* refer to the long-term development of this world-system, including such things as expansion, commodification, and urbanization (see Section 2.6).
3 For Wallerstein, *contradictions* are a key law of motion of the modern world-economy. He defines them as circumstances in which there is a clash between action that is rational over the short term and over the long term. The most famous example is the tendency of the capitalist world-system towards under-consumption: while it is in the capitalists' short-term interest to keep wages down, over the long term, this leads to a decline in purchasing power and thus to reduced profits.
4 In contrast to the common use of the term, for Wallerstein *crises* are unique events in the history of every world-system and lead to its replacement by another system. They come about through an unfavourable combination of the other three dynamics and lessen the systemic restrictions on actors, enabling them to break out of the framework constraining them (see Section 2.6).

2.3 The role of the state and of international politics in the modern world-system

World-system theory, however, is not just a theory of global economic development, but a theory of international politics (though many, especially Marxian, observers of world politics would underline the indivisibility of politics and economics and the eminently political character of economic and distributive processes). Central to Wallerstein's assumptions about the role of politics in the capitalist world-system is the stabilization of the system through the form of political organization. For Wallerstein, the stability of this system over the past 500 years is remarkable, despite all the internal contradictions, wars, famines, and so on. For him, one of the keys to its stability is the role of the sovereign state and of the international state system (on what follows, see Hobden and Jones 1997: 134–140).

States play an essential role in the functioning of the capitalist world-economy in a dual sense. First, they provide a framework for the realization and securing of property rights. Without secure property rights, the capitalist economy is unable to function, with respect, for example, to the long-term refinancing of investments or repayment of loans. Such property rights can be secured in various ways, not only through a law-governed state of the Western type, but also through corresponding measures by authoritarian regimes. The second key function of the state within capitalism arises from the internal contradictions produced by this economic system (see Section 2.2). These contradictions are particularly apparent in the reluctance of the capitalist mode of production to provide the infrastructure necessary to its functioning. For each individual capitalist enterprise, it would be irrational to organize and finance such things as primary education or a comprehensive transport network. It is the state that takes on such tasks.

It is not just the existence of states that is essential to the functioning of the capitalist world-system, but also their organization as an international system in which – and there are similarities here with the realist concept of anarchy – no state can exercise total dominance over the others. The existence of rival power centres ensures that no state can exercise excessively restrictive control over the enterprises located within its polity, as these would otherwise move to other states, undermining the abandoned state's revenue base. Were a single world state to emerge, however (a world-empire, in Wallerstein's terminology), it would be capable of exercising such control and thus effectively undermining the basis of the capitalist world-economy. But precisely because the political organization of this economy consists of a competitive international structure, the formation of such a world state is highly unlikely. The key reason for this is that the competition between capitalist enterprises regularly leads to such fluctuations in the relative power distribution between different states and regions within the system that no state manages to control all the others. In this respect, not only is the international system necessary to the functioning of the capitalist world-economy, but the economy is vital to maintaining the international system. This close connection with the world-economy makes world-system theory quite different from neorealism, which is otherwise similar in emphasizing the significance of the sovereign state and anarchical international system.

2.4 The state in the centre, the semiperiphery and the periphery

Alongside these general connections between state system and capitalism, Wallerstein assumes that the state plays a specific role in the centre, the semiperiphery and the periphery. This marks a further difference from neorealism, which assumes a functional equivalence of states in different world regions. (See the contribution by Niklas Schörnig in this volume.) States in the centre have a special dual function in maintaining the structures of the modern world-system. First, certain of these states have taken on a hegemonic leadership role within the international system (see Shannon 1996: 136–146; Wallerstein 2000: 253–263). The Netherlands in the mid-seventeenth century, Great Britain in the mid-nineteenth century and the USA in the mid-twentieth century have played such a role because they were well ahead of their rivals in economic terms. The key significance of these hegemons for the existence of the capitalist world-system consisted in their leadership role, through which they enforced certain standards with which all international transactions had to comply – as when the United States initiated the Bretton Woods system towards the end of the Second World War. As a rule, these standards chiefly reflected the interests of a given hegemon, but they also created the predictability so essential to the functioning of a capitalist economy – and which, in the case of Bretton Woods, was partly responsible for the post-war economic boom. Many of these standards continue to exist even if a hegemon has passed the peak of its military and economic power, so over a longer period these hegemonic cycles, which last around a century, create the stability that keeps capitalism going, somewhere in the middle ground between a world state and anarchy.

The second key function of states in the centre for the stabilization of the system lies in the (potential) use of their military power vis-à-vis the periphery and semiperiphery in order to maintain their dominant position within the world-economy. This is not just a matter of access to essential raw materials and markets, but of disciplining states that threaten to undermine the stability of this economic system. As examples of such activities, exponents of world-system theory identify "Operation Desert Storm" (1991) against Iraq, as well as the overthrow of left-wing governments in Latin America, such as that of Allende in Chile (1973).

As mentioned earlier, the semiperiphery also plays a vital role in stabilizing the capitalist world-system. Here too the state plays a key role. Compared with those of the periphery, states of the semiperiphery have fairly functional administrative structures. In the first instance, these structures are there to organize the project of national development, in other words to attempt to shift the country from the semiperiphery to the centre. More important to the functioning of the capitalist world-system, however, is the authoritarian character of these states: though they may be ostensibly democratic, they are usually ruled by a small elite, mostly under the watchful eyes of the military. This authoritarian character is important as it enables these states to control trade union activity. This in turn is important as a means of enforcing lower wage and social standards than in the centre, thus ensuring suitable conditions for those traditional industries no longer competitive in the centre.

Within the periphery, the existence of a dominant class closely tied to the state apparatus, whose behaviour ultimately serves the interests of the centre's dominant classes rather than its own population, also has an important function for the stability of the capitalist world-system. This so-called "comprador class", like the elites of the semiperiphery, thus receives support from the centre in order to dampen down at least some of the potential tensions arising from the exploitative relationship between centre and periphery. This support may take the form of direct military aid but may also mean tolerating brutal and repressive regimes in these states.

2.5 Geoculture

Recently, Wallerstein has increasingly focused on the concept of geoculture (see Wallerstein 1991, 1995; Shannon 1996: 204–207; Hobden and Jones 1997: 139f.). Geoculture is

Wallerstein's term for the cultural framework of the modern world-system; he uses a very broad concept of culture that takes in values and ways of thinking. In contrast to the economic and political dimensions of the world-system, the geoculture is less tangible, but like that dimension it contributes substantially to the stabilization of the system, chiefly by legitimizing it. There are two central aspects to Wallerstein's reflections on the geoculture within the modern capitalist world-system: the role of liberalism as its dominant ideology and the function of scientism as its prevailing knowledge system.

If an established order is supported by a widely disseminated ideology, this secures the order much more effectively than mere coercion (see the chapter by Andreas Bieler and Adam David Morton on neo-Gramscianism in this volume). Wallerstein argues that for around two hundred years the modern world-system has been legitimized by an extraordinarily successful ideology in the shape of liberalism, which is commonly held to be the only rational mode of societal organization. Liberalism is in fact so successful that even the competing ideologies of conservatism and socialism have adopted central postulates of liberalism and now represent mere variants of liberal ideology (see Wallerstein 2000: 416–422). Particularly important to the stabilizing role of liberalism is its legitimization of the state:

> Liberalism is the only ideology that permits the long-term reinforcement of the state structures, the strategic underpinning of a functioning capitalist world-economy. Conservatism and socialism appeal beyond the state to a "society" which finds its expression in other institutions. Liberalism, precisely because it is universalistic and contractual, finds the ultimate resolution of conflicts in state decisions, the state alone being presumed to have no "interests" of its own but to be the vector of the majority compromise and consensus.
>
> (Wallerstein 1991: 10)

As the dominant knowledge system, scientism arose in the context of secularization and came to reign supreme due to the triumph of the modern natural sciences. Not only were natural scientific laws applied, with great success, in the production process, thus advancing the accumulation of capital, but these laws claim to be universally valid, regardless of time, space and epistemological interest. This model of knowledge representation was not limited to the natural sciences but was subsequently applied to other disciplines as well, including the social sciences. Here scientism suppresses normative and critical alternatives, thus helping stabilize the modern world-system.

For Wallerstein, the common denominator of liberalism, scientism and capitalism is their universalizing character. But this stands in striking contrast to the massive inequalities in the capitalist world-system. In order to explain these inequalities while preserving its universalizing character, the geoculture entails other crucial elements such as racism and sexism (see Wallerstein 2000: 272–289, 344–352). The different qualities of "races" and sexes explain why, despite the universal character of the world-system, some people are "more equal" than others (Hobden and Jones 1997: 140); at the same time, within the framework of a *divide et impera* strategy, these supposed differences serve to undermine potential antisystemic resistance.

2.6 The crisis of the modern world-system

Though Wallerstein identifies a number of precisely interlocking factors that secure the remarkable stability of the modern world-system, he assumes that this stability is being increasingly undermined and that the world-system is approaching its crisis phase. At first sight this idea seems paradoxical, given the collapse of the Soviet Union and the ostensible triumph of capitalism. But Wallerstein identifies key eroding factors that extend not just to economic aspects but also, in close connection with them, to political and geocultural aspects of the world-system (see Shannon 1996: 149–151; Hobden and Jones 1997: 140–142; Wallerstein 2000: 428–434).

Tendencies towards economic crisis are a direct result of the internal contradictions of the capitalist world-system addressed earlier (see Section 2.2). Wallerstein argues that this system has so far managed to offset these contradictions through a process of continual expansion. This process of expansion has taken two main forms (see also Shannon 1996: 127–131). Fairly obvious is the process of spatial expansion, in which capitalism spreads across the entire globe. Less obvious, meanwhile, is the intensification of capitalist economization, achieved mainly through urbanization and commodification. As a result of urbanization, an increasing proportion of the world population has left rural areas and moved into urban agglomerations, often abandoning its previous mixture of production for the market and for private use in favour of a pure market orientation. Commodification means a process in which an ever greater proportion of daily life is covered by market processes – when, for example, childcare is provided by a service sector enterprise rather than grandparents. Wallerstein asserts that this process of expansion has reached its limits, both in geographical terms and because almost every aspect of life has been commodified. Finally, as a result of several hundred years of uninterrupted capitalist development, the ecosystem is in increasingly bad shape. The structure of the capitalist mode of production, however, Wallerstein tells us, prevents the necessary, highly expensive process of "repair": enterprises cannot pay as this would set back their capital accumulation and the state cannot do so either as this could only happen at the expense of social welfare, thus undermining the social stability of the system.

The inequalities and contradictions of the capitalist world-system have frequently led to the formation of opposition groups. The emergence of such groups, however, has never caused a fundamental crisis of the system. On the contrary, these antisystemic movements have in fact generally helped stabilize the system. This paradoxical development is due to the fact that these movements were co-opted into the capitalist world-system such that they themselves developed an interest in maintaining the system. According to Wallerstein, this form of stabilization too is now coming up against its limits. First, the costs of the approach used hitherto are too high, particularly in the case of the various labour movements, which were incorporated into the system by means of an ever more complex welfare system. Due to a combination of demographic developments and economic stagnation, this welfare state is now increasingly beset by crisis, such that it can no longer be maintained without reducing current levels of capital accumulation. Reduced welfare provision and a marked reduction in support for the periphery diminish the legitimacy of the prevailing order. Wallerstein expects further political crisis triggers to result from the current development of antisystemic movements, which cannot be straightforwardly co-opted. This is because they refuse to organize themselves into the disciplined, centralized form of political parties or because, other than rejecting the system, the goals they pursue are too heterogeneous (the example he mentions here is the development of "rainbow coalitions" in a number of societies of the centre). These crisis tendencies are further reinforced by the dramatic development of global communication systems, which make it increasingly difficult to conceal the massive inequalities in the capitalist world-system while also facilitating global political mobilization. The most recent example of such antisystemic movements is the protests against the WTO (the Seattle movement). The economic and political causes of crisis are ultimately joined by those within the prevailing geoculture. Wallerstein sees a turning point for the dominant ideology of liberalism in the unrest of 1968, which brought together coalitions of students and workers in a number of different places across the world, resulting in strikes, demonstrations and unorthodox, unco-optable forms of political organization (see also Wallerstein 2000: 355–373). Wallerstein sees the attack on the state, as the main pillar of the prevailing order, as the most serious aspect of these events. The state was depicted as paternalistic and repressive, shaking citizens' faith in the legitimacy of the prevailing order. In addition to this undermining of the prevailing geoculture, the crisis of scientism has increasingly seen a questioning of the ideal of absolute truth, even within the natural sciences.

If we accept Wallerstein's assumption that we are now living through the crisis of the prevailing world-system, the question arises as to how long this crisis phase will last and what kind of world-system will emerge from it. Wallerstein himself assumes that this crisis will extend over the next 20–40 years (see Wallerstein 2000: 435–453; 2009) but that its outcome is almost impossible to predict at present. Wallerstein's key argument here is that in phases of crisis systemic constraints are loosened, constraints that otherwise direct actors along fixed channels, so the present generation will play a significant role in structuring the new system. In this situation, it is above all the social sciences that have a responsibility to develop alternatives for this new order. Wallerstein himself hopes for the establishment of a democratic and relatively egalitarian world state, but also thinks it possible that social inequalities, armed conflicts and authoritarian tendencies will intensify.

3 Internal theoretical developments

Wallerstein's world-system theory is a self-contained theoretical edifice, one constantly being developed further by its creator. But this has not prevented other authors from helping develop it. On the contrary, like few contemporary theorists in International Relations, Wallerstein has been in a position to establish a school that has done much to build on his work. Ragin and Chirot (1984: 276) go as far as to refer to an "academic cult". Here I can highlight just a few examples of the broad application of the world-system paradigm as understood in this sense, in contrast to Wallerstein's own world-system theory. I focus on contributions that make reference at least indirectly to International Relations, while largely ignoring studies on anthropology, archaeology, geography, and so on (see Hall 2000).

3.1 Methodological refinements

Many internal theoretical developments concentrate on refining and formalizing the sometimes vague analytical toolkit provided by Wallerstein (see Shannon 1996: 202–204). Particularly impressive in a visual sense is the use of network analysis to determine the position of states within the modern world-system (see Grimes 2000: 36). The first writings to use these mathematical techniques in the social sciences were concerned with the power structure in small communities. People were asked who they turn to (and how often) when problems crop up in their local area. On the basis of systematic surveys, the power structures within these communities can then be depicted mathematically and graphically. In analogous fashion, instead of phone calls, world-system theorists use diplomatic contacts, trade volume and military interventions to depict the position of individual states in the centre, periphery and semiperiphery (see Snyder and Kick 1979; Knoke 1990: 175–202; Kick and Davis 2001). As the comprehensive data needed for network analytical studies is available for all states only for a relatively short period, other researchers have limited themselves to more simple data covering a longer interval, such as gross national product. All these studies, however, confirm the basic assumptions of world-system theory, namely the possibility of a tripartite division of the world into centre, semiperiphery and periphery and the constantly growing inequality between these status groups (Grimes 2000: 38).

All world-system theorists agree that world-systems are subject both to cycles and to long-term trends (see Section 2.2). Building on Wallerstein's theory, however, there has been a marked expansion in the spectrum of trends and cycles subjected to examination and in the corpus of relevant data (see Shannon 1996: 177–180; Grimes 2000: 38–49). We now have significantly better data on the trends mentioned above relating to demography, acquisition of technology and commodification. In addition, the research on economic cycles has become more sophisticated. All important cycles are underpinned by the same logic:

> [A] new set of products are introduced that sell well, the market expands, and related employment swells, allowing for an expansion of worker/"consumer" spending. The market eventually becomes saturated, sales drop, income contracts, and workers are laid off. The effect of the contraction is prolonged by the extended feedback loop through those firms producing capital goods. These manufacturers of the means of production take orders in advance, which means that they are producing machinery for constructing the end product long after the slump in sales of that product has started. This long feedback only prolongs the downturn. But eventually, the excess inventory is sold out, production resumes, and renewed growth is possible.
>
> (Grimes 2000: 42f.)

This regularity applies not just to the "normal" six- to eight-year business cycle (or "Juglar cycle"), which is linked with the acquisition of new capital goods and their depreciation, but also to the 20–25-year "Kuznets cycles" and the Kondratiev cycles mentioned earlier, of such importance to Wallerstein. "Logistics" are an even longer term phenomenon than Kondratiev cycles, though they are rather vague conceptually (see Shannon 1996: 135f.). Methodologically sophisticated studies on all these cycles have appeared over the last few years. Alongside these economic cycles, cycles of hegemony play a major role in the analysis of the capitalist world-system. Again, nuanced empirical studies have appeared on this topic in recent years. The relevant authors disagree not just about the connection between economic cycles (particularly Kondratiev cycles) and the rise of new hegemons, but also about how many states of the centre play the role of hegemonic powers. Diverging from Wallerstein's triad of the Netherlands, Great Britain and the United States, Modelski and Thompson (1996) also identify Portugal (sixteenth century) and ascribe to Great Britain a "dual" hegemonic cycle (200 years).

3.2 A "world-system" or several "world systems"?

Not all world-system theorists limit themselves to merely refining the categories laid down by Wallerstein. Some of them question certain elements of his theoretical edifice and attempt to reconstruct them or his theory as a whole (for a good overview, see Denemark *et al.* 2000). For exemplary purposes I shall describe one of these attempts here. One of the topics debated with particular intensity among Wallerstein's successors is how to "correctly" define a world-system. Different definitions result in quite different perspectives on world history, for example, with respect to when the present-day system began and how to distinguish it from earlier world-systems (see Shannon 1996: 195–202; Grimes 2000: 31–33; Chase-Dunn and Anderson 2005). Wallerstein works on the assumption that because of its capitalist character the modern world-system is unique and that capitalism arose in sixteenth-century Europe for the first and only time before going on to spread to other regions of the world. André Gunder Frank and Barry Gills (2000), meanwhile, argue that for at least 5000 years we have been living in one continuous Afro-Eurasian world system – without a hyphen, in order to distinguish it from Wallerstein's version – that has featured capitalist elements for millennia. In light of this basic idea they set out similarly far-reaching theoretical aspirations, which they sum up as follows:

> (1) the existence and development of the world system stretches back not just five hundred but some five thousand years; (2) the world-economy and its long-distance trade relations form a centerpiece of this world system; (3) the process of capital accumulation is the motor force of world system history; (4) the center–periphery structure is one of the characteristics of the world system; (5) alternation between hegemony and rivalry is depictive of the world system, although system wide hegemony has been rare or non-existent; and (6) long economic cycles of ascending and descending phases underlie economic growth in the world system.
>
> (Frank and Gills 2000: 3)

In this debate there is disagreement, first, over how crucial the upheaval in the early sixteenth century was – that is, whether the "ceaseless" accumulation of capital in fact began then (as Wallerstein assumes). Further, the question arises as to whether a highly developed international division of labour is necessary to the existence of a world system (as Wallerstein assumes) or whether the significantly freer definition put forward by Frank and Gills (2000: 4) is sufficient: "A criterion of systemic participation in a single world system is that no part of this system would be as it is or was if other parts were not as they are or were." With respect to historical (archaeological and anthropological) data, the relevant authors are also at odds over the extent of long-distance trade in the region lying between Egypt and Central Asia around 3000 BC and the impact of this trade on the societies involved. Frank and Gills and Wallerstein also diverge with respect to the role of markets in pre-modern societies. While Wallerstein characterizes these societies as dominated by military coercion ("world empires", see Section 2.1), Frank and Gills assume that markets played a far greater role. The scale of global hegemonies, the start date of cyclical developments, and so on, are also subject to dispute; "continuationists" assume the continuous existence of capitalism (including, alongside Frank and Gills, Kajsa Ekholm-Friedman, Jonathan Friedman, and George Modelski), while "transformationists" assume that a significant turning point occurred in Europe in the sixteenth or seventeenth century (including, alongside Wallerstein, Samir Amin, Christopher Chase-Dunne, and Thomas D. Hall). From the perspective of the dominant theories of international politics, meanwhile, these disputes are trivial if we turn to the radically different perspective on world politics shared by both "world system" and "world-system" theorists. Ultimately, these lively debates about the course – and future – of world history demonstrate the fruitfulness and enduring topicality of the theory building inspired by Wallerstein and others over the last three decades. At the same time, we should keep in mind that the disputes described here are just an example of contemporary empirical and theoretical developments in world-system theory. The theory of global capital accumulation put forward by Giovanni Arrighi (1994, 2008; Arrighi and Silver 1999) should inspire greater interest in the analytical potential of world system theories, particularly the argument that finance capitalism, the currently dominant developmental phase of capitalism (Nölke 2009), is not a novel phenomenon but a recurrent transitional phase between two successive accumulation regimes; compared with conventional interpretations of the financial crisis, this sheds a quite different light on contemporary economic developments (Schmalz 2009: 6).

4 External criticisms

Fundamental criticisms of world-system theory start either with the structure of Wallerstein's theory or its empirical foundation. Besides this, many observers reject his theory because it was influenced by Marxian thought and has a terminology to match. Because this critique is not usually based on an intensive engagement with world-system theory, however, I will not be paying it too much attention here. Critics generally refer to Wallerstein's magnum opus, so it will be my key focus here as well (for an in-depth survey, see Shannon 1996: 155–186).

4.1 Criticisms of Wallerstein's theoretical edifice

As a structuralist theory, Wallerstein's conceptual system attracts the same kind of criticism as other structural schemes (such as neorealism), namely that it is excessively deterministic, leaving insufficient room for the "agency" of individual actors. This criticism is sometimes reinforced by the claim that Wallerstein is an economic reductionist who tries to trace every phenomenon of international politics back to economic factors (see Skocpol 1977: 1078f; Zolberg 1981: 255; Shannon 1996: 155–159). Wallerstein does in fact formulate his theory in a highly deterministic way by assuming that the structure of a given world-system – with the exception of its crisis stage – imposes quite major restrictions on the potential actions of a given state, social class or even household, leaving them very little room for manoeuvre. With respect to the state's capacity for action, this perspective is largely incompatible with the basic assumptions of other theories of International Relations such as classical realism (see the chapter by Andreas Jacobs in this volume) or liberal theory (see the chapter by Siegfried Schieder). Wallerstein recognizes only a few exceptions to the rule that state action is greatly hemmed in by structural economic constraints. Apart from the less-structured transitional phase from one world-system to another, he believes that individual states can move from one position within the world-economy – centre, semiperiphery or periphery – to another only in very specific circumstances, as Japan has done, perhaps to be followed by other East Asian states in the near future. To put it differently, the question of whether governments possess enough autonomy to choose a given path of economic development continues to be highly significant in the context of the contemporary debate on globalization. While the answer to this question is still greatly disputed in empirical terms, Wallerstein must be recognized for his pioneering role in formulating it – and he has provided a great deal of evidence to back up his view of governments in the periphery and semiperiphery (Hobden and Jones 1997: 135).

While some observers regard Wallerstein's perspective as overly Marxian, for others it is not Marxian enough. The key question here is whether Wallerstein defines capitalism correctly, a particularly important question from a Marxian perspective. For Wallerstein, the core hallmark of capitalism is the ceaseless accumulation of capital through the appropriation of profit within the framework of exchange relations, with capitalists selling goods at a price higher than the purchase price (or production costs). Critics have suggested that this definition is imprecise. Brenner (1977: 32), for example, points out that production for exchange is an attribute of many economic systems not usually referred to as capitalist. He goes much further than this, however, suggesting that Wallerstein fails to grasp the core of capitalism, which from a Marxist perspective is not an exchange relationship but a mode of production controlled by a class of property owners and managers, in which labour is bought and sold like any other good (Brenner 1977: 31f.). Profits are obtained by exploiting the working class, with capitalists failing to pass on to them the full value of the goods and services they produce. These differing assumptions about the origin of profit and thus the core of capitalism engender quite different perspectives on the developmental dynamics and crises of the economic system (Hobden and Jones 1997: 135; see also Shannon 1996: 162–165).

Another criticism which is made fairly often relates to the potentially teleological or functionalist character of world-system theory (see Skocpol 1977: 1088; Boeckh 1985: 60f; Shannon 1996: 180–182). Those making this argument point out that Wallerstein superimposes on certain historical realities a significance that is not necessarily objectively justifiable. For example, in light of the contemporary world-system, Wallerstein interprets the events of the past in such a way that they could only have had *one* conceivable outcome (the modern-day world-system). For these critics, he not only attributes too much coherence to world history but also neglects a wide range of potential developmental and explanatory alternatives (Hobden and Jones 1997: 135). This often goes hand-in-hand with criticism of the research strategy deployed by world-system theorists. On this view, such theorists consciously seek out empirical cases that support their theory ("soft cases") and shy away from addressing evidence that – at least at first sight – contradicts their assumptions ("hard cases") and might cause them to modify their theoretical edifice.

4.2 Criticisms of world-system theory's empirical foundations

Beyond claims of functionalism and the associated criticism that Wallerstein has a one-sided perception of historical realities, some critics also cast doubt on his empirical assertions. A key focus here is the conditions for the emergence of capitalism in the sixteenth century. Critics contest both that capitalism in fact arose in the sixteenth century (see Section 3.2) and the causes of the transition to capitalism – accepted by many observers – at this point in time. Of the wide range of explanations of capitalism (Marx, Polanyi, Schumpeter, Weber), I shall briefly present one alternative that approaches Wallerstein's model in terms of the complexity of theoretical argument and breadth of empirical detail and that emphasizes the global dimension of capitalism in much the same way as Wallerstein. I am referring to the work of Hartmut Elsenhans (for a brief summary of his argument, see Elsenhans 1991: Chapter 1). Elsenhans agrees with Wallerstein that capitalism arose in Europe in the sixteenth century. He doubts, however, that the exploitation of the South was necessary to its emergence (much like Brenner 1977; see also Shannon 1996: 169–172). Wallerstein, and many other observers, particular dependency theorists, see a close connection between the emergence of this economic system and the discovery of the New World (1492) and of the sea routes around the Cape of Good Hope (1498), which facilitated the establishment of European long-distance trade and thus the accumulation of capital through exploitation – forced labour, the slave trade, appropriation of monopolistic profits from trade, influx of precious metals, and so on. This exploitation certainly occurred, but, according to Elsenhans, it was no more necessary to the emergence of capitalism than was later colonialism. The money concentrated in the hands of the major overseas trading companies was not used to finance industrial growth in Europe, but to buy land and high office and wage wars. For him, industrial development in Europe was a result of the expansion of small-scale industrial production and was actually hampered by the trading companies (Elsenhans 1991: 18). After all, capitalism did not emerge in Portugal, Spain or northern Italy, but in England. There the Poor Laws introduced towards the end of the sixteenth century ensured the creation of mass purchasing power. This was absorbed primarily by the rapidly growing small businesses run by the lower ranking members of the aristocracy and former peasants in guild-free areas (ibid.: 31). For Elsenhans (from a modified Keynesian perspective), this combination of redistribution to the benefit of the poor and small-scale industrial production is the key to the emergence of capitalism.

Such disputes over the origin of capitalism are of more than merely historical value. Depending on how we think capitalism emerged – through capital accumulation on the basis of exploitation or through the production of mass-produced commodities to meet mass demand – we will have different ideas about how it functions today and what needs to be done to stabilize or do away with it. There are some things, however, that Elsenhans and Wallerstein agree on: intellectually, they agree on the necessity for transdisciplinary, particularly transhistorical and transregional analyses, and in practical political terms they both see it as tremendously important to reduce the massive inequalities that exist across the globe.

Despite the criticisms, which sometimes take a highly polemical form, many observers are united in their admiration for the work of Immanuel Wallerstein. At a time of academic fragmentation and specialization, Wallerstein's contribution stands out, particularly in light of his ability to combine visionary scope and provocation with an almost encyclopaedic mastery of historical detail (Buzan and Little 2001: 30). The fact that a conceptually parsimonious theory that seeks to explain the broad outlines of world history over the last few centuries with reference to a fairly small number of variables cannot always do justice to the empirical minutiae is something that its exponents should be able to live with. And at a time when economic globalization and the tensions between the West and the South dominate the international agenda, it is especially valuable to take a look at Wallerstein's ideas, which have become somewhat unfashionable over the last decade. Even if Wallerstein is wrong – and there is some reason to think he may be with respect to the origins of capitalism – there is a special fascination to his complex work and his vision of the social sciences, particularly for students of International Relations. The subprime mortgage crisis highlights the contemporary relevance of theories that make capitalism and its global character central to the analysis of international politics.

5 Notes

1 The *Annales* School gets its name from its most important organ of publication, the *Annales d'histoire économique et sociale*. Its distinguishing feature vis-à-vis traditional historiography is its focus on longer-term socio-economic developments rather than detailed accounts of political events and personalities.

2 The concept of the *longue durée* describes the influence of environmental changes on human development in contrast to the medium-term impact of social structures (such as capitalism, patriarchy and racism) and the short-term focus of conventional historiography.

6 Bibliography and recommended reading

6.1 Primary texts

Wallerstein, Immanuel 1974: *The Modern World-System I: Capitalist Agriculture and the Origins of the European World-Economy in the Sixteenth Century*. New York: Academic Press.

Wallerstein, Immanuel 1979: *The Capitalist World-Economy*. Cambridge: Cambridge University Press.

Wallerstein, Immanuel 1980: *The Modern World-System II: Mercantilism and the Consolidation of the European World Economy*. New York: Academic Press.

Wallerstein, Immanuel 1989: *The Modern World-System III: The Second Era of Great Expansion of the Capitalist World-Economy*. New York: Academic Press.

Wallerstein, Immanuel 2000: *The Essential Wallerstein*. New York: The New Press.

Wallerstein, Immanuel 2004: *World-Systems Analysis: An Introduction*. Durham, NC: Duke University Press.

Wallerstein, Immanuel 2011: *The Modern World-System IV: Centrist Liberalism Triumphant, 1789–1914*. Berkeley, CA: University of California Press.

The reader is also referred to the two journals of world-system research, the *Review* of the Fernand Braudel Center at the State University of New York (SUNY), Binghamton, formerly headed by Wallerstein, and the *Journal of World-Systems Research* (http://csf.colorado. edu/jwsr/), only available online.

6.2 Secondary texts

Blaschke, Jochen (ed.) 1983: *Perspektiven des Weltsystems. Materialien zu Immanuel Wallerstein: "Das moderne Weltsystem"*.: Frankfurt a. M.: Campus Verlag.

Godfrank, Walter R. 2000: Paradigm Regained? The Rules of Wallerstein's World-System Method, *Journal of World-Systems Research* 6(2): 150–195.

Hall, Thomas D. (ed.) 2000: *A World-System Reader: New Perspectives on Gender, Urbanism, Cultures, Indigenous Peoples, and Ecology*. Lanham, MD: Rowman & Littlefield.

Palumbo-Liu, David, Robbins, Bruce W. and Tanoukhi, Nirvana 2011: *Immanuel Wallerstein and the Problem of the World-System: Scale, Culture*. Durham, NC: Duke University Press.

Shannon, Thomas R. 1996: *An Introduction to the World-System Perspective*, 2nd edn. Boulder, CO: Westview Press.

6.3 Other texts used in this chapter

Arrighi, Giovanni 1994: *The Long Twentieth Century: Money, Power, and the Origins of Our Times*. London: Verso.

Arrighi, Giovanni 2008: *Adam Smith in Beijing: Lineages of the Twenty-First Century*. London: Verso.

Arrighi, Giovanni and Silver, Beverly (eds) 1999: *Chaos and Governance in the Modern World System*. Minneapolis, MN: University of Minnesota Press.

Boeckh, Andreas 1985: Dependencia und kapitalistisches Weltsystem, oder: Die Grenzen globaler Entwicklungstheorien, in Nuscheler, Franz (ed.) *Dritte Welt-Forschung. Entwicklungstheorie und Entwicklungspolitik*. PVS-Sonderheft 16. Opladen: Westdeutscher Verlag, pp. 56–74.

Brenner, Robert 1977: The Origins of Capitalist Development: A Critique of Neo-Smithian Marxism, *New Left Review* 104: 25–93.

Buzan, Barry and Little, Richard 2001: Why International Relations Has Failed as an Intellectual Project and What to Do About it, *Millennium* 30(1): 19–39.

Chase-Dunn, Christopher and Anderson, E. N. (eds) 2005: *The Historical Evolution of World Systems*. Houndmills: Palgrave Macmillan.

Denemark, Robert A. *et al.* (eds) 2000: *World System History: The Social Science of Long-term Change*. London: Routledge.

Elsenhans, Hartmut 1991: *Development and Underdevelopment: The History, Economics and Politics of North–South Relations*. London: Sage.

Frank, André Gunder and Gills, Barry K. 2000: *The Five Thousand Year World System in Theory and Practice*, in Denemark, Robert A. *et al.* (eds) *World System History: The Social Science of Long-term Change*. London: Routledge, pp. 3–23.

Grimes, Peter 2000: Recent Research on World Systems, in Hall, Thomas D. (ed.) *A World-System Reader: New Perspectives on Gender, Urbanism, Cultures, Indigenous Peoples, and Ecology*. Lanham, MD: Rowman & Littlefield, pp. 29–58.

Hall, Thomas D. 2000: *World-Systems Analysis: A Small Sample from a Large Universe*, in Hall, Thomas D. (ed.) *A World-System Reader: New Perspectives on Gender, Urbanism, Cultures, Indigenous Peoples, and Ecology*. Lanham, MD: Rowman & Littlefield, pp. 3–28.

Hobden, Stephen 1998: *International Relations and Historical Sociology: Breaking Down Boundaries*. London: Routledge.

Hobden, Steve and Jones, Richard Wyn 1997: World-System Theory, in Baylis, John and Smith, Steve (eds) *The Globalization of World Politics: An Introduction to International Relations*. Oxford: Oxford University Press, pp. 125–145.

Kick, Edward L. and Davis, Byron L. 2001: World-System Structure and Change. An Analysis of Global Networks and Economic Growth across Two Time Periods, *American Behavioral Scientist* 44(10): 1561–1578.

Knoke, David 1990: *Political Networks: The Structural Perspective*. Cambridge: Cambridge University Press.

Modelski, George and Thompson, William R. 1996: *Innovation, Growth and War: The Coevolution of Global Economics and Politics*. Columbia, SC: University of South Carolina Press.

Nölke, Andreas 2009: Finanzkrise, Finanzialisierung und Vergleichende Kapitalismusforschung, *Zeitschrift für Internationale Beziehungen* 16(1): 123–139.

Ragin, Charles and Chirot, Daniel 1984: The World System of Immanuel Wallerstein: Sociology and Politics as History, in Skocpol, Theda (ed.) *Vision and Method in Historical Sociology*. Cambridge: Cambridge University Press, pp. 276–312.

Schmalz, Stefan 2009: Spielarten der Weltsystemtheorie: Der Ansatz von Giovanni Arrighi, Paper for the joint conference "Kapitalismustheorien" of the ÖGPW and DVPW, 24 and 25 April, Vienna.

Skocpol, Theda 1977: Wallerstein's World Capitalist System: A Theoretical and Historical Critique, *American Journal of Sociology* 82(5): 1075–1102.

Snyder, David and Kick, Edward L. 1979: Structural Position in the World System and Economic Growth, 1955–1970: A Multiple-Network Analysis of Transnational Interactions, *American Journal of Sociology* 84(4): 1096–1126.

Viotti, Paul R. and Kauppi, Mark V. 1993: *International Relations Theory: Realism, Pluralism, Globalism*. New York: Macmillan.

Wallerstein, Immanuel 1991: *Geopolitics and Geoculture: Essays on the Changing World-System*. Cambridge: Cambridge University Press.

Wallerstein, Immanuel 1995: *After Liberalism*. New York: The New Press.

Wallerstein, Immanuel *et al.* 1996: *Open the Social Sciences: Report of the Gulbenkian Commission on the Restructuring of the Social Sciences*. Stanford, CA: Stanford University Press.

Wallerstein, Immanuel 2009: Follow Brazil's Example. Reimagining Socialism, *The Nation*, March 23.

Zolberg, Aristide R. 1981: Origins of the Modern World System. A Missing Link, *World Politics* 33(2): 253–281.

Neo-Gramscian perspectives

Andreas Bieler and Adam David Morton

1 Introduction

The global political economy is undergoing profound change. This is evident in developments since the global economic crisis of the 1970s, while the collapse of real existing socialism in the early 1990s marked the end of the post-World War II order.

The post-WWII world order was characterized by the Bretton Woods system, which was crucially influenced by the United States. On the basis of fixed exchange rates and the US dollar as lead currency, this system steered international financial relations through the International Monetary Fund (IMF) and shaped international trade relations through the General Agreement on Tariffs and Trade (GATT). This order was based on so-called embedded liberalism, whose core principle was liberalization and international free trade. But it also legitimized governments' efforts to intervene to regulate the national economy: to redistribute the national wealth in order to ensure internal stability and social peace (Ruggie 1982). Embedded liberalism was achieved through the Western welfare state.

There is broad agreement that the structural characteristics of embedded liberalism have ceased to pertain since the early 1970s and that the so-called Pax Americana no longer exists. The global economic crisis of the early 1970s, above all, the abolition of gold–dollar convertibility by President Nixon and the subsequent "oil price shocks", plunged the Western industrial states into deep recession. The Fordist accumulation regime based on mass production and mass consumption seemed to have outlived its usefulness. A Keynesian policy of demand management on the national level was clearly no longer capable of stimulating the economy. Against the background of the transnationalization of production and the activities of transnational companies (TNCs) as new and important international actors, along with the development of a global financial market, the question arose as to whether states now had any capacity at all to manage their own economies. In the context of the decline of American hegemony, which seemed confirmed by "Vietnam", and the economic resurgence of Japan and Europe, this was primarily a question of the United States' capacity to lead the international system and thus of whether cooperation was possible "after hegemony"[1] (see also the chapters by Manuela Spindler and Bernhard Zangl in this volume).

These empirical developments prompted many to question established, or orthodox, approaches within International Relations (IR). As far as "critical" authors were concerned, neither institutionalist approaches, such as interdependence analysis or regime theory, nor neorealism, seemed to offer acceptable explanations for these changing structures. As a result, in the early 1980s, what are sometimes referred to as "traditional" approaches within IR faced a fundamental challenge from critical perspectives, which include feminist and postmodern approaches as well as the critical theory of historical materialism (see the chapters by Barbara Finke, Thomas Diez and Christoph Humrich in this volume). The development of *neo-Gramscian perspectives* in the early 1980s must also be regarded as part of the rejection of established approaches within IR. Based on a historical materialist understanding of social change and drawing on the insights of the Italian Marxist Antonio Gramsci[2] (hence the term neo-Gramscian perspectives, Italian School or even *transnational historical materialism*; see Bieling *et al.* 1998: 7), Robert Cox[3] developed a *critical theory of hegemony, world order and historical change* (see especially Cox 1981, 1983 and 1987). While Gramsci was mainly interested in explaining the mechanisms of bourgeois domination within Western states, various neo-Gramscian perspectives extend this interest to transnational relations of power and domination and develop a critique of global capitalism. This is done through a critical examination of neorealism (especially Waltz 1979), neoliberal institutionalism (especially Keohane 1984) and world-system analysis (especially Wallerstein 1974). Neo-Gramscians criticize the "static" character of these approaches and their resulting inability to explain change. Cox criticizes neorealism for its conception of international relations of power and domination, which is fixated on the state and in which the structure of the international system compels states to behave in the same way at all times (see also the chapter by Niklas Schörnig in this volume). According to Cox, neoliberal institutionalism too (and above all regime theory) is based on the assumption that states should be regarded as the most important actors (see the chapter by Bernhard Zangl). For Cox, world-system analysis works on the assumption of a static world system composed of states of the periphery, semi-periphery and core (see the chapter by Andreas Nölke). This, Cox believes, makes it impossible to analyse structural *change*. Further, these approaches help maintain prevailing social relations of power, with all their injustices, within an existing order. Cox, therefore, describes these approaches as *problem solving*. A critical theory, on the other hand, "does not take institutions and social and power relations for granted but calls them into question by concerning itself with their origins and whether they might be in the process of changing" (Cox 1981: 129).

Cox's theory is critical in the sense that it is fundamentally interested in how a world order comes to be, what structures of power and domination are characteristic of a given world order, how these are reproduced and secured and what "forces" (in the sense of class actors) within an existing world order have the emancipatory potential to change it. Cox's critical theory is based on a dialectic conception of history that is centred on the constant process of historical change and investigates the potential for alternative developments (Cox 1981: 129, 133–134). The relations of production play an important role in this perspective.[4] In what follows, we set out Cox's approach step-by-step.

2 Hegemony, world order(s) and historical change: the neo-Gramscian perspective of Robert Cox

To gain some initial purchase on neo-Gramscian perspectives, it is helpful to shed some more light on the concept of *hegemony*. In colloquial speech, hegemony means pre-eminence, supremacy or even leadership. Neorealism also uses this term. Here, however, hegemony is viewed straightforwardly as a state's dominance, based on its economic and military capacity. The rise and fall of hegemonic powers follow certain iron (and timeless) laws (hegemonic cycles) (see the chapter by Niklas Schörnig in this volume). Neo-Gramscian perspectives, on the other hand, try to understand the development of hegemony historically. They view hegemonic structures as the product of social processes, which also include social, cultural and ideological dimensions in their definition of hegemonic structures. Here hegemony implies prevailing structures of power and domination secured by a combination of coercion and consensus. The latter finds expression in the general acceptance of certain ideas by a large number of actors and is also undergirded by material resources and institutions. Hegemony thus establishes a relationship of power and domination in the sense of a (world) order underpinned by consensus and coercion.

> Hegemony at the international level is . . . not merely an order among states. It is an order within a world economy with a dominant mode of production which penetrates into all countries and links into other subordinate modes of production. It is also a complex of international social relationships which connect the social classes of the different countries. World hegemony is describable as a social structure, an economic structure and a political structure; and it cannot be simply one of these things but must be all three. World hegemony, furthermore, is expressed in universal norms, institutions and mechanisms which lay down general rules of behaviour for states and for those forces of civil society that act across national boundaries – rules which support the dominant mode of production.
>
> (Cox 1983: 171–172)

Neo-Gramscian perspectives work on the assumption that hegemony develops on three levels of action within a highly specific "historical structure"[5]:

1 on the level of *social relations of production*, which comprise the totality of social relations in material, institutional and discursive terms and generate social class forces as key actors;
2 on the level of the state or *state forms*, which are based on historically determined and interwoven complexes of state and civil society; and
3 on the level of various *world orders*, which not only represent phases of peace and conflict, but also prompt reflection on how alternative forms of world order might come about. The levels of action are presented schematically in Figure 1 (Cox 1981: 138).

As actors, "social forces" are active on each level and concurrently on all three levels. Because the relationship between the levels of action is conceived in a dialectic rather than linear way, in analytical terms *each* of these levels may form the starting point for an examination of historical processes (ibid.: 153).

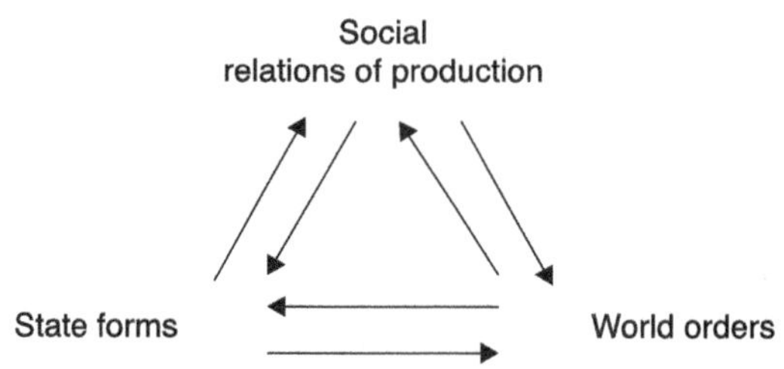

Figure 1

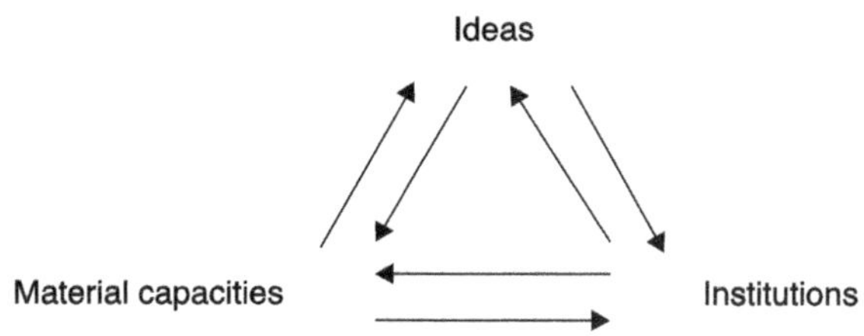

Figure 2

Cox argues that on each of the three levels of action three more reciprocal elements combine to form historical structures, which are important to understanding how hegemony arises. These are:

1 *ideas*, which are understood as intersubjective conditions or collective notions of social order;
2 *material capacities* based on resources; and
3 *institutions*, through which ideas and material conditions are linked with one another in a specific way and that function to stabilize a particular order.

This dialectically conceived relationship between material conditions, institutions and ideas may be shown schematically in Figure 2.

So the goal of this perspective is to reconstruct hegemonic historical structures by laying bare the social and international realities of production, power and domination. In this view a historical structure consists of a specific constellation of social relations of production, form of state and world order (Cox 1987: 396–398).

So far we have provided only a rough outline of Cox's approach by presenting its fundamental components. Let us now take a closer look.

2.1 Relations of production and social forces

For Cox, the structures expressed in the social relations of production must be our point of departure if we wish to understand and analyse the development of hegemony. But this does not mean that his approach endorses economic reductionism or determinism. As a historical materialist, he does view the production of the material conditions of existence as a fundamental human activity. Despite this, Cox rejects the assumption that social structures and different state forms are simply determined by the economic relations of production. His concept of production is far more broadly conceived:

> Production . . . is to be understood in the broadest sense. It is not confined to the production of physical goods used or consumed. It covers the production and reproduction of knowledge and of the social relations, morals and institutions that are prerequisites to the production of physical goods.
>
> (Cox 1989: 39)

He thus refers to the structures found in the sphere of production as "modes of social relations of production", which comprise the configuration of social forces involved in the production process. Examples include subsistence-level agricultural production as well as "internationalized" forms of production organized through multinational companies. The objective of describing different forms of social relations of production is to identify what promotes the appearance of these forms and how these forms are connected and transformed (Cox 1987: 103). For Cox, the reciprocal relationship between production and power is of crucial importance. In order to investigate this relationship, he develops an approach focused on how specific social relations of production generate specific social class forces, how these forces establish the basis of their power through state forms and how this in turn influences world order. This approach builds on the social ontology of historical structures (ibid.: 4). It refers to the "persistent social practices, made by collective human activity and transformed through collective human activity" (ibid.: 4). So this approach attempts to comprehend "the reciprocal relationship of structures and actors" (Cox 1995a: 33; Cox 2000: 55–59; Bieler and Morton 2001b).

In contrast to established approaches such as neorealism and regime theory, which understand the state as a homogeneous actor and as the only significant actor, neo-Gramscian perspectives identify social classes ("social forces" is the usual term) as key actors. Here hegemony is understood as a form of class domination. Rather than a static analytical category, Cox understands class as a historical category, and he uses it heuristically (Cox 1987: 355–357; [1985] 1996: 57). For him – in contrast to "orthodox" Marxist approaches – class identity does not result automatically from the place of various social forces within the relations of production, but is always the outcome of specific situations of historical conflict (see Thompson 1978). "Bring back exploitation as the hallmark of class, and at once class struggle is in the forefront, as it should be" (Ste. Croix 1981: 57). This focus on exploitation and resistance to it guarantees that social forces are not simply reduced to material aspects, but include other forms of identity that are bound up with struggles – such as ethnic affiliation, nationality, religion and gender. To sum up, we might say that " 'non-class' issues – peace, ecology, and feminism – are not to be set aside but given a firm and conscious basis in the social realities shaped through the production process" (Cox 1987: 353). Kees van der Pijl has elaborated on this conception of class struggle. Neoliberal capitalism, he argues, has now extended exploitation to the processes of social reproduction – as exemplified in the application of capitalist profit criteria to health systems – and to the environment. Resistance to this, whether from progressive social movements, green parties or populist nationalist movements may be understood as class struggle just as much as the conflict between employers and employees in the workplace (van der Pijl 1998: 36–49).

2.2 State forms and the concept of the historical bloc

The conceptual framework we have set out so far analyses how the social relations of production within certain state forms (such as mercantilist, welfare state, state capitalist, neoliberal, and so on) are established. Changes in the relations of production lead to new configurations of social forces. State power in turn builds on these configurations. Rather than treating the state as a given or already constituted institutional category, the analyst considers the historical constructions of various state forms and the social contexts of political struggles. This is achieved by referring to the concept of the historical bloc, thus expanding the theory of the state to include relations within civil society.

The term historical bloc refers to the manner in which leading social forces establish dominance over subordinate social forces within a specific national context. This is more than a simple political alliance between classes or class fractions. The term "historical bloc" refers to the integration of a variety of class interests that are propagated throughout society, "bringing about not only a unison of economic and political aims, but also intellectual and moral unity . . . on a 'universal' plane" (Gramsci 1971: 181–182). The nature of the historical bloc as such necessarily entails the existence of hegemony. Hegemony is established "if the relationship between intellectuals and people-nation, between the leaders and the led, the rulers and the ruled, is provided by an organic cohesion" (ibid.: 418).

These concerns are inherent in the emphasis on the various state forms, which – as Cox states – differ fundamentally in terms of the characteristics of their historical blocs, that is, the configuration of social forces on which state power ultimately rests. "A particular configuration of social forces defines in practice the limits or parameters of state purposes, and the modus operandi of state action, defines, in other words, the *raison d'état* for a particular state" (Cox 1987: 105). To sum up, by analysing various state forms we can examine the social basis of a state and comprehend the historical "content" of different states. This concept also helps us recognize alternative developmental possibilities by pointing out the contradictions within the historical bloc on which a state form was established, and elaborating what potential there may be to form a rival historical bloc and a different state form (ibid.: 409).

In contrast to conventional state-centred approaches within IR, a broader theory of the state is inherent in this neo-Gramscian perspective, which includes investigation of the complex of state and civil society. Instead of underestimating state power and declaring that it does not exist, our attention is directed towards social forces and processes and how they behave with respect to the development of states (Cox 1981: 128).

Gramsci understood the state not simply as an institution limited to the "government of the functionaries" or to the "top political leaders and personalities with direct governmental responsibilities"; instead "the state is the entire complex of practical and theoretical activities with which the ruling class not only justifies and maintains its dominance, but manages to win the active consent of those over whom it rules" (Gramsci 1971: 244). Here the state is understood not just as the apparatus of government operating within the "public" sphere (government, parties, the armed forces). It is also understood as part of the "private" sphere of civil society (church, media, education) through which hegemony functions (Gramsci 1971: 261). The state, then, is not defined uncritically as a kind of institutional category or as a "thing in itself", but is the expression of a form of social relations through which capitalism and hegemony are expressed. It is this combination of political and civil society, which is referred to as the "integral state", through which the ruling classes organize intellectual and moral functions, as well as coercion, as part of the political and cultural struggle over hegemony (Gramsci 1971: 258, 271).

Different social relations of production generate different social class fractions. Transnational foreign capital is not simply an autonomous force outside of state influence, but represents certain classes or class fractions within the state apparatus. These contradictory and heterogeneous relations within the state are a result of the antagonism between national and transnational fractions of capital and labour. So the state is a condensed form of the hegemonic relationship between the dominant class and other class fractions. This condensation of a hegemonic relationship occurs when a leading class develops a "hegemonic project" that goes beyond its own economic interests and is capable of binding together the differing aspirations and shared interests of different social classes and class fractions. This is a process of the "most purely political phase" of the class struggle, which occurs on a " 'universal' plane" and results in the formation of a historical bloc (ibid.: 263).

2.3 Hegemony and world order(s)

Though originally a national phenomenon, the hegemony of a social class may in principle spread beyond the nation when a particular form of the social relations of production is extended to other countries, ultimately leading to a situation in which the national organization of production is integrated into a hierarchy of globally intertwined structures of production (Cox 1983: 171; 1987: 149–150). Such a process of expansion makes it possible to link the social forces in different countries: "A world hegemony is thus in its beginnings an outward expansion of the internal (national) hegemony established by a . . . social class" (Cox 1983: 171). This highlights the capacity of hegemonic forces to universalize their interests via generally accepted ideas, norms, rules and institutions, backed by their political and military geopolitical capabilities.

The outwardly directed expansion of a particular form of social relations of production and of the interests of a leading class may also be supported by international institutions. Gramsci (1971: 243) called this the "internal and international organisational relations of the state", which include associations and organizations such as the Rotary Club or the Roman Catholic Church that have a transnational character but are nonetheless firmly anchored within a particular state.

Hegemony, then, "operates" on two levels. First, through the construction of a historical bloc and the creation of social cohesion within a state form and second through the international "projection" of hegemony on the level of world order. One example that occurred in Gramsci's day was the expansion of Fordist assembly plants beyond the borders of the United States, through which the power of "Americanism and Fordism" was established from the 1920s and 1930s on, ultimately culminating in global hegemony (Gramsci 1971: 277–318; see also van der Pijl 1984).

2.4 The Pax Americana and globalization

It is one of the main aims of neo-Gramscian perspectives to explain processes of structural change. The transition, roughly outlined in the introduction to this chapter, from the post-war order of embedded liberalism to globalization, is a key field of empirical study in Cox's work. In what follows we discuss in depth his perspective on these processes of change, our main goal being to cast more light on his theoretical approach, as set out in earlier sections, by reference to an empirical example.

Cox argues that until the early 1970s a hegemonic world order led by the United States – also known as the Pax Americana – held sway. This rested on the principle, mentioned earlier, of embedded liberalism. Its concomitant expression at the level of state form was the so-called Keynesian welfare state – a model characterized by state intervention in the economy (i.e. a policy of full employment through budget deficits and an expansive welfare system) (Gill and Law 1988: 79–80).[6] The social relations of production underpinning this state form were organized around a Fordist regime of accumulation based on mass production, mass consumption and tripartite corporatism (a coalition of government, industry and employers) (Cox 1987: 219–230). The global economic crises of the 1970s shook this order, along with the social relations of power that supported it within the Western welfare states. Cox identifies two tendencies as the main causes of this structural change: the internationalization of production and the internationalization of the state.

Since the erosion of the world ordering principles inherent in the Pax Americana in the 1970s, the *internationalization of the structures of production* has intensified, a process unfolding at the top of an emerging global class structure and propelled by a "transnational managerial class" (Cox 1981: 147). By using differences in wage levels and systems of social security between individual states, transnational companies have fostered the integration of production structures on a transnational level: they have organized the production of various elements of a single production process in different geographical locations. Alongside the "transnational manager class" that has developed in the course of this process, the internationalization of the structures of production has been supported by other actors in the sphere of productive capital – particularly manufacturing industry. This includes small and medium-sized enterprises that function as contracting partners and suppliers, import-export businesses, and sections of finance capital active in banking, insurance and finance.

These processes have been fostered by state elites active in international organizations and supported by the perspectives of industry, state officials and representatives of international organizations, which have converged as a result of these processes and clearly privilege the "logic of capitalist market relations". These processes have ultimately increased the structural power of transnational capital (Gill and Law 1988: 484). They have been shaped by the contradictions between *transnational* forces of capital and *national* capital fractions. Because of their great dependency on national or regional protective measures (protectionism), national capital fractions, rooted in structures of production organized on the national level, have resisted global competition. For Cox, the working class is split along two lines. First, there are conflicts between people working for transnational and national companies. Second, there are conflicts between workers who generally have secure jobs, members of the core workforce of transnational companies, and those on the "periphery" of the labour market who have only short-term contracts or work part-time (Cox 1981: 235). In short, through the internationalization of the structures of production globalization has led to the fragmentation of capital and labour into transnational and national social class forces.

As Cox sees it, now that the Pax Americana is over, international hegemony is no longer linked so strongly to the role of a leading nation state, but is the expression of the hegemony of social forces – above all, transnational capital and the support it receives from the transnational section of the working class.

From a neo-Gramscian perspective, the internationalization of production equates to a fundamental change in the social basis of the state. This change is often referred to as the "retreat of the state" (Strange 1996). Robert Cox, conversely, argues that while the internationalization of the structures of production may not be eroding the role of the state (in the sense of a "retreat"), it is changing it fundamentally. He seeks to capture this dynamic by referring to the "internationalization of the state". He shows how the internationalization of the structures of production – together with accompanying transnational processes of consensus-forming and geopolitical power supported by international institutions such as the World Bank and International Monetary Fund – is "mediated" by the state. As a consequence these processes lead to the privileging of those state organs and institutions within a state apparatus that have a special connection to the global economy. These include presidents' and prime ministers' offices, finance ministries and central banks. This privileging occurs at the expense of institutions with a more national focus such as labour and industrial ministries (Cox 1992: 31). Regardless of whether we are talking about the state forms of Western industrialized countries or states on the periphery, the state is understood as a "transmission belt" through which the national and regional levels are adapted to the neoliberal logic of capitalist competition (ibid.: 31).

3 From the internationalization of the state to globalization: the differentiation of neo-Gramscian perspectives

In the 1980s and 1990s, apart from Cox, the most important studies from a neo-Gramscian perspective probably came from Stephen Gill, also at York University in Toronto, and from scholars at the University of Amsterdam (especially Otto Holman 1996; Henk Overbeek 1990; and Kees van der Pijl 1984, 1998).[7] Further, a number of multi-authored volumes appeared in the 1990s that brought together a broad spectrum of theoretical and empirical analyses of contemporary globalization (Gill 1993a; Hettne 1995; Overbeek 1993; Gill and Mittelmann 1997).[8] In order to present the different forms taken by neo-Gramscian theory and its further development, we had to make a selection from the wide range of studies now available. In what follows we can therefore consider only the most important theoretical trends that diverge from Cox's work. In making this selection, our main goal has been to show that neo-Gramscian perspectives, as a diverse plurality, can inform empirically productive investigations of a broad range of globalization-related issues.

Stephen Gill has given the thesis of the internationalization of the state a more solid theoretical foundation. His approach differs somewhat from that of Cox. Like Cox, Gill places the global restructuring of production in the context of structural changes in the 1970s. According to Gill, during this period a transition occurred from the "international historical bloc" of social forces established in the period following the Second World War to a "transnational historical bloc". This linked and integrated the interests and identities of social forces across national boundaries and classes. Further, though, it established very specific conditions under which a *hegemony of transnational capital* might take shape. It is apparent here that for Gill economic and political elites such as the "transnational managerial class" are of far greater significance than they are for Cox (see also Gill's empirical study of the Trilateral Commission: Gill 1990). Gill focuses on transnational networks of production and investigates how national governments lose their political autonomy through the process of transnationalization, while at the same time having become an integrated part of this process and to some extent its agents.

Gill sees a restructuring of relations of production and finance propelled by transnational capital and thus the emergence of a new transnational regime of accumulation. This development revolves around two key processes: the so-called "new constitutionalism" of "disciplinary neoliberalism" and the concomitant spread of market society.

The core of "new constitutionalism" is the spread of "market discipline" – in other words, macroeconomic principles such as market efficiency, discipline and competitiveness – along with associated political-institutional support. What this camouflages is "the move towards the construction of legal or constitutional devices to remove or insulate substantially the new economic institutions from popular scrutiny or democratic accountability" (Gill 1992: 165). This process is reinforced by the policies of international institutions, which have now shifted in a neoliberal direction, particularly the IMF, the GATT/WTO and G-7, and by processes of regional integration such as the EU and the North American Free Trade Agreement (NAFTA) (Gill 2001). Through the spread of the concept of market society, based on the ideology of capitalist progress, and the concomitant establishment of exclusionary and hierarchical political structures, the "new constitutionalism" aims to present neoliberalism as the only possible developmental model (Gill 1995: 399).

Gill – diverging from Cox – points out that the consolidation of neoliberalism is based on *supremacy* rather than hegemony. Supremacy entails the dominance of a historical bloc over a fragmented opposition (Gill 1995: 400, 402, 412). This idea is matched by a conceptual difference that distinguishes Gill from Cox: a historical bloc "may at times have the potential to become hegemonic" (Gill 1993b: 40). Gill thus implicitly assumes that a historical bloc may exist even without hegemony – in other words, without consensual safeguards.[9]

Other authors have used the concept of supremacy to analyse the United States' policies towards the Third World in the context of demands for a "new international economic order" in the 1970s (Augelli and Murphy 1988). For Augelli and Murphy, the spread of the ideology of American liberalism, based on individualism and free trade, played a fundamental role in securing US supremacy in the 1970s and 1980s. For these authors, however, this supremacy is not based simply on American dominance. They introduce a distinction between supremacy, dominance and hegemony, in which it is only through dominance or hegemony that supremacy arises (Augelli and Murphy 1988: 132). Gramsci (1971: 57) himself stated that "the supremacy of a social group manifests itself in two ways, as 'domination' and as 'intellectual and moral leadership' ". While the first variant of supremacy entails subordination through force, the second refers to an alliance led by a hegemon. Through this distinction, Augelli and Murphy highlight the coercive character of US hegemony in its Third World policies – in contrast to its hegemonic leadership role vis-à-vis allies.

Rupert (1995) investigates the development of the Fordist accumulation regime in the USA, based on mass production, and shows how this new mode of production underpinned US hegemony in the post-war era. In an earlier work (Rupert 1990), he investigated the role played by trade union disputes as the new mode of production was being established within the mass production industries in the United States. Building on these studies, Rupert also investigated the clash of social forces over the North American Free Trade Agreement in the US (Rupert 2000).

Processes of transnational class formation in Europe and problems of European integration in the context of globalization, especially conflicts over the best model of capitalism for Europe in the future, are also classical theoretical and empirical foci of neo-Gramscian perspectives (Holman 1992, 1996; Bieler 2000, 2006; Bieler and Morton 2001a; van Apeldoorn 2002; Cafruny and Ryner 2003; Overbeek 2003; van Apeldoorn *et al.* 2009; Nousios *et al.* 2012). Other key topics include the eastward expansion of the EU and the concomitant neoliberal restructuring of the new member states (Bohle 2002, 2006; Holman 2004; Shields 2012).

Robinson (2004) has made a detailed study of the internationalization of structures of production and the concomitant development of transnational state structures. This led to a debate within neo-Gramscian perspectives in which Morton (2007a), in particular, analysed the continuing importance of state forms to capitalism and asserted that "the manner in which the rule of capital is maintained is thus advanced best through a nodal appreciation of state formation processes" (Morton 2007a: 150).

With respect to the spread of capitalism through processes of "uneven and combined development" (see several of the chapters in Anievas 2010), the concept of "passive revolution" has also become increasingly important. This concept relates to processes of restructuring prompted "from above" that displace the class demands "from below" within civil society (Morton 2007a: 150–170; 2007b; 2010a; 2010b; Hesketh 2010). A passive revolution refers to processes in which aspects of the social relations of capitalist development are either instituted and/or expanded, resulting in both "revolutionary" rupture and a "restoration" of social relations. Also important is the formulation of a critique of the "varieties of capitalism" literature, which attempts to explain structural change primarily with respect to national institutions (Bruff 2008; Macartney 2009a). Finally, a number of studies tackle US interventions in countries of the periphery (e.g. Robinson 1996) or scrutinize processes of state formation and the construction and contestation of hegemony in Mexico (e.g. Morton 2011).

So there are now a large number of neo-Gramscian perspectives that seek to shed light on the problems of the global political economy through a critical theory of hegemony, world order and historical change.

4 Welcome discussions: controversies over neo-Gramscian approaches

Criticisms of neo-Gramscian approaches began in the 1990s. But the IR mainstream has not really responded to these approaches (Scherrer 1998: 161). Those authors who have put forward criticisms have generally been ones whose own perspectives are close to historical materialism. Their criticisms cannot therefore be regarded as "external" in any straightforward sense.

For *critics arguing from an "orthodox" Marxist standpoint*, neo-Gramscian perspectives lack historical-material "rigour". For Peter Burnham (1991), the neo-Gramscian definition of hegemony, for example, represents a "pluralist empiricism" that overlooks the central importance of relations of production. For Burnham, because neo-Gramscian approaches attribute equal importance to ideas and material conditions, they overlook the contradictions of the social relations of production as the fundamental structural constraints of capitalism, which is tantamount to lapsing into a purely idealist explanation of economic policies (ibid.: 81). For him, neo-Gramscian perspectives fundamentally overstate the potential for political strategies and thus conscious action. For Burnham, it is above all economic laws, particularly the law of value, that are of relevance to the reproduction of dominance within a society and within international relations (see also Burnham 1994).[10] In our own work, we have responded to this criticism by highlighting the material structure of ideas, i.e. the way different discourses are rooted in the material reality of class struggles (Bieler and Morton 2008).

Scherrer (1998: 165–166), in turn, criticizes the fact that neo-Gramscian perspectives, though they highlight the fundamental importance of relations of production to the development of hegemony, fail to explore to what extent functional economic realities (he mentions the example of the balance of payments) influence the actions of political agents. This criticism applies above all to Gill (Scherrer also mentions counterexamples from the wide range of neo-Gramscian approaches), who clearly works on the assumption that elites possess greater freedom of action than others (for a critique of this fixation on elites, see the detailed argument put forward by Scherrer 1998: 169).

The neo-Gramscian *thesis of the internationalization of the state* has also come in for criticism. Leo Panitch in particular argues that neo-Gramscian approaches seek to explain the role of the state in a way that is too "top-down" with respect to the emergence of power relations: globalization is understood as a process involving a movement from the global to the national or from "outside" to "inside". On this view, as the core of the thesis of the internationalization of the state, the metaphor of a "transmission belt", moving from the global to the national level, overlooks the fact that globalization is brought about actively *by states themselves* (Panitch 1994). Panitch thus disputes Cox's assertion that the nation state is undergoing a functional shift that is turning it into a mere transmission belt between the global economy and national societies, as this underestimates the role of the nation state in contemporary processes of globalization. For Panitch, this is to view the state as a kind of "victim" of the structural and organizational power of capital (Panitch 1996: 89–96).

Other authors also dispute the thesis of the internationalization of the state (e.g. Baker 1999) and suggest that greater account must be taken of such things as the mutual interactions between the global and local level (Ling 1996). For these critics, it is above all class conflicts within national social formations that neo-Gramscian perspectives ignore (Moran 1998). The role of the state, as Panitch among others states (1994: 74), is still determined by struggles between social forces within specific national social formations, though this is not to deny that social forces are of great importance within transnational structures.

In response, Cox himself has pointed out that the internationalization of the state and the role of transnational elites in forging a consensus has yet to be fully understood and thus requires further research (1992: 30–31; he has also called this a "nébuleuse"). The thesis of the internationalization of the state, Cox states, is based merely on a number of interlinked hypotheses that point to areas requiring empirical research (Cox [1993] 1996: 276).

From a broader perspective, critics have suggested that the hegemony of transnational capital has been overestimated and that it actually has far less potential to bring about a transformation of the world order. They question the impression often made of a largely smooth and consistent neoliberal restructuring of the global economy. Such analyses, according to André Drainville (1994: 125), "must give way to more active sorties against transnational neo-liberalism, and the analysis of concepts of control must beget original concepts of resistance". Thus, as Paul Cammack (1999) also believes, it is important to bring out not just the coherence of neoliberalism but also the potential for *counterhegemonic movements*. Far too often, Cammack asserts, the issue of counterhegemonic movements and thus the potential for a transformation of the existing order is left for future research. The mobilization against the World Trade Organization (Seattle, November 1999), the unrest during the G8 meeting in Genoa (July 2001) as well as the ongoing processes of resistance within the World Social Forum, demonstrate the need to view globalization as an arena of highly contested social relations. A number of authors have responded to these criticisms by analysing both the possible role of trade unions as part of this resistance (Bieler 2006; Bieler and Lindberg 2010) and by scrutinizing the situation of unprotected workers within the global economy (Bieler *et al.* 2008; Davies and Ryner 2006). Studies have also been made of resistance to neoliberal restructuring in Mexico (Morton 2011; Hesketh 2013). Macartney (2009b) has looked at the contemporary financial crisis from a neo-Gramscian perspective.

A final significant criticism of neo-Gramscian perspectives highlights the necessity of engaging more intensively with Gramsci's work, and above all of gaining a correct conception of the Italian thinker's complex methodological, ontological and epistemological concerns (Germain and Kenny 1998). There is a risk, some critics assert, that some of Gramsci's concepts, which have been detached from their historical-political context, might lose the theoretical significance they once possessed. But this call for a re-examination of Gramsci's own historical situation should not prevent us from understanding ideas both within as well as beyond their specific historical context, without insisting on the need to "scale-up" Gramsci's concepts to the international level (Morton 2007a: 15–38; Morton 2007b; Ives and Short 2013).

> [What matters] is the way . . . in which Gramsci's legacy gets interpreted, transmitted and used so that it [can] remain an effective tool not only for the critical analysis of hegemony but also for the development of an alternative politics and culture.
>
> (Buttigieg 1986: 15)

It is vital to engage constructively with these criticisms if neo-Gramscian perspectives are to continue to develop in a conceptually and empirically productive way. Equally important is critical engagement with other recent historical materialist advances, including work by historical geographical materialists on the spatial logistics of state power and the contradictions of space (see, for example, Harvey [1982] 2006), discussions of Leon Trotsky's notion of "uneven and combined development" (Rosenberg 2006; Morton 2011; Bieler 2013) and debates about the role of states in globalization and a perceived new imperialism (see, for example, Callinicos 2009; Panitch and Gindin 2012). Only by remaining open to other developments in historical materialist scholarship, by reaching beyond established concepts, will neo-Gramscian perspectives be able to retain their intellectual vibrancy.

5 Notes

1 To quote the title of Keohane (1984) in which – building on interdependence analysis – he did much to establish regime theory.

2 Antonio Gramsci (1891–1937) was active in the workers' councils movement – a radical labour movement – in Turin towards the end of the First World War, primarily as editor of the newspaper *L'Ordine Nuovo* (New Order) and was later involved in the founding of the Italian Communist Party, of which he was president until his arrest by the fascist regime in 1926. During his imprisonment, he composed 33 notebooks, first published as the *Prison Notebooks* in Italian in the 1950s, and later in many other languages.

3 From 1977 on, Robert Cox taught political science and carried out research at York University in Toronto, Canada. He was formerly director of the International Institute for Labour Studies, part of the International Labour Organization (ILO) and professor at Columbia University in New York. Cox (1996) contains a brief autobiographical account of Cox's intellectual influences.

4 Cox thus adheres to the "productionist paradigm" of critical theory. See also the chapter on critical theory by Christoph Humrich in this volume. In the introduction to his chapter he makes a clear distinction between the "communicative paradigm" of critical theory in the wake of Habermas and the "productionist paradigm" of critical theory.

5 Cox borrows the concept of "historical structure" from Fernand Braudel.

6 It is important to note here that Cox calls the Keynesian welfare state the "neoliberal state". We do not follow Cox's usage here in order to avoid confusion with the conventional understanding of neoliberalism, which relates to processes in the late 1970s and 1980s that Cox calls "hyperliberalism".

7 The latter group are often referred to as the "Amsterdam School". On this group and for an overview of their work, see especially van Apeldoorn (2004). The establishment of such schools should, however, be avoided, as it entails the risk of simplifying internal contradictions and often leads to the formation of orthodoxies. This in turn undermines the relevant authors' theoretical diversity and critical intentions. For the same reason we should speak of neo-Gramscian perspectives, plural, rather than neo-Gramscianism (Morton 2001).

8 The reader is also referred to the handbook of international political economy by Stephen Gill and David Law, which compares the theoretical foundations, methodology and empirical application of neo-Gramscian perspectives with those of the mainstream (Gill and Law 1988).

9 For a multi-authored volume featuring essays by Stephen Gill, see Gill (2008).

10 For an in-depth discussion of these and other criticisms, see Bieler *et al.* (2006).

6 Bibliography and recommended reading

6.1 Primary texts

Cox, Robert W. (with Timothy Sinclair) (ed.) 1996: *Approaches to World Order*. Cambridge: Cambridge University Press.

Gill, Stephen (ed.) 1993a: *Gramsci, Historical Materialism and International Relations*. Cambridge: Cambridge University Press.

Gill, Stephen 2008: *Power and Resistance in the New World Order*, 2nd edn. London Palgrave.

Gramsci, Antonio 1971: *Selections from the Prison Notebooks*, ed. and trans. Q. Hoare and G. Nowell Smith, London: Lawrence and Wishart.

Morton, Adam David 2007a: *Unravelling Gramsci: Hegemony and Passive Revolution in the Global Political Economy*. London: Pluto Press.

6.2 Secondary texts

Bieler, Andreas, Bonefeld, Werner, Burnham, Peter, and Morton, Adam David 2006: *Global Restructuring, State, Capital and Labour: Contesting Neo-Gramscian Perspectives*. Basingstoke: Palgrave.

Bieler, Andreas and Morton, Adam David (eds) 2006: *Images of Gramsci: Connections and Contentions in Political Theory and International Relations*. London: Routledge.

Bieling, Hans-Jürgen and Deppe, Frank 1996: Gramscianismus in der Internationalen Politischen Ökonomie: Eine Problemskizze, *Das Argument* 217: 729–740.

Overbeek, Henk (ed.) 1993: *Restructuring Hegemony in the Global Political Economy: The Rise of Transnational Neoliberalism in the 1980s*. London: Routledge.

Scherrer, Christoph (1998): Neo-gramscianische Interpretationen internationaler Beziehungen, in Hirschfeld, Uwe (ed.) *Gramsci-Perspektiven, Argument-Sonderband Neue Folge* AS 256, Hamburg: Argument-Verlag, pp. 160–174.

van der Pijl, Kees 1998: *Transnational Classes and International Relations*. London: Routledge.

6.3 Other texts

Anievas, Alexander (ed.) 2010: *Marxism and World Politics: Contesting Global Capitalism*. London: Routledge.

Augelli, Enrico and Murphy, Craig 1988: *America's Quest for Supremacy and the Third World: A Gramscian Analysis*. London: Pinter.

Baker, Andrew 1999: *Nébuleuse* and the "Internationalisation of the State" in the UK?, *Review of International Political Economy* 6(1): 79–100.

Bieler, Andreas 2000: *Globalisation and Enlargement of the EU: Austrian and Swedish Social Forces in the Struggle over Membership*. London: Routledge.

Bieler, Andreas 2006: *The Struggle for a Social Europe: Trade Unions and EMU in Times of Global Restructuring*. Manchester: Manchester University Press.

Bieler, Andreas 2013: The EU, Global Europe and Processes of Uneven and Combined Development: the Problem of Transnational Labour Solidarity, *Review of International Studies*, 39(1): 161–183.

Bieler, Andreas and Lindberg, Ingemar (eds) 2010: *Global Restructuring, Labour and the Challenges for Transnational Solidarity*. London: Routledge.

Bieler, Andreas, Lindberg, Ingemar and Pillay, Devan (eds) 2008: *Labour and the Challenges of Globalisation: What Prospects for Transnational Solidarity?* London: Pluto Press.

Bieler, Andreas and Morton, Adam David (eds) 2001a: *Social Forces in the Making of the New Europe: The Restructuring of European Social Relations in the Global Political Economy*. London: Palgrave.

Bieler, Andreas and Morton, Adam David 2001b: The Gordian Knot of Agency-Structure in International Relations: A Neo-Gramscian Perspective, *European Journal of International Relations* 7(1): 5–35.

Bieler, Andreas and Morton, Adam David 2008: The Deficits of Discourse in IPE: Turning Base Metal into Gold?, *International Studies Quarterly* 52(1): 103–128.

Bieling, Hans-Jürgen, Deppe, Frank and Tidow Stefan (1998): Soziale Kräfte und hegemoniale Strukturen in der internationalen politischen Ökonomie. Vorwort, in Cox, Robert (ed.), pp. 7–27.

Bohle, Dorothee 2002: *Europas neue Peripherie. Polens Transformation und transnationale Integration*. Münster: Westfälisches Dampfboot.

Bohle, Dorothee 2006: Neoliberal Hegemony, Transnational Capital and the Terms of the EU's Eastward Expansion, *Capital & Class* 88: 57–86.

Bruff, Ian 2008: *Culture and Consensus in European Varieties of Capitalism*. London: Palgrave.

Burnham, Peter 1991: Neo-Gramscian Hegemony and the International Order, *Capital & Class* 45: 73–93.

Burnham, Peter 1994: Open Marxism and Vulgar International Political Economy, *Review of International Political Economy* 1(2): 221–231.

Buttigieg, Joseph A. 1986: The Legacy of Antonio Gramsci, *Boundary* 214(3): 1–17.

Cafruny, Alan W. and Ryner, Magnus (eds) 2003: *A Ruined Fortress? Neoliberal Hegemony and Transformation in Europe*. Lanham, MD: Rowman & Littlefield.

Callinicos, Alex 2009: *Imperialism and Global Political Economy*. Cambridge: Polity Press.

Cammack, Paul 1999: Interpreting ASEM: Interregionalism and the New Materialism, *Journal of the Asia Pacific Economy* 4(1): 13–32.

Cox, Robert W. 1981: Social Forces, States and World Orders: Beyond International Relations Theory, *Millennium: Journal of International Studies* 10(2): 126–155.

Cox, Robert W. 1983: Gramsci, Hegemony and International Relations: An Essay in Method, *Millennium: Journal of International Studies* 12(2): 162–175.

Cox, Robert [1985] 1996: Realism, Positivism, Historicism, in Cox, Robert W. (with Timothy Sinclair) (eds) *Approaches to World Order*. Cambridge: Cambridge University Press., pp. 49–59.

Cox, Robert 1987: *Production, Power and World Order: Social Forces in the Making of* History. New York: Columbia University Press.

Cox, Robert 1989: Production, the State and Change in World Order, in Czempiel, Ernst-Otto and Rosenau, James N. (eds) *Global Changes and Theoretical Challenges: Approaches to World Politics for the 1990s*. Toronto: Lexington Books.

Cox, Robert 1992a Global Perestroika, in Panitch, Leo and Miliband, Ralph (eds) *The Socialist Register: New World Order?* London: Merlin Press.

Cox, Robert [1992b] 1996: Towards a Posthegemonic Conceptualisation of World Order: Reflections on the Relevancy of Ibn Khaldun, in Cox, Robert W. (with Timothy Sinclair) (ed.) *Approaches to World Order*. Cambridge: Cambridge University Press, pp. 144–173.

Cox, Robert [1993] 1996: Production and Security, in Cox, Robert W. (with Timothy Sinclair) (ed.) *Approaches to World Order*. Cambridge: Cambridge University Press, pp. 276–295.

Cox, Robert 1995: Critical Political Economy, in Hettne, Björn (ed.) *International Political Economy: Understanding Global Disorder*. London: Zed Books, pp. 31–45.

Cox, Robert 2000: The Way Ahead: Towards a New Ontology of World Order, in Wyn Jones, Richard (ed.) *Critical Theory and World Politics*. Boulder, CO: Lynne Rienner, pp. 45–59.

Davies, Matt and Ryner, Magnus (eds) 2006: *Poverty and the Production of World Politics: Unprotected Workers in the Global Political Economy*. London: Palgrave.

Drainville, André 1994: International Political Economy in the Age of Open Marxism, *Review of International Political Economy* 1(1): 105–132.

Germain, Randall D. and Kenny, Michael 1998: Engaging Gramsci: International Relations Theory and the New Gramscians, *Review of International Studies* 24(1): 3–21.

Gill, Stephen 1989: Global Hegemony and the Structural Power of Capital, *International Studies Quarterly* 33(4): 475–499.

Gill, Stephen 1990: *American Hegemony and the Trilateral Commission*. Cambridge: Cambridge University Press.

Gill, Stephen 1992: The Emerging World Order and European Change: The Political Economy of European Union, in Panitch, Leo and Miliband, Ralph (eds) *The Socialist Register: New World Order?* London: Merlin Press, pp. 157–196.

Gill, Stephen 1993b: Epistemology, Ontology and the "Italian School", in Gill, Stephen (ed.) *Gramsci, Historical Materialism and International Relations*. Cambridge: Cambridge University Press, pp. 21–48.

Gill, Stephen 1995: Globalisation, Market Civilisation and Disciplinary Neoliberalism, *Millennium: Journal of International Studies* 24(3): 399–423.

Gill, Stephen 2001: Constitutionalising Capital: EMU and Disciplinary Neoliberalism, in Bieler, Andreas and Morton, Adam David (eds) *Social Forces in the Making of the New Europe: The Restructuring of European Social Relations in the Global Political Economy*. London: Palgrave, pp. 47–69.

Gill, Stephen and Law, David 1988: *The Global Political Economy: Perspectives, Problems and Policies*. London: Harvester Wheatsheaf.

Gill, Stephen and Mittelmann, James H. (eds) 1997: *Innovation and Transformation in International Studies*. Cambridge: Cambridge University Press.

Gramsci, Antonio 1971: *Selections from the Prison Notebooks*. Ed. and trans. Quintin Hoare and Geoffrey Nowell-Smith. London: Lawrence and Wishart.

Harvey, David [1982] 2006: *The Limits to Capital*, new edn. London: Verso.

Hesketh, Chris 2010: From Passive Revolution to Silent Revolution: Class Forces and the Production of State, Space and Scale in Modern Mexico, *Capital & Class*, 34(3): 383–407.

Hesketh, Chris 2013: The Clash of Spatialisations: Geopolitics and Class Struggle in Southern Mexico, *Latin American Perspectives*, 40(4): 70–87.

Hettne, Björn (ed.) 1995: *International Political Economy: Understanding Global Disorder*. Halifax: Fernwood.

Holman, Otto 1992: Introduction. Transnational Class Struggle and the New Europe, in Holman, Otto (ed.) European Unification in the 1990s: Myth and Reality, *International Journal of Political Economy* (Special Issue) 22(1): 3–22.

Holman, Otto 1996: *Integrating Southern Europe: EC Expansion and the Transnationalisation of Spain*. London: Routledge.

Holman, Otto 2004: Integrating Peripheral Europe: The Different Roads to "Security and Stability" in Southern and Central Europe, *Journal of International Relations and Development* 7(2): 208–236.

Ives, Peter and Nicola Short 2013: On Gramsci and the International: A Textual Analysis, *Review of International Studies*, DOI: http://dx.doi.org/10.1017S0260210512000526.

Keohane, Robert O. 1984: *After Hegemony: Cooperation and Discord in the World Political Economy*. Princeton, NJ: Princeton University Press.

Ling, L.H.M. 1996 Hegemony and the Internationalising State: A Post-Colonial Analysis of China's Integration into Asian Corporatism, *Review of International Political Economy* 3(1): 1–26.

Macartney, Huw 2009a: Variegated Neo-Liberalism: Transnationally Oriented Fractions of Capital in EU Financial Market Integration, *Review of International Studies* 35(2): 451–480.

Macartney, Huw 2009b: Disagreeing to Agree: Financial Crisis Management within the "Logic of No Alternative", *Politics* 29(2): 111–120.

Moran, Jonathan 1998: The Dynamics of Class Politics and National Economies in Globalisation: The Marginalisation of the Unacceptable, *Capital & Class* 66: 53–83.

Morton, Adam David 2001: The Sociology of Theorising and Neo-Gramscian Perspectives: The Problems of "School" Formation in IPE, in Bieler, Andreas and Morton, Adam David (eds) *Social Forces in the Making of the New Europe: The Restructuring of European Social Relations in the Global Political Economy*. London: Palgrave, pp. 25–43.

Morton, Adam David 2007b: Waiting for Gramsci: State Formation, Passive Revolution and the International, *Millennium: Journal of International Studies* 35(3): 597–621.

Morton, Adam David 2010a: Reflections on Uneven Development: Mexican Revolution, Primitive Accumulation, Passive Revolution, *Latin American Perspectives* 37(1): 7–34.

Morton, Adam David 2010b: The Continuum of Passive Revolution, *Capital & Class* 34(3): 315–342.

Morton, Adam David 2011: *Revolution and State in Modern Mexico: The Political Economy of Uneven Development*. Lanham, MD: Rowman & Littlefield.

Nousios, Petros, Overbeek, Henk and Tsolakis, Andreas (eds) 2012: *Globalisation and European Integration: Critical Approaches to Regional Order and International Relations*. London: Routledge.

Overbeek, Henk 1990: *Global Capitalism and National Decline: The Thatcher Decade in Perspective*. London: Allen & Unwin.

Overbeek, Henk (ed.) 2003: *The Political Economy of European Employment: European Integration and the Transnationalisation of the (Un)Employment Question*. London: Routledge.

Panitch, Leo 1994: Globalisation and the State, in Panitch, Leo and Miliband, Ralph (eds) *The Socialist Register: Between Globalism and Nationalism*. London: Merlin Press, pp. 60–93.

Panitch, Leo 1996: Rethinking the Role of the State, in Mittelmann, James H. (ed.) *Globalization: Critical Reflections*, Boulder, CO: Lynne Rienner, pp. 83–113.

Panitch, Leo and Gindin, Sam 2012: *The Making of Global Capitalism: The Political Economy of American Empire*. London: Verso.

Robinson, William I. 1996: *Promoting Polyarchy: Globalisation, US Intervention and* Hegemony. Cambridge: Cambridge University Press.

Robinson, William I. 2004: *A Theory of Global Capitalism: Production, Class, and State in a Transnational World.* Baltimore, MD: Johns Hopkins University Press.

Rosenberg Justin 2006: Why Is There No International Historical Sociology?, *European Journal of International Relations* 12(3): 307–340.

Ruggie, John G. 1982: International Regimes, Transactions and Change: Embedded Liberalism in the Postwar Economic Order, *International Organisation* 36(2): 379–415.

Rupert, Mark 1990: Producing Hegemony: State/Society Relations and the Politics of Productivity in the United States, *International Quarterly* 34: 427–456.

Rupert, Mark 1995: *Producing Hegemony: The Politics of Mass Production and American Global Power*. Cambridge: Cambridge University Press.

Rupert, Mark 2000: *Ideologies of Globalisation: Contending Visions of a New World Order*. London: Routledge.

Shields, Stuart 2012: *The International Political Economy of Transition: Transnational Social Forces and Eastern Central Europe's Transformation*. London: Routledge.

Ste. Croix, G.E.M. de 1981: *The Class Struggle in the Ancient Greek World from the Archaic Age to the Arab Conquests*. London: Duckworth.

Strange, Susan 1996: *The Retreat of the State: The Diffusion of Power in the World Economy*. Cambridge: Cambridge University Press.

Thompson, E.P. 1978: Eighteenth-Century English Society: Class Struggle Without Class?, *Social History* 3(2): 133–165.

van Apeldoorn, Bastiaan 2002: *Transnational Capitalism and the Struggle over European Integration*. London: Routledge.

van Apeldoorn, Bastiaan 2004: Special Issue: Transnational Historical Materialism: The Amsterdam International Political Economy Project, *Journal of International Relations and Development* 7(2): 110–236.

van Apeldoorn, Bastiaan, Drahokoupil, Jan and Horn, Laura (eds) 2009: *Neoliberal European Governance and Beyond: The Contradictions of a Political Project*. London: Palgrave.

van der Pijl, Kees 1984: *The Making of an Atlantic Ruling Class*. London: Verso

Wallerstein, Immanuel 1994: *The Modern World-System I: Capitalist Agriculture and Origins of European World-Economy in the Sixteenth Century*. San Diego, CA: Academic Press.

Waltz, Kenneth N. 1979: *Theory of International Politics*. Reading, MA: Addison-Wesley.

International Political Economy

Hans-Jürgen Bieling

1 Introduction

In the 1950s and 1960s, when only a small number of isolated studies appeared that we might attribute to International Political Economy (IPE), the discipline did not exist in any meaningful sense. It not only lacked a clearly defined field of study, but issues in security policy were very much to the fore within the discipline of International Relations. Towards the end of the 1960s, the Western European and Japanese economies began to catch up with that of the United States; European integration advanced; international interdependence increased; transnational companies (TNCs) became more important; the Bretton Woods system collapsed and the world was plunged into recession in 1974/75. Only in this context of a changed global economic constellation did IPE undergo a kind of refoundation (see Strange 1995a; Murphy and Nelson 2001; Bieling 2011: 10ff.). During this period, a considerable number of scholars, including Robert Gilpin, Steven Krasner, Peter Katzenstein, Robert Cox, Edward Morse, David Baldwin, Robert Keohane and Joseph Nye turned their attention to issues in political economy (see Cohen 2008). They investigated the changed relationship and interaction between states, markets, international institutions and social relations, each with their own specific set of analytical concepts (see also the chapters by Manuela Spindler and Bernhard Zangl in this volume).

Within this debate, Susan Strange's (1923–1998) key contribution was to focus on the historical-critical analysis of international and transnational power structures and probe how and why state action and the functioning of markets change. The investigative approach she developed is difficult to locate within the paradigms generally applied to International Relations and IPE (see Gill and Law 1988; Biersteker 1993; Ravenhill 2008). Most points of contact are with the advocates of neo-Gramscian perspectives – such as the critique of the neorealist mainstream, a historical perspective and the importance placed on nonstate actors (see Bieling 2011: 50ff., and the chapter by Andreas Bieler and Adam David Morton in this volume). The focus of her interest, however, is not so much on capitalist accumulation, in other words, the relations of production, as on changes in international monetary and credit relations.

Susan Strange always resisted any comprehensive theoretical canonization of her concepts. Instead she aimed to tear down the barriers that exist between disciplines and between different schools of thought (see Strange 1970). She overcame the strict division between economics and politics as well as that between national and international political economy. Against a narrow analytical focus on the decisions made by state actors, she consistently emphasized the influence of (trans-)national social actors; and against a deterministic perspective, she analysed the transformation of international economic relations – of relations of production as well as monetary and financial relations – as a process shaped and advanced on the basis of given power configurations by means of political decisions and non-decisions. Against institutionalist or regime theoretical studies that focus too heavily on formal international arrangements, she highlighted the structuring force of (socio-)economic power imbalances (see Strange 1982). Finally, she provocatively claimed that rather than International Political Economy being a subset of International Relations, we should turn this on its head and regard International Relations as a key dimension of a society-centred rather than state-centred and thus more comprehensive, integral IPE (see Strange 1989a: 435; 1994b: 218).

Never shy of conflict, this original and unorthodox but always creative analytical approach to issues in IPE is no doubt in part the result of a rather unusual biography (see Strange 1989a). After studying economic and social sciences at the London School of Economics (LSE), Strange pursued a career as a journalist, first as economics correspondent at the *Economist*, then as a reporter for the *Observer* in Washington (White House) and New York (United Nations). When she returned to the United Kingdom in 1949, she continued to work as a journalist. She had six children and also taught International Relations at University College London. Between 1965 and 1978, she was a researcher at Chatham House (formerly known as the Royal Institute of International Affairs). As well as her first monographs, *Sterling and British Policy* (Strange 1971) and *International Monetary Relations* (Strange 1976a), a number of essays appeared during this period in which she already began to outline her heterodox research program (see also: Cohen 2008: 44ff.). In 1974, together with Alastair Buchan, she founded the British International Studies Association (BISA). It was not until 1978 that she took up her chair in International Relations at the LSE. She subsequently not only supervised countless doctoral students, but also wrote those books – *Casino Capitalism* (Strange [1986] 1994a, and *States and Markets* (Strange [1988] 1997a) – that made her known across the world. Her zest undiminished, she remained active even after her retirement. In 1989, she moved to the European University Institute in Florence for five years, establishing a chair in International Political Economy there, and with John Stopford she published *Rival States, Rival Firms* (see Stopford and Strange 1991). Finally, there were further periods of teaching and research in Milan, Tokyo and Warwick as well as two more books: *The Retreat of the State* (1996) and, shortly before her death, *Mad Money* (1998a).

2 Theoretical description: structural power in the international political economy

The analytical perspectives developed by Strange, informed by theories of power and structure, stand in stark contrast to the American, in other words largely positivist, quantitative and economically liberal mainstream debate within IPE (see Cohen 2007; Maliniak and Tierney 2009). This debate certainly deals with the interaction between states and markets, particularly the management of world trade, exchange rates, foreign debt and direct investment, but it does not examine more deeply whether, and if so how, the interests and strategies of the actors involved are shaped by their specific structural circumstances – both social and international. This limits IPE to an approach that primarily if not exclusively considers the economic action of state actors, above all governments, and which Strange (1995a: 164; Strange 1975 was already making similar points) criticized as the PIER approach ("Politics of International Economic Relations") (see also Palan 2003). What she was rejecting here was not just neorealist approaches but also pluralist theories of interdependence. These certainly pay greater attention to transnational actors and strategies, so they have a certain sensitivity to the fact that economic aspects and interests are articulated within political structures, for example, in the negotiation of international regimes. At the same time, however, they lack awareness of the political processes occurring beneath the level of international regimes, that is, within transnational economic and social structures of power and authority (see Strange 1982: 495f.; Tooze and May 2002; see also the chapter by Manuela Spindler in this volume).

2.1 Analytical perspective and epistemological interest

This of course has epistemological consequences, though these are often not explicitly spelt out. For the most part, participants in the mainstream debate are concerned only with comprehending the location of political power and authority and perhaps, in an attempt to answer the Lasswellian question "Who gets what?", with determining very roughly the distributive consequences that follow in the wake of international institutions or conflicts for states or national economies (see Strange 1995a: 165). For Strange, however, such a perspective is far too narrowly focused and beholden to the status quo. When she asks "Cui bono?" (Who benefits?), she does so from a far broader perspective. The starting point of her analysis is not simply international actors and regimes but the profound *socioeconomic* changes that shed light on historical changes in – socially anchored – inter- and transnational power relations (see Strange 1976b; 1984: 272ff.). Alongside primary power structures such as security, production, money and finance, as well as knowledge, she also pays attention to the secondary structures of transport, trade, energy and welfare organizations (see Strange 1994a). For her, it is only on the basis of these various components of power and structure that we can understand why and in what direction the nexus of authority and market or of market and authority stabilizes or changes.

The research program developed by Susan Strange in this context differs from the common analytical frames of US-dominated IPE in a number of respects. First, Strange problematizes the research practice of unreflective comparative analysis that loses sight of overarching contextual conditions, in other words the functioning of the international political economy, as it compares specific national developmental trajectories and institutional systems. This does not mean that she considers comparative studies superfluous and meaningless. But they can enhance our understanding only if their focus extends beyond the nation state or national economy and if they are embedded in a conception of the transformation of inter- or transnational power structures (see Strange 1997b). Second, she repeatedly criticizes the interpretive frame put forward by the neorealist school and its assumption of an autonomous power politics based on the nation state (see, for example, Strange 1996: 66ff). For her, such a perspective is highly questionable *analytically* as it is underpinned by an artificial separation between economics and politics. It entails a very narrowly defined state-centred analytical perspective that is incapable of grasping multidimensional transnational power structures and the diverse range of forms taken by non-nation state authorities – such as TNCs, international organizations, (criminal) networks, and so on. It is also *politically* problematic as it clings to traditional concepts of political power and political order – the Westphalian system of states and domestically focused US politics – through which the United States reacts to global processes of transformation not cooperatively but through a unilaterally defined claim to domination. Third and finally, Strange criticizes the methodology of those approaches within IPE that, inspired by the debate within economics, develop game theoretical models before going on to subject the associated hypotheses to rigorous empirical testing (see Strange 1995a: 167f.). For her, such an approach is inappropriate because it focuses primarily on "measurable phenomena", presupposes a "static world" and assumes a detached scientific observer who thinks he or she can analyse "objective reality".

But despite her remarks on the changes in the transnational structure of knowledge, Strange (1994a: 136) was ultimately little interested in such meta-theoretical issues. Her conception of science is far more pragmatic in nature (see Palan 2003). Though she sets great store by the idea that science should not just describe but always explain as well (see Strange 1994a: 10f.), she essentially sees science as a medium for correcting or expanding on "common sense" (see also May 1996: 168ff.) or more specifically as a bridge between the understanding of the "real world" and the potential to change it (see Morgan *et al.* 1993: 9). In this sense, her focus is on developing a "new realist ontology" (see Strange 1997d; Cox 1996: 183ff.) or a new "radical ontology" (see Tooze 2000a, 2000b) with the help of a historically open conceptualization of power structures. This ontology is distinguished above all by the fact that, in contrast to the state-centred realist ontology, it understands international structures of authority as a highly dynamic and highly complex web of social power relations – shaped by economic, state and social factors.

2.2 Structures and forms of the exercise of power

The conception of power that underpins Strange's work is a highly comprehensive one. It includes direct coercion and force as well as diverse forms of authority and influence: "Power is simply the ability of a person or group of persons to affect outcomes that their preferences take precedence over the preferences of others" (Strange 1996: 17). Just how this happens depends on a large number of factors: on social and international structural changes and on historically specific processes of negotiation within a network of (trans-)national and intergovernmental interactional relations (see Strange 1994a: 39ff).

Power may be but is not inevitably linked directly to the pursuit of specific interests. Power also has an impact in cases where we cannot identify a specific pressure group. On this view, power is not simply a thing, a quality associated with specific actors. Instead, it is a constitutive component of social relations that may engender relational or structural effects. We may understand *relational power*, as in the work of Max Weber or of the realist school, as the capacity of an actor (country *a*) to impose its will on another actor (country *b*) or to influence its behaviour in its own interest. For Strange, this kind of exercise of power is not meaningless but is far less important than the impact of structural power. By *structural power* she means "the power to shape and determine the structures of the global political economy within which other states, their political institutions, their economic enterprises and (not least) their scientists and other professional people have to operate" (Strange 1994a: 24f.). In this context, structural power is not limited solely to the explicitly political dimension of international relations or, for example, to the agenda-setting or organizing of international regimes. It also extends to the relative control of international structures of production and financial relations, including the asymmetric patterns of economic reproduction safeguarded by them, and to the organization, characteristics, and distribution of knowledge, information and beliefs.

This structural analysis has three significant implications. First, it is difficult to make a sharp distinction between political and economic or between political and ideological power. The distinctions made by Strange (1994a: 25f.; 1975) are more analytical in nature, as the different dimensions of power often reinforce and sometimes even determine one another.

> It is impossible to have political power without the power to purchase, to command production, to mobilize capital. And it is impossible to have economic power without

> the sanction of political authority, without the legal and physical security that can only be supplied by political authority.
>
> (Strange 1994a: 25)

Second, power is primarily determined functionally and non-territorially. The crucial factor is not control over land and people, but rather – in both social as well as inter- and transnational terms – influence on the structural parameters, rules and thus results of international political economy. Third, Strange explicitly underlines that none of the structural dimensions of power, each of which refers to specific and basic social needs, takes precedence or is necessarily determinative. Power relations within the structures of security, finance and knowledge, regardless of how they are mediated, cannot be derived from power relations within the structure of production. To quote Strange (1994a: 26): "structural power is to be found not in a single structure but in four separate distinguishable but related structures".

1 For Strange, the *security structure* forms the framework of power within which certain protective and defensive mechanisms are put in place to ward off natural disasters, environmental risks, or violent conflicts. Not all social groups have equal opportunity to control the use or avoidance of force. It is specific, primarily state elites that have this power. Disputes within the security structure result chiefly from the fact that different authorities do not simply coexist peacefully but come into conflict beyond the boundaries of the protective tasks they have taken on. They may flare up between two or more states, but also within one state: between central and provincial governments and between the government and social actors such as trade unions, sects or criminal organizations. A sharp distinction is often made between the security risks that arise within nation states (criminality, terrorism or civil war) and those that affect the international state system (war or trade embargoes). For Strange (1994a: 48), such a perspective is problematic because security risks often cannot be reduced to either the social or the international dimension.

   So this conception of the international security structure certainly exhibits parallels with the interpretive framework of the neorealist school, which focuses above all on the balance of power between states (see May 1996: 179; Strange 1994a: 50ff.). But the differences are no less important. First, for Strange the international security structure is not shaped exclusively by nation states but also by countless nonstate actors. Second, in comparison to realist views, her concept of security is more comprehensive. For her, security refers not just to immediate political dangers but includes the monitoring of other risks, such as environmental problems, monetary and financial market crises, unemployment, famines or developments in (weapons) technologies (see Strange 1996: 33f.). Third, Strange discusses the social asymmetries of power that are inscribed into security policy arrangements – through the relationship between protectors and protected. Fourth and finally, for her the security structure does not automatically take precedence over other power structures. To a large extent, its significance depends on whether the internal or external dangers perceived – including by protected groups – are so acute that other values and goals such as prosperity, freedom and justice are adversely affected.

2 The *production structure* is the sum of all those arrangements that stipulate which goods are produced "by whom and for whom", which methods and technologies are used to this end, how this process is organized and "by whom". As the foundation of societal wealth, it is in the structure of production that all the key decisions relating to the

production and distribution of economic resources are made (Strange 1994a: 64). The consequences for the distribution of social and international power that flow from the nature of production are undoubtedly important. Changes in the structure of production often find expression in a very direct way in social relations of power and class. The effects on inter- and transnational relations are more indirect, though by no means less significant, since the conditions, forms and character of state action change along with production. This applies for example to the pattern of interaction between governments and TNCs (see Stopford and Strange 1991: 214ff.), the forms of state control and generally to the political potential to respond to international economic risks and instabilities (see Strange 1994a: 84ff.).

For Strange, the internationalization of the economy is an expression of a fundamental transformation of the structure of production. According to Strange (1984: 273), the transnationalization of power and control structures that goes hand-in-hand with this is not satisfactorily expressed by official economic figures on foreign trade or foreign investment. Ultimately, many other developments are embedded in this process – such as the growing importance of high-tech products and new services or the privatization of former state enterprises. As a consequence, the power of the unionized workforce is eroded (see Strange 1996: 52) and a "triangular diplomacy" takes shape between national governments, between governments and TNCs, and between TNCs (see Stopford and Strange 1991: 19ff.). To the extent that the struggle for world market share becomes the leading principle of action here, the strategic orientation of states and governments also changes. For them, in contrast to the colonial and imperial stage, what matters is no longer the mobilization of power in order to acquire economic resources and thus wealth and prosperity but rather deploying economic resources to expand their own potential for power, control and influence (see Strange 1991).

The concept of a structure of production permeated by class and power relations put forward by Strange displays a number of parallels with (neo-)Marxist analyses. But there are certain dimensions of Strange's work that differ from them. First, she emphasizes that the structure of production is just one among several dimensions of structural power, not the primary foundation in light of which we can decipher the other forms of power and power resources (see Strange 1994a: 26). Second, while she regards cost relations as an important determinant that has an impact on how the structure of production develops, for her, this structure is concurrently exposed to other economic and noneconomic influences, such as technological change, market dynamics and security policy considerations, or cultural and ideological factors. Third, contrary to certain traditional Marxist analyses, she understands financial relations, above all the provision of credit, as an autonomous phenomenon within the capitalist economy rather than one derived from accumulation. The issuing of credit and the creation of money, on this view, is in principle unlimited; in other words, it does not depend on whatever profits may have been accumulated in advance. For her, this is the only way to explain why capitalist development is proceeding in such an extraordinarily dynamic fashion (see Strange 1994a: 30; 1997c: 244).

3 Susan Strange (1971, 1976a, 1997a, 1998a) carried out particularly in-depth examination of the *financial structure*. In contrast to many conventional perspectives, she sheds light on the way that those who are in the position to provide credit also have considerable power to control the functioning and development of the economy. As we have already seen with respect to the structure of security and production, national and international aspects are closely bound up with one another in the structure of finance as well. At first sight, the domestic stability of the value of money (inflation) and the

criteria and costs of the issuing of credit (interest rates) are above all the outcome of national economic, fiscal and monetary policies, in other words of the interplay of government and central bank. As a rule, however, in most countries the potential to organize and decide on the national level is in fact highly restricted, since inter- and transnational influences – other governments, central banks and the financial markets – have an impact on monetary and fiscal relations through external changes in the stability of monetary value (exchange rates). Susan Strange (1994a: 90) defines the financial structure in this sense as the sum of all those arrangements through which the provision of credit and currency relations are regulated.

Historically, it was only with the banks that a regulated system of credit took shape. This gave private actors and the state the option of borrowing money in order to invest or provide public goods. Through the diversification and extension of financial transactions – and the increasing importance of other financial market actors, above all institutional investors such as insurance companies or investment and pension funds (see Huffschmid 2002) – the financial structure has become more differentiated. On the whole, this development has been conducive to economic growth, investment and innovation. But negative accompaniments have also been apparent (see Strange 1994a: 96ff.). Social inequalities and power imbalances have got worse while the instability within the financial system has grown markedly as a result of the diminishing power of state authorities. Susan Strange (1997a, 1998a) has repeatedly subjected this development to sharp criticism. For her, the globalized financial structure has gained a life of its own, that is, it has detached itself from the functional requirements of the real economy. The associated problems were and to some extent still are keenly felt in the highly indebted developing countries, which have no choice but to submit to the criteria of a largely US-dominated financial structure.

For Strange, these tendencies are an expression of the fact that the balance of power has shifted in favour of the financial markets within the authority-market or market-authority nexus. But she interprets this not simply as a systemic, let alone deterministic or inexorable process but as a development brought about, to some extent consciously, by political negotiations and (non-)decisions (see Strange 1997a: 25ff.; Helleiner 1994: 81ff.; Scherrer 1999: 185ff.). Alongside the emergence of the Eurodollar market in the 1960s and the carefully considered decision by the Nixon administration to abandon the Bretton Woods system of fixed exchange rates, she also mentions the subsequent policies of deregulation with respect to private financial market actors. Essentially, in contrast to claims still common within the scientific debate until recently, she does not put this down to the hegemonic decline of the United States but to a *change of form* in US hegemonic politics:

> [I]t was not the decline of American hegemonic power in the 1970s and 1980s so much as its misuse, exploiting the system rather than managing it, giving too much freedom and responsibility for credit creation to banks, that was at the root of subsequent troubles. It was the pursuit of short-term instead of long-term national interest that sowed the seeds of monetary disorder and financial instability.
>
> (Strange 1994a: 104; similar remarks appear in 1997a: 22f.)

The global economic and financial crisis unfolding since 2007 may be understood as an expression of this potential for instability examined so precociously by Strange (see Bieling 2009). The analytical perspective that she developed is shaped above all by (financial) Keynesian considerations (see Strange 1998b: 10ff). On this view, a developed financial system is certainly highly advantageous to the dynamic development of a capitalist economy, but without sufficient – national and international – political controls, it runs the risk of producing socially destructive effects and instabilities.

4 Finally, the *knowledge structure* may at first sight appear to be a "foreign body" within the "new realist ontology" put forward by Strange (see Guzzini 2000) as it introduces elements into this perspective that make it interesting to social constructivists (see Tooze 2000a). For Strange, knowledge and information are sources of power that are all too often overlooked and undervalued within IPE (see Strange 1994a: 119). At the same time, however, the knowledge structure and the power constituted by it are extremely difficult to grasp. In comparison to the other structures, it not only includes a broad range of phenomena, but in terms of theories of power it is defined in a basically negative way, that is, chiefly through the sequestering of information and stocks of knowledge. The knowledge structure comprises beliefs in the sense of key moral principles and dogmas, generally valid practical knowledge but also channels of communication – universities, elite networks, and (mass) media – through which knowledge, beliefs and ideas are "transported". Control over all these dimensions provides a power that should not be underestimated as the knowledge structure lays down what kind of knowledge is accessed, stored and socially communicated (see ibid.: 121).

Strange does not work on the assumption that technological developments – such as new information and communication technologies – are automatically and directly relevant to the balance of power within the authority-market or market-authority nexus. But to the extent that they can be used in the struggle over market share, in monetary transactions or military strategies, they have substantial social and international effects on the structure of production, finance and security (see ibid.: 133ff.). For Strange, the structure of knowledge as a whole seems to be gaining in importance, not least because it is changing rapidly and pervading all other areas. Among other things, this is apparent in the fact that states – the United States being particularly successful in this regard – are increasingly competing to lead the knowledge structure in technological, informational and cultural terms. Further, knowledge-based power resources are also becoming more important within national societies. The influence of individuals and social groups is more and more determined by their access to knowledge and information, not necessarily by how much capital they possess.

5 Supplementary to the primary power structures listed above, Strange (ibid.: 139ff.) also looks at a number of secondary power structures or "issue areas". These include transnational transport systems, international trade, the provision of energy and welfare and development systems. For Strange, all these areas, which tend to be central to theories of interdependence (1994a: 139), are secondary chiefly because they are decisively shaped and organized by the primary structures. The secondary structures help operationalize the functioning of the primary structures, but are themselves scarcely determined by the system of value preferences (see May 1996: 183). Nonetheless, their ordering structure and mode of operation – and this also applies to international law and the global food system – are by no means irrelevant to the options and potential power of enterprises, states, social groups and individuals.

2.3 Towards a different world (dis-)order?

The notion of structural power is more than an abstract, purely formal theoretical concept. It is a historical-heuristic interpretive framework with the help of which Strange seeks to systematically decipher key developments and processes of upheaval within the international political economy. In her books and essays she discusses a large number of specific aspects and facets of these developments. But she sees the novelty of transnational developmental dynamics as due to three tendencies in particular.

1 In very general terms, Strange (1984: 273ff.; 1995b: 64ff.; 1996) has long noted the *transnationalization* of all four power structures. This development is undoubtedly at its strongest in the financial structure. Here, countless acts of deregulation and liberalization have increasingly removed monetary and credit relations from the sphere of national control, while transnational actors within the private financial market – major banks, insurance companies, pension and investment funds, and rating agencies (see Strange 1996: 122ff.) – are more and more able to define and organize politics. The structure of production has also been strongly transnationalized. In the context of advancing international competition, TNCs increasingly place national economic, tax, fiscal, infrastructure, and social policies under pressure – through trade and investment as well as investment-related bargaining (see Stopford/Strange 1991). The knowledge structure has also gained a strongly transnational dimension because of the new information and communication technologies, globally-oriented media and marketing enterprises, and the cross-border networking of scientific know-how. It is in the security structure that transnationalization is least advanced. Even here, however, as a result of international networks of organized criminality – including (drugs) mafias, money-laundering and international terrorism – the nation state's potential for control seems to be on the wane (see Strange 1996: 110ff.; 1995c: 305ff.).

   Strange interprets all of this to the effect that within the authority-market or market-authority nexus, the balance of power is shifting away from (central) state actors. She observes a diffusion of power as private (market) actors – in collaboration with state actors or in parallel to them – gain increased room for manoeuvre and potential for control (see Strange 1996: 73ff.; 1995b: 68ff.). This by no means renders the power of states and governments obsolete, but cooperation and competition with non-state actors changes the character of this power. First, the territorial ties and anchoring of state power are loosened, and second, this power is geared more and more towards the criteria of market and competition.

2 Though states are becoming fundamentally more vulnerable through this process, the diffusion of power – both "upward" and "downward" (see Strange 1995b: 67f.) – does not result in the weakening of power asymmetries within the international political economy. For Strange (1988 and 1995c: 300f.), the opposite is the case. As she sees it, power is becoming concentrated in the hands of those actors and social groups that – with respect to international competition among other things – make investment decisions (TNCs), issue credit (major banks and other financial enterprises), and have at their disposal market-relevant stocks of knowledge (research centres, universities). Governments and states are involved in this process in as much as they play a crucial role in laying down the conditions and parameters for this kind of market-based exercise of power. The options open to them and their room for manoeuvre differ greatly and are increasingly unequal. Strange (1995b: 65) repeatedly shows that the emerging "international business civilization" is largely dominated by the United States. She refers here to the United States' "non-territorial empire" (see Strange 1989b). Through the interplay between market and government actors – American financial metropolises, the headquarters of TNCs, and the centre of political decision-making in Washington – this

empire exercises a major influence on international power structures, shaping how they change and are reproduced; at the very least, it controls them in a structural sense.

3 As intimated above, these observations boil down to the thesis that US hegemony is changing form. Strange highlights three key dimensions or developments. For her, first of all, as a virtual consequence of the diffusion of the capacity for power, state and government action is no longer primarily territorial but functional, that is, determined by rivalry over world market share and productivity resources (see Strange 1996: 73ff.). Second, as mentioned earlier, within this new logic the United States has at its disposal incomparable power and organizational potential: not just within the security and production structure but particularly within the financial and knowledge structure (see Strange 1987; 1988). Third and finally, the United States no longer makes much effort to deploy its power resources to coordinate and stabilize international structures on a cooperative basis and in harmony with the interests of its political allies and economic partners. For Strange (1988: 13; see also Helleiner 1994: 101ff), since the late 1960s the United States' inter- and transnational economic and fiscal policies have primarily been determined by short-term national interests, which explains why she agrees with Robert Gilpin's (1987: 90) claim that the United States has turned from a "benevolent to a predatory hegemon". Strange does not agree with the thesis, commonly expounded in the late 1980s, that this is due to the United States' (relative) decline. On the contrary, she often criticizes the decline debate, very sharply, as an attempt to justify, politically and intellectually, the United States' refusal to enter into closer international economic and fiscal policy cooperation by highlighting the supposed weakness of the US economy (see Strange 1987, 1988, 1994a: 237ff., 1996: 194ff.).

Of course, the transformational dynamics of the international political economy include a number of other aspects: accelerated change in technologies and market structures, the growing importance of modern service companies, the increased significance of the knowledge structure and the undermining of democratic decision-making mechanisms (see Story 2000). All of them provide further confirmation of Susan Strange's key claims. The collapse of real existing socialism and the end of the opposition between capitalism and communism also fit into the analytical framework she developed. These developments are particularly striking testimony to the fact that the core political and intellectual problems have changed (see Strange 1997c). From the late nineteenth century on, scholars were primarily concerned with the questions "socialism or capitalism?" and "peace or war?". For Strange, the first question has been more or less settled since 1989. This also applies to moderate versions of the "third way": even the concept of a capitalist economy regulated by collective agreement and a welfare state has faced strong opposition. For her, the question of "peace or war?" is no longer of much relevance either, at least not in the conventional form of wars to expand territorial possessions. This does not mean that violent conflicts – civil wars, ethnic conflicts, and so on – are simply outmoded, but they now exhibit a very different motivational structure and tend to proceed in a quite different way.

For Strange (1997c: 237), the key problems and issues that will dominate the twenty-first century result primarily from the internationalization of production and the political inadequacy of the state system (see also Strange 1999). In her view, the internationalization of production, which is being greatly accelerated by technological change and the independent momentum of monetary and credit relations, is driving a wedge between the social and ecological reproductive needs of national societies and the interests of the transnational economy (see Strange 1997c: 242). At the same time, the international state system lacks the political means to respond adequately to this. The state system may guarantee democratic decision-making structures on the foundation of mutual recognition of formal rights of sovereignty, but there is no sufficiently stable regulatory arrangement that might impose political control on the lightning-fast process of economic transnationalization to the benefit of social reproduction.

3 Further developments and criticisms of Strange's theoretical design

Despite the central (pioneering) role played by Susan Strange in refounding and developing IPE not just in the UK but worldwide and the wide reception of her writings, no "Strange School" has emerged in the narrow sense of the term. Strange (1989a) always took a sceptical view of school formation. She was predominantly concerned to encourage students, whether undergraduate or postgraduate, to come to their own conclusions and develop their own ideas. Further, the analytical framework she developed, which was very open in historical and conceptual terms, is of only limited use to school formation. It is difficult to derive canonized theorems or hypotheses from her basic conceptual framework that might then be tested with reference to a specific object of study. Nonetheless, the heuristic interpretive concept delivered by Strange and her historical reconstruction of key processes of transformation provide endless stimulation. They have been put to productive use and developed by a large number of scholars within the heterodox IPE debate (see Morgan *et al.* 1993; Lawton *et al.* 2000).

Some, for example, have looked at the significance of the knowledge structure to the processes of transformation within the other power structures and investigated how and in what form transnational "epistemic communities", such as the Bank for International Settlements or the Delors Committee, tasked with preparing the conceptual ground for European economic and monetary union, have influenced key decisions affecting the financial structure (see Helleiner 1994; Verdun 2000) or indeed the structure of production (see Mytelka 2000). Others have been inspired by Strange in their analyses of global production structures (see Lawton and Michaels 2000). Yet others have sought to include competition between employees in the negotiated competition between states and firms ("triangular diplomacy") (see, for example, Allen 1993). And more than a few have been stimulated and inspired by her – then – provocative statements critiquing the notion of US decline or, in the contemporary context, the thesis of the "retreat of the state" (see Gilpin 2000).

When it comes to analysing the contemporary era, studies of recent developments in the structure of global finance are also of interest. Strange (1997a: 175ff.) herself had long assumed that the exceptional structural power of the United States persists in this field. This idea was confirmed by later neo-Weberian studies that highlighted the embedding of the American state in a web of social actors (see Seabrooke 2001) and examined the global appeal of the US economy (see Panitch and Konings 2008). In light of the prevailing constellation of power, Strange believed that the re-regulation of monetary and credit relations could be achieved only through long-termist, enlightened US policies. Only towards the end of her career did she consider the possibility that Western Europe and Southeast Asia might push for new transnational structures of control, though in collaboration with the United States (see Strange 1995c: 71; 1998a: 55). Eric Helleiner (2000) has taken up these ideas. In his view, over the course of the 1990s, the Western European and Southeast Asian economies have increasingly sought to escape US dominance. Economic and monetary union and financial market integration within the European Union (see Bieling

2006) point in this direction, as do initiatives aimed at achieving greater regional crisis and currency management in Southeast Asia.

It is of course very difficult to predict how the interpretive concept developed by Strange will be received and developed over the next few years. In the aftermath of the global currency and financial crisis, scholars may well return to her concept of "casino capitalism" and her ideas on currency and financial markets. It is possible, however, that the relevant – empirical and conceptual – endeavours will focus less on her "new realist ontology" than on the epistemological aspects of her analytical perspective. Key sources of stimulation here include the concept of the knowledge structure, which Strange herself left undeveloped. By largely equating knowledge with information, she ended up with an instrumental concept of knowledge tailored towards the exercise of power. She generally paid little attention to customs, values and beliefs, though these also have an influence on options, decisions, and negotiations. Paying more attention to these elements would allow us to achieve a more comprehensive and systematic understanding of how the knowledge structure interacts with other power structures: first by elaborating a social politics of objectivity and truth (see May 1996: 184f.) and second – with respect to the functioning of academic communication structures – through the reflexive self-positioning of academic theories, methods and empirical analysis (see Guzzini 2000; Tooze 2000a). The latter also implies a more precise epistemological positioning as the precondition for the critique of science and society.

4 IPE: theoretical heuristic of power or theory of global capitalism?

Though the work of Susan Strange has played a central and pioneering role in the refoundation of a critical and heterodox IPE, some scholars have been less than impressed with her attempt to tear down the conventional disciplinary boundaries between politics, economics, history and geography (see Earnest *et al.* 2000: 412). In this "no man's land" of an academic landscape strictly divided into different disciplines, she often came up against ignorance, misunderstanding, or sheer defensiveness. On those occasions when her ideas were considered at all, they generally triggered highly stereotypical responses. Some accused her of being too sweeping in her judgements, particularly in her criticisms of US foreign economic policies. Others made fundamental criticisms of her holistic analytical perspective, claiming that it was inadequately differentiated intellectually and that it impeded clearly defined and verifiable statements and hypotheses. Some critics highlighted methodological problems such as an unsophisticated, eclectic collection of theoretical fragments (see Buzan 1989) or weaknesses in the provision of empirical evidence that cast doubt on the explanatory potential of the relevant data. Apart from the last point, none of these criticisms made much impression on Strange. Because of their ahistorical perspective, she was always highly critical of scientistic concepts that propose unrealistic models and seek to verify the hypotheses derived from them according to natural scientific-mathematical criteria. For Susan Strange, theory – taking account of structural parameters – must always refer to concrete social reality, to concrete history or concrete social and international conditions (see Palan 1999: 123).

In line with this, we may describe the relationship that existed between Susan Strange and mainstream IPE (i.e. neorealism, interdependence analysis and regime theory), with its focus on the state and institutions and its arguments couched in terms of models and game theory, as one of disregard and mutual incomprehension. The basic theoretical assumptions and analytical perspectives were clearly too different to allow for a productive clash (see Cohen

2007). This does not apply, however, to the fundamental criticisms made by scholars within heterodox IPE, whose arguments are also historical and informed by theories of power and capitalism. To simplify somewhat, these amount to the criticism that while Strange developed an interesting theoretical heuristic of power for the historical-empirical reconstruction of the international political economy, she failed to produce any systematic theory of global capitalism (see Palan 2003). This is evident among other things in three theoretical weaknesses or problem areas.

1 The first criticism is that Strange failed to adequately theorize the state. In her historical-descriptive analyses, Strange tends to conceive of the state in formal terms, that is, as a rule-setting institution with its own authority. While this is not entirely false, it often leads to a view of state and economy as functionally differentiated and opposing spheres. The idea here is that this implicit dichotomy undermines her own claim to present an integrated understanding of international political and economic processes (see Cutler 2000). In order to avoid this, so the argument goes, she herself would have to work on the basis of an integrated analytical concept: either a governance structure that includes the interactional patterns of both arenas as a "state-market condominium" (see Underhill 2000) or an understanding of the state that conceives of it far more broadly, that is, as an institutionalized ensemble for the pursuit of public and (private) social interests and thus as an inherently contradictory social relationship. This would have major consequences in two key respects. First, the specific division between state and economy would itself have to be understood as the result of political processes, and second, the "retreat of the state" observed by Strange would not be analysed primarily as a weakening of the state but as a process of state transformation.
2 In connection with this, a second criticism relates to the lack of any conceptualization of upheavals and transformation processes within the international political economy. Accelerated change is undoubtedly centre stage in her analyses. But in order to explain its momentum, she "only" mentions very general determinants such as technological development, competition and the change in market relations or specific historical aspects such as decisions and non-decisions by the central state (see May 1996: 185). The basic forces propelling and validating these factors and determinants tend to remain obscure. Strange does not explain, for example, why in the late 1960s and early 1970s the United States used its structural power in a more domestically focused way against its own long-term interests, thus making a large number of "mistakes" – such as dissolving the Bretton Woods system (see Deppe 1991: 115f.). Strange was clearly resistant to putting forward a concept anchored in social theory and – by linking national and inter- or transnational processes – determining more precisely which interactional patterns and forms of mediation exist between the primary power structures (see, for example, Cox 1996: 180f.).
3 Third and finally, the first two criticisms taken together amount to the claim that Susan Strange has an underdeveloped or one-sided concept of the "social". This is not to say that she sets little store by social processes and developments. On the contrary, again and again she refers to unequal power structures, distributive relations and social injustices. Ultimately, however, she discusses all these dimensions primarily as a consequence of upheavals and (non-)decisions within the power structures that she studies and only very vaguely as the precondition and foundation for the transformation of international political economy. This blank spot could be filled, among other things, by two conceptual additions. The first would be the systematic inclusion of the knowledge

structure or, to be more precise, a conception that not only seeks to describe but also to define theoretically how, by whom, and to what extent (trans-)national structures are constructed discursively, that is, through the imparting of knowledge, information and beliefs. The second addition would be a conception that, in light of ongoing processes of social construction, is capable of deciphering more precisely, in terms of class and political theory, the social struggles and transformative perspectives inherent in patterns of economic reproduction and social structures.

Strange was always very sceptical about such ambitions, at least when they were taken too far. She was dubious about the prospect of developing a grand theory that could explain everything (see Palan 1999, 2003; Tooze 2000b). The world seemed to her too complex and specific historical developments too contingent for there to be any way of systematizing the numerous factors involved in a theoretically adequate way. In order to avoid monocausal or deterministic explanatory models, she exercised self-restraint. The historical, open character of her concepts as well as the always refreshing and frequently inspiring character of her arguments, seem to suggest that she was right to do so.

5 *Bibliography and* recommended reading

5.1 Primary texts

Stopford, John and Strange, Susan (with John S. Henley) 1991: *Rival States, Rival Firms: Competition for World Market Shares*. Cambridge: Cambridge University Press.

Strange, Susan [1986] 1997a: *Casino Capitalism*. Manchester: Manchester University Press

Strange, Susan [1988] 1994a: *States and Markets*, 2nd edn. London: Pinter.

Strange, Susan 1996: *The Retreat of the State: The Diffusion of Power in the World Economy*. Cambridge: Cambridge University Press.

Strange, Susan 1998a: *Mad Money: When Markets Outgrow Governments*. Manchester: Manchester University Press.

5.2 Secondary texts

May, Christopher 1996: Strange Fruit: Susan Strange's Theory of Structural Power in the International Political Economy, *Global Society* 10(2): 167–189.

Lawton, Thomas C., Rosenau, James N. and Verdun, Amy C. (eds) 2000: *Strange Power: Shaping the Parameters of International Relations and International Political Economy*. Aldershot: Ashgate.

Morgan, Roger, Lorentzen, Jochen, Leander, Anna, and Guzzini, Stefano (eds) 1993: *New Diplomacy in the Post-Cold War World: Essays for Susan Strange*. New York: St. Martin's Press.

5.3 Other texts

Allen, Michael H. 1993: Rival Workers: Bargaining Power and Justice in Global Systems, in Morgan, Roger, Lorentzen, Jochen, Leander, Anna, and Guzzini, Stefano (eds) *New Diplomacy in the Post-Cold War World: Essays for Susan Strange*. New York: St. Martin's Press, pp. 45–54.

Bieling, Hans-Jürgen 2006: EMU, Financial Integration and Global Economic Governance, *Review of International Political Economy* 13(3): 420–448.

Bieling, Hans-Jürgen 2009: Wenn der Schneeball ins Rollen kommt: Überlegungen zur Dynamik und zum Charakter der Subprime-Krise, *Zeitschrift für Internationale* Beziehungen 16(1): 107–121.

Bieling, Hans-Jürgen 2011: *Internationale Politische Ökonomie. Eine Einführung,* 2nd updated edn. Wiesbaden: VS-Verlag.

Biersteker, Thomas J. 1993: Evolving Perspectives on International Political Economy: Twentieth-Century Contexts and Discontinuities, *International Political Science* Review 14(1): 7–33.

Buzan, Barry 1989: States and Markets, *International Affairs* 65(2):, 331.

Cohen, Benjamin 2007: The Transatlantic Divide: Why Are American and British IPE so Different?, *Review of International Political Economy* 14(2): 197–219.

Cohen, Benjamin 2008: *International Political Economy: An Intellectual History*. Princeton, NJ: Princeton University Press.

Cox, Robert W. 1996: "Take Six Eggs": Theory, Finance, and the Real Economy in the Work of Susan Strange, in Cox, Robert W. (with Timothy J. Sinclair) *Approaches to World Order*. Cambridge: Cambridge University Press, pp. 174–188.

Cutler, Claire A. 2000: Theorizing the "No-Man's-Land". Between Politics and Economics, in Lawton, Thomas C., Rosenau, James N. and Verdun, Amy C. (eds) *Strange Power: Shaping the Parameters of International Relations and International Political Economy*. Aldershot: Ashgate, pp. 159–174.

Deppe, Frank 1991: *Jenseits der Systemkonkurrenz. Überlegungen zur neuen Weltordnung*. Marburg: VAG-Verlag.

Earnest, David C. *et al.* 2000: Reflections: Blurring the Boundaries and Shaping the Agenda, in Lawton, Thomas C., Rosenau, James N. and Verdun, Amy C. (eds) *Strange Power: Shaping the Parameters of International Relations and International Political Economy*. Aldershot: Ashgate, pp. 409–420.

Gill, Stephen and Law, David 1988: The *Global Political Economy: Perspectives, Problems, and Politics*. New York: Harvester Wheatsheaf.

Gilpin, Robert 1987: *The Political Economy of International Relations*. Princeton, NJ: Princeton University Press.

Gilpin, Robert 2000: The Retreat of the State?, in Lawton, Thomas C., Rosenau, James N. and Verdun, Amy C. (eds) *Strange Power: Shaping the Parameters of International Relations and International Political Economy*. Aldershot: Ashgate, pp. 197–214.

Guzzini, Stefano 2000: Strange's Oscillating Realism: Opposing the Ideal – and the Apparent, in Lawton, Thomas C., Rosenau, James N. and Verdun, Amy C. (eds) *Strange Power: Shaping the Parameters of International Relations and International Political Economy*. Aldershot: Ashgate, pp. 215–228.

Helleiner, Eric 1994: *States and the Reemergence of Global Finance: From Bretton Woods to the 1990s*. Ithaca, NY: Cornell University Press.

Helleiner, Eric 2000: Still an Extraordinary Power, But for How Much Longer? The United States in World Finance, in Lawton, Thomas C., Rosenau, James N. and Verdun, Amy C. (eds) *Strange Power; Shaping the Parameters of International Relations and International Political Economy*. Aldershot: Ashgate, pp. 229–247.

Helleiner, Eric, Pagliari, Stefano and Zimmermann, Hubert (eds) 2010: *Global Finance in Crisis: The Politics of International Regulatory Change*. London: Routledge.

Huffschmid, Jörg 2002: *Politische Ökonomie der Finanzmärkte*, updated and expanded edn. Hamburg: VSA-Verlag.

Lawton, Thomas C. and Michaels, Kevin P. 2000: The Evolving Global Production Structure: Implications for International Political Economy, in Lawton, Thomas C., Rosenau, James N. and Verdun, Amy C. (eds) *Strange Power: Shaping the Parameters of International Relations and International Political Economy*. Aldershot: Ashgate, pp. 57–74.

Maliniak, Daniel and Tierney, Michael J. 2009: The American School of IPE, *Review of International Political Economy* 16(1): 6–33.

May, Christopher 2000: Addendum: Fifty Years of International Affairs Analysis: An Annotated Bibliography of Susan Strange's Academic Publications, in Lawton, Thomas C., Rosenau, James N. and Verdun, Amy C. (eds) *Strange Power: Shaping the Parameters of International Relations and International Political Economy*. Aldershot: Ashgate, pp. 421–443.

Murphy, Craig N. and Nelson, Douglas R. 2001: International Political Economy: A Tale of Two Heterodoxies, *British Journal of Politics and International Relations* 3(3): 393–412.

Mytelka, Lynn K. 2000: Knowledge and Structural Power in the International Political Economy, in Lawton, Thomas C., Rosenau, James N. and Verdun, Amy C. (eds) *Strange Power: Shaping the Parameters of International Relations and International Political Economy*. Aldershot: Ashgate, pp. 39–56.

Palan, Ronen 1999: Susan Strange 1923–1998: A Great International Relations Theorist, *Review of International Political Economy* 6(2): 121–132.

Palan, Ronen 2003: Pragmatism and International Relations in the Age of Banker's Capitalism: Susan Strange's Vision for a Critical International Political Economy, in Bauer, Harry and Brighi, Elisabetta (eds) *International Relations at LSE: A History of 75 Years*. London: Millennium Publishing Group, pp. 117–138.

Panitch, Leo and Konings, Martijn (eds) 2008: *American Empire and the Political Economy of Global Finance*. New York: Palgrave Macmillan.

Ravenhill, John (2008): International Political Economy, in Reus-Schmit, Christian and Snidal, Duncan (eds) *The Oxford Handbook of International Relations*. Oxford: Oxford University Press, pp. 539–557.

Scherrer, Christoph 1999: *Globalisierung wider Willen? Die Durchsetzung liberaler Außenwirtschaftspolitik in den USA*. Berlin: Sigma.

Seabrooke, Leonard 2001: *U.S. Power in International Finance: The Victory of Dividends*. New York: Palgrave Macmillan.

Story, Jonathan 2000: Setting the Parameters: A Strange World System, in Lawton, Thomas C., Rosenau, James N. and Verdun, Amy C. (eds) *Strange Power: Shaping the Parameters of International Relations and International Political Economy*. Aldershot: Ashgate, pp. 19–37.

Strange, Susan 1970: International Economics and International Relations. A Case of Mutual Neglect, *International Affairs* 46(2): 304–315.

Strange, Susan 1971: *Sterling and British Policy: A Political Study of an International Currency in Decline*. Oxford: Oxford University Press.

Strange, Susan 1975: What is Economic Power, and Who Has It?, *International Journal* 30(2): 207–224.

Strange, Susan 1976a: International Monetary Relations. Vol. 2 by Shonfield, Andrew (ed.) *International Economic Relations in the Western World 1959–71*. New York: Oxford University Press.

Strange, Susan 1976b: The Study of Transnational Relations, *International Affairs* 52(2): 333–345.

Strange, Susan 1982: Cave! Hic Dragones: A Critique of Regime Analysis, *International Organization* 36(2): 479–497.

Strange, Susan 1984: The Global Political Economy, 1959–1984, *International Journal* 39(2): 267–283.

Strange, Susan 1987: The Persistent Myth of Lost Hegemony, *International Organization* 41(4): 551–574.

Strange, Susan 1988: The Future of the American Empire, *Journal of International Affairs* 42(1): 1–17.

Strange, Susan 1989a: I Never Meant to be an Academic, in Kruzel, Joseph and Rosenau, James N. (eds) *Journeys Through World Politics: Autobiographical Reflections of Thirty-Four Academic Travelers*. Lexington, MA: Lexington Books, pp. 429–436.

Strange, Susan 1989b: Toward a Theory of Transnational Empire, in Czempiel, Ernst-Otto and Rosenau, James N. (eds) *Global Changes and Theoretical Challenges. Approaches to World Politics for the 1990s*. Lexington: Lexington Books, pp. 161–176.

Strange, Susan 1991: New World Order. Conflict and Co-operation, *Marxism Today* 44(1): 30–33.

Strange, Susan 1994b: Wake up, Krasner! The World *Has* Changed, *Review of International Political Economy* 2(1): 209–219.

Strange, Susan 1995a: Political Economy and International Relations, in Booth, Ken and Smith, Steve (eds) *International Relations Theory Today*. Cambridge: Polity Press, pp. 154–174.

Strange, Susan 1995b: The Defective State, *Daedalus* 124(2): 55–74.

Strange, Susan 1995c: The Limits of Politics, *Government and Opposition* 30(3): 291–311.

Strange, Susan 1997b: The Future of Global Capitalism, or Will Divergence Persist Forever?, in Crouch, Colin and Streeck, Wolfgang (eds) *The Political Economy of Modern Capitalism*. London: Sage, pp. 182–191.

Strange, Susan 1997c: The Problem or the Solution? Capitalism and the State System, in Gill, Stephen and Mittleman, James H. (eds) *Innovation and Transformation in International Studies*. Cambridge: Cambridge University Press, pp. 236–247.

Strange, Susan 1997d: Territory, State, Authority and Economy. A New Realist Ontology of Global Political Economy, in Cox, Robert W. (ed.) *The New Realism: Perspectives on Multilateralism and World Order*. Basingstoke: Macmillan, pp. 3–19.

Strange, Susan 1998b: *What Theory? The Theory in Mad Money*. CSGR Working Paper No. 18. Warwick: CSGR.

Strange, Susan 1999: The Westfailure System, *Review of International Studies* 25(3): 345–354.

Tooze, Roger 2000a: Ideology, Knowledge and Power in International Relations and International Political Economy, in Lawton, Thomas C., Rosenau, James N. and Verdun, Amy C. (eds) *Strange Power: Shaping the Parameters of International Relations and International Political Economy*. Aldershot: Ashgate, pp. 175–194.

Tooze, Roger 2000b: Susan Strange, Academic International Relations and the Study of International Political Economy, *New Political Economy* 5(2): 280–289.

Tooze, Roger and May, Christopher (eds) 2002: *Authority and Markets: Susan Strange's Writings on International Political Economy*. Houndmills: Palgrave Macmillan.

Underhill, Geoffrey R.D. 2000: Global Money and the Decline of State Power, in Lawton, Thomas C., Rosenau, James N. and Verdun, Amy C. (eds) *Strange Power: Shaping the Parameters of International Relations and International Political Economy*. Aldershot: Ashgate, pp. 115–135.

Verdun, Amy 2000: *European Responses to Globalization and Financial Market Integration. Perceptions of Economic and Monetary Union in Britain, France and Germany*. New York: St. Martin's Press.

Social constructivism

Cornelia Ulbert

1 Introduction

Constructivist approaches have become firmly established within the spectrum of IR theories.[1] The term covers a diverse range of theoretical perspectives whose common denominator is the assumption that we have no direct access to "reality". Instead the "social world", as accessible to us, is constructed through the way in which we deal with others, the ideas we share about the "world" and how we experience our environment. Beyond that, it becomes more difficult to define what "constructivism" in International Relations actually means (see Fierke and Jørgensen 2001: 4). This is bound up with the fact that social scientific constructivism[2] is not just a theory in the narrower sense of the term. According to Jørgensen, the term "constructivism" is used in four different ways, depending on the level on which a given author engages with it: philosophical constructivism, constructivism as metatheory, constructivist theory building and constructivist empirical research (Jørgensen 2001).

The first level, philosophy, revolves around debates within the theory of science over whether there is a reality outside of our perception and how we can make statements about the "world" in the first place. On this level, we might apply the term "constructivist" to postmodern, social constructivist and even certain critical approaches. Metatheory is a theory about theories that surveys alternative explanatory approaches and possible systematic research programmes. With the help of a metatheory we can specify epistemological goals and gain insights into how we might formulate, apply and verify theories. In the first instance, constructivism as a metatheory does not make statements about specific phenomena within international politics or how they might be explained. Based on a number of key premises, the constructivist perspective instead opens up possible ways of comprehending an object of study and making statements about its character. But this means that different authors have different ideas about what constructivism actually is.

The first thing we can say is that constructivist approaches in International Relations are underpinned by ideas about its objects of analysis (ontology) based on the assumption that the social world is constructed. This goes hand-in-hand with the epistemological insight that knowledge is socially constructed. Ultimately, all constructivist writings aim to describe and explain, with the aid of various methods, how these constructions are produced. Constructivist approaches thus comprise a triangle of ontology, epistemology and methodology (see Figure 1).

There is consensus that constructivism – like rationalism – is not in the first instance a *substantial* theory within International Relations, in other words one with a particular content. Substantial theories that make statements about the phenomena of international politics would include deterrence theory or theories of the "democratic peace".

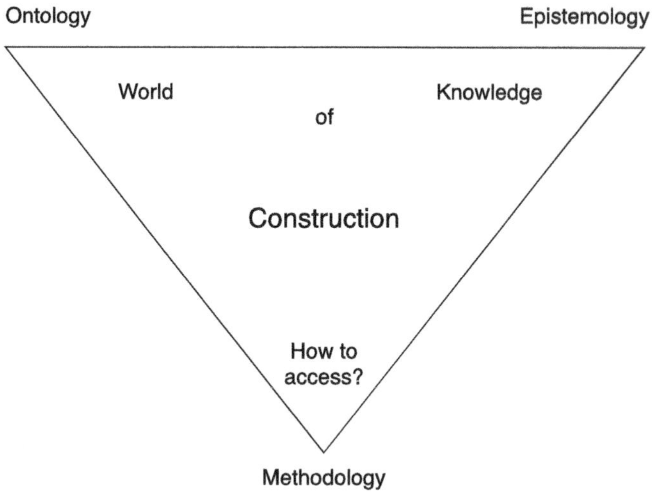

Figure 1 The constructivist triangle.

There are real historical reasons, as well as reasons related to the history of science or the discipline itself, why constructivist approaches have been accepted so rapidly within International Relations. As early as the 1980s, a theoretical debate began to take off within International Relations that Yosef Lapid described as the "third great debate" following those between realism and idealism and between traditionalism and behaviourism (Lapid 1989). This debate between positivist and "post-positivist" approaches saw an intensive effort to get to grips with the epistemological foundations of the discipline, an endeavour that called into question many assumptions about the nature of its objects of study such as anarchy or sovereignty (see, for example, Ashley 1988). In the 1980s, neo-institutionalism entered the theoretical debate within IR (see also the chapters on interdependence and regime theory by Manuela Spindler and Bernhard Zangl in this volume). It was in this context that Robert Keohane introduced the distinction between rationalist and reflexive institutionalist approaches in a much discussed essay (Keohane 1988), a distinction that was fundamental to subsequent debates on all approaches characterized by a nonpositivist conception of science or by interpretive and *Verstehen*-based methods.[3] Only in the second half of the 1990s did the term "constructivism", which appeared in the work of Nicholas Onuf (1989), become established to refer to those approaches that underline the intersubjective quality of the social world and the reciprocal constitution of actor and structure, and that make the role of ideas, constitutive rules and norms, and the endogenous development of interests and identities, central to their analyses.[4] The events of 1989 accelerated the search for new theoretical explanatory models, since the discipline had to admit that it had not predicted the end of the Cold War with its existing analytical toolkit (Lebow and Risse-Kappen 1995). Socioeconomic and political changes such as globalization, environmental changes, an awareness of the rise of knowledge societies and the changed role of the state also confronted the discipline of International Relations with new theoretical challenges.[5]

Alexander Wendt, who will play a key role in the following discussion as our reference theorist, has been a source of stimulus for the theoretical debate on constructivist approaches since the appearance of his first essay on the "Agent-Structure Problem in International Relations Theory" in 1987 in the journal *International Organisation*. From the outset his conception of constructivism was marked by an attempt to define its boundaries with rationalism. Framed like this, it is claimed that constructivism occupies the middle ground between rationalist and postmodern approaches (see, for example, Checkel 1998; Christiansen *et al.* 1999; Reus-Smit 2009; for an in-depth analysis, see Adler 1997). An alternative view regards postmodern approaches as a variant of constructivism (Katzenstein *et al.* 1998; Adler 2013), if constructivism is understood in a broader sense as an epistemological stance.[6]

2 Constructivism as *via media*: Alexander Wendt

Although Alexander Wendt deliberately got "out of the constructivist business" (Schouten 2008: 2) some years ago, he is still one of the most prominent figures to have introduced constructivism to International Relations. He is now regarded as one of the discipline's most important theorists, having developed a model of international politics anchored in a theory of science (see Jackson 2001) twenty years after Waltz's *Theory of International Politics* (Waltz 1979). At the height of his influence critics warned against regarding Wendt's work as representative of the full range of constructivist approaches, thus establishing a new "orthodoxy" (Kratochwil 2000). Despite all the criticisms of his version of constructivist theory,[7] there is no denying that Wendt has consistently discussed crucial issues in highly regarded essays, which have sparked off intensive debates and led to the establishment of constructivist approaches within the theoretical spectrum of International Relations.

One of the central foundations of Wendt's work is his critical examination of neorealism as formulated by Kenneth Waltz (see the chapter by Niklas Schörnig in this volume). In his studies, Wendt too seeks to explain the phenomena of international politics in light of the structure of the international system. So in terms of the analytical level, Wendt, like Waltz, is operating on the systemic level. The structure of the international system, which Wendt regards as the foundation of action, is the starting point for his explanations, which is why his approach may be described as *structuralist*. The crucial difference from Waltz, however, lies in the fact that for Wendt it is not just material but also *immaterial factors* that are crucial to explaining international politics. In 1999 he brought together the ideas he had formulated over a decade in numerous essays in a book whose title both borrows and distinguishes itself from Waltz's earlier work, *Social Theory of International Politics* (abbreviated as STIP in what follows). Following the appearance of STIP, Wendt was increasingly concerned with issues in the theory of science and philosophy of consciousness and started working on the theoretical foundations of a "quantum social science". As yet, however, this exists only as a rough conceptual outline (Wendt 2006). In the following discussion, Alexander Wendt's theoretical work as collated in STIP will play a central role.

Building one on the other, we can essentially identify three key issues that characterize his structuralist approach. The first is the question of how "structure" must be conceptualized in order to adequately explain processes within international politics; this led him to discuss the actor-structure problem (Wendt 1987). Second, based on the neorealist assumption that anarchy is the crucial structural ordering principle guiding the action of states within the international system, Wendt then turned to the broader issue of the importance of anarchy in explaining state action. For him, this discussion culminated in the oft-cited insight that "anarchy is what states make of it" (Wendt 1992a). But if anarchy is not the crucial explanatory factor in state action within international politics, then – and this was the third step – Wendt inevitably had to confront the question of what state action is based on. These ideas and the formulation of models of international politics derived from different cultures of social interaction form the core of STIP.

2.1 The actor-structure problem

The debate on the relationship between actors and structures that began in International Relations in the second half of the 1980s is often regarded as one of the theoretical starting points for the constructivist turn within International Relations and as one of the key substantive debates. First, Wendt discussed "The Agent-Structure Problem in International Relations Theory" (Wendt 1987). This essay and another one by David Dessler (1989) gave rise to a lively debate.[8]

At the heart of the actor-structure problem lies the fact that from a social scientific perspective action is always embedded in specific structures. Because of this there are essentially two approaches to explaining social phenomena: either with reference to various actors and their attributes (individualist explanation) or with reference to the structures in which actions are embedded (structuralist explanation). Right from the start, Wendt's interests lay in structural explanations. He considers these so crucial because for him they are the only way we can get at the ultimate bases of social action (Wendt 1987: 363). But there are different variants of explanatory approaches among the theories of International Relations, all of which assume the explanatory force of structures but that differ in how they view the importance and character of structure (its so-called ontological status) and how far-reaching its effects may be. Though anarchy and the international distribution of power are important structural elements of the international system for neorealists, Wendt rightly points out that neorealist explanations are essentially based on an individualist ontology and explain behaviour in terms of attributes on the actor level. The structure of the international system is defined, with regard for example to the distribution of power, according to specific attributes of member states ("distribution of capabilities"). These determine what the structure looks like, for example whether we are dealing with a bipolar, multipolar or even unipolar system. Logically, these attributes are ontologically antecedent to structure and impact on the behaviour of actors via the structure. World-system approaches, conversely, adopt a holistic perspective.[9] For them the structure of the international system is based on the organizing principles of the capitalist global economy, especially the form of the international division of labour (see also the chapter by Andreas Nölke in this volume). So this structure is based not on the characteristics of actors but is instead responsible for the characteristics actors develop in the first place. From a holistic (or, better, structuralist) perspective, then, structures exercise constitutive rather than merely causal effects on actors and their behaviour (Wendt 1999: 165–178).[10]

Wendt, however, criticizes both perspectives for taking an overly narrow view of the complexity of international politics (reductionism). They either make actors the basic units and regard them as given, so that they precede structures ontologically (ontological individualism) or, as in world-system theory, make structures the basic units, which are ontologically antecedent to actors (ontological structuralism). But they fail to adequately explain the characteristics and causal effects of these different basic units. Both standpoints work on the assumption that their basic units are pre-given and unproblematic. Essentially, neorealism lacks a theory of the state, in other words an appropriate theory of action, while the world system approaches lack a corresponding system theory.

Wendt's proposal for overcoming this dilemma is based on Anthony Giddens' theory of structuration (see Giddens 1984), the basic assumption here being that actors and structures determine one another. This means on the one hand that structures are constitutive of actors and their interests while on the other hand actors constantly reproduce and maintain but may also change structures through their action. In this way structures not only act to limit behaviour. They also contain the "rules" that lay down for actors a particular repertoire of action options and thus constitute the foundation of social interaction. Each of these perspectives provides a different type of explanation as each provides answers to different questions. If structures are the point of departure, then the key question is how certain actions or certain patterns of action are possible in the first place. If we adopt the actor perspective, then the crucial issue is *why* a particular action *x* rather than action *y* occurred. In contrast to the structuralist variant, Wendt calls this actor-focused form of explanation "historical". But the fact that Wendt links both perspectives to these questions also shows that he ultimately gives precedence to structures. It is structures that make action possible in the first place though they do not determine it. The choice of a particular action option becomes explicable from the actor-centred, historical perspective, according to which certain – exogenously pregiven – identities and interests of actors influence which of the structurally possible action variants is in fact selected. If we assume this reciprocal constitution of actor and structure there are consequences for how we might understand, for example, anarchy as a structural attribute of the international system and what this might mean for the action of states.

2.2 *Cultures of anarchy within the international system*

If Wendt's ideas were initially informed by the insights of structuration theory, which is based on the interplay between actor and structure, then his essay "Anarchy Is What States Make of It" reveals a clear development in his work towards *processes* of social interaction and the endogenous development of interests and ideas. In this essay, borrowing from the term coined by Nicholas Onuf (Onuf 1989), Wendt for the first time refers to his theoretical approach as "constructivist" (Wendt 1992a: 393). The starting point for this theoretical development is the attempt to get to grips with neorealist and neoliberal approaches that shaped the theoretical debate in International Relations from the second half of the 1980s. Wendt asserts that both schools within this debate are incapable of explaining the development of interests and identities despite the fact that this is ultimately the foundation for understanding change within international politics. After the end of the Cold War, the discipline had to concede that its main analytical instruments had failed to recognize the processes that lead to this fundamental change in the structure of the international system. Wendt suggests that the rationalist orientation of both neorealism and certain neoliberal approaches was responsible for failing to acknowledge the complex learning processes that had brought about a redefinition of actor interests and identities. The dominant approaches had worked on the assumption that interests and identities are exogenously pre-given and focused on the behaviour-determining necessities produced by the structure of the international system as a seemingly anarchical self-help system. This diagnosis points up the attractiveness of "reflexive" or "constructivist" approaches since these were in a position to fill these very gaps and explain changes in interests and identities. Right from the outset, however, Wendt connects the turn to constructivism with the clear objective of building bridges both between the various "fringes" of the rationalist and constructivist camps and between "modern" and "postmodern" variants of constructivism (Wendt 1992a: 394). It is this aspiration to find an intermediary position, a *via media* (Wendt 1999: 47) between different and sometimes seemingly incompatible theoretical and epistemological positions that gives Wendt's constructivist approach a very specific character while at the same time opening him up to attack from all sides.

Wendt grounds his analysis of the significance of anarchy within the international system in a number of key constructivist assumptions. He links this with the goal of proving the liberal-institutionalist thesis that international institutions are in fact in the position to change state identities and interests. Wendt thus assumes that actors act vis-à-vis objects or other actors on the basis of the meanings that these objects and actors have for them. Collectively shared meanings are constitutive of all the structures underpinning our action. Because meanings are collectively shared, actors experience a certain amount of identity formation, in other words, they achieve a relatively stable, role-specific understanding of themselves and the expectations others have of them. Identity formation is thus a process of the *social* definition of actors, which is based on actors' collective notion of themselves and the world. The study of identity is so crucial because identities underlie the development of interests. In contrast to the assumptions made by rationalist approaches, actors define their interests *at the same time* as they define the underlying situation. We may understand institutions as the relatively stable totality or "structure" of these interests and identities. Institutions are, as it were, congealed collective knowledge about oneself and the world and never exist independent of underlying identities. In other words, institutions and identities determine one another.

Based on these assumptions, Wendt criticizes the neorealist reading of anarchy, according to which the lack of a superordinate regulatory authority necessarily means that the international system is a self-help system in which states rely on power politics in order to survive. For Wendt, self-help is just one possible institution that may develop under conditions of anarchy – but it does not inevitably do so. As a result, Wendt doubts that there is just one inevitable "logic of anarchy" on the macro-level of the international system. Once it is clear, Wendt claims, that the foreign policy behaviour of states varies, then the question arises as to whether it is really true that this one form of international system, the anarchical self-help system, always develops on the micro-level of international interaction (Wendt 1999: 247). Wendt examines this question mainly in the final third of STIP. For him the answer is clear. According to his structuralist understanding, the anarchical structures do in fact constitute the key units, but these structures may very well differ in character on the macrolevel, which is why the international system may be organized in different ways.

This perspective on anarchy opens up if we understand the structure of the international system as a *social* rather than material structure. In line with this, Wendt works on the assumption that we can distinguish between at least three different structures within the international system, depending on which shared conception of rules actors are guided by. Within international politics, this conception of rules is shaped by how determinative violence is in the relationship between actors and their environment, which will influence whether states perceive one another as enemies, rivals or friends (see Figure 2).

Drawing on the concepts of the English School, Wendt calls the corresponding structures – which may then develop within the international system – the Hobbesian, Lockean or

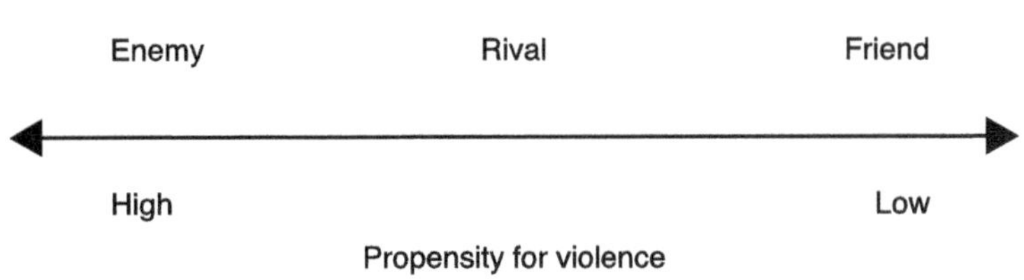

Figure 2 Conceptions of the roles of international actors.

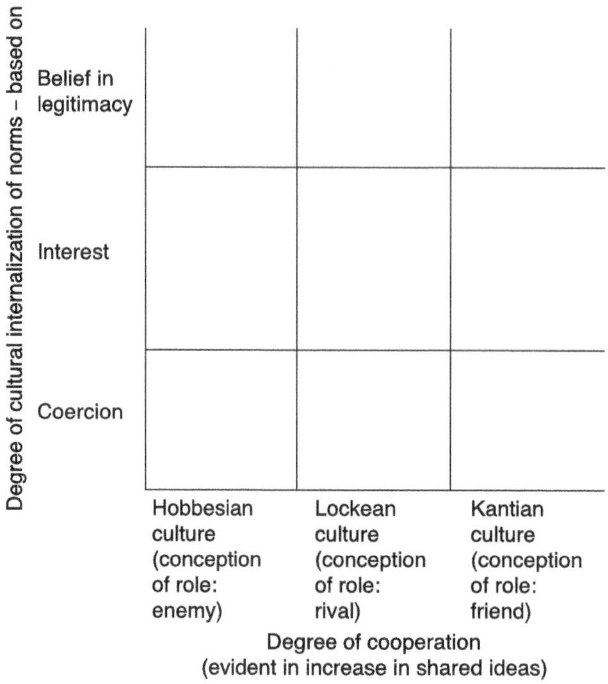

Figure 3 The development of different international cultures.

Source: Wendt (1999: 254), expanded version

Kantian structure (see Wight 1991). These structures, and the norms they entail, embody different cultures of anarchy. Which type of structure is realized depends on two factors. The first is the extent to which these norms are internalized by the various actors. The degree of internalization can be determined by whether actors adhere to norms because they are forced to do so (neorealist perspective on norm compliance), because it is in their interest to do so (neoliberal perspective) or because they regard the norms as legitimate (sociological or constructivist understanding of norm compliance) (Wendt 1999: 250). For Wendt, the second key factor is the degree of cooperation. This finds expression in an increasing number of shared ideas, which in turn lead to a situation in which something like an international society or even community may develop (see Figure 3).

According to this distinction, only the Hobbesian structure would lead to an anarchical self-help system, because states perceive one another as enemies. The more states that do so, the more this perception shapes the dominant culture within the international system. As a result, the famous "war of all against all" would be due to ideas, not to the reality of anarchy, in other words the lack of a superordinate regulatory authority or human nature itself (Wendt 1999: 260).

A developmental process is inherent in the different cultures, and Wendt believes he can discern this process in the historical record. For him, the Hobbesian culture is characteristic of the period before the signing of the Peace of Westphalia (1648). With the development of the modern system of sovereign states, a qualitative structural shift occurred towards a legally safeguarded system of mutual recognition of the right to exist and the right to property. This system is not free of violence, but its use occurs within the framework of international law, which makes states' behaviour predictable to a certain extent (ibid.: 279–281). For Wendt, historical developments since the end of the Second World War indicate the latest change in the quality of the international system. At least within the so-called OECD world, patterns of interaction appear to have developed that go beyond legally safeguarded cooperation. It is characteristic of this new culture that states deal with emerging conflicts without the use of violence and security is no longer a matter for the individual state but is regarded as a good to be produced jointly. Kant already described such a system in his *Toward Perpetual Peace: A Philosophical Sketch* (Kant [1795] 2006), which is why this form of international system is also referred to as Kantian (Wendt 1999: 297).

Wendt's different cultures of anarchy demonstrate that states' action within the international system is embedded not just in material but also in ideational structures. It is these ideas that ensure that states' interests are defined in terms of content, that abstract concepts such as "power" are made meaningful and that states gain a clear idea of the strategies through which they are pursuing their interests. Which of these cultures dominates and to what extent a given culture is internalized is something that can only be clarified empirically. But we are still left with the question of how these cultural structures can be produced, maintained and reproduced through actors' action. In other words, how do we explain structural change within the international system?

2.3 Identity formation and structural change within the international system

The development of and changes in collective identities are key topics in constructivist research. As I briefly set out above, from a constructivist perspective identities determine actors' interests. Should these identities change, then actors' perspective on certain situations may also change, which may prompt a redefinition of interests. We can explain structural change within the international system in light of these processes. Wendt works on the assumption that processes of identity formation occur through interaction with other actors. This means that states are essentially constituted through engagement with other actors, not just on the state level but also – and, for Wendt, this is the starting point for all subsequent reflections – through interaction between states on the international level (Wendt 1994, 1996). In this context Wendt distinguishes, among other things, between so-called corporative and collective identity. States possess certain common attributes that are the foundation of their corporative (or individual) identity and through which they distinguish themselves as states. These common attributes can be traced back to certain material characteristics (political system, monopoly on violence, sovereignty, citizenry, territory) and motives for action (ensuring survival, autonomy, welfare, sense of collective self-worth), which are the same for all states and which lead to the state being understood as a coherent actor (Wendt 1999: 193–245). Wendt was later to defend this view vehemently against critics (Wendt 2004). Consequently, Wendt is no longer interested in how individual state identity comes about, now that he believes he has identified certain attributes of the "state as such". He now turns to the level of the international system and examines processes of cultural selection, which, he believes, lead to the development of collective or social identities. Here, two mechanisms of cultural selection – imitation and social learning – play an important role (Wendt 1999: 313–321). With reference to the fictional example of the first meeting between two actors who have never previously had contact, Wendt brings out how he believes social identities take shape (ibid.: 328–331, Wendt

1992a: 404f.). What emerges is that through social interaction actors do more than merely gain new information about one another. Through the mutual processes of role attribution in which they engage, and which they may accept through the way they respond to one another, they also reciprocally construct each other's key characteristics. This results in the development of specific actor identities. In terms of international politics, this means that a Hobbesian culture could become established only because, in their first encounter, states adopted a hostile stance towards one another. If we want to escape from the logic of this Hobbesian anarchy of the self-help system, what we need to do is redefine identities. In historical terms Wendt assumes that a shift has occurred away from a Hobbesian towards a Lockean culture and sees indications of a Kantian culture in at least parts of the international system. How might the requisite shift in identity take place?

Wendt identifies four explanatory factors as he searches for causal mechanisms that might explain in concrete terms the shift he discusses in certain parts of the international system away from a Lockean culture towards a Kantian one: interdependence (mutual dependence), shared fate, similarities in institutional characteristics and self-restraint (Wendt 1999: 343–363). The first three factors are necessary but in themselves or in combination they are not sufficient to change the identity of collective actors. Only when one or all three of these factors are coupled with self-restraint will identity begin to change. It is only when states impose rules of conduct upon themselves that we have evidence that they do not feel threatened by an "other" and will not necessarily cling to their current identity.

In his later work, Wendt goes so far as to predict that a world state is "inevitable" within 100 to 200 years (Wendt 2003, 2005). Again, what he sees at work here is a "logic of anarchy", though one that differs from the scenarios portrayed in STIP. On the micro-level of human action, this process is neither linear nor does it appear deterministic. Yet Wendt again emphasizes the structural factors on the macro-level as a result of which, he believes, a world state with a global monopoly on violence will ultimately and inevitably emerge. Wendt sees as a key driving force the development of military technologies that are making wars ever more destructive. But this material factor alone is not enough to convince states to transfer the monopoly on violence to a world state. A world state would develop only if, in addition, the identity of states was to change in such a way that the loyalties of their own citizens were transferred to all the peoples of the world. Wendt sees the mechanism that could help bring about this shift in identity as grounded in individuals' desire for recognition. As soon as this aspiration is satisfied by mutual recognition, a collective identity will arise (Wendt 2003: 507–516).

The way in which Wendt conceptualizes identity change is characteristic of his constructivist approach. His epistemological assumptions, which are shaped by scientific realism, entail a positivist standpoint: he assumes that there is a reality beyond the observable and that science is especially well suited to producing knowledge about this reality. On an ontological level he counts himself a member of the constructivist camp since he assumes that ideas play a prominent role within the social world. Yet his goal is to achieve social scientific explanations of the effects of non-observable ideational factors (Wendt 1999: 47–91; 1998). Yet this concern to uphold a certain conception of science, a concern shared by most of his academic colleagues, also lays the foundation for a certain tension within Wendt's approach that invites criticism both from other constructivist approaches as well as non-constructivist ones. The key difference between the two camps lies in the fact that constructivists (broadly conceived) question the key scientific and especially epistemological views expressed by Wendt, while non-constructivist critics welcome Wendt's views in this regard for opening up points of contact with the mainstream debate.

3 Constructivism beyond the *via media*

It is striking that Wendt's understanding of constructivism is limited to a purely ontological perspective. As a result he tends to lose sight of the core of constructivist endeavours in philosophy and the social sciences, namely the question of how we ultimately obtain knowledge. In contrast to traditional epistemological positions, which focus on finding ways to narrow the distance between the object of knowledge and "reality" as much as possible, on the epistemological level constructivist approaches foreground the role of the knowing subject within the process of obtaining knowledge. From a constructivist perspective, then, all processes of understanding and perception are relevant so that cognitive and discursive processes and especially language as a vehicle of thought and knowledge play a prominent role (see also Zehfuß 1998; Onuf 2001). But the role of language cannot be reduced to the intersubjective mediation of "reality". One key departure point for constructivist approaches is the assumption that all knowledge is "theory-laden", that is, located within a specific linguistic frame of reference characterized in part by specific social practices. This casts doubt on the notion that reality can be grasped independent of our point of observation. Language thus becomes a key medium through which "reality" becomes accessible *and* at the same time constituted through the speech act. On the level of a philosophical conception of constructivism concerned with epistemological issues, postmodern approaches might also be described as "constructivist" (see also the chapter by Thomas Diez in this volume). Taking the "linguistic turn" in international relations seriously, a growing body of conceptual and empirical studies now focuses on the role of social communication from a "radical" constructivist approach either rooted in systems theory (e.g. Albert *et al.* 2008) or in different variations of poststructuralist discourse theory and analysis (e.g. Epstein 2008; Holzscheiter 2010). More recently, constructivist authors have drawn upon pragmatist approaches to conceptualize knowledge generation as a social and discursive activity (Friedrichs and Kratochwil 2009). All constructivist approaches in this broadly conceived sense that work on these epistemological premises have a perspective on the actor-structure relationship, the issue of anarchy within the international system and how identities take shape and change that differs from that of Wendt with his "moderate" social constructivism.

3.1 The co-determination of actors and structures as practice: rules and norms within international politics

The mutual determination of actors and structures is one of the central starting points for constructivism. Though Wendt has popularized this idea within International Relations, in his theory building he ultimately privileges structures. Underlying this is the fundamental problem that in the actor-structure relationship as described in Giddens' theory of structuration it is unclear which mechanism serves to facilitate this mutual influencing. The answer implicit in the work of Nicholas Onuf and Fritz Kratochwil[11] is: rules and norms are the key connecting link between actors and structures. But they gain this status only if we do not regard them as part of structure but instead grant them independent ontological status. From a constructivist perspective, actors are always rule-guided actors. Norms and rules lay down for actors what they should do. But this "should" is not to be understood solely as constraining action. On the contrary, because rules *open up* possible actions and choices to actors, they endow them with the quality of actor in the first place. Rules are thus not only regulatory in character but are also constitutive of actors. At the same time, rules and the practices associated with them often form identifiable patterns of action that create an institutional context, in other words the structure in which actors' action is embedded.

Sovereignty is one of the key practices within the international system. It is characterized by specific rules such as the precept of non-intervention and the attribution of particular rights and obligations, and these lay down certain action options. But at the same time sovereignty establishes key characteristics of states and constitutes states as actors within the international system. This is bound up with a bifurcation of political space into "external" and "internal" spheres. What this example demonstrates is that rules and norms make the process of the mutual determination of actors and structures comprehensible in the first place. In this process, language and communication must be understood as key social *actions* by means of which shared meanings are created. "Indeed, saying is doing: talking is undoubtedly the most important way that we go about making the world what it is" (Onuf 1998: 59). From this point of view, international relations are "structured by practices, which give meaning to international action" (Adler and Pouliot 2011: 1). Subsequently, constructivist scholars have increasingly engaged with cultural theories of social practices (Reckwitz 2002), "returning practice to the linguistic turn" (Neumann 2002).

3.2 Anarchy and authority in the international system

As we saw during the discussion of Wendt's constructivist approach, anarchy is considered the central ordering principle within the international system from which neorealism derives the inevitable logic of action known as self-help. Wendt accepts the assumption of anarchy in the sense of the lack of a central source of order and merely argues that the structure of the international system, as it forms under these conditions, depends on which conception of roles states are guided by. Onuf and Kratochwil, meanwhile, for whom rules are the main point of departure, or Richard Ashley from a postmodern perspective, arrive at a fundamentally different assessment of anarchy (Ashley 1988; Kratochwil 1989; Onuf 1989; Onuf and Klink 1989). As rationalist regime analysis has shown, there are many international institutions that regulate interactions between states. Though there may be no central regulatory authority within the international system, this system is nonetheless far from devoid of order. The opposition between anarchy as the ordering principle within the international system and hierarchy as the ordering principle characteristic of states in the domestic sphere casts a veil over what we see when we assume that different rules may lead to different forms of authority (*Herrschaft*). Political communities are distinguished by authority, but hierarchy is just one form of authority that is also found within the international system because of the power differences between states. So if we emphasize the rule-bound nature of international politics, there is no need to explain that anarchy is what states make of it. "Order" within the international system is based merely on a number of different forms of authority that go beyond hierarchy. For constructivist theorists, the fact that Wendt continues to make anarchy the starting point of his ideas is the key criticism of his conception of identity.

3.3 Identity formation and change as communication process: "Ideas all the way down"

Wendt's conception of how collective state identities develop is that this occurs through an interactional process between states on the level of the international system. What matters to the unfolding of this process and the "culture" of the international system is how states encounter one another for the first time. Wendt's constructivist critics point out that communication plays no role in these interactional processes as a meaning-creating element, which is why actors' first encounter seems to entail specific moves of the kind familiar from game theoretical models (see also Zehfuss 2001, 2002: Chapter 2). What Wendt leaves out of account here is that no social action takes place in a "pre-social" space, so actors do not interact "presuppositionlessly" even during their first encounter. But Wendt must work on the assumption of this anarchical state of nature if he wishes to explain social actions causally.

This tension between a traditionally positivist conception of science that seeks causal explanations and predictions and a constructivist ontology that assumes that the world is constructed socially is particularly apparent in Wendt's conceptualization of identity. Wendt is unable to penetrate theoretically the construction of social identities in any complete way ("ideas all the way down"), which has partly to do with his dichotomous contrast between ideas and material factors, though he puts human nature down to the satisfaction of certain basic needs such as physical survival (Wendt 1999: 130–132). Consequently, he has to make certain fixed assumptions about his actors. This leads him to ascribe to states a particular form of corporate identity and thus to justify his idea of the state as a homogeneously acting actor. It is this decision that attracted sharp criticism. To simplify somewhat, this amounts to the claim that he "reifies", in other words objectifies the state by attributing to it certain character traits, and anthropomorphizes it by attributing to it certain tasks and intentions (Jackson 2004; Neumann 2004). Wendt's constructivist critics point out that while it is possible to say that a state acts, what is actually meant by this is that individuals act within a particular structural context (in this case the state) because every social explanation requires a structure (context) and actors (Wight 2004). Wendt's specific action theoretical assumptions, of course, also place major limitations on the concept of social construction, as Wendt's postmodern critics in particular have pointed out (e.g. Campbell 2001; see also the chapter by Thomas Diez in this volume).

Wendt's "Anarchy" essay of 1992 already attracted the criticism that he cannot adequately explain the construction of state interests and identities as long as he conceptualizes the state in realist fashion as a uniform actor while every domestic political process disappears into this "black box" (Weldes 1996: 280). Wendt regards the problem of identity formation merely from the perspective of the system, not that of an individual state or representatives of a state as other constructivist authors do.[12] As a consequence, he has not developed an action theory from which we might derive causal mechanisms responsible for the choice of a particular identity or role.[13]

In the last few years Wendt has turned to the development of a "quantum social science" (Wendt 2006), motivated in part by the desire to provide a theoretical foundation for a conceptualization of the "state as person" (Wendt 2004). The goal of this endeavour is to apply to the "body–mind problem" the findings of quantum physics about the character and behaviour of the smallest particles, the so-called "wave-particle dualism", which deals with the relationship between mental and physical conditions. Ultimately, Wendt seeks to construct a coherent argument that there is something like a "collective consciousness" that makes states autonomous actors (Wendt 2006: 203f.). In the early version of this argument he still maintained the division between facts and ideas, something which attracted criticism from a radical constructivist perspective. According to critics, we are still left with the problem that even body and mind are first constituted by language and the distinction between physical and mental worlds is possible only through language (see Kessler 2007: 260–265). Therefore, in a more elaborate version of his "quantum mind",

Wendt conceptualizes social objects like the state or the international system as constituted by language, which for him is analogous to quantum mechanics:

> In its wave aspect the state (or international system) is a socially shared structure of potentiality, and as such not real in the standard, classical sense. As wave function the state can be actualized in many ways, no one of which constitutes the "true" state of the state. In its particle aspect, in contrast, the state does have an actual, definite reality, but this reality only manifests itself in the material behaviour of individuals.
>
> (Wendt 2010: 293)

Although Wendt's new metaphysical insights from the world of quanta have already been taken up in a cautiously positive way (Keeley 2007), in the foreseeable future these are likely to have less influence on empirical research than his STIP.

As far as his positioning in philosophy of science is concerned, critics have also highlighted Wendt's own location within the tradition of scientific realism. In the opinion of critical or radical constructivists it is exactly this point of view that causes him to neglect the role of language and argumentation processes in the scientific determination of "truth". Why, as Fritz Kratochwil asked in his critique of Wendt's conception of science, has Wendt not sought to develop *a* social theory of international politics instead of a *singular* "social theory" (Kratochwil 2000: 89–90)? We can find an answer to this if we look at the other side of the *via media*, namely the camp of traditional theorists of international relations.

4 The *via media* as a bridge to mainstream theories in International Relations

Having crucially shaped the debate on constructivism within International Relations for many years, Wendt's STIP received a great deal of attention. The book was not only discussed at academic conferences; the *Review of International Studies* devoted a special issue to exploring it.[14] Wendt's constructivist approach met with a largely positive response from the exponents of traditional theories within International Relations. Though some suggested that Wendt's work puts too much emphasis on clarifying the ontological question of the nature of the international system rather than analysing international politics, they still identified "points of contact" with the key debates in the discipline. His approach was viewed as a positive "strategy of engagement" (Jackson 2001: 109) in the sense of a systematic engagement with theoretical assumptions shared by mainstream researchers within International Relations. The discipline has taken to heart the idea that "ideas matter" at least since the appearance of *Ideas and Foreign Policy* (1993) by Judith Goldstein and Robert Keohane. To put it in somewhat simplistic terms, from the perspective of those who would locate themselves beyond the *via media*: if we reduce constructivism to an engagement with the role of ideas, if we ascribe an independent status to material and immaterial factors and make the search for causal explanations a significant component of our conception of science, then constructivism becomes far less frightening than it is if informed by the kind of epistemological assumptions to which postmodern or radical constructivist approaches are so attached. The kind of "moderate", "soft" or "conventional" constructivism on the level of theory building that Wendt's social constructivism represents is not regarded as a refutation of or danger to existing theoretical assumptions, but instead as a complimentary alternative to or further development of existing approaches. This opens up new perspectives on familiar subjects such as anarchy, the security dilemma or questions of cooperation under conditions of anarchy. But it also allows us to tackle new research problems such as the development and impact of collective identities (Hopf 1998, 2002; Copeland 2000). It comes as no surprise, then, that the criticisms of Wendt's theoretical approach are less fundamental than those made by constructivist critics. Certainly, a few mainstream voices suggest that the dichotomous contrast between idealism and materialism is untenable in the form presented by Wendt. But this does not inspire them to problematize his approach in any more extensive way; they merely emphasize that classical realism or neoliberal institutionalism cannot be regarded as purely materialist theories (Keohane 2000: 126–129).

For some time, accounts of the theoretical landscape within International Relations focused on the formation of "camps" that privilege constructivist or rationalist theories (Katzenstein *et al.* 1998). But the thrust of this discussion was that constructivist approaches sought to demonstrate their "surplus value" vis-à-vis the established rationalist approaches (see, for example, Adler 1997; Checkel 1998; Ruggie 1998). Though reference was often made to a constructivist challenge to rationalist approaches, the exponents of such approaches did not really feel that their assumptions were being questioned. They responded either by expanding on their own rationalist assumptions[15] or pushing for a division of labour between the two schools of thought. A symptomatic example of this was the contribution by James Fearon and Alexander Wendt in the first edition of the *Handbook of International Relations* on the basic assumptions of rationalist and constructivist approaches, which teased out the commonalities and differences as well as the strengths and weaknesses of both perspectives (Fearon and Wendt 2002). Interestingly, this article was deleted in the second edition of the *Handbook of International Relations* (Carlsnaes *et al.* 2013). Instead, in his revised contribution on "Constructivism in International Relations" Emanuel Adler celebrates the fact that "the so-called debates of the 'isms', including a debate between constructivism and rationalism, have decreased markedly" (Adler 2013: 112) and that constructivism has become "naturalized", i.e. the idea that social reality is constructed or that social action has to be assessed in context "has become received wisdom even among rationalists" (ibid.: 112).

From this point of view, Alexander Wendt's attempts to build bridges with traditional political science research in International Relations have certainly been successful in the sense that the discipline is returning to its "idealist roots" and paying more attention to social processes. That this sometimes involves old wine in new bottles is evident in the renaissance of the English School (see also the chapter by Christopher Daase in this volume). And in fact, at least in International Relations in the United States, Wendt's moderate constructivism has established a certain orthodoxy of the kind that Kratochwil warned about (Kratochwil 2000). As the debate has advanced, "Wendt (even) meets East" (Rother 2012), in other words Wendt is influencing IR communities in other parts of the world (see Cho 2012; Flawith 2011).

Wendt's efforts to achieve a synthesis between a positivist epistemology and constructivist (ideational) ontology (see also Guzzini and Leander 2006a) have prompted him to produce a steady outflow of new scientific ideas up to and including the project of a social theory based on the findings of quantum physics (Wendt 2003, 2006, 2010). Although he consciously left the framework of constructivism (Schouten 2008: 2), the debate he instigated on the ontological and epistemological premises or non-premises of the discipline opened up space for a new generation of researchers who rediscovered *social* processes in international and global politics. The discipline's new interest in furthering research on the transformation of social, political and global orders has also resulted in the establishment of a new journal on *International Political Sociology* under the auspices of the International

Studies Association in 2007. Wendt himself was one of the founding editors of a new journal on *International Theory*, which was first issued in 2009 to foster a dialogue between international political theory, international relations and international law (Snidal and Wendt 2009: 5). Opening up the various disciplinary "silos" has produced new empirical research, not only on norms and identities, but also on power and practices. Theoretical approaches following Foucault and Bourdieu – to name but two former "strangers" to IR theory – have appeared even in mainstream journals like *International Organization*. Critical Theory, poststructuralism, and postcolonialism, which were missing as distinct theoretical approaches in the first edition, are referred to in a separate chapter of the second edition of the *Handbook of International Relations* (Zehfuss 2013), which also acknowledges the new theoretical pluralism in International Relations (Checkel 2013).

Even if the turf war over which "ism" is best suited to explaining and understanding international relations and global politics seems to have lost its acridity, theoretical cleavages still remain: "In fact, theoretical fragmentation now seems deeply embedded within the field, and explicit attempts to build research programs across theoretical approaches are limited" (Wight 2013: 46). Thus, although some authors see the discipline "beyond paradigms" and celebrate its analytic eclecticism (Sil and Katzenstein 2010), the new theoretical pluralism seems to come at a very high price, as Colin Wight laments: "The idea that one has to declare which tribe one belongs to and that this determines one's ontological frame of reference, epistemology, and appropriate methods seems a bizarre way for a discipline to proceed" (2013: 47). But ultimately, scholars embracing the idea that the "world out there" is deeply social should not be astonished to discover that even science is a social process.

5 Notes

1 My sincere thanks to Siegfried Schieder and Manuela Spindler for their helpful comments on the first version of this chapter.

2 Seminal and standard texts on constructivism in the social sciences include Berger and Luckmann (1966) from a sociology of knowledge perspective and Searle 1995 within a philosophy of language framework. These texts illuminate both the sociological, philosophical and analytical philosophical roots of constructivism.

3 This discussion was initially strongly focused on the distinction between "explanation" and "understanding" (for the essentials, see: Hollis and Smith 1990). For an overview of the beginnings of this debate and its various facets, see Schaber and Ulbert (1994).

4 For recent accounts of constructivism, see Adler (2013); Barnett (2011); Hurd (2008); Krell (2009: Chapter 11); Reus-Smit (2009). For a survey of constructivist research in International Relations, see Ulbert and Weller (2005) and Risse (2009), who looks at constructivism in the analysis of European integration.

5 For a more in-depth examination of points of contact with the social sciences and an attempt to locate these developments within the history of science and identify pioneering thinkers, see Adler (2013) and Ruggie (1998).

6 In the German discipline of International Relations too it was the desire to distance oneself from the rationalist paradigm that prompted many scholars to engage with constructivist approaches. The so-called "ZIB debate", kicked off by an article by Harald Müller (Müller 1994) in the *Zeitschrift für Internationale Beziehungen*, was an original take on these issues that explored the importance of communication and agreement-oriented action, drawing on Jürgen Habermas (see also Risse 2000; Müller 2004; Herborth 2007).

7 See Sections 3 and 4.

8 See especially Hollis and Smith (1990, 1991); Wendt (1991, 1992b). An overall summary of the first phase of the debate is provided by Gould (1998). For later contributions, see Doty (1997); Jabri and Chan (1996); Suganami (1999); Wight (1999); Herborth (2004); for the essentials, see Wight (2006).

9 Holism is a school of thought within philosophy that emphasizes that the whole is greater than the sum of its parts. Parts can be understood only in the context of the whole.
10 On the essential features of causal and constitutive explanations, see Wendt (1998) and Wendt (1999: 77–88), see also Ulbert (2005: 19–22).
11 Central to the approaches of Onuf and Kratochwil are their magnum opuses *World of Our Making* (Onuf 1989) and *Rules, Norms, and Decisions* (Kratochwil 1989). Because they focus on philosophical and epistemological matters, however, neither text can really be recommended as introductory reading.
12 See, for example, the contributions in Katzenstein (1996) or the very different approaches of Campbell (1992) and Checkel (1999).
13 See, for example, Shannon's critique of Wendt's prognosis that the development of a world state is inevitable (Shannon 2005).
14 See the contributions by Alker, Doty, Keohane, Krasner and Smith, and Wendt's reply in *Review of International Studies* 26(1), 2000.
15 This was apparent in the German debate on communicative action in the *Zeitschrift für Internationale Beziehungen* in Otto Keck's replies (Keck 1995, 1997) to Harald Müller (Müller 1994).

6 Bibliography and recommended reading

6.1 Primary texts

Wendt, Alexander 1987: The Agent-Structure Problem in International Relations Theory, *International Organization* 41(3): 335–370.

Wendt, Alexander 1992a: Anarchy Is What States Make of It, *International Organization* 46(2): 391–425.

Wendt, Alexander 1999: *Social Theory of International Politics*. Cambridge: Cambridge University Press (esp. ch. 4, 5, 6).

6.2 Secondary texts

Adler, Emanuel 2013: Constructivism in International Relations: Sources, Contributions, and Debates, in Carlsnaes, Walter, Risse, Thomas and Simmons, Beth A. (eds) *Handbook of International Relations*, 2nd edn. Los Angeles: Sage, pp. 112–144.

Fierke, Karin M. and Jørgensen, Knud Erik (eds) 2001a: *Constructing International Relations: The Next Generation*. Armonk, NY: M.E. Sharpe.

Guzzini, Stefano and Leander, Anna (eds) 2006: *Constructivism and International Relations: Alexander Wendt and His Critics*. London: Routledge.

Onuf, Nicholas 1998: Constructivism: A User's Manual, in Kubálková, Vendulka, Onuf, Nicholas and Kowert, Paul (eds) *International Relations in a Constructed World*. Armonk, NY: M.E. Sharpe, pp. 58–78.

6.3 Other texts

Adler, Emanuel 1997: Seizing the Middle Ground: Constructivism in World Politics, *European Journal of International Relations* 3(3): 319–363.

Adler, Emanuel 2013: Constructivism in International Relations: Sources, Contributions, and Debates, in Carlsnaes, Walter, Risse, Thomas and Simmons, Beth A. (eds) *Handbook of International Relations*, 2nd edn. Los Angeles: Sage, pp. 112–144.

Adler, Emanuel and Pouliot, Vincent 2011: International Practices, *International Theory* 3(1): 1–36.

Albert, Mathias, Kessler, Oliver and Stetter, Stephan 2008: On Order and Conflict: International Relations and the "Communicative Turn", *Review of International Studies* 34: 43–67.

Ashley, Richard K. 1988: Untying the Sovereign State: A Double Reading of the Anarchy Problematique, *Millennium: Journal of International Studies* 17(2); 227–262.

Barnett, Michael 2011: Social Constructivism, in Baylis, John, Smith, Steve and Owens, Patricia (eds) *The Globalization of World Politics: An Introduction to International Relations*, 5th edn. Oxford: Oxford University Press, pp. 148–165.

Berger, Peter L. and Luckmann, Thomas 1966: *The Social Construction of Reality: A Treatise in the Sociology of Knowledge*. Garden City, NY: Doubleday.

Campbell, David 1992: *Writing Security: United States Foreign Policy and the Politics of Identity*. Manchester: Manchester University Press.

Campbell, David 2001: International Engagements: The Politics of North American International Relations Theory, *Political Theory* 29(3): 432–448.

Carlsnaes, Walter, Risse, Thomas and Simmons, Beth A. (eds) 2013: *Handbook of International Relations*, 2nd edn. Los Angeles: Sage.

Checkel, Jeffrey T. 1998: The Constructivist Turn in International Relations Theory, *World Politics* 50(2): 324–348.

Checkel, Jeffrey T. 1999: Norms, Institutions, and National Identity in Contemporary Europe, *International Studies Quarterly* 43(1): 84–114.

Checkel, Jeffrey T. 2013: Theoretical Pluralism in IR: Possibilities and Limits, in Carlsnaes, Walter, Risse, Thomas and Simmons, Beth A. (eds) *Handbook of International Relations*, 2nd edn. Los Angeles: Sage, pp. 220–241.

Cho, Young Chul 2012: State Identity Formation in Constructivist Security Studies: A Suggestive Essay, *Japanese Journal of Political Science* 13(3): 299–316.

Christiansen, Thomas, Jørgensen, Knud Erik and Wiener, Antje 1999: The Social Construction of Europe, *Journal of European Public Policy*. Special Issue 6(4): 528–544.

Copeland, Dale C. 2000: The Constructivist Challenge to Structural Realism, *International Security* 25(2): 187–212.

Dessler, David 1989: What's at Stake in the Agent-Structure Debate?, *International Organization* 43(3): 441–473.

Doty, Roxanne Lynn 1997: Aporia: A Critical Exploration of the Agent-Structure Problematique in International Relations Theory, *European Journal of International Relations* 3(3): 365–392.

Doty, Roxanne Lynn 2000: Desire All the Way Down, *Review of International Studies* 26(1): 137–139.

Epstein, Charlotte 2008: *The Power of Words in International Relations: Birth of an Anti-Whaling Discourse*. Cambridge, MA: MIT Press.

Fearon, James and Wendt, Alexander 2002: Rationalism v. Constructivism: A Skeptical View, in Carlsnaes, Walter, Simmons, Beth A. and Risse, Thomas (eds) *Handbook of International Relations*. London: Sage, pp. 52–72.

Fierke, Karin M. and Jørgensen, Knud Erik 2001: Introduction, in Fierke, Karin M. and Jørgensen, Knud Erik (eds) *Constructing International Relations: The Next Generation*. Armonk, NY: M.E. Sharpe, pp. 3–10.

Flawith, Robert William 2011: The Regressing "Culture of Anarchy" in Ancient China and its Implications for Wendt's Progressive Constructivism, *Australian Journal of International Affairs* 65(3): 263–282.

Friedrichs, Joerg and Kratochwil, Friedrich 2009: On Acting and Knowing: How Pragmatism Can Advance International Relations Research and Methodology, *International Organization* 63(4): 701–731.

Giddens, Anthony 1984: *The Constitution of Society*. Berkeley, CA: University of California Press.

Goldstein, Judith and Keohane, Robert O. (eds.) 1993: *Ideas and Foreign Policy: Beliefs, Institutions, and Political Change*. Ithaca, NY: Cornell University Press.

Gould, Harry D. 1998: What *Is* at Stake in the Agent-Structure Debate?, in Kubálková, Vendulka, Onuf, Nicholas and Kowert, Paul (eds) *International Relations in a Constructed World*. Armonk, NY: M.E. Sharpe, pp. 79–98.

Guzzini, Stefano and Leander, Anna 2006a: Wendt's Constructivism: A Relentless Quest for Synthesis, in Guzzini, Stefano and Leander, Anna (eds) *Constructivism and International Relations: Alexander Wendt and his Critics*. London: Routledge, pp. 73–92.

Herborth, Benjamin 2004: Die *via media* als konstitutionstheoretische Einbahnstraße. Zur Entwicklung des Akteur-Struktur-Problems bei Alexander Wendt, *Zeitschrift für Internationale Beziehungen* 11(1): 61–87.

Herborth, Benjamin 2007: Verständigung verstehen: Anmerkungen zur ZIB-Debatte, in Niesen, Peter and Herborth, Benjamin (eds) *Anarchie der kommunikativen Freiheit: Jürgen Habermas und die Theorie der internationalen Politik*. Frankfurt a. M.: Suhrkamp, pp. 147–172.

Hollis, Martin and Smith, Steve 1990: *Explaining and Understanding International Relations*. Oxford: Clarendon.

Hollis, Martin and Smith, Steve 1991: Beware of Gurus: Structure and Action in International Relations, *Review of International Studies* 17(4): 393–410.

Holzscheiter, Anna 2010: *Children's Rights in International Politics: The Transformative Power of Discourse*. Houndmills: Palgrave Macmillan.

Hopf, Ted 1998: The Promise of Constructivism in International Relations Theory, *International Security* 23(1); 171–200.

Hopf, Ted 2002: *Social Construction of International Politics: Identities & Foreign Policies, Moscow, 1995 and 1999*. Ithaca, NY: Cornell University Press.

Hurd, Ian 2008: Constructivism, in Reus-Smit, Christian and Snidal, Duncan (eds) The *Oxford Handbook of International Relations*. Oxford: Oxford University Press, pp. 298–316.

Jabri, Vivienne and Chan, Stephen 1996: The Ontologist Always Rings Twice: Two More Stories about Structure and Agency in Reply to Hollis and Smith, *Review of International Studies* 22(1): 107–110.

Jackson, Patrick Thaddeus 2001: Constructing Thinking Space: Alexander Wendt and the Virtues of Engagement, *Cooperation and Conflict* 36(1): 109–120.

Jackson, Patrick Thaddeus 2004: Hegel's House, or "People are States Too", *Review of International Studies* 30(2): 281–287.

Jørgensen, Knud Erik 2001: Four Levels and a Discipline, in Fierke, Karin M. and Jørgensen, Knud Erik (eds) *Constructing International Relations: The Next Generation*. Armonk, NY: M.E. Sharpe, pp. 36–53.

Kant, Immanuel [1795] 2006: Toward Perpetual Peace. A Philosophical Sketch, in Kant, Immanuel: *Toward Perpetual Peace and Other Writings on Politics, Peace, and History*. New Haven, CT: Yale University Press, pp. 67–109.

Katzenstein, Peter (ed.) 1996: *The Culture of National Security: Norms and Identity in World Politics*. New York: Columbia University Press.

Katzenstein, Peter J., Keohane, Robert O. and Krasner, Stephen D. 1998: International Organization and the Study of World Politics, *International Organization* 52(4); 645–685.

Keck, Otto 1995: Rationales kommunikatives Handeln in den Internationalen Beziehungen. Ist eine Verbindung von Rational-Choice-Theorie und Habermas' Theorie des kommunikativen Handelns möglich?, *Zeitschrift für Internationale Beziehungen* 2(1):: 5–48.

Keck, Otto 1997: Zur sozialen Konstruktion des Rational-Choice-Ansatzes. Einige Klarstellungen zur Rationalismus-Konstruktivismus-Debatte, *Zeitschrift für Internationale Beziehungen* 4(1): 139–151.

Keeley, James F. 2007: To the Pacific? Alexander Wendt as Explorer, *Millennium* 35(2): 417–430.

Keohane, Robert O. 1988: International Institutions: Two Approaches, *International Studies Quarterly* 32(4): 379–396.

Keohane, Robert O. 2000: Ideas Part-Way Down, *Review of International Studies* 26(1): 125–130.

Kessler, Oliver 2007: From Agents and Structures to Minds and Bodies: Of Supervenience, Quantum, and the Linguistic Turn, *Journal of International Relations and Development* 10(3): 243–271.

Kratochwil, Friedrich V. 1989: *Rules, Norms and Decisions: On the Conditions of Practical and Legal Reasoning in International Relations and Domestic Affairs*. Cambridge: Cambridge University Press.

Kratochwil, Friedrich 2000: Constructing a New Orthodoxy? Wendt's "Social Theory of International Politics" and the Constructivist Challenge, *Millennium* 29(1): 73–101.

Krell, Gert 2009: *Weltbilder und Weltordnung. Einführung in die Theorie der internationalen Beziehungen*, 4th revised and updated edn. Baden-Baden: Nomos.

Lapid, Yosef 1989: The Third Debate: On the Prospects of International Theory in a Post-Positivist Era, *International Studies Quarterly* 33(3): 235–254.

Lebow, Richard N. and Risse-Kappen, Thomas (eds) 1995: *International Relations Theory and the End of the Cold War*. New York: Columbia University Press.

Müller, Harald 1994: Internationale Beziehungen als kommunikatives Handeln. Zur Kritik der utilitaristischen Handlungstheorien, *Zeitschrift für Internationale Beziehungen* 1(1): 15–44.

Müller, Harald 2004: Arguing, Bargaining and All That: Communicative Action, Rationalist Theory and the Logic of Appropriateness in International Relations, *European Journal of International Relations* 10(3): 395–435.

Neumann, Iver B. 2002: Returning Practice to the Linguistic Turn: The Case of Diplomacy, *Millennium* 31(3): 627–651.

Neumann, Iver B. 2004: Beware of Organicism: The Narrative Self of the State, *Review of International Studies* 30(2): 259–267.

Onuf, Nicholas 1989: *World of Our Making: Rules and Rule in Social Theory and International Relations*. New York: Columbia University Press.

Onuf, Nicholas 1998: Constructivism: A User's Manual, in Kubálková, Vendulka, Onuf, Nicholas and Kowert, Paul (eds) *International Relations in a Constructed World*. Armonk, NY: M.E. Sharpe, pp. 58–78.

Onuf, Nicholas G. 2001: The Politics of Constructivism, in Fierke, Karin M. and Jørgensen, Knud Erik (eds) *Constructing International Relations: The Next Generation*. Armonk, NY: M.E. Sharpe, pp. 236–254.

Onuf, Nicholas and Klink, Frank F. 1989: Anarchy, Authority, Rule, *International Studies Quarterly* 33(2): 149–173.

Reckwitz, Andreas 2002: Toward a Theory of Social Practices. A Development in Culturalist Theorizing, *European Journal of Social Theory* 5(2): 243–263.

Reus-Smit, Christian 2009: Constructivism, in Burchill, Scott *et al.* (eds) *Theories of International Relations*, 4th edn. Houndmills: Palgrave, pp. 212–236.

Risse, Thomas 2000: "Let's Argue!" Communicative Action in World Politics, *International Organization* 54(1): 1–39.

Risse, Thomas 2009: Social Constructivism and European Integration, in Wiener, Antje and Diez, Thomas (eds) *European Integration Theory*, 2nd edn. Oxford: Oxford University Press, pp. 144–160.

Rother, Stefan 2012: Wendt meets East: ASEAN Cultures of Conflict and Cooperation, *Cooperation and Conflict* 47(1): 49–67.

Ruggie, John G. 1998: What Makes the World Hang Together? Neo-Utilitarianism and the Social Constructivist Challenge, *International Organization* 52(4): 855–885.

Schaber, Thomas and Ulbert, Cornelia 1994: Reflexivität in den Internationalen Beziehungen. Literaturbericht zum Beitrag kognitiver, reflexiver und interpretativer Ansätze zur dritten Theoriedebatte, *Zeitschrift für Internationale Beziehungen* 1(1): 139–169.

Schouten, Peer 2008: Theory Talk #3: Alexander Wendt on UFOs, Black Swans and Constructivist International Relations Theory. Available at: http://www.theory- talks.org/2008/04/theory-talk-3.html (accessed 21 April 2009).

Searle, John R. 1995: *The Construction of Social Reality*. London: Penguin.

Shannon, Vaughn P. 2005: Wendt's Violation of the Constructivist Project: Agency and Why a World State is *Not* Inevitable, *European Journal of International Relations* 11(4): 581–587.

Sil, Rudra and Katzenstein, Peter 2010: *Beyond Paradigms: Analytic Eclecticism in the Study of World Politics*. New York: Palgrave Macmillan.

Smith, Steve 2000: Wendt's World, *Review of International Studies* 26(1): 151–163.
Snidal, Duncan and Wendt, Alexander 2009: Why There is International Theory Now, *International Theory* 1(1): 1–14.
Suganami, Hidemi 1999: Agents, Structures, Narratives, *European Journal of International Relations* 5(3): 365–386.
Ulbert, Cornelia 2005: Konstruktivistische Analysen der internationalen Politik. Theoretische Ansätze und methodische Herangehensweisen, in Ulbert, Cornelia and Weller, Christoph (eds) *Konstruktivistische Analysen der internationalen Politik.* Wiesbaden: VS Verlag für Sozialwissenschaften, pp. 9–34.
Ulbert, Cornelia and Weller, Christoph (eds.) 2005: *Konstruktivistische Analysen der internationalen Politik.* Wiesbaden: VS Verlag für Sozialwissenschaften.
Waltz, Kenneth N. 1979: *Theory of International Politics.* New York: McGraw-Hill.
Weldes, Jutta 1996: Constructing National Interests, *European Journal of International Relations* 2(3): 275–318.
Wendt, Alexander 1987: The Agent-Structure Problem in International Relations Theory, *International Organization* 41(3): 335–370.
Wendt, Alexander 1991: Bridging the Theory/Meta-Theory Gap in International Relations, *Review of International Studies* 17(4): 383–392.
Wendt, Alexander 1992a: Anarchy is What States Make of It, *International Organization* 46(2): 391–425.
Wendt, Alexander 1992b: Levels of Analysis vs. Agents and Structures: Part III, *Review of International Studies* 18(2): 181–185.
Wendt, Alexander 1994: Collective Identity Formation and the International State, *American Political Science Review* 88(2): 384–396.
Wendt, Alexander 1996: Identity and Structural Change in International Politics, in Lapid, Yosef and Kratochwil, Friedrich (eds) *The Return of Culture and Identity in IR Theory.* Boulder, CO: Lynne Rienner, pp. 47–64.
Wendt, Alexander 1998: On Constitution and Causation in International Relations, *Review of International Studies* 24: Supplement, 101–117.
Wendt, Alexander 1999: *Social Theory of International Politics.* Cambridge: Cambridge University Press.
Wendt, Alexander 2003: Why a World State is Inevitable, *European Journal of International Relations* 9(4): 491–542.
Wendt, Alexander 2004: The State as Person in International Theory, *Review of International Studies* 30(2): 289–316.
Wendt, Alexander 2005: Agency, Teleology and the World State: A Reply to Shannon, *European Journal of International Relations* 11(4): 589–598.
Wendt, Alexander 2006: Social Theory as Cartesian Science: An Auto-Critique from a Quantum Perspective, in Guzzini, Stefano and Leander, Anna (eds) *Constructivism and International Relations: Alexander Wendt and His Critics*, London: Routledge, 181–219.
Wendt, Alexander 2010: Flatland: Quantum Mind and the International Hologram, in Albert, Mathias, Cederman, Lars-Erik and Wendt, Alexander (eds) *New Systems Theories of World Politics.* Basingstoke: Palgrave Macmillan, pp. 279–310.
Wight, Colin 1999: They Shoot Dead Horses Don't They? Locating Agency in the Agent-Structure Problematique, *European Journal of International Relations* 5(1): 109–142.
Wight, Colin 2004: State Agency: Social Action without Human Activity? *Review of International Studies* 30(2): 269–280.
Wight, Colin 2006: *Agents, Structures and International Relations: Politics as Ontology.* Cambridge: Cambridge University Press.
Wight, Colin 2013: Philosophy of Social Science and International Relations, in Carlsnaes, Walter, Risse, Thomas and Simmons, Beth A. (eds) *Handbook of International Relations.* 2nd edn, Los Angeles: Sage, pp. 29–56.

Wight, Martin 1991: The Three Traditions in International Theory, in Wight, Gabriele and Porter, Brian (eds) *International Theory: The Three Traditions – Martin Wight*. Leicester: Leicester University Press, pp. 7–24.

Zehfuß, Maja 1998: Sprachlosigkeit schränkt ein. Zur Bedeutung von Sprache in konstruktivistischen Theorien, *Zeitschrift für Internationale Beziehungen* 5(1): 109–137.

Zehfuss, Maja 2001: Constructivism and Identity: A Dangerous Liaison, *European Journal of International Relations* 7(3): 315–348.

Zehfuss, Maja 2002: *Constructivism in International Relations: The Politics of Reality*. Cambridge: Cambridge University Press.

Zehfuss, Maja 2013: Critical Theory, Poststructuralism, and Postcolonialism, in Carlsnaes, Walter, Risse, Thomas and Simmons, Beth A. (eds) *Handbook of International Relations*, 2nd edn. Los Angeles: Sage, pp. 145–169.

Critical theory

Christoph Humrich

1 Introduction

In the afterword to the essay that established critical theory as a distinct approach in the social sciences, Max Horkheimer writes that critical theory is concerned with "people and *all their potential*" (Horkheimer 1970: 58; my emphasis). Critical theory sees it as its task to identify, critique and overcome any social mechanisms and structures that systematically prevent people from realizing their potential. In other words, it identifies and criticizes *systems of exclusion* and seeks emancipation from them. To this end, critical theory engages both with social practice and with other social science theories.

On the level of social practice, numerous kinds of exclusion need to be tackled, from the lack of opportunity to live a decent life, to the curtailment of rights, or limited prospects of a professional career as a result of gender, race or nationality. On the level of theory, critical theory actively delimits itself from what it views as non-critical theory. It refers to these theories as *traditional, positivist* or "*problem-solving*" theories. The charge here is that in attempting to explain the social world in terms of general causal relationships and put forward solutions to acute problems on this basis, these theories merely help reproduce existing systems of exclusion. Treating the social world as a research object susceptible to explanation and technical manipulation means treating it as *quasi-natural.* Some components of the social world thus necessarily appear as unchangeable regularities or parameters. Critical theory seeks to expose such false *naturalizations* both through theoretical reflection and empirical studies. It attempts to expose and explain the historical contingency and fundamental changeability of social conditions previously regarded as natural. Unmasking the contingency of existing social orders makes it possible to conceive of alternatives that might help emancipate us from exclusionary systems, in other words help to create *more inclusive* orders.

A number of very different approaches are placed under the rubric of "critical theory".[1] They differ according to the type of exclusionary systems they are concerned with, how they conceive of emancipation and thus of alternatives to the existing social order. They also differ in how they assess the prospects for emancipation generally and where they look for emancipatory potential within the existing social order. As a critical theory, feminism, for example, is distinguished by its focus on gender-specific exclusion (see the chapter by Barbara Finke in this volume). Postmodern approaches differ from other currents within critical theory in their scepticism about alleged emancipation: because every social order is constituted through the exclusion of alternative possibilities, every order is necessarily a system of exclusion and postmodernists refuse to endorse any of these systems (see the chapter by Thomas Diez in this volume). Modernist approaches within critical theory, meanwhile, are geared towards the objective of emancipation within an at least roughly definable, more inclusive social order. Here we may distinguish between the *communicative* and *productionist* paradigms of critical theory. The productionist paradigm can be traced back directly to Marx's criticism of political economy. Marx saw the potential for emancipation as arising directly from the development of the social forces of *production*. The communicative paradigm was developed by Jürgen Habermas. For him, the potential for emancipation lies in uncircumventable conditions of language use that always keep communication open to critique and moral learning.

Within International Relations (IR) theory, Andrew Linklater has sought to systematically import the communicative paradigm of critical theory as developed by Habermas. I explore Linklater's critical theory in the following sections of this chapter.[2] Initially, however, the term "critical theory" became known in IR mainly through the work of Robert Cox, which comes under the rubric of the productionist paradigm. It was in an oft-cited article from 1981 that he introduced the above-mentioned distinction between critical and problem-solving theory into American IR (Cox 1981; see the chapter by Andreas Bieler and Adam David Morton in this volume).

With their critical theories, Cox and Linklater were part of a broader movement within IR that emerged in the early 1980s as a response both to changes in the practice of international politics and to developments within IR theory.[3] In terms of political practice, in the late 1970s the two superpowers reversed the progress made through the policy of détente between East and West. Once again Cold War tensions mounted and the nuclear arms race intensified. It was during this period that Kenneth Waltz published his neorealist theory of international politics. In view of the anarchical structure of international relations, it referred to an *unchanging* "self-help system". By naturalizing anarchy and self-help, Waltz's neorealism made it seem imperative to learn to live with them. He thus positively underscored the idea that the bipolar distribution of power between East and West provided the system with relative stability (see also the chapter by Niklas Schörnig in this volume). But the perception of a growing risk of nuclear war spurred many scholars to develop theoretical alternatives with the practical intent of overcoming the Cold War international system (Kubálková and Cruickshank 1986: 165).

Like other critical theorists of international relations, then, Linklater emphasizes the contrast between his work and neorealism, which he regards as the embodiment of a positivist, "problem-solving" theory (see Hoffman 1987: 236; Linklater 1998b: 15). Linklater's studies have gained a great deal of attention within English-speaking IR, and have been included in many introductory texts. In this sense, they may be regarded as exemplary of the critical theory of international relations in general and its communicative paradigm in particular.

2 The critical theory of international relations: Andrew Linklater

2.1 Linklater's communicative paradigm of critical theory

Linklater first presents his theoretical programme in the book based on his PhD dissertation, *Men and Citizens in the Theory of International Relations* (Linklater 1982). Though he did not explicitly refer to critical theory at the time, he later elaborated this programme as the critical theory of international relations within the framework of the communicative paradigm. In *Men and Citizens*, Linklater examines the difference between moral obligations towards one's *fellow citizens* and those towards one's *fellow human beings*. His reflections here ultimately seek to establish moral universalism as the only possible normative perspective for an international political theory and to dismiss the idea that it is our obligations to fellow citizens that should take precedence. In so doing, he criticizes the state as an exclusionary system. The state is premised on the distinction between fellow citizens and other human beings with the effect of including the former in its moral obligations while excluding the latter.

In the 1980s, Linklater went on to grapple both with realism and the productionist paradigm of critical theory. The result was *Beyond Realism and Marxism: Critical Theory and International Relations*, in which he began to think for the first time about a critical theory of international relations within the framework of the communicative paradigm. According to Linklater, both Marxism and realism neglect "the significance of moral development and . . . the main advances in the evolution of universal moral norms" (Linklater 1990a: 7). What we must do, then, is incorporate these into theories of social evolution. One of the ways Linklater does this is by borrowing the idea of the central importance of learning processes from Habermas' "reconstruction of historical materialism" (Habermas 1991). These learning processes are mediated by linguistic interaction. Learning becomes possible through so-called *communicative action*, which is based on achieving mutual understanding through the "forceless force" of the better argument (Habermas 1984–87).

Because it looks not just at production processes but also communicative interaction, Linklater's critical theory can examine exclusion in the spheres of morality and law, for example, in the way that *political communities* deal with one another. It is law and morality that distinguish between included and excluded and thus constitute political communities as systems of exclusion – be it on the level of the state, international society or entire civilizations (Linklater 1998b: 123ff.). As in *Men and Citizens*, what interests Linklater here is "the significance of . . . differences between insiders and outsiders for the conduct of external relations" (Linklater 1990c: 146). "Outsiders" are individuals whose opportunities to realize their potential are ruled out as completely or largely irrelevant through the thinking and action of "insiders". Emancipation from exclusionary systems that privilege the particularist interests of "insiders" (for example, those of citizens, men, Germans or whites) over those of "outsiders" (the rest of humanity, in each case), means more inclusive, more universal moral and legal forms and norms that expand the circle of "insiders" or at least mitigate the exclusion of "outsiders".

At present, the law-based exclusionary systems of citizenship and state sovereignty make the state a dual system of exclusion (Linklater 1996b: 88). Both domestically and with respect to the external world, citizenship and sovereignty make a distinction between "insiders" and "outsiders". Citizenship establishes inclusion in a state's system of decision-making and distribution but of course also exclusion from them. It gives the rights of citizens priority over the rights of the rest of humanity. Within the state, national or ethnic minorities or even women may be "outsiders" in that they lack full citizenship or citizenship lacks the institutional means to help them realize their potential. So the state may also be bound up with systems of moral exclusion such as patriarchy, nationalism, racism or cultural chauvinism. The institution of state sovereignty safeguards these exclusionary systems vis-à-vis the rest of the world on the international level. Through their sovereignty, states are not only protected from interference in their own affairs. In addition, they can neither be forced to consider the rest of humanity when making national decisions nor can they be prevented from exclusively privileging their own citizens at the expense of others through their foreign and international policies.

The communicative paradigm of critical theory underlines that exclusionary systems may be changed through processes of moral-practical learning. Building on Habermas, Linklater distinguishes between three other concepts of learning: (1) the *technological-instrumental* learning centred on the control of nature; (2) the *strategic* learning involved in the manipulation of other actors; and (3) the *diplomatic* learning based on rules of coexistence within international society. In analysing all the various forms of learning, the goal is

> to understand how the relationships among the different forms of social learning . . . shape the moral boundaries specific to individual communities; it is to comprehend the latter's potential for organizing their external relations in accordance with universalistic principles as opposed to norms that are particularistic and exclusionary.
>
> (Linklater 1990c: 277)

The analysis of forms of learning and their interaction as propagated by Linklater forms part of his magnum opus, *The Transformation of Political Community: Ethical Foundations of the Post-Westphalian Era* (Linklater 1998b). Here Linklater elaborates his critical theory of international relations with reference to three dimensions.

Through the *normative* dimension, Linklater seeks to establish the validity of certain "nonarbitrary principles that can be used to criticize existing social practices and to imagine improved forms of life" (Linklater 2001a: 25). In other words, these principles form the normative ground for a critique of exclusionary systems by explaining why this critique is legitimate. The non-arbitrary principles he establishes lead Linklater to make three normative demands for more *universal inclusion*, greater *sensitivity to difference* and a *more just distribution* of material goods. The *sociological* dimension is concerned with social structures and mechanisms of exclusion and their historical evolution. In Linklater's terminology, here we examine how forms of inclusion and exclusion are learned or unlearned through social processes and how political communities are constituted or transformed as a result. Linklater seeks to show that there has been a triple transformation of political communities in the Western world – in line with his normative demands – as a result of moral-practical learning processes and thus that international society can change as well. Because this transformation calls into question the present-day international system of sovereign nation states, which is traced back to the Peace of Westphalia (1648), Linklater refers to his explicitly normative theory as an "ethics for the post-Westphalian era". Through the *praxeological* dimension, Linklater then seeks to identify the emancipatory potential within the existing order that might be developed in practice to further advance the triple transformation of the "Westphalian system". Linklater calls this potential "moral capital". This capital is, as it were, at our disposal to invest in the realization of a more inclusive order.

2.2 The dimensions of critical theory

The normative dimension

It is difficult to deny that the state is a dual system of exclusion. But to criticize this system in a morally sound way is a significant challenge when we consider that most political theories have sought to provide normative justification for legitimate forms of statehood. To meet this challenge, Linklater claims, one needs to rely on the normative foundation of *moral universalism*: "Universalism . . . desires what *no* morally exclusive community can supply, namely a politics of *impartiality* which takes the welfare of *all* humans into account"

(Linklater 1990b: 49; my emphasis). If his critique is to endure, he must be able to justify this foundation in moral terms. In doing so, however, Linklater relies mainly on a negative argumentational strategy. Instead of a positive justification, he only indirectly argues *for* moral universalism by rejecting criticisms of it. He tackles three closely linked arguments against universalism that he identifies in the work of the nineteenth-century historicists (Meinecke, Treitschke), postmodernists (including Foucault, Lyotard and Rorty) and feminist authors (such as Gilligan and Fraser).

Linklater quotes Friedrich Meinecke to underline that the historicists were attempting to demonstrate that universalist ethics "always bring with them a clump of native soil from the national sphere, a sphere that no individual can completely leave behind" (Linklater 1998b: 65). This means that alleged universalist ethics are ultimately still particularist and may be abused to justify one's own particular interests in the name of humanity. This is an argument shared by postmodern critics, who assert – on the basis of epistemological reservations – that a non-exclusive ethics applicable to all human beings is fundamentally impossible.

Feminist critics in particular have assailed universalism for its blindness to difference. They maintain that universalist ethics exclude a so-called ethics of care that considers the needs of the "concrete other". Caring for the needs of a concrete other is primarily associated with the everyday moral practices of women (Linklater 1996a: 291). These feminist critics argue that universalist ethics itself may become an exclusionary mechanism. Because it envisages welfare for all without bias, universalism sees merely "generalized others", in other words, abstract individuals who have certain rights regardless of the differences in their actual needs (see Linklater 1992: 32ff.). Further, precisely because universalist ethics must abstract from specific conditions, it is accused of being too abstract to prompt people to take action. It is thus very unlikely to be politically effective.

In rejecting criticisms of moral universalism Linklater uses discourse ethics as a theoretical tool.[4] Discourse ethics postulates that a norm can lay claim to validity only if it gains the consent of all those affected by it in a non-exclusive, domination-free discourse. The fact that individuals are excluded from decisions that affect them thus contradicts the discourse ethical notion of legitimate norms. Letting only members of a specific community (such as citizens) decide cannot be justified in discourse ethical terms if the consequences of this decision also affect individuals outside of this community (Linklater 1996a: 193).

Equipped with discourse ethics, Linklater can counter the historicists' critique by asserting that one of discourse ethics' main strengths is to help prevent a particularist morality dressed up in universalist concepts. By calling for the uncoerced agreement of all those affected, discourse ethics seeks to guarantee genuine universality: particularist arguments would be unable to achieve consensus within a domination-free discourse.

Linklater takes the wind out of the sails of the postmodern critique by showing that its practical proposals actually reflect the principles of discourse ethics. At least implicitly, many postmodern theorists share the discourse ethical conviction that "the legitimacy of systems of exclusion ought to be decided in open dialogue" (Linklater 2001a: 28ff.). The feminists' charge of blindness to difference can be countered with two key arguments. First, the demand that we must pay due regard to difference in our moral reflections entails its own universalist moral aspiration: it is morally imperative for everyone to take account of differences in an unbiased way (Linklater 1990c: 140). Second, Linklater argues that within a discourse, empathetic understanding and inclusion of the interests of the "concrete other", in other words sensitivity to difference, is one of the vital prerequisites for all mutual understanding. Linklater therefore regards many of the postmodern and feminist objections less as critique than as a more complete description of how discourse ethics must function in practice (Linklater 1996a: 291).

The criticism that universal norms are overly abstract applies to discourse ethics because it is merely a kind of test of the validity of norms. Discourse ethics cannot itself generate normative prescriptions. But precisely because it makes the legitimacy of norms dependent on the uncoerced consent of all those affected, it entails the vision of an *ideal communication community*, the possibility of participating in a non-exclusive and domination-free discourse. In other words, discourse ethics calls for of the "realization, within the real communication community, of the ideal communication community characterized by non-repressive consultation" (Apel 1997: 38; Linklater 2001a: 30). This implies the moral prescription of measures necessary to achieve ideal communication communities (see, for example, Linklater 1998b: 106).

In rejecting the critique of discourse ethics, Linklater is defending universalism as a legitimate normative ground for his critical theory. Furthermore, if we conceive of political communities essentially as communicative communities, discourse ethics demands greater universality and sensitivity to difference along with a just distribution of material goods as prerequisites for ideal communication communities. This amounts to the above-mentioned triple transformation of the "Westphalian system". So what Linklater has done here is to use discourse ethics to justify the triple transformation as a political programme.

The sociological dimension

The universalist critique of the state as a dual system of exclusion would be pointless if there was no possibility of changing the system. So critical theory must show that this exclusionary system is historically contingent and thus fundamentally changeable. In this vein, Linklater reflects critically on the foundations of traditional International Relations theory: for him, IR theory so far has examined only the relations between states while assuming in advance and thus naturalizing the *existence* of states and a particular form of *coexistence* within the international system.

Linklater understands the rise of the state as an exclusionary system as a case of the *strategic learning* of control in the form of state monopolies and the *moral-practical unlearning* of loyalties beyond the state. Crucial here are the three monopolies of the legitimate use of the means of violence, tax raising and the demand for loyalty. These highlight the three social forces that were in play during the formation of the state and that the state had to learn to control in order to ensure its survival or sovereignty: war, economy and culture (Linklater 1995: 183ff.). It was above all the first two monopolies that brought the development of citizenship in their wake. Subjects whose rulers demanded that they do military service and pay taxes called for matching rights. But it is the monopoly on loyalty that is especially important to Linklater (see Waller and Linklater 2003). The emergence of a state monopoly on loyalty meant that people could no longer be primarily loyal to subnational (for example, regional or occupational) or transnational communities (such as the Catholic Church in the Middle Ages). This led both to the repression, persecution or assimilation of communities that might require alternative loyalties, such as ethnic minorities, as well as to the development of new communities, particularly of citizens in the sense of "nation building".

For Linklater, space for the triple transformation is emerging in the Western world because state monopolies are being eroded by the demise of the very forces whose control was so central to the emergence of the state. In the West, the importance of the three state monopolies is diminishing as a result of the pacification of international relations, the privatization of the economy and the cultural pluralization of societies. As a result, Linklater claims, the state too is losing significance as the key entity that determines the moral difference between "insiders" and "outsiders" (Linklater 1995: 184ff.; 1996b: 83ff.).

On the international level as well, the "state" as a dual system of exclusion is coming under pressure. Here Linklater identifies four ideal typical stages of inclusion or exclusion between which transitions occur through learning processes. Following the state of *Hobbesian anarchy* in which sovereignty is not institutionalized, states enter into a *pluralist international society* when they achieve the development and recognition of rules of coexistence through *diplomatic* learning. These rules, which include state sovereignty, at least ensure that smaller, militarily inferior states are not prevented from realizing their potential within their own borders. At the same time, sovereignty codifies power imbalances and the unequal distribution of material resources. It is primarily the West that profits from this. In what Hedley Bull calls the "revolt against the West", the established international order of coexistence is attacked by non-Western states – partly because it is regarded as an expression of the West's cultural hegemony (Linklater 1992: 30). Further, as states become increasingly interdependent, conflicts arise over the appropriate practice and limits of the right of sovereignty (Linklater 1990c: 194). As a result of economic globalization and ecological interdependence, national decisions frequently impact on other states' room for manoeuvre. The challenges to sovereignty lead to what Linklater calls "cosmopolitan harm conventions" (Linklater 2001b). These are constructions that regulate the relationship between "insiders" and "outsiders" and thus mitigate exclusion. These include those multilateral conventions that oblige states to avoid causing harm and suffering to people, whether in the sphere of the environment, human rights or with respect to rules intended to limit war and its consequences. By negotiating and agreeing such conventions, states find themselves engaged in the moral-practical learning of universal norms. This marks the transition to a *solidarist international society*, which becomes more inclusive through a shared stock of universal moral objectives among states. Finally, in a *post-Westphalian world*, both state sovereignty and the exclusionary mechanisms of citizenship are superseded by universal loyalties (Linklater 1998a: fn. 27; 1998b: 167ff.).

The praxeological dimension

The sociological dimension has revealed that the erosion of state monopolies or sovereignty on the international level has made alternative orders conceivable. Turning to the normative dimension, we are faced with the question of how we might use this development in order to help realize *ideal* communication communities. What "moral capital" within the existing order might be invested in order to organize political communities in a more universal, difference-sensitive and egalitarian way? Linklater's stance here is that this moral capital is already present: domestically in the institution of citizenship and internationally in the cosmopolitan harm conventions.

Inherent in the institution of citizenship are liberties that guarantee "insiders" a sphere of individual freedom for the realization of their potential while at the same time, through rights of participation, giving them the chance to collectively set the social limits of this sphere vis-à-vis the spheres for realization of all other fellow citizens. The guaranteeing of liberties is closely linked to the monopolies enjoyed by the nation state. This means that liberties are affected when these monopolies are eroded. Political rights come under pressure as powers are transferred to international organizations, while social rights are challenged by economic globalization. While internationalization and globalization may lead to a more inclusive *international* society as a result of the moral capital of the cosmopolitan harm conventions, on the national level they may threaten individual freedom at the state level because they are removing key supervisory decisions from citizens, in other words, those affected. But people can use their citizenship rights both to counter the forces threatening these same rights and even to extend their scope. Linklater's assessment is that:

> [Democratic states] by virtue of their commitments to constitutional democracy . . . are increasingly drawn into discussions about how the achievements of national citizenship can be retained and consolidated as the logics of globalisation and regionalisation transform modern political life.
>
> (Linklater 1998b: 198)

One way of countering the threats to civil liberties is the *transnationalization of citizenship*, which is already happening in the European Union (EU). Here we see the influence of the "moral capital" of citizenship: while the transferral of decisions to the European level threatened the effective safeguarding of liberties, there were increasing demands for the democratization of the European Union, which then led to the granting of transnational civil and political rights. At the same time, of course, this transnationalization means a more inclusive order, because the political community of "insiders" is enlarged. Liberal freedom from the state is strengthened by extensive rights of appeal before international courts. Through the right to vote in local elections for EU citizens in all member states, along with the increasing influence of the elected EU Parliament, political rights on the EU level are becoming more substantial. The redistribution of resources to structurally weak regions can, moreover, be interpreted as the beginnings of transnational social rights (see Linklater 1996b; 1998b: 184ff.; 2001b).

But citizenship can also become more inclusive through greater *sensitivity to difference*. People invest the moral capital of rights in a different way when they use it to achieve greater sensitivity to difference through legal procedures or political action. In Western societies, indigenous peoples and minorities, but also women, no longer merely demand the equal safeguarding of their human rights, but call for the recognition of their particular concept of the good life by the dominant colonial, national or patriarchal culture. To this end, they demand group-specific rights that guarantee them the opportunity to live this difference within the dominant culture or to realize their potential as they see fit (Linklater 1998b: 186ff.; 2001a: 30).

2.3 The development of Linklater's critical theory after the Transformation of Political Community

Following publication of the *Transformation of Political Community*, Linklater's thoughts have increasingly revolved around the cosmopolitan harm conventions (Linklater 2001b). This has implications for all three dimensions of his critical theory. It is most clearly evident in the fact that Habermas' communicative paradigm has become less influential in grounding Linklater's ideas theoretically – though it remains present in the background.

First, the cosmopolitan harm conventions have become central to Linklater's sociological dimension (see Linklater 2007a: Chapter 9). In search of theoretical tools for a sociology of cosmopolitan harm conventions, Linklater discovered German sociologist Norbert Elias (2007a: Chapter 10). Linklater is interested in the hypothesis that violence and unnecessary suffering are reduced through the process of civilization, and that, concomitant to this process, members of society increasingly identify with one another emotionally. Elias postulates that such a process occurs in all societies, since all societies must solve the problem of how members of society can satisfy their own needs without harming others. This emphasis on the process of civilization avoids the distinction between civilized and uncivilized, since there is no relevant threshold level.

One problem involved in applying Elias' ideas, however, is that Elias saw no process of civilization at work within international society. Because of this, Linklater links his references to Elias with an intense engagement with the English School, in which he finds a sociology of the civilizing of international relations in embryonic but conceptually underdeveloped form. The result is a typology, developed with Elias' help, of forms of suffering or harm, to be used when comparing international societies (Linklater 2007a: 174ff.; Linklater and Suganami 2006; see the chapter by Christopher Daase in this volume).

This intensified sociological engagement with the cosmopolitan harm conventions gives rise to changes in the normative dimension as well: the focus on conventions in a sense weakens the strongly universalist and reason-centred assumptions of discourse ethics. The recognition of autonomous civilizing processes leads Linklater, first, to distinguish between a "thin" and a "thick" reading of discourse ethics (Linklater 2005): while the "thick" reading demands that in all societies norms are validated only through procedures that have been institutionalized in accordance with discourse ethics, the "thin" reading is limited to including in decision-making processes those who might be affected by decisions beyond national boundaries. Linklater rejects the "thick" reading because it might result in gross interference in social traditions. Yet the "thin" reading that he prefers still explicitly includes the potential for outsiders to legitimately criticize internal traditions – as part of a genuine universal dialogue.

Linklater, second, not only makes the avoidance of harm the focus of his sociology, but also brings it into play as the core element of a global ethics (see, for example, Linklater 2006). In the *Transformation of Political Community*, Linklater still tried to normatively justify the fairly demanding programme of triple transformation, whose ultimate goal is a more inclusive, difference-sensitive and just world order, as a means of approaching the ideal communicative community. Now he replaces the method of discourse ethics with a materially defined principle as the normative ground of criticism (see Eckersley 2008): the "no-harm principle". Though Linklater gives the concept of harm a very broad reading, this principle is significantly less demanding than the triple transformation envisioned by the discourse ethical foundation. Still, the avoidance of unnecessary harm remains a universal principle, and it is hard to deny that if it was respected it would mean significant changes in world politics. It also represents a more realistic programme:

> Perhaps the principle "above all, do no harm" should be regarded as the most fundamental and least demanding way in which the citizens of one state can respect duties to humanity in the face of clashing conceptions of the good.
>
> (Linklater 2007a: 130)

This principle can be further justified if we assume that sociologically the development of morality has something to do with moral feelings or empathy. Because empathy tends to form as a result of the experience of suffering rather than, for example, through rational discourse, an ethics that aims to motivate actors should also focus on this. It is true that rational discourses may determine what is morally imperative, but they may not adequately motivate people to put this into effect. Again, it is the sociology of Elias and the early critical theory of Horkheimer and Adorno that have inspired this idea rather than Habermas' reason-centred discourse ethics (Linklater 2007b).

Finally, Linklater returns once again to "the indispensable Elias" in his praxeological dimension (2009: 3). Here he reflects on the role of theory and "grand narratives". Elias, according to Linklater, believed in the possibility of a grand narrative of human history. Such a narrative might influence the prevailing short-term perspective of politics, pushing it in the direction of long-term thinking. Linklater believes the theory of international relations can play a key role in the construction of such a narrative.

3 Habermas' communicative paradigm in International Relations

Linklater's work has been broadly received and comes up whenever the critical theory of international relations is mentioned. But in contrast, for example, to the neorealist theory of international politics developed by Kenneth Waltz, his work has not triggered the development of an intellectual school. This is regrettable for two reasons. First, Linklater's work provides a theoretical framework that – if used and developed by a broad range of researchers working on a common basis – would bear comparison with the IR classics. Second, there are many ways in which researchers currently working with the communicative paradigm of critical theory could create a more comprehensive and coherent school-like context, which might lead to productive collaboration. While Linklater has moved away from Habermasian ideas, International Relations theorists have become far more interested in Habermas' communicative paradigm. A by now extensive body of research, which has made use of Habermas' key ideas in one way or another, can provide valuable building blocks for a critical theory of International Relations based on the communicative paradigm.[5]

Those studies within International Relations that refer to Habermas may be assigned to four theoretical fields. These are (1) the *theory of action*; (2) *discourse ethics*; (3) the *theory of political institutions*; and (4) the *theory of society*. The research that has been done in each of these fields and Linklater's theoretical programme may usefully complement each other.

1 The *theory of action* built on the concept of communicative rationality is the foundation of the communicative paradigm (Habermas 1984–87). Habermas asserts that the rational use of language by competent speakers entails the idea of reaching agreement via the noncoercive imperative of the better argument. Actors act communicatively when they coordinate their interests solely through the "forceless force" of the better argument. Here actors communicate *as if* they find themselves within the kind of *ideal* communication community for which discourse ethics calls. But does communicative action occur at all in *real* political processes? Because of the crucial role of dialogue and learning processes in his theory, Linklater requires concrete evidence of this. Numerous studies, which typically examine the role played by communicative action in international interactions, have now provided this evidence.[6] Within the broader context of this debate, a number of authors have brought out the specific functions of communicative action in international negotiations (e.g. Gehring 1995). They have also shown that we cannot explain specific results of negotiation without referring to communicative action. The research group on human rights around Thomas Risse has discovered that under certain conditions states find themselves in a process of "argumentative self-entrapment"; through communicative action, this may lead step-by-step to a recognition of human rights (Risse *et al.* 1999). Whether in the numerous committees of the

European Union (see, for example, Joerges and Neyer 1998), the dialogue of cultures within the international public sphere (Lynch 2000, 2005), the negotiations on the Kyoto Treaty (Eckersley 2004), ILO conventions on child labour (Ulbert and Risse 2005) or the statute of the International Criminal Court (Deitelhoff 2006, 2009): argument, dialogue and the process of reaching agreement also occur in international politics.[7]

2 The second theoretical field in Habermas' work on the communicative paradigm is *discourse ethics*. As a yardstick of the validity of norms, it can help us critically evaluate the communication that actually takes place. In the relevant studies, indicators derived from discourse ethics help to determine the degree of legitimacy in evaluations of political processes (see, for example, Jones 1999; Bjola 2005; Finke 2005; Gehring 1995; Nanz and Steffek 2004; Steffek 2004). For Linklater, discourse ethics has primarily functioned to morally justify his general critique of the state as exclusionary system. But he has not carried out critical analyses of specific norm-setting processes and thus has not applied his theory to immediate practical questions. The studies mentioned above show what such application might look like. Though in some cases this literature can identify signs of discursive legitimacy (for example, through transparent processes of decision-making, the participation in decision-making of those affected, public deliberation and an orientation towards finding agreement), international politics continues to fail major tests of legitimacy. Legitimacy deficits can be ameliorated through the institutionalization of communicative rights and through rules and procedures that foster communicative action and at least temporarily eliminate power asymmetries.

3 Habermas' third theoretical field aims to achieve the same effect within the nation state. For the *theory of political institutions*, the central question is how legitimate procedures in the discourse ethical sense can be established given the decision-making pressures of the political system and the motivational, cognitive and organizational limitations of political actors (Habermas 1996). Habermas calls a democracy whose institutional structure and political practices are geared towards the discourse ethical notion of legitimacy a "deliberative democracy". The basic idea of this model is that decisions within the executive, legislative and judicial branches must be supported by *deliberation* (the collective consideration of reasons for or against particular policies) in the public sphere and key institutions. This requires institutionalization of appropriate communicative rights, rules and procedures. Habermas is able to show that functioning modern, democratic, constitutional and welfare states require such procedures and have institutionalized them with varying degrees of success.

In International Relations, Habermas' theory of institutions can be applied in two possible ways: as a theory of transnational and/or cosmopolitan democracy, and as a theory of the institutional design of international institutions. Reflections on the theory of cosmopolitan democracy fit neatly with Linklater's studies. For Linklater, the transnationalization of citizenship rights represented one possible route to universal inclusion. But how should we conceive of the political structures in which these rights are enacted? Here Linklater points to David Held's theory of *cosmopolitan democracy*, which puts forward a concrete model of such structures (Held 1995). But Held's model is that of a typical liberal parliamentary democracy. A better match with Linklater's discourse ethical foundation are studies geared towards the model of deliberative democracy in a transnational context (Schmalz-Bruns 1999; Dryzek 2006; Bohman 2007; Smith and Brassett 2008). Proposals of this kind have been made chiefly with respect to the democratic deficit in the EU (Eriksen and Fossum 2003). Neyer (2006) goes so far as to refer to a "deliberative turn" in studies of the EU polity.

The second application of Habermas' theory of political institutions relates to the international legal order, namely, international law and the design of international instututions. Linklater, of course, applies his discourse ethical criteria explicitly to the level of international interactions, in other words international society. But he focuses chiefly on the *material content* of the norms institutionalized through cosmopolitan harm conventions – not on the internationally institutionalized communicative *processes* of generating applying and enforcing these norms. These processes in international regimes and international organizations may of course correspond to discourse ethical ideals to a greater or lesser degree (see Ellis 2002; Mitzen 2005; Payne and Samhat 2004). Again, the discourse ethical function of institutionalized rules is to minimize the effects of power asymmetries within international interactions. Such rules may place procedural limits on the deployment of power resources in negotiations (e.g. through sequencing, majority decisions or court-like procedures) or enmesh states in a tightly knit web of justificatory obligations (e.g. through rules of transparency, reporting systems or monitoring) (Steffek 2003; Payne and Samhat 2004; Risse 2004). Studies focused on such issues have emerged chiefly in the wake of International Relations scholars' increased interest in the process of legalization (see Neyer 2004; Humrich 2011). Overall, however, Harald Müller seems right to state that we have yet to see any equivalent of Habermas' theory of political institutions on the international level (Müller 2007: 223).

4 Finally, in his *communication theory of society* Habermas has described the historical evolution of the democratic constitutional and welfare state (1984–87, 1995). One of the key ideas here is that the political and economic systems have become detached from the *lifeworld*. In the lifeworld, action is co-ordinated through communicative action and processes of agreement, but within the system this is done through the exchange media of power and money. Systems rely on legitimation through communicative agreement. At the same time, however, they increasingly infiltrate the lifeworld. Through this "colonization of the lifeworld", they threaten the basis of their own legitimacy. The second key idea is that in the lifeworld of successfully modernizing societies moral-practical learning processes occur that make it possible to re-attach lifeworldly processes of agreement with the system through the democratization of law.

Linklater does not consider the first idea. Yet the system-life world distinction might help us investigate problematic developments such as conflicts between the globalized economic system and local lifeworlds. Another example would be the legitimacy deficits within political systems that presuppose rationalized lifeworld structures but are institutionalized in what are still largely traditional societies (Jones 2001; Jung 2001; Anievas 2005).[8]

But Linklater also makes very limited use of the second idea. Rather than tracing the process of legalization, he is more concerned to demonstrate a broad macrosociological tendency for change within international society. He does not offer any direct analyses of the development of international law or of concrete moral-practical learning processes. Within a broadly Habermasian framework, Neta Crawford has carried out a detailed study of decolonization as a learning process (2002). An analysis of the evolution of international law along the lines of Habermas' social theory has already been identified as a desideratum though no one has attempted the task so far (Albert 2002; see Humrich 2011).

Last but not least, it should be noted that Habermas himself has tackled topics in international politics in greater depth over the last few years. His contributions can be located within the field of the theory of political institutions and theory of society. His studies of the "postnational constellation" are an attempt to process theoretically the dissolution of national forms of societization (Habermas 1998, 2001). His works on the constitutionalization of international law can be regarded as interventions in the debate on world order (Habermas 2006, 2008a, 2008b). It is interesting to note that, unlike the authors mentioned above who have applied his theory within International Relations, Habermas himself does not see communicative action or deliberation as having much empirical or normative significance beyond the state (see the critique by Johnson 2008, Scheuermann 2008; Humrich 2011). His vision of world order is based on a materially (rather than procedurally-discursively or deliberatively) justified UN monopoly of force and on strategic compromises negotiated between those actors having the potential for global action. But as argued above, Linklater and the "Habermasians" within International Relations have already provided concepts and empirical evidence that make Habermas' reserve about applying his own theory to international politics seem unjustified.

4 Criticisms of critical theory: wolf in sheep's clothing and sheep in wolf's clothing[9]

Linklater has faced criticisms relating to all three dimensions of his theory. I focus here on two related criticisms of the normative dimension, which boil down to the idea that Linklater's discourse ethical justification for universalism cannot provide a solid basis for a critical theory. This leads on to the question of whether Linklater has succeeded in responding to the critique of discourse ethics when defending his normative foundations.

First, despite its sensitivity to difference, Beate Jahn condemns discourse ethics as an "imperialistic project" (Jahn 1998: 641). In her view, Linklater's positing of an ideal typical sequence of ever more inclusive stages of social development necessarily goes hand-in-hand with a devaluation of the lower stages, as these are further away from the normative goal. But the notion of an *equal* discourse is mere window-dressing if one of the parties to dialogue is assumed from the outset to be lower down the developmental ladder (ibid.: 633ff.). If Linklater is providing argumentational support for Western hegemony and interventions through an implicit postulate of moral superiority, then he is helping maintain the related exclusionary mechanisms just as much as traditional theories. Despite cloaking himself in the garb of critical theorist, on this view, Linklater is merely a wolf in sheep's clothing.

A second criticism directed against the communicative paradigm of critical theory is the claim that it so far has failed to produce concrete empirical analysis of international politics (see, for example, Elshtain 1999; Eckersley 2008). Precisely because discourse ethics is concerned not with specific content but with the *general* and *ideal* form of communication, the critics assert, it lacks the theoretical and conceptual toolkit that would allow it to properly analyse *real* discourses. It thus neglects the level of exclusionary practice and remains praxeologically irrelevant. So, on this view, Linklater appears as a sheep in wolf's clothing with respect to the contribution that a critical International Relations theory might make to the triple transformation of the "Westphalian system".

On the one hand, Linklater counters both criticisms with reference to his new focus on cosmopolitan harm conventions. The typology of forms of harm that he develops with Elias' help provides a direct route into analysis of the content of relevant political discourses. His retreat to the morally weaker call for the avoidance of suffering and his emphasis on processes of civilization specific to different societies certainly take some of the wind out of Jahn's sails.

On the other hand, however, it is open to question whether Linklater really refrains from judging others' stage of moral development. We can illustrate this problem by looking at the example of his position on NATO's intervention in the Kosovo conflict. Here he asks, "whether Europeans can reasonably lay claim to what might be called regional exceptionalism" (Linklater 2007: 86). By "exceptionalism" Linklater means the right to intervene in other societies. This is justified through the doctrine of "progressivism", while "statism" puts a higher normative value on sovereignty than human rights. Because Europe has gone furthest towards institutionalizing cosmopolitan communities, the question is "whether a Europe that espouses a doctrine of regional exceptionalism is being true to itself" (ibid.: 86). The answer, according to Linklater, is that Europe "cannot adopt statism without contradicting [its] universalistic commitments" (ibid.: 88). This criterion of authenticity, rather than, for example, that of moral correctness, seems to serve here as the justification for intervention. As if to underline the inherent danger of an imperialism with a moral mission, he states: "Significantly, many who supported NATO's actions . . . did so . . . also because they thought that Kosovo might be the catalyst for a new era of 'cosmopolitan law enforcement' " (ibid.: 89).

The problem, as a diehard exponent of the communicative paradigm of critical theory would probably respond, can only be solved through the institutionalization of procedures that bring political decisions beyond the nation state into line with discourse ethical criteria. If we were to focus on the development of such procedures, we might also make a substantive contribution to the transformation of political communities. Such a focus could build on the extensive empirical research on the institutions of political opinion formation and decision-making which has been done within the communicative paradigm. The exponents of this paradigm keep up the hope that improved procedural institutionalization of political opinion formation and decision-making would make learning more likely and that this in turn would lead to enhanced cosmopolitan norms.

5 Notes

1 Because of the context of its emergence, in Anglo-Saxon International Relations, the term "critical theory" often refers to the totality of *postrealist* and *postpositivist* approaches. In German, the term is associated only with the Frankfurt School founded by Horkheimer and Adorno. The tendency has taken hold to refer to critical approaches as a whole as "critical theory" and the work of the Frankfurt School as "Critical Theory" with initial capital letters.

2 I therefore refer frequently to concepts developed by Habermas in this chapter, but for reasons of space I am unable to explain them in detail. I refer the reader instead to the introduction by Ingram (2010) and the *Cambridge Companion to Habermas* (White 2005).

3 In West German IR, critical theory had already appeared by the late 1960s in the form of *critical peace research*. This chapter is nonetheless limited to the anglophone debate because critical theorists and critical theory no longer play any role in German IR (see Humrich 2006).

4 Discourse Ethics was developed by Karl-Otto Apel and Habermas. See Apel (1997), Habermas (1993) and Linklater (1998b: 85–108).

5 Though there is also great interest in Habermas' work within German International Relations, Linklater has received very little attention as yet. This confirms rather than contradicts the earlier statement that critical theory no longer plays any role in German IR. Habermas' concepts are used in a non-critical, explanatory way (cf. Deitelhoff 2006, 2009) and thus Linklater's critical theoretical usage is of less interest.

6 Harald Müller has put forward the more far-reaching argument that achieving agreement on cooperative arrangements and stable cooperation on the international level is not even possible without

communicative action. This has sparked off an interesting debate in German-speaking IR on communicative action within international politics (2001; for a summary of the debates, see Humrich 2006: 79–85).

7 For critical summaries of the results of this research, see Deitelhoff and Müller (2005), Herborth (2007), Müller (2007) and Saretzki (2007).

8 Martin Weber (2005) thus correctly sums things up by stating that as a theoretical resource Habermas' theory of society has so far played a merely subordinate role within International Relations.

9 This play on words comes from Jahn's critique (1998: 637).

6 Bibliography and recommended reading

6.1 Primary texts

Linklater, Andrew 1998b: *The Transformation of Political Community: Ethical Foundations of the Post-Westphalian Era*. Cambridge: Polity Press.

Linklater, Andrew 2007a: *Critical Theory and World Politics: Citizenship, Sovereignty and Humanity*. London: Routledge.

Rengger, Nicholas and Thirkell-White, Ben (eds) 2007: *Critical International Relations Theory after 25 Years*. Cambridge: Cambridge University Press.

6.2 Secondary texts

Eckersley, Robyn 2008: The Ethics of Critical Theory, in Reus-Smit, Christian and Snidal, Duncan (eds) *Oxford Handbook of International Relations*. Oxford: Oxford University Press, pp. 346–358.

Jahn, Beate 1998: One Step Forward, Two Steps Back. Critical Theory as the Latest Edition of Liberal Idealism, *Millennium* 27(3): 613–641.

Shapcott, Richard 2008: Critical Theory, in Reus-Smit, Christian and Snidal, Duncan (eds) *Oxford Handbook of International Relations*. Oxford: Oxford University Press, pp. 327–345.

6.3 Other texts

Albert, Mathias 2002: *Zur Politik der Weltgesellschaft. Identität und Recht im Kontext internationaler Vergesellschaftung*. Weilerswist: Velbrück Wissenschaft.

Anievas, Alexander 2005: Critical Dialogues: Habermasian Social Theory and International Relations, *Politics* 25(3): 135–143.

Apel, Karl-Otto 1997: *Diskurs und Verantwortung. Das Problem des Übergangs zur postkonventionellen Moral*, 3rd edn. Frankfurt a. M.: Suhrkamp.

Bjola, Corneliu 2005: Legitimating the Use of Force in International Politics: A Communicative Action Perspective, *European Journal of International Relations* 11(2): 266–303.

Bohman, James 2007: *Democracy Beyond Borders: From Demos to Demoi*. Cambridge, MA: MIT Press.

Cox, Robert W. 1981: Social Forces, States and World Orders: Beyond International Relations Theory, *Millennium* 10(2): 126–155.

Crawford, Neta C. 2002: *Argument and Change in World Politics: Ethics, Decolonization, and Humanitarian Intervention*. Cambridge: Cambridge University Press.

Deitelhoff, Nicole 2006: *Überzeugung in der Politik. Grundzüge einer Diskurstheorie internationalen Regierens*. Frankfurt a. M.: Suhrkamp.

Deitelhoff, Nicole 2009: The Discursive Process of Legalization: Charting Islands of Persuasion in the ICC Case, *International Organization* 63(1): 33–65.

Deitelhoff, Nicole and Müller, Harald 2005: Theoretical Paradise – Empirically Lost? Arguing with Habermas, *Review of International Studies* 31(1): 167–179.

Dryzek, John S. 2006: *Deliberative Global Politics: Discourse and Democracy in a Divided World*. Cambridge: Polity Press.

Eckersley, Robyn 2004: Soft Law, Hard Politics, and the Climate Change Treaty, in Reus-Smit, Christian (ed.) *The Politics of International Law*. Cambridge: Cambridge University Press, pp. 80–105.

Ellis, Jaye 2002. International Regimes and the Legitimacy of Rules: A Discourse-Ethical Approach, *Alternatives* 27(2): 273–300.

Elshtain, Jean B. 1999: Really Existing Communities, *Review of International Studies* 25(1): 141–146.

Eriksen, Erik Oddvar and Fossum, John Erik (eds) 2003: *Democracy in the European Union: Integration through Deliberation?* London: Routledge.

Finke, Barbara 2005: *Zur Legitimation globaler Politik durch NGOs. Frauenrechte, Deliberation und Öffentlichkeit in der UNO*. Wiesbaden: VS Verlag für Sozialwissenschaften.

Gehring, Thomas 1995: Regieren im internationalen System. Verhandlungen, Normen und Internationale Regime, *Politische Vierteljahresschrift* 36(2): 197–219.

Gehring, Thomas, Krapohl, Sebastian, Kerler, Michael and Stefanova, Sachka 2004: *Rationalität durch Verfahren in der Europäischen Union. Europäische Arzneimittelzulassung und Normung technischer Güter*. Baden-Baden: Nomos.

Habermas, Jürgen 1984–87: *Theory of Communicative Action*, Vols 1 and 2. London: Heinemann.

Habermas, Jürgen 1991: *Communication and the Evolution of Society*. Cambridge: Polity.

Habermas, Jürgen 1993: *Justification and Application: Remarks on Discourse Ethics*. Cambridge: Polity.

Habermas, Jürgen 1996: *Between Facts and Norms: Contributions to a Discourse Theory of Law and Democracy*. Cambridge: Polity.

Habermas, Jürgen 1998: *The Inclusion of the Other: Studies in Political Theory*. Cambridge, MA: MIT Press.

Habermas, Jürgen 2001: *The Postnational Constellation: Political Essays*. Cambridge: Polity.

Habermas, Jürgen 2006: *The Divided West*. Cambridge: Polity.

Habermas, Jürgen 2008a: *Between Naturalism and Religion*. Cambridge: Polity.

Habermas, Jürgen 2008b: The Constitutionalization of International Law and the Legitimation Problems of a Constitution for World Society, *Constellations* 15(4): 444–455.

Held, David 1995: *Democracy and the Global Order: From the Modern State to Cosmopolitan Governance*. Cambridge: Polity Press.

Herborth, Benjamin 2007: Verständigung verstehen. Anmerkungen zur ZIB-Debatte, in Niesen, Peter and Herborth, Benjamin (eds) *Anarchie der kommunikativen Freiheit. Jürgen Habermas und die Theorie der internationalen Politik*. Frankfurt a. M.: Suhrkamp, pp. 147–172.

Hoffman, Mark 1987: Critical Theory and the Inter-Paradigm Debate, *Millennium* 16(2): 231–249.

Horkheimer, Max 1970: *Traditionelle und kritische Theorie. Vier Aufsätze*. Frankfurt a. M.: Fischer.

Humrich, Christoph 2006: Germany, in Joergensen, Knud Erik and Knudsen, Tonny Brems (eds) *International Relations in Europe: Traditions, Perspectives and Destinations*. London: Routledge, pp. 72–99.

Humrich, Christoph 2011: Facts Without Norms? Does the Constitutionalization of International Law Still Have a Discourse-Theoretical Chance?, in Ungureanu, Camil, Guenther, Klaus and Joerges, Christian (eds.), *Jürgen Habermas*, Vol. 2. Farnham: Ashgate, pp. 323–338.

Ingram, David 2010: *Habermas: Introduction and Analysis*. Ithaca, NY; Cornell University Press.

Joerges, Christian and Neyer, Jürgen 1998: Von intergouvernementalem Verhandeln zur deliberativen Politik: Gründe und Chancen für eine Konstitutionalisierung der europäischen Komitologie, in Kohler-Koch, Beate (ed.) *Regieren in entgrenzten Räumen*. PVS Sonderheft 29, 1998. Opladen: Westdeutscher Verlag, pp. 207–234.

Johnson, Pauline 2008: Globalizing Democracy: Reflections on Habermas's Radicalism, *European Journal of Social Theory* 11(1): 71–86.

Jones, Deiniol Lloyd 1999: *Cosmopolitan Mediation? Conflict Resolution and the Oslo Accords*. Manchester: Manchester University Press.

Jones, Deiniol Lloyd 2001: The Global and the Local: "System" and "Life-World" in the Study of World Order, *Cooperation and Conflict* 36(3): 297–305.

Jung, Dietrich 2001: The Political Sociology of World Society, *European Journal of International Relations* 7(4): 443–474.

Kubálková, Vendulka and Cruickshank, Arthur A. 1986: The "New Cold War" in "Critical International Relations" Studies, *Review of International Studies* 12(1): 163–185.

Linklater, Andrew 1986: Realism, Marxism and Critical International Theory, *Review of International Studies* 12(3): 301–312.

Linklater, Andrew 1990a: *Beyond Realism and Marxism: Critical Theory and International Relations*. Basingstoke: Macmillan.

Linklater, Andrew 1990b: *Men and Citizens in the Theory of International Relations*, 2nd edn. Basingstoke: Macmillan.

Linklater, Andrew 1990c: The Problem of Community in International Relations, *Alternatives* 15(2): 135–153.

Linklater, Andrew 1992: What is a Good International Citizen?, in Keal, Paul (ed.) *Ethics and Foreign Policy*. Canberra: Allen & Unwin, pp. 21–43.

Linklater, Andrew 1995: Community, in Danchev, Alex (ed.) *Fin de Siècle: The Meaning of the Twentieth Century*. London: I. B. Tauris, pp. 177–197.

Linklater, Andrew 1996a: The Achievements of Critical Theory, in Smith, Steve, Booth, Ken and Zalewski, Marysia (eds) *International Theory: Positivism and Beyond*. Cambridge: Cambridge University Press, pp. 279–298.

Linklater, Andrew 1996b: Citizenship and Sovereignty in the Post-Westphalian State, *European Journal of International Relations* 2(1): 77–103.

Linklater, Andrew 1998a: The Idea of Citizenship and the Development of the Modern State, in Preuss, Ulrich K. and Requejo, Ferran (eds) *European Citizenship, Multiculturalism and the State*. Baden-Baden: Nomos, pp. 51–66.

Linklater, Andrew 1999: Transforming Political Community: A Response to the Critics, *Review of International Studies* 25(1): 165–175.

Linklater, Andrew 2001a: The Changing Contours of Critical International Relations Theory, in Wyn Jones, Richard (ed.) *Critical Theory and World Politics*. Boulder, CO: Lynne Rienner, pp. 23–44.

Linklater, Andrew 2001b: Citizenship, Humanity, and Cosmopolitan Harm Conventions, *International Political Science Review* 22(3): 261–277.

Linklater, Andrew 2005: Dialogic Politics and the Civilising Process, *Review of International Studies* 31(1): 141–154.

Linklater, Andrew 2006: The Harm Principle and Global Ethics, *Global Society* 20(3): 329–343.

Linklater, Andrew 2007b: Towards a Sociology of Global Morals with an Emancipatory Intent, *Review of International Studies* 33: Special Issue, 135–50.

Linklater, Andrew 2009: Grand Narratives and International Relations, *Global Change, Peace and Security* 21(1): 3–17.

Linklater, Andrew and Suganami, Hidemi 2006: *The English School of International Relations: A Contemporary Reassessment*. Cambridge: Cambridge University Press.

Lynch, Marc 2000: The Dialogue of Civilizations and International Public Spheres, *Millennium* 29(2): 307–330.

Lynch, Marc 2005: Transnational Dialogue in an Age of Terror, *Global Society* 19(1):, 5–28.

Mitzen, Jennifer 2005: Reading Habermas in Anarchy: Multilateral Diplomacy and Global Public Spheres, *American Political Science Review* 99(3): 401–417.

Müller, Harald 2001: International Relations as Communicative Action, in Fierke, Karin M. and Joergensen, Knud Erik (eds) *Constructing International Relations: The Next Generation*. Armonk, NY: M.E. Sharpe, pp. 160–178.

Müller, Harald 2007: Internationale Verhandlungen, Argumente und Verständigungshandeln. Verteidigung, Befunde, Warnung, in Niesen, Peter and Herborth, Benjamin (eds) *Anarchie der kommunikativen Freiheit. Jürgen Habermas und die Theorie der internationalen Politik*. Frankfurt a. M.: Suhrkamp, pp. 199–223.

Nanz, Patrizia and Steffek, Jens 2004: Global Governance, Participation and the Public Sphere, *Government and Opposition* 39(2): 314–335.

Neyer, Jürgen 2004: *Postnationale politische Herrschaft. Vergesellschaftung und Verrechtlichung jenseits des Staates*. Baden-Baden: Nomos.

Payne, Rodger A. and Samhat, Nayef H. 2004: *Democratizing Global Politics: Discourse Norms, International Regimes, and Political Community*. Albany, NY: State University of New York Press.

Risse, Thomas 2004: Global Governance and Communicative Action, *Government and Opposition* 39(2): 288–313.

Risse, Thomas, Ropp, Stephen C. and Sikkink, Kathryn (eds) 1999: *The Power of Human Rights: International Norms and Domestic Change*. Cambridge: Cambridge University Press.

Saretzki, Thomas 2007: Argumentieren, Verhandeln und Strategie. Theoretische Referenzen, begriffliche Unterscheidungen und empirische Studien zu *arguing* und *bargaining* in der internationalen Politik, in Niesen, Peter and Herborth, Benjamin (eds) *Anarchie der kommunikativen Freiheit. Jürgen Habermas und die Theorie der internationalen Politik*. Frankfurt a. M.: Suhrkamp, pp. 111–146.

Schmalz-Bruns, Rainer 1999: Deliberativer Supranationalismus. Demokratisches Regieren jenseits des Nationalstaats, *Zeitschrift für Internationale Beziehungen* 6(2): 185–244.

Scheuermann, William E. 2008: Global Governance without Global Government? Habermas on Postnational Democracy, *Political Theory* 36(1): 133–151.

Smith, William and Brassett, James 2008: Deliberation and Global Governance: Liberal, Cosmopolitan, and Critical Perspectives, *Ethics and International Affairs* 22(1):, 69–92.

Steffek, Jens 2003: The Legitimation of International Governance: A Discourse Approach, *European Journal of International Relations* 9(2): 249–275.

Steffek, Jens 2004: Sources of Legitimacy Beyond the State: A View from International Relations, in Joerges, Christian, Sand, Inger-Johanne and Teubner, Gunther (eds) *Transnational Governance and Constitutionalism*. Oxford: Hart, pp. 81–102.

Ulbert, Cornelia and Risse, Thomas 2005: Deliberately Changing the Discourse: What Does Make Arguing Effective?, *Acta politica* 40: 3.

Waller, Michael and Linklater, Andrew (eds) 2003: *Political Loyalty and the Nation State*. London: Routledge.

Weber, Martin 2005: The Critical Social Theory of the Frankfurt School, and the "Social Turn" in IR, *Review of International Studies* 31(1): 195–209.

White, Stephen K. (ed.) 2005: *The Cambridge Companion to Habermas*. Cambridge: Cambridge University Press.

Postmodern approaches

Thomas Diez

1 Introduction

In an article widely known within political science circles in the German-speaking world, Max Kaase once compared the analysis of political culture to an attempt "to nail a pudding to the wall" (Kaase 1983). Kaase's polemical metaphor also applies, though with an ironic twist, to any introductory overview of postmodern approaches in International Relations, in two respects. First, what Kaase would call "culture" is a key object of postmodern analyses. Second, most postmodern theorists repudiate such simple categorizations (Campbell 1998a: 4). They are, in other words, interested in taking a look at the pudding without attempting to pin it down. They are aware that, like all labels, the term "postmodern" cannot do justice to the complexity of arguments and is often used to blithely dismiss them as irrelevant or even dangerous because of their relativism (on the latter point, see the discussion in Section 4).[1]

But postmodern theorists see this problematizing even of one's own identity not as a drawback but as liberation from stereotypical thinking. They regard categorization as suspect. They also see it as a virtue to constantly question one's own assumptions because, as we will see, they consider the objective comprehension of reality impossible. This is why we hear so much about "reflexive" approaches (Smith 2001, though he includes other approaches under this rubric; Wæver 1998). So while Kaase would like to nail the pudding to the wall but is unable to, postmodern theorists view Kaase's project as such as nonsensical and restrictive.

1.1 Two understandings of "postmodern"

To provide us with a first taste of this particular pudding, it is helpful to distinguish between two interrelated but very different understandings of the term "postmodern": the epochal and the analytical. The first, namely the concept of postmodernity as an era, is probably far more familiar to us from the media, but is less relevant with respect to developing a theory of international relations.

For many people, postmodernity as an *era* is characterized by a profoundly complex reality in which processes of globalization go hand-in-hand with the dissolution of the familiar reference points through which life was formerly organized, such as – of particular importance to International Relations – modern territorial states (see Cooper 1998). In this connection the concept of the "postmodern war" is particularly important, and here changes in weapons technologies, including the emergence of so-called high-tech weapons, as well as the increasingly diverse range of actors involved in armed conflicts, play a key role (see Gray 1997 and Kellner 2002). In a more positive sense, in light of its overlapping decision-making authorities, lack of centralization and hierarchy and the ongoing process of its development, we might refer to the European Union as a "postmodern polity" (Ruggie 1993). If we follow John Gerard Ruggie, we can better understand the novel form of international system that is emerging if we embed it in the analysis of parallel, far-reaching changes in various spheres of life, and compare these with the changes that accompanied and facilitated the development of the modern territorial state. We might think, for example, of the development of the Internet and the complex forms of communication that it has made possible, of changes in financial markets and the emergence of a purely virtual market, detached in many respects from material or territorial points of reference (and whose consequences were dramatically laid bare by the financial crisis of 2008/9), the multi-dimensional narratives of films such as *Pulp Fiction* or the increasing playfulness of architecture.

One of Ruggie's central arguments is that analysis of such changes helps us understand political transformations without requiring us to use a specifically "postmodern" method (Ruggie 1993: 170). What the social constructivist Ruggie has in mind here is the dispute between postmodern – in the *analytical* sense – and positivist approaches. Essentially, this dispute revolves around epistemological questions, above all whether and if so how it is possible to analyse reality as an external observer. Ruggie himself criticizes the unquestioned acceptance of a number of basic assumptions about international politics in many International Relations theories, such as sovereignty, anarchy or the notion of the territorial state. He thus calls for the more in-depth analysis of those structures that make such things as the modern territorial state possible in the first place. For him, however, as for Alexander Wendt (1999; see also Fearon and Wendt 2002), there is ultimately a describable reality and our objective must at least be to understand, if not explain, it. Postmodern theorists do not deny the existence of this reality but they argue that it is ultimately only ever accessible within a particular *discursive context* (see, for example, Foucault 1984a; Laclau and Mouffe 1985: 105–114).

1.2 Discourse and reality

This enables us to explain two core characteristics of postmodern approaches in the analytical sense: first, their focus on the analysis of texts and other representations of events (such as images or symbols) rather than on the events themselves – one of the first standard works of postmodern International Relations thus bore the title *International/Intertextual Relations* (Der Derian/Shapiro 1989). Second, such approaches are distinguished by a deep scepticism about "objective" truths and thus categorizations, because if what we know about events is discursively mediated, then there must always be more than one version of these events.

Which version becomes established is a question of power. In other theoretical approaches, this power is generally linked to actors: those in a more favourable position because of resources or their place within (international) society dominate at least the official perspective. But from a postmodern perspective, discursive representations are not merely the *expression* of power. Instead power is inherent *in* discourse itself in that it allows us to capture events in words – but at the same time it limits what we may describe as reality. In other words, the roots of power do not lie within the individual actor but in the discursive context in which a (speech) act takes place and from which we can never entirely free ourselves (see Guzzini 1993: 472). We may change a discourse by means of our (speech) acts, but we do not decide to act on the basis of a single, valid objectivity. Neither can we control change, since someone else will "read" our "text" in his or her specific context. This stands in sharp contrast to the positivist objective of making International Relations a modern science focused on the formulation of explanatory theories and the testing of causal hypotheses.

This epistemological standpoint is linked with the conception of postmodernity as an era in the sense that both highlight diversity (that of postmodern reality or postmodern portrayals of reality). Further, in light of the proliferation of political spaces within an epochally post-modern world, some authors have come to the problematic conclusion that analysis of this world requires a specifically postmodern approach that does justice to the new diversity. By now the reader will have noticed that these two things are not necessarily connected, even if we can assume that new technologies such as the Internet are in fact leading us towards the "end of grand narratives", as predicted by French philosopher Jean-François Lyotard (1984), who coined the term "postmodernity" as applied to the social sciences.

1.3 Postmodern approaches as the critique of neorealism in particular

Let us return to International Relations. From a postmodern perspective we can describe neorealism in the 1970s and 1980s as a "grand narrative", and it was above all in response to neorealism that a number of International Relations scholars first began to draw on postmodern thought. Richard K. Ashley played a key role here. In his essay on the "Poverty of Neorealism" (Ashley 1986), he criticized Kenneth N. Waltz's "theory of international politics" in light of its state-centredness, utilitarianism, positivism and structuralism. Instead he gave precedence to classical realism because, he argued, it leaves more room for the transformation of international politics as it does not subject states"men" to the universal laws of a systemic structure (see also the chapter by Niklas Schörnig in this volume). The "poverty of neorealism", then, lay in its determinism, which left no room for political alternatives. Ashley, drawing on the work of Foucault, claimed that this determinism was largely the result of a positivist conception of science.

Subsequent to Ashley's work, postmodern critics' main target was the enshrining of the notion of the international system as a system of states in which states act on the basis of cost-benefit calculations, a system whose anarchical structure is contrasted with the secure domestic sphere of the state. Ashley himself, but above all R. B. J. Walker (1988, 1993), Michael Shapiro (1991, 1997) and – as set out in more detail below – David Campbell "deconstruct" core texts of the discipline of International Relations such as Waltz's "theory" with the help of documents central to international politics such as speeches, treaty texts and foreign policy decisions, but also with reference to a broader set of societally relevant texts, including popular culture. They attempt to show how these texts treat certain assumptions as unproblematic givens. As soon as we question these assumptions, however, the theoretical edifice often collapses, opening up new political perspectives. The problematization of such assumptions thus not only destroys (French: *détruit*) but also facilitates construction. In other words, it "deconstructs" by laying bare texts' internal contradictions and unfounded assumptions and relating them to other texts, thus opening up new perspectives.

These authors draw not just on the work of Foucault, but also on that of other so-called "poststructuralists", above all, Jacques Derrida. Their main borrowing from him is the notion that all identity requires difference. In other words, I cannot refer to "a" without simultaneously making a distinction between "a" and "b", because if we did not distinguish "a" from something else, we would be unable to identify "a" in the first place. So the existence of "a" presupposes "b" and vice versa – each gains its significance only through the discourse in which they are distinguished. This is not a new argument as such, having already been put forward by structuralists such as Ferdinand de Saussure. But where the poststructuralists differ from Saussure is that they do not regard differences as firmly anchored within a linguistic structure but as discursively reproduced and thus, at least potentially, in constant motion. This is why I referred earlier to the impossibility of permanently fixing meaning. Instead meaning is subject to a process of constant (though never arbitrary) shift (see Frank 1983: 94–95). In significant part, political disputes consist in attempts to articulate meanings and differences in meaning and establish them as universally valid through discourse (Laclau and Mouffe 1985; Connolly 1993). One of the central aims of postmodern approaches is to depict such political disputes and question semantic hegemonies, in other words explain temporarily successful attempts to lay down meaning, to reconstruct those semantic alternatives that have been lost because they were "defeated", and shed light on the practices that have marginalized these alternatives.

Once we have accepted the basic features of such an approach, it is not hard to understand how it is applied to international relations. Most conventional theories of international relations presuppose the existence of a system of states and draw a clear line between the anarchical character of international politics and a hierarchical domestic politics that is viewed as regulated or at least as potentially amenable to regulation. On this view, there is an opposition between state sovereignty and international anarchy, between the order of the "internal" and the dangers of the "external" sphere. Again borrowing from Derrida, postmodern writings show that these two concepts not only determine one another and consequently that the sovereign state emerges largely through its delimitation from the anarchical international sphere, but that both spheres are value-laden: sovereignty is good, anarchy is a problem (see Ashley 1988). So danger always comes from outside, justifying measures that oppose this external world. From the perspective of postmodern theorists, however, we cannot presuppose the existence of the state, which only gains its identity when we draw the boundary between the "internal" and "external", constructing a state (or even national) identity that is opposed to the external world. Many postmodern writings focus on the analysis of texts in which such boundary-drawing between "internal" and "external" always implies a danger emanating from outside (see, for example, the work of David Campbell, which I will be discussing later). Conversely, a number of authors have emphasized that we do not necessarily have to construct identities in opposition to threatening others, but that we may also conceive of others as equally valid, or have asserted that we construct difference through a temporal understanding of our own past (see Rumelili 2003; Diez 2004; Hansen 2006: 38–54). For example, German identity after the Second World War was constructed in significant part by marking it off from past excessive nationalism, while European identity was largely constructed by emphasizing its difference from the ceaseless armed conflicts that occurred before 1945.

Because both international politics and International Relations (as a discipline) take the state as their unproblematic point of departure, they are entangled in the same discourse. At the very least this limits freedom of movement across boundaries and perpetuates security dilemmas, while marginalizing alternative forms of political organization and rendering them almost impossible to imagine. So from a postmodern perspective, in its obsessive drive to explain prevailing political conditions, a positivist science of International Relations of this kind is an accomplice to the "statesman" of international politics. Conversely, as we saw earlier, postmodern writings are far more interested in questioning prevailing political conditions and thus, at the very least, opening our eyes to alternatives. In this sense we can understand postmodern approaches as a form of critical theory of international relations (see also the chapter by Christoph Humrich in this volume), though as we shall see below this critical aspiration is contested (see Section 4.2).

1.4 Other contexts in which postmodern approaches have emerged

Before turning to David Campbell as an exemplary exponent of postmodern approaches, I must highlight at least two other contexts in which postmodern writings have emerged. Like Ashley's writings, they too are connected with the critical examination of neorealism, but exhibit very specific points of contact with earlier theoretical developments. Michael Shapiro, for example, originally became known through studies produced in association with the research group around Robert Axelrod. In the 1970s, this group attempted to portray the intellectual world of foreign policy decision-makers through so-called "cognitive maps" in order to understand the genesis of specific decisions that do not necessarily seem "rational" (see Axelrod 1976). In a contribution to the journal *Cooperation and Conflict* that is well worth reading, Shapiro, along with a number of his colleagues, comes to the conclusion that these "maps" are produced solely on a textual basis; what they can do, therefore, is depict a given foreign policy discourse rather than peer into a politician's internal world (Bonham *et al.* 1987). In line with this, in later writings Shapiro devoted himself to deconstructing representations of international politics, often by pairing foreign policy documents with texts, images or symbols that would not usually make it into studies in International Relations. It is not without a certain irony that in 1997 he returned to the topic of maps, but this time in order to show how different forms of human life are forced into a particular schema through cartographic representations (Shapiro 1997).

The creative selection of analytical material is characteristic of many postmodern studies and is engendered by scepticism about the notion that particular, narrowly delimited "political" documents are more relevant to the understanding of political processes than, for example, everyday texts and objects, including TV programmes and pop music. We find ourselves faced with the problem of drawing boundaries once again. Apart from Shapiro, the most conspicuous contributions here have been made by James Der Derian, who rose to prominence through his writings on the shift in the understanding of "diplomacy" and the "genealogy" of this concept, which he traced all the way back to antiquity (Der Derian 1987). Der Derian's writings on contemporary "antidiplomacy" include such things as a diary he kept in the mid-1980s, before the collapse of the Soviet Union, on a cruise for peace along the coast of the Baltic states, as well as an analysis of CNN reporting in the Gulf War of 1990/91 (Der Derian 1992). In recent times Der Derian has turned to the interweaving of war, media and the entertainment industry (2009). His interest in the transformation of diplomacy, meanwhile, underlines the fact that Der Derian, as a student of Hedley Bull, is also working in the tradition of the English School. Its interest in theory building beyond American positivism (see the chapter by Christopher Daase in this volume) was another context in which postmodern ideas could be productively deployed, though the influence of these writings (and here we might also mention the work of Iver Neumann 1996, 1999) on the English School itself has generally been marginal so far (but see Der Derian 1995).

2 Foreign policy, identity and the possibility of an international ethics: the work of David Campbell

Among postmodern writings within International Relations, those of David Campbell are among the best known. There are probably a number of reasons for this. Campbell's style is relatively simple and clear for a postmodern text. But above all, his monographs have dealt with three key problems of contemporary international politics: (1) the foreign policies of the United States (*Writing Security*, 1992, new edition 1998); (2) the Gulf War of 1990/91

(*Politics without Principle*, 1993); and (3) the conflict as well as Western intervention in Bosnia in the early to mid-1990s (*National Deconstruction*, 1998a). Here Campbell draws chiefly on "traditional" analytical material (official documents, media reports, interviews) and fuses theoretical reflections with a critique of specific policies. In what follows, I present his work with reference to three major thematic complexes: (1) the role of foreign policy in the construction of state identity; (2) the ethical consequences of "radical interdependence"; and (3) deconstruction as the foundation of the political.

2.1 Foreign policy and identity

Writing Security exemplifies most of the characteristics of postmodern approaches identified above, particularly in its focus on discursive representation and here above all the construction of identity through difference. The latter prompts Campbell to write a new account of foreign policy. It is a notable feature of the book's genesis that it was written partly during Campbell's stint as lecturer at Johns Hopkins University in Baltimore, where Derrida sometimes ran courses, and where Campbell was in close contact with political theorist William Connolly, who published one of the key works on the relationship between identity and difference during the same period (Connolly 1991).

The very title of Campbell's book clearly indicates his postmodern approach: *Writing Security*. This may make no sense from a traditional standpoint. In light of our discussion so far, however, it is clear what this means: "security" is not an objective state of affairs, so it cannot simply be equated with the shielding of a territory from military threats as in conventional studies in International Relations. Instead, "security" is in fact defined through these studies, though they never state this explicitly. As explained above through the example of the modern territorial state, "security" is a concept that both analysts and practitioners tend to blithely but wrongly presuppose. Texts on security policy bring security into play in a particular way, in other words, they "write" it. Campbell's book traces this process of the "writing" of "security", and thus fits the pattern of a number of other successful attempts made chiefly since the 1990s to open up the concept of "security" within International Relations to dimensions that lie beyond military threats (see Krause and Williams 1997; Terriff *et al.* 1999; Booth 2005; Peoples and Vaughan-Williams 2010). What interests Campbell, like other postmodern analysts, is what effect these discursive representations have, in particular, which political decisions they facilitate and which they exclude (Campbell 1998a: 5, 117).

For Campbell, security is written through foreign policy. A key function of foreign policy, then, is the construction of state identities. The foundation of this argument is the relationship, discussed above, between identity and difference. Security presupposes something that must be rendered secure: in Campbell's case study, this is the United States. But if its securing is to be meaningful, then a specific identity must be attached to it. But from a postmodern perspective, this identity cannot be presupposed but is instead (re)constructed at the moment of its articulation.

In order to properly understand the new account of foreign policy associated with this, we must probe just what the term means. On the traditional view, foreign policy is "the shield of the republic", protecting it from external threats, as Walter Lippmann (1943) once put it. From Campbell's perspective, meanwhile, foreign policy is enmeshed in a discursive practice that distinguishes the internal from the external and thus defines what is "foreign" – a practice, in other words, that makes things "foreign". The state's foreign policy, then, is just one particular form of foreign policy; Campbell (1992: 76)[2] distinguishes between a foreign policy that comprises "all practices of differentiation or modes of exclusion", "which constitute their objects as 'foreign' in the process of dealing with them", and foreign policy as the specific state form of such practices. On this view, one crucial function of foreign policy is "the reproduction of an unstable identity at the level of the state, and the containment of challenges to that identity" (ibid.: 78).

In *Writing Security*, Campbell shows how the identity of the United States in this sense was reproduced over the centuries through a chain of foreign policies, from the encounter with indigenous Americans through the mythology of the "frontier" to the Cold War and the evocation of new dangers following the end of the East–West conflict; from this perspective, this conflict was merely a specific historical manifestation of the deeper discourse of identity/difference. This discourse continued after 1990 and has "written" security anew, for example, through the war on drugs. Through foreign policy, this has been shifted away from the contradictions of (post)modern U.S. society to the jungles of Latin America (ibid.: 198–215).

This example lays bare the critical aspiration of Campbell's work: for him (as for many other postmodern authors) what matters is ultimately not *that* identity is constructed through difference, but rather the exclusionary and marginalizing *consequences* of specific forms of identity. Above all, this includes the question of the extent to which foreign policy suppresses alternative ways of life, evokes dangers, restricts freedom of movement and legitimizes social exclusion – from the persecution of the indigenous peoples of North America through the harassing of "communists" during the McCarthy era to the marginalization of drug addicts in the slums of the major cities. In a later work, Campbell summed up his new account of foreign policy as follows: "Foreign policy can consequently be understood as an ethical power of segregation, the purpose of which is to constitute agency in the form of the state and to assign responsibility through the inscription of a geography of evil" (Campbell 1993: 27).

But it is also typical of Campbell that, in light of his critique, he sees the potential for change. According to him, the aim must be to achieve a foreign policy approach that respects an "inherently plural world" and is not built "upon the desire to contain, master and normalize threatening contingencies through violence" (Campbell 1992: 252). This, according to Campbell, requires us to recognize that we owe our identity to the very "other" that our foreign policies seek to fight through the writing of security. This basic idea already contains the seeds of Campbell's later works, which intensify his focus on international ethics.

2.2 Radical interdependence and the possibility of international ethics

One of the central problems that Campbell sees in international politics is already evident in *Writing Security*, and he elaborates it even more clearly in his later works: the "alignment between territoriality and the various dimensions of identity, so that it becomes possible to speak of a particular state with a definable character" (Campbell 1993: 24). He pays particular attention to the drive to bring territory, national identity and moral claims into line with one another. The resulting "discourse of moral certitude" (ibid.: 67) is often most clearly evident in the United States, so in *Politics Without Principle* Campbell again focuses on U.S. foreign policy, this time the reaction to Iraq's occupation of Kuwait in August 1990 and the ensuing Gulf War.

Campbell's core argument, which we can also straightforwardly apply to the U.S.-led interventions in Afghanistan and Iraq, is a critique of the "discourse of moral certitude". What he would like to see is a foreign policy not based on incontrovertible principles and ultimately implemented by force, but one informed by the understanding that our own identity cannot be detached from the associated network of relations between us and others, between identity and difference. Here Campbell links the epochal and analytical conception of postmodernity when he writes that nowadays "the extent and nature of the vast network of relations within which states are sequestered as subjects disturb the efficaciousness of any one-dimensional representation of agency, power, responsibility, or sovereignty" (ibid.: 84). But his main argument is based on a theoretical notion taken from his reading of the philosopher Emanuel Levinas.

For Levinas, the right to existence only ever arises with reference to the other (see Campbell 1998a: 173–174). This undermines the modern categories of subject and object, with each individual being made absolutely responsible for the other. Levinas focuses on immediate face-to-face personal relations. Campbell, meanwhile, develops this notion into the concept of "radical interdependence" – interdependence not in the sense of neo-liberal theory, which uses the term chiefly in the sense of economic networks between states and their resulting vulnerability (see the chapter by Manuela Spindler in this volume), but in a radicalized form that poses the question of responsibility within international politics (though not only there) in a new way:

> There is a prior and more fundamental sense of interdependence that is significant here: the sense in which the origin of an agent or subject – whether that agent or subject be an individual or a state – is to be found in the relationship between self and Other, and not in the uncovering of some autonomous sovereign ground of being removed from that relationship.
>
> (ibid.: 95)

This has clear consequences for the prospect of formulating an international ethics. Attempts to do so usually invoke universal principles. Campbell and other postmodern theorists regard such universalism as problematic because they of course always work on the fundamental assumption of a plurality of perspectives. To paraphrase Rob Walker: in "one world" there are always "many worlds" (Walker 1988). The invocation of universal principles is thus an attempt to impose order on the world by force, all too often literally. Campbell, therefore, not least in opposition to the thesis of "just war", calls for a "politics without principles" – not in the sense of being "unprincipled", but as a call for us to put our own house in order and re-conceptualize foreign policy (as already intimated in *Writing Security*). In particular, this means understanding that "we" always already find ourselves within an ethical context. So judging action depends not so much on which rules regulate action, but on the ways in which the mutual dependencies in our relations with others are taken seriously (Campbell 1993: 93, 1998a: 176).

Campbell's account of the Gulf War shows with exemplary clarity the practical consequences that would flow from such a "principled absence of principles". His main focus is on the involvement of the American and other Western governments, secret services and industrial firms in the Iraqi dictatorship, for example, through the military support for Saddam Hussein in his war against Iran in the 1980s, Iraqi investments in Europe, the acceptance of military exports to Iraq in violation of the law or loans made to Iraq. While this involvement would suggest that it is "impossible" "to draw any clear boundary that would clarify where agency and responsibility reside" (Campbell 1993: 43), according to Campbell American diplomacy concentrated on forging an international coalition against Saddam Hussein as an incarnation of "evil" (ibid.: 57). In opposition to this other, the identity of the

United States was cleansed of its involvement in Saddam's dictatorship and assured of its moral superiority.

As Campbell lays bare, in this case the concept of radical interdependence does not mean that the invasion of Kuwait was not in breach of the law. But rather than setting in motion the machinery of war, postmodern international ethics calls for the long-term rethinking of foreign policy objectives, acceptance of our own involvement and thus a focus not just on the responsibility of others but also with respect to our own action. To put it in concrete terms, this means, for example, ceasing to support violent dictatorships or guerrilla movements, long regarded by American governments as an effective means of tackling communism or radical Islam, and supporting those local political organizations that are aware of their hybrid identity, even if this is not necessarily beneficial to their supposed self-interest. From this perspective we can in a sense see the terrorist attacks of 11 September 2001 and former US President George W. Bush's subsequent characterization of the conflict as a struggle between "good" and "evil", in which the world had to come out either "for" or "against" the United States, as an intensified repetition of the events of ten years earlier.

2.3 Deconstruction as the foundation of the political

The linkage of territory and identity is also prominent in Campbell's (1998) book *National Deconstruction*, in which he examines the war in Bosnia following the collapse of Yugoslavia. Here his critique focuses on the adoption of a territorial representation of the conflict throughout much of the international political sphere. This led to an acceptance of the argument that different ethnic groups could not live together in the same area. The outcome was that while Bosnia looked like a state on paper, it was *de facto* divided up in line with the plans put forward openly by Croatian and Serbian politicians as well as Western intellectuals. For Campbell, this was an "ethnic strategy [that] overlooked the dimensions of the conflict . . . that problematized ontopological accounts" (Campbell 1998a: 114), in other words, those representations in which territoriality (*topos* – place) was *not* made an essential feature (*ontos* – being) of identity. This strategy did a huge disservice to those Bosnians "who pursued non-nationalist options in both their daily lives and their desires for the future" (ibid.: 114).

One of the book's key arguments is that deconstruction is a practice that facilitates the articulation of such non-national options. Deconstruction thus contributes to a democracy that is based not just on institutions but that entails a specific democratic ethos. For Bosnia, the deconstruction of unquestioned identities and their linkage with territoriality would have been a prerequisite for moving towards a truly multicultural state but, as Campbell argues, this was never seriously attempted. Such deconstruction would have created space for alternative constructions of identity of the kind articulated by independent radio stations such as Belgrade's B-92, ones that largely correspond to the Bosnian government's official position, the kind of constructions generated by the complexity of identitarian affiliation in the former Yugoslavia and that Campbell encountered again and again in conversation during his travels in Bosnia. But it is crucial that such alternative constructions of identity do not themselves make any claim to absoluteness that would in turn subvert the democratic ethos that Campbell has in mind.

Campbell counters the criticism that a deconstructive ethos must ultimately degenerate into absolute relativity and, because it questions all representations, cannot underpin political decisions, by arguing that it is in fact deconstruction that makes politics and responsible action possible. This is because if there really were

> secure foundations, privileged epistemological grounds, and unquestionable ontological bases "somehow removed from the strife, investments, and contamination regularly associated with them", then social action would be no more than the automatic operation of a knowledge, and ethics and politics would be no more than technology".
>
> (Campbell 1998a: 183–184)

In this sense, deconstruction is the precondition for politics.

In place of the "ethnic strategy" practised by the West, Campbell calls for the articulation of "conceptions of community that refuse the violent exclusions and limitations of identity politics" (ibid.: 208). Relevant strategies might consist, for example, of strengthening non-state perspectives that already exist, the more precise analysis and questioning of how identities and particular conceptions of history arise, supporting the peace initiatives of local non-governmental organizations, developing a multinational civil society and constructing new criteria for international responsibility (ibid.: 232–240).

3 The diversity of postmodern approaches

While it would be wrong to reduce postmodern approaches to the ideas of Campbell, the latter may nonetheless be considered typical of a significant current of postmodernism that is centrally concerned with the constitution of national identities and the national interest, particularly by marking off boundaries with the "other". One example of this is R. B. J. Walker's (1993) oft-cited main work, *Inside/Outside: International Relations as Political Theory*, in which Walker problematizes the boundary between the internal and external sphere of the state, views international relations as a significant element in the genesis of the modern state and thus, in a sense, provides a comprehensive political-theoretical grounding for Campbell's work (Walker 1993). In addition to this set of themes, there are at least two other important trends worth mentioning.

The first consists of writings that, while anchored in the analytical conception of postmodernity, are concerned chiefly with changes in the present era often regarded as characteristic of postmodernity in the epochal sense. This includes, for example, the development of the Internet and other new forms of communication or weapons technology. The question that arises here is to what extent such developments change our view of international politics. Is speed, for example, playing an increasing role in determining international events? Have the new media technologies enduringly changed our conception of "war" and, if so, with which political and ethical consequences? Which new political spaces are emerging through the increasing mobility of people, capital, goods and services? How is the nature of violent conflicts changing in the age of computer simulations, intelligent bombs and the proliferation of actors who possess such technologies?

James Der Derian (1992, 2009), as well as authors such as Mathias Albert (1996), have often examined these issues in a creative way.[3] They increasingly agree that we cannot understand discourse solely as written text since this would be to reproduce the problematic dichotomy between ideas (or in this case text) and objective reality. We can instead conceive of discourse as the context and process of the representation of reality, whether with respect to identity or, for example, sovereignty (Weber 1995). This primarily means texts but also a large number of other practices that construct reality (Williams 2003; Campbell 2010).

The second trend is the increasing number of discourse analytical studies on foreign policy. These focus not so much on the identity/difference issue as on how the conceptualization of specific concepts, which are central to the formulation of foreign policy, facilitates foreign policy decisions in a variety of discursive contexts in the first place – or eliminates them from what is regarded as the realm of the possible. Particularly popular objects of investigation here are the European policies of EU member states. Ole Wæver and his colleagues in Copenhagen have produced a number of studies in which they attempt to show how in the national contexts of Germany, France, the UK and certain Scandinavian countries, the fundamental conceptions of "state" and "nation" (and the relationship between them) exercise a crucial influence on European policies by pre-determining how the future of Europe can be imagined within a given national discourse (Larsen 1997; Wæver 1998; Hansen and Wæver 2001; see the overall survey in Wæver 2009).

Essentially, the only thing that such an approach has in common with the writings of Campbell is that it attaches great importance to the discursive construction of reality. Otherwise, however, it is strongly geared towards explanatory (and quite non-critical) objectives and scarcely questions the state as an analytical unit, though this might be justified with reference to the ongoing discursive centrality of the state. The question, however, is whether the key discourses, for example, with respect to European policy, are in fact those of "state" and "nation" and whether these discourses can be delimited along the lines of the nation state. At least with respect to certain conceptions of Europe, other discourses, such as economic discourse, are significant and these are clearly transnational in nature. Further, even in debates within the framework of the nation state, there are always a large number of such conceptions (see Diez 1999) and it is certainly in the spirit of the postmodern call for plurality to highlight this diversity rather than focusing solely on the dominant discourses.

Overall, however, it is striking that formal discourse analyses, some of which use quantitative methods to analyse a text, have as yet scarcely been used within International Relations. This may have something to do with the fact that such studies risk falling into the trap of the text/reality opposition and of overstating texts' determinative character (see Campbell 1998b: 219). Despite this, some authors have been insistent about the need to define more precisely the methods used in discourse analysis (see Milliken 1999). Hansen (2006) and Diez (1999) do not see poststructuralist approaches as in any way freed from the obligation to formulate their methods clearly and reflect on them, and in line with this they make space within their writings to discuss the development of their methodological approach. This, however, is not uncontested as it might limit the creativity of some of the authors discussed above and "domesticate" postmodern approaches, in other words, integrate them into the mainstream by watering them down.

This brings us to the broader discussion of postmodern approaches. First, though, I would like to at least adumbrate two other trends. Feminist approaches that draw on postmodern ones play an important role in theoretical debates. They probe, for example, the extent to which the representation of the modern state system entails certain "masculine" characteristics (see the chapter by Barbara Finke in this volume). Lastly, there are works that, like Der Derian, render the boundaries between "culture", "politics" and "science" fluid by making poems, films and images central to their analyses of international politics (see Shapiro and Alker 1996; Bleiker 2000; Danchev and Walker 2006). Hansen (2006), for example, shows how foreign policy decisions are partly influenced by travelogues and memoirs, or what she refers to as "literary non-fiction" (2006: 68–70 & passim).

4 Critical theory or charlatanism?

Of the various critical and constructivist approaches that have emerged within International Relations since the 1980s in response to neorealism and the subsequent dominance of rationalist approaches, postmodern writings are widely regarded as the most radical, and they have therefore provoked the greatest resistance. Cooperation between "traditionalists" and "postmodernists" is the exception (though see Sterling-Folker and Shinko 2005) – the best-known example here is the so-called "Copenhagen School" of security studies, the key figures here being Ole Wæver and Barry Buzan. The members of this school view security as a (speech) act that presents a problem as a fundamental danger to a "self", thus legitimizing the use or at least preparation of extraordinary means – including war in extreme cases (see Buzan *et al.* 1998).

Criticisms of postmodern approaches can essentially be reduced to three points: (1) that they amount to nothing more than meaningless word games; (2) that they fail to uphold scientific standards; and (3) that they are relativist. These criticisms come both from those who espouse positivist scientific ideals (in other words, the advocates of rationalist approaches, though also social constructivists in certain respects), as well as exponents of critical theory (on the latter, see also the chapter by Christoph Humrich in this volume). These three criticisms share a common point of departure, namely, the postmodern rejection of a single comprehension of reality with the status of absolute truth.

4.1 Social science?

A key consequence of this is that the project of a science that seeks to *explain* prevailing conditions becomes problematic because of the impossibility of gaining objective access to reality. Further, a postmodern approach seems to provide us with no helpful means "to differentiate knowledge from nonsense" (Wight 1999: 313; see Biersteker 1989: 265). And if this is the case, why should we put our faith in a postmodern approach if it is merely affirming one of many possible truths? Here, according to John Vasquez (1995: 225), the essentially welcome critique of positivism provided by postmodern approaches turns into negative self-contradiction. As a result, social constructivists keep their distance from postmodern currents and generally insist on adhering to an approach that seeks to explain or understand the world. At the very least, they wish to uphold the notion of a material reality that is in principle comprehensible, which places them in an intermediate position between rationalist and postmodern approaches (see Adler 1997 and the chapter by Cornelia Ulbert in this volume). Vasquez himself sees postmodern approaches as highlighting the need to rethink the aspiration to produce scientific theories within International Relations and to rethink their formulation. On this view, as Mathias Albert (1994: 59) once put it, postmodern approaches would have a "corrective function" rather than having the capacity or aspiration to occupy a new, dominant position within the discipline.

Yet if we follow Hansen (2006: 17–36) we might also view postmodern writings as embodying an alternative conception of science that eschews causal analysis and instead demonstrates how such things as identitarian discourses and political action are mutually constituted. For Hansen, rejecting a conception of science as the analysis of causes does not lead to a rejection of all kinds of science, but instead requires us to rethink the categories of scientific theory, with the ultimate goal of producing a "discursive epistemology" with a specific focus on the interplay between the construction of identity and politics.

4.2 Relativistic?

Critique, as exemplified in Critical Theory's upholding of Enlightenment ideals, has always been partly associated with the desire to achieve emancipation, an aspiration that underpinned the notion of an alternative world order (see the chapter by Christoph Humrich in this volume). But from a postmodern perspective, how are we to decide which world order is better than any another? To quote Colin Wight again: "What is unclear is how they go about making choices and on what grounds" (Wight 1999: 315). Further, it is inherent in the conception of power found within postmodern approaches that responsibility is in essence located within discourse and is therefore difficult to localize within a concrete political context (Rosenau 1990: 96). Finally, Ruggie (1993: 145–146), for example, mentions the personal political engagement of a number of postmodern philosophers (particularly Paul de Man and Martin Heidegger as "pioneers" of postmodern ideas) during the Nazi period as an argument against postmodern normative deracination.

Two responses to these criticisms seem particularly compelling. First, Foucault (1984b) saw his work as lying more in the tradition of the Enlightenment than that of its opponents. What this dispute boils down to is the interpretation of emancipation and Enlightenment. At this point it is sufficient to underline that for many postmodern authors such as Campbell (1998a: 213–214) a central aspect of the Enlightenment consists in the constant questioning of unquestioned "realities". Equally, with respect to the facilitation of emancipation, for them it is crucial to create space for the articulation of political alternatives, though not by setting specific alternatives in stone (George 1995: 222). This last point also means that ethics can only ever be justified in specific local contexts (Cochran 1999: 136). Second, as we saw above, it can be argued that the absence of principles actually entails a principle that exhorts us to combat all forms of totalitarianism – in other words, that a postmodern ethics does ultimately result in a kind of problematized and moderated universalism (see Cochran 1999: 136). In the literature, things generally seem to have calmed down following the initial conflicts over the future path of critical theory (for a summary, see Rengger and Hoffman 1992; Brown 1994); most of the relevant authors seem to believe that there is no insurmountable contradiction between critical theory, on the one hand, and postmodern approaches, on the other (see George 1994: 163–166). Summing up in this vein, Peter Lawler (2008: 388) states that many postmodern authors are not interested in rejecting the Enlightenment but rather in advancing the ethos of the Enlightenment, an ethos directed chiefly towards the constant critique and questioning of prevailing realities.

4.3 Incomprehensible?

The third criticism, that postmodern writings amount to meaningless word games, is aimed above all at the often perplexing concepts that pervade them. In a famous-notorious passage, Robert Gilpin (1986: 303), for example, claimed that he had not received Ashley's critique of neorealism from the journal *International Organization*, which had originally commissioned this response to Gilpin, in the "English translation". But what seems to some like a mass of words without meaning is for others a result of the necessity of portraying a different reality. It would be very difficult to pursue this key goal by using conventional vocabulary – particularly if you believe in the centrality of the text. Certainly, some authors might often express certain things more straightforwardly and clearly, though the present chapter is probably adequate testimony to the difficulties that this involves.

Postmodern approaches are now part of the standard repertoire of International Relations. One indication of this is the appearance of an increasing number of books and articles and even introductory texts (see for example Edkins and Zehfuss 2009) that analyze the problems of international politics from a postmodern perspective without going to great trouble to justify this explicitly. This is a positive development. It was necessary to hold up a mirror to International Relations and question the discipline's epistemological foundations. By the same token, this process of problematization cannot remain centre stage forever. When all is said and done, David Campbell (1999: 318) is surely right to state that postmodern critique is ultimately less a matter of epistemology than of ethical-political engagement. But this engagement calls on us to get to grips with the problems of violence or hunger and our entanglement in them, even if we consistently eschew a single representation of these problems.

5 Notes

1 I thank Stefano Guzzini and Jürgen Haacke for their valuable comments. The editors of the present volume, along with Julia Grauvogel, provided particularly helpful suggestions for the revision of this chapter for the present edition.
2 Quotations from the first edition. The second edition (1998) differs from the first mainly in the addition of an epilogue.
3 Also of interest in this context is Der Derian's "Information Technology, War and Peace Project", available at: www.watsoninstitute.org/infopeace.

6 Bibliography and recommended texts

6.1 Primary texts

Ashley, Richard K. 1988: Untying the Sovereign State: A Double Reading of the Anarchy Problematique, *Millennium: Journal of International Studies* 17(2): 227–262.
Campbell, David 1992: *Writing Security: United States Foreign Policy and the Politics of Identity*. Minneapolis, MN: University of Minnesota Press [2nd rev. edn 1998].
Der Derian, James and Shapiro, Michael J. (eds) 1989: *International/Intertextual Relations: Postmodern Readings of World Politics*. New York: Lexington Books.
Hansen, Lene 2006: *Security as Practice: Discourse Analysis and the Bosnian War*. London: Routledge.
Walker, R. B. J. 1988: *One World, Many Worlds: Struggles for a Just World Peace*. London: Zed Books.

6.2 Secondary texts

Campbell, David 2010: Post-Structuralism, in Dunne, Tim, Kurki, Milja and Smith, Steve (eds) *International Relations Theories: Discipline and Diversity*, 2nd edn. Oxford: Oxford University Press, pp. 213–237.
Lawler, Peter 2008: The Ethics of Postmodernism, in Reus-Smit, Christian and Snidal, Duncan (eds) *The Oxford Handbook of International Relations*. Oxford: Oxford University Press, pp. 378–390.

6.3 Other texts

Adler, Emanuel 1997: Seizing the Middle Ground: Constructivism in World Politics, *European Journal of International Relations* 3(3): 319–363.
Albert, Mathias 1994: "Postmoderne" und Theorie der internationalen Beziehungen, *Zeitschrift für Internationale Beziehungen* 1(1): 45–63.
Albert, Mathias 1996: *Fallen der (Welt-)Ordnung. Internationale Beziehungen und ihre Theorien zwischen Moderne und Postmoderne*. Opladen: Leske + Budrich.
Ashley, Richard K. 1986: The Poverty of Neorealism, in Keohane, Robert O. (ed.) *Neorealism and Its Critics*. New York: Columbia University Press, pp. 255–300.

Axelrod, Robert (ed.) 1976: *Structure of Decision: The Cognitive Map of Political Elites*. Princeton, NJ: Princeton University Press.

Biersteker, Thomas J. 1989: Critical Reflections on Post-Positivism in International Relations, *International Studies Quarterly* 33(2): 263–267.

Bleiker, Roland (ed.) 2000: Poetic World Politics. Sonderheft der Zeitschrift *Alternatives* 25: 3.

Bonham, Matthew G., Jönsson, Christer, Persson, Stefan and Shapiro, Michael J. 1987: Cognition and International Negotiation: The Historical Recovery of Discursive Space, *Cooperation and Conflict* 22(1): 1–19.

Booth, Ken 2005: *Critical Security Studies and World Politics*. Boulder, CO: Lynne Rienner.

Brown, Chris 1994: "Turtles all the way down". Anti-foundationalism, Critical Theory and International Relations, *Millennium: Journal of International Studies* 23(2): 213–236.

Buzan, Barry, Waever, Ole and de Wilde, Jaap 1998: *Security: A New Framework for Analysis*. Boulder, CO: Lynne Rienner.

Campbell, David 1993: *Politics without Principle: Sovereignty, Ethics, and the Narratives of the Gulf War*. Boulder, CO: Lynne Rienner.

Campbell, David 1998a: *National Deconstruction: Violence, Identity and Justice in Bosnia*. Minneapolis, MN: University of Minnesota Press.

Campbell, David 1998b: The Disciplinary Politics of Theorizing Identity, in Campbell, David: *Writing Security: United States Foreign Policy and the Politics of Identity*, 2nd edn. Minneapolis, MN: University of Minnesota Press, pp. 207–227.

Campbell, David 1999: Contra Wight. The Errors of Premature Writing, *Review of International Studies* 25(2): 317–321.

Cochran, Molly 1999: *Normative Theory in International Relations: A Pragmatic Approach*. Cambridge: Cambridge University Press.

Connolly, William E. 1991: *Identity/Difference: Democratic Negotiations of Political Paradox*. Ithaca, NY: Cornell University Press.

Connolly, William E. 1993: *The Terms of Political Discourse*, 2nd edn. Princeton, NJ: Princeton University Press

Cooper, Robert 1998: *The Postmodern State and World Order*. London: Demos.

Danchev, Alex and Walker, R.B.J. 2006: Art and Politics. Special Issue of *Alternatives: Global, Local, Political*, 31: 1.

Der Derian, James 1987: *On Diplomacy: A Genealogy of Western Estrangement*. Oxford: Basil Blackwell.

Der Derian, James 1992: *Antidiplomacy: Spies, Terror, Speed, and War*. Oxford: Basil Blackwell.

Der Derian, James (ed.) 1995: *International Theory: Critical Investigations*. New York: New York University Press.

Der Derian, James 2009: *Virtuous War: Mapping the Military-Industrial-Media-Entertainment Network*, 2nd edn. Boulder, CO: Westview Press.

Diez, Thomas 1999: *Die EU lesen. Diskursive Knotenpunkte in der britischen Europadebatte*. Opladen: Leske + Budrich.

Diez, Thomas 2004: Europe's Others and the Return of Geopolitics, *Cambridge Review of International Affairs* 17(2): 319–335.

Edkins, Jenny and Zehfuss, Maja (eds) 2009: *Global Politics: A New Introduction*. London: Routledge.

Fearon, James and Wendt, Alexander 2002: Rationalism vs. Constructivism: A Skeptical View, in Carlsnæs, Walter, Risse, Thomas and Simmons, Beth A. (eds) *Handbook of International Relations*. London: Sage, pp. 52–72.

Foucault, Michel 1984a: The Order of Discourse, in Shapiro, Michael J. (ed.) *Language and Politics*. Oxford: Basil Blackwell, pp. 103–138.

Foucault, Michel 1984b: What is Enlightenment?, in Rabinow, Paul (ed.) *The Foucault Reader*. New York: Pantheon, pp. 32–50.

Frank, Manfred 1983: *Was ist Neostrukturalismus?* Frankfurt a. M.: Suhrkamp.

George, Jim 1994: *Discourses of Global Politics: A Critical (Re)Introduction to International Relations*. Boulder, CO: Lynne Rienner.
George, Jim 1995: Realist "Ethics", International Relations, and Postmodernism: Thinking beyond the Egoism-Anarchy Thematic, *Millennium: Journal of International Studies* 24(2): 195–223.
Gilpin, Robert G. 1986: The Richness of the Tradition of Political Realism, in Keohane, Robert O. (ed.) *Neorealism and Its Critics*. New York: Columbia University Press, pp. 301–321.
Gray, Chris Hables 1997: *Postmodern War: The New Politics of Conflict*. London: Routledge.
Guzzini, Stefano 1993: Structural Power: The Limits of Neorealist Power Analysis, *International Organization* 47(3): 443–478.
Hansen, Lene and Wæver, Ole (eds) 2001: *European Integration and National Identity*. London: Routledge.
Kaase, Max 1983: Sinn oder Unsinn des Konzepts "Politische Kultur" für die Vergleichende Politikforschung, oder auch: Der Versuch, einen Pudding an die Wand zu nageln, in Kaase, Max and Klingemann, Hans-Dieter (eds) *Wahlen und Politisches System. Analysen aus Anlass der Bundestagswahl 1980*. Opladen: Westdeutscher Verlag, pp. 144–172.
Kellner, Douglas 2002: Postmodern War in the Age of Bush II, *New Political Science* 24(1): 57–72.
Krause, Keith and Williams, Michael C. (eds) 1997: *Critical Security Studies*. Minneapolis, MN: University of Minnesota Press.
Laclau, Ernesto and Mouffe, Chantal 1985: *Hegemony and Socialist Strategy: Towards a Radical Democratic Politics*. London: Verso.
Larsen, Henrik 1997: *Foreign Policy and Discourse Analysis: France, Britain and Europe*. London: Routledge.
Lippmann, Walter 1943: *U. S. Foreign Policy: Shield of the Republic*. Boston: Little, Brown and Co.
Lyotard, Jean-François 1984: *The Postmodern Condition: A Report on Knowledge*. Manchester: Manchester University Press.
Milliken, Jennifer 1999: The Study of Discourse in International Relations: A Critique of Research and Methods, *European Journal of International Relations* 5(2): 225–254.
Neumann, Iver B. 1996: Self and Other in International Relations, *European Journal of International Relations* 2(2): 139–174.
Neumann, Iver B. 1999: *Uses of the Other: The "East" in European Identity Formation*. Minneapolis, MN: University of Minnesota Press.
Peoples, Columba and Vaughan-Williams, Nick 2010: *Critical Security Studies: An Introduction*. London: Routledge.
Rengger, Nick and Hoffman, Mark 1992: Modernity, Postmodernity and International Relations, in Doherty, Joe, Graham, Elspeth and Malek, Mo (eds) *Postmodernism and the Social Sciences*. London: Macmillan, pp. 127–147.
Rosenau, Pauline 1990: Once Again into the Fray: International Relations Confronts the Humanities, *Millennium: Journal of International Studies* 19(1): 83–110.
Ruggie, John Gerard 1993: Territoriality and Beyond: Problematizing Modernity in International Relations, *International Organization* 47(1): 139–174.
Rumelili, Bahar 2003: Constructing Identity and Relating to Difference: Understanding the EU's Mode of Differentiation, *Review of International Studies* 30(1): 27–47.
Shapiro, Michael J. 1991: *Reading the Postmodern Polity*. Minneapolis, MN: University of Minnesota Press.
Shapiro, Michael J. 1997: *Violent Cartographies: Mapping Cultures of War*. Minneapolis, MN: University of Minnesota Press.
Shapiro, Michael J. and Alker, Hayward R. (eds) 1996: *Challenging Boundaries*. Minneapolis, MN: University of Minnesota Press.
Smith Steve 2001: Reflectivist and Constructivist Approaches to International Theory, in Baylis, John and Smith, Steve (eds) *The Globalization of World Politics: An Introduction to International Relations*, 2nd edn. Oxford: Oxford University Press, pp. 224–249.

Sterling-Folker, Jennifer and Shinko, Rosemary E. 2005: Discourses of Power: Traversing the Realist-Postmodern Divide, *Millennium: Journal of International Studies* 33(3): 637–664.

Terriff, Terry, Croft, Stuart, James, Lucy and Morgan Patrick M. 1999: *Security Studies Today*. Oxford: Polity.

Vasquez, John A. 1995: The Post-Positivist Debate. Reconstructing Scientific Enquiry and International Relations Theory after Enlightenment's Fall, in Booth, Ken and Smith, Steve (eds) *International Relations Theory Today*. Cambridge: Polity, pp. 217–240.

Wæver, Ole 1998: Explaining Europe by Decoding Discourses, in Wivel, Anders (ed.) *Explaining European Integration*. Copenhagen: Copenhagen Political Studies Press, pp. 100–146.

Wæver, Ole 2009: Discursive Approaches, in Wiener, Antje and Diez, Thomas (eds) *European Integration Theory*, 2nd edn. Oxford: Oxford University Press, pp. 163–180.

Walker, R. B. J. 1993: *Inside/Outside: International Relations as Political Theory*. Cambridge: Cambridge University Press.

Weber, Cynthia 1995: *Simulating Sovereignty: Intervention, the State and Symbolic Exchange*. Cambridge: Cambridge University Press.

Wendt, Alexander 1999: *Social Theory of International Politics*. Cambridge: Cambridge University Press.

Wight, Colin 1999: MetaCampbell: The Epistemological Problematics of Perspectivism, *Review of International Studies* 25(2): 311–316.

Williams, Michael C. 2003: Words, Images, Enemies: Securitization and International Politics, *International Studies Quarterly* 47(4): 511–531.

Feminist approaches

Barbara Finke[1]

1 Introduction

More clearly than other currents within political theory, feminist approaches are linked with a political-social movement, namely, the women's movement. In line with this, feminist theory and the political practice of the women's movement have been constant sources of mutual stimulation. Like the labour movement, the women's movement is one of the "old" social movements that emerged in Europe and North America in the wake of nineteenth-century modernization. The Second World War and the associated changes mark the turning point between old and new social movements, with the latter usually associated with the political-social upheavals of the 1960s and 1970s. The European and American civil rights and student movements of the 1960s were the starting point for the renewal of the women's movement,[2] which gained particular momentum in the 1970s. The slogan "the private is political" played a central role here, and to this day it serves as a key point of reference in discussions of equality and gender issues.

While public awareness of the women's movement has declined since the late 1970s, feminist political theory has been developed in crucial ways since then and has made it into International Relations, albeit rather belatedly.[3] The slogan coined within the new women's movement concerning the political character of the private sphere challenged antiquated political forms, content and boundary lines and culminated in greater feminist interest in the foundations of political thought (see Elshtain 1981; Pateman 1988; MacKinnon 1989). Unsurprisingly, the critique of the division between the private and public spheres has become a key element in feminist political analysis. Modern statehood is based on separate spheres, a "rational" political public sphere, on the one hand, and an "emotional" private domestic sphere, on the other (see Pateman 1988). This division between the private and public spheres is also a modern political theoretical concept of relevance to international relations. As a result of the assignment of women and "feminine" characteristics to the supposedly nonpolitical private domestic sphere, "women as actors in international politics have remained largely invisible" (Ruppert 1998: 28).

Cynthia Enloe has applied the notion of the political character of the private sphere to International Relations and shown where the "invisible" women are to be found within international politics (Enloe 1989, 2000). Her 1989 book, *Bananas, Beaches & Bases: Making Feminist Sense of International Politics* is considered a "classic" of feminist literature within International Relations. For Enloe, the private is not just political but international. She develops an unusual perspective on international politics and calls into question our traditional notions of the scope of the political (Locher-Dodge 1998: 435). She investigates the significance of female labour, as manifested in the everyday experiences of millions of women in every part of the world and the role played by such labour in the "men's world of big politics" (Krell 1996: 153). Enloe explains, for example, how prostitution in proximity to British and American military bases – particularly in Third World countries – is organized and controlled by the military authorities. She highlights the importance of domestic labour and cheap female workers to multinational companies and analyses the gender-specific division of labour in the United States' diplomatic service. Enloe brings out the importance of women, particularly women's (ancillary) work, to the functioning of international politics. At the same time, the examples she adduces shed light on how the existing international system is maintained through the construction and reproduction of traditional notions of femininity and masculinity.

The examples identified by Enloe show that the division between private and public is closely bound up with the opposition between "femininity" and "masculinity". At the same time this defines what is perceived as "political" and what is not. A chain of dualistic oppositions reflects repetitive structures of thought both in the political theory of the state and in the theory of international relations. Feminist analysts seek to expose these structures because they believe that a more in-depth understanding of power and power mechanisms is possible only through a perspective informed by feminism (Enloe 2007a). Recent feminist approaches examine the gender-specific construction of the political based on the dualism female/male, but at the same time question the association of particular qualities or principles of action with women's or men's nature. The foundation of this strand of research, which is described as *gender research*, is the concept of gender. *Gender* – which is centred on the relationship *between* genders – relates to social rather than biological gender. When referring to "gender", feminism (as well as critical research on men, which also works with this category) refers to the social construction of relations between genders (for an overview, see Whitworth 2008). Gender in the sense of a socially mediated notion of typically female or typically male qualities and principles of action is central to feminist analysis because "as a structural concept it impacts every area of social, political and thus also international action" (Locher-Dodge 1998: 425, see also Section 3).

Feminist gender research and the associated notion of socially mediated structures of thought reflected an epistemological[4] upheaval within political theory that began to make an impact in the late 1980s within the theory of International Relations, triggering the so-called "third debate" (see Section 2.3). This debate, which was centrally concerned with epistemological issues, was accompanied by the end of the Cold War, which brought new patterns of conflict and cooperation under the purview of International Relations and raised doubts about the explanatory power of the prevailing theoretical approaches. Beginning in the Anglo-American world, *post-positivist* theoretical approaches have entered into International Relations, including recent feminist approaches. The premise of the social construction of reality may be considered the basic assumption common to post-positivist approaches, one espoused with particular vigour by postmodernists (see Locher-Dodge 1998: 433; Ruppert 1998: 28). More than in the German-speaking world, in the United States, International Relations is dominated by a modern positivist conception of science, and this became the point of departure for post-positivist critique. The neorealist school in particular has exercised a significant influence on the theory and practice of International Relations in the United States.

In line with this, the post-positivist approaches that have fanned out from the Anglo-American world initially grappled mainly with the neorealist paradigm. *Feminist approaches* have underlined that the neorealist theoretical edifice, which is centrally informed by the assumption that the international system has an anarchical structure and that there are such things as rationally acting state actors, presents itself as gender-neutral, but is implicitly based on a male-defined world-view. Post-positivists thus refer to the *androcentrism* within a supposedly objective and gender-neutral theoretical approach. According to feminist critics, androcentric approaches are implicitly geared towards male interests and criteria. Locher-Dodge concludes that in neorealism "characteristics associated with masculinity, such as strength, aggressiveness and instrumental rationality . . . are projected onto the behaviour of states, whose success as actors depends on the possession of and use of these masculine qualities" (Locher-Dodge 1998: 431; see also Grant 1991; Peterson 1992; Tickner 1992; Whitworth 1994). *Postmodern approaches* have focused on the characteristics of modern Western thought within the neorealist paradigm. They assert that neorealism is intertwined with the linguistic and cognitive schemas of a *modern* Western philosophy that tends to construct reality through an opposition between hierarchical dualisms. These dualisms are characterized by conceptual pairs, the first of which is implicitly presented as superior. The binary conceptual pairs of relevance to the construction of (international) politics include inside/outside, identity/difference, public/private and of course – as postmodern feminist approaches underline – male/female.

Since the "third debate", the linkage of feminism and postmodernity has been a frequent occurrence in International Relations. Christine Sylvester, for example, whose magnum opus will serve as an example in what follows, already makes it clear in the title of her book that she is indebted to the postmodern paradigm. We may thus consider her a typical representative of those feminist theoretical approaches influenced most prominently by postmodern ideas (see Zalewski 1994: 415).

2 Feminism and international relations within postmodernity: Christine Sylvester

In *Feminist Theory and International Relations in a Postmodern Era*, Christine Sylvester explicitly addresses a specialist readership with an interest in theory, placing epistemological issues at the centre of her analysis (Sylvester 1994a). Her approach involves a number of key steps. First, she presents a classification of feminist theoretical approaches, locating her *postmodern feminism* in this context. Her main focus here is on the epistemological differences between feminist approaches that – as in the case of Cynthia Enloe – make women central to their analysis of international politics, and postmodern approaches that question the category "woman" as the foundation of feminist analysis. A number of texts have worked with and discussed this classification (see Keohane 1989; Weber 1994). Sylvester then examines the three theoretical debates within International Relations from a feminist perspective. She does this through the genealogical critique of key source texts in political theory and through analysis of the established discourses of International Relations that draw on these sources. Finally, Sylvester attempts to develop her own feminist method of *empathetic cooperation*, buttressed with examples from political practice.

2.1 Feminist theoretical approaches in International Relations

The term *feminism* covers a large number of approaches whose common normative goal is to uncover gender-specific inequality and achieve equality for women (see Locher-Dodge 1998: 425). Differences are found mainly on the epistemological level. Christine Sylvester, for example, has completed a "decisive theoretical turn" (Locher 1996: 381) away from research on women, which focuses on the role and perspective of women within international politics, towards gender research, which is centred on the significance of gender ascriptions to the social construction of reality. Unlike Enloe, who opens up a new perspective on International Relations by making women visible within international politics, Sylvester problematizes the very category of "woman" on which Enloe bases her analysis.

Sylvester seeks to highlight the *cultural production* of our notions of femininity and masculinity, so her work comes under the rubric of postmodern feminist approaches in a broad sense. She draws on the work of American philosopher Judith Butler (esp. Butler 1990), who regards "classification into two genders as an act of cultural production. This means that gender is a discursive construct rather than part of a natural process" (Sylvester and Bleiker 1998: 413). From this perspective, the categories "man" and "woman" are "part of a nexus of language, knowledge and power through which relatively small biological differences become a key criterion of social relations" (ibid.: 416; see Sylvester 1998: 189). In this connection, Butler (2004) refers to the "performativity" of gender, in other words the insight that our gender is not determined solely through biological parameters, that we in fact produce it through our speech and action. Sylvester makes this epistemological stance clear in her publications by generally placing the term "woman" in inverted commas.

For Sylvester, the first level of classification of feminist approaches depends on how the relevant authors approach the category of "woman" and their attitude towards the *women/"women" question in International Relations* (see Zalewski 1994). Sylvester distinguishes between (1) approaches that make the difference between men and women, between masculine and feminine characteristics, the basis of their analysis; and (2) those approaches that problematize this gender difference – like Sylvester herself:

> [The first approach deals with] activities of average people, as interpreted by feminist analysts. This form *outlines* women, power and international politics where this gender triangle was not presumed to exist . . . A second, radically sceptical approach, *inlines* identity in international politics with respect to shapes that surround men and women in theories and in practices, leaving behind in the middle, so to speak, shadows of gender and boundaries of gender transgressed.
>
> (Sylvester 1996: 262–263; original emphasis)

On the second level of the classification of feminist approaches, Sylvester refers to Sandra Harding (Harding 1986), who distinguishes between *feminist empiricism, feminist standpoint* and *feminist postmodernism*.[5] Sylvester adds the category of *postmodern feminism*, locating her own approach within it. While *feminist empiricism* and *standpoint feminism* adopt the modern distinction between female and male characteristics, the two postmodern variants of feminism regard the categories of "man" and "woman" as socially constructed and politically produced. In line with this, Sylvester underlines that:

> When speaking of "men" and "women", it is important to establish . . . that I do not pose these gender categories as permanent, immutable, determinant and essential. Rather, I see "men" and "women" as socially constructed subject statuses that emerge from the politicization of different anatomies in ways that support given divisions of labor, traits, places, and power.
>
> (Sylvester 1994a: 4)

Feminist empiricism builds on quite different assumptions, assuming the existence of an objectively identifiable category of "woman" and, according to Sylvester, is particularly deeply rooted in the modern positivist conception of science. This approach works on the assumption that it is sufficient to expose the androcentrism within mainstream theoretical approaches and to "add women" to the familiar approach to research in order to generate a complete and undistorted picture of reality (see ibid.: 31–36). As Sylvester sees it, the political-practical manifestation of this conception of science is *liberal feminism*, which regards the liberal state as the appropriate framework for the goal of women's equality, if only existing laws were consistently interpreted and enforced in line with the imperative of equality. Sylvester sums up these parallels as follows: "In short, just as feminist empiricists accept certain premises of science, even as they critique other premises, liberal feminism basically accepts liberalism in a state activist form and critiques its application to women" (ibid.: 39).[6]

In its critique of the established approaches in political theory, *standpoint feminism* goes much further than liberal feminism. Feminist approaches of this kind advocate the view that the experiences of women must be the point of departure for feminist research. This is not just a matter of offsetting the androcentrism of existing theoretical approaches. Instead the expectation is that the feminine perspective on international politics will lead to different, potentially superior insights into the character of international relations. Implicit here is the concept of a "feminine morality" (see Nunner-Winkler 1991), though this entails the risk of absolutizing "typically" female characteristics and thus enshrining the hierarchical gender opposition found in established theoretical approaches in reverse. Here the superiority of feminine morality is justified sociologically and sometimes biologically and is primarily related to a supposed connection between motherhood and a peaceable nature. This essentialist line of argument,[7] which postmodern feminists criticize, is particularly palpable in *radical feminism*, which Sylvester regards as a political-practical variant of *standpoint feminism* (Sylvester 1994a: 49–52; see also Krell 1996: 155).

Feminist postmodernism is characterized by a radical scepticism about the categories and intellectual structures of modern theoretical approaches, which include approaches such as *feminist empiricism* and *standpoint feminism*. The categories called into question from the perspective of feminist postmodernism include the subject that acts in a coherent and independent way and a neatly defined gender identity, along with the associated binary intellectual structures based on hierarchical oppositions. Feminist postmodernists lay bare the social constructedness of these modern categories and intellectual structures through deconstruction. As discussed earlier, it is the existence of a homogeneous category of "woman" that is being denied here. The emphasis is instead on the *differences* between women and the diversity of their experiences. In this connection, Sylvester refers to the arguments put forward by an important exponent of feminist postmodernism:

> Sandra Harding, a leading light of postmodernism, suggests that we should expect differences in cognitive styles and world views from people engaged in different kinds of social activities . . . Are we more alike than different? Do we have a standpoint? Harding thinks not . . . It is, theoretically, preferable [for Harding] to accept the notion of permanent partiality and to explore intersecting, contradictory and simultaneous realities within a pro-women framework.
>
> (Sylvester 1990: 246)

Feminist postmodernism of this stripe is often criticized for taking an arbitrary normative stance. Critics claim that along with the uniformly acting subject and the category "woman", this kind of feminism eliminates the subject that might pursue emancipatory aspirations (see

Section 3). On the basis of these criticisms, Sylvester distances herself to some extent from radical postmodernism and characterizes her own theoretical approach as *postmodern feminism*, which is located between *standpoint feminism* and *feminist postmodernism*. Sylvester, however, emphasizes that these feminist theoretical approaches are not mutually exclusive and that each approach contributes to the interpretation of international politics (see Sylvester 1994a: 66–67).

2.2 The postmodern feminism of Christine Sylvester

For Sylvester, we can develop the feminist theory of International Relations and find a way out of the dilemma of "women" (as a socially constructed category) and women (as politically acting subjects) by linking an enlightened *standpoint feminism* with *feminist postmodernism*, which she believes she can do by constructing a *postmodern feminism*. Postmodern analysis is associated with the dilemma of the lost subject or the problem of the "vanishing woman" (Zalewski 1994: 415). Sylvester's analysis too is based on the assumption that "women" as a category is a social construction and that there can be no question of any natural opposition between masculine and feminine qualities. In line with this, the question that arises for feminist theory is "How can we simultaneously put women at the center and decenter everything including women?" (Sylvester 1994a: 12).

Sylvester takes the view that we can dissolve the boundaries between an enlightened *standpoint feminism*, which eschews both essentialist arguments and the notion of *the* feminine standpoint, and postmodern thought. Recent approaches informed by standpoint feminism underline the *diversity* of female experiences and standpoints. This reflects their scepticism about the construction of universalist, monopolizing categories for political scientific analysis, scepticism that is also characteristic of postmodern theoretical approaches. In contrast to radical postmodern approaches, Sylvester emphasizes that a *feminist* theory of International Relations must accept the fact that women identify with their gender, making this identity, alongside others, the foundation of their social action: "If gender is a home for some 'women', then it makes no sense to refuse them that identity because, technically, it is not real" (ibid.: 53). Postmodern feminism, however, is characterized by the assumption that there is a great diversity of female experiences and standpoints and that the subjective standpoint is defined by a large number of different identities, including gender identity: "Hence the emphasis [of postmodern feminism] on multiple standpoints, on being (. . .) several things at once in a prismatic postmodern world – rural-black-mother-agriculturalist-socialist-cooperator – and, therefore, being homeless as a single-identity knowing Self" (ibid.: 59).

Another element in Sylvester's approach is her critical examination of the established discourses of International Relations. Here Sylvester exposes key discourses of modern Western thought and analyses the impact of these theoretical source texts on the classical theoretical approaches of International Relations.

2.3 Discourse analysis and genealogical critique

Discourse analysis is a method used both by feminist approaches of various kinds and postmodern theoretical approaches. The goal is to unearth discursively founded mechanisms of domination, because, according to Sylvester, "language is never neutral. It reflects specific social values, ideas, entire ways of life. Language is always politics, even if it doesn't seem that way at first sight" (Sylvester and Bleiker 1998: 412). In this context, Sylvester underlines that the uncovering of linguistically grounded mechanisms of domination has an emancipatory function (1994a: 318): "Postmodern feminism can usefully raise 'strange' questions about stories we have accepted about 'his' world that deny 'us' agency in IR" (ibid.: 62; see also Sylvester 1994b: 318). According to Sylvester, established discourses within International Relations create "conceptual filters that make masculine values look like a social norm and feminine ones like deviations from it" (Sylvester and Bleiker 1998: 413). Discourses in all three theoretical debates have contributed to the exclusion of women from international politics. In line with this, Sylvester concludes: "Though international politics, which is saturated with masculine values, is presented as gender-neutral, women can enter this sphere only briefly, as visitors . . . Women, prevailing international discourses teach us, are at home elsewhere" (Sylvester and Bleiker: 1998: 412). In order to expose the origins of this exclusion and find out where women are "at home", Sylvester takes a look at the source texts on which modern International Relations theories draw.[8]

The systematic exclusion of women from (international) politics and their banishing to the private sphere begin with the *classics of political theory*. Sylvester refers to Jean-Jacques Rousseau, who explains in *Emile* that women are captives of their sexual passions and lack the rationality necessary to participation in public political life. Correspondingly, the private domestic sphere is the proper setting for women, while public life is the reserve of men. Niccolò Machiavelli, a classical figure of political theory and a key source for realism with its concept of the national interest, devotes an entire chapter of the *Discorsi* to examining how women tempt (states-)men into mixing public and private affairs, thus bringing disaster on the state. According to Machiavelli, (states-)men can therefore be judged only in light of their action in the public interest of the state, and women according to their action within the private sphere. Thomas Hobbes, another classical figure of the realist school, uses the "state of nature" as an analogy for the state system. He views the (natural) role as mother and the associated tasks of caring and nurturing as reasons for limiting women to the domestic sphere. As a result of this disadvantageous position in the war of all against all, which Hobbes presupposes as the natural human condition, women are enslaved and captured more often than men. But the parties to the "social contract", which according to Hobbes brings the state of nature under control, can only be full and free citizens, and this does not include the subjugated women (see Sylvester 1994a: 5, 80–81).

With an analysis of the three major theoretical debates within International Relations from a feminist perspective, Sylvester makes it clear that the gender-specific construction of the political in the classic texts of political theory is an important source on which the dominant theories of International Relations directly or indirectly draw. The *first debate* in International Relations between classical realism and idealism was concerned with the question of whether – as realism underlines – independent, interest-led states within an anarchical environment are the object of International Relations or whether the discipline should concern itself with the relations between state and nonstate actors and with the potential for cooperation and peace, which was the point of departure for the idealist school. Despite all the differences, both theoretical approaches worked with the division between the public and private sphere and the associated implicit exclusion of women from international politics. Central to the classical realist school was the concept of the (male) public interest in the tradition of Machiavelli, which should be kept separate from (female) private affairs (Sylvester 1994a: 80). In this way, an implicitly masculine concept of externally pre-given interests arose and this underlies the assumption of the rationality of state actors in realism and neorealism. Classical idealism, meanwhile, probed the possibilities and preconditions for the peaceful coexistence of states. It drew on theories of political contract that, as Sylvester explained with respect to Hobbes' "social contract", exclude women as parties to contract and draw on masculine concepts of reason in the tradition of Rousseau. From any perspective geared towards the work of Rousseau or Machiavelli, it is imperative to keep female emotionalism out of the kind of public political affairs embodied in contractually regulated, peaceful cooperation between states (ibid.: 82).[9]

The *second debate* scrutinized whether a positivist conception of science is appropriate to International Relations. Neorealism, in particular, aims to provide a model of international politics that is as simple as possible and features clearly verifiable hypotheses. Such a model is based on the assumption that natural scientific methods are applicable to international relations. Neorealism places the assumption that the international system has an anarchical structure at the centre of its theoretical reflections. It is true that this places limits on the state actor's room for manoeuvre, but as Sylvester emphasizes: "States were at least given rationality and capabilities by the neorealists (and realists before them) whereas 'women' inside states were outside the public sphere of rationality" (ibid.: 114). Neorealism is interested only in the *outside* of the international system, while the *inside* of the state is left explicitly out of account. Like the private sphere within the political theory of the state, the neorealist theory of international relations regarded the internal sphere of the state as irrelevant or nonpolitical. This had another consequence for the visibility of women within neorealism: "Placed outside politics in the private civil sphere of the nation, 'women's' actions would surely be incapable of affecting the capabilities of socially isolated neorealist states" (ibid.: 115). Neorealism thus banishes women from international politics in a dual sense, excluding them from the international system and limiting them to domestic politics (which is of no relevance to international politics) and then further restricting them to the (nonpolitical) private sphere.

In the *third debate* within International Relations, post-positivist theoretical approaches mount a challenge to the formerly dominant theories of International Relations. The postmodern critique of neorealism and other approaches in the tradition of modern Western philosophy has attracted particular attention. In theoretical terms the premises and methods of postmodern approaches offer a great deal of space for feminist issues and in their mode of argument they overlap with postmodern feminist approaches, among others. Feminist and postmodern theory have a shared interest in exposing linguistically normalized mechanisms of domination. Yet despite the fact that an openness to feminist issues is, as it were, an *a priori* feature of postmodern paradigms, such issues have rarely been actively explored. Postmodern approaches point to the problematic universalization of modern Western traditions of thought and argue that we must view knowledge as historically, culturally and socially determined and thus as variable. In line with this, they call for a softening of the rigid boundaries between the scientific disciplines and a questioning of pre-given identities. But the *gender-specific* construction of the political, which determines that modern theories of international relations present themselves as gender-neutral, is often overlooked. Postmodern authors rarely discuss feminist issues. Feminist authors appear in the bibliographies of post-positivist texts almost as rarely as they do in those of the established theoretical schools. Sylvester remarks: "Yet the third debate can sound like its predecessors in one key respect: despite thirty years of feminist theorizing, 'women' do not appear in the citation list and gender is not among the categories of contestation" (Sylvester 1994a: 8).

2.4 Empathetic cooperation as feminist method

The questioning of modern schemas of thought through genealogical critique and discourse analysis is an important tool of postmodern theoretical approaches. This method certainly helps uncover linguistically founded structures of domination, but – it is often argued – it can make no constructive contribution to the theory of International Relations or to feminism. In light of this, Sylvester seeks to go beyond the critique of established theoretical approaches and make good on feminism's emancipatory aspirations by constructing a feminist method of "empathetic cooperation". This method is intended to help overcome the binary and exclusionary intellectual structures of modernity and advance the feminist project of equality between the genders in both theory and practice. Pairs of conceptual opposites such as we/others, West/East, North/South and inside/outside determine our ideas about the character of international politics. The method of empathetic cooperation is intended to show that "we" have more in common with "the other" than it may seem at first sight. Identities are less clear-cut than we might think in view of the oppositions underpinning our ideas.

The *method of empathetic cooperation* is aimed at theorists of international relations and calls on them to actively question their own identity and associated standpoint, and to listen to other voices, in order to overcome the traditional binary structures of thought. The idea here is to soften up the seemingly so unambiguous boundaries between the intellectual and analytical categories found in International Relations. Sylvester defines the concept of cooperation as "negotiating respectfully with contentious others" (Sylvester 1994a: 96). Here she is addressing all those concerned with International Relations theory and its future development (see Sylvester 1994b, and 1994a: 96–99). Further, according to Sylvester, this method can open up political scientists' minds to examples of "empathetic cooperation" in political practice. Again, this can help open up a different perspective on international politics and heighten our awareness of events that lie outside the realm of the political as conventionally perceived (see Sylvester 1994b: 328).

For Sylvester, one example of the *politics of empathetic cooperation* involves establishing a connection between a masculinist security policy and feminine sphere of the everyday in political practice. Sylvester illustrates this with reference to a group of British women in the early 1980s who called themselves "Women for Life on Earth" and initiated a protest march to an American airbase at Greenham Common where medium-range missiles were to be stationed. They were unable to prevent the arrival of the missiles but vividly expressed their protest and the consequences of the missiles' presence on their personal lives by camping on the grounds of the base for several days and celebrating their everyday life. They attempted to tear down the fence surrounding the base in an effort to symbolically overcome the boundaries between the bellicose elements inside the base and the peaceful elements outside it (Sylvester 1994a: 184–197 and 1994b: 330–331; see also Sylvester 2005). In this case, it was the actors themselves who sought to question the dualism of security policy and the private sphere and to forge a link between security policy and women's personal, everyday lives.

3 Between postmodernity and claims of emancipation: internal theoretical critique and differentiation

Sylvester's attempt to walk the tightrope between postmodernity and feminist emancipatory claims must be seen as a response to the debate triggered by the growing influence of postmodern thought within feminist theory since the late 1980s. Judith Butler is an important representative of postmodernity and Sylvester draws on her work when she rejects the idea of a natural gender identity. It was above all Butler who provoked resistance from feminist theorists such as Nancy Fraser and Seyla Benhabib.[10] As they see things, the postmodern deconstruction of the subject is no substitute for critique of existing social realities. Nancy

Fraser believes that "feminists do need to make normative judgments and to offer emancipatory alternatives" (Fraser 1994: 71). And Seyla Benhabib suggests that the loss of the subject may mean that "anything goes", destroying the foundations of feminism as a political theory. "Interpreted thus, postmodernism undermines the feminist commitment to women's agency and sense of selfhood" (Benhabib 1994: 29). Sylvester has addressed these criticisms; despite the deconstruction of a natural feminine gender identity and the associated rejection of any unambiguous category of "woman", she seeks to develop a feminist method and salvage the capacity for feminist action.

This aspiration to unite postmodernity and female subjectivity was bound to lead to contradictions, which have been elaborated by critics. According to *postmodern critics*, the feminist method of empathetic cooperation and the examples of its implementation mentioned above have laid bare the dilemma inherent in Sylvester's approach. In her critique, Nancy Massotto notes that because of the opposition between a masculinist conception of security and feminine efforts to achieve peace, the example of the women of Greenham Common tends to reinforce the modern dualism between male and female qualities rather than calling it into question (Massotto 1999: 240–241).

Expounding similar arguments, Marysia Zalewski (1994) points out that underlying the method of empathetic cooperation and the selection of empirical examples (in which it is generally women who practise the politics of empathetic cooperation) is a specific view of women and associated notion of typically female attributes. On this view, Sylvester is far closer to *standpoint feminism* than her assumption of the socially constructed nature of the category of "woman" would lead us to believe (1994a: 420–421). The examples of the practice of empathetic cooperation put forward by Sylvester are intended to overcome the division between high politics and the everyday world of women. So Sylvester is working with the feminist notion of the political character of the private sphere that informs Cynthia Enloe's analysis of the interactions between international politics and women's everyday lives. The criticisms put forward by Zalewski or Massotto, who analyse Sylvester's work from a postmodern perspective, demonstrate that it is very difficult to maintain a balance between postmodernity and standpoint feminism, and that in light of the case studies she selects, Sylvester shows an implicit proclivity for conventional standpoint feminism of the kind espoused by Cynthia Enloe.

Gender research within International Relations can lead to innovative questions and very different results if the premise of the socially constructed nature of female and male gender identities is consistently followed through. The diversity of methodological approaches, from ethnographic methods through normative ethics to the analysis of the performing arts with respect to international relations is evident in Ackerly *et al.* (2006).

One example of the new horizons that are opening up is critical *research on men*. Rather than placing women at the centre of its analyses, this research problematizes the role of men and investigates the political function of the construction of masculinity (see also Janshen 2000). The multi-authored volume by Zalewski and Parpart (1998) brings together a number of essays that consciously address the "question of men" and analyse the significance of traditional notions of masculinity within International Relations.

The dispute between postmodern and standpoint feminists over the dilemma of the "disappearing woman" and how best to realize feminist emancipatory aspirations dominated the feminist debate of the 1980s and 1990s. Zalewski discusses whether the analysis of men might mark a new phase in feminist theory building. We might consider authors' increasing engagement with the "question of men" to be evidence of the acceptance of postmodern gender research within political scientific analysis, which would constitute progress from a feminist perspective. Zalewski also remarks:

> Is moving to the "man" question the fourth stage in this typology? Some feminist postmodern approaches would . . . imply that the move is evidence of progression. But feminist approaches that remain loyal to an emancipatory feminism based on the subject of woman would stress the importance of keeping men out of the center of feminist analysis and insist on the insertion of women as subjects and objects.
>
> (1998: 12)[11]

The empirical investigation of male action and the further deconstruction of the category of "man" might serve as a starting point for new analyses of international relations now that feminist authors of various stripes have demonstrated how international relations build on male action, male subjectivity and specific constructions of masculinity (see, for example, Hooper 2001, Dean 2001; for a recent work, see Parpart and Zalewski 2008 *et al.* on "white male privilege" in International Relations). Research on men does not necessarily have to be seen as an example of progress in feminist theory building, but may supplement theoretical and empirical studies that are centrally concerned with women (see Zalewski 1998: 12).

The insights of gender research have found expression in public debates over the last few years, while in the form of "gender mainstreaming" they have been integrated into the strategies of international bureaucracies (Whitworth 2008: 399–402; Shepherd 2010, see also Locher and Prügel 2009, True 2010). Gender mainstreaming *as a strategy* aims to build the different realities of men and women into the process of policy formulation in an attempt to ensure the equality of those affected. Critics assert, however, that gender mainstreaming within global institutions serves chiefly to solve problems more effectively rather than contributing to any fundamental change in gender relations and that images of men or women are used in a strategic-instrumental way within (military) policy discourses (Whitworth 2004: 120, Hunt 2002). Feminists are sceptical of the depoliticization of the concept of gender associated with problem-oriented "gender mainstreaming" (Sjoberg 2007).

In line with this, feminist approaches continue to use the concept of gender to analyse international conflicts and concrete situations of violence in order to unearth power structures and point up the political impact of constructions of femininity and masculinity (Whitworth 2004; Eichler 2006; Hunt and Rygiel 2006). Here, the torture scandal in Abu-Ghraib and the events in Guantanamo Bay in the wake of the Iraq War of 2003 have attracted a great deal of attention (Enloe 2007b; Richter-Montpetit 2007; Philipose 2007; Butler 2009b).[12]

4 Critique, co-optation, points of contact: the external reception of feminist approaches in International Relations

Making a distinction between the theory-internal and external reception of feminist approaches within International Relations is difficult since feminist critique may also be regarded as external if expressed by the exponents of a different theoretical perspective. This was evident in my earlier remarks on the debate between modern and postmodern feminists (see Benhabib *et al.* 1994). The critical reception of feminist analyses of international relations from a nonfeminist perspective is a fairly rare event – a fact that has itself been the subject of feminist critique (see Section 2.3).

The two most prominent examples of nonfeminist reception are two older essays. These examine feminist approaches within IR in the context of the "third debate", which was going on at the time they were published. The first is an essay in German by Gert Krell in *Zeitschrift für Internationale Beziehungen* (Krell 1996), but most important is an essay by Robert Keohane that appeared in *Millennium* (Keohane 1989). Both authors begin by surveying feminist approaches within International Relations, drawing on the classification used by Sylvester, who drew on the work of Sandra Harding (though Krell uses different terms for his categories): *feminist empiricism, feminist standpoint* and *feminist postmodernism*. Krell's article is a survey with a critical undertone. The main target of his criticism is radical feminism – a variant of standpoint feminism that draws on the essentialist argument that there exists a superior feminine morality. Krell rejects this argument by pointing to the "involvement or complicity of women in colonialism, militarism and imperialism" (Krell 1996: 156). But he concedes that this criticism scarcely applies to more recent feminist approaches, which largely reject the essentialist argument of a superior female morality. According to him, however, even postmodern authors sometimes fail to free their arguments entirely from essentialist tropes, as evident in the work of Sylvester and her method of empathetic cooperation (see ibid.: 155). This critique demonstrates that Krell's arguments are not fundamentally different from those of feminist authors such as Zalewski or Massotto.

An interesting case of external critique is Robert O. Keohane's engagement with feminist approaches in International Relations, since he looks for potential points of contact between feminism and mainstream approaches within the discipline. A number of authors arguing from a feminist perspective, however, reject this approach as co-optation. And Keohane's proposal to link the neoliberal institutionalism that he himself espouses (see the chapters by Bernhard Zangl and Manuela Spindler in this volume) with standpoint feminism does in fact go hand-in-hand with a very sweeping critique of feminist approaches of a postmodern character (see Weber 1994). With his interest in the conditions and potential for cooperation between states through international regimes, Keohane, like the exponents of postmodern and feminist approaches, is certainly among the critics of neorealism. But he roundly rejects the postmodern project of deconstructing modern subjectivity as pursued by Sylvester and others:

> It seems to me that this postmodernist project is a dead-end in the study of international relations – and that it would be disastrous for feminist international relations to pursue this path. I . . . object to the notion that we should happily accept the existence of multiple incommensurable epistemologies, each equally valid. Such a view seems to me to lead away from our knowledge of the external world, and ultimately to a sort of nihilism.
>
> (Keohane 1989: 249)

Keohane does see possible points of contact, however, between standpoint feminism and institutional theories. He takes up the feminist critique of the "gendered concepts" of neorealism and identifies common ground with regime theory. Central here is the concept of power found in realism and neorealism, which defines it as control. More recent approaches within International Relations, above all institution-centred approaches, in contrast, emphasize the relational character of power (ibid.: 246). Regime theory is interested in the conditions and possibilities for international cooperation through international regimes. In line with this, it works with a concept in which power is defined as the "ability to act in concert". This "feminine" concept of power, Keohane tells us, establishes an important connection between institutional theory and standpoint feminism and directs the epistemological focus of International Relations to spheres of politics lying beyond (male-dominated) security policies, spheres in which cooperation is necessary and possible: "Emphasising power as the ability to act in concert would call attention to areas of world politics in which human beings seek to collaborate to cope with collective problems, such as those arising from ecological and economic interdependence" (ibid.: 246).

Keohane makes much the same argument with respect to the concepts of state sovereignty and reciprocity, which also exhibit a masculinist character within neorealism. Reciprocity is an important element in the modern concept of sovereignty and in neorealism it is based on a rationalist model of action that functions in line with the principle of "tit-for-tat". Though regime theory does not reject the rationalist model of action, alongside rational considerations of utility, it too examines the impact of norms and diffuse processes of socialization within international relations. Keohane suggests that a feminine reformulation of state reciprocity that underlines the significance of empathy and mutual obligation in the relationship between states may be helpful in explaining these processes.

Like standpoint feminism, then, Keohane assumes that the rationalist model of the state as egotistical utility maximizer has masculinist connotations, while he views cooperation on the basis of empathy as a feminine model of action (ibid.: 247). Keohane's argument is anchored in the *natural* opposition between masculine and feminine action orientations, which many recent feminist approaches informed by postmodernism are highly sceptical about. But even Sylvester, as the exponent of a postmodern feminism, succumbs to the inherent attractions of this line of argument and bases her method of empathetic cooperation on the assumption that cooperation and empathy are typically feminine principles of action. For Keohane, the coexistence of male and female models of action is not a theoretical problem. On the contrary, it is part of his notion of the reality of international politics: the relevance of standpoint feminism for International Relations, according to Keohane, arises from the fact that *both* models of action are important to analysing the laws of motion of international politics (see Keohane 1989: 250). Both in feminist and mainstream theoretical approaches within International Relations, the implicit notion of "typically" feminine or masculine action orientations seems to be widespread, to the point where it has become an important point of reference both for feminist theory building as well as the internal and external critique of feminist approaches within International Relations. Postmodern feminist theoretical approaches reject these intellectual structures, but they do not always manage to free themselves from the "modernist" categories of binary thought.

What this chapter has shown is that we can no more refer to feminist theory within International Relations in the singular than we can to feminism itself as a homogeneous political-social phenomenon. Feminists constantly underline that we should really refer to "feminisms" in the plural (Whitworth 2008: 392). One development evident in the postmodern feminism of Christine Sylvester is the linkage of a feminist perspective with other theoretical approaches in International Relations since the 1990s. Further evidence of this trend can be found in the work of Sandra Whitworth (1994, 2004, 2008) and Tordis Batscheider (1993). Whitworth fuses a neo-Gramscian approach of the kind espoused within International Relations by Robert Cox (see the chapter by Andreas Bieler in this volume) with a feminist perspective. Batscheider examines the significance of gender relations to a critical peace research informed by Critical Theory in the tradition of the Frankfurt School. Despite the diversity of feminist approaches, we can discern common issues and a shared objective: overcoming the exclusion, disadvantaging and oppression of women within international politics. This essentially means that feminist approaches have a normative interest in unearthing and eliminating gender-specific inequality. The most important issue here is *the significance of gender relations* to (international) politics, which can in turn be traced back to the question of the existence and origins of "typically" feminine or masculine action orientations. How authors respond to these questions depends on which feminist perspective they espouse. Nonetheless, *gender as a concept* now plays an important role in most feminist theoretical approaches (and not just in International Relations). Beyond feminist theory and empirical research, the co-optation of the concept of gender through the "gender mainstreaming" practised in international bureaucracies illustrates that gender research is making an impact within international relations.

5 Notes

1 This chapter has not been revised and the translation reflects the version in the German edition printed in 2010.

2 In the German context, a distinction is usually made between the old and new women's movement, while Anglo-American writers tend to refer to a first and second wave, thus placing more emphasis on continuities than ruptures. For an in-depth study, see Gerhard (1999: 12–38).

3 The starting point of the English-language feminist debate within International Relations is considered to be the 1988 special issue of the journal *Millennium*, "Women and International Relations", parts of which appear in Grant and Newland (1991). For up-to-date analyses, see, for example, Tickner (2005),Whitworth (2008) and Sjoberg and Tickner (2012).

4 Epistemology is concerned with the nature, origin and limits of our knowledge.

5 The literature includes a number of attempts to provide an introduction to feminist theories. Tickner (2008) distinguishes between liberal, critical, social constructivist, postmodern and postcolonial feminist theory, while Whitworth (2008: 392–395) expands on the approaches inspired by Harding by adding radical feminists, feminist critical theory and postcolonial feminist theory. Many authors focus on just three main currents: liberal, radical and post-modern feminism (see, for example, Ruppert 1998).

6 A further development of this feminist approach can be found in transnational feminism; see, for example, the contributions in Ferree and Tripp (2006).

7 The tendency to absolutize and naturalize unchanging female and male characteristics is referred to as "essentialism", and Sylvester also uses the term in this context. Marysia Zalewski remarks: "Any feminist theory which is taken to imply 'essential woman', meaning that women have something inherent, unchanging and shared that defines them as women, is held in particular disregard by contemporary postmodern feminist theory" (1994: 409).

8 Sylvester draws on feminist analyses of the state and of classical political theory, such as those of Carole Pateman (1988) and Jean Bethke Elshtain (1981).

9 As an example of this attitude, Sylvester identifies the election campaign of American President Woodrow Wilson – the leading protagonist of political idealism during and after the First World War:

> Woodrow Wilson . . . campaigned for the US presidency on a platform advocating peace and disfavoring women's suffrage, ostensibly because the people – the voice of idealist reason – opposed this extension of the franchise. "The people" opposing "women's" vote while favoring peace, however, had voice only through the socially contracted citizen "men" of the country.
>
> (Sylvester 1994a: 82)

10 A good overview of this debate can be found in the multiauthored volume by Benhabib *et al.* (1994). Though Fraser and Benhabib argue as feminists here, they are essentially critical theorists rather than feminist political theorists.

11 Here Zalewski bases her remarks mainly on the typology of feminist approaches used by Sylvester (feminist empiricism, feminist standpoint and feminist postmodernism). She views these three types as successive tendencies in feminist theory building.

12 The events in the prisons at Abu Ghraib and Guantanamo have, for example, been interpreted as signs of "gender confusions" that served to mask imperialistic masculinity. The relevant authors here underline that the armed forces are well acquainted with the manipulation of gendered images (Whitworth 2008: 403).

6 *Bibliography and* recommended reading

6.1 Primary texts

Enloe, Cynthia 1989: *Bananas, Beaches & Bases: Making Feminist Sense of International Politics*. Berkeley, CA: University of California Press.

Shepherd, Laura J. (ed.) 2010: *Gender Matters in Global Politics: A Feminist Introduction to International Relations*. London. Routledge.

Sylvester, Christine 1994a: *Feminist Theory and International Relations in a Postmodern Era*. Cambridge: Cambridge University Press.

Tickner, J. Ann 1992: *Gender in International Relations: Feminist Perspectives on Achieving Global Security*. New York: Columbia University Press.

6.2 Secondary texts

Enloe, Cynthia 2007a: Feminism, in Griffith, Martin (ed.) *International Relations Theory for the Twenty-First Century: An Introduction*. New York: Routledge.

Keohane, Robert O. 1989: International Relations Theory. Contributions of a Feminist Standpoint, *Millennium* 18(2): 245–254.

Krell, Gert 1996: Feminismus und Internationale Beziehungen. Zwischen Dekonstruktion und Essentialisierung, *Zeitschrift für Internationale Beziehungen* 3(1): 149–181.

Locher, Birgit 1996: Feminismus ist mehr als "political correctness". Anmerkungen und Ergänzungen zu Gert Krells Literaturbericht, *Zeitschrift für Internationale Beziehungen* 3(2): 381–397.

Weber, Cynthia 1994: Good Girls, Little Girls and Bad Girls: Male Paranoia in Robert O. Keohane's Critique of Feminist International Relations, *Millennium* 23(2): 337–349.

Whitworth, Sandra 2008: Feminism, in Reus-Smith, Christian and Snidal, Duncan, *The Oxford Handbook of International Relations*. Oxford: Oxford University Press, pp. 319–407.

Zalewski, Marysia 1998: Introduction: From the "Woman" Question to the "Man" Question in International Relations, in Zalewski, Marysia and Parpart, Jane (eds) *The "Man" Question in International Relations*. Boulder, CO: Westview Press, pp. 1–13.

6.3 Other texts

Ackerly, Brooke, Stern, Maria and True, Jacqui (eds) 2006: *Feminist Methodologies for International Relations*. Cambridge: Cambridge University Press.

Batscheider, Tordis 1993: *Friedensforschung und Geschlechterverhältnis. Zur Begründung feministischer Fragestellungen in der kritischen Friedensforschung*. Marburg: BdWi-Verlag.

Benhabib, Seyla 1994: Feminism and Postmodernism, in Benhabib, Seyla, Butler, Judith, Cornell, Drucilla and Fraser, Nancy (eds), *Feminist Contentions: A Philosophical Exchange*. London: Routledge, pp. 17–34.

Benhabib, Seyla, Butler, Judith, Cornell, Drucilla and Fraser, Nancy (eds) 1994: *Feminist Contentions: A Philosophical Exchange*. London: Routledge.

Butler, Judith 1990: *Gender Trouble: Feminism and the Subversion of Identity*. London: Routledge.

Butler, Judith 2004: *Undoing Gender*. London: Routledge.

Butler, Judith 2009b: *Frames of War: When is Life Grievable?* London: Verso.

Dean, Robert D. 2001: *Imperial Brotherhood: Gender and the Making of the Cold War*. Amherst, MA: University of Massachusetts Press.

Eichler, Maya 2006: Russia's Post-Communist Transformation: A Gendered Analysis of the Chechen Wars, *International Feminist Journal of Politics* 8(4): 486–511.

Elshtain, Jean Bethke 1981: *Public Man, Private Woman: Women in Social and Political Thought*. Princeton, NJ: Princeton University Press.

Enloe, Cynthia 2000: *Maneuvers: The International Politics of Militarizing Women's Lives*. Berkeley, CA: University of California Press.

Enloe, Cynthia 2007b: Feminist readings on Abu Ghraib: Introduction, *International Feminist Journal of Politics* 9(1): 35–37.

Ferree, Myra Marx and Tripp, Aila Mari (eds) 2006: *Global Feminism: Transnational Women's Activism, Organizing, and Human Rights*. New York: New York University Press.

Fraser, Nancy 1994: False Antitheses, in Benhabib, Seyla, Butler, Judith, Cornell, Drucilla and Fraser, Nancy (eds) *Feminist Contentions: A Philosophical Exchange*. London: Routledge, pp. 59–74.

Gerhard, Ute 1999: *Atempause. Feminismus als demokratisches Projekt*. Frankfurt a. M.: Fischer.

Grant, Rebecca 1991: Hans Morgenthau's Principles of Political Realism: A Feminist Reformulation, in Grant, Rebecca and Newland, Kathleen (eds) *Gender and International Relations*. Milton Keynes: Open University Press, pp. 27–40.

Grant, Rebecca and Newland, Kathleen (eds) 1991: *Gender and International Relations*. Milton Keynes: Open University Press.

Harding, Sandra 1986: *The Science Question in Feminism*. Ithaca, NY: Cornell University Press.

Hooper, Charlotte 2001: *Manly States: Masculinities, International Relations, and Gender Politics*. New York: Columbia University Press

Hunt, Krista (2002): The Strategic Co-optation of Women's Rights: Discourse in the "War on Terrorism", *International Feminist Journal of Politics* 4(1): 116–121.

Hunt, Krista and Rygiel, Kim (2006): *(En)Gendering the War on Terror: War Stories and Camouflaged Politics*. Aldershot: Ashgate.

Janshen, Doris (ed.) 2000: *Blickwechsel: Der neue Dialog zwischen Frauen- und Männerforschung*. Frankfurt a. M.: Campus.

Locher, Birgit and Prügl, Elisabeth 2009: Gender and European Integration, in Wiener, Antje and Diez, Thomas (eds) *European Integration Theory*, 2nd edn. Oxford: Oxford University Press, pp. 181–197.

Locher-Dodge, Birgit 1998: Internationale Politik – Geschlechtsneutrale Paradigmen?, in Kreisky, Eva and Sauer, Birgit (eds) *Geschlechterverhältnisse im Kontext politischer Transformation*. Opladen: Westdeutscher Verlag, pp. 425–449.

MacKinnon, Catharine A. 1989: *Towards a Feminist Theory of the State*. Cambridge, MA: Harvard University Press.

Massotto, Nancy L. 1999: Elephants as Artists: Postmodernism, Gender, and International Relations. A Review Essay, *Social Politics* 6(2): 230–244.

Nunner-Winkler, Gertrud (ed.) 1991: *Weibliche Moral: die Kontroverse um eine geschlechtsspezifische Ethik*. Frankfurt a. M.: Campus.

Parpart, Jane and Zalewski, Marysia (eds.) 2008: *Rethinking the Man Question: Sex, Gender and Violence in International Relations*. London: Zed Books.

Pateman, Carole 1988: *The Sexual Contract*. Stanford, CA: Stanford University Press.

Peterson, V. Spike 1992: Security and Sovereign States: What is at Stake in Taking Feminism Seriously?, in Peterson, V. Spike (ed.) *Gendered States: Feminist (Re)Visions of International Relations Theory*. Boulder, CO: Lynne Rienner, pp. 31–64.

Philipose, Liz 2007: The Politics of Pain and the End of Empire, *International Feminist Journal of Politics* 9(1): 60–81.

Richter-Montpetit, Melanie 2007: Empire, Desire and Violence: A Queer Transnational Feminist Reading of the Prisoner "Abuse" in Abu Ghraib and the Question of "Gender Equality", *International Feminist Journal of Politics* 9(1): 38–59.

Ruppert, Uta 1998: Theorien internationaler Beziehungen aus feministischer Perspektive, in Ruppert, Uta (ed.) *Lokal bewegen – global handeln. Internationale Politik und Geschlecht*. Frankfurt a. M.: Campus, pp. 27–55.

Sjoberg, Laura 2007: Agency, Militarized Femininity and Enemy Others: Observations from the War in Iraq, *International Feminist Journal of Politics* 9(1): 82–101.

Sjoberg, Laura and Tickner, Ann J. 2012: Feminist Perspectives on International Relations, in Carlsnaes, Walter, Risse, Thomas and Simmons, Beth A. (eds) *Handbook of International Relations*, 2nd edn. London: Sage, pp. 170–194.

Sylvester, Christine 1990: The Emperor's Theories and Transformations: Looking at the Field through Feminist Lenses, in *Pirages*, Dennis, Mary and Sylvester, Christine (eds) *Transformations of the Global Political Economy*. London: Macmillan, pp. 230–253.

Sylvester, Christine 1994b: Empathetic Cooperation. A Feminist Method for IR, *Millennium* 21(2): 315–336.

Sylvester, Christine 1996: The Contributions of Feminist Theory to International Relations, in Smith, Steve, Booth, Ken and Zalewski, Marysia (eds) *International Theory: Positivism and Beyond*. Cambridge: Cambridge University Press, pp. 254–278.

Sylvester, Christine 1998: "Masculinity", "Femininity", and "International Relations": Or Who Goes to the "Moon" with Bonaparte and the Adder, in Zalewski, Maryisa and Parpart, Jane (eds) *The "Man" Question in International Relations*. Boulder, CO: Westview Press, pp. 185–198.

Sylvester, Christine 2005: The Art of War/The War Question in (Feminist) IR, *Millennium: Journal of International Studies*, 33(3): 855–878.

Sylvester, Christine and Bleiker, Roland 1998: Meine Stimme ein Vogellaut. Sprachkritik, Empathie und internationales Geschlechterregime, in Kreisky, Eva and Sauer, Birgit (eds) *Geschlechterverhältnisse im Kontext politischer Transformation*. Opladen: Westdeutscher Verlag, pp. 411–424.

Tickner, J. Ann 2005: What is Your Research Program? Some Feminist Answers to International Relations Methodological Questions, *International Studies Quarterly* 49: 1–21.

True, Jacqui 2010: Gender Mainstreaming in International Institutions, in Shepherd, Laura J. (ed.) *Gender Matters in Global Politics: A Feminist Introduction to International Relations*. London. Routledge, pp. 189–203.

Whitworth, Sandra 1994: *Feminism and International Relations: Towards a Political Economy of Gender in Interstate and Non-Governmental Institutions*. Basingstoke: Macmillan.

Whitworth, Sandra 2004: *Men, Militarism, and UN Peacekeeping: A Gendered Analysis*. Boulder, CO: Lynne Rienner.

Zalewski, Marysia 1994: The Women/"Women" Question in International Relations, *Millennium* 23(2): 407–423.

Zalewski, Marysia and Parpart, Jane (eds) 1998: *The "Man" Question in International Relations*. Boulder, CO: Westview Press.

Critical geopolitics

Mathias Albert, Paul Reuber and Günter Wolkersdorfer[1]

1 Introduction

The use of geopolitical analytical categories, indeed the use of the term "geopolitics" itself, long seemed to be something of a taboo in the still fairly young discipline of International Relations, particularly in the German-speaking world. This explicit disregard for "geopolitics", as a school of thought well established in the late nineteenth century and in the first decades of the twentieth, is not primarily due to the "objective" status that the authors of "classical" geopolitics – chiefly Friedrich Ratzel and Karl Haushofer in Germany – ascribe to the role of geographical realities in the functioning of international politics. It is mainly a result of the adaptation of geopolitical thought found in the National Socialists' geographical ideology – though this theoretical objectivism did foster such adaptation. It is only since the end of the East–West conflict that political geography and International Relations have once again begun to pay more attention to geopolitical issues. This applies to the field of so-called "critical geopolitics", which questions the objectifying geographical notions of classical politics and highlights the social construction of space, and it applies also to the basically restorative revival of classical geopolitical categories for the analysis of structure formation within the international system.

So far, the majority of theories in International Relations have conceived of space as state territory. Only in the wake of the development of "critical" theoretical approaches since the late 1980s and early 1990s and in response to debates on globalization have a number of approaches begun to pay attention to the contingency of territoriality as *one* of many possible ways of constructing and organizing social and political space.

Building quite seamlessly on a "classical" geopolitical perspective, *political realism* views control over territory and the (geo-)strategic predicament entailed in a territory's physical-geographical characteristics as one of the state's key power resources. As states vie for power, control over territories achieved through the formation of alliances or through conquest represents a crucial factor. Only with John H. Herz's (1957) famous thesis of the "end of the territorial state", triggered by the development of a global system of nuclear deterrence, has state control over territory lost at least some of its importance, even in realist thought, though it remains an important factor in the perception of global structures of conflict below the level of the nuclear "balance of terror" (the key term here being "domino theory"; see also the chapter by Andreas Jacobs in this volume).

As political realism has developed into *structural realism* or *neorealism*, it has retained this reference to space, but by emphasizing the *international system* as the primary analytical level this aspect has been pushed further into the background, at least theoretically (see the chapter by Niklas Schörnig in this volume). Control over territory remains relevant with respect to the distribution of power resources between the units of the international system, but does not impact on system structure or system differentiation.

Increasingly, the broad spectrum of *institutionalist approaches* seem to get by without making any reference to space. Analyses of international relations anchored in interdependence and regime theories give precedence to the conditions in which functionally specific cooperation arises within the international system in the absence of the guaranteed stability provided by a hegemon (see also the chapters by Manuela Spindler and Bernhard Zangl in this volume). Focusing on the at least partial taming – though not overcoming – of anarchy within the international system relativizes the significance of classical power resources, and the significance of territoriality is left largely out of account. It only remains present in the background because institutionalist approaches leave in place the basic realist model of the international system as one based on sovereign territorial states. The end of the East–West conflict and attempts to get to grips empirically and theoretically with processes of denationalization and globalization led to a qualitative shift in the international system itself (through the increasing significance of nonstate actors, for example). Only in the wake of these developments have scholars once again begun to pay new attention to the dimension of territoriality (see Brock and Albert 1995). The "world of states" is diminishing in importance vis-à-vis the "world of society" (Czempiel 1991). Borders are beginning to dissolve, which primarily means that territoriality is losing its capacity to shape the structure of political processes. But to the extent that structures of "global governance" (that rest partly on the activities of private actors) are taking shape, in which states continue to play an important role, it seems that the development of a "post-Westphalian" system by no means results in territoriality losing all significance, but in a change in the meaning of territoriality for (international) politics. This insight is linked with a final turning away from the objectivist conception of space based on the assumption that the territorial form of statehood is a kind of pre-given fact of nature. John G. Ruggie (1993) made a landmark contribution in this vein with his essay on "Territoriality and Beyond" by highlighting the status of territoriality as epistemic and social construct. To some extent this meant that the mainstream of the discipline was now building on post-positivist and postmodern writings whose main goal is epistemological critique. Sometimes inspired by contributions from geography and urban sociology, these had already highlighted the specifically *modern* forms of the representation of space that underlie realist notions of an international system constitutively differentiated by territory.

At the risk of simplifying and overstating things slightly, we might say that in the wake of internal theoretical developments and of the upheavals that have occurred within the global system (the end of the East–West conflict, processes of globalization), the tendency to "forget space" within the discipline of International Relations has diminished since the early 1990s. But within the discipline this insight into the constructed nature of territoriality as a perceptual and structural model of space within international relations has done no more than jump-start the discourse on space. The way in which the spatial dimension is discussed and utilized in contemporary analyses of the international system varies substantially, extending from notions of de-territorialization of varied provenance (see Newman 1999) up to and including the use of classical categories of geopolitical thought (see Gray and Sloan 1999). Between these two poles, however, a broad spectrum of analytical options has also opened up. Where they seem most likely to make a substantial contribution is in reassessing the international system as one that is *partly* constituted by space. Simply put, a variety of authors have sought to determine the form of newly emerging, structurally and epistemologically impactful representations and constructions of space within the global context. The work done in this regard extends from attempts to redefine the concept of "political space" on the global level (see Walker 1993) to the conceptual and empirical identification of a new "regionality" within global space (see Joenniemi 1997). These endeavours increasingly draw on the ideas of political geography and particularly "critical geopolitics". Beyond this, the emergence of critical geopolitics, which arose through critical examination of the "classical" geopolitics of the late nineteenth and early twentieth centuries is particularly instructive. This subfield has systematically discussed and described the shift described above in views of space within theories of international relations. Understanding the emergence and content of "critical geopolitics" thus provides us with a number of stimuli that can help us get to grips with the spatial dimension of the contemporary global system in a conceptually and empirically substantive way.

To investigate the structural change in international relations, discussed nowadays primarily in terms of upheaval in the "Westphalian system" of sovereign territorial states, it thus seems essential to examine more closely the significance of "space" as a factor in the structuring, perception and construction of the international system. As stated at the beginning of this chapter, it is true that International Relations is increasingly getting over its long-standing "blindness to space" and that this process is occurring in analogy to and in connection with research in political geography, which has subdivided into "classical" and "critical" approaches. But despite increasing agreement within the discipline that the dimension of space should play an important role in the analysis of international relations, there remain significant, theoretically founded differences regarding the nature and extent of this role. The present chapter intends to help readers make their own minds up about this by systematically relating ways of considering space when conceptualizing the international system and investigating global structural change to the various concepts of (critical) geopolitics discussed within political geography. In light of this, it seems inappropriate to try to shed light on "geopolitics" and its influence on International Relations or its applicability within International Relations by presenting the work of a reference theorist. So the present chapter aims to provide a systematic rather than author-focused account. If we had to identify a reference theorist, it would be Gearóid Ó Tuathail with his critical geopolitics, though the latter has by now divided into a number of different subfields. The next section provides an overview of the central hypotheses of "classical" and "critical" geopolitics. We then examine the significance of the various geopolitical models to International Relations and ask how they might contribute to the investigation of the international system. The chapter concludes with a number of critical remarks on critical geopolitics.

2 Classical and critical geopolitics

2.1 The history of geopolitics

The heyday of classical geopolitics was the late nineteenth century. As a form of academic support for imperialism and naval policies, it served the state in specific ways. The world was divided up, conquered and measured. The quantification of the world by means of specific spatial units (such as degrees of latitude and longitude) was only possible through a view of the world "as a differentiated, integrated, hierarchically ordered whole" (Gregory 1994: 36). The geopolitical construction of the world entailed a dichotomous notion of space. Both ends of this dichotomous model were constructed in contrast to what they were *not*, in contrast to their specific other: West versus East, North versus South, Orient versus

Occident and maritime empire versus continental empire, to mention just a few examples of this dichotomous geopolitical conception.

The antagonism between sea and land, between maritime power and continental empire led to the first influential argument in geopolitics, namely Mackinder's pivot area thesis. This dichotomous notion of power, presented before the Royal Geographical Society by British geographer and geopolitician Halford J. Mackinder (1904), divided the nations of the world into states with maritime possessions and states with territorial possessions. This approach provided the foundation for many geopolitical models used to this day, the dualism between land and ocean being the key discursive figure in their construction. The specific ideas entailed in this approach took on tremendous power-political relevance with respect to the situation of the various nation states at the time. Here, Russia represents the classical power centre of a continental empire, a so-called pivot area with no direct access to the sea. This is surrounded by a fringe of territories with ocean access. These are distinguished by an ambiguous conflict-inducing position equally determined by oceanic and continental influences. The rest of the world is arranged around this fringe. The external territories of Japan, the United Kingdom and United States, – according to Mackinder – are purely oceanic in character. For him the *balance of power* or shifts in power within this dual world structure are the driving force behind all developments, with conflicts being settled in the transitional or fringe area.

Quite different in character from Mackinder's ideas are the arguments put forward in German geopolitics, which must be seen in relation to the specific position of Germany.[2] The key German exponents of geopolitics, Friedrich Ratzel and Karl Haushofer, developed their ideas within the nationalistic intellectual climate that held sway at the time. So there was no great stretch between their geopolitical models and Hitler's *Lebensraum* ("living space") policies.

Ratzel's model of the state as organism

The fundamentally new aspect of Ratzel's political geography was his attempt to construct a more dynamic model of the natural dependency of states than Mackinder's rather static conception. This he did by drawing on Darwin's ideas about biological selection, which enjoyed great popularity at the time. Ratzel, who had come to geography from zoology, constructed his political geography on a thoroughly natural scientific view of the world. Because of this, his construction of the relationship between space and politics is determined by the state's physical foundations, while he virtually ignores how societies, culture and economy affect the territory of the state. Another core aspect of his work, also borrowed from Darwinist theory, is his biologistic analogy of the state as an "organism rooted in the soil". Here the state is endowed with the characteristics of a living being, of an organism, which can be considered healthy and strong only if it is capable of constant growth, in other words ceaseless territorial expansion. Ratzel thus sees the core role of political-geographical investigation as tracking the historical movement and counter-movement of peoples and states: in line with its basic Darwinist thesis, this political geography legitimizes every case of imperialism and expansionism so long as it is geographically determined. Ratzel sees the reasons for the growth and contraction of specific states in the cultural stage reached by a given people and in the natural potential of the territory over which it rules. In his work, this insatiable need for space inherent in life contrasts with the limited surface of the Earth. As he sees it, this "contradiction" gives rise to a struggle of "life with life over space" "all over the world" (Ratzel 1901: 153). Again and again, Ratzel constructs a close connection between a "growing people" and "increasing space" and then makes this claim more specific by relating it to the German Empire in the run-up to the First World War:

> Everywhere we look, then, territory is being won and lost. We see retreat and progress in every corner; there will always be ruling and servile peoples. A people too must be either hammer or anvil. Under no circumstances must Germany restrict itself to Europe; among world powers, it is only as a world power itself that it stands any chance of securing for its people the land it requires for growth
>
> (Ratzel 1906: 377)

With scientifically reputable arguments, Ratzel thus provides the political-geographical basis for the German Empire's colonial and naval policies. After the First World War, the connection made here between politics and science led to the rapid development of political geography at universities. Ultimately, Ratzel's dynamic political geography based on the "law of growing territories" also provided crucial stimulus to the *Lebensraum* ideology. "Ratzel's theory was thus compatible not just with the classical concept of geography, but also with the Third Reich's ideology of *Lebensraum*. The reorientation that made race the crucial force of history is already inherent in his work" (Schultz 1998: 217).

The actual term "geopolitics" for arguments of this kind was first used in 1905 by Swedish political scientist Rudolf Kjellén. But his concepts were already informed by Ratzel's ideas and it was on this basis that they established the core concepts of geopolitical discourse valid to this day.

Karl Haushofer and geopolitics

It was Karl Haushofer, Professor of Geography in Munich, who then took the decisive step of instrumentalizing geopolitics for use in Nazi ideology (see Haushofer *et al.* 1928). Historians put the fact that his ideas were able to exercise such a crucial influence on Hitler's views primarily down to his biographical connections. The intermediary role played by Haushofer's student Rudolf Hess is likely to have been particularly important in the development of Hitler's concept of *Lebensraum*. Following the failed putsch in Munich in 1923, Haushofer hid Hess in his home for a number of months, and there Hess and his mentor engaged in an intensive exchange of views that resulted in the incorporation of Haushofer's geopolitical world-view into the ideology of National Socialism. It was during their incarceration in Landsberg that Hitler and Hess then formulated such foundational features of Nazism as the mythology of the *Führer* and the demand for *Lebensraum*, ideas committed to paper in Hitler's *Mein Kampf*. According to Hipler (1996), the fact that Haushofer played a quite inconspicuous role within the Nazi machinery of power is due in part to his view of himself. Haushofer saw himself as the man of ideas "in the background", an *éminence grise* (ibid.: 79ff., 177).

After the Second World War, Haushofer's role and influence were received and reconstructed very differently in the German and Anglo-American worlds. In the German-speaking countries, the historical entanglements of geography were "dealt with" almost exclusively through an emphasis on Haushofer as an individual, while a significant part of American geopolitics in the post-war era was inspired by the mythology surrounding the Geopolitical Institute (*Geopolitisches Institut*) and its director. In the United States, Haushofer was viewed as the "scientific brain behind Hitler". The discursive exaggeration of his role led all the way to Hollywood, where one American propaganda film depicted

Table 1 Classical geopolitics

Geopolitical order:	*Geopolitical discourse:*
Hegemonic geopolitical order brought about by the United Kingdom, 1815–1875	Geopolitics as harmonious-static structure comprising People and territory (Herder)
International conflicts in the imperialist era, 1875–1945	Geopolitics as dynamic "natural" struggle over Lebensraum (Ratzel, Haushofer)
The geopolitical order of the Cold War, 1945–1990	Geopolitics as ideology, Realpolitik (Kissinger, Waltz)
Transnational liberalism, ecological collapse, clash of civilizations 1990–?	Diversification of geopolitical discourses (Fukuyama, Kaplan, Huntington, Brzezinski)

Source: Agnew (1998), Ó Tuathail (1996), Schultz (1998), Wolkersdorfer (2001).

Haushofer and his Geopolitical Institute as the nerve centre of National Socialism. As Ó Tuathail sets out in his *Critical Geopolitics*, the belief that "geopolitics was something America has to know" (Ó Tuathail 1996: 113) goes back to Haushofer and his imaginary Geopolitical Institute in Munich. In Germany, meanwhile, because of the historically burdensome falsehoods propagated by geopolitics, political geography led a shadowy existence until the early 1990s.

To this day the legacy of classical geopolitics persists: the creation of difference through territorial metaphors has remained a significant element even in many recent geopolitical approaches (see Table 1). Again and again theorists have deployed a dichotomous geopolitical rhetoric to air conceptions of a future territorial order. In the early 1990s, this led to a more profound conceptual critique within the discipline of geography and to a new, more radical reconceptualization of the concepts, tropes and patterns of thought that had characterized geopolitical analysis for almost a century. In other words, it led to the establishment of *critical geopolitics.*

2.2 The conception of critical geopolitics

Through its view of the state as organism, based on supposedly "objective" spatial criteria, classical geopolitics examined the "natural" strengths and weaknesses of nation states. Its political recommendations were derived from the constraints of these deterministic, geography-based arguments. The present-day school of critical geopolitics distances itself from such traditional concepts, constructed "in proximity to real-world events" (Fiedler 2000: 7). The new geopolitics takes a radically different course, subjecting these concepts themselves to investigation: "Geopolitics, for us, engages the geographical representations and practices that produce the spaces of the world" (Ó Tuathail and Dalby 1998: 2). Critical geopolitics seeks to critically examine the contexts in which geopolitical arguments and world-views emerge.

The key question with which it is concerned is thus how actors' discourse linguistically constructs geopolitical world-views, how geographical regionalization and boundary-marking construct new political spaces and how these discursive concepts then impact on the political arena. Critical geopolitics demonstrates how political actors safeguard their territorial-political interests with the tools of geopolitical argument and the rhetoric of geographical connection and separation in order to "demonstrate" how right and plausible their interests are.

By focusing its attention on the linguistic (and cartographic) production of space, critical geopolitics adheres to a guiding principle derived from Said's *Orientalism* (1978), one that Gregory has reformulated and expressed more precisely in geopolitical terms for use in cultural geography in his *Geographical Imaginations* (1994): rather than objective entities, geopolitical constructions, including their cartographic representations, are always "regionalizations" constructed from a one-sided perspective and disseminated to political ends. They are active forms of geopolitics (see also Albert and Reuber 2007).

A transformed conceptual frame is necessary for such a research perspective. If we want to look at the differences and the impact of different geopolitical discourses, we require a meta-framework that, in epistemological terms, not only opens up a broader perspective but adopts a *different* perspective. To this end, political geography required a paradigmatic shift, an understanding that geopolitics cannot be politically and morally neutral:

> The sign "geopolitics" does not have any essential meaning over and above the historical web of contextualities within which it is evoked and knowingly used . . . We should not be mesmerized by the deployment and use of the sign geopolitics but look toward the more important problematic it marks. That problematic is the problematic of geopolitics, the politics of the production of global political space by dominant intellectuals, institutions, and practitioners of statecraft in practices that constitute "global politics".
>
> (Ó Tuathail 1996: 146)

By rejecting essentialist concepts in this way, political geography spotlights geopolitical discourses and the construction of political actors' geopolitical representations. The goal here is to interpret these in a Foucauldian sense as linguistic formations of power and space and thus to show in which ways "political elites have depicted and represented places in their exercise of power" (Dodds and Sidaway 1994: 515ff.). The way to do this is through deconstruction. Informed by a constructivist ontology, deconstruction works on the assumption that geography and especially political geography cannot be an objective description of the world, that geographical descriptions (re-)produce specific conceptions of order and power relations. Inevitably, then, research in critical geopolitics focuses on the relationship between geography, politics and power.

As a kind of poststructuralist political geography, critical geopolitics conceives of key geopolitical models as linguistic constructions featuring geographical-territorial semantics and modes of representation (see Ó Tuathail 1996; Ó Tuathail and Dalby 1996; Dalby 2003; Dodds and Sidaway 1994; Gregory 1994, 1998 *et al.*). Reflecting the *linguistic turn*[3] in the social sciences, from this perspective the diverging geopolitical notions held by political actors underpin the argumentational models that linguistically construct new political geographies.

Poststructuralist-discursive political geography deconstructs geopolitical discourses and conceives of them as elements in strategic action. The aim here, then, is not to construct a factually founded, supposedly "more objective" or even "better" counterargument to existing geopolitical models (see, for example, the many responses to Huntington's ideas on the clash of civilizations). Instead critical geopolitics shows, from a meta-perspective, how geographical arguments about connection and separation as well as key geopolitical principles are formulated as linguistic constructions and deployed as discursive strategies in political disputes. A good example of this can be seen in the discipline of geography. The production of strictly delimited cultural areas for use in school geography classes was long one of the discipline's basic tasks. In the 1960s, geographer Albert Kolb (1962) put forward a theory of cultural areas almost identical to Huntington's ideas. Kolb intended his earlier attempt at demarcation to foster a geography of peace. Huntington's approach, on the other hand, is centrally concerned with border-drawing and thus entails an immanent rhetoric of war. What is interesting here is not that a near-identical model existed thirty years ago. The crucial point is that different scholars could produce a geography of peace and a rhetoric of war on the basis of the same model.

Such a perspective brings out the inevitably normative character of key geopolitical models. The more clearly we see the relativity and strategic role of political-geographical language games, cartographic representations and regionalization, the less – both within political discourse itself and in terms of the polarization and instrumentalization of the public – they can play their at times manipulative role within geopolitical conflicts over power and territory. From this perspective, every form of active geopolitics appears as a construction that arose in a specific historical and political context and is thus bound up with this context. In line with this, the deconstruction of leading geostrategic models in the contemporary academic arena is opposed to the renaissance of traditional ideas, sometimes informed by a virtually naturalistic determinism, for which "geopolitics [is] a theory of the influence of geographical space on a state's politics" (Brill 1994: 21). This positivist, historically burdened form of geopolitics gained a certain impetus in the first half of the 1990s after the "lifting of the iron mantle of Stalinist communism" (Lacoste 1990: 19). The poststructuralist turn in political geography, in contrast, shows clearly how quickly such an understanding of geopolitics can lead us to an ideological dead-end, and points to the extent to which such concepts themselves are merely the active normative "doing of geopolitics" (for an in-depth study, see Lossau 2000; Wolkersdorfer 2001). In conceptual terms, there are no "right" and "wrong" language games within the "conflict of discourses" (Lyotard 1988). From an academic perspective, attempts to draw on geographical-geopolitical arguments from the sphere of "position, territories and borders" are best understood as a discursive strategy used by politically acting subjects, one that serves to legitimize and enforce political objectives.

Though a critical geopolitics with these intentions cannot deny that it entails an action theoretical perspective, it is the constructivist, relational ontology that remains at its core. This is a key difference from the many strands of political geography in the post-war era that sought to identify "objective" boundaries by drawing on analytical-scientistic procedures to underline the supposed neutrality of the discipline and "the contrast between scientific research and propagandistic use, trends and predictions" (Boesler 1983). It is only from this perspective that the shift in perspective embodied in critical geopolitics becomes fully visible. This is not a matter of looking for "objective" boundaries, but of investigating "those geographies that . . . are made and reproduced by acting subjects on the basis of differing power positions" (Werlen 1995: 6). Such deconstruction of central geopolitical models unmasks their function as targeted geostrategic discourses concerned with territorially-bound concepts of them-and-us. It shows how political actors engage in geopolitics through the skilful linguistic and sometimes symbolic cartographic linkage of religion, culture and/or ethnicity with territorial identity, how they use language to generate territories in which certain characteristics are desirable and others are not, in which some people may live while others are expelled.

With reference to examples, critical geopolitics shows that a geopolitical-territorial semantics can be used not just to shape collective sentiments and foster solidarization, but also to rhetorically legitimize borders and exclusion. This is the point of departure for dangerous forms of political instrumentalization, for the strategic abuse of geopolitical worldviews. These reduce the complexity of the social sphere to a catchy spatial code. Through these dubious connections and simplistic analyses, key actors can practise geopolitics, incite ethnic persecution, expulsion and cleansing and wage bloody wars for other purposes.

What geopolitical world-views present as "regional identity" and "differences between groups" are largely deliberate strategic constructions. This becomes particularly clear at times of armed conflict. All parties to war evoke one-sided geopolitical scenarios to justify their actions and encourage loyalty among the general population (an example being CNN news coverage of the Gulf War or of the Kosovo conflict). Often, political actors use relatively small differences to construct geopolitical images that enable them to pursue their own interests.

By laying bare these characteristics, critical geopolitics adopts a very different perspective than classical geopolitics in terms of its relevance to practice. Within a political and media landscape that increasingly privileges rapid, polarizing, sweeping and polemical constructions of geopolitical realities, particularly in cases of conflict, the deconstruction undertaken by critical geopolitics points to the relativity and inevitably intentional, strategic character of these staged – and often linguistically and visually compelling – representations.

3 Additional perspectives: what does geopolitics do for International Relations?

There is always a certain risk involved in attempts to relate an abstract theoretical discourse directly to current problems of international politics. Nonetheless, in the wake of 9/11, it seems vital to gauge the extent to which it is the perspectives of classical or critical geopolitical thought that are best suited to describing global political structures and conflicts. The key concept of a "clash of civilizations" is constantly invoked in this connection (Samuel P. Huntington). It embodies a geopolitical model that told us, more than a decade after the loss of the secure geopolitical notions of order that went hand-in-hand with the East–West conflict, that world politics is once again wracked by conflicts anchored in specific geographical locations. It is undeniable that geopolitical arguments have been more openly deployed in political debates, particularly in recent discussions of energy policies. But events in the aftermath of the terror attacks of 11 September 2001 might also be read as delegitimizing classical geopolitical ideas within global political practice more profoundly than all the theoretical critiques put forward by critical geopolitics. The increased visibility of a diverse range of military and political coalitions, one rapidly succeeded by the next, as well as processes of ethnic and religious differentiation and the ensuing conflicts, which do not occur between nation states or even world regions but cross-cut individual states across the world, potentially make simple geopolitical models seem useless.

As cautious as we should be about making an overly direct connection between different levels of observation, for theory building in International Relations this can only mean continuing the work already begun by some participants in the theoretical debate, namely scrutinizing how spatial-territorial ordering principles operate and probing the political mechanisms inherent in the construction of key spatial-geopolitical models. But economic globalization, global migration flows, the emergence of new forms of transnational law, and so on, constantly suggest that it is not just the meaning of the territorial state's boundaries and thus the usefulness of the analytical categories ("state-as-actor") that ultimately rest upon it, that are changing. These processes certainly indicate that we must strive to come up with new – critically self-reflective – spatial concepts, but also that the drawing of territorial boundaries, the establishment of order, changes in prevailing orders and the construction of collective identities are inseparably bound up with one another (see Albert *et al.* 2001) and must therefore be subjected to critical deconstruction (see Reuber and Wolkersdorfer 2004). As we begin to grasp how complex these realities are, it becomes self-evident that we cannot do justice to this complexity within a single discipline. We must increasingly seek to establish dialogue between political science and neighbouring disciplines.

Despite this insight into the significance of space to understanding international relations, we can of course pose the critical question, "*How much space* is necessary to the processes of international politics and their analysis?" (von Bredow 2000: 435). After all, one of the most influential approaches within International Relations, neoliberal institutionalism or regime theory, suggests that because of the processes of international organization and institutionalization (regime formation), the structural transformation of international relations is largely geared towards the needs of functional problem-solving and tends to attenuate those conflicts of interest amenable to territorial depiction. In other words, this transformation is mitigating the "anarchy" of the international system (see the chapters by Manuela Spindler and Bernhard Zangl in this volume). And from this perspective, by developing mechanisms of "governance beyond the nation state" (Zürn 1998), international politics does in fact appear to be generating appropriate problem-solving structures in a context of increasing denationalization or globalization. Given that not just global problems but also their resolution are increasingly geared less towards territorial boundaries and more towards functionally specific schemas and requirements, is the category "space" not diminishing in importance – quite regardless of whether we are working with a basically naturalistic or socially constructed conception of space?

If we bring together those approaches in critical political geography outlined in the preceding sections with attempts to break away from the limitations of "methodological nationalism" or the "territorial trap" (Agnew 1994) when describing a global system, then the exact opposite would appear to be the case. Attempts to comprehend the object of International Relations – while explicitly crossing the boundaries of neighbouring disciplines – not as a system of states but as a global system or alternatively as an international or world society, make it particularly important to get to grips with the *relationship* between functional and regional/spatial distinctions as we attempt to establish new theoretical definitions. In no way does this entail a demand for the "primacy of space" when studying global structures and processes. Instead what we need to do is use nuanced accounts of the construction of space and notions of spatial order, particularly those facilitated by political geography, in order to determine the effectiveness of these constructions in comparison to functional principles of order. The approaches in political science and political geography addressed in this chapter might help us highlight the newly emerging *diversity of forms* of regional differentiation and regional orders under the conditions of functional differentiation in world society.

In the past few years, as scholars have drawn on sociological systems theory in particular, a lively debate has taken off over the extent to which, from the perspective of world society theories, we might refer to the primacy of functional and segmentary re-differentiation, whether there is a conflict between these processes and to what extent they should be understood in geographical terms (see, for example, Japp 2007). With a few exceptions (such as Stetter 2008), however, these discussions continue to suffer from a lack of empirical research. A productive response would be to pay more attention to the literature on the "new regionalism" in world politics (such as Hettne and Inotai 1994).

But none of this is just a matter of looking at the new territorial distinctions of world society through the lens of realpolitik or a realist ontology. More profoundly, the "continued relevance of critical geopolitics" (Dalby 2008) has to do with the efficacy of territorial semantics, representations and discourses in society, politics and media. Drawing on Michel Foucault, this geopolitics is centrally concerned to deconstruct the symbolic archaeology of power encoded within these constructions – an archaeology that seems indispensable to the structuring of society, particularly its political sphere.

There are two aspects to the role and benefits of factoring in space and – primarily "critical" – geopolitical thought into theory building, and to the transgression of disciplinary boundaries between political science and political geography which this inevitably entails.

On the one hand, within the theoretical discourse of International Relations in the narrower sense, considering space and incorporating critical geopolitical thought may exercise a corrective effect on those theoretical models that – whether because they build on the world-views of classical geopolitics in realist thought, or because they focus on the functional problem-solving found in neoliberal institutionalism – either suffer from a tendency towards an "obsession with space" or "blindness to space". On the other hand, as this discourse moves away from the observational schemas characteristic of a "Westphalian" world informed by the "territorial state" towards a "post-Westphalian" and "global" world, considering space and incorporating critical geopolitical thought push it not only to pin down the relationship between different principles of differentiation and structuring (such as regional versus functional), but also require the deconstruction of classical territorial semantics on a metalevel.

4 The critique of "critical geopolitics"

Like every concept, critical geopolitics has its inconsistencies and obscurities. Problems exist on a number of levels and range from fundamental ontological issues to specific aspects of methodological implementation in the context of empirical research. In what follows, reflecting the arguments of Müller and Reuber (2008), we shall briefly discuss some of the key points that have emerged from what is by now a broad-based critical examination of the foundations of critical geopolitics.

4.1 The problem with the concept of discourse

Critical geopolitics' emphasis on a discourse-oriented approach conceals a fundamental misunderstanding typically associated with the fashionable word "discourse", namely that different philosophical schools use the concept on virtually opposite theoretical foundations. Discourse theory as used in the context of critical geopolitics builds on Foucault and is an aspect of postmodern deconstructivism (see also the chapter by Thomas Diez in this volume). This contrasts with the concept of discourse geared towards finding agreement and influenced by Jürgen Habermas, whose framing world-view is shaped by modernization theory (see also the chapter by Christoph Humrich in this volume). The Habermasian concept of discourse is incompatible with critical geopolitics; it is in fact opposed to it. If we ignore this fundamental distinction we not only risk semantic obscurities but more far-reaching misunderstandings about the basic epistemological presuppositions of critical geopolitics.

4.2 The problem of conceptual vagueness and heterogeneity

One of the core problems of critical geopolitics that has been discussed in the German-speaking context in particular is its conceptual heterogeneity. This leads to theoretical inconsistencies (see Lossau 2002; Redepenning 2006: 76ff.). Critics' main line of attack here is that the approach combines elements from a number of grand theories and that because these theories' basic assumptions differ, these elements are only partially compatible. This conceptual criticism is especially important with regard to the use of critical geopolitics within International Relations and political geography because it has implications for the issues considered in, and the scope of, empirical studies. In what follows, we therefore take a closer look at this criticism, with a focus on three key aspects.

(a) *The difficulties involved in reconciling different social macrotheories:* the conceptual problems of critical geopolitics result from the combination of action-oriented and post-structuralist theoretical approaches. These difficulties are already inherent in aspects of the programmatic publications that appeared in the mid–1990s, and their roots lie in the two levels of examination at the core of critical geopolitics' research programme: the understanding of actors' geopolitical action, and how this understanding is informed by geographical and/or geopolitical representations. The first level is implicitly underpinned by theoretical approaches that make statements about the action of individual and collective actors. On the second level, the explicit goal is to deconstruct geopolitical representations, notions and models, and the relevant authors here borrow from Foucault's more linguistically oriented poststructuralist approaches. The problems to which this combination gives rise are especially apparent in the different concepts of actor that result.

(b) *The problem of differing concepts of actor under the umbrella of critical geopolitics:* whether in the form of political elites or "intellectuals of statecraft", the concept of the actor is a key element in critical geopolitics. Yet key authors have failed to subject it to more than superficial theoretical reflection. If they work on the assumption of actors who act strategically (as part and parcel of their geopolitical power politics and by deploying geopolitical representations), then some of their publications are undergirded by a concept of actor inspired by the kind of methodological individualism propagated by modern action theories. Others, meanwhile, work with concepts of actors more informed by poststructuralism. We now take a brief look at this distinction.

As in other fields, *theories of action* in critical geopolitics always presuppose the action of individual actors, in other words, social phenomena are explained as the aggregate of individual actions. This is the case, for example, when studies focus on key actors – whether historical or contemporary – from the field of geopolitics and analyze their geopolitical concepts and models. Though such reconstructions implicitly take greater account of an overall constructivist perspective with respect to their concepts of actor, what both have in common is that they fail to question acting subjects as the basic building blocks on the theoretical level.

The tendency to frame actors theoretically in this way is undoubtedly part of the reason for the success of critical geopolitics, since it offers a perspective on conflicts over space and power quite close to a narrative typical of late modern democratic societies, that of the self-determining individual. It is this proximity of critical geopolitics to everyday narratives that enables it to portray specific geopolitical conflicts, as well as conflicts over geopolitical representations and models, within a conceptual framework that the general public can easily understand. At the same time, however, this compatibility with society's self-representation has a crucial disadvantage. In this form of scientific reconstruction, it is assumed *a priori* that actors act according to the principles of "bounded rationality". While this assumption of utilitarianism may often serve as a plausible convention, it is a normative postulate not amenable to epistemological verification.

(c) *Concepts of the actor informed by poststructuralism and discourse theory* seek to avoid this rash assumption, which is why they collide with those models informed by action theory. The differences here derive among other things from Foucault's approach, which features a quite different view of the actor far more geared towards language and discourse. From this perspective, the notion of an *a priori*, classical, pre-given subject disappears, and humanity is "erased, like a face drawn in sand at the edge of the sea" (Foucault [1966] 2002: 422). This ontologically and epistemologically fundamental difference becomes blurred in the concept of critical geopolitics. When Dodds and Sidaway (1994: 515ff.), for example, remark that this field is all about "deconstructing the ways in which political elites have depicted and represented places in their exercise of power", we see clearly that the actor-oriented perspective is the conceptual fundament onto which the deconstruction of geopolitical representations has been "grafted". Similar arguments have been put forward by a number of other authors who regard discourses as linguistic resources that actors can deploy strategically to further their own objectives (see, for example, Browning and Joenniemi 2004: 708). Ackleson (2005; see also Adams 2004) works with a conception of discourse close to speech act theory to show how political elites deploy discourses as "scripts" to frame security problems linguistically and thus position them within public debates. Against this background, it seems justified to worry that a number of studies "give empirical compatibility . . . precedence over conceptual acuity" (Redepenning 2006: 95).

(d) *The limited groups of actors investigated:* in addition to conceptual difficulties with actors, researchers tend to be narrowly focused on certain types of actor. Much of the literature focuses quite strongly on geopolitically relevant actors, structurally located within the framework of administrative and political institutions. In this context, Redepenning (2006: 98) rightly points to the contradiction of "wishing to discuss geopolitics and geo-power as a widespread social phenomenon while *de facto* limiting oneself to the governmental sphere". There are approaches here and there that make more effort to incorporate into their analyses the role of transnational networks of businesses, NGOs, civic actors, media and their geopolitical representations. Often, however, these are to be found not so much under the label of critical geopolitics than in the subfields of post-colonialism or political ecology, which operate with a quite different conceptual framework.

4.3 Nascent developments informed by poststructuralist conceptions

In both the German-speaking context and further afield, a number of the criticisms addressed above have inspired debates on the prospects for both the conceptual and methodological framework of a poststructuralist political geography beyond critical geopolitics. The possibilities that have been aired – in terms of their theoretical perspective and conceptual foundations – can be grouped under communication-oriented sociological system theories (Redepenning 2006) and language-oriented poststructuralist approaches (see, for example, Reuber and Wolkersdorfer 2007; Mattissek 2008; Glasze and Meyer 2008; Müller 2008; Glasze and Mattissek 2009).

5 Notes

1 Günter Wolkersdorfer passed away in 2008. He co-authored this chapter in the first German edition of the book.

2 This historical peculiarity has been widely discussed with reference to a German *Sonderweg* or "special path": "German thought and German feeling finds expression first and foremost in the unanimous rejection of anything that even begins to approximate English thought and feeling or indeed Western European thought and feeling as a whole" (Sombart, quoted in Sprengel 1996: 162). Sombart thus gave an implicitly negative assessment of liberalism, positivism and subjectivism, which he contrasted with the idea of community, wholeness and the organism.

3 The turn to a conceptual framework grounded in the philosophy of language that assumes that the relationship between words and things is laid down by language communities. In brief, language orders and creates reality. See, for example, Rorty (1991).

6 *Bibliography and* recommended reading

6.1 Primary texts

Agnew, John A. (ed.) 1997: *Political Geography: A Reader*. London: Arnold.

Agnew, John A. 1998: *Geopolitics: Re-Visioning World Politics*. New York: Routledge.

Ó Tuathail, Gearóid 1996: *Critical Geopolitics: The Politics of Writing Global Space. Borderlines*, vol. 6. Minneapolis: University of Minnesota Press.

Ó Tuathail, Gearóid, Dalby, Simon and Routledge, Paul (eds) 1998: *The Geopolitics Reader*. New York: Routledge.

6.2 Journals

Geopolitics

Political Geography

6.3 Secondary texts

Agnew, John A. 1994: The Territorial Trap: The Geographical Assumptions of International Relations Theory, *Review of International Political Economy* 1(1): 53–80.

Albert, Mathias, Jacobson, David and Lapid, Yosef (eds) 2001: *Identities, Borders, Orders: Rethinking International Relations Theory*. Minneapolis, MN: University of Minnesota Press.

Dalby, Simon 2008: Imperialism, Domination, Culture: The Continued Relevance of Critical Geopolitics, *Geopolitics* 13(3): 413–436.

Dodds, Klaus J. and Sidaway, James 1994: Locating Critical Geopolitics, *Environment and Planning D: Society and Space* 12(5)): 515–24.

Redepenning, Marc 2006: *Wozu Raum? Systemtheorie, Critical Geopolitics und raumbezogene Semantiken*. Leipzig: Leibniz-Institut für Länderkunde.

Reuber, Paul and Wolkersdorfer, Günter 2007: Politische Geographie, in Gebhardt, Hans, Glaser, Rüdiger, Radtke, Ulrich and Reuber, Paul (eds) *Geographie. Physische Geographie und Humangeographie*. Heidelberg: Elsevier, pp. 751–772.

6.4 Other texts

Ackleson, Jason 2005: Constructing Security on the US-Mexico Border, *Political Geography* 24(2): 165–184.

Adams, Paul C. 2004: The September 11 Attacks as Viewed from Quebec: The Small-Nation Code in Geopolitical Discourse, *Political Geography* 23(6): 765–795.

Albert, Mathias and Reuber, Paul (eds) 2007: Strategic Regionalisations: New Perspectives on Regions in a Global System (special issue of *Geopolitics* 12: 4).

Boesler, Klaus-Achim 1983: *Politische Geographie*. Stuttgart: Teubner.

Brill, Heinz 1994: *Geopolitik heute. Deutschlands Chance?* Berlin: Ullstein.

Brock, Lothar and Albert, Mathias 1995: Entgrenzung der Staatenwelt. Zur Analyse weltgesellschaftlicher Entwicklungstendenzen, *Zeitschrift für Internationale Beziehungen* 2(2): 259–285.

Browning, Christopher S. and Joenniemi, Pertti 2004: Contending Discourses of Marginality: The Case of Kaliningrad, *Geopolitics* 9(3): 699–730.

Brzezinski, Zbigniew 1997: *The Grand Chessboard: American Primacy and Its Geostrategic Imperatives*. New York: Basic Books.

Czempiel, Ernst-Otto 1991: *Weltpolitik im Umbruch*. Munich: C.H. Beck.

Dalby, Simon 2003: Calling 911: Geopolitics, Security and America's New War, *Geopolitics* 8(3): 61–68.

Fiedler, Werner 2000: Vorwort, in Janssen, Manfred and Sibom, Frank (eds) *Perspektiven der europäischen Integration. Sozioökonomische, kulturelle und politische Aspekte*. Opladen: Leske + Budrich.

Foucault, Michel 2002 [1966]: *The Order of Things: An Archaeology of the Human Sciences*. London: Routledge.

Glasze, Georg and Mattissek, Annika 2009: *Handbuch Diskurs und Raum. Theorien und Methoden für die Humangeographie sowie die sozial- und kulturwissenschaftliche Raumforschung*. Bielefeld: transcript.

Glasze, Georg and Meyer, Aika 2008: Das Konzept der "kulturellen Vielfalt" – Protektionismus oder Schutz vor kultureller Homogenisierung?, in Kessler, Johannes and Steiner, Christian (eds) *Facetten der Globalisierung: Zwischen Ökonomie, Politik und Kultur*. Mainzer Kontaktstudium Geographie, vol. 12. Wiesbaden: VS Verlag.

Gray, Colin S. and Sloan, Geoffrey (eds) 1999: *Geopolitics: Geography and Strategy*. London: Frank Cass.

Gregory, Derek 1994: *Geographical Imaginations*. Oxford: Blackwell.

Gregory, Derek 1998: The Geographical Discourse of Modernity, in Gebhardt, Hans and Meusburger, Peter (eds) *Explorations in Critical Human Geography*. Hettner-Lecture, vol. 1. Heidelberg: Selbstverlag des Geographischen Instituts Heidelberg, pp. 45–70.

Haushofer, Karl, Obst, Erich, Lautensach, Herrmann and Maull, Otto (eds) 1928: *Bausteine zur Geopolitik*. Berlin: Vowinckel.

Herz, John 1957: Rise and Demise of the Territorial State, *World Politics* 9(4): 473–493.

Hettne, Björn and Inotai, András (eds) 1994: *The New Regionalism*. Helsinki: World Institute for Development Economics Research of the United Nations University.

Hipler, Bruno 1996: *Hitlers Lehrmeister – Karl Haushofer als Vater der NS-Ideologie*. St. Ottilien: Eos.

Japp, Klaus P. 2007: Regionen und Differenzierung, in Baecker, Dirk, Hutter, Michael, Romano, Gaetano and Stichweh, Rudolf (eds) *Zehn Jahre danach. Niklas Luhmanns "Die Gesellschaft der Gesellschaft". Sonderheft der Zeitschrift Soziale Systeme*. Stuttgart: Lucius & Lucius, pp. 185–195.

Joenniemi, Pertti (ed.) 1997: *Neo-Nationalism or Regionalism? The Restructuring of Political Space around the Baltic Rim*. Stockholm: NordRefo.

Kolb, Albert 1962: Die Geographie und die Kulturerdteile, in Leidelmair, Adolf (ed.) *Hermann von Wissmann-Festschrift*. Tübingen: Geographisches Institut der Universität Tübingen.

Lacoste, Yves 1990: *Geographie und politisches Handeln. Perspektiven einer neuen Geopolitik*. Berlin: Wagenbach.

Lossau, Julia 2000: Anders denken. Postkolonialismus, Geopolitik und Politische Geographie, *Erdkunde* 54(2): 157–167.

Lossau, Julia 2002: *Die Politik der Verortung: Eine postkoloniale Reise zu einer Anderen Geographie der Welt*. Bielefeld: transcript.

Lyotard, Jean-François 1988: *The Differend: Phrases in Dispute*. Minneapolis, MN: University of Minnesota Press.

Mackinder, Halford J. 1904: The Geographical Pivot of History, *Geographical Journal* 23: 421–444.

Mattissek, Annika 2008: *Die neoliberale Stadt. Diskursive Repräsentationen im Stadtmarketing deutscher Großstädte*. Bielefeld: transcript.

Müller, Martin 2008: Situating Identities: Enacting and Studying Europe at a Russian Elite University, *Millennium: Journal of International Studies* 37(1): 3–25.

Müller, Martin and Reuber, Paul 2008: Empirical Verve, Conceptual Doubts: Looking from the Outside in at Critical Geopolitics, *Geopolitics* 13(3): 437–457.

Newman, David (ed.) 1999: *Boundaries, Territory and Postmodernity*. London: Frank Cass.

Ó Tuathail, Gearóid and Dalby Simon 1996: Editorial Introduction: The Critical Geopolitics Constellation: Problematizing Fusions of Geographical Knowledge and Power, *Political Geography* 15(6–7): 451–456.

Ó Tuathail, Gearóid and Dalby, Simon 1998: Introduction, in Ó Tuathail, Gearóid and Dalby, Simon (eds) *Re-Thinking Geopolitics: Towards a Critical Geopolitics*. London: Routledge, pp. 1–15.

Ratzel, Friedrich 1901: *Der Lebensraum. Eine biogeographische Studie*. Tübingen: Laupp Verlag.

Ratzel, Friedrich 1906: *Kleine Schriften*. Vol. 2. Munich: Oldenbourg.

Reuber, Paul and Wolkersdorfer, Günter 2004: Auf der Suche nach der Weltordnung? Geopolitische Leitbilder und ihre Rolle in den Krisen und Konflikten des neuen Jahrtausends, *Petermanns Geographische Mitteilungen* 148(2): 12–19.

Rorty, Richard 1991: *Objectivity, Relativism and Truth*. Cambridge: Cambridge University Press.

Ruggie, John Gerard 1993: Territoriality and Beyond. Problematizing Modernity in International Relations, *International Organization* 47(1): 139–174.

Said, Edward 1978: *Orientalism*. New York: Routledge and Kegan Paul.

Schultz, Hans-Dieter 1998: Herder und Ratzel: Zwei Extreme, ein Paradigma?, *Erdkunde* 52: 212–233.

Sprengel, Rainer 1996: *Kritik der Geopolitik. Ein deutscher Diskurs 1914–1944*. Berlin: Akademie-Verlag.

Stetter, Stephan 2008: *World Society and the Middle East: Reconstructions in Regional Politics*. Houndmills: Palgrave.

von Bredow, Wilfried 2000: Internationale Politik und Raumordnung, in Diekmann, Irene, Krüger, Peter and Schoeps, Julius H. (eds) *Geopolitik. Grenzgänge im Zeitgeist*. Vol. 1.2, *1945 bis zur Gegenwart*. Baden-Baden: Nomos, pp. 433–452.

Walker, R. B. J. 1993: *Inside/Outside: International Relations as Political Theory*. Cambridge: Cambridge University Press.

Werlen, Benno 1995: *Sozialgeographie alltäglicher Regionalisierungen*. Vol. 1: *Zur Ontologie von Gesellschaft und Raum. Erdkundliches Wissen*, Heft 116. Stuttgart: Steiner.

Wolkersdorfer, Günter 2001: Politische Geographie und Geopolitik: Zwei Seiten derselben Medaille?, in Reuber, Paul and Wolkersdorfer, Günter (eds) *Politische Geographie. Handlungsorientierte Ansätze und Critical Geopolitics*. Heidelberger Geographische Arbeiten, vol. 112. Heidelberg: Selbstverlag des Geographischen Instituts Heidelberg, pp. 33–56.

Zürn, Michael 1998: *Regieren jenseits des Nationalstaates*. Frankfurt a. M.: Suhrkamp

Index

Locators shown in *italics* refer to tables.

PASSIONATE PAINT

PASSIONATE PAINT
THE ART OF LYS HANSEN

Edited by **Giles Sutherland**

MAINSTREAM PUBLISHING

EDINBURGH AND LONDON

First published in 1998 by
MAINSTREAM PUBLISHING COMPANY (EDINBURGH) LTD
7 Albany Street
Edinburgh EH1 3UG

ISBN 1 84018 096 X (hardback)
ISBN 1 84018 095 1 (paperback)

A catalogue record for this book is available from the British Library

Designed by Janene Reid
Photographs of Lys Hansen's artwork by Colin Ruscoe
Photograph of Lys Hansen on p.2 by George Sutherland
Typeset in 10 on 17pt Gill Sans Light
Printed in Hong Kong by H&Y

CONTENTS

ACKNOWLEDGEMENTS

I am grateful to the following for help in the preparation of this volume: Veronica Cordeira, Lys Hansen, Susan Hopkin, Anne McKelvie, Steve Robb, Mhairi Scott, Lisa Sibbald, Aris Thayne and John Wilson. George Sutherland gave valuable advice and assistance with reading the texts at an early stage. Also of assistance were Jacqui Sergeant and Karen Greenan of Edinburgh College of Art, Valerie Fiddes of the Talbot Rice Gallery, Edinburgh, and Glasgow Print Studio. A special note of gratitude must go to Judy Diamond at Mainstream Publishing for advice and valued assistance.

Additionally, I should like to thank the writers who have given so willingly of their time and effort and without whose contributions this book would not have been possible. I also acknowledge with gratitude Colin Ruscoe, whose patience and professionalism have resulted in excellent photographic reproductions of the works.

Finally, special thanks must go to all collectors and owners of Lys Hansen's work for their help towards the compilation of the *catalogue raisonné*, for allowing the works to be borrowed for the purposes of photography and for giving their permission to reproduce them.

Giles Sutherland

This book is dedicated to the memory of my grandparents,
Alfred William Hansen and Agnes Hansen

EDITOR'S PREFACE

Lys Hansen is undoubtedly an artist of some importance, a fact confirmed by the collection of work and views presented in this publication. As editor, my approach has been to garner views which reflect on the diverse aspects of Lys Hansen's career as an artist which has spanned over forty years to date. The result is, I believe, a fascinating and revealing insight into the work of an extremely prolific painter, sculptor, printmaker and maker of *assemblages* – the *catalogue raisonné* lists almost six hundred entries, from 1956 to the present. The titles of the essays in this book are, for the most part, self-explanatory, and the subject-matter reflects the specialisms and interests of the writers concerned. I have deliberately solicited contributions from as wide a cross-section of people as possible; here are the views of an arts impresario, a collector, a gallery curator, an art historian, poets, lecturers, journalists and critics. The result is a collection of voices which ranges from the academic to the lyrical. This diversity celebrates and complements the diversity of the work and the life of the artist. It allows for differences of opinion, insight and approach which a monograph, however well intentioned, cannot. Where there are overlaps, of either fact or opinion, I hope they act as useful cross-references; many of them also represent important points in Lys Hansen's career. Several writers mention, for example, *Performance* (1983) (Pl.52) which is undoubtedly a seminal work, as is *The Divided Self* which reflects the transition from the personal to the political with a sketch in gouache (Pl.57) and a later version in oil (Pl.46)

As well as these voices, the artist's own voice is to be heard in a detailed interview which touches on many aspects of her career: her family background, her response to the Dunblane tragedy and on her most recent work based on experiences of her grandfather's birth-place, the Danish island of Bornholm in the Baltic Sea.

Over the years, a substantial body of criticism has built up around Lys Hansen's work – in journals, newspapers, catalogues and on television and radio. A selection of this has been reproduced as an appendix to the main body of text.

Giles Sutherland,
Edinburgh, 3 May 1998

WARPAINT AND WOMANFLESH

LIZ LOCHHEAD

because the flesh can be
tortured
because the flesh can be
raped
because the flesh can be
mutilated
because the flesh can be
burned
because the flesh can be
scorned
because the flesh can be
corseted within the skin
because the rage can be
held in
the flesh must be painted.

because the skin can be
displayed
because the skin can be
flayed
because the skin can be caked with make-up
be bruised gorgeously gored gilded
pierced grafted grazed greased
split slit skelped scuffed stretched scratched scored stroked
tanned tattooed tabooed
because the skin
can be the tip of the iceberg
because
the skin
can be the bag with all the boiling blood and bones within
the skin must be painted.

because the lip can be
any of your and all of your
old lip
because the lip is tender
because the lip can slip
because the lip can kiss and tell
because the lip can frame the mouth that is the mouth of hell
because the lip can be
lipsticked slicked smeared larded lauded glossed bossed breached
because the lip can be zipped
the lip must be painted

because of the white of the eye
because of the white lie
because of the truth of the colour of fire
because of the iris of desire
because
the limb can be akimbo
the limb can be dismembered
because the love can be remembered
because the lady can be sawn in half
because the lady can bellylaugh
because the lady's got guts
because the lady's not for turning
because of the good times
because of the war crimes
because of the iron maiden
because of the presidential wink
because of everything except the kitchen sink
Lys Hansen must always be painting.

FOREWORD

PROFESSOR RICHARD DEMARCO OBE

Lys Hansen is an artist I have known over the last three decades. I regard this as a privilege, because in that time she has developed a recognisable and authentic personality as a painter giving little regard to passing fashion in Scotland. Lys Hansen's subject-matter is the mystery of the human body as expressed in female sensuality, and it could be said that she has invested her own experience as a painter and as a woman in creating a new kind of landscape or perhaps *inscape*. She knows instinctively that the human body is mainly an expression of the larger world of landscape and that the human presence in nature is not something separate.

She has protected herself from the weaknesses inherent in all too many aspects of feminist art. She has done so by striking a celebratory note and developing an objective viewpoint on the power and mystery of the female form, often *in extremis*.

She handles paint in the Scottish tradition so that her paintings, large or small, can give delight in their often glorious and basically expressionistic, confident and risk-taking brushwork. When you add her delight in colour in the tradition of the Scottish Colourists, you often have in her work the proof that she is indisputably an artist of the Scottish tradition. That is a term lacking in accuracy, however, because when all is said and done she belongs to an international tradition which can be defined as north European and is linked to her Scandinavian origins. Often, therefore, one can link her work to Munch and the German Expressionists.

Like these northern European modernists, she is dealing with the mystery of the human psyche in travail and, in addition to this, the problems of being a woman as the expression of the very life-giving force of Mother Earth. Lys Hansen is very often painting the earth mother in herself, but more than that she is expressing a deep longing for that which the earth itself cannot satisfy, that which belongs to the spiritual realm. It can be said that her art aspires to the condition of prayer, that her sensuous and sinuous female figures are in a state of transmogrification capable of assuming the form of angels or even devils. Robert Burns would have recognised his 'cutty sark' in many of her more outrageous images.

Lys Hansen has the attitude of the long-distance runner; although her output of work is prodigious she has paced herself well and the work has developed in a slow, natural and inevitable organic process, changing with the years into what can be termed nowadays as a quieter mood – more reflective, more compassionate. She and Germaine Greer would have much to talk about with regard to the contribution that womankind must make in a world that is becoming overly concerned with scientific data, and the idea that art is a form of entertainment to be linked automatically with leisure and sport. You do not look at Lys Hansen's paintings in moments defined as leisure time, but in those moments when you are asking serious questions of your own bodily presence in the challenging, inevitably terrifying and unremitting daily experience of life. Every now and again she paints an iconic image which will call to mind the Medieval and Renaissance images of the sorrowful Magdalene and the Virgin Mother. Lys Hansen's achievement is that she has attended to the business of painting, come what may, and now belongs to that small band of Scottish artists of her generation who willingly inhabit not only the world of Scottish contemporary art but also the art world at large, while remaining quintessentially European.

LYS HANSEN AND THE MACLAURIN ART GALLERY

MIKE BAILEY

When we write the history of any gallery, it is a truism that key figures will emerge in the narrative, figures who had a significant influence on the development of the gallery, through their unique contributions to the exhibition programme or their representation within a permanent collection. Typically, we only recognise the significance of these contributors in retrospect.

The Maclaurin Art Gallery[1] is no exception to this dictum. Opened in 1976, it was recognised as a major exhibition venue which offered an innovative and challenging programme throughout the 1980s and into the present decade. In those golden years, the gallery – often in association with other venues in south-west Scotland – presented major exhibitions by Alan Davie, Bridget Riley, Henry Moore, Patrick Heron, John Bellany, June Redfern and many others. It is no surprise to find Lys Hansen within this company.

Since 1988, Lys Hansen has been a frequent exhibitor at the Maclaurin Art Gallery and her recent work is represented in the permanent collection by the diptych *Look and Listen* (Pl.7) (and an associated pencil study, Pl.2) developed during her second Berlin residency. This essay explores a fruitful collaboration between the artist and curatorial staff.

After study in Edinburgh, leading to a diploma in art and a degree in drama, Hansen pursued postgraduate studies (completed in 1963) embracing fine art, drawing and painting. Awards took her to France, Holland and Germany, and to the British School in Rome; experiences that would contribute to the quality and content of her work over the next thirty-five years. Settling with her husband, initially in London and later in central Scotland, she devoted her time to

2. ***Look and Listen*****, 1993**
cat 470

bringing up their young family. By the early-1980s, she was active again, winning a series of awards which culminated in a Scottish Arts Council Major Award in 1984, a studio in Berlin the following year and a prize in the Smith Biennial, also in 1985. Solo exhibitions at the Third Eye Centre, Glasgow, and in Dublin and in Belfast, showed an artist of substance who might represent her generation with contemporaries such as John Bellany and Bruce McLean.

By 1985 the Maclaurin Trust had formulated exhibition and collecting policies which embraced a wide range of contemporary art from all parts of the British Isles. They forged links with galleries in the west of Scotland, in Northern Ireland and England. Curatorial staff visited Manchester, London, Newcastle or Bath more often than Edinburgh or Glasgow. At the same time, an increasing interest in contemporary work from Germany, Poland and Italy broadened the programme, and allowed visitors to set the work of Scottish artists in an international dimension. It is fascinating to recall these eventful years, and to record how a particular artist left her very personal, but important and enduring, mark on the gallery.

For the Maclaurin Gallery staff, the first encounter with Hansen's work came in 1984. Seen in a variety of locations, including the London and Bath Art Fairs, and the Edinburgh Festival Demarcation exhibition,[2] the work made an immediate impact. An exhibition preview in Glasgow facilitated the first meeting with Hansen, and the beginning of an enduring friendship. Essentially feminine, the work was intriguing, self-assured and confident. In an era dominated by Young Turks, it was refreshing to discover this less bombastic work by a mature artist from an older generation.

As the Maclaurin Gallery took its first steps towards the formation of a permanent collection, we noted Hansen, in the gallery records, as an artist to be pursued, both as a potential exhibitor and for inclusion in the permanent collection – objectives that we did not achieve until eight years later.

The late-1980s was a time of great ferment in society and the arts. The realisation that the abrasive new Britain could not engage with the social and political values of most Scots displaced the euphoria of the Falklands War. Parallels can be found with the smouldering political situation of Clydeside in 1919 which artist Ken Currie referred to, for example, when he wrote: 'The possibility now exists, as John Maclean said way back in 1919 "to make Glasgow a revolutionary centre second to none".'[3] An increasing social awareness, in part a reaction to the cultural decadence of the Thatcher years, was driving Scottish artists forward, as they renewed and reinforced links with European partners.

In the 1980s, Glasgow School of Art nourished a group of young painters (dubbed the 'Glasgow Pups'[4]) who embraced a raw social realism, informed by the *Neue Sachlichkeit*[5] movement of Weimar Germany. Predominately male, this group included painters who had experience of working in the failing heavy industries of Clydeside. Meanwhile, in England, many art schools were in disarray, emaciated by the constant shifts in educational policy which had resulted, for example, in a reduction of the teaching of the basic skills still valued in the Scottish schools.

3. *Courting Pleasures*, 1987
cat 289

This artistic movement from Scotland filled a cultural vacuum in Britain, appealing to the *nouveau riche* of the flourishing South-East. New money was invested in Scottish painters who were taken up by enthusiastic London dealers. This enthusiasm for Scottish art encouraged a renaissance for some of the older generation and, as worn canvases were recovered from grubby storerooms, fortunes were made overnight.

In that time, with a thriving art market driven by affluence and fashion, it was too easy to fall into the popular mode and promote the fashionable artists. Exhibitions such as 'The Vigorous Imagination' in Edinburgh set the new agenda, highlighting some of 'the most interesting artists to have emerged in the 1980s [demonstrating] the view that Scotland had a coherent new movement in the visual arts'.[6] By way of a counter-blast, another show, entitled 'Continuing the Tradition', emphasised the continuity of style and purpose that might be found through four generations of Edinburgh painters: 'essentially a claim by the 369 Gallery and those who exhibit there, to a

TOP
4. *Act I Scene I (Duet)*, 1987 *cat 295*

BELOW
5. *Act I Scene II (Duet)*, 1988 *cat 296*

place in an evolution of painting that owes much to a strong sense of community, place and common heritage'.[7] Although Hansen had contributed to the programme at the 369 Gallery,[8] she was not included in this review.

The battle lines had been drawn and, as gallery-owners flocked to the cause, many mid-career artists felt excluded. Hansen's reaction to this trend, which favoured irreverent youth, was characteristic. With limited exhibition opportunities at home, forays outwith Scotland offered greater expectation. Dublin and Belfast had provided solo exhibition opportunities. Now, in London, space was found at the Camden Arts Centre.[9] This show attracted favourable interest from the London critics, notably Waldemar Januszczak of *The Guardian*, who noted 'the presence of an important artist in terms which are indisputable'.[10]

I was fortunate to see the content of that London show at the planning stage, in company with the enthusiastic curator, Zuleika Dobson. The position of the work in the mainstream of European art could not be doubted. The candid, expressionist images, in a predominantly cool and acid palette, paid homage to the works of Käthe Kollwitz, while drawing on some of the imagery of Italian religious painting. In so many works, the constraint of contorted figures within the bounds of the canvas, demonstrated an acute awareness of the female dilemma: this was no matriarchal society – despite an increasing consciousness of female artists and their numerical dominance within the student body of Scottish art colleges.[11]

The 1985 residency in Berlin had a profound effect on Hansen. Awareness of the

6. *How Wisdom and Folly meet, mix and unite; how Virtue and Vice blend their black and their white* (three panels), 1987
cat 294

wall which divided the city allowed her to consider the desolation of the eastern sector and draw contrasts with the affluent west. The barrenness of that killing-ground, a violation of landscape, both physical and social, recurring throughout the world in those areas where ideologies were in conflict, became a source of sorrow and inspiration. Her depiction of the human misery attached to this political and social exploitation, and her interest in the poetry and drama of survival in such slavish circumstances, reinforced her concerns for the position of women and children in contemporary society. Seeing women as the losers, her response was to paint canvases that made a direct attack upon the senses – and while an interpretational note might explain time and place, the works did not require explanation. The bold statements demanded an immediate and unconditional emotional response. Clare Henry, in her review of the 1988 Edinburgh exhibition, refers to 'female form into spiritual contortions; Picasso-esque figures with life blood to give'.[12]

The content and rationale of these works were close to the particular interests of the Maclaurin staff. Travel to various parts of Europe, and awareness of impending political change on the continent, favoured inclusion of Hansen's work in the gallery programme. When the idea of presenting an exhibition ('For a' That') inspired by the poetry and ideas of Robert Burns was developed, it was envisaged that Hansen would obviously be a key contributor.

This intriguing show featured thirteen artists[13] – all but two with a Scottish background – who were commissioned to prepare works which explored the romanticism or the socialist ideals enshrined in Burns's writing. Contributions from the seven male artists were mostly political in outlook, often humorous, drawing on links with contemporary society. John Houston, for example, included a work depicting the Royal Scottish Academy as a jelly mould[14] – an oblique attack on the English influence that is rife in Edinburgh institutions. In contrast to these 'manly' interests, the women, for the most part, explored the romanticism and hedonism in Burns's works. Hansen's painting, the largest canvas in the exhibition, found a middle road and was the most profound contribution in the show.

Hansen selected some lines from a poem entitled 'Sketch. Inscribed to The Rt. Hon. Ch. J. Fox Esq. –' which formed the title of a triptych *How Wisdom and Folly meet, mix and unite; How Virtue and Vice blend their black and their white* (Pl.6).[15]

'These lines,' Hansen wrote, 'state clearly the duality in human nature which Burns was well aware of. His work always acknowledges the human condition, its dilemmas and conflicts. The work is allegorical; with the heads, limbs and bodies of Virtue and Vice blended and entwined, with the head of the poet seen at the breast of Virtue, his eye closed in contemplation and understanding.' This exhibition, shown at the Maclaurin Art Gallery and Rozelle House, Ayr, in November 1989 toured to five venues in central and eastern Scotland in the following months.

It is fascinating to record that this painting returned to Ayr in an exhibition of Hansen's work linked to the bicentenary of Burns's death in 1997.[16] One feature of that show was further work inspired by Hansen's Berlin experiences, renewed in the years between 1988 and 1995, with other works inspired by writing on romantic themes.

In the autumn of 1988 Hansen had developed sufficient work from her Berlin residency, some three years earlier, to mount a major exhibition in the City Art Centre, Edinburgh.[17] When the canvases were on the gallery walls, the show's curators suggested that this could be a touring exhibition and invited the Maclaurin Art Gallery to participate in the touring arrangements. Although the tour was not realised, the Maclaurin retained their interest in the work and, in January 1990, some twenty works selected from the material remaining in the artist's studio were presented in rooms at the Maclaurin Art Gallery.

For the gallery, this was a fitting exhibition to launch an eventful year, which included shows by Henry Moore, a major installation by Jason Bowman and a show by three artists working from Berlin: Margaret Hunter, Carla Fioravanti and Inge Husemann.[18] These exhibitions, including Hansen's show, were part of the gallery's contribution to the visual arts programme of Glasgow City of Culture 1990 with linked exhibitions at Pollok Park (Henry Moore) and the Goethe Institute in Glasgow. (Interestingly, Inge Husemann was to become a close friend of Lys Hansen, introducing her to further contacts in Berlin and the former Eastern Länder of that country.)

The preliminary notes describing the 1990 Hansen exhibition refer to 'feminist, expressionist and very direct figurative works'. This was later expanded:

> Following a major Scottish Arts Council award in 1985, Lys Hansen was able to take up painting full time. She spent several months working in a studio in Berlin, becoming aware that her experience of the city was overlaid by memories of films or written accounts of the horrors of war and division. Working on a large scale, she brought her long-standing concern with individual relationships into a framework of ideas which increasingly embraced universal themes, an awareness of political and social realities activated by visits to Dublin and Belfast.
>
> Today, as our social and political identity moves closer to Europe, and as the political and physical structures in a divided Germany are tested and breached, it is appropriate to show work that had its beginnings in Berlin. This show, which follows our previous links with Europe, will be our first show in the 1990s to highlight the European mainland influences in Contemporary Art . . .

Writing of her exhibition, Lys Hansen states, 'The timing was right for me. My children had grown up, I needed to paint and my re-evaluation for myself of the human body coincided with the figurative explosion . . . I wanted my paintings to look people in the eye and say "I know what I'm doing and why I'm doing it" . . . I wanted to be unshakeable.'[19]

Looking back on that show one recalls the drama and vigour of the works masking a feminine sensitivity. Yet, below the drama, there is a more passive quality – a sense of waiting for the expected and the unexpected. By the time these works were presented in Ayr the Berlin wall was breached and the eastern borders were open. Perhaps the figures in *Berlin Trilogy* (Pl.24) are free to speak at last.

Hansen returned to Berlin in 1992, in a privately arranged exchange with another German artist, Karin Christiansen. Working from an atelier overlooking the wall, close to the former Checkpoint Charlie, Hansen produced a series of works that illuminated the history of human misery, and hope, that came from those years of separation. Gleaning her ideas from careful observation of the still-derelict sites, and by considering the many stories of heroism and failure, brutality and indifference that the conflicting political systems spawned, Hansen produced a body of work that was compelling and harrowing. It was a moving interpretation of John F. Kennedy's words '*Ich bin ein Berliner!*'.

Hansen developed an exhibition – 'In Place of the Wall'[20] – from this residency, in collaboration with Stirling artist Peter Russell, who was in Berlin during the same period. While Russell's work illuminated the severed networks and arteries of the city, Hansen presented her characteristic figurative works, weighted by a narrative of those years of isolation and deprivation. They showed these works at the Maclaurin Art Gallery, as part of a national tour, in April 1993.

'In Place of the Wall' was opened by Douglas Gifford, who drew fascinating parallels between the political and cultural conditions in Scotland and Berlin. His speech proffered alluring images of Scots gaining a greater freedom, as the audience recalled the heady days when the wall was breached and the Berlin Philharmonic Orchestra played Beethoven's Ninth Symphony in celebration of the climactic event. Later, Hansen lectured on her work and her experiences in Berlin. In a moving talk, she provided compelling insights into her response to the remnants of those border marches within a modern city.

This lecture encouraged contemplation of Hansen's contribution to art education in Scotland. Her understanding of human misery and her distinctive approach to composition, enhancing an idea through dramatic gesture and the hyperbole of the classical actor, has distinguished her as a teacher. Her capacity quietly to lead students to the contemplation of their subjects from unusual viewpoints, her conduct of life-drawing classes and her positive criticism of their efforts, has informed the work of many students over recent years, notably in the department of ceramics at Glasgow School of Art, where she worked as a visiting lecturer in the late-1980s. The fruits of this guidance were clearly visible in an exhibition of student work, presented at the Maclaurin in the summer of 1987.[21]

One work in the 1993 exhibition, *Look and Listen* (Pl.7), was destined to remain in Ayr as part of the Maclaurin's permanent collection. During her time in Berlin, Hansen had visited the site of the wartime Gestapo Headquarters, now established as a museum. Drawing on her memories of this place of misery and oppression, she distilled the detail into an illuminating diptych, contrasting the remnants of the deserted cells with a lingering crowd on the outside. This work echoes, in a

7. *Look and Listen* (diptych), 1993
LEFT PANEL
Look and Listen
RIGHT PANEL
Look and Listen
cat 466

sense, the earlier work *Berlin Trilogy*, in the passivity of the watching mass, struck dumb by the horror of man's capacity for inhumanity towards his fellows.

For this writer, the painting recaptured the pervading ambience of Germany in the second half of the twentieth century. (A personal visit to East Berlin in 1971 had included views of the wall from the east.) By 1989 there was a sense of waiting, of expectancy; and, in the border areas, on barred road and tracks leading to the east, people were looking eastwards into forest and heathlands, awaiting the arrival of fugitives and refugees. When they finally breached the wall, the euphoria was tangible and the intuition of a beginning for the new millennium was overwhelming. For me, the painting encapsulated forty years of history and suffering.

Hansen was to return to Berlin in 1996, in company with other Scottish artists, to present an exhibition of new work.[22] Taking the theme of a suitcase, the artists' journeys and their work, perhaps unintentionally, emulated the experience of those displaced persons fifty years earlier, who had flocked to the safer havens in Germany. In 1997 Hansen included some of these later Berlin works in an exhibition presented at Rozelle House in Ayr.[23]

Looking back on Hansen's work over the past fifteen years, her contribution to Scottish art and the development of the Maclaurin Art Gallery is clearly substantial. There is consistency throughout the development of her style, showing a sense of history, both social and artistic. At the core of her work are humility and humanity, echoing the work of many Great Masters. In choosing subjects from the recent history of Berlin, Hansen is working in the tradition of Callot, Goya and Dix, whose images of war profoundly affect the viewer. While writers have drawn parallels with the imagery in Picasso, we should not overlook the influence of Beckmann, notably his triptych *Departure* (1932–33) and *Fish Ride* (1934).[24] Hansen, like these Great Masters, tells it as it is.

Today, as Hansen prepares for a major exhibition on the Danish island of Bornholm, she is returning to a spiritual home. The new works, some inspired by more recent human calamities, show her continuing concern for humanity and, in particular, the children who will be our future. I look forward to seeing these works in Lys Hansen's next exhibition at the Maclaurin Art Gallery planned for the autumn of the year 2000.

LYS HANSEN'S WORK FROM A DANISH PERSPECTIVE

METTE BLIGAARD

In the summer of 1996 Lys Hansen made her first visit to Bornholm, the Baltic island where her paternal ancestors lived and from where her grandfather, as a fourteen-year-old boy, ran away to sea. Eventually, Ludwig Andreas Hansen ended up in Grangemouth, settled down and raised a family of Scots, and apart from his name nothing gave away his Danish origin, nor was it ever stressed.

Bornholm is a rocky island in the middle of the Baltic Sea. Its scenery is different from any other Danish landscape. Inland moors and woodland are strewn with granite rock formations furrowed by glacial striae. Nestled in along the coast, the small fishing villages with their red-tiled roofs contrast with the blue of the sea. The characteristic angular chimneys of the herring smoke-houses are the only vertical elements here. Higher up in the hinterland, the unusual round Medieval churches, particular to Bornholm, built for the defence of the island as well as for worship, stand isolated in the fields. From the cliffs of the northernmost promontory where the impressive ruins of the fortress Hammershus towers, you can see the Swedish coast on a clear day. The Danish mainland is a six-hour boat trip away.

Apart from its natural beauty, it is also primarily the light that has attracted generations of Danish artists to this island. In 1911 a group of young painters newly returned from Paris arrived at Bornholm. Absorbed in matters of colour theory brought about by their recent encounter with the work of Cézanne and Cubism, they were drawn by the extraordinary luminous atmosphere of the island and, of course, by the rocky scenery – unique in Denmark. They gathered on the small island of Christiansø off the east coast of Bornholm, where the cubic architecture of the military fort and the geometric forms of the granite rocks provided them with abundant motifs in spite of the diminutive size of the island. Here, at the eastern extremity of Denmark with the line of the horizon as the only constant point of focus, there seemed to be a closer connection to the cosmos. Human beings are conspicuously absent from their paintings.

Now, a rocky island should not overly excite a Scottish artist, nor should the works of a group of painters dedicated to landscape necessarily arouse the interest of an artist whose entire work is centred on depicting human beings. Lys Hansen's visit to Bornholm was spurred by curiosity. She felt the urge to explore her ancestors' past as well as that of the islanders in general. She was 'invading her past', as she put it. In seeking her roots she was at the same time looking for inspiration.

The outcome of this Scottish artist's visit

8. Carl-Henning Pedersen: *Man and Woman*, 1944, oil on canvas, 100.5 x 81cm. Statens Museum for Kunst, Copenhagen

turned out to be a series of works spiritually related to another group of artists who also found their way to Bornholm, some of whom were to form the COBRA group just after the Second World War. Along with the Danes Richard Mortensen (1910–93), Ejler Bille (b.1910), Asger Jorn (1914–73), Carl-Henning Pedersen (b.1913) and others, came the Dutch painters Eugène Brands and Anton Rooskens and the Belgian, Constant. In spite of the fact that the COBRA movement was an international phenomenon, nationality was strongly stressed, not least by Asger Jorn, the leading figure of the Danish COBRA artists. According to Jorn:

> Being his own centre, no artist is provincial. If he lives in Denmark then foreign art is provincial to him, but I am convinced that the task of the artist is to find general human truths, to transcend local jargon in order to find a human common language.[1]

During visits to Bornholm in the late 1930s and during the war – when foreign travel was prohibited and Bornholm was a substitute for the south of France – these artists found inspiration not so much in the scenery as such but in the abundance of things left behind by the island's former inhabitants. They were preoccupied with the old Nordic myths and imagery which they encountered in the rock carvings, on runic stones and in the frescoes of the Medieval churches. This primitive, 'tribal' art – testimony to the eternal need of man for artistic expression – constituted their main source of inspiration. Provocatively, and with great spontaneity, they created fabulous beings

ABOVE
9. *Catch*, 1984
cat 183

RIGHT
10. *Masticator*, 1984
cat 173

in sparkling colours and in images applied to the canvas with a conspicuous sense of textural effect. The sculptor Sonja Ferlov Mancoba (1911–84) collected tree roots and twigs, subsequently turning them into anthropomorphic or zoomorphic sculptures during her stay at Bornholm in 1935. The idea of the *objet trouvé* developed by the Surrealists was to be pursued by Lys Hansen half a century later. These artists seldom resorted to pure abstraction, but they transformed the human image into amoeba-like shapes and the human face into masks mirroring all kinds of emotional states of mind, for, as Carl-Henning Pedersen proclaimed in 1948:

> The truth we are seeking must be connected with man – it cannot be something outside man. It must be a chain in the development of culture which is made up of the combined achievements of individuals.[2]

The human condition is the subject-matter of Lys Hansen's work. The isolation of man, human emotions, existential anguish and tormented human beings are her motifs. 'My work is about taking an issue and opening it up. Art is about truth,' she explains, paraphrasing Carl-Henning Pedersen's dictum. Her imagery, however, is completely different from his and that of his contemporaries. Hansen's human beings are not like the limbless personae of the COBRA painters. On the contrary, they are all faces and limbs. Whether her point of departure is a historical person or event or a contemporary issue, her powerful comment is expressed through human bodies. Conflicts are ultimately a question of human relations, of passion and pain, suppression and isolation, and Hansen treats her subjects so that they become universal statements.

The titles of her works say it all: *Lust, Greed, Desire, Hunger (The Four Demons Within)*, *Catch*, *Grip*, *Reject*, *Pain and Sorrow*, *Woman and Man*, *Two in One*, *Love Bites*, *Greater Spotted Lover*, *Allein (Alone)*, *The Sadness of Men without Women*, *Say Nothing, Hear Everything, See All* and so on. She depicts the fugitive with distorted limbs trying to escape, the lovers devouring each other as love bites turn into mastication, the aggressor assaulting and pawing his prey, the recumbent female figure trying in vain to pose nicely to comply with convention, the passive spectator frantically shielding his eyes to avoid seeing, and yet seeing it all. Eyes are reduced to slits or to the black holes of a skull or they are blindfolded, as in *The Pity* (Pl.12). Screams are suppressed because the mouth is stuffed with limbs, feet or hands, as in *Ich Habe Hunger II* and *III* (Pl.13 and Pl.15), or speech is made impossible because the mouth is simply missing. Tongues are stuck out sensually with lust or greedily with hunger, as in *Four Demons Within* (Pl.47). For Hansen's beings, gesticulation is the main means of expression. Hands are spread out to act as wings by the person falling into the abyss, or they are used as aids for the balancing act of the tightrope walker. Hands are also instrumental in the passionate encounter of man and woman. Lovers struggle, fingers clutching fingers and fingers clutching toes. In the gouache *She Has Found His Hands for Him* (Pl.17) from 1985, a man with enormous hands is caressing a woman, or is he holding her back? A recurrent motif in

11. ***Pain and Sorrow*, 1984**
cat 182

Hansen's work is the hands used as a shield to protect the face. These images are akin to Käthe Kollwitz's figures who cover their faces to avoid seeing the unbearable atrocities of war, and to Edvard Munch's screaming creature in a desolate landscape – an icon of expressionistic art – whose hands are protecting its ears in order not to hear its own cry.

Expressionism is a convenient label to stick on Hansen's art. Her mature work came into being simultaneously with the revival of figurative expressionism on the continent and in Britain, but she was of course also familiar with Munch and Nolde from having visited Norway and Germany as early as 1959. During the 1980s she made several trips to Germany, becoming well acquainted with the German neo-expressionists; their works share certain similarities with her own: the large formats, the shrill colours and the obsession with the human body. But while *Die neue Wilde* created images of coarse, mocking or clowning figures, they also maintained an

ABOVE
12. *The Pity* (diptych), 1993
cat 465

OPPOSITE
13. *Ich Habe Hunger III*, 1992
cat 456

ironic distance from their subjects.

In Denmark as in Germany – and Scotland – figurative painting was revived at the beginning of the 1980s. Inspired by the Italian *Transavantgarde* and the new primitive German painting, the Danish painters adopted either an extremely realistic formula or a coarse, untamed expressionism. At first this art was considered a reaction against the previous decades' conceptual and minimal art; later it was seen rather as a continuation of conceptual art – although the concept had changed. Though from the outset Hansen's art was fundamentally expressive, she was not familiar with this aspect of Danish art, which was created by a generation of artists born in the late 1950s, when she was attending Edinburgh College of Art. In her student days artistic inspiration was sought almost exclusively in France and Italy. When she resumed painting in the late-1970s, however, she was caught by the *Zeitgeist*, and she directed her attention mainly towards northern Europe, particularly Germany.

Hansen's work has a conspicuous affinity with that of another Danish artist, Svend Wiig Hansen (1922–97), a giant in twentieth-century Danish art, who is sometimes

regarded as a forerunner of the young *wild* Expressionists of the 1980s. Like his Scottish namesake, Wiig Hansen's art deals with the great existential questions, and his pictorial universe is dominated by the human figure. On large canvases, in sculpture and in various graphic techniques, he depicts mutilated and tormented figures concerned with the basic human instinct of survival, not unlike Lys Hansen in her Belfast[3] and Berlin[4] trilogies. Wiig Hansen's frightened human beings are abandoned in grey, bare landscapes as if they were left on a desolate planet. In the gigantic *The Earth Weeps*, executed in 1981 in front of an audience at the Munch Museum in Oslo, the whirling masses of bodies seem to have been deprived of their protective skin and the network of nerves laid bare.

In contrast, Lys Hansen's figures are generally set out against a nondescript background, enclosed in a narrow space close to the surface of the picture as if they are going to burst out of the canvas. In her post-Bornholm works she is still pursuing the same subject-matter as before, and her pictorial universe has not changed. The experience of the island scenery did not make her turn to landscape, although the line

LEFT
14. ***Fingering II*****, 1989**
cat 328

RIGHT
15. ***Ich Habe Hunger II*****, 1992**
cat 455

FAR RIGHT
16. ***Self-portrait: Finger, Features, Foot*****, 1987**
cat 266

of the horizon is now occasionally introduced. Like Jorn, she is preoccupied with the 'continuity of motifs', the chain of people passing, those who have gone and those who are to come. She aims to bridge past and present. The imagery of the past appears as an accessory in her canvases inspired by the visit to Bornholm: the round churches, the prehistoric megaliths, the runic inscriptions, Viking ornamentation and the sun wheel or wheel of life so often to be found also in Jorn's work.

In a series of nine gouaches from 1996, quite exceptionally without figurative subject-matter, she has created variations on the shape of the cross of Saint Andrew and the circle. In one of the nine images she pays homage to her grandfather. It is the vision of his shroud stretched out to form a simple open shape. In her rendering of the earthy, mouldy linen she has obtained a striking textural effect. *We Are Each Other* is the title of a large painting from 1997, whose main feature is three upright shapes inspired by the megaliths in the Bornholm countryside. Another is *Bodypiece/Landpiece* (Pl.22), an equally large canvas in predominantly deep-red colours symbolising the red of the earth

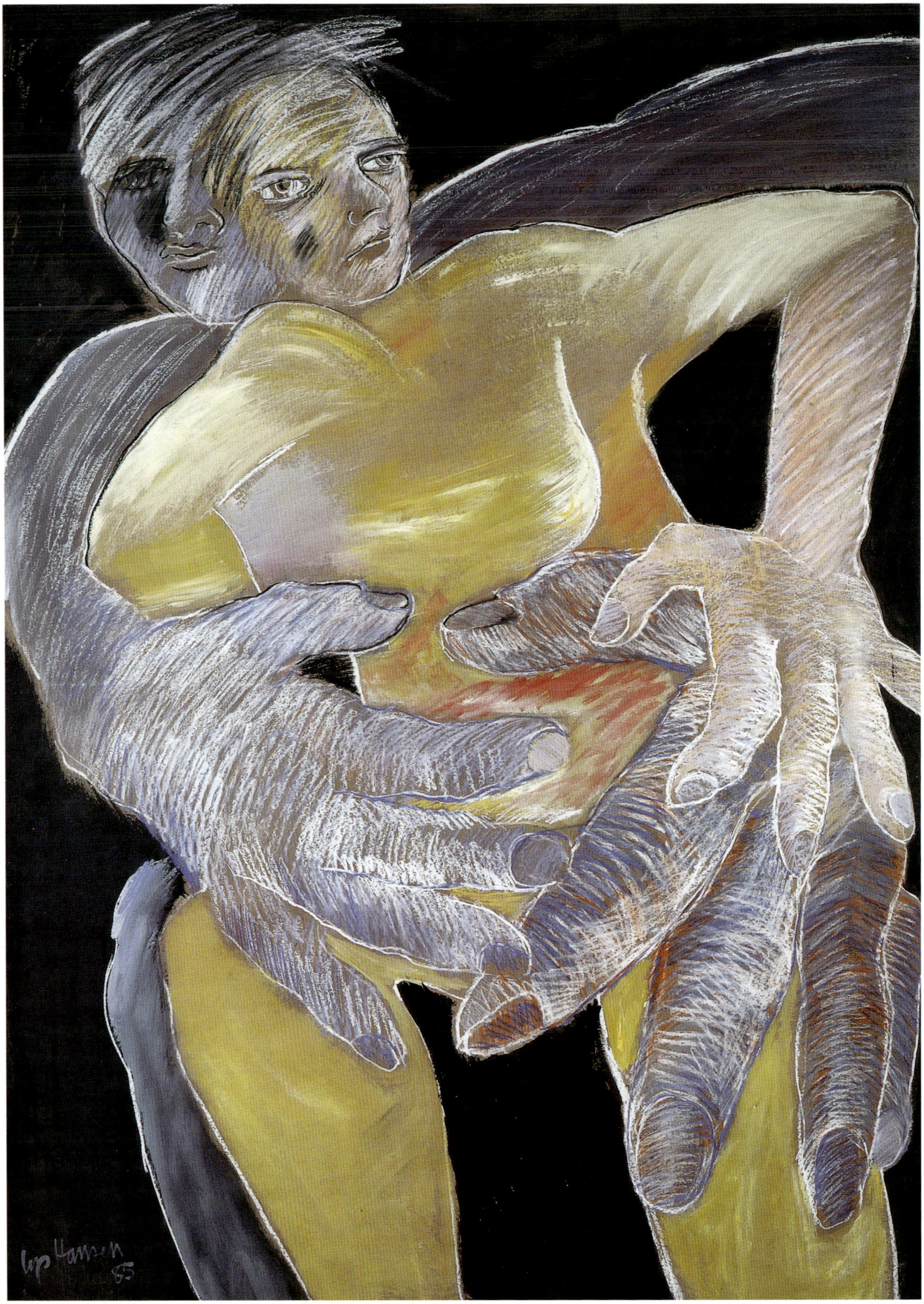

and red as energy and the force of life. The earth and man are one. The body of a (female?) figure is discerned, its life-giving parts laid bare. The pelvis and the spine are delicately outlined. Small, frail, blue hands are holding the spinal column, trying to protect the vulnerable parts and 'keeping its life force coming through the spine'. It is the image of growth, of the female principle. She is filled with energy yet vulnerable at the same time.

Wiig Hansen treated the same subject in an early sculpture. His *Mother Earth* (Pl.21) from 1953 is a seated female figure – both hands on her chest and her womb impudently exposed – shockingly violating the classical canon although the face is a distant descendant of archaic Greek sculpture. It is a man's vigorous, and at the same time almost tender, vision of woman as the incarnation of creation. Originally, the sculpture was painted in a bright red colour.

The Sacrifice (Pl.23) is another result of Lys Hansen's Danish visit. To rest from pure colour work she created a powerful image in a subdued palette quite unique in her *oeuvre*. Against a background of predominantly ochre and earthen colours an imposing figure is delineated in dark contours. This image is inspired by the Bronze Age bog bodies found in peat bogs in various parts of Denmark. Like the Bog Queen in Seamus Heaney's poem,[5] she has risen from the dark. The abundant mane of hair is cut off from the head and transformed into flames. The head is shaved bare, its leather cap turned into a helmet, 'the chin is a visor'. She/he epitomises the link between past and present, at the same time a bog person and one of our contemporaries, a warrior and a punk.

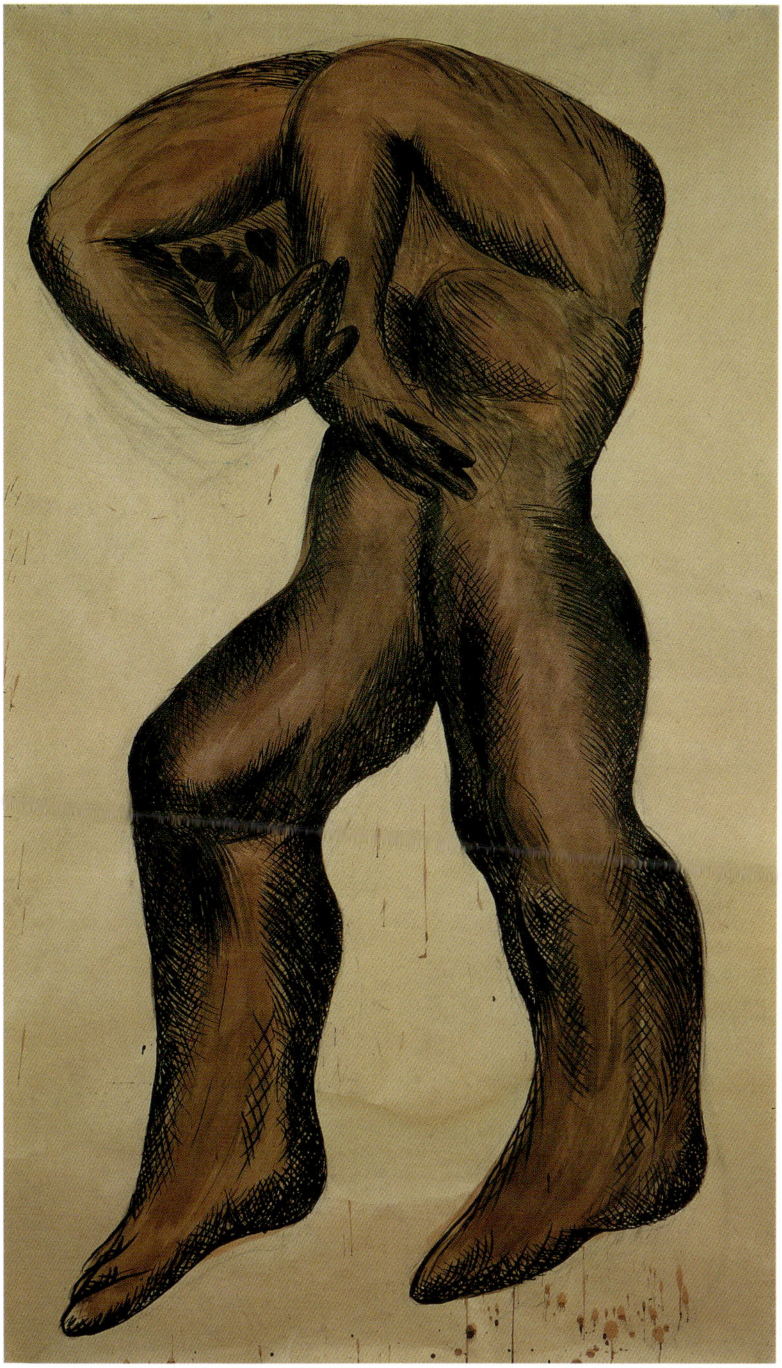

ABOVE
18. Svend Wiig Hansen: *Man, the Human Animal*, 1991, sepia, Indian ink on paper, 240 x 160cm. Private Collection

OPPOSITE
17. *Love Suite II: She Has Found His Hands for Him*, 1985
cat 201

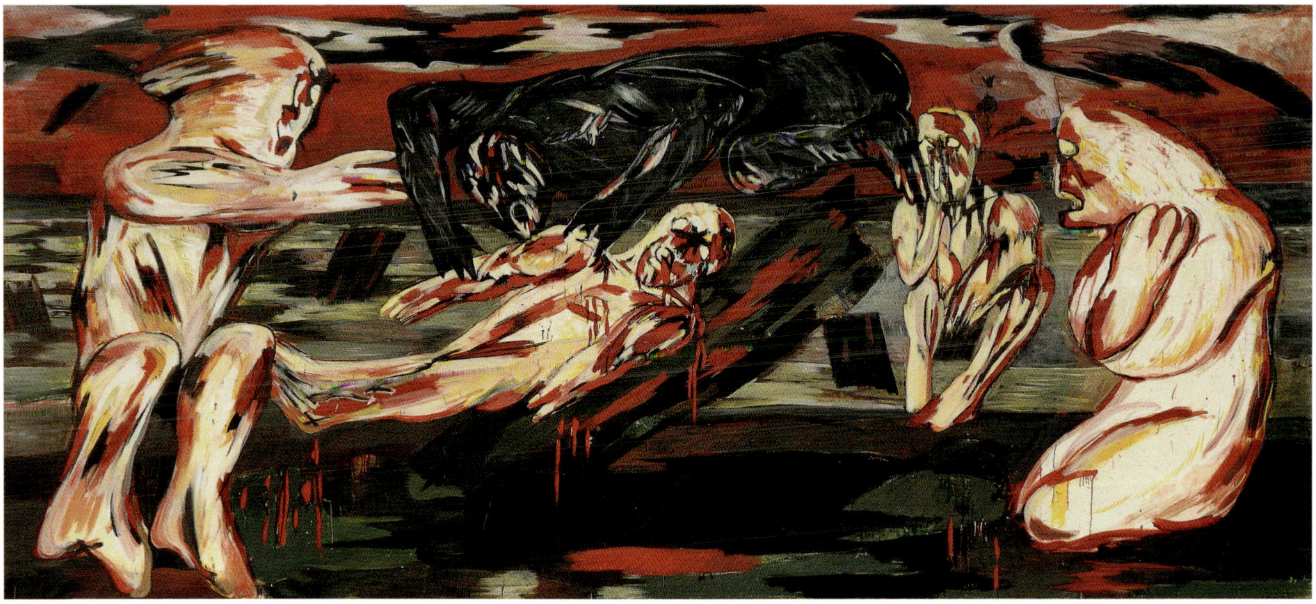

ABOVE
19. Svend Wiig Hansen: *The Victim of Fear*, 1974–86, oil on canvas, 201 x 438cm. Aarhus Art Museum

RIGHT
20. Svend Wiig Hansen: *Couple*, 1974–78, oil on canvas, 210 x 145cm. Private Collection

21. Svend Wiig Hansen: *Mother Earth*, 1953, concrete, originally painted red. 130cm high. Herning Kunstmuseum, Denmark

There is nothing timid in Hansen's pictorial universe. Uncompromisingly, she continues creating powerful images in the idiom she has developed simultaneously with the neo-expressionistic painters of the 1980s and '90s. But for Lys Hansen it is not a question of a conscious choice of style. As Hayden Murphy pointed out in 1985: 'Lys Hansen's part in "neo-expressionism", in my visual experience of art, is not so much "neo" as fundamentally expressive.'[6]

The natural outlet for her creative energy is – considering her intellect and her temperament – through a spontaneous expressionism of a 'Northern' kind, which to a continental beholder seems quite unique in Scottish art.

22. *Bodypiece/Landpiece*, 1998
cat 583

23. *The Sacrifice*, 1998
cat 584

24. *Berlin Trilogy* (triptych), 1985
LEFT PANEL
Say Nothing
CENTRE PANEL
Hear Everything
RIGHT PANEL
See All
cat 198

25. *Death in a Red Dress*, 1992
cat 458

HANSEN AND BERLIN

RICHARD CARR

Berlin, the divided city; Lys Hansen, the divided self: a woman with an allegiance to a man, a mother with an allegiance to two sons, an artist with an allegiance to her own creativity and self-expression – demands that are difficult and perhaps impossible to reconcile. Were she a male artist, there would be no problem. But, being female, society pressures her to conform to the conventional and domestic roles expected of her. And, as a female artist, there are no role models for her to follow: even as a student at Edinburgh College of Art, Lys Hansen had no access to Joan Eardley or Anne Redpath. And, after college and at a time when she was considering a full-time commitment to her art, she realised that the artistic emphasis in Scotland was upon portraiture, landscape and still-life. Revealing feelings in an expressionistic way was not encouraged.

During the years 1985 and 1986, Lys Hansen went to Berlin twice – visits made possible by a grant from the Scottish Arts Council which released her from nine months of teaching. These visits, first for two months and then for one month, were to a divided city where she felt cut off and isolated, unknown without either language or identity. Her reasons for wishing to travel and work there were complex and deep-rooted. Lys was always fascinated by Berlin. She had grown up during the war when the city was both a symbolic and an actual threat, and became for her an embodiment of early childhood fears and worries. Then, in 1983, Richard Demarco organised a conference that revealed both the number and variety of museums and galleries in the USA, Australia and Germany.[1] This had provoked a strong interest in Lys in the way that art was given a much higher priority in other countries, particularly Germany, than it was in Scotland. In Germany, she was able to deepen her experience of artists like Paula Modersohn-Becker and Käthe Kollwitz – with whom she had felt a deep artistic affinity for many years – making a special trip to Bremen to visit the Modersohn-Becker house and State Collection. She observed that, reflecting the importance of these artists in Germany, their work was to be found in most major galleries and museums throughout the country. Although geographically and linguistically isolated, she felt paradoxically at home in a culture which took art seriously and valued artists and the contribution they had to make to society.

So, during these two visits, the pattern of her life was broken and, being in retreat in Berlin, she had a chance to consider the place of a woman artist in society while visiting museums and entering the Eastern Sector.

That too was the crossing of a divide, whether via Checkpoint Charlie or on the Underground.

East Berlin: the frightening face of a divided city. Going through the wall at Checkpoint Charlie meant returning by the same route as you left, past an area where, even in the middle of the day, there were no people, no cars, no shops, no life. And, once in East Berlin, a visit to *The Threepenny Opera* reminded Lys of the tough, sinister underbelly of the city, while the fact that visitors were given a single sheet of toilet paper on entering museums said a lot about its poverty. As a result, there was an immediate change in her painting. *Licking and Biting* (Pl.41), a collage in acrylic shown at the Third Eye in Glasgow in 1984, had plenty of ferocity and animation, but in Berlin the artist developed and explored her use of oils, discovering a greater sense of depth and form. The result was *The Berlin Trilogy: See All, Hear Everything, Say Nothing* (Pl.24). Here, fingers fill a mouth or close one eye and the face is enclosed by arms and hands. The mouth is stopped up by fingers in expressionistic close-ups where reds, yellows and blues are swept on to the canvas in thick, broad strokes. As Bill Hare has written:

> Hansen's large-scale paintings, with their expressive use of anatomical distortion, vivid non-naturalistic colour, claustrophobic composition and overwhelming immediacy, work on many levels . . . Hansen's women dare to have a life of their own, even if they seem to be involved in heightened

26. ***The Fall I*, 1985**
cat 199

moments of frantic moral and psychological crisis.[2]

In Berlin, Lys Hansen's paintings showed both fear and the desire to look. The visits marked a crossroad in her life: no longer could she avoid the dilemma caused by domestic responsibilities on the one hand and artistic need on the other.

The first visit to Berlin had given her an opportunity to consider both her upbringing, during which she had been taught to submerge her feelings, and her subsequent life when, as a wife and mother, she had been the only female in an otherwise all-male household. It had made her realise that she could not resist the urge to paint and that she could express on canvas feelings she couldn't put into words. The result was an upsurge in violent imagery, long before related manifestations by artists like Peter Howson, for example, were seen. The force of the imagery was recognised when she talked about her work at a conference on women's art organised by Timothy Neat at Duncan of Jordanstone College of Art. Her exhibition in the Third Eye Centre in Glasgow in 1984 was the direct result of this exposure.

At the same time, Lys returned to drawing, often in black and white, frequently depicting figures bereft of many of their limbs. She comments that many people fail to function fully, neglecting parts of their body or their intellect. Following her second visit to Berlin, she returned to large canvases where the whole body appeared again, often with emphasis upon the hands and feet. Paintings from this period were shown in the City Art Centre in Edinburgh in 1988.

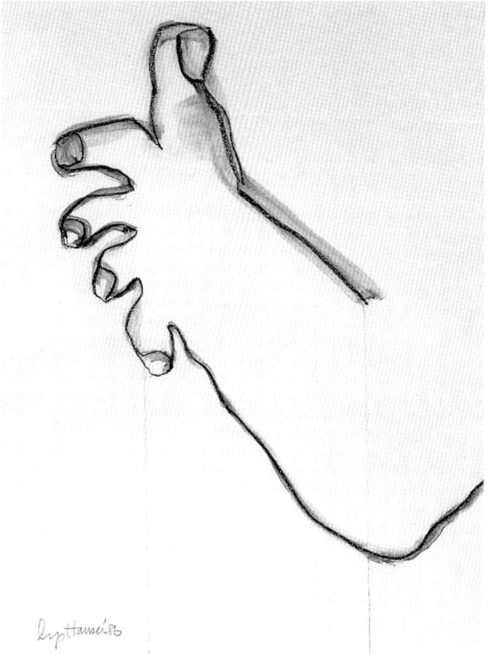

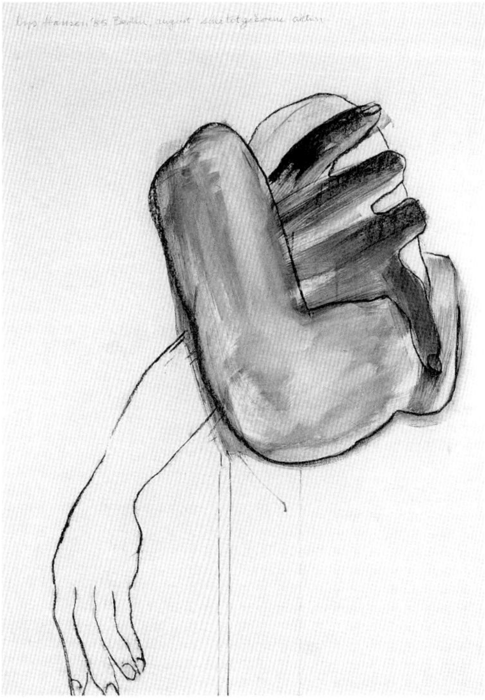

TOP
27. *Foot (Your Foot)*, 1986
cat 269

BELOW
28. *Still-born Action*, 1985
cat 205

ABOVE
29. ***Help Me!*****, 1992**
cat 440

OPPOSITE
30. ***Moment of Truth*****, 1993**
cat 468

In 1992 she returned to Berlin – this time to a liberated city following the destruction of the wall in 1989 and the reunification of Germany. In Berlin, a joint project had been arranged with Peter Russell and Lys Hansen by Karin Christiansen who, along with a small group of artists, ran the Produzenten Galerie Broschwitz in Berlin. Hansen and Russell were invited to work at this gallery and to exhibit their work.[3] Lys lived at the Kunstlerhaus[4] in Christiansen's atelier at Checkpoint Charlie while, in a spirit of reciprocal exchange, Christiansen came to Scotland and lived and worked at Lys's home and studio. Despite the immense changes that had taken place in the intervening years, Checkpoint Charlie and the area along the line of the wall remained a wasteland – a place of ghosts where people had planned and carried out so much killing.

The violence that she sensed was expressed in *Death in a Red Dress* (Pl.25), where a female figure is shown, her head at a severe angle to her body, blood pouring from her mouth, uttering a scream that cannot be heard as opposed to one that can. The scream represents all the people whose torture or death – in soundproofed rooms in the grim ministerial buildings along the line of the Berlin wall or in the underground bunkers close by – left their torturers and executioners unmoved: a reminder of man's inhumanity to man and particularly of man's inhumanity to women.

The red pigment that pours from the mouth down to the valley between the woman's breasts looks like dried blood – like using one's own blood, the artist says, and watering it down to paint with it. And the rubbing down of the pigment on the heavy

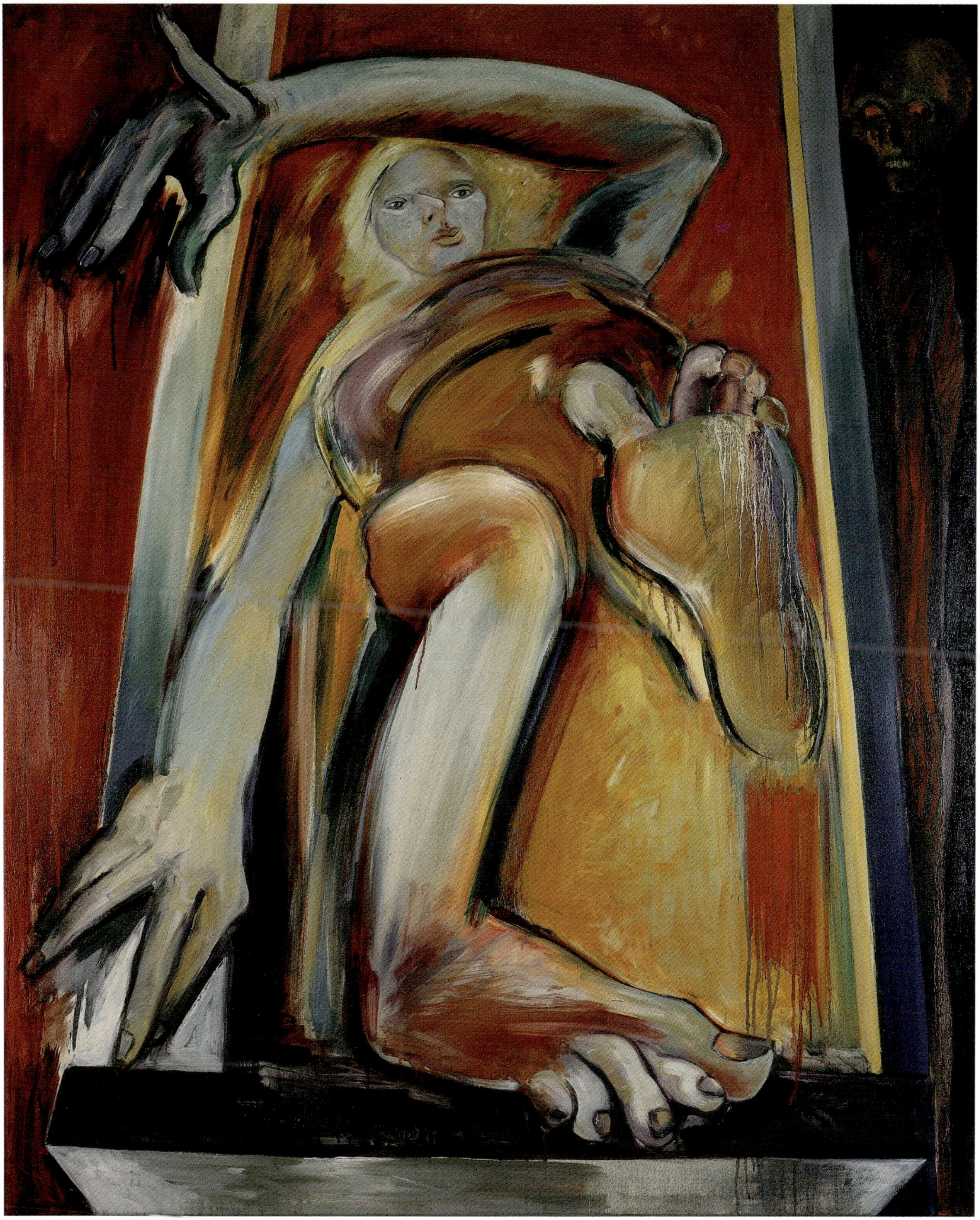

paper is a reference to the Berlin wall, itself stained with the dried blood of the people who died trying to escape over it. *Death in a Red Dress*, inspired by a female drug addict the artist saw in Berlin, is about wasted life in a wasteland of wasted life – a closed, doomed figure like the Knight in Bergman's *The Seventh Seal*.

Another painting, *Moment of Truth* (Pl.30), shows a female nude who appears to be struggling to free herself from a box-like structure, her hands and feet distorted as they try to feel their way out. To one side is a thin skeletal figure – that of Death, who awaits us all. But *Moment of Truth* also draws upon vivid and tangible recollections of Lys's mother's wasting body as she died of cancer. The artist has commented:

> My mother's body is imprinted on my flesh from handling and bathing her as she slowly died over a period of months. What is important (for me) is not the seeing with my eyes but the sense and memory of it from the inside of my flesh, nerves, heart, senses. I don't have to look to draw – I just draw.[5]

Connected to this is the idea that out of death comes new life, expressed politically in the museum about the people who escaped (as well as those who didn't) from East Berlin which opened at Checkpoint Charlie in 1987. As she wrote about her visit to Berlin in 1992:

> Only a short distance away from where I lived was the *Topographie des Terrors.* Here was once the most dreaded address in all Berlin: Prinz Albrechtstrasse 8. It was the head-quarters of the Gestapo and the SS. From this address was planned 'the persecution of all political enemies and all unwanted social groups, ranging from homosexuals to religious minorities, the exploitation and enslavement of millions of people who, next to the Jews, were likewise considered racially inferior, predominantly the Russian and Polish populations'. Heavily bombed by the Allied Forces, the terrain has now been flattened. Grasses, bushes and wild flowers grow there now and, since 1987, a small museum has been built above which includes the interrogation cells. There is now a memorial to all who died under the Gestapo régime. The visitors are few, the faces are pale and voices are hushed as one examines the photographs and documentations of the terrible events that took place here and elsewhere.[6]

But, of course, *Moment of Truth* may also represent Lys Hansen herself, the moment of liberation from restriction and confinement, of escape from a lifetime of compromise to a new period when she can return to being a full-time artist.

She visited Berlin again in the summer of 1996, a visit arranged as part of an exchange between members of the Berufsverbandes Bildender Künstler Berlins (BBK) and members of the Society of Scottish Artists while she was its president, when members of the BBK showed in the SSA's hundredth annual exhibition which was held in the Royal Scottish Academy in Edinburgh in 1995. Then, bonds between the Berlin artists (among whom were non-Germans) and members of the SSA (among whom were non-Scots, including former president Reinhard Behrens, who had encouraged Lys to go to Berlin in the first place) were forged during the foreign artists' stay in Edinburgh. So, when she returned to Berlin a year later, she was both accompanied by other members of the SSA and welcomed by artists living in the city.

This time Berlin had changed yet again: the city that had caused so much havoc during the twentieth century was being rebuilt, its centre described as the biggest building-site in Europe, if not the world. Also notable was the lack of any frontier between the former Eastern and Western Sectors. For the artist, the recently reunified Berlin represented the reunification of her own personality, a process of great significance, because she saw German confidence being expressed in its intellectual and artistic life, as well as its economic and technological prowess. Nevertheless, despite the towering cranes and half-completed buildings, and the Red Box demonstrating Germany's belief in Berlin's future, there were still ghosts behind the new façades. The exhibition held jointly between members of the BBK and SSA was shown in both Scotland and Berlin, in the former entitled 'What is a Suitcase?' and in the latter 'Shopping and More'.

In her part of the exhibition, she showed three pieces of work. The first consisted of a disjointed diptych and an object (a suitcase) and was called *Ich habe einen Koffer in Berlin* ('I have a suitcase in Berlin') (Pl.31 and Pl. 32). The left-hand panel was titled *Leiben Lust* ('Lust for Life') and the right-hand panel *Dead Men Tell No Tales*, the odd juxtaposition of the two canvases symbolising the fact that the two Germanies have still not managed to merge.

The left-hand panel expresses the new Berlin with new constructions and an opened suitcase looking into the old, concealed secrets. The right-hand panel shows a huge skull head and descending, bound figures representing the problem of trying to bury the past. A burlesque catman sits on another suitcase – a reminder of when Berlin was the artistic centre of Europe during the Weimar Republic. Below the diptych sits an actual suitcase as a 'travelling companion' to the piece. It contains an old blanket and gas-mask, found in the flea-market; on the outside are drawings of people, mainly heads of refugees, both male and female. The rich symbolism inherent in the suitcase allows one to ascribe various meanings to the work, but foremost is surely the idea of domicile, albeit transient, and a place where one can feel at least partly at home.

Above the suitcase was another piece entitled *'Tis Never Too Late to Tell Her You Love Her*: when the work was shown in Berlin, the gallery wall was painted sky-blue in the shape of a smock Lys's seafaring grandfather had worn. Fourteen small three-dimensional rectangular panels containing bric-à-brac found in Berlin were placed on this blue-painted shape, including a compact disc with the title *The Essential Monroe* (meaning: is this what that icon has been reduced to?), a pierrot's head encased in rose petals suspended in a net bag, a tin heart and an ear-shaped growth taken from the scum that had formed on some stale liquid. Below the smock-shaped patch of blue was a narrow canvas scroll which had been unrolled and placed on a shelf and on it the words, 'It's never too late to tell her . . . It's never too late to tell her . . .' repeated as a plea of longing. The work referred obliquely to Lys's paternal grandmother who had attempted suicide on a number of occasions. The third piece of work was called *Everyone Has a Cross to Bear*, a suite of nine drawings inspired by the amalgam of feelings, memories and experiences which had accompanied the artist on her continental journeys.

It was as if, after all the anguish and rebellion experienced during her previous visits to Berlin, Lys was back in the city as someone returning home, happy at last to be a beachcomber making use of whatever she happened to find there. And, again, there was both an external, objective connection and an internal, subjective connection. Lys Hansen describes herself as not wholly Scottish, certainly European, a traveller across the seas like her Danish grandfather. While staying in Berlin, she had visited the Danish island of Bornholm to seek out her Danish ancestry. There, she not only found connections with many other Hansens, but the Bornholms Kunstmuseum offered her an exhibition as a daughter of the island. And, again, through this cathartic process, she perhaps made yet another reconciliation, this time with the memory of her father.

RIGHT
31. ***Suitcase*, 1996**
cat 531

OPPOSITE
32. ***Ich Habe einen Koffer in Berlin (I Have a Suitcase in Berlin)* (diptych), 1996**
LEFT PANEL
Lieben Lust
RIGHT PANEL
Dead Men Tell No Tales
cat 530

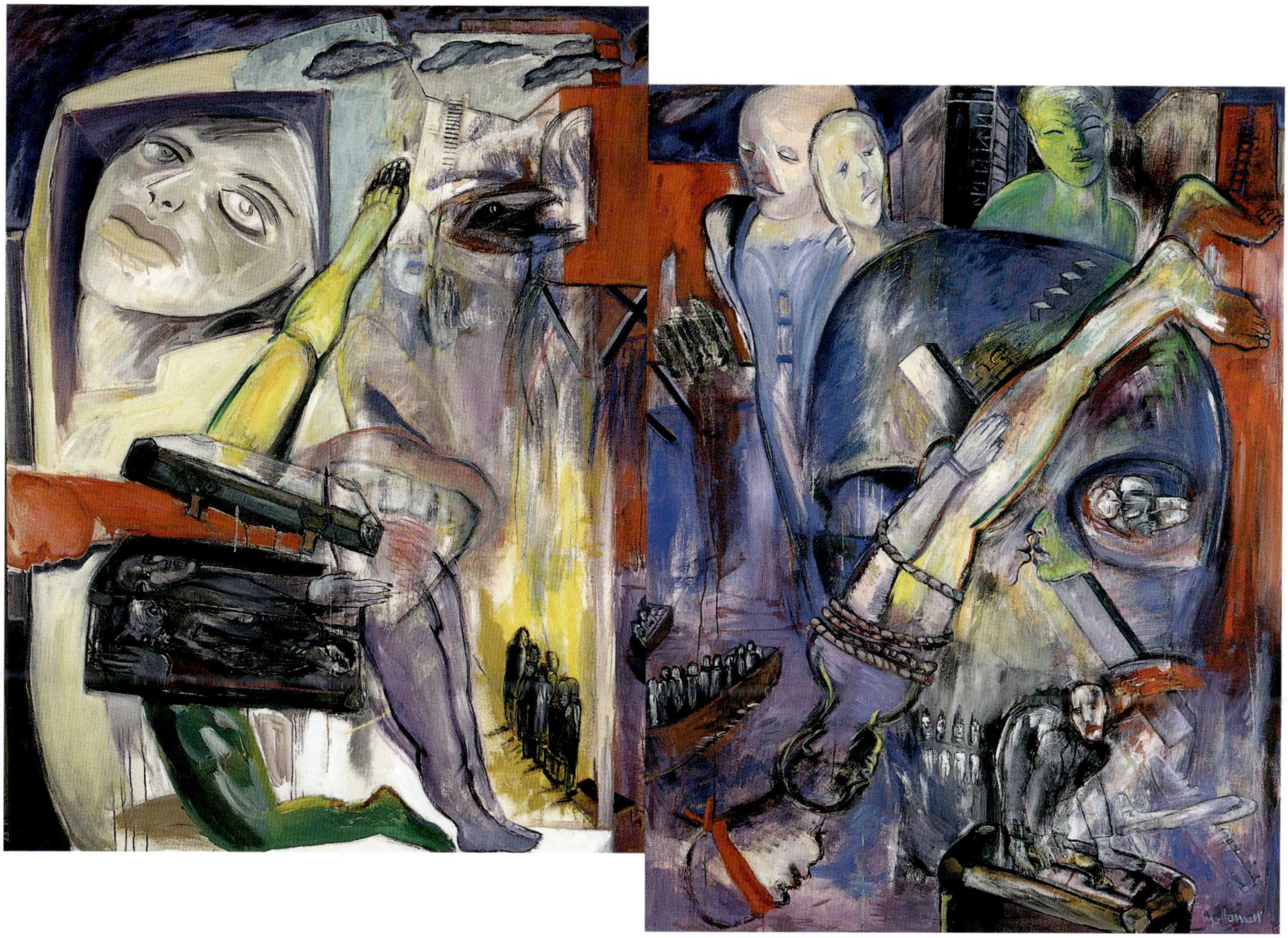

33. *Surrender, Never*, 1980
cat 109

LYS HANSEN: RECENT WORK

IAIN GALE

To stand before a painting by Lys Hansen is to come face to face with your deepest, darkest fears. Look longer and the feeling grows in intensity as the picture begins to suck you in. You may start to panic. You may want to avert your eyes, as if from the edge of some vertiginous drop. But if you stay; if you look; if you can bear to confront everything the artist has to tell you, then, when at last you do turn away, it will be to a world which seems somehow more precious. A world that you now instinctively want to preserve. A world in which every human form holds the unexpected promise of new hope and where the actual and psychological horrors which inspire Hansen's imagery need not be allowed to continue. For these are works of great compassion. Pleas from the heart which through their very savagery and despair are uniquely able to reach into our souls and change the way we feel.

It is hard to know where they come from, the monsters which populate these extraordinary paintings. You might as well ask Mary Shelley how she conjured the idea of Frankenstein. They are, in a sense, allegorical. But their true genesis lies deep in the artist's mind. For they are also, surely, cathartic, a means by which she is able to release her own personal demons. In terms of their artistic evolution, they are easier to explain. It is as if the powerful expressionist tradition present in Scottish landscape for the last half-century – in particular in the work of MacTaggart, Robin Philipson and John Houston – has taken another quarter-century to mature in figure painting.

For Hansen her present paintings are a natural development over the last twenty years. Hansen's early work was made in an assured, draughtsmanlike manner, which some might argue is more aesthetically pleasing than the style which she has today made her own. But to do so is to miss the point. These are not easy images. No one ever said that art was going to be easy. Art exists to tell us about ourselves – to ask and to answer the big questions. And this Hansen does with some effect, opening our eyes and our hearts to the world and all its great, glorious, ghastly and mysterious truths.

Nevertheless, even today, in her pastel drawings, she reveals a fine draughtsmanship – an ability to convey mood in a single continuous line of black crayon. And this, apart from deriving from a natural talent, also reveals something of her training at Edinburgh College of Art under such masters as William Gillies.

It was partly in reaction to this education, however, that Hansen began to make her first truly independent works, far removed from such pleasant lyricism and even from the colourful expressionism of the Edinburgh School.

These early paintings have something of the dynamism of Russian avant-garde semi-abstraction of the 1920s. The theme, as ever, is the human figure, seen here in great, statuesque maidens, composed of tubes – pseudo-cubist machine-age goddesses which offer a clue to her later development. From them Hansen moved on to organically mutated female bodies, in the most extreme of which the inner self explodes through the outer, the breasts being pushed aside, the pudenda the source of creation. Some of these images are distorted – almost as if the flesh has been pressed hard against a piece of glass between figure and viewer.

They are also beautifully and luxuriously sensual – addressing an implicitly feminist agenda without any of the concomitant severity we might usually expect. Particularly effective in this context is a 1980 painting of a female torso set against a blue arc, *Surrender, Never* (Pl.33). Another, *Split Torso* (Pl.34), offers an exquisite arrangement of flesh against a blue luminous ground – a cross between abstraction and figuration achieved with bold brush marks and drips. It is an essentially sexual painting and one which only a woman might have painted. It is possible in these works to detect two themes which point the direction forward and offer a way into Hansen's work. One is the idea of monumentality – of the human form as that of a metaphorical 'goddess'. The other is contained in the spirit of the work – an irrepressible burgeoning urge to life. It is perhaps significant that this latter idea seems to be an extension, in terms of Scottish art history, of what J.D. Fergusson had managed to achieve in the 1920s. Indeed it seems at times almost as if Hansen has taken up where Fergusson left off. Fergusson's 'Rhythm' movement had espoused the idea – largely derived from Bergson – of energy being present in musical harmony and dance, its principal manifestation and means of expression being the female form. For Hansen, too, the figure is everything – and not just the figure, but the female figure, in its raw, naked state. If this appears perhaps to go against traditions within Scottish painting, which has ever been constrained from addressing the nude and exploring the body and sexuality, we should perhaps look again to Fergusson. For, as he explained in 1948, in his seminal work, *Modern Scottish Painting*: 'Calvinism has produced a state of mind in Scotland that makes the Scots artist afraid to paint a nude.' Hansen displayed no such fear when, almost half a century later, she took up Fergusson's call.

The monumentality of her nudes, with their huge, square-toed feet and massive limbs, suggests a homage to some neo-classical 1920s Picasso nereid, transported to the end of the century and crazily out of control. Closer to home, in stylistic terms they link her yet again to Fergusson. There is a similar sense of the primeval in their figures. They are more than human: allegorical gods who tap into our darker side with a sense of life force which seems to echo the driving *leit-motif* of the age of Wagner and the sublime vision of German and Nordic romanticism. Thus, essentially northern paintings, they also, in this context, perpetuate the idea of a specifically northern school of art, an art

34. *Split Torso*, 1979
cat 88

35. *Day of the Jackal, March 13 1996 Dunblane* (triptych), 1996–97
cat 534

created straight from the soul, with an intensity rarely seen in Scotland and perhaps more readily associated with Scandinavia. It comes as no surprise to learn that Hansen herself is quarter Danish.

Consider Hansen's works within this tradition and there quickly emerges a further, essentially Romantic, quality. We might refer to it most simply as the perpetual mystery of how easily and how often we destroy the very things we love. And, with this in mind, observe how, gradually, Hansen's work begins to mature. Most noticeably it becomes bigger. The scale of the paintings is inevitable, unavoidable and absolutely necessary to their function. Her subject-matter, the central – if at times unpalatable – themes of the human condition, demand such monumentality. At the same time her bodies become more violent. Sensuality gives way to aggression. The split within the form, running from sex to head, appears and widens – a cutting through of the body, effectively obscuring its subtle eroticism. This ancient construct of a paradoxical dichotomy of the sensual and the violent informs all of Hansen's work as it does much of northern culture.

It is at once the fine line between genius and madness, the narrow margin which divides pain and pleasure – the duality of the persona – and, ultimately, the conflict which rages within us all.

The eventual culmination of this impetus within Hansen's early work was manifested in an orgy of paint in which the forms of full-breasted women emerge in an explicitly sexual way and which call to mind most immediately the monumental paintings of female figures made by Willem De Kooning during the 1950s – the gaping, grinning gashes of their open mouths echoing those of their equally threatening vulvas. The difference, of course, between these expressionist icons and the women made by Hansen lies in the very fact that Hansen herself is a woman. And so they contain none of that sense of intimidation present in the De Koonings. You will find no *vagina dentata* here.

There is, nevertheless, the underlying idea of an aggressive sexuality, both here and in the series of works in which tongues become intertwined as open-mouthed kisses. Implicit in these works is a reflection upon the sex act itself – the idea of penetration cutting into the female and the invasion of the body. Here, once again, Hansen explores the slim boundary between love and aggression.

While though it may appear to form the essence of her subject-matter, it is not simply the idea of personal physical and psychological conflict with which Hansen concerns herself, but the way in which that conflict is mirrored throughout other aspects of our existence in a world on the brink of the twenty-first century. Every one of these paintings can in a way be seen as part of a continuing human tragedy – a *Lear*-esque cataclysm translated on to canvas – unremitting and apparently without hope. The underlying theme is the way in which division tears at the fabric of society, whether racial, ideological or based upon some inner, personal dysfunction. It is this which links themes in Hansen's work which might at first appear disparate, from the death of Mary Queen of Scots (the idea of duality in a nation both loving and destroying its queen) to cities torn apart by religion and politics (principally Belfast and pre-unification Berlin and, most powerfully and most recently, the Dunblane massacre). It seems ironic that in the past she has had to travel to experience the human misery of the world – to visit its tortured places and to journey in her mind into the past – that Hansen's studio should itself be located so close to Dunblane. Stays in Berlin and Ireland and her studies of Scottish history revealed just how easily lives can be torn apart. Suddenly, with Dunblane, the horror was there on her own doorstep.

The triptych *The Day of the Jackal* (Pl.35), which is her response to that outrage, is one of the most moving works of art that I have ever experienced. It is numbing, harrowing, its three component panels each distinct yet mutually insistent in their unrelenting cry of pain. Reading from left to right we see a mother cradle her dead child while a figure hangs its head in grief and the black crow of death descends. In the centre are a huge head with an open mouth and a falling child, with behind them a searing line of light. In the third and final panel, on the right, parents are shown, vainly asking 'Why?', while a child issues from the mouth of a huge head in a grotesque parody of birth. Most of all, though, it is the image which qualifies the triptych itself which completes the effect. The smaller piece – what Hansen calls *The Jackal* (Pl.36) – is necessarily quite separate. It is an almost monotone, framed collage of a hideous mask, made from the covering of a bicycle seat in the stylised shape of an animal's head. It is quite simply horrific, and as a well-weathered critic I am still constantly surprised to find my mind haunted by the singularity of this image, so simple yet so grim. It has become for me the anonymous and inevitable face of the bringer of death – at

36. ***The Jackal*****, 1996**
cat 535

once Thomas Hamilton and everyman, the face of evil, of man and the devil which, once seen, imprints itself on the memory with the grip of a gorgon. This could not have been achieved by a lesser artist, and defines Hansen's position within the art not only of contemporary Scotland, but of the world.

Hansen is a Scottish artist. She is also a European artist. Yet, although her images can be seen as belonging within specific lines of tradition (they are fundamentally of the late-twentieth century and they could not have been made at any other time in the history of art or by anyone other than a woman), they are post-holocaust in their imagery, post-modernist in their form. With them Hansen has taken the image of the woman in art out of Olympia's bedchamber and given her back her dignity. But to do so she has had to have the courage to come to terms with the often unpleasant truth of the human condition and, perhaps more frighteningly, to explore the unfathomable depths of her own psyche.

37. *One and the Other*, 1980
cat 102

DIVIDED SELF – UNIFIED VISION: THE EXPRESSIONIST ART OF LYS HANSEN

BILL HARE

'Painting is Dead' has been the verdict handed down from the courts of fashionable art criticism throughout this ultimate decade of our century. To be more accurate, it is figurative painting which is now judged to be completely obsolete and redundant. Scottish artists, however, seem not to have got the message and human subject-matter is still the central focus of concern for many of our leading painters. The art of Lys Hansen is a notable example of this determined and continuing commitment to humanist values in contemporary Scottish art.

If one were asked to single out the most significant trend that has emerged on the Scottish art scene over the last twenty years in which Lys Hansen has been a leading professional painter, this would have to be the spectacular rise in the number of women artists coming to prominence. What is also remarkable is that a high number of these artists have made the figure, or more specifically the female body, their primary subject. Lys Hansen, along with other women painters such as Gwen Hardie, Margaret Hunter, June Redfern and Alison Watt are a loose but distinctive force in recent Scottish figurative art. Before focusing on the work and career of Lys Hansen, therefore, a brief discussion of the wider significance of this phenomenon is necessary.

In contrast to the history of art in most other countries, the depiction of the nude figure, male or female, is conspicuous by its almost total absence in Scottish painting. In the early-eighteenth century Richard Waitt exceptionally presented himself in a self-portrait, painting a rather naïve version of *Venus at her Toilet*. Needless to say, he did not find any takers amongst his prudish patrons for such a *risqué* subject. Even in the nineteenth century when Scottish artists were granted a little more freedom in what they might be allowed to paint, the figure in the landscape was well and truly clothed against the cauld blast of conventional morality. J.D. Fergusson apart, this cultural apartheid against the nude was still forcibly evident as late as the 1950s. When the hapless Joan Eardley, for instance, exhibited a picture of a sleeping male nude figure (now in the National Galleries of Scotland collection) she was ridiculed in the Scottish popular press with such juvenile headlines as 'Oh, he's got no clothes on'. Predictably, Eardley never repeated such an exposure again!

In the late-1970s and early-1980s, when Lys Hansen returned to full-time painting after bringing up her young family, the art scene in Scotland was changing radically. After the predominance of conceptionalism and minimalism, raw painting was back with a

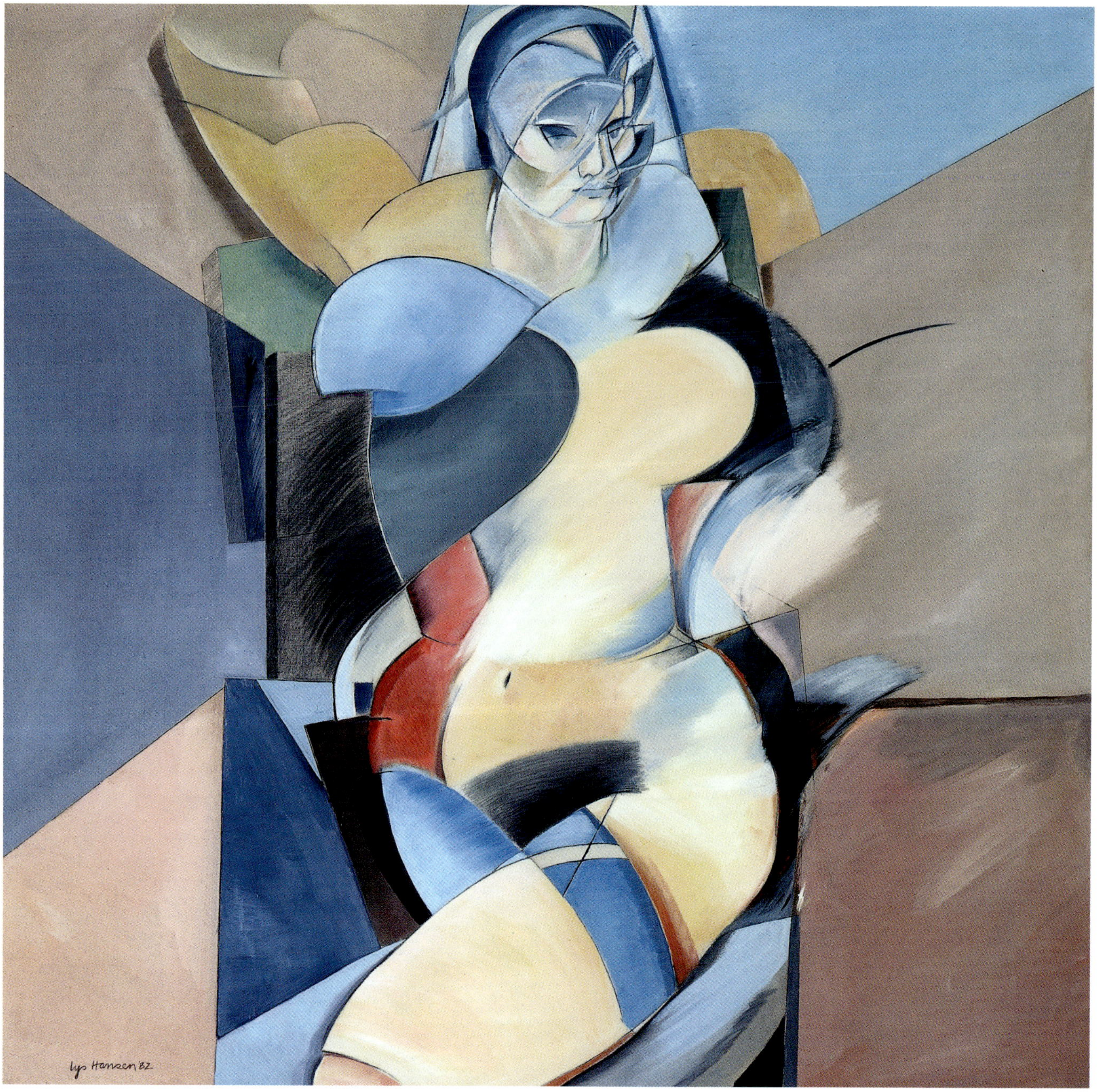

38. *Athena*, 1982
cat 138

39. *Electric Torso*, 1980
cat 105

vengeance. And even though Lys Hansen was never part of any specific art movement, her style of painting could readily be linked with what became known as Scottish neo-expressionism. There were strong affinities between her depictions of female figures in highly agitated and contorted poses and the dominant characteristics of much of the art of the young Scottish painters of the 1980s. For instance, the male painters such as Ken Currie and Peter Howson, sometimes called the 'New Glasgow Boys', also concentrated on the human figure, but usually in an overtly social or even political context. Hansen, on the other hand, as with a number of her fellow Scottish women artists, tended to disconnect her figures from any particular social or domestic environment and instead dealt with much more universal (and at the same time, deeply subjective) themes. For these women artists, and especially Lys Hansen, the female body became the scene for a whole range of disturbing discourses on our physical and emotional condition which the eminent writer and psychologist R.D. Laing had earlier diagnosed as the 'Divided Self'.

Similar to the dominant characteristic in much figurative painting in the 1980s, Lys Hansen's early works tended to have a mythic dimension. This can be found in her version of *Athena* (1980) (Pl.38), for instance.

Compared with her later free, expressionistic mode of painting, this rather Pop Art-style picture has a strong sense of graphic design in which the female anatomy is subjected to cubistic division and rearrangement in the fashion of Richard Hamilton, for example. Yet, even in such a relatively academic piece of work, one senses that just underneath the surface powerful emotional forces could split apart this veneer of cool intellectual order.

This split immediately occurs in a subsequent work from this period – *One and the Other* (1980) (Pl.37). It is almost as if the artist is now rewriting the mythical birth of Athena from a woman/mother's point of view. In the ancient Greek version, the head of Zeus, Athena's father, is split open with an axe and the goddess is created fully formed as the original brain child. Clearly in such a story the emphasis is exclusively on the male intellectual aspect of creativity. With *One and the Other*, however, Lys Hansen wishes to present a very different version of events.

Creativity and birth for an artist who is also a mother is a very potent topic in Lys Hansen's paintings. She continually returns to different ways of expressing what this means and feels for her. The prevalent characteristic of her treatment of this theme is to emphasise the physical and emotional experiences involved. In *One and the Other*, therefore, it is not the male head, but the female body which is being split apart. The colour here is much more austere compared with the erotic *Athena* (Pl.38). The spinal area of the torso is torn wide open to reveal a dark chasm, while the rest of the body shudders in great convulsions, with breasts and buttocks quivering with seismic tremors of sexual pleasure and physical pain. That experience of cathartic ecstasy is most powerfully expressed in *Electric Torso* (1980) (Pl.39).

As images of convulsive sensual experiences, these paintings of the early 1980s are very compelling. Yet they still tend to rely on a decidedly graphic mode of representation and so the intrinsically expressive potential of the painting medium itself is not fully utilised. Throughout the mid-1980s, however, Hansen developed her own distinctive style of painting by concentrating on bridging the gap between form and expression in her work.

This begins in a relatively tentative manner, as can be seen in a picture like *Woman with Man* (1979–82) (Pl. 40). Here colour is no longer restricted to being used in the flat and circumscribed manner of the earlier paintings, but is much more freely applied, with the whole surface of the picture plane being worked over by aggressive brushstrokes. This gives more all-round unity to the work, although there is still a sense of a figure firmly placed in front of a fixed background. The figure itself is a commanding presence; like a not-too-distant cousin of one of Willem De Kooning's 'Women'. Lys Hansen's 'Woman', however, represents a more primeval nature with her gigantic, overflowing breasts recalling the monumental sexuality of the *Venus of Willendorf*. Not surprisingly, the head of the male presence, perched precariously on the woman's chest, looks decidedly uneasy about his predicament. Yet powerful as this painting is, it still tends to have an over-reliance on drawing and graphic outline. In fact, the most resolved area in the picture is the massive

40. *Woman with Man*, 1979–82
cat 97

41. *Licking and Biting*, 1984
cat 176

42. *The Fall II: Agony in the First Garden*, 1985
cat 211

43. ***Love Bites*****, 1984**
cat 180

right thigh which is a *tour de force* in the use of colour to suggest form and yet at the same time convey sensual energy.

From the mid-1980s onwards, that energisation of the painting medium becomes one of the outstanding features of Lys Hansen's work. The division between medium and message is successfully bridged by the animated manner with which she appears to activate the all-over surface of her canvases. This can be fully appreciated in a group of paintings she produced around 1984–85 in which two human heads seem to be submerging themselves into each other in the manner of Brancusi's *Kiss*. Here the highly charged dialectical tension, between tender attraction and brutal aggression, is underlined in the pictures' titles such as *Licking and Biting* (Pl.41), *Love Bites* (Pl.43) and *Agony in the First Garden* (Pl.42). In these works, the rapacious, devouring heads practically fill the whole canvas and so almost eliminate the foreground/background dichotomy which dogged some of the earlier works. Furthermore, there is now a real dramatic conflict involved which has an all-consuming focus of attention, as soft vulnerable tongues or fingers are lured into the gaping trap of the bared-teethed mouth of the ambivalent lover. In these highly charged paintings, mouths, teeth, tongues, fingers and lips are all sucked into a great vortex of sexual passion which recalls the 'battle of the sexes' work of Picasso and Giacometti of the early-1930s.

Lys Hansen is in fact one of the few Scottish artists who has been able to develop a meaningfully creative dialogue between her work and that of a Modern Master like Picasso, especially with his surrealist period of the late 1920s and early 1930s. The fruits of this scrutiny of Picasso can further be seen in the single-figure pictures, which she was also producing in the mid-1980s, as for example *Allein (Alone)* (Pl.45) or *Signals* (Pl.44), both 1985. Such works recall the great *Bather* paintings by Picasso, especially *The Swimmer* of 1929. Yet while Picasso's figures feel like giant puppets activated by the Master's outside string-pulling control, Lys Hansen's women are surely animated by their own disturbing internal emotional and psychic energy. In paintings like *Allein*, the figure appears to be trapped within the narrow confines of the picture frame. The space that the woman occupies seems less like a physical dimension and more like a psychological one, created by the obsessive mind of the protagonist herself. This results in any room for manoeuvre being reduced almost to the shallow surface of the picture plane, thus forcing the figure into a grotesque posture powerfully suggesting the turbulent mental condition of the woman herself. This figure generates a disturbing presence which, through contorted and displaced limbs, challenges and threatens the viewer's normal attitude to the representation of women within a whole range of artistic, sexual and social contexts.

While at this time many of the women figures in Lys Hansen's paintings are presented with a marked feeling of isolation and entrapment, the artist herself was eager to open out her work to a wider social and political environment. This first came to the fore after she went to Berlin in 1985. There she could see for herself not only individual people, but a whole society which was divided from itself and its own recent history. One of the major achievements of her Berlin experience was that she now had the confidence and ability to elevate her art to the dimensions of modern history painting. This resulted firstly in the monumental *Berlin Trilogy* (Pl.24) (1985) in which the three panels treat, in human form, the allegorical tale of the Three Wise Monkeys. While the mythical monkeys deliberately cut themselves off from the outside world around them, the condition of the humans in Lys Hansen's triptych is that they 'Hear Everything', 'See All' but 'Say Nothing' – as indicated by the separate titles for each panel. Thus the ironic situation in our contemporary society is that we are ever bombarded with a never-ending stream of sounds and images but, despite all our mass-media technology of communication, we are unable, or unwilling, to make any real contact with each other in a one-to-one relationship.

As with much of Lys Hansen's later work, the *Berlin Trilogy* strongly suggests a pervasive atmosphere of suppression which is expressed through the self-imprisoning posture of the figures, acting as a metaphor for the wider context of social discontinuity in the body politic at large. The deep divisions in our society are reflected in the way that the human hands in the *Trilogy* do not act as agents of response to what we see and hear, but instead work against their communicative role to become suppressive forces that enclose us from the world outside. The deeply injurious effect that this civil war of the senses can have on us is dramatically expressed in another work of 1985, the appropriately entitled *Divided Self Trilogy* (Pl.46), where the human head and body are literally tearing each other apart.

In *Grip*, the central panel from the *Divided Self Trilogy*, the initial onslaught on the viewer's sensibilities is created by the violent distortions to which the highly mutable face is being subjected. On closer inspection, however, one begins to appreciate that these facial mutilations have a strong pictorial authenticity to them as well a psychological one. In the internal narrative of the picture, the fingers of the half-hidden hand manipulate the features to suggest powerfully the psycho-social ritual of 'putting on a public face'. While this psychological narrative is what most forcibly impacts on our immediate attention, *Grip* also rewards a more sustained and critical analysis. Here I would suggest that this involves the variety of pictorial languages that are at work within the painting. *Grip* is rich in the multilingual range of modern painting's modes of representation – from allusions to cubistic fragmentation and multi-viewpoints, to surrealist biomorphic transformancies, to expressionist primitivistic distortions – all adding many layers of visual complexities to a haunting image of the human experience. Lys Hansen's work has evolved into a highly intelligent and personal version of the language of

RIGHT
44. *Signals*, 1985
cat 208

FAR RIGHT
45. *Allein (Alone)*, 1985
cat 206

expressionism. Her paintings are the product of an extremely articulate artist who is well skilled in the art of picture-making. She is able to communicate the emotional reality of her imagination in a manner that can appeal not only to the viewer's emotional sympathies, but also their aesthetic sensibilities.

During the 1990s, despite marked changes in taste and fashion, Lys Hansen's humanist commitment to, and faith in, the intrinsic power of painting to express an authentic vision of human affairs has remained steadfast. This is strongly evident in her triptych *Witness with Evidence* (Pl.47) (1994) which possesses a truly mythic quality. This work has a strong catastrophic theme, so that the dark ominous threat which stalks most of her work now reaches apocalyptical dimensions. There are obvious biblical overtones, with such panel titles as *Where were you, God, when I needed you?*. Yet, although there is a heart-rending despair running through all the panels and the accompanying sculptures, there is also an energy and vitality animating the work. The symbolic imagery may, like Dürer's *Four Horsemen of the Apocalypse*, spell out doom and disaster; yet like the German master, Hansen infuses her vision with such dedication to her painterly craft and such commitment to the grand rhetoric of her theme, that this work in the end expands the viewer's outlook on human life and history.

In her most recent major work, Lys Hansen has attempted to deal with a human tragedy that occurred frighteningly close to home. The artist's studio is near Dunblane, where sixteen schoolchildren and their teacher were murdered by a crazed gunman. Like the rest of the country, Lys Hansen was deeply distressed by this horrendous event, especially as the plight of the children (born and unborn) is a recurring theme in her work. Despite certain reservations, she committed herself to making a large painting entitled *Day of the Jackal* (Pl.35).

With such a subject, which instantly recalls the Massacre of the Innocents, a strong biblical theme is again suggested in the painting. In the right-hand panel, two figures look pleadingly to the heavens for an answer to the artist's earlier question, 'Where were you, God, when I needed you?' On the left side of the painting there is the artist's own version of the *pietà* scene. Above the grieving group is the ominous presence of a threatening black crow, recalling the old Scots ballad, 'Twa Corbies'.[1] Appropriately, the deadly bird spreads its wings like a black crucifix. Next to the *pietà* group is the giant figure of a child who, like many of the heads in the artist's earlier paintings, is torn between looking out and covering up its terrified eyes with its hands clasped protectively round its face. The central panel seems to take us on to a bleak inhospitable landscape with a vivid yellow escarpment on the horizon. A terrifying skull-like head dominates the immediate foreground while just behind is a figure of a wailing woman etched in bare outline into the dark-blue ground. From the woman's arms falls the white silhouette of the innocent dead child, drawn out like a police murder-scene diagram. Such a graphic device as a reference to forensic imagery adds to the particular potency of the work in the same way as Picasso's documentary allusions in *Guernica*. In the *Day of the Jackal*, Lys Hansen has, with skill and sensitivity, managed to negotiate the

46. *The Divided Self' trilogy* (triptych), 1985
LEFT PANEL
She is She
CENTRE PANEL
Grip
RIGHT PANEL
Goodbye
cat 194–196

47. *Witness with Evidence* (triptych), 1994
LEFT PANEL
Where were You, God, when I needed You?
CENTRE PANEL
The Near Death of Hope
RIGHT PANEL
Four Demons Within: Lust, Greed, Desire, Hunger
cat 489

difficult divide between responding to the specific circumstances of the actual event, and at the same time fulfilling the need to elevate this local tragedy onto the level of universal significance.

Day of the Jackal is painted on three separate panels, but unlike the earlier triptychs these are butted together to create a much greater visual coherence for the work. That sense of unity is also felt in the inter-relatedness of the picture's consistent iconography of pain and death which allows the stridently discordant colours to play off against each other in an extremely highly charged fashion. This, for me, is what the whole development of Lys Hansen's work seems to have been striving to achieve. She is truly a courageous artist, who is prepared to acknowledge and address the deep and troubling divisions which wrack not only our own physical and mental life but also the whole fabric of modern society. Yet Lys Hansen the artist, although distressed, is not daunted by what she sees around her. The overall unity of her artistic vision, as evidenced by her major works, gives her the creative power to exorcise the demons which can terrorise our lives and haunt our imaginations. As with high tragedy, the paintings of Lys Hansen ultimately have a cathartic power, which is able to rejuvenate our senses and revitalise our spirit. Such painting is never dead.

LYS HANSEN: ROLE MODEL

CLARE HENRY

They used to call them gods and goddesses; later heroes and heroines. Today's fashionable expression for an inspirational figure is less glamorous: 'role model'. I hate the term, but it does fit Lys Hansen. By virtue of her work (brave, powerful, dynamic, ambitious in scale, heroic in attitude – all noticeably male accolades in times past) and her theme (the female body), she is not only a considerable artist but has become a key role model for younger Scottish women artists.

She finds this rewarding. 'Working with people and other artists is a vital part of my philosophy,' she says. 'Teaching has always been my strong love. To open minds and eyes, extend hopes and aspirations – what a challenge. I consider it a privilege and a joy. Being a token woman does leave one out on a limb – but I'm not in an ivory tower; I'm out there. I trust even my three-year presidency of the SSA from 1992 to 1995 made a contribution. Today's art students can't imagine how rare a full-time, female professional artist was even thirty years ago. Girls were expected to make nice wives, mummies and homes. Early Scottish women artists can be counted on the fingers of one hand. As a student in the late-1950s I had no women tutors. I think most girls want to relate to women who have travelled the course and succeeded. How fine it would have been to have heard Joan Eardley or Anne Redpath speaking about their work; but they were rarefied beings, merely glimpsed via their pictures in the RSA.' Yet even that fact was encouraging and led the young Hansen to aim high.

Hansen has always been fearless; a woman in a hurry. This goes hand in hand with singleminded, committed effort. 'Unrelenting hard work is essential. Not to use your skills and abilities is unforgivable. And I differ from most of my contemporaries in that I see art as a political voice, not a domestic pursuit.'

This is where Hansen's long track record of vigorous, meaningful painting coupled with sparky teaching sets her apart. Ahead of her time in questioning women's role and tackling the subject of their sexual identity (she sees the female body as a field of love and war with often bitter conflict), her pioneering has been dedicated – and perhaps more difficult than those who follow in her footsteps may realise – to embracing issue-based art.

Three decades of blazing a trail have run parallel to nurturing – not just her many students but her own family of husband and two sons. As for so many women, this juggling act has not been easy, a fact reflected in paintings which shout their raw message: fingers tearing at pent-up frustrations; bodies struggling, scrambling, torn asunder. When I first got to know her work in 1980, her own divided loyalties and personal debate were being obsessively reflected in paint.

Outspoken and honest to a degree, she is an intuitive painter who tries to balance emotion with intellect. 'By the late 1970s I was feeling so suppressed by this domesticity that I felt a bit of me was dying. I had a full life – but much was missing. If it's in you, art must have its life. The only way to rid myself of the ache was with a brush in my hand.'

In 1979 she started painting the female torso, but found 'I couldn't get her to lie down, my psyche wouldn't allow it. She kept getting up, bursting out of the canvas!' These autobiographical gyrating figures with their obvious 'family/career split' symbolism were captured in slippery blue/mauve hues which could veer to the vulgar – but their intention carried the day.

The images were highly personal and exposed a great deal. 'I began by looking at gender; the male/female sides of us all; the need for a woman to be strong and sure yet also loving and gentle. Lovers, husbands, children have your body from the inside. They dominate by sheer physical possession. Soon your confidence shrinks. Being a wife and mother – that's your world. In the 1960s that was not questioned; identity, self, she as she, was not a familiar concept. There was very little material around on women artists. I remember finding a monograph on Paula Modersohn-Becker in the Third Eye[1] and falling on it avidly. Likewise Käthe Kollwitz.' As with Modersohn-Becker, Hansen sees painting as the 'Runic script' for the expression of innermost emotions.

'Gradually I realised that my experience as a woman, wife and mother gave me a powerful understanding of the world and that I could bring that special quality into paint. I had access to the amazing energy and force of the female psyche, her sexuality and all that is the begetter of the life force – if only I could harness it!'

As her work developed, Hansen was asked to talk about it. 'I never had a problem in verbalising my aims. The pictures are a way of looking honestly at myself; trying to get to the core of truth. The nakedness is not simply for the sake of it but represents a nakedness of the psyche. A male artist may paint a female form because he enjoys it: it's attractive, sensual, erotic. My nudes are not intended as titillation. We come into the world naked and with raw needs and desires. It's only later that clothes, manners, inhibitions, protocol, are imposed on us. I try to strip everything away: bare body and soul.'

This elimination of the accidental, and her instinctive grasp on the essence of form expressed by means of utmost simplicity and economy of line, was to come to the fore in an impressive series of monochromatic works on paper done in Berlin in 1985. Inspired by Richard Demarco's conference at the Edinburgh Festival[2] which focused on the explosion of new German museums (Hansen is a great supporter of Demarco), she decided she had to see for herself. Four months there alone, working flat out, produced a remarkable series of stark, angry pictures. Suppressed fears, emotions and desires are everywhere.

But before Berlin, enter Mrs Harris, the subject of – in Hansen's eyes – her seminal

48. *The Rivals – Scarsdale (Mrs Harris I)*, 1982
cat 140

49. *Stagefright*, 1984
cat 181

work. 'Mrs Harris hit the headlines in 1982. A respectable headmistress in Scarsdale, upstate New York, she flipped when her lover, a famous doctor, took a younger mistress. Little Mrs Harris got out her gun and shot him – four times. I was so taken with her rage! In court she was triumphant. She'd found the courage to do it; discovered a kind of power. She created an earthquake; she had defied the rules of society. We all know killing is more acceptable by a man. Women are taught to be docile, how to weep. I was busy on a figure painting at the time, so I just grabbed at newspaper and magazine photos of her, then ripped, tore and collaged them onto the canvas. Mrs Harris inspired me to take a great artistic leap!'

This painting, *The Rivals – Scarsdale (Mrs Harris I)* (Pl.48), represents Hansen's transition, providing the link into a more violent human sexuality where she pushes the viewer right up against the lovers, so close you can feel their hot breath and hear the panting groans. Her tangle of heads, hands, mouths, lips, feet, torsos, eyes, fingers – all apparently involved in frantic exploration of the human physique – include female fingers which interlock with a male foot; lips which lick and bite as they gobble up another's knuckle. Hansen grabs at the senses; senses hungry for pleasure and pain. She captures both the reality and dream of life and love.

The boldly fragmented, rapidly painted *The Rivals* and all that followed are the antithesis of *Athena* (Pl.38), completed only weeks earlier. While *Athena*, symbolising wisdom, is an elegant, stylised, pale cubist figure, outwardly voluptuous yet impervious to sexual mores, and painted in a smooth, stylish manner, *The Rivals* is violent in form and lush in colour.

The Rivals was the start of a series of wild women, from harridan to seductress, whose fractured surfaces and red lipstick reflected the changing roles of the 1980s as, displaced and dissatisfied, women reinvented themselves and moved on.

Hansen moved on to paint *Stagefright* (Pl.49) which won a prize at the famous 1985 Stirling Smith Biennial which also toured to London. Hansen subsequently shared a two-person Camden Arts Centre show in 1986, getting formidable reviews from those tough critics Waldemar Januszczak and Sarah Kent. The latter homed in on Hansen's debt to De Kooning while highlighting the *Divided Self Trilogy* (Pl.46):

> whose horror has a fierce authenticity that clearly emanates from internal pain. The twisted double face which forms the central panel is also a hand wrenching its own features apart – a powerful evocation of inner conflict and one of the most compelling portrayals of psychic suffering that I have seen for a long time. The kind of bravery required to make a picture that raw should enable Hansen to proceed; she has so much that is valuable to say.[3]

Januszczak heralded Hansen's appearance as an 'indisputably important artist from Scotland – where else?' thus:

> her painting seems to circumnavigate the mind entirely and speaks directly to the nerves in your legs. But such sensuality alone would not make these paintings as remarkable as they are. The sound of flesh colliding with flesh is common enough in art, from Rubens to Utamaro and Picasso. What makes Hansen's oils so interesting is that they introduce a note of introspection into the proceedings. This is a woman's view. And however dense the tangle of limbs, there always seems to be an eye somewhere in the background, peeping out from between parted fingers, watching, speculating, a thoughtful witness to its own climax.[4]

Despite these accolades for her impressive, aggressively expressionist paintings, amid all the 1980s' interest in Scottish art and Glasgow Boys hype, Hansen failed to hit the jackpot. Why? Because she was female? Because she didn't live in Glasgow? Because she wasn't thirty-something? Who knows. Certainly the work merited attention, no question of that. Other mid-career women, Beth Fisher, Jacki Parry, June Redfern, Victoria Crowe, Sam Ainslie and many more, suffered a similar fate and only now are acknowledged. Happily for younger women artists, they are not the first to tread Scotland's misogynistic cultural minefield, and as a result should not be marginalised in the same way.

Needless to say, Hansen gets a bigger,

better response in Europe. She is not alone here; Scots are often without honour in their own country. First Berlin, now Bornholm welcomes this outspoken painter.

Germany inspired *Birthing Blind, Berlin* which shows a huge skull birthing a defective child from the mouth. From the eye-sockets emerge other skulls. This is one of many disquieting Hansen images of the emergent new Germany retaining the embers of the old state within.

Always concerned and fearful for the young, in the 1990s high-profile reports on child abuse propelled Hansen to tackle this subject – and it was while actually working on a picture on this topic that the radio announced the tragedy of Dunblane. 'Just miles down the road; too close. We knew the people, the parents. Horror. I picked up my brush and inscribed the canvas "March 13th".' That picture grew into a memorial triptych, *Day of the Jackal* (Pl.35), where figures explode with terrible grief in dramatic gesture (Hansen studied both drama and art). Hopefully, this major work will find a home in one of Scotland's civic museums.

If women are now eventually beginning to take their meaningful place in society and in the art world alongside men as dynamic beings with different and yet complementary input, we must not forget that much of this is due to people like Hansen who have fought long and hard along the way.

However, with one son's marriage on the horizon, Hansen is at a stage to look both back and forward. 'My mother encouraged me in every way. She was extremely direct; both my parents were people of no nonsense but also people of dreams and imagination. They enjoyed expressing themselves in word and song. But I worry that the next generation, however gifted, just want late marriages and careers. Pop a pill and kill a child. The pendulum has swung too far. It's symbolised by the big boots girls wear. They think it's just a fashion statement but it says a whole lot more: 'no one's going to mess with me'. And if the women are making all that fine art, who is making the homes and the new babies? Future generations must inherit artistic genes or else what has it all been for?'

With imminent exhibitions in Bornholm and London plus a period working in Poland and Berlin, Hansen continues to do battle, 'winning some, losing others! You just hope you achieve a few of the things you set your heart on.'

LIVING WITH THE WORK

JUDITH MACRAE

I love paintings. I love looking at them. I love the way they make me feel. I get too emotional and I know it, but it can't be helped. Sometimes the need for them makes me go into debt for them. I hang them wherever I am living and I feel a bit more centred.

Many paintings – no, most paintings – are beyond my grasping for them and I can only look at prints of them and suck them in and remember. Small bits, intimately: the curving sheen of Marthe Bonnard's back as she rests upon a bed, a sleeve of the guessed-at bridegroom in *The Jewish Bride*, the writhing gash of Soutine's hanging carcase, the pearly lustre of Cleopatra caught luring Anthony in the huge blue Tiepolo, the translucent flesh and refulgent light of Della Francesca's *The Baptism of Christ*. And there are many more. Recently I added the plaited bodice of a grey silk dress which Raeburn miracled out of scurries of paint. A special store. A private rejoicing. These I cannot have. I pretend which paintings I could have if they awaited my choosing . . . I've got quite a collection.

I don't like printed copies much, they are always so mean. Flattened and squashed and mean. So, I try and buy what I like, what I can find. Now, one of the things I particularly like in painting is the paint. I mean the colour shapings: squashy, smeared and very brave. I enjoy the unabashed sensuality of pigment and the excitement of the act of putting it down just so, just there. I admire that courage, letting it speak for itself.

Lys Hansen does that. She lets it shout and roar and is not afraid to have it scream and sing, and sometimes the colours, the laying down of the pigment and the emotional intent coalesce. I have some of these. I met Lys at a school.[1] She taught Art and I taught bits other people had left. It was a tough place. The kids were so honest it hurt and they didn't give a damn about school. They knew the score and I was ignorant coming as I did from the paradisical Antipodes. They taught me a lot. Lys and I came together and grew into friendship. I didn't know she was a painter.

When I went to her council house in Clackmannan there was a lot hanging on the walls, small walls pushed down by lowish ceilings, all white. I remember the sense of the paintings shoving the space, yelling for air. I was surprised; they were bold and vigorous and big. I did not expect this.

I liked them instantly, a sort of visceral jump that is entirely physical. I had no money so I couldn't buy anything, and anyway I didn't like to ask.

I went to Strathclyde University to study English; Lys taught and painted and birthed

50. *The Body Electric*, 1980
cat 111

Giles, her first son; and we just lived our lives. She started the Blairlogie exhibitions[2] and at one of them I bought *Rainbow House*. There's no date on it but I'm sure it's about 1967. It is a house much like a child's house and the hills behind are the Ochils. In its window hangs a rainbow. It seems to me to be a domestic, gentle vision but the window is blind except for the rainbow and I am not sure if it is a reflection or if the colours come from inside. It's a gouache and rather subdued in its dark greeny browns and it always reminds me of Lys's own house at Blairlogie.

A little while later she agreed to hang some of her work in the café where we ate cheese rolls and drank a sort of coffee between lectures.[3] It was an ugly space, empty and somehow hostile to anything but the utilitarian. I got help, and together we lied and bluffed our way to getting permission, told Lys the weekend we had chosen, and she and her husband George came loaded with canvases. In the empty, echoing caff we hung her work and had a great time. It was 1968. Anything seemed possible and a great deal was.

These paintings met with such hostility from the student sippers you would have thought they were a personal affront to each individual, so we were totally vindicated in the act of bringing in real live art. We never admitted it was us, it was too much fun listening to the outrage. Later we had the Scottish Arts Council find John Connolly's *The Kiss*, a great sculpture in metal, and had them place it at the foot of the steps of the Livingstone Tower. Much better to be seen than stand shrouded in some Arts Council basement. John wholeheartedly agreed.

51. *Night Torso*, 1981
cat 120

Now the Collins Gallery fills the deadness outside the Livingstone Tower and there is art right at the heart of Strathclyde University. Lys plans an exhibition there some time in the future. A nice irony.

The next painting was a gift, a special one, a watercolour. I was very pregnant and Lys painted me wearing a brilliant dress lolling on a couch. It was for my unborn child. He has it in his bedroom right now. *For Corydon, 1971.* This may be one of Lys's first moves towards figuration which came to be so important in her development. It is rather conservative in style and no one would really know it was me unless they knew the patterns of the dress. The face is non-existent – that wasn't what interested her as a painter; she loved the colour and the red shoes and that is what the painting really is, a study of pattern and colour.

Then I left Scotland and returned to Australia. On one of my return trips I took back *Yellow Stretch*, a female nude kneeling in profile, her left arm raised. This drawing is in pastel on a yellow paper and you can see the power of the woman's heavy body as she stretches, the heavy, full breasts pendulous. This hangs in a yellow-and-sage-green bedroom and glows against its wall. Another painting made the long journey in 1980, *The Body Electric* (Pl.50). This work vibrates with energy, its femaleness a pulsing magical presence shimmering in its own forcefield. The strong orange yellow of the torso arches to a fiery head, pale green and alight with energy. Behind stream rivers of colour, deep blues are fireworked by flashes of red, lime green, cobalt and ultramarine. The paint flies and sings and is of such confident bravado it always makes me smile. This was a different order of painting: no longer the spaces left, this electric torso is barely contained in its silver frame, its powerful thighs press outward into space. It is just temporarily pinned and will fly, given half a chance.

A little painting came as a surprise. In 1981 *Night Torso* (Pl.51) arrived, an oil of a powerful body; pink and rich against the dark, full of strength and a heavy energy. Like *The Body Electric* it is another powerful female figure exultant, but it is a great deal heavier, somehow more primitive. Both these paintings give me a continuing feeling of pleasure and I think this pleasure is in the recognition of a powerful female sexuality. And she paints as if she is in love with the stuff, rich slides and flourished strokes, smears and sweeps. It is like looking at a controlled and mastered explosion.

Then I returned permanently to Scotland and acquired *Performance* (Pl.52). Or should I say *Performance* acquired me. Living with this astonishing work is a great gift. The wicked eye of its striding woman looks to us with a melancholy knowingness, her breasts bulge and flare; who belongs to those hands and feet stretching into its forward space? A man is enmeshed in her, she in him; together, they merge in a flurry of limbs. But always she looks at me, saying, 'You know what this is about, don't you?', and I do. The performance of the expected, ghosts of our other selves shimmering behind our actions. And that performance with a man, out of bed and in bed; sex and all its pretences and terrible honesties. And then there is the wonderful rest, the canvas is a territory of textures, pasted paper, bits of cloth and always the ever-present paint – an active presence –

lively and confident and daring. *Performance* covers nearly a whole wall in my sitting-room; and I love it.

Talking about painting as a non-expert is a bit silly. It's the vocabulary, I expect. I know about the movements and the names and I've done a lot of looking and I suppose I can hold my own talking about what I see, but it stops there. I can see Lys Hansen as an 'expressionist', but the word gets a little vague around the edges when you look at her work. Writing about *Performance* is even sillier because much of what I respond to is its emotional clout. It is a big painting in many ways and can be savoured over years of looking. Oddly, it doesn't dominate, it just looks supremely at ease.

I really do think *Performance* is a terrific painting and it gives me a charge of energy every time I look at it, wickedly grinning out of the dissolves and merges of its sexuality.

The next painting of hers to force me into debt was the beautiful *Death in a Red Dress* (Pl.25). This was one of the paintings resulting from work done in Berlin in 1992. I went to the Dundee opening[4] and I just couldn't stop looking at it. *Death in a Red Dress* is a haunting work, the lolling head with it heavy-lidded shut eyes suggests a great endurance; the folded arms, resignation. I find it very touching: the little tender feet, the drooping shoulder and its thin left arm, the ambivalence of reality and heightened reality, the quality of the pigment, the red dress the same colour as the stream of blood from the smear of her carmine mouth and, most of all, the sense of heart-rending sadness which, for me, is its primary force. There are resonances, such as the Otto Dix painting of the prostitute in her slippery red satin, sexually aggressive in its nastiness, but the feeling in Lys Hansen's dead girl is light years away from this icon of a past, decadent Berlin. This woman has been used and left to die. Again, this is a big painting which needs a whole wall. Some remark they couldn't live with it, 'too overpowering', 'too devastating', 'too bloody piteous'. And then there are those who envy me her presence and are drawn to looking for a long time. As for me, now that she is in my life, I can't imagine her not being there.

And so I come to the last, a gift and a safekeeping. *Tender Regrets*, is a gouache; two heads twist to look to each other, but both seem blind. Against a red background, the faces float as ghosts. The man's arm encloses the woman as if to enfold her, but the distance remains. Strong heads, sad heads struggling still. Dark lines run like tears from each face. It hangs opposite *Death in a Red Dress* and this conjunction pleases, for both are full of an honest, unflinching humanity.

So there you are. That's the collection. A group of paintings which mean a great deal to me and give me the greatest pleasure. Not a lot, but you can't have everything you want, can you?

52. *Performance*, 1983
cat 155

LYS HANSEN: PAINTER

JUDITH MACRAE

There are some painters who confront us with images we do not wish to see, images too painful, too close to a psychic bone for comfort, which tell us a truth too disturbing for equanimity. Lys Hansen has grown to become such a painter.

With honesty and without compromise, she gives us a disconcerting and difficult vision of our personal and sexual personae without costumes or props, naked upon the stage of her own choosing, the painting itself.

Such a confrontation creates conflict. When faced with a painting wrenched from the acceptable, when confronted by imagery of assertive sexual power, we are over-whelmed by our own physical responses; a holding of breath, perhaps, or a skin shiver of sensual recognition; a suspension of thought or an internal lurch, barely discernible, of vertigo. The comfortable world is displaced by another reality; we are flung into one barely palatable and distinctly disturbing.

Our response to this initial physical displacement is two-fold. At first we are fascinated and look with obsessive attention, saturating ourselves with the painting's image, its symbols and signs. In a real sense we are held by the power of the painting and our critical ability is suspended, we are disarmed. Ambivalence also pervades us for we are both fascinated and repelled, at once moving inward and drawing back. We search for clues as we look at the painting, clues to make sense of our own response, to come to control and understanding. With paintings of powerful sexual ambiguity we are ill at ease, embarrassed as if publicly exposed by our own slight rise in blood heat, the quickening of pulse.

We then seek to control our first physical response and fascinated looking by making intellectual sense of what we have experienced. This second response brings our critical armoury to bear upon the painting, to distinguish, categorise and enumerate its values in both style and content. Often it is our own self-knowledge, our accumulated experience of such works, which will decide our critical attitude. Too often our defences are readymade.

We avoid what the paintings tell us about ourselves by saying what the painting is not rather than what it is; it is as if we have not developed a vocabulary to help us under-stand what these paintings actually do to us, how their gestures work upon our own psyche. We do not create the conditions in which a particular and unique dialogue can freely take place – between the painting and its audience. For the paintings are not passive; they are active and coruscate with energy, demanding from us an active response, a meeting, a recognition of our own behaviour in such paintings, a form of truth-telling we do not like to accept as our own. This involved and open looking, leading to recognition of ourselves, is exciting; it is the action of revelation. Nothing ever appears quite the same again.

There are many images filed and stored in our Pantheon of Art, images that once shattered perceptions and infuriated the arbiters of taste. Once reviled, they are now revered. Defused by familiarity, they have become acceptable and are now symbols of our own aesthetic sophistication. Paintings centrally concerned with the revelation of our own secret natures are met with initial hostility. The language of the painting has to be learnt, we must learn to see without preconceptions, we must allow the painting to act upon us.

There are those who would argue that the second process of bringing to bear the informed analytic intelligence on the chaos of an emotional response is an essential to all that makes us civilised. Of course; but not at the expense of the recognition of our own human behaviour as revealed by those who struggle to shape such a reality. Then, it is a failure of nerve.

Hansen's major works sit squarely in this struggle of revelation and understanding. She has chosen the human body as a paradigm for the exploration of emotional and sexual conflict, the human body transformed by the force and pressure of needs, emotions and desires from deep within itself.

Lys Hansen was initially concerned with the world as 'out there', a world of objects placed in space, of houses and skies, of landscapes translated through windows, abstracted and reorganised. Primarily, her painting represented the world as a continual still-life to be arranged by the artist into pleasing or arresting conformities, to organise reality as an aesthetic function. She relied on her formal strengths: draughtsmanship, a strong sense of design, her sure and often brilliant use of colour. Above all, they were paintings concerned with order and control – traditional painterly works recognisably within the traditions of Scottish painting, rather cool and highly skilled – distinctly works of a painter about to realise her talent. But it seemed as if Hansen lacked a true focus, as if her ability and experience could not find its model. Through a long and arduous working, she has come to the figure as a metaphor for this experience.

Figures are in many of the earlier paintings as part of the construction and design element. Pale, vaguely realistic figures of women, passive as if waiting, anonymous and decorative. The vivid colour, flattened and controlled, gave its vigour to the surroundings; the milky sky, the vegetable phallic shapes, the breast of a hill, the hidden, secret body of landscape. Like ghosts, the nude female figures floated in her paintings without real presence, but still insisting on their place; their sexuality a decorative addition in the tradition of the female nude. She rediscovered the torso, exploring its possibilities through extensive figure drawings from life – pastels, gouache, oils, acrylic – in an absorbing and fascinating struggle with the power of the form.

The paintings resulting from her explorations are exercises in tone and structure, the paint more fluid and spontaneous; warm pinks and creams stretching and leaning into the surrounding darkness, shoulders merging into breasts, a new muscular strength in thighs and hips. Small paintings of impressive scale as in *Night Torso* (Pl.51), its peach and pink resplendent in a growing power. Confidence expanded, she experimented further with the form, not as an intellectual exercise, but more as allowing herself freedom to be spontaneous, intuitively feeling her way, splitting the body, merging male and female, the erotic element of fusing, of flesh combining. Bodies are activated by passions, no longer passive, they explode and reform into curves and patterns, shapes of suggestibility and subtlety.

Her exhibition in 1980 can be seen as a watershed,[1] for these paintings took her into new possibilities. She realised the erotic ambiguities of such forms; the shapes are vigorous, the sexuality palpable, sometimes strangely androgynous. Her palette is wide and varied, ranging from the softest tones of blues and pinks to the jungle brilliance of the painting, *Soaring*, irradiated and gleaming, an orange torso cometing across a parrot-streaked background, its femaleness alive with sexual joy.

Hansen had found her focus: the making of public images distilled from private experience and private pain, the human body transformed and reshaped by her own aesthetic logic, a process of exploration and discovery.

The heart of her working is always in the making of the painting itself, the application of the paint to the canvas for, as she says, 'Each piece of paint is there for a specific function'. There is dynamism in the paint surface – a broth of paint slashes, smudges and layers out of which the images thrust. Nothing is hit and miss, she works doggedly and persistently, each colour has its position, each blur of paint has a purpose in the unity of the painting. For the surface is a unified surface through the energy of the paint; it reaches into and across all the canvas and the eye finds this dynamism actively pulling disparate elements into a whole.

Always in Hansen's work there is the recognition of the obduracy of the paint and the tensions this obduracy creates upon the surface of the canvas. She struggles to allow the paint its own nature yet still control it, to mould it to her own needs. If you look closely at the surface of a Hansen painting you will see it is alive with this struggle. There are spurts, smears, congestions of paint. It is alive with creative intent; it is dynamic. There is not an inch of submissive, static surface; it crackles, bristles with energy. Her figures grow from this, working in a symbiotic relationship, their energy the paint's energy, their power pulled from the intense depths of the paint's working. There is no blocking out or filling in, of background or foreground; it is as if we watch the creation of the form in the paint itself, forced by the power of the working into being, into object.

Hansen pushes the technical restraints to extremes, setting problems of scale and surface, as in *The Divided Self trilogy – She is She*, *Grip* and *Goodbye* (Pl. 46), where, for example, the lunging figure of *Goodbye* looks back, hauntingly, to an unknown protagonist and nearly throws the three works out of unity. It is the position of the head, eyes swivelled, that pulls the three paintings

53. *Enfold*, 1980
cat 104

together – Hansen set herself a difficult technical problem and solved it. One of the reasons for this lies in her technical ability, but she is also able, through ruthless self-criticism, to reject what she sees as inadequate to what she intends and, through a strict discipline, to work until she achieves what she wants. If she finds her considerable battery of skills insufficient, she is not afraid to experiment; to tear and cut paper and paste it to her canvas, to combine media and to extend the boundaries of her frames. This willingness to experiment and change as the painting's life dictates, gives her work added gusto and daring, a sense of play and delight in the actual process of painting itself.

Like many other contemporary painters, she uses painting's long history of skills and conventions. She uses her knowledge of the past as a natural source of reference, not as an adroit and manipulative cultural pastiche but as an acknowledgement and understanding of those authoritative painters of history who still remain potent for us in the present. So a painter who reorganises the form into new shapes reminds us of Picasso with his protean plastic rearrangements of the body; while a woman lashed by lines makes us

54. *Getting in on the Act* (diptych), 1984
cat 177

think of De Kooning, a painter with whom Hansen has some affinities especially in the vigour of the paint and the primordial presence of some of her women. But it is the area of concern, the female body charged by the electricity of its needs and emotions, that is similar – not the intent. Hansen does not plagiarise. She transforms the reference by the intensity of her own experience, her own conflicts, her own grappling with the body as metaphor. *Mrs Harris 2* strides out like a latter-day Willendorf Venus, chunky thighs streaming with black power. This is brilliant figure painting at the extremes of the form as realism, as if *Mrs Harris 2*, torn and re-assembled by her own pain, transmutes into an icon for those who have lost all in the sexual game but dare to remain, implacably, still there. This painting is a statement about the pain of loss, the recognition of a disturbing sexual self demanding its own life – the torso breaking up upon itself, disintegrating yet continuing to survive.

Progressively, her work has grown darker in content and colour. Most recently, this deepening has been paralleled by an increase in the canvas's actual size. When faced with Hansen's paintings there is an immediate sense of their large-scale, irrespective of their actual measurements. Figures appear monumental, space is filled or pushed away by these forms, they burst down or push upwards, straining, as in *Drowning* or heads twisted, eyes sliding, mouths agape as in *Grip* (part of Pl.46). Torsos are powerful and vigorous, their flesh tones lambent, brushstrokes forceful and confident. The figures violently surge from the scorings and seethings of their surrounding storm of paint and collage. In the intensity of her working and the resultant febrile quality of the paint surface, she images forth her own magical talisman, figures signalling her psychic direction in ambiguous and mysterious gestures.

Her paintings are powerful and disturbing in size and concept; they compel our attention: they can make us uncomfortable, even uneasy. The grasping and grappling of hands, the groping into mouths of *Love Bites* (Pl.43), or the virtuoso display of technique in the blackly humorous and sharply sexual *Performance* (Pl.52), force us to look. These images release their emotions like a controlled explosion.

In some works there is a deliberate sense of theatre, a performing distance. *Curtain Call*, *Performance*, *Getting in on the Act* (Pl.54). This last painting is a large, strutting work, its tongue firmly in its cheek. There is a sense of conscious performance, an audience watching the glitter of eye and slash of red mouth in the near parody of female sexuality of the major figure with its air of sly, humorous awareness that comes close to a burlesque show, a parade of clichéd sexiness with a brittle nervous edge. It is a painting of sexual absurdities and it cleverly uses the social mores out of which it is formed. Hansen shows us what it is to be a woman on the hunt, on show and yet powerless. Only the gleam in the eyes lets us in on the perennial joke of appearance and reality. To get in on the act we must play the roles allotted for the performance. This female figure plays it to the hilt but saves herself from humiliation by self-mockery as she struts her stuff shadowed by a partnered male. It is sexual comedy wrought from sexual despair.

The largeness of these canvases is necessary, as if her figures and faces, heads and hands need the room to be, as if they would fill the world if ever they finally screamed free. They have filled the diptych and the triptych, reaching and running, bodies broken and impossibly arched, reassembled into harsher shapes and more accurate paradigms for her purpose.

Her purpose is the exploration of what she feels and what she has lived. She tears apart in apparent discord to speak with a greater honesty, a truer voice. It is in one of her most assured and accomplished works, *Stagefright* (Pl.49), that she shows what that reshaping can become. Its wholeness of technique and purpose, its tense unity as the figures fly and are pinned by the press of paint and ripped paper, its ordering of disintegration into a study of desperation, make it a painting of insight and power. In this work, emotion, idea and technique fuse into an image of what it is to be bodied and fleshed, what it is to suffer and yet continue the struggle to become complete and whole.

This struggle to be complete and whole shows itself in many of her later pieces. Hansen's figures intertwine and dissolve upon themselves and each other. It is as if we watch a spiritual metamorphosis from the flesh inward, the external form moulded to shape the internal perceptions, and extremes of emotion necessitate the extremes of physical distortion we experience in her work.

There is a growing impulse to harmony, to a calmness in the probing of her own responses to an acutely felt life and in the shaping of forms to express these responses. Hansen is gradually moving toward painting which has a quality of stillness, where the figures and faces seem to hover, to wait as if in the act of meditation on what it is to exist. For beyond the need to express the struggle lies her understanding of the unity she senses somewhere hidden at the heart of things, a unity which can make the journeying at least bearable. Her paintings may scream their pain but they are not works of aridity or black despair. Their vitality and their exuberant derring-do deny such pessimism.

But writing about the paintings themselves is an exercise in another form of description and is finally unnecessary. For they exist in their own right as unique and original objects. It is in a void of silence and of stillness they will make their power felt. It is this aura of stillness and silence that allows us to feel the presence of the painting. It is not that we should venerate a painting as some sort of holy object but rather that we be ready to accept what the painting does, and any dialogue that takes place will be of a pictorial nature: of symbol, of shape, of resonances of feeling and ultimately, essentially private. This is not to discard knowledge or deny criticism and fall into the mumbo-jumbo of a barbarous mysticism; rather it accepts the fact that art acts upon us in mysterious ways and at best we can only fumble to describe its effect in the alien medium of words, to describe that which defies and escapes description.

The babble of words can do more to muddle than clarify. Words become more than notes and signs toward an understanding; they become an obeisance to their own jargon and obscurities that exclude both the painting and its audience. This is not to accept ignorance and naïvety, nor to deny the human impulse to share and order by the description of that which moves, delights or alarms us. Rather, it is to recognise that the vibrations that emanate from a painting can only be fully understood in an alert and informed silence. What we say afterwards, how we explain the mystery of the experience, may be rewarding or satisfying, but compared with the significance of the active communion between the painting and the viewer, it is irrelevant.

Lys Hansen's work is redolent with the power of the unique object and in her finest achievements she transcends the personal and deeply intimate well-spring of their initial impulse. She continues to work with unfailing determination – for working is fundamental to wholeness and it is the means she has to press her deepest perceptions into a necessary order. It is a continuous struggle for her and one most of us do not have the courage to acknowledge or the strength to explore.

In her painting she offers us the imagery of her own fierce journeying. How we deal with such an honesty is how we deal with our own leap of blood.

55. *Self, Mouthless*, 1991
cat 397

VISIONS AND THE WORD: A POET'S RESPONSE TO THE WORK OF LYS HANSEN

HAYDEN MURPHY

She said she
woke up with him
in her head

So started Liz Lochhead's atypical poem of the 1980s, 'Dreaming Frankenstein'.[1] It is dedicated to Jacki Parry, June Redfern and Lys Hansen. Artists. Visual recorders of visions. Scottish interpreters of contemporary dilemmas. Diversifiers. The inclusion of Hansen had particular resonance for this commentator. It was 1984 and I was compiling a catalogue for an exhibition that would travel to Belfast and Dublin. As 'Arts in Scotland' columnist for *The Irish Times*, I had written in the previous year of my initial reaction to Hansen's work in the Open Eye Gallery, Edinburgh:

> (it has an) even curiously innocent level . . . Here were well-built pictures. Nudes, female. The catalogue notes (culled from a *Studio International* interview/article with Jonathan Benthall) spoke of 'armoured . . . inner aspects . . . (of) spiritual, physical and emotional strength'. I saw pictures of torsos well portrayed, with a glimpse of an imagination really working in the one large piece on show. I felt rather than saw 'continuity and growth' (Benthall). There was the presence of ambition; craft as opposed to contrived art.[2]

The following year I moved through a more expansive exhibition. Larger canvases, themes enlarged, a palette extended. This was in Glasgow's Third Eye Centre, as the CCA was then known. In her succinct introduction to the catalogue the Scottish writer and critic Cordelia Oliver wrote:

> Women, having discovered a new self-esteem and an articulate voice to defend themselves with in this male orientated world, have begun to make use of the various art media for purposes of propaganda. Nothing wrong with that: but it must be said that some, in doing so, are in danger of getting their priorities wrong, as artists, and of losing the very quality that can make a woman's art significant, as such.
>
> Hansen's art is not feminist in the accepted sense: rather it depends on an inner strength which seems to accompany a deeply subjective experience of being female, not merely feminine. The difference is basic: some men who paint are more 'feminine' than truly male in the sort of taste and

sensitivity they bring to bear on the work they do.

Lys Hansen's paintings involve the female nude form, but never seen as the passive object of sexual or tactile titillation which is how most men regard it. Here, on the contrary, is a living, organic entity experienced from within as a fusion of physical reality and psychological mystery which is far from passive and anything but static.

Now in early middle age (*b.* Falkirk, 1936), having reared a male family to young adulthood and finding herself able and ready to beam all her creativity back into art, Lys Hansen speaks of herself as a woman in a hurry. 'My painting has a great deal to to say about my own relationships and my own place within these relationships.' But to see what she is doing as propaganda is to miss the point: as for any good artist, the marrying of content with form is what matters first and last.

Feelings necessarily bottled up for years are now being released on canvas; complex neo-expressionist images, aggressive and angry at times, but with more than a touch of humour.[3]

I quote at length as, not for the first or last time, Oliver was to be my guidestar in Scottish, gender and artistic matters. A palimpsest on paintings becoming familiar. A selection of the Glasgow paintings, fused with 'new work of primal vitality and comparable size', made up the collection that travelled to Ireland. The exhibition was entitled 'She is She'.

Mnemonic for an Imagination:

In the arid days of early 1989 H is meeting a train to take him away from Edinburgh. Work. A poetry reading and lecture on 'The Critic's Function' on Campus. Trains are late due to the delay of the incoming one from Stirling. Suddenly there is an arrival. Passengers bump in an urgent Noon overflow and influx.

Lys, black tip-topped emerges. Disappears. 'Exhibition' she echoes.

On the journey landscapes with boulders heave into wrestling images. Flesh and tan countenanced haystacks merge through furrowed sinews tattoo in a crop of circular movements.

'Woman is the landscape and the landscape is in the woman'
Willem De Kooning

Almost a decade later it is a house in the Wicklow mountains. H is a house guest following a lecture on 'The Place of Art in the Palaces of Ireland'. He has mentioned the change of emphasis in the later work of Hansen. Many in the company reminisce about her show in the Project Arts Gallery, Dublin. H associates change, through the presence as President of Ireland of a woman who quotes poetry and once long ago read Law and Fine Arts as a contemporary.

'And for all this, nature is never spent, there lives the dearest freshness deep down things'
G.M. Hopkins

It is Easter Monday in Dublin's GPO. 1991. The 75th anniversary of Insurrection. Over a hundred artists, poets, painters, actors, pundits, politicians, have gathered to make statements.

Afterwords H sips with a group including an artist and printmaker.

'You know Lys Hansen, you wrote a bit about her. A real artist. She's got Vision.'

'She put the frighteners on me. Not her personally. I never met her. The figures. They put the Word on me.'

A moment of imaginative stagefright allows the tableaux to move in memory. Surrounded by armoured Knights and distorted heads of Queens H sits. The Red and Black of life. In this tapestry emaciated Adam becomes distanced from the apple-embracing fingers of Eve. No contest. Conflict creating Art. Fusion.

56. *Portrait Bust with Pedestal*, c.1990
cat 373

So to the internal world of the pictures both then and now. Hansen's image for Lochhead's poem is a face agape. Eyes and mouth are open and aslant to the body. There is space between the mind and the matter therein. A minefield. Such illustration is not portraiture. It is not decorative. Nor is it simply interpretative. It is reflective. It delves into the 'deep down things' of Gerard Manley Hopkins. In fact, the priest would find a soul-companion with the Scottish icon maker.

This element of her art, a secular spirituality, was given to exciting further exploration as the depth and strength of her canvases, her boards, her screens, became inhabited by gyres and spirals of extended colouration in her later work. The peacock mating with the phoenix.

Evidence of a motivation towards this expression of an 'emotive urge' can be surmised in the way she approvingly quotes from Hannah Arendt:

> . . . the modern age in its rebellion against society has discovered how rich and manifold the realm of the hidden can be under the conditions of intimacy; but it is striking that from the beginnings of history to our own time it has always been the bodily part of the human existence that needed to be hidden in privacy. All things connected with the necessity of the life process itself.[4]

Evolution's energy and, as Oliver pointed out, creative pleasure, permeate the paintings. If epitomised by one specific work it would be the maelstrom of eclectic caricature caged in

Installation, Wall of Faces. Then there is the fierce intimacy of the contemporary *Licking and Biting* (Pl.41). Carnality exciting cannibalism is the first reaction.

Then it becomes more the story of resigned (lapsed?) Christian, face to face, being tongued in the pagan Coliseum by a lion with cultivated tastes. Hansen's early work, in Richard Demarco-curated exhibitions, come to mind with *Getting in on the Act* (Pl.54). The impresario's interactive relationship with the late, great theatre director Kantor enlarge the sensibility. It is in the eyes. Here are Mother Courage's embittered European troops become History's actors. Primed characters for canvas. The eyes direct the attention. Guide the unwary viewer's eye to accept ideas convoluting unconsciously in the mind.

Further communication across the arts is aroused by *Mother's Child*. It associates both directly and in an enlightening fashion the remarks made by John Berger in a similar, familial reflective context:

> A woman must continually watch herself . . . from earliest childhood she has been taught and persuaded to survey herself continually. And so she comes to consider the surveyed and surveyor within her as two constituent yet always distinct elements of her identity as a woman.[5]

So to where Identity becomes revelation for this commentator. A triptych, *Trilogy for a New Ireland* (Pl.57), is a natural starting place. Narrative moves left to right, from *She is She* to *Grip* to *Goodbye*. Images grown up within rural Ireland re-emerge.

The gloriously exhibitionist stone carvings Sheela na Gig in church and castle niches are source references. In these gloriously happy, often masturbating figures, always female, lies an awareness of the mischief of gender differences . . . and reaction to same. In those Celtic mnemonics to servitude and in the themes of Hansen – the shapes of breasts, pudenda, fingers and continual flight from 'Christian' proprieties – have common root. As the Irish poet Nuala Archer wrote of those carvings in 1994, they are 'as rude as truth'.

These later paintings dispel the self-proclaimed 'bottled-up' approach of earlier work. The release of Dame Harridan, a confident Genie, is fulsome. When shown in Dumfries's Gracefield Studios in the early 1990s a fellow studio artist of Hansen's complained that they were 'complex, too clustered, muddied'. Maybe. So is 'rude truth'. To me, they, and subsequent large canvases, are to the eye and mind straightforward expressions of womanhood. Statements of a humane separateness without distorting distancing from humanity. Her females are both voluptuous and vulnerable. A gay – if 'sometimes hetereosexually experimental' – artist friend of mine said of her work: 'They are the better elements of a good dream.' Her males are fugitives. Not chased but distanced. Her groupings, with the expressive use of wide splayed limbs and fingers, sometimes initially suggest groping. On longer, closer concentrated observation they can be seen as terminal embraces. Familial. Etched leaves from Dante's 'Dark Wood'.

The classifiers designate her work as 'being within late-twentieth-century neo-

57. Sketch for 'The Divided Self'. Trilogy for a New Ireland (triptych), c.1985
LEFT PANEL
She is She
CENTRE PANEL
Grip
RIGHT PANEL
Goodbye
cat 255

expressionism'. In my visual experience of what faces me empirically – rather than what is presented to me by label – there is in Hansen's work not so much of the 'neo' as substantial, old-fashioned, focused narratives that are fundamentally expressive. She is Shaman.

Is she aggressive? She was certainly accepted, positively so, as such in far from gentle Ireland. So, yes. Her pictures would be failures, map-line-lies, if they failed in their representation of human aggression. She stirs.

Are her pictures 'angry'? Such was a question put to me on an arts programme . . . on radio. Wireless. No, they are not so. Always. Thematically and chronologically, they depict anger at waste. But, as I said thirteen years ago, they have a 'curiously innocent' sensuality in their portraiture of events. It is the colours that illustrate the itch, the irritation that is anger. The figurative pieces flush as if separation sheets over well-posed photographs lit by a flickering flame. Then the formal artistry takes over. Framed bodies gnaw their way as etched third-dimensional primates. And glow to glare. She is Lamplighter.

Commenting on this aspect of her work, I concluded in that ever-so-fading catalogue note:

> As an artist She is She, individually inhabiting and recreating an imaginative world that cannot be simply

58. *Archaic Sensation*, 1991
cat 409

clichéd by the word 'feminist'. I respond to the strength of womanhood. Whether she is important is really up to her own view of herself. That her paintings give me pleasure is my sense of her immediate importance to me.[6]

Still stays communication now. Her human landscapes pulse. Roots flower among barren stretches of cliff-faces. There are tales being told. Exposed. Experienced. Not always shared. But the imperative of art is to stimulate curiosity. Excite a sense of an unknown. Diversify emotion.

Visions create irrational conundrums. Words simply wound the silence about them.

LYS HANSEN: A WOMAN IN A HURRY

CORDELIA OLIVER

Thirty years or so ago, when some of us were reading books by Jack Burnham and Theodore Roszak and *The Glass Bead Game* by Hermann Hesse, a work which triggered that era of questioning accepted facts in all the arts, some of us found ourselves wondering uneasily whether it might, indeed, be true that painting, as such, was in its dying throes if not actually dead. There's no doubt that we relished the work of Marcel Duchamp and that some of us were undoubtedly excited by many of the conceptualist products brought to the 1970 Edinburgh Festival by Joseph Beuys, Günter Uecker, Klaus Rinke and the rest of the Düsseldorf artists in the exhibition 'Strategy-Get-Arts', which was organised by Richard Demarco in Edinburgh College of Art. Yet we tended to remain unconvinced by all the arguments being promoted among the forcefully proselytising avant-garde.

It must have been at that time, in the early 1970s, that a young front-rank English painter, Albert Irvin, was interviewed by a journalist who clearly hoped to push him firmly into an unwelcome corner with a statement that went something like this: 'You must admit that painting is dead and that what you are doing is no longer valid.' With his reply, heartfelt as it was, and not without humour, Bert Irvin turned the tables with a vengeance. 'Only for eunuchs,' he growled in his rich cockney voice.

Were that question to be put to Lys Hansen today, more than twenty years later, her answer might not be framed in precisely the same form, but I suspect that her put-down would be equally terse and no less convincing. Lys remains, above all, a painter for whom imagery created on a flat surface with brush and pigments is the paramount method of reflecting and, more importantly, attempting to understand and come to terms with, her own experience of life in all its aspects.

And Lys Hansen's life has indeed been a rich source of experience for a painter of her type, capable of responding to, confronting and eventually finding ways of filtering through a wealth of often striking imagery, all that fate can throw at a given individual, male or female; all the infinitesimal shades of comfort and misery that lie in between the extremes of joy and sadness.

Lys was born in Falkirk, in the central belt of Scotland, and her decision to make a life in the visual arts took her to Edinburgh College of Art for several years of study in the mid-1950s. That this was a significant choice she could scarcely have known at the time, but in fact it was so. Edinburgh College of Art was a hotbed of painterly activity, with members of the so-called 'Edinburgh School of Painting' –

the late William Gillies and William MacTaggart and, by no means least, Robin Philipson (all three knighted in later life for services to the visual arts) – leading the teaching staff in the department of drawing and painting. MacTaggart and Philipson, in particular, became known for the freedom and energy of their brushwork allied to a notable chromatic brilliance. As Lys Hansen's tutor, Philipson must have exerted a certain influence on her way of working, on the forcefulness of her brushwork and the expressive determination in the use of pigments which still invests her canvases; even, dare one say, on her courage in often attempting to send her messages in full voice and on a massive scale. The content of their work, of course, has little or nothing in common. Philipson's painting, for all the colourful, indeed energetic, bravura which immediately strikes the viewer, tends to remain largely decorative *au fond*. But Lys Hansen is a story-teller, powerful as such, and capable, at best, of arousing disquiet, even on a small scale and even in the absence of striking colour.

As her surname suggests, Lys has ancestral roots which are not Scottish. Her paternal grandfather was born on the Danish island of Bornholm in the Baltic Sea, and in several visits over recent years she has discovered to her delight that even the visual appearance of the little houses with their colour-saturated exteriors strikes a deep, responsive chord.

But this deep emotional relationship with Bornholm is a comparatively recent discovery. Her upbringing was undoubtedly Scottish, and those years at art college, surrounded by the work of the Edinburgh Colourists, must have helped to give her confidence in her own ability, consolidating that innate relish in using brush and potent colours to maximum effect. Even then, as she will tell you, she wasn't interested in the decorative side of domestic subjects, flowers and still-lifes, so dear even to her gifted contemporaries. At college Lys Hansen was undoubtedly a front-runner, winning prizes and scholarships which enabled her to travel in Europe. Yet, in common with many other gifted individuals in Scotland at the time, she decided to earn her living as a teacher, a career into which she threw herself with energy and enthusiasm, eventually lecturing part-time to art students at Glasgow School of Art and Stirling University. Energy, indeed, might be Lys Hansen's middle name. For most young women, the normal load of work involved in a teaching career, with a husband and two young sons to care for, would have left neither time nor energy, creative or otherwise, to spare for painting. But plenty of evidence exists that here is someone capable of expanding time and recharging energy *ad infinitum*.

Lys Hansen's paintings almost inevitably involve the human form to some degree, nowadays dramatically distorted more often than not. But fairly early in her career I remember seeing and admiring an attractive female nude of buxom beauty, all iridescent pinks and blues, plumply curvilinear amid exotic foliage, the whole image suggesting an affectionate nod in the direction of Matisse. Other similar, equally painterly, canvases followed, deceptively easy on the eye until, on a closer look, the image stealthily delivers its own sharp shock, rousing sensations of expansions and contractions, penetrations, splittings apart – extremes of agony and ecstasy, of primal energy and forces close to nature's own. Reminded of those split-body paintings, Lys is certain that they arose out of 'a need to take myself apart and somehow re-form myself'. In fact there is a later, more obviously stressful trilogy painted in the mid-1980s, which has been given *The Divided Self* (Pl.46 and Pl.57) as its title. Since those early years Lys Hansen has continued to search for, and find, an individual voice; increasingly potent images seem almost to erupt from the volcano of an imagination fired by a mix of anger and pity at human misery plus a kind of affectionate sorrow at human frailties.

By the early 1980s, Lys Hansen's paintings were familiar, first of all in group shows throughout Scotland and occasionally from participation in group exhibitions held overseas. For the most part, however, her reputation grew by means of a succession of solo exhibitions, mostly seen in smaller Scottish galleries. By that time, too, she had found a large studio in a converted warehouse within easy reach of her home at Blairlogie, near Stirling – a space which allowed her to realise a growing need to create some of her images on a truly monumental scale. So in 1984 she held a major show of her recent work at the former Third Eye Centre in Glasgow, an event which, to my mind, marked a milestone in her career as a serious artist.

I remember visiting her studio at that time and being struck – taken aback, almost – by the violence as well as the sheer scale of the new imagery. Even at the time I remember feeling that here was an artist who, having reared her two sons to young adulthood and finding herself able and ready to beam all her creativity back into painting, might be seen as a woman in a hurry. Here, I felt, were feelings necessarily bottled up for years being suddenly released on canvas in a rush of complex neo-expressionist images, aggressive and angry at times, but with more than a touch of gentle humour. 'These big paintings,' I wrote at the time, 'will doubtless shock the faint-hearted by the primal vitality they exude, whereas, in fact, they represent a giant step forward for an artist with half her working life in front of her, and with the creative energy plus the courage of her convictions to make best use of her talent.'[1]

One memorable canvas from that period was entitled *Performance* (Pl.52): I recall two fiercely thrusting naked figures, all huge hands and feet in wild activity, born, was it, of anger – or frustration. But even without that title, even, indeed, without knowing the artist, one might have guessed that the essential Lys Hansen has always been a physical creature, a natural performer easily roused to dance and vigorous movement. Nothing in her work seems passive. Few if any of her Scottish contemporaries seemed to me to share her brand of passionate commitment to expression at all costs. Joan Eardley was, of course, the obvious exception, not least in the late seascapes, those sometimes desperate – and surprisingly often triumphant – attempts to give powerful expression to a hyper-sensitive response to the theatre of the elements. Eardley, of course, was at the height of her short career while Lys Hansen was still a student at Edinburgh.

It was soon after that memorable Third Eye exhibition that Lys won the Scottish Arts Council award which offered her nine

LEFT
60. *Consuming and Consummation: Bridesmaid IV*, 1994
cat 485

RIGHT
61. *Consuming and Consummation: Bridesmaid V*, 1994
cat 486

OPPOSITE
59. *Bride from the East*, 1994
cat 481

months' precious freedom from teaching. Her choice of Germany as the source of the new experiences turned out to be nothing less than cathartic. As she herself has said, more than once, 'That stay in Berlin put me out into the real world. It's not just that when you go away you can see yourself, your life at home and your country, in a different way. Working like that, in a very different place, entirely on your own for nearly a year, you find yourself desperately trying to capture everything that's coming towards you. And you really do get time to explore yourself – without feeling that somebody else is invading you.' Since 1985 Lys has returned to Berlin several times in the years before and after the collapse of the Wall. It was from that experience in 1992, when she stayed in an Atelierhaus beside the former Checkpoint Charlie, that she conceived a major, meaningful painting, *Bride from the East* (Pl.59), with its smaller companion series, *Consuming and Consummation: Bridesmaids* (Pl.60 and Pl.61), in monoprint.

As a painter, Lys Hansen exhibits immense confidence in handling her media, wielding large brushes and relishing her pigments like a different kind of sustenance. Nobody, seeing her work, can possibly doubt this fact. There are times, indeed, when her paintings seem like a performance, that they tend to trigger off a muscular response, to grab you, to set you back on your heels, so to speak. 'Oh, but it isn't just about grabbing,' she insists. 'Paint is such a marvellous vehicle for expression. I also mean to whisper and caress, to lick and touch. Painted hands can protect or wound. I'm painting about emotions, about the human experience; about the four demons within all of us – greed, lust, desire and hunger.' That was the name given to one panel in a vast, impressive triptych, *Witness with Evidence* (Pl.47), which was first shown in 1994 at the Society of Scottish Artists annual exhibition.[2]

So, in her work, avid mouths with tongues and teeth feature again and again, suggesting powerful sensory as well as communicative organs. One of the panels of another large triptych *Very Human* (Pl.62), the subject derived from potent memories of a visit to a Moroccan village, conjures up and conveys her vivid memory of two heavily veiled women ululating. Every brushmark on the canvas conveys the high, painful sound; the memory of that endless ululation is the painting.

Though almost all her work is figurative, with the figures nude and often presented in more or less violent action, Hansen works from keen and constant observation, never from models in or out of the studio. Neither are her figures 'placed' in 'real' settings. They are, as she herself has said, 'in a psychic state of being'. The titles she gives them are strongly emotive rather than descriptive: for example, the head of the screaming woman in *Birthing Blind, Berlin*, with skulls reflected in her terrified eyes, vomits forth an infant; yet another triumvirate of huge, distorted heads, also painted in Berlin in 1985 and known as the *Berlin Trilogy*, scarcely need their titles, *Say Nothing, Hear Nothing, See All* (Pl.24). And one recent major work, already begun on canvas before the news of that fatal morning broke in all its horror and pity, was immediately given a new impetus, and a new dedication, *March 13 1996 Dunblane*, and a new title, *Day of the Jackal* (Pl.35). It is impossible to attempt to describe the wealth of imagery, the endless demands on one's response, when confronted by a work of this complexity.

Not all Lys Hansen's work is, or has been, on a mural scale. The *Mary Queen of Scots* series (Pl.78, Pl.79 and Pl.80) (which also, like others in recent years, has involved some three-dimensional objects) is largely modest in scale and, in terms of colour, what might even be called *sotto voce*, red pigment falling like watery blood across the paper with its often exquisite linear imagery. On a larger scale, *Death in a Red Dress* (Pl.25) carries the same chilling effect – no visual shouting necessary.

It is in recent years, however, that Lys has discovered the full power of her Nordic heritage, not least a knowledge at first hand of a seafaring ancestry that seems to have opened new windows on her life and her art. This boundless wealth of imagery, from sculptured standing-stones to the bones of big sea-creatures, from the activities of lives spent through the ages in hunting and fishing to the northern need for warmth and enclosure; all this and a great deal more besides, brought together in the net of an artist's inborn serendipity, has been taking monumental shape on the walls of her studio.

GROWING WITH THE WORK: A PERSONAL REFLECTION

GILES SUTHERLAND

If attempting to write critically about the work of a living artist has its inevitable pitfalls, then to engage in such a process when, additionally, one is related to the artist would seem to complicate the situation even further. That the artist Lys Hansen is my mother further disrupts the potential for any dispassionate and 'objective' art historical analysis. But why should writing about art lack passion or feeling – particularly when so much of the work in question seems to mix pain and compassion with the very paint with which it has been brought in being? No, this is not the place for art history – a discipline where the tools and techniques of analytical process seem curiously at odds with something so close, familiar and yet paradoxically unknown.

I can't remember when I first became aware of being surrounded by paintings, as I was from an early age. Perhaps I first remember seeing an image of myself in a large oil, painted on hardboard and framed by that angled aluminium which was so common in the 1960s. I appeared – fringed and dressed in a blue and white striped T-shirt – somewhere off-centre among a still-life composition of fruit, a table and a jug with flowers. It was a painting whose perspectives were deliberately unsettling. I can rationalise it now, but at the time this strangeness somehow rendered painting as a familiar yet unknowable quantity. And I was in the painting, but somehow not its subject.

Growing up in central Scotland was a curious business for one who had seen and been seen from such perspectives. I attended a small school in Alloa but soon after moved to the local primary school in Menstrie. It may be a trick of memory or the product of repeated telling but the first question I can remember being asked was: 'What team do you support?' (the choice was not vast – either Rangers or Celtic). The second question was: 'Are you a Catholic or a Protestant?' In Scotland, the two questions were – and to a large extent still are – synonymous. Despite my brief attendance at Episcopalian St John's, I had no idea what either was. I now realise that my parents had never mentioned or succumbed to the petty, tribal, pseudo-religious loyalties which had infected so many of my very young classmates, who had been turned overnight into five-year-old bigots.

None of this seemed to have much to do with the fringed boy in the stripey T-shirt in that bright but strange painting. I kept quiet about the art, sensing that was the best position to adopt to ensure survival. Occasionally bits of the truth slipped out: 'Was that your sister who brought you to school?', I was asked one day. My mum didn't look like the other mums. Often I wished or prayed that I could be 'the same'. I didn't really like all this art stuff. It set me apart. I was ashamed.

Later, at secondary school, the world of the imagination was marginalised, though its nourishing flame was kept alive by a few precious souls who recognised its importance. So, in those days at least, art was mostly an alien thing here too. I cringed when, in the interest of social investigation, one of our teachers asked us all, in turn, the respective professions of our parents. Doubtless there were others who dreaded this imposition, but as I mouthed the word 'artist', I wished for deliverance.

Why was I so embarrassed by this association? Undoubtedly, being an artist – and the son of an artist – is not a run-of-the-mill thing. But there was more to it than that. It was Freud who first defined the Oedipus complex as the son's sexual impulse towards the mother, who is the first embodiment of sexual desire. Lys Hansen's paintings are undoubtedly sexual and the predominance of the female nude in my early life undoubtedly confirmed this association. Following a large spread in the then *Glasgow Herald* which showed my mother posed beneath a voluptuous blue female nude, there was much innuendo and blunt comment in the classroom as to the effect of these pictures on adolescent sexuality. Nakedness, nudity and sexuality all merged into one frightening but simultaneously alluring and forbidden world of adult knowingness. I was confused

62. *Very Human* (triptych), 1995
LEFT PANEL
The Greater Spotted Lover
CENTRE PANEL
The Sadness of Men without Women
RIGHT PANEL
Speaking in Tongues
cat 505

and maybe even angered, but I didn't know it.

Things changed, though. My first girlfriend was overawed and full of admiration on her first visit to our house, its walls festooned with paintings. Her view gave me strength and pride. And at university things got better. Suddenly it was *cool* to have a mother as an artist. I took pride in the work and strove to understand it. Lys Hansen's show at the Third Eye Centre in 1984 was a turning point. I was twenty and wrote:

> . . . the art has been moulded, more than anything, by life itself; the most voluminous source materials are the artist's own experiences . . . the paintings deal with interactions between people and the emotions and responses provoked by these interactions. The most accomplished and important painting is *Performance* (1983) – it has evolved over a year or more; worked and reworked, its conclusion is definite, forceful. *Performance* is many things – it remains deliberately ambiguous, open to interpretation . . .[1]

The piece is signed 'Giles Hansen Sutherland' and, despite its self-consciousness, it was, I now realise, a brave effort for someone barely emerged from their teenage years. I was coming to terms with the work, and growing up from it and with it. Doubtless the performance threw up in my own mind not only generalised human sexual relations but also reflected my own uncertain forays into the complexities of sexual encounter.

At the time of this exhibition I was editing

63. *Dreaming Frankenstein*, 1984
cat 175

(along with the now accomplished writer Duncan McLean) a literary broadsheet, *Clanjamfrie*,[2] which featured new and established writers from Scotland and further afield. I went along to a reading by Liz Lochhead and was surprised and pleased when she read out a poem 'Dreaming Frankenstein' dedicated to the artists Jacki Parry, June Redfern and Lys Hansen. We asked Liz for permission to reproduce the poem alongside a charcoal-wash illustration by Lys Hansen, one of a series which she made for *Clanjamfrie*:

> She said she
> woke up with him in
> her head, in her bed
> . . . she knew – oh that was not how –
> but he'd entered her utterly.[3]

64. Ludwig Andreas Hansen

The poem conflates the creative process with the sexual one – here a violent and penetrative act. It was a strong combination of word and image and one which gave *Clanjamfrie* a credibility and strength which belied the youthfulness and inexperience of its editors. I have the image of this 'monster' (*Dreaming Frankenstein*) (Pl.63) in my home – sometimes its sadness and pathos makes me take it from the walls. I cannot look at it. It is not an illustration to the poem any more than the poem seeks to illustrate the visual work. The two are symbiotically linked, but separate. When I see this face, the phrase *qui tollis peccata mundi* moves through my mind. A friend from Alabama once told me that it was the face of a slave in thrall for a lifetime. Mary Shelley's 'monster' was not the pieced-together being whose pain and betrayal led to murder and revenge; it was rather the impulse within all of us to create that which we cannot control. In that sense we are all 'monsters', and the agonised face makes me confront these impulses within myself. Is it perhaps a mirror for all who look within?

What makes one ascribe national characteristics to a work of art? Is there such a thing as 'Scottish art' other than art which has been created in Scotland or by Scottish people? At times, in moments of misplaced nationalism, I had wondered why Lys Hansen's work did not seem more 'Scottish'. Maybe I longed for it to be so and perhaps this feeling had come from partially misconstrued notions about the importance of a nationally defined art as espoused by MacDiarmid and his followers. I have become increasingly uneasy with the notion of cultural nationalism which seeks to create or recreate a 'tradition' which has a tenuous and often spurious genealogy. There is very little that is specifically 'Scottish' about Lys Hansen's work and I feel that this is the way it should be. The work fits more happily into a wider European tradition which, as other writers in this collection point out, embraces the likes of Munch, the German Expressionists and contemporary painters like Wiig Hansen in Denmark. Elsewhere, Mette Bligaard explores these connections in more detail, conscious of my mother's Danish ancestry of which she and my grandfather were both proud and curious.

My great-grandfather, Ludwig Andreas Hansen (Pl.64), left the island of Bornholm in 1888 at the age of fourteen and eventually settled, after years at sea, in Scotland, first in Leith and then in Grangemouth. I myself live on the River Forth, Scotland's huge inviting mouth, which has seduced many a seafarer, and so I trace Hansen's voyage into the womb of my country. He was a huge man by all accounts and had to have his smocks specially made. He spoke eight languages and in the evenings, smoking a gentle pipe, he could be found turning the wireless dial to Warsaw, Stockholm, Moscow, Cologne and Oslo, his ear tuned to the tongues that had colonised, traded with and in turn been ousted from his own native island. In Lys Hansen's *Requiem for a Sailor* (Pl.65) I sense the spirit of this man.

So what should we make of Lys Hansen's treatment of Scottish subject-matter? Undoubtedly, this was a late, perhaps unexpected and for me a welcome, development in a corpus of work whose boundaries were constantly expanding and whose subject-matter was continuously evolving.

Agnes Hansen (*née* Burns) (Pl.67) and Alfred William Hansen (Pl.66), my

65. *Requiem for a Sailor*, 1989
cat 324

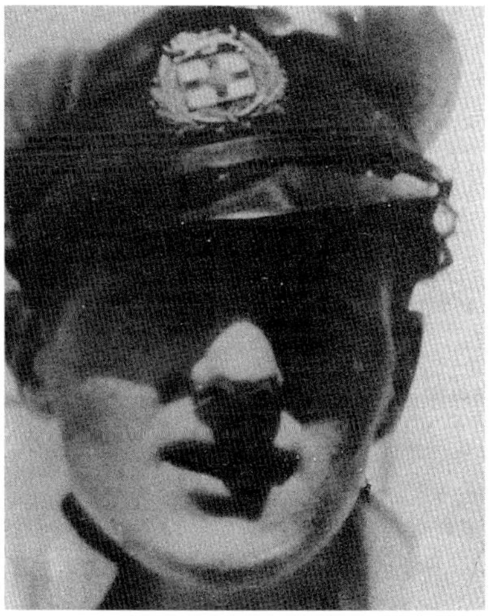

TOP
66. Alfred William Hansen

MIDDLE
67. Agnes Hansen (*née* Burns)

BOTTOM
68. James Burns

grandparents, died within a few months of each other in 1990. We were a close family, emotionally and physically, and their deaths affected me profoundly. The sense of grief and loss was intense, because they had always been there. At my grandparents' funerals I read poems by Robert Burns (Pl.76) – 'A man's a man for a' that' for my grandfather and 'Afton Water' for my grandmother. This poet's work has a particular resonance in my mother's painting. Burns was an important presence in my mother's life: my grandfather was a devotee and would quote passages with passion and sincerity, particularly after a couple of glasses of *uisge beatha*. My grandmother was born and grew up in rural Ayrshire. Her father, James Burns (Pl.68), a shoemaker and piper, born in 1874, must have been only the third or fourth generation since Robert Burns's death in 1796. Burns had therefore died within the living memory of my great-grandfather's time. Robert Burns wasn't a dim and distant historical figure, like Shakespeare or Milton. He was alive. Doubtless my mother felt this link too and the combination of this kind of familial immersion and the unarguably tragic nature of Burns's life and untimely death at the age of thirty-seven made him seem very close. Perhaps it is part of an increasing desire to re-assess Scottishness that artists in Scotland feel able to tackle subjects such as these; certainly the exploding of some of the shabby myths surrounding Burns is a welcome development.

I have a number of Lys Hansen's works in my home besides the Frankenstein image. One of these is called *The Angel at the Crossing* (Pl.69)

RIGHT
69. *The Angel at the Crossing*, 1990
cat 337

BELOW
70. *The Crossing*, 1990-91
cat 380

and it is one of those images which Richard Demarco in the foreword to this collection rightly points out 'aspire to the condition of prayer'. It is a small piece – uncharacteristically so, only perhaps eight inches by ten inches. The palette is dark and heavy – a kind of sonorous *gravitas* in oil. In it, a central form – the image of the crucifixion – structures the work and lends it both narrative and metaphor. My grandfather once told me that having placed five large stones on the lane which led to his house, he had imbued them with meaning: *birth*, *life*, *death*, *resurrection* and *ascension*. In that intimate and private description, he revealed himself to be a man of deeply spiritual values who, despite a limited education, strove to make sense of the world around him. It seemed fitting, therefore, that my mother had also turned, in the series of works of which *The Angel at the Crossing* is a part, to Christian metaphor in order to try to come to terms with the loss of her parents. As with any work of art worthy of the name, *The Angel at the Crossing* has a resonance beyond the particular associations it has for me. It stands as a more universal statement on its subject-matter and acts as a potential prayer for those who might seek meaning and solace from its substance.

The grief surrounding my grandparents' death was almost unbearable for my mother. But this deeply painful but inevitable and human experience was explored repeatedly in a number of works; grief was worked out on the canvas, a catharsis through the medium of paint. The grief *is* the work. The Crossing is the movement from our world to another – what should we call it? – the world of the spirit and the soul. In Norse mythology it was called Valhalla and I think this is as good as any for my grandfather. In his large life he had been sailor, soldier, labourer, baker, fisherman, gardener. He gave me a love of the land and something of a self-sufficiency of the spirit. I miss him terribly but he lives on and this painting is one of the places in which I find him.

In Scotland you are never far from the landscape. Even in the midst of its cities it is difficult not to catch a glimpse of a hill from the streets. My grandparents had a number of my mother's works on their walls, all landscapes, curiously the least explored area in my mother's painting. Recently I rescued one of these from the lock-up which acts as the store for her work. It is a painting done in 1956 of a Norwegian fiord (Pl.71) and is a record of my mother's first trip abroad. It had hung in my grandparents' house for as long as I can remember. Done when my mother was nineteen, it struck a chord with my grandparents and was an image which obviously held a great deal of meaning for them. I had it glazed and reframed and it hangs in my kitchen. Another work was the view which one gets looking due west from my grandparents' home in Blairlogie – trees, hills, field. The wood actually surrounds a now silted-up curling pond, part of the former Blair estate. Besides the native birch and oak is evidence of more exotic planting – huge poplars, cypresses and rhododendron. I knew the woods well as a boy and it always struck me as a curious double-vision looking out of my grandparents' window to a view which simultaneously existed as a painting on the walls.

Once, I had been salmon-fishing with my

grandfather on the River Dochart and had fallen asleep while he fished further downstream. Concealed beneath the bank there had been no sign of me and I now think of the desperate afternoon he must have spent wandering up and down the swollen river looking for the drowned corpse, his hopes of a fine spring-run fish in ruins as he framed the words he would give to my parents and the police. We drove home in silence until the hills behind the village loomed in a squash of purple and I remarked that they reminded me of my mum's painting in his house. There was no response.

A friend once said that growing up surrounded by paintings must have had a strong impact. It has – how could it not? The externalisation of such on-the-edge emotion in a culture which is traditionally buttoned-up – thin-lipped, even – gives you a different slant on life. But there were gentler images. You know these terrible difficulties and pleasures are there and sometimes you wanted to shut them up, shut them out. But you step back, take stock, and consider this rawness. You need the distance, not least to assert and become yourself.

71. Norwegian Fiord, 1956
cat 1

LEFT
72. *Self-portrait*, 1959
cat 8

BELOW
73. *Boatmaker's Fish Garden*, 1966
cat 19

INTERVIEW WITH LYS HANSEN

GILES SUTHERLAND

Braco, Perthshire, 8 and 23 March 1998

1. EDINBURGH COLLEGE OF ART

Can you describe the ambience and atmosphere at Edinburgh College of Art? Did your teachers share some particular characteristics in their methods and approach to painting?

On the whole they were very kindly as teachers and very pleasant to work with. Most of them belonged to a much more decorative or 'female' tradition in art. Working from a post-war point of view, they also made a connection with France and the *joie de vivre* in French painting. As students we were required to look at a lot of artists' work, particularly Bonnard's; I saw it in Paris on one of my scholarships. His work is brilliant in terms of beauty of paint and his concept of light.

One of my teachers, Charles Pulsford, tended to be more rebellious and angry than the others; he was very well respected by the students and I found him an interesting teacher, particularly in my post-graduate year. Philipson was flamboyant, of course. Gillies had a very pawky sense of humour and would point to a piece of colour and say, 'Aye, bonnie colour!' Johnny Maxwell talked about his garden. I was in MacTaggart's still-life class. They were all splendid painters. Philipson was certainly a very enthusiastic teacher, as was Jimmy Cumming. None of them had political aspirations, however – art wasn't for politics or for changing the world. It was, I suppose, for celebrating its beauty. Maybe this was because of the harsh reality of the war and the restrictions it imposed – the lack of joy.

Did you make a conscious decision to go to Edinburgh or was it something that happened by default?

I come from a working-class background where my parents knew nothing about art or really all that much about education, except that education was valuable. I applied to both Edinburgh and Glasgow and when I received the acceptance from the former, my mother advised me to go there. The decision was taken like that; perhaps she thought at that time Glasgow was maybe a bit rough . . .

You had some contemporaries or near-contemporaries at Edinburgh College of Art. They have all taken their own directions but perhaps you've taken a very different direction from many of them.

A lot of people haven't continued to paint or haven't decided to develop their skills. Kenny Dingwall is one exception; he also comes from Alloa, so there's a marginal connection there. He was a very introverted person and this is why his work tends to cover everything up; it makes a celebration of hiding. I haven't got that kind of character. I want to open everything up; I want to look at everything, which is a very vulnerable position. But I find that if I open it up and I look at it, I can understand. I try to understand myself, the world and other people better.

Other contemporaries included Bob Callender who was in the year above me. There was Peter Stitt who went off to Australia and is working most interestingly and very well. Additionally, David Harding went on to significant things at Glasgow School of Art. Eric Hilton left Scotland and went to America – he's important in terms of carrying his vision and achieving it in an entirely different society and different culture.

You come from a working-class background, but your parents supported you in your education. Where did the art come from and why did you pursue that particular direction?
It wasn't really a poor background – it was rich in many ways: in feeling, expression, love and warmth. Both my parents were expressive and gifted in music. My upbringing was rich in poetry; my father was very keen on Robert Burns. The arts were very strong in my family; there was a love of stories, dreams and imagination.

How would you characterise your parents' attitude towards your work? It couldn't have been easy for them to accept a lot of the work . . .
They clearly didn't understand it, but they loved me unconditionally; they certainly would never stop me. They watched and let me achieve in my own way. They had faith in me because I was so focused and so strong that if they tentatively interfered or suggested I might be wasting my time they knew this would just make me more determined.

In 1956 you made a trip to Norway. That seems to have been a significant event . . .
Yes. There were Norwegian students studying in Edinburgh and some of my friends and I got to know some of them. Norway was the first foreign country I ever went to – before Paris – and I saw the work of Edvard Munch. Although I liked his work, however, I didn't analyse it at that stage.

Why was the cultural and intellectual orientation in Scotland towards France?
Well, these teachers were Celts – they had a love of colour and were passionate. They also had a desire for sunny living; painting is also about dreaming too. I think all of this had a strong influence on them. Unfortunately, it caused a lot of Scottish art from that period to go into a very domestic *cul de sac*. This is still the case today, although there are some wonderful painters. But the paint isn't being used like a sword or a lance of the mind to probe into a different level. That's where I felt I really didn't fit because I knew I had other important reasons for painting.

2. GERMANY

You've used the terms 'lance' or 'probe' to describe how painting enters the mind as a political act. That's certainly embodied, at least on the surface, much more forcibly in the German tradition. You went to Germany in 1985 . . .
I had been there as a student in 1959–60. I had a travelling scholarship in Europe and I

had gone to the museums. However, 1985 was a very significant journey. We have to think very much about the northern European character; we have a dismal climate and it's often very grey. We spend a lot of time in the cold in winter and there is a great deal of angst. Scotland itself has been in a poor political state for many years. In the past there has often been a tendency to bury our heads in the sand and paint pretty pictures. I think there's a new consciousness that's come through the arts in the 1980s: that Scotland has its own particular political identity, its own problems and has really got something to say, and I think I'm part of that.

What was it about Germany that attracted you? Why didn't you go to France or somewhere else?
I had been at a Housing of the Arts conference put on by Richard Demarco during the Edinburgh Festival.[1] I had heard many speakers discussing their buildings and their new art, particularly in Germany. There were also delegates from Australia and the United States. The German situation was the most impressive: their buildings, their collections and their attitude that art and artists were an important and intelligent political force. This is not the situation in Scotland. People here often want art to be pretty and uncontentious; there's nothing wrong with it being attractive and beautiful – something you admire in your home – but that's not *only* what art is about. Scotland is small and dominated by the four art schools. The majority of successful artists in Scotland taught in these colleges and dominated the concept of art as they were training young people. Those who left – for example, John Bellany and Alan Davie, who soon got out of Scotland – realised that there was a bigger world that they wanted to explore in terms of art.

You went to Berlin in 1985 for two months with a Scottish Arts Council award. This experience profoundly affected your work . . .
For the first time since I had been a student I was on my own and I didn't have a family to look after and no one else to consider except myself. It was extremely dramatic. For the first time in twenty-odd years I could just be an artist. That meant I could get up and work all day, go to the museums, come back and be totally alone. It was gruelling because we need other people to endorse our identities. Being alone day after day meant that I could go very deep inside myself, which was important. I did a lot of work and let everything come out. I made enormous headway for myself in terms of exploring and gaining confidence and power in my work.

Where did some of the images that you made come from, and what did they relate to?
The *Berlin Trilogy* (Pl.24) stemmed from the saying 'Speak no evil, hear no evil, see no evil'. This work is about suppression, which is with us all of our lives whether it is personal or political. I was thrust into central Europe and the extraordinarily isolated city of West Berlin. It seemed to heighten my own isolation. You pick up something in the airwaves – it was highly stimulating to be alone in a country where I didn't know the language. It was lonely, terrifying and I needed my paint and my expression very strongly.

Because I use the human form, I started to

LEFT
74. *Where am I? (Wir bin Ich?)*, 1985
cat 207

OPPOSITE
75. *It Happened at the Wall*, 1992
1 *Shaft*
2 *Man Searching for a Thread*
3 *I Spy*
4 *Tooth and Nail*
5 *Moment of Truth*
6 *I Have my Dead Ones*
7 *Run Rabbit Run*
8 *Don't Look Down*
cat 445–452

focus very strongly on the parts of the body. These can be highly significant – whether it's a finger and a fingernail over the mouth, or a hand over the eye or a hand covering the ears. These are strong gestures of humanistic dilemma and my psyche was very in tune with this because I had been suppressing my needs and my desires as an artist. Creatively, I had almost died because I wasn't pursuing these.

Why is the human body the inevitable vehicle for these expressions in your work?

It's all that you have when you come into this world and you have to live in it. We are conditioned by it in so many ways. It's something I know best of all from the inside. In Berlin it seemed I was right inside something. That was important that I and the paint were inside, coming out, rather than taking a landscape or a view of a city and being detached from it.

The experience of Berlin enabled you to look inside yourself, not inside that very different culture. Later you did begin to explore the political arena in Germany . . .

I decided that I was linked in a way to all humanity. It was important to develop the 'masculine principle', that strong constructive side, that is energetic, can be aggressive and is certainly powerful. In the early 1980s I started feeling much more whole because I felt a better balance between my feminine and masculine sides.

You visited Berlin on a number of occasions. Did you find that your work changed when you were there or did it change in the intervening periods?

I think it's about a feeding ground – plants and people all need to be where they can grow, and I work very well in Berlin. I like my responses when I'm there. I don't know why that is – it's very curious. On my last visit to Berlin I also went from there to Bornholm where my grandfather came from.

3. ANCESTORS

Was that another significant turning point?

Yes. It was important for me to see myself in a much broader European context. When you are away from the place where you normally live you can look back at yourself and your country in a much more objective way, with perspective. Bornholm was a place I had heard about but had never visited. I feel a strong attraction for that particular area and I am responding to something that's deep inside myself.

I wanted to see this island because of my grandfather, who had been a sailor. When I saw Bornholm I started to realise why he wanted to leave: to find out what was across the sea. There is a connection between his sense of adventure and my own need to travel and to explore with paint. It is an extraordinary adventure and takes a lot of courage. If a student were to ask me what would be most useful to them in their journey in being an artist, I would say it's courage.

Can you tell me a bit more about the work you've been doing subsequent to your visit to Bornholm?

I've been looking at the connections between the Vikings and the Celts. I see these peoples as being highly imaginative and passionate visionaries. They left a lot of artwork and expressions of their culture. I question my own education and the emphasis on the Renaissance in Italy. This rich Celtic and Viking culture has not been given adequate emphasis in the education system.

I'm working at the moment on a large triptych. There's a central image derived from a photograph of human remains in an archaeological excavation in Denmark.[2] She now looks like a warrior figure – a woman with her skull like some kind of helmet, an amazing mane of flaxen hair streaming out behind her. Part of her torso has decomposed to reveal ribs and her spine and pelvic girdle. But the skin has remained intact on her thighs so that we have this extraordinary image of modernity.

It's like she's almost sort of walked into the studio today and yet she's so ancient and has been preserved in peat. I suppose it's my fascination with life and death. The spinal column or backbone is important – you need 'backbone' to get through everything in life.

There is also the story of Eve and how God took one of Adam's ribs and formed her. Women have always been held up as an icon for their beauty, their flesh and their form. This young woman is still extraordinarily beautiful and yet she's been carved away but she still retains her spirit and energy. In a strange way I've resurrected her so she's a symbol of the ancient and the modern coming together. From the past we learn about the future.

These paintings will be exhibited in Bornholm in the autumn of 1998. How do you anticipate the reaction to these works?
Bornholm is well known for its landscape painting and portraiture. I don't think it has a heritage of strong figurative art apart from portraiture, so I'm hoping that the people of the island will find this aspect new and interesting. I hope they will recognise themselves in the images. There is another piece I am working on which I haven't resolved yet; it's provisionally titled *We Are One Another*. We are each other – this is what makes our links with the past and helps us go on to the future; it is what makes us human.

4. IRELAND AND CONFLICT

You visited Ireland a number of years ago . . .
I had an exhibition in Belfast and Dublin in 1985.[3] I was very moved by my visit – the country was tearing itself apart.

An important work in this show was The Divided Self (Trilogy for a New Ireland), *which is a metaphor for the body politic being torn apart . . .*
Absolutely. *She is She* was one panel, *Grip* was the centre panel with the head ripping itself apart, and *Goodbye* was the dream, I suppose, that conflict – both political and personal will be resolved.

You made a trip to Jerusalem a number of years ago. You seem to be attracted to areas of political difficulty.
The Middle East is an area which is invariably in conflict and people seem to focus on the differences rather than what they have in common. We all have a connection with each other, but peoples and governments seem to emphasise our differences and fight over these aspects. I'm concerned with the conflict and I try to resolve it in my work as well as I can. I face the problem and try to find an image to resolve it. I know it's only just paint, but that's where my skill lies.

Do you think that making art can make a difference? Joseph Beuys, for example, believed this.
Yes. People have said to me after looking at my work, 'That is how I feel.' I am not the only one who feels this way – there are others coping with these problems but when I put it into paint I can reflect on it in an extraordinarily powerful way.

Do you feel that, as the artist, you are acting as some kind of emotional conduit for society?
Yes. I have a specific function: to pick up on the things that other people find difficult to deal with. I can take shapes and colours and give them some kind of physical form, although at times it remains strangely abstract and elusive.

Do you think you feel more than other people – more intensely?
I think I am required to tune into these things whereas other people might push them away and perhaps not deal with them. I have specifically acquired the skills to respond in a highly sensitive way.

5. TEACHING

You have done a significant amount of teaching. How important is that to you?
One of the most exciting things about being an artist is surprising yourself. Working with students also allows this to happen: they can surprise and delight themselves. I've always been very keen to pull wonderful things out of them and free an area that has been not developed or has not been considered valuable. I see each student as a tremendous challenge – the live debate between teacher and student can be highly creative. It is exciting to work with another person whose ideas are continually evolving. I evolved myself and that was exciting too. I learned to be a dynamic teacher and that has integrated very much into my work.

I put my whole self and energy into it. I attempt to open up the students so they examine themselves. I've taught students who were timid and unsure of themselves to develop a confidence, a power and a skill – that was miraculous to watch. I've seen it happen in hours, in a few days, sometimes over a number of years. I was able to help them get access to themselves. You'd almost have to ask one of them what the process was, it was so magical.

You have or have had many roles in life: mother, wife, daughter, teacher, artist. Where do you find the time?
If it's important, you find the time for what you want. Everybody has the same time in the world – it's how you use it. Women are very good at juggling time because they have to deal with the families, make the tea, answer the children's questions, do many things at the same time. They're very agile with time because they've had to be. I've always had to carve out an area for myself after work and after my responsibilities of my home and children. I wouldn't like to have been without this because it equipped me with an understanding of love and knowledge. The recent power and confrontation in the work is because I've grown up. I know what I want to paint. I have a reason for painting, not just wanting to push paint around but to do something specific with it.

6. SCOTLAND: FAMILY, ROBERT BURNS AND MARY QUEEN OF SCOTS

Your mother, Agnes Hansen (née *Burns) grew up in Ayrshire as did Robert Burns. In 1986 you were asked to explore Burns and his work . . .*
Mike Bailey of the Maclaurin Gallery in Ayr[4] invited me, along with a dozen other artists, to look at the work of Robert Burns. Although Burns was very familiar to me, I nevertheless spent a whole week reading the poems, seeing where my spirit could click and fit for that particular piece. I fastened on a poem entitled 'Sketch. Inscribed to The Rt. Hon. Ch. J. Fox Esq. –', written in English:

How Wisdom and Folly meet, mix and unite;
How Virtue and Vice blend their black and their white;[5]

This appealed to me enormously because it's a struggle that exists within all of us: the good and the not-so-good and all the grey areas. This was an amazing piece of language for me to focus on. I had been dealing with the non-isolated figure – for example, a woman's body is occupied by many, her husband, her children. It's a body strongly related to the earth and so the painting evolved as one person, but at the same time acknowledging the dilemma of virtue, vice, wisdom and folly.

LEFT
76. Alexander Nasmyth: *Robert Burns*
Scottish National Portrait Gallery

BELOW
77. *Thou know'st that Thou hast formed me with passions wild and strong; and list'ning to their witching voice has often led me wrong (No.1)*, 1996
cat 532

Burns is so relevant. The work may have been written in the eigtheenth century but even today its meaning is profound. It's disappointing that it wasn't taught at school but the echoes of it in my own home were rich and good. Recently I looked at Burns again, once again by invitation from Cyril Gerber at the Compass Gallery.[6] I chose a poem called 'A Prayer, in the Prospect of Death' and used these lines from it as the title of my painting (Pl.77):

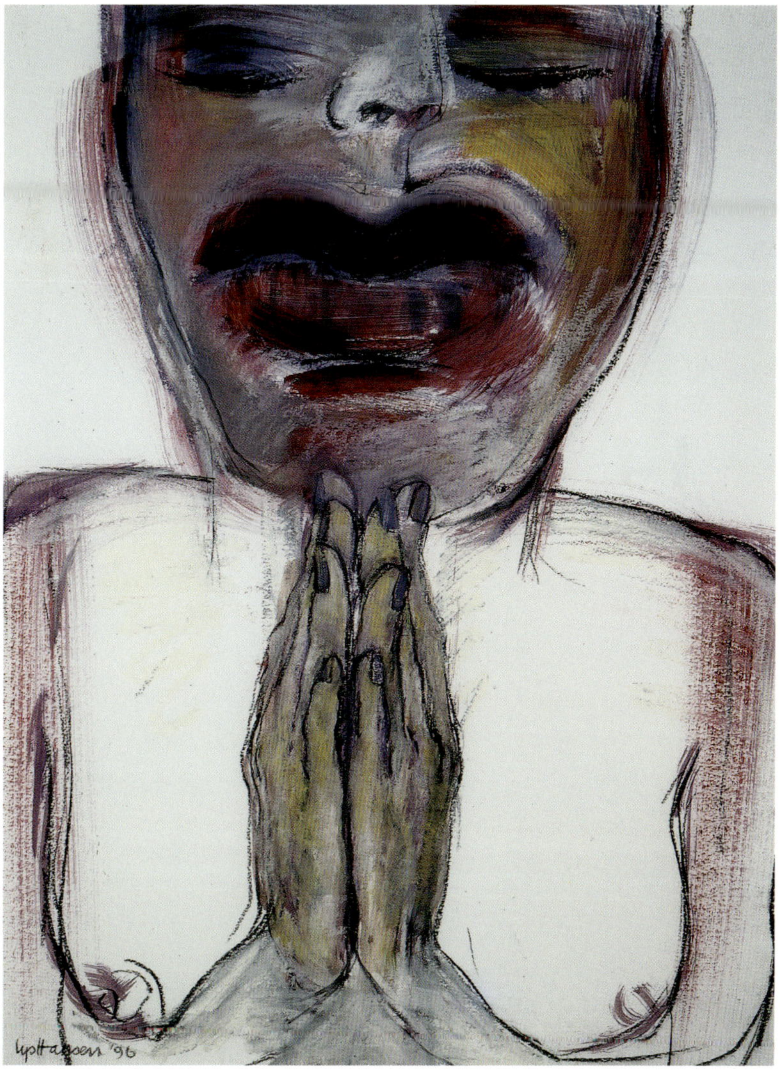

Thou know'st that Thou hast formed me,
With Passions wild and strong;
And list'ning to their witching voice
Has often led me wrong.[7]

Burns is able to put into so few words such profundity of meaning and human emotion. I like his work enormously – it rings true from deep inside. The painting focused on the mouth and the hands. The mouth is saturated in terms of the experience of life – food or love – or is party to deception. The clasped hands represent the touching of the self and asking for forgiveness of oneself for one's inadequacies.

Other writers have influenced my work – D.H. Lawrence, tremendously so. I have always found his work highly sensitive and very oriented towards the female aspects. Also the work of Sylvia Plath, Ted Hughes[8] and Virginia Woolf. It is the minds of these people that I relate strongly to. I take great inspiration from their words and their thoughts.

Your father, Alfred Hansen, he had a passion for Burns. Where do you think that came from?
It came largely from his passion for life; he recognised himself in many ways in Burns – perhaps he would have liked to have been a poet. He certainly sang extremely well. He was a 'man's man' but he also had a highly romantic side. He quoted not only from Burns but also from Omar Khayyám. He tried to find a philosophy that suited his spirit. He certainly was larger than life, volatile and was full of energy. I miss him and his largeness of spirit – he was generous, raucous and quite unforgettable.

As well as Burns you've also looked at some other aspects of Scottish life – in particular Mary Queen of Scots. This has been a fairly recent development in your work . . .
It was 1991 and I was, I suppose, grieving for both parents at the time. I was invited to take part in an exhibition about Mary Stuart organised by Emily Ash.[9] This focused my reading on Mary. Once again I feel the teaching of Scottish history which I had experienced at school had been somewhat lacking and we passed over Mary quickly. As a mature woman I was able to interpret her life, her suffering and her tragic end and that was a tremendous challenge.

I tried to do the work – particularly my representation of the execution in as delicate a manner as possible. As an expressionist painter, I have learned to relate to emotion – and the great pain that Mary was undoubtedly experiencing – in much the same way as an actress interpreting a part. I found it very exciting to do; I loved doing it. I was brought up in the Church of Scotland but they've taken everything away; they've left the walls bare and sometimes they've left the spirit and the soul somewhat blank. Making things gives the hands a purpose and the heart comfort; I found it good to put my grief into these pieces. I also did *A Banner for Mary* (Pl.79), with the huge Scottish rampant lion. Scotland devoured and mauled Mary and did not come to her aid – but then she was a political pawn. It was embarrassing having this woman as the head of a country; it was convenient for some members of the Scottish nobility to get rid of her.

Robert Burns and Mary Queen of Scots both endured great personal suffering in different ways. Do you feel somehow that you are able to connect with these people? Is this necessary to make art?
I don't think it's necessary to connect with them to make art. Some people can form their art in a more distant way, but that's just not how I am. There are people in the world who perhaps feel too much, or they take it upon themselves to attend to these areas in life for others. It's like people perhaps who

OPPOSITE
78. ***Mary Queen of Scots: The Execution*****, 1991**
cat 412

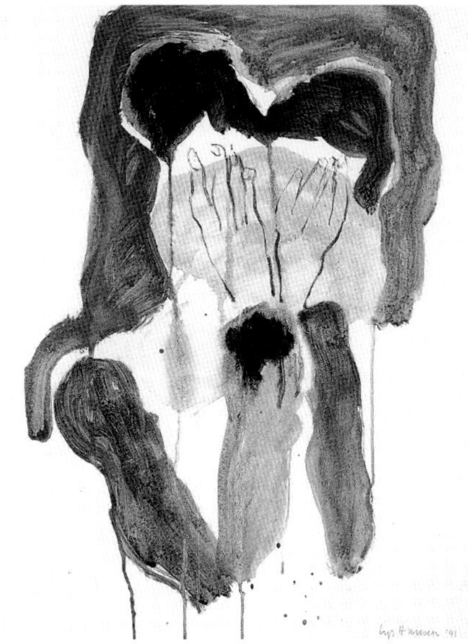

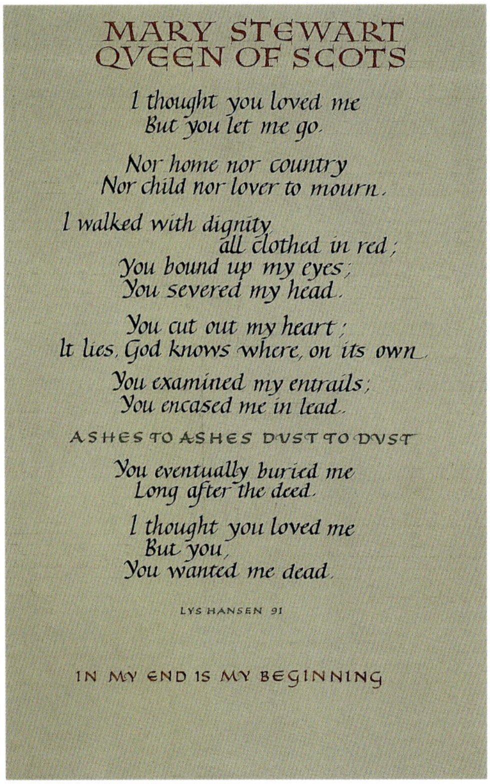

TOP
79. *A Banner for Mary*, 1991
cat 413

BELOW
80. *Mary Queen of Scots*, 1991

are good at gardening: they make the flowers grow for the rest of us. A lot of people feel these things too without a doubt. I have always felt I had a gift to reflect on these areas. It's important in life to feel the extremes. There are great joys and great sorrows and often they are inter-mixed. That is what it is to be human and that's what it is to make your art.

Have any other things been of significance in your upbringing?
Yes. I have been profoundly influenced by the fact that my brother, Louis (Ludwig) Hansen, experienced learning difficulties and had special educational needs. This made me aware from a young age that whatever talent one had – even 'average' talent – it should not be squandered. I couldn't understand, for example, why talented people at art school wasted their time going to the pub. As a child I felt I had to achieve for both Louis and myself. His disability caused a lot of pain and disappointment in the family.

One of my paintings, *The Mother's Child* relates specifically to my feelings about my brother. When a woman is pregnant she thinks constantly about the baby and if it will be healthy. If the child is not 'perfect' it is inevitably the woman who carries the burden of guilt, as I think my mother did.

7. LANDSCAPE AND NATURE

You have painted landscape in Norway, France and Scotland. It has been a recurrent if not always prominent aspect of your work. Do you feel that it is an important presence?
Yes. I've used landscape but usually through the human form. I live directly under the

Ochil Hills: these forms are usually black and huge at night; sometimes they are smooth and voluptuous like velvet. It doesn't matter where you are in the area, your eyes are drawn to them. They change with the weather, the light and relative to one's own position. Some of these forms have featured in my work. Many of the huge forms and figures in my work are intertwined, like an enormous hill range.

Landscape painting in Scotland has been so well done by so many artists. I chose to turn my attention to an inner landscape where I felt I could make some contribution. It is most challenging to try and work with what is on the inside.

These painters were painting inner landscapes through the external landscape. The best landscape painters were really painting themselves . . .

Projecting themselves in their landscapes – yes, I would agree with that. I always return to people. For me, they are the most fascinating. They are the land, the country, the nation.

TOP
81. Louis Hansen

BELOW
82. Lys Hansen as a child

In your upbringing there was a certain closeness to nature and there are aspects of your work which touch on the natural world – animals, for example. Does this mean a great deal to you?

Yes. I was brought up in the country, walking the land and watching its changing seasons, its changing light and shapes. Nature was always pointed out to me as I walked the fields with my father. These were strong and vital lessons in learning – to use one's eyes and to enjoy the world around.

The goose features in my work. We used to keep geese and the head of a goose just appeared in my painting, *One and the Other* (Pl.37). It's also the Chinese symbol of creativity. The goose and the wild-goose-chase – I think painting is a bit like that too. The torso was about reforming my own body, my own physicality, my own attitude, my own ideas, my own expectancy of myself and what I could achieve. This is the responsibility of each individual to themselves: to dig in, go in and find out what is valuable. Nobody else can do this except yourself. Each of us has to take on our own responsibilities from what we want in life and try to get access to it, and I did that through paint.

8. DUNBLANE

Another aspect of your work which has been continuous if not prominent, is your use of construction, assemblage and sculpture . . .
I've always collected. Many artists collect things when they're out walking: shells, stones, feathers, bric-à-brac, colours, things washed up on the beach. You just have a fascination for examining things and gradually they accumulate. Often there comes a time when you want to use them or piece them together. It also can be a refreshing change from paint to turn your hand to touching materials. Painting is such a passion and a time-consuming occupation – I would like to do many more things but solving problems with paint is very demanding.

One recent piece is called *The Jackal* (Pl.36). The material is the canvas cover of an old bicycle seat which was part of my collection of bric-à-brac which I use for collage. I used the inside of it as an inspiration for heads for the warring factions in the piece called *The Pity* (Pl.12). Then I had just painted from it and adapted it almost like a war helmet or war mask. I returned to it shortly after the Dunblane shooting and found that the inside of this material seemed like the inside of a head gone mad. I don't know what was in the head and mind of the killer that day but I felt that this particular piece summed it up. It was placed on the canvas and I added a few lines – particularly the small, white, sharp teeth. It seemed to sum up that day of madness. It complements the triptych which is dedicated to Dunblane – *The Day of the Jackal*. This piece has been done to commemorate that tragedy and to commiserate with the parents and the community. Dunblane is only a few miles from my studio and I know a lot of people who were affected by that terrible tragedy.

APPENDIX I

CATALOGUE RAISONNÉ, 1959–97

Compiled by VERONICA CORDEIRO and MHAIRI SCOTT
Edited by MHAIRI SCOTT

CATALOGUE NOTES

Works are listed in chronological order. For each year, securely dated works are listed first, followed by those that are approximate, and then by those which bridge more than one year. Those to which it has not been possible to assign an approximate date have been listed together at the end. Dimensions are in centimetres. Height precedes width, followed by depth where applicable.

Only the present or most recent known owner is given. Where the date, size, medium or collection is unknown these have been omitted from the catalogue.

Every effort has been made to ensure this catalogue of works is as complete as possible, but it is acknowledged that it is not exhaustive, since many works remain untraced. Included in the notes are additional details supplied by the artist regarding the circumstances of the creation of the work, and cross-references to related works, where applicable. The following abbreviations are used:

c.	*circa* (about)
b/w	black and white
Excl.	Excluding
Incl.	Including
PC	Private Collection
COA	Collection of the Artist
LP	Left panel or element of a compound work (e.g. triptych)
CP	Centre panel or element of a compound work
RP	Right panel or element of a compound work
RSA	Royal Scottish Academy
SSA	Society of Scottish Artists
RSWA	Royal Society of Women Artists

1. *Norwegian Fiord*, 1956
(plate 71)
oil on canvas
50 x 41
PC

2. *Aix-en-Provence*, 1959
gouache on tinted paper
48 x 64
COA

3. *Aix-en-Provence*, 1959
watercolour on paper
48 x 64
COA

4. *Paris Sketch I*, 1959
watercolour on paper
20 x 17
COA

5. *Paris Sketch II*, 1959
watercolour on paper
20 x 17
COA

6. *Paris Sketch III*, 1959
watercolour on paper
20 x 17
COA

7. *Paris Sketch IV*, 1959
watercolour on paper
36 x 17
COA

8. *Self-portrait*, 1959
(plate 72)
details unknown

9. *Untitled (woman on a balcony)*, c.1959
oil on board
74 x 51
Edinburgh College of Art, School of Drawing and Painting Collection

10. *Mulatto Woman*, 1959–60
gouache
81 x 61
PC, Lancaster

11. *Still-life with Stripes*, 1960
gouache on paper
36 x 51
Cyril Gerber Fine Art Gallery, Glasgow

12. *Still-life with Blue Plate*, 1960
gouache on paper
36 x 51
Cyril Gerber Fine Art Gallery, Glasgow

13. *Still-life with Jugs, Flowers and Chinese Newspaper*, 1960
collage, pen and ink
43 x 53
PC, Lancaster

14. *Still-life with Jar, Jug and Fruit*, 1960
watercolour and pastel on paper
58 x 71
PC, Edinburgh

15. *Untitled (two abstracted figures)*, c.1960
oil and sawdust on board
96.5 x 76
Edinburgh College of Art, School of Drawing and Painting Collection

16. *Abstract Exercise*, 1962
gouache on paper
18 x 20
COA

17. *Abstract Exercise with Figures*, 1962
gouache on paper
25 x 20
COA

18. *Aku-Aku*, 1962
oil on board
122 x 104
PC, London

19. *Boat-maker's Fish Garden*, 1966
(plate 73)
oil on board
152 x 122
University of Stirling Collection

20. *Rainbow House*, 1967
gouache and acrylic
61 x 51
PC, Dunoon

21. *Red Kettle and Dead Fish*, 1967
oil on board
122 x 91
PC, Edinburgh

22. *Boy Standing*, c.1967
charcoal
53 x 35
PC, Edinburgh

23. *Untitled (still-life)*, 1968
PVA on canvas

132 x 99
PC, Bridge of Allan

24. *Arabesque*, c.1968
oil on board
152 x 122
PC, Edinburgh

25. *Still-life with Cherries*, c.1968
oil on board
122 x 152
PC, Bridge of Allan

26. *Garden Table – Red Chair*, c.1969
oil on board
122 x 152
PC, Bridge of Allan

27. *Bow Window*, c.1969
pastel on green paper
24 x 38
PC, Edinburgh

28. *Curling Pond Wood, Blairlogie*, 1970
ink and wash
56 x 74
PC, Stirling

29. *Girl with Poppy Head*, 1970
oil
81 x 69
PC, Stirling

30. *The Ochils*, 1970
pastel
26 x 38
PC, Culross

31. *The Bottle*, c.1970
oil on canvas
91 x 61
PC, Edinburgh

32. *Blue Stocking*, c.1970
acrylic on canvas
29 x 25
PC, Edinburgh

33. *Nude – Water Woman*, c.1970
pastel
17 x 15
PC, Bridge of Allan

34. *Wood, Blairlogie*, c.1970
watercolour
66 x 53
PC, Edinburgh

35. *Red Nude II*, early 1970s
pastel
30 x 23
PC, Inverness

36. *Magenta Night*, early 1970s
pastel/gouache mix
20 x 30
PC, Edinburgh

37. *For Corydon*, 1971
acrylic on canvas
53 x 51
PC, Dunoon

38. *Figure with Stars and Stripes*, c.1971
acrylic on canvas
25 x 25
COA

39. *Weighted (Small Torso)*, c.1971
acrylic on canvas
17 x 14
COA

40. *Still-life with Teapot*, c.1971
gouache on black paper
51 x 76
PC, Bridge of Allan

41. *Through a Window*, 1972
pastel
96.5 x 71
PC, Fife

42. *Blue Nude and Aircraft*, 1972
acrylic and pastel with pencil
23 x 27
PC, Stirling

43. *From My Window*, 1972
gouache
46 x 51
PC, Culross

44. *Large Space in a Window*, 1972
gouache and pastel on paper
51 x 76
PC, Bridge of Allan

45. *Untitled (sectional nude with aeroplane)*, 1972
oil and pastel
34 x 30
PC, Clackmannanshire

46. *Theme on a Doll's-House*, 1972
oil on canvas
61 x 51
PC, Falkirk

47. *View from a Window*, 1972
pastel and gouache
23 x 29
PC, Stirling

48. *Circus Girl*, 1972
PVA on board
25 x 20
PC, Clackmannanshire

49. *Landscape from a Window*, 1972
PVA on canvas
84 x 102
PC, Bridge of Allan

50. *View of Hills*, c.1972 (unfinished)
oil on canvas
91 x 89
PC, Stirling

51. *View from Studio Window I*, c.1972
gouache and acrylic
24 x 30
PC, Larbert

52. *View from Studio Window II*, c.1972
gouache and acrylic
24 x 30
PC, Larbert

53. *Trees at Logie*, c.1972
46 x 28
PC, Aberdeen

54. *Veronica x 2*, 1973
acrylic on canvas
34 x 45
PC, Belfast

55. *Window, Sunset, House*, 1973
gouache and acrylic
25 x 30
PC, Larbert

56. *Stars and Stripes*, 1973
gouache on card
13 x 13
PC, Belfast

57. *Ochre Thoughts*, 1973
mixed media on canvas
61 x 61
PC, Edinburgh

58. *Untitled (three views of nude)*, c.1973
acrylic on canvas
64 x 64
PC, Dunblane
Painted at the same time as *Ochre Thoughts* (cat 57)

59. *Night House Plants*, c.1973
oil on canvas
48 x 48
PC, Edinburgh

60. *Studio Window*, c.1973
oil on canvas
51 x 40.5
PC, Dollar

61. *Yellow Group and Tree*, c.1973
acrylic on canvas
61 x 51
PC, Edinburgh

62. *Plant Reflection*, c.1974
oil
41 x 37
PC, Inverness

63. *Red Night Figures*, c.1974
acrylic on canvas
61 x 61
PC, Dollar

64. *Nude Through a Cloud*, 1975
oil on canvas
104 x 94
PC, Prestwick
Part of a rejected painting by the artist on the reverse.

65. *Untitled (landscape with confined female figures)*, 1975
pastel
36 x 27
PC, Inverness
Executed during or just after a stay in Altandhu, near Achiltibuie

66. *Untitled (landscape with rainbow and large female figure in a box)*, 1975
pastel
36 x 27
PC, Inverness
Executed during or just after a stay in Altandhu, near Achiltibuie

67. *Blue Nude with Totem*, c.1975
oil on board
122 x 122
COA

68. *Stride*, c.1976
oil on canvas
30 x 30
PC, Gourock

69. *Yellow Stretch*, c.1976
pastel
29 x 22
PC, Dunoon

70. *Moving Sideways*, 1977
acrylic and pencil on canvas
91 x 91
COA

71. *Untitled (window figure)*, 1977
oil on canvas
91 x 89
PC, Stirling

72. *Blue Life*, 1977
PVA on canvas
94 x 94
PC, Alloa

73. *Stride*, 1977
oil on canvas
56 x 45
PC, Edinburgh

74. *Cloud Islands*, 1977
pastel
46 x 38
PC, Stirling

75. *Sleep Walker*, 1978
oil and acrylic on canvas
30 x 25
PC, Glasgow

76. *Shadows Across the Night*, 1978
pastel, watercolour and pencil
46 x 39
PC, Bridge of Allan

77. *House, Hill, Tree and Cloud*, c.1978
acrylic on canvas
144 x 99
PC, Glasgow

78. *Flight Out*, c.1978
oil on canvas
12.5 x 12.5
PC, Edinburgh

79. *Red Still-life*, c.1978
oil on canvas
122 x 122

80. *Blue Narcissus* (diptych), 1979
acrylic on canvas
91 x 91
PC, Australia
Part of the 'Torso' series

see cat 81–85, 87–89, 99, 100, 102–105, 112, 120–122

81. *Split Torso with Lily*, 1979
acrylic on canvas
46 x 46
COA
This is a small version of *Blue Narcissus* (cat 80)

82. *Night and the Lilies*, 1979
acrylic on canvas
41 x 41
COA
see cat 80

83. *Back to Front Torso*, 1979
acrylic on canvas
41 x 41
COA
see cat 80

84. *Flying Torso*, 1979
acrylic on canvas
66 x 66
COA
see cat 80

85. *Exploding Torso*, 1979
acrylic on canvas
63.5 x 63.5
COA
see cat 80

86. *Night Figure*, 1979
acrylic on paper
28 x 43
COA

87. *Torso in the Night Wind*, 1979
oil on canvas
38 x 36
PC, Edinburgh
see cat 80

88. *Split Torso*, 1979
(plate 34)
acrylic on canvas
68.5 x 68.5
COA
see cat 80

89. *Summer Torso*, 1979
oil on canvas
35 x 35
see cat 80

90. *Coat of Many Colours (Nude)*, 1979
acrylic on canvas
94 x 124
PC, Belfast

91. *Untitled (woman from the back)*, 1979
gouache and acrylic on card
84 x 66 (excl. frame)
PC, Newbury

92. *Baggage and General*, 1979
mixed media on chipboard
23 x 25
COA
Created for the 'Packaged Art' exhibition in Edinburgh

93. *Blue Package and Drawing*, 1979
mixed media on chipboard
28 x 13 (overall size)
COA
Mounted drawing of a small package with the package suspended below.
see cat. 92

94. *Cream and Brown Package and Drawing*, 1979
mixed media on chipboard
28 x 13 (overall size)
COA
see cat. 92

95. *Vase of Colours*, 1979
mixed media on canvas on board
51 x 30
COA
see cat 92

96. *Resurrection*, c.1979
51 x 41
PC

97. *Woman with Man*, 1979–82
(plate 40)
acrylic on canvas
111 x 56
COA

98. *Turbulent Figure*, c.1979
pastel
37 x 25
PC, Dunblane

99. *Torso Rising*, c.1979
acrylic and collage on canvas
PC, Bridge of Allan
see cat 80

100. *Swooning Torso*, c.1979
acrylic on canvas
74 x 51
PC, Dunblane
see cat 80

101. *Leaping Figures*, 1979–80
ceramic and steel on a wooden plinth
46 x 15
COA

102. *One and the Other*, 1980
(plate 37)
acrylic on canvas
102 x 91
COA
see cat 80

103. *Stance*, 1980
acrylic on canvas
56 x 51
PC, Australia
see cat 80

104. *Enfold*, 1980
(plate 53)
acrylic on canvas
46 x 40.5
see cat 80

105. *Electric Torso*, 1980
(plate 39)
acrylic on canvas
86 x 76
COA
see cat 80

106. *Resting*, 1980
acrylic on canvas
61 x 51
PC, Glasgow

107. *Leap for Joy*, 1980
oil
38 x 30
PC, Glasgow

108. *Bursting*, 1980
oil and collage on canvas
75 x 74
PC, Larbert

109. *Surrender, Never*, 1980
(plate 33)
acrylic on canvas
49 x 42
PC, Tayport

110. *Night Viewed*, 1980
oil or acrylic on canvas
66 x 56
PC, Newbury

111. *The Body Electric*, 1980
(plate 50)
acrylic on canvas
61 x 61
PC, Dunoon

112. *Boxed Torso*, c.1980
acrylic on canvas
30 x 25
PC
see cat 80

113. *Advancing Male*, c.1980
acrylic on card
112 x 81
COA

114. *Island Woman I*, c.1980
acrylic on canvas
30 x 20

115. *Island Woman II*, c.1980
acrylic on canvas
30 x 20
PC

116. *That Pink Feeling*, c.1980
acrylic on canvas
30 x 30
PC, Edinburgh

117. *Strutting*, c.1980
acrylic on canvas
35.5 x 30
COA

118. *Venus Rising*, c.1980
oil on canvas
20 x 18
PC, Stirling

119. *Venus Displaced*, c.1980
oil, acrylic and collage on canvas
127 x 158
COA

120. *Night Torso*, 1981
(plate 51)
acrylic on paper
25 x 20
PC
see cat 80

121. *Night Torso II*, 1981
oil and collage on canvas
19 x 18
PC, Dunoon
see cat 80

122. *Moving On*, 1981
acrylic on canvas
51 x 46
PC, Australia
see cat 80

123. *Splintered*, 1981
acrylic on canvas
42 x 36
PC, Belfast

124. *Seated*, 1981
acrylic on canvas
23 x 20
PC, Glasgow

125. *Presenter II*, 1981
acrylic on canvas on wood
19 x 24
PC, Belfast

126. *A Little Night Music*, 1981
mixed media collage
53 x 48
PC

127. *Dreaming Letters, Loving Words*, 1981
mixed media collage and acrylic on canvas
32 x 24
PC, Brechin

128. *Poetic Night*, 1981
oil on canvas
29 x 24
PC, Stirling

129. *Appeal*, 1981
oil or acrylic
107 x 91
PC, Glasgow

130. *Standing Nude*, 1981
PVA on canvas
15 x 10
PC, Dunfermline

131. *Stance*, c.1981
acrylic on canvas
46 x 39
PC, Glasgow

132. *Bound*, c.1981
acrylic and collage on canvas
25 x 20

133. *Break and Burst*, c.1981
acrylic and collage on canvas
25 x 20

134. *Black Jug with Flowers*, c.1981
acrylic on canvas

30 x 25
PC

135. *Nude at Window, Reflected*, c.1981
mixed media and collage
33 x 24
PC, Dollar

136. *Reclining Nude*, c.1981
acrylic on canvas
23 x 20
PC, Edinburgh

137. *Blue Nude*, 1982
oil on canvas
61 x 61
PC, Stirling

138. *Athena*, 1982
(plate 38)
oil on canvas on board
122 x 122
PC, Falkirk

139. *Athena*, c.1982
acrylic on canvas
20 x 15
PC, Edinburgh
study for *Athena* (cat 138)

140. *The Rivals – Scarsdale (Mrs Harris I)*, 1982
(plate 48)
acrylic and collage on canvas
122 x 116
Glasgow Vennel Museum, Glasgow
This painting bridges the gap between the investigation of the nude (the 'torso' series) and the subsequent large collage panels, e.g. 'Stagefright' (cat 181)

141. *Blue Split Torso on Red*, c.1982
acrylic and collage on canvas
126 x 126
COA
see cat 80

142. *Dropped Torso*, c.1982
acrylic on canvas
35.5 x 25
PC
see cat 80

143. *Fruit Bowl and Tulips*, c.1982
acrylic
17 x 14
PC, Stirling

144. *Running This Way and That*, c.1982
acrylic on canvas
51 x 35.5
PC

145. *Sun*, c.1982
acrylic on canvas
76 x 61
PC, Edinburgh

146. *Departing*, c.1982
acrylic on canvas
30 x 25
PC

147 *Wired Stance*, c.1982
acrylic on canvas
PC, Falkirk

148. *Les Filles*, c.1982
acrylic on canvas
30 x 25
PC, Edinburgh

149. *Survivor*, c.1982
mixed media collage on canvas
53 x 63.5
PC, Glasgow

150. *Nude and Door*, c.1982
oil on canvas
19 x 14
PC, Fife

151. *Night Fruit*, c.1982
oil on canvas
66 x 61
PC, Stirling

152. *Red Formula*, 1983
oil and collage on canvas
39 x 32
PC, Edinburgh

153. *Dark Formality*, 1983
acrylic and oil on canvas
40.5 x 30
PC, Falkirk

154. *Wired Movement*, 1983
acrylic and oil on canvas
30 x 29
PC, Falkirk

155. *Performance*, 1983
(plate 52)
acrylic, oil and collage on canvas
175 x 221
PC, Dunoon

156. *Songstress*, 1983
acrylic on canvas
29 x 24
PC, Falkirk

157. *Volatile*, 1983
oil and collage on canvas
28 x 22
PC, Glasgow

158. *Blue Formula*, 1983
oil and collage on canvas
35 x 30
PC, Glasgow

159. *Bust*, 1983
oil and collage on canvas
35.5 x 29
PC, Stirling

160. *Speaker*, 1983
oil and collage on canvas
35.5 x 29
PC, Stirling

161. *Models Resting*, 1983
oil and mixed media
25 x 20
PC, Glasgow

162. *The Performers*, 1983
oil on canvas
30 x 23
PC, Greece

163. *Birthday Boy*, c.1983
acrylic and collage on canvas
201 x 233
PC

164. *Struggle*, c.1983
acrylic on canvas
61 x 51
PC, Edinburgh

165. *Leaving*, c.1983
acrylic on canvas
40.5 x 30

166. *Striving*, c.1983
acrylic on canvas
61 x 51

167. *Trellis*, c.1983
acrylic on canvas
30 x 30
PC

168. *Night Ladies*, c.1983
acrylic and oil on canvas
43 x 38
PC, Edinburgh

169. *Carousel*, c.1983
acrylic on canvas
29 x 18
PC, Dunblane

170. *Dark Swing*, c.1983
acrylic on canvas
30 x 25
PC, Glasgow

171. *Mrs Harris II – The Trial*, 1983–84
mixed media and collage on canvas
122 x 109
PC, London

172. *Mother's Child*, 1983-84
acrylic and collage on canvas
152 x 122
COA

173. *Masticator*, 1984
(plate 10)
oil on canvas
51 x 51
COA
Developed from *Woman with Man* (cat 97). Considered by the artist to be one of her most important works, although never exhibited because it was 'possibly too painful for people to look at'.

174. *Reject*, 1984
acrylic and collage on canvas
167.5 x 175
COA

175. *Dreaming Frankenstein*, 1984
(plate 63)
black pastel on paper
31 x 46 each
PC
Series of drawings based on the Liz Lochhead poem of the same title

176. *Licking and Biting*, 1984
(plate 41)
collage and gouache on paper on board
124 x 124
COA

177. *Getting in on the Act* (diptych), 1984
(plate 54)
oil on canvas
183 x 305 in total
COA

178. *Woman as Fish*, 1984
oil on canvas
59.5 x 46
PC, Glasgow

179. *Mother and Child*, 1984
pastel on paper
74 x 53
COA

180. *Love Bites*, 1984
(plate 43)
oil on canvas
102 x 102
COA

181. *Stagefright*, 1984
(plate 49)
acrylic and mixed media collage
201 x 236
COA
Smith Biennial – Prizewinner

182. *Pain and Sorrow*, 1984
(plate 11)
gouache and collage on paper
102 x 102

183. *Catch*, 1984
(plate 9)
acrylic and collage on canvas
206 x 235
COA

184. *Wall of Faces*, c.1984
244 x 457
Executed on site at the Third Eye Centre, Glasgow

185. *Arette*, c.1984
oil on canvas
167.5 x 46
COA

186. *Mother's Child*, c.1984
acrylic
152 x 122

187. *Curtain Call*, c.1984
acrylic and collage
152 x 122

188. *Rock A Bye*, c.1984
acrylic and collage
152 x 122

189. *Crash*, c.1984
acrylic and collage on canvas

76 x 76
PC, Edinburgh

190. *Drowning*, c.1984
acrylic on canvas
122 x 122
PC, Ireland

191. *Fish Woman*, c.1984
acrylic on canvas
25 x 20
PC

192. *Man Hero*, c.1984
black pastel
74 x 53

193. *Man Head*, c.1984
black pastel and charcoal on paper
71 x 53 (excl. frame)
PC, Sheffield

194. *The Divided Self trilogy* (triptych), 1985
(plate 46)
She Is She (LP of trilogy)
oil on canvas
183 x 152
COA

195. *The Divided Self trilogy* (triptych), 1985
(plate 46)
Grip (CP of trilogy)
oil on canvas
183 x 152
COA

196. *The Divided Self trilogy* (triptych), 1985
(plate 46)
Goodbye (RP of trilogy)
oil on canvas
183 x 152
COA

197. *Steady Girl*, 1985
gouache on card
112 x 81
PC, London

198. *Berlin Trilogy*, 1985
(plate 24)
Say Nothing (LP of trilogy)
Hear Everything (CP of trilogy)
See All (RP of trilogy)
oil on canvas
each panel 183 x 152
COA

199. *The Fall I*, 1985
(plate 26)
oil on canvas
222 x 175
COA
Painted after the artist's father suffered a cerebral thrombosis

200. *Love Suite: Now She Has Brought His Feet*, 1985
pastel with gouache on paper
187 x 136
COA
One of a suite of five inspired by the Ted Hughes poem, 'Bride and Groom lie hidden for three days'. The first four created at the same time
see cat 201–204

201. *Love Suite: She Has Found His Hands For Him*, 1985
(plate 17)
pastel on paper
187 x 136
COA
see cat 200

202. *Love Suite: She Gives Him His Eyes, She Finds Them in the Rubble*, 1985
pastel on paper
187 x 136
COA
see cat 200

203. *Love Suite: He Gives Her Her Skin*, 1985
pastel on paper
186.5 x 136
COA
see cat 200

204. *Love Suite: They Take Each Other to the Sun*, 1985
pastel on paper
186.5 x 136
PC, Glasgow
Created after the first four and not exhibited.
see cat 200

205. *Still-born Action*, 1985
(plate 28)
gouache and black pastel on paper
122 x 86
COA

206. *Allein (Alone)*, 1985
(plate 45)
pastel with wash and gouache on paper
122 x 86
COA
One of a suite of three: other two works entitled *Where Am I?* and *Signals*.
see cat 207 and 208

207. *Where Am I? (Wir bin Ich?)*, 1985
(plate 74)
pastel with wash and gouache on paper
122 x 86
COA
One of a suite of three.
see cat 206

208. *Signals*, 1985
(plate 44)
pastel with wash and gouache on paper
122 x 86
COA
One of a suite of three
see cat 206

209. *Sieh Alles (See Everything)*, 1985
pastel, charcoal and gouache on paper
180 x 123
COA

210. *Holding*, 1985
screenprint
66 x 53
PC, Edinburgh

211. *The Fall II: Agony in the First Garden*, 1985
(plate 42)
acrylic and collage on canvas
135 x 135
COA

212. *Night Runner*, c.1985
acrylic on card
112 x 84

213. *Hear Nothing*, c.1985
acrylic on paper
178 x 122
Sketch for a panel in the *Berlin Trilogy*
see cat 198

214. *Still-born Idea*, c.1985
b&w gouache on paper
119 x 84
PC

215. *Self, Old*, c.1985
b&w gouache on paper
approx. 91 x 71

216. *Self, Middle*, c.1985
b&w gouache on paper
approx. 91 x 71

217. *Self, Young*, c.1985
b&w gouache on paper
approx. 91 x 71

218. *Men Performing I*, c.1985
b&w gouache on paper
20 x 14
PC, London
see cat 219–221

219. *Men Peforming II*, c.1985
b&w gouache on paper
20 x 14
PC, London
see cat 218

220. *Men Performing III*, c.1985
b&w gouache on paper
20 x 14
PC, London
see cat 218

221. *Men Performing IV*, c.1985
b&w gouache on paper
20 x 14
PC, London
see cat 218

222. *Woman and Toilette*, c.1985
black pastel
63.5 x 48

223. *Am I*, c.1985
black pastel on paper
117 x 81
PC

224. *What Now*, c.1985
black pastel on paper
122 x 84
PC, Aberdeen

225. *Who Am I*, c.1985
black pastel on white paper
114 x 91
PC

226. *Handstand*, c.1985
gouache
112 x 84
PC, London

227. *Waiting*, c.1985
gouache
188 x 132

228. *Artist and Sailor*, c.1985
gouache
190.5 x 132
Part of the 'Artist and Sailor' series. The sailor is an alter ego, the adventurer. Also a gender challenge: the sailor, like a doctor, is traditionally assumed to be male.

229. *The Player*, c.1985
gouache
190.5 x 137

230. *Bête Noire*, c.1985
gouache
61 x 48
PC

231. *Serenade*, c.1985
gouache
178 x 123
COA

232. *Small Self I*, c.1985
gouache on card
21 x 29
PC

233. *Small Self II*, c.1985
gouache on card
21 x 29
PC

234. *Small Head*, c.1985
gouache on card
18 x 10
PC, Stirling

235. *The Blue Lips*, c.1985
gouache on paper
178 x 132
COA

236. *Ledge*, c.1985
gouache on paper
112 x 84
PC

237. *In the Park*, c.1985
gouache on paper

238. *Holding On*, c.1985
gouache on paper
183 x 122

239. *All Fours*, c.1985
gouache on paper

112 x 84
PC

240. *Kiss*, c.1985
gouache on paper
119 x 86
PC

241. *Swan Song*, c.1985
gouache on paper
183 x 244
Painted in Berlin
see cat. 259

242. *Duet I*, c.1985
gouache on paper
183 x 122

243. *Fingers Features Face*, c.1985
gouache on paper
86 x 71

244. *Stepping Out*, c.1985
gouache on paper
190.5 x 132

245. *Solo*, c.1985
gouache on paper
185 x 160
COA
Sketch for oil of same title (cat 265)
Painted in Berlin.

246. *Boule Player*, c.1985
gouache on paper
193 x 132

247. *Head in the Park*, c.1985
gouache on paper
190.5 x 132

248. *Duet II*, c.1985
gouache on paper
190.5 x 132

249. *Pink Sailor*, c.1985
gouache on paper
190.5 x 132

250. *Lady Light*, c.1985
gouache on paper
63.5 x 48
PC

251. *Angel of Mercy*, c.1985
gouache on paper
190.5 x 137

252. *Hanging Fire*, c.1985
gouache or acrylic on card
112 x 84
PC, London

253. *Turkish Night*, c.1985
gouache and pastel on card
29 x 21
PC, Stirling

254. *Running Man*, c.1985
oil on board
14 x 11.5
PC, Brechin

255. *Sketch for 'The Divided Self': Trilogy for a New Ireland* (triptych), c.1985
(plate 57)
She is She (LP)
Grip (CP)
Goodbye (RP)
gouache on card
each panel 115 x 85
COA

256. *Flying In*, c.1985
oil on canvas
203 x 178
COA

257. *Two of a Different Kind*, c.1985
oil on canvas
152 x 152
COA

258. *Spring*, c.1985
oil on canvas
183 x 152
PC

259. *Swan Song*, c.1985
oil on canvas
213 x 274
COA
Developed from earlier painting of same title (cat 241) This version painted in Scotland.

260. *Hands*, c.1985
pencil on paper
119 x 94
Executed in Berlin

261. *My Foot*, c.1985
pencil on paper
112 x 84
LP of group of three drawings, see cat 262 and 263

262. *Our Hands*, c.1985
pencil on paper
112 x 84
CP of group – see cat 261

263. *Your Feet*, c.1985
pencil on paper
112 x 84
RP of group – see cat 261

264. *The Object of Renewal*, 1985–86
oil on canvas
203 x 178
COA

265. *Solo*, 1985–87
oil on canvas
203 x 178
COA

266. *Self-portrait: Fingers, Features, Foot (one of a pair)*, 1985–87
(plate 16)
oil on canvas
91 x 71
PC, Bath
Commissioned by Sean Kelly of Artsite, Bath, as part of a group show. Artists were invited to submit a self-portrait in a prescribed size.

267. *Self-Portrait: Fingers, Features, Foot (one of a pair)*, 1985–87
oil on canvas
91 x 71
COA
see cat 266

268. *William Wallace*, 1986
oil on canvas
203 x 127
COA

269. *Foot (Your Foot)*, 1986
(plate 27)
pastel and water on paper
74 x 56
COA
One of a pair with cat 270

270. *Foot (My Foot)*, 1986
pastel and water on paper
74 x 56
One of a pair with cat 269

271. *Palm Sunday I*, 1986
black gouache and pastel on paper
190.5 x 132
Part of the Jerusalem Suite: six works executed in Jerusalem at Christmas

272. *Palm Sunday II*, 1986
black gouache and pastel on paper
190.5 x 132
Part of the Jerusalem Suite, cat 271

273. *A Foot in Jerusalem*, 1986
black gouache and pastel on paper
190.5 x 132
Part of the Jerusalem Suite, cat 271

274. *Holding – Jerusalem*, 1986
black pastel and gouache on paper
190.5 x 132
Part of the Jerusalem Suite, cat 271

275. *Wait, Don't Go!*, 1986
gouache on paper
190.5 x 132
Part of the Jerusalem Suite, cat 271

276. *Falling For You*, 1986
gouache on paper
190.5 x 132
Part of the Jerusalem Suite, cat 271

277. *The Fall II*, c.1986
gouache on paper
PC, London

278. *The Fall III*, c.1986
gouache on paper
142 x 102
PC, London

279. *Toes*, c.1986
graphite on paper
119 x 94
Executed in Berlin

280. *Foot*, c.1986
graphite on paper
119 x 94
Executed in Berlin

281. *She Holding Him*, c.1986
pastel and watercolour on paper
122 x 84
PC
Executed in Berlin

282. *Foetal Distress*, c.1986
pastel on paper
119 x 84

283. *Sculpture in the Park I*, c.1986
pastel, wash and gouache
122 x 86
COA

284. *Sculpture in the Park II*, c.1986
pastel, wash and gouache
122 x 86
COA

285. *Head in the Dark*, c.1986
pencil on paper
112 x 84
Executed in Berlin

286. *Winter*, 1987
acrylic, pastel and watercolour
40 x 48
PC, East Lothian

287. *Sketch for 'Act I Scene I or II'*, 1987
gouache on two joined sheets of paper
188 x 151
COA
Painted in Berlin
see cat 295

288. *Sketch for 'Act I Scene I or II'*, 1987
gouache on paper
187 x 136
COA
Painted in Berlin
see cat 295

289. *Courting Pleasures*, 1987
(plate 3)
graphite on paper
COA
Executed in Berlin.

290. *Two of a Kind*, 1987
oil on canvas
152 x 152
COA

291. *Katrina in the Boat (diptych)*, 1987
oil on canvas
178 x 406 (each panel 178 x 203)
COA

292. *Duet III*, 1987
oil on canvas
203 x 178
COA
Painted in Berlin

293. *Holding*, 1987
screenprint A/P
approx. 23 x 20
Various PCs/COA
A co-edition print with Peacock printmakers. Exhibited with. SSA in 1988 and sold to raise funds for the society

294. *How Wisdom and Folly meet, mix and unite, how Virtue and Vice*

mix their black and their white (three panels), 1987
(plate 6)
oil on canvas
244 x 366 (each panel 244 x 122)
Robert Burns piece. Title from Burns poem 'Sketch. Inscribed to the Rt. Hon. Ch. J. Fox. Esq. M—'. Commissioned by the Maclaurin Gallery, Ayr

295. *Act I Scene I (Duet)*, 1987
(plate 4)
oil on canvas
203 x 178
COA
First 'Duet'. The title refers to 'the performance of love (as well as sorrow) – "'singing it out".' Painted in Berlin.

296. *Act I Scene II (Duet)*, 1987
(plate 5)
oil on canvas
203 x 178
COA
see cat 295

297. *Striding Male*, c.1987
blue gouache on buff card
51 x 43
PC, London

298. *Holding You*, c.1987
gouache and wash on paper
122 x 122

299. *Holding You*, c.1987
print
30 x 25
PC, Glasgow

300. *The Kiss*, c.1987
30 x 24
PC, Glasgow

301. *Still-life with Plant*, c.1987
30 x 51
PC, Glasgow

302. *The Kiss*, 1988
acrylic
81 x 122
PC, Glasgow

303. *Madonna I*, 1988
black pastel on paper
63.5 x 48
COA
Executed in France.

304. *Plate – 'Eve and the Serpent'*, 1988
glazed ceramic plate
diameter 48cm
PC
One of a series of 10 ceramic plates. Signed and dated (incised on base)
see cat 305–310

305. *Plate – 'Ripple'*, 1988
glazed ceramic plate
diameter 48cm
COA
see cat 304

306. *Plate – 'Face Plate I'*, 1988
glazed ceramic plate
diameter 48cm
COA
see cat 304

307. *Plate – 'Pool I'*, 1988
glazed ceramic plate
diameter 48cm
COA
see cat 304

308. *Plate – 'Steinbeck'*, 1988
glazed ceramic plate
diameter 48cm
Glasgow Museums and Art Galleries
see cat 304

309. *Plate – 'Pool II'*, 1988
glazed ceramic plate
diameter 48cm
PC, Glasgow
see cat 304

310. *Plates – titles untraced*, 1988
glazed ceramic plate
diameter 48cm
Four ceramic plates of a series of ten
see cat 304

311. *The Old Song and Dance Act*, 1988
gouache on card
113 x 83
COA

312. *November Thoughts*, 1988
acrylic on canvas
33 x 20
PC

313. *Devouring You*, 1988
oil on canvas
182 x 136
COA

314. *Boy on a Swing*, c.1988
b&w gouache drawing on paper
195.5 x 135
COA
Painted in France

315. *The Boule Player*, c.1988
b&w gouache on paper
195.5 x 135
COA
Painted in France.

316. *Mine (Foot)*, c.1988
black pastel
61 x 51
PC, Bathgate

317. *Head in the Dark*, c.1988
gouache on paper
190.5 x 136
COA
Painted in France

318. *Loving You I*, c.1988
gouache on paper
185 x 135
COA
Painted in France. One of a pair – see cat 319

319. *Loving You II*, c.1988
gouache on paper
183 x 132
see cat 318

320. *Resting Together*, c.1988
gouache on paper
193 x 132
Painted in France

321. *Waiting*, c.1988
gouache on paper
198 x 136
COA
Painted in France

322. *Resting with You*, c.1988
gouache on paper
190.5 x 132
Kirkcaldy Art Gallery and Museum

323. *Head of a Sailor*, c.1988
oil on canvas
27 x 22
PC, Glasgow

324. *Requiem for a Sailor*, 1989
(plate 65)
b&w gouache on paper
195.5 x 135
COA
Painted in France

325. *Good Morning Lady (Woman I)*, 1989
black pastel on paper
40.5 x 28
PC, Ashfield

326. *Smile Lady Smile (Woman II)*, 1989
black pastel on paper
40.5 x 28

327. *Girl with Bird*, 1989
oil on canvas
46 x 46
COA

328. *Fingering II*, 1989
(plate 14)
oil on paper
55 x 46
PC, Dunblane

329. *Fingering III*, 1989
pastel
63.5 x 48
PC

330. *Sailor with Flowers*, 1989
screenprint A/P
122 x 96.5
Various Private Collections
see cat 228

331. *Fingering*, c.1989
gouache on paper
40.5 x 28
PC, London

332. *Artist, Sailor and Brush*, c.1989
oil on canvas
81 x 55
COA
see cat 228

333. *Madonna II*, c.1989
black pastel on paper
63.5 x 48
PC, Glasgow

334. *Artist and Sailor*, c.1989
gouache
203 x 132
see cat 228

335. *Sailor and Artist Dancing*, c.1989
gouache
190.5 x 132
see cat 228

336. *Embrace*, c.1989
oil on board
12.5 x 10
PC, Blackpool

337. *The Angel at the Crossing*, 1990
(plate 69)
mixed media on canvas on board
27.5 x 31
PC, Edinburgh
Part of the 'Crossing' series

338. *Agnus Dei: Ram of Death I*, 1990
monoprint with gouache
63.5 x 48
One of a suite of four, painted for the artist's mother, Agnes Hansen.

339. *Agnus Dei: Ram of Death II*, 1990
monoprint with gouache
63.5 x 48
see cat 338

340. *Agnus Dei: Ram of Death III*, 1990
monoprint with gouache
63.5 x 48
see cat 338

341. *Agnus Dei: Ram of Death IV*, 1990
monoprint with gouache
63.5 x 48
see cat 338

342. *Seated Woman*, 1990
acrylic
approx. 48 x 43
PC, Guildford

343. *Getting Ready*, 1990
acrylic on paper
63.5 x 48
PC, Edinburgh

344. *Give Me Water I*, 1990
charcoal and oil on paper
64 x 48
PC, Stirling
Part of the 'Libation' (healing water) series: an attempt by the artist to come to terms with the death of her parents in 1990

345. *Holding*, 1990
gouache
approx. 18 x 12.5
Barbican Art Gallery, London

346. *Torso and Wall*, 1990
oil
approx. 48 x 43
PC, London

347. *Classic Fellow II*, 1990
oil
approx. 48 x 43
PC, London

348. *Listening for the Angels*, 1990
oil on board
30 x 30
PC, Aberdeen
see cat 337

349. *Monochrome Self*, 1990
oil on canvas
61 x 51
COA

350. *Self-portrait with Brush*, 1990
oil on canvas
152 x 122
COA
Part of the 'Artist/Self-portrait' series, a themed series painted after being in France in 1988–89.

351. *Sketch for 'Self-portrait with Brush'*, 1990
oil on canvas
66 x 57
COA

352. *Artist with Brush and Tube*, 1990
oil on canvas
96.5 x 81
COA
see cat 350

353. *Artist with Brush*, 1990
oil on canvas
66 x 56
COA
see cat 350

354. *Blue Mood*, 1990
oil on canvas
18.5 x 15
PC, Stirling

355. *Man Walking*, 1990
pastel
approx. 18 x 12.5
PC, London

356. *Touching II*, 1990
pastel
approx. 48 x 43
Maclaurin Art Gallery, Ayr

357. *Figurine*, 1990
plaster and acrylic
PC, London

358. *Berlin Beckons*, c.1990
oil on canvas
183 x 152
COA

359. *Features, Fingers, Foot*, c.1990
gouache on paper
95 x 74
COA

360. *Artist and Sailor*, c.1990
oil on canvas
152 x 122
COA
see cat 228

361. *Memento Mori*, c.1990
oil on canvas
84 x 84
COA

362. *Bête Noire*, c.1990
acrylic on paper
63.5 x 48
PC, Edinburgh

363. *Untitled*, c.1990
oil crayon on paper
18 x 25
PC, Bridge of Allan

364. *Healing Jar*, c.1990
black and white drawing
48 x 58
PC
see cat 344

365. *In Need of Libation*, c.1990
black pastel on paper
63.5 x 48
PC
see cat 344

366. *Feeling*, c.1990
black pastel on paper
40.5 x 28
PC
see cat 344

367. *Untitled*, c.1990
medium and size unconfirmed
PC, Bridge of Allan

368. *Artist and Alter Ego*, c.1990
gouache
190.5 x 132
see cat 350

369. *The Water Carrier*, c.1990
oil on canvas
30 x 20
PC, London
see cat 344

370. *Crossing Over II*, c.1990
oil on canvas
34 x 24
PC, Staffordshire.
see cat 337

371. *Artist with Palette*, c.1990
oil on canvas
122 x 46
COA
see cat 350

372. *Artist, Sailor and Flowers*, c.1990
oil on canvas
63.5 x 56
COA
see cat 228

373. *Portrait Bust with Pedestal*, c. 1990
(plate 56)
oil on canvas
60 x 48

374. *Self-portrait with Palette*, c.1990
oil on canvas
66 x 61
PC, London
see cat 350

375. *Classic Fellow I*, c.1990
oil or acrylic
18 x 15
PC, Glasgow

376. *Quiet Consideration* c.1990
pastel on paper
48 x 58
see cat 344

377. *Blue Expression* c.1990
PVA on canvas
17 x 15
PC, Staffordshire.

378. *Head Apart* c.1990
watercolour
16.5 x 18
PC, Staffordshire.

379. *Tender Regrets* c.1990
gouache
57 x 46
PC, Dunoon

380. *The Crossing*, 1990–91
(plate 70)
oil on canvas
185 x 259
COA
One in a three-part series dealing with the deaths of the artist's parents in 1990

381. *Crossing Back*, 1990–91
oil on canvas
203 x 178
COA
see cat 380

382. *Crossing Over*, 1990–91
oil on canvas
203 x 178
COA
see cat 380

383. *In Preparation*, 1990–91
gouache on paper
66 x 51
PC, London

384. *Receiving*, 1991
acrylic
25 x 19
PC, London

385. *Bearer*, 1991
acrylic
18 x 15
PC, London

386. *Aquarius*, 1991
acrylic
PC

387. *Orpheus & Euridice*, 1991
acrylic
approx. 48 x 43
PC

388. *Remembrance Jar*, 1991
acrylic
58 x 48
PC, London

389. *Woman and Jug*, 1991
black pastel
63.5 x 48
PC, Bridge of Allan
Water / Libation series

390. *Come the Water Come the Wine*, 1991
black pastel on white paper
63.5 x 48
PC, Aberdeen
see cat 344

391. *Waiting*, 1991
graphite
64 x 48
PC, Nassau

392. *Keeper of the Vessels*, 1991
gouache
66 x 48
PC, Aberdeen

393. *Seeking Libation*, 1991
gouache
approx. 66 x 51
PC, London
see cat 344

394. *I Remember You Well*, 1991
gouache on paper
63.5 x 48
PC, Aberdeen

395. *Afloat and Dreaming II*, 1991
oil
20 x 30
PC, Nassau

396. *Hand of Love*, 1991
oil on board
15 x 10
PC, Aberdeen

397. *Self, Mouthless*, 1991
(plate 55)
oil on canvas
68.5 x 58
COA

398. *In Libation*, 1991
oil on canvas
94 x 94
COA
see cat 344

399. *Bearing the Jars*, 1991
oil on canvas
96.5 x 81
COA
see cat 344

400. *The Water Carrier*, 1991
oil on canvas
approx. 18 x 12.5
PC, London

401. *Secret Love*, 1991
oil on paper
51 x 56
PC, Aberdeen

402. *Woman and Vessel*, 1991
oil on paper
62 x 48
PC, Nassau

403. *Orpheus & Euridice*, 1991
pastel
approx.48 x 43
PC, London

404. *Classic Flow*, 1991
pastel
approx. 48 x 43
PC, London
see cat 344

405. *Au Jardin*, 1991
pastel
approx. 48 x 43
PC, London

406. *At the Well*, 1991
pastel and gouache on paper
63.5 x 48
PC, Stirling

407. *Receiving*, 1991
pastel and gouache on paper
66 x 45
COA
see cat 344

408. *Pleasure Jar*, 1991
pastel and PVA
60.5 x 13
PC, Kent

409. *Archaic Sensation*, 1991
(plate 58)
acrylic and oil on canvas
30 x 25
PC, Bridge of Allan

410. *Be Still My Heart*, 1991
gouache on paper
212 x 142
COA
Part of the Mary Queen of Scots series/installation, commissioned and produced for an exhibition in Edinburgh

411. *I Thought You Loved Me*, 1991
b&w photographs
all 10 x 6 unframed
Various PC incl. USA
Set of twelve photographs.
Part of the Mary Queen of Scots series
see cat 410

412. *Mary Queen of Scots: The Execution*, 1991
(plate 78)
pastel and gouache
PC, Edinburgh
Suite of nine works, part of the *Mary Queen of Scots* series
see cat 410

413. *A Banner for Mary*, 1991
(plate 79)
gouache on paper
193 x 132
COA
see cat 410

414. *Mary Dreaming of a Helping Hand*, 1991
oil on board
30 x 30
PC, Edinburgh
see cat 410

415. *Prisoners I*, 1991
mixed media construction/collage
12.5 x 10
PC
One of a pair of panels (see below) produced for the Mary Queen of Scots exhibition, Edinburgh, 1991. Three further panels added to group for tour, 1994, see cat 478–480

416. *Prisoners II*, 1991
mixed media construction/collage
12.5 x 10
PC
see cat 415

417. *The Hand That Betrayed*, 1991
acrylic and oil on canvas
30 x 30
PC, Bridge of Allan
see cat 415

418. *Exercise Before Death: 1. 'Union'*, 1991
lead on canvas mounted on board
approx.30 x 30
COA
One of six pieces in a group entitled 'Can this not be said to be, then, an exercise before death?'. Part of cat 410

419. *Exercise Before Death: 2. 'Prayers'*, 1991
plaster on canvas on board
approx. 30 x 30
COA
see cat 418

420. *Exercise Before Death: 3. 'Prayers'*, 1991
plaster on canvas on board
approx.30 x 30
COA
see cat 418

421. *Exercise Before Death: 4. 'Prayers'*, 1991
plaster on canvas on board
approx.30 x 30
COA
see cat 418

422. *Exercise Before Death: 5. 'Mask with Skull'*, 1991
lead on canvas mounted on board
approx. 30 x 30
COA
see cat 418

423. *Exercise Before Death: 6. 'Vagina'*, 1991
lead and plaster relief
6 deep x 26.5 x 26.5
COA
This panel represents a shrivelled womb
see cat 418

424. *Above and Beyond the Call of Duty*, 1991–92
oil on canvas
183 x 152
COA
Painted in homage to the artist's parents after their deaths in 1990. Includes four small 3D panels to go underneath
see cat 425–428

425. *Above and Beyond* panel, 1991–92
mixed media including child's dress on panel
30 x 30
COA
see cat 424

426. *Above and Beyond* panel, 1991–92
mixed media
30 x 30
COA
see cat 424

427. *Above and Beyond* panel (depicting hands), 1991–92
paint and earth pigment
30 x 30
COA
see cat 424

428. *Above and Beyond* panel (depicting figure), 1991–92
paint and earth pigment
30 x 30
COA
see cat 424

429. *Is It Water or Is It Wine*, c.1991
black pastel on white paper
all 63.5 x 48
COA / PC
Series of ten drawings. Part of the Libation / Healing series, cat 344

430. *Untitled (grey head)*, c.1991
oil
28 x 24
PC, Perthshire

431. *Spring to Life*, c.1991
oil on canvas
12.5 x 9
PC, Bridge of Allan

432. *Dispensing Libations II*, c.1991
b&w gouache on paper
63.5 x 48
see cat 344

433. *Watering the Parts*, c.1991
b&w gouache on paper
see cat 344

434. *Quiet Consideration*, c.1991
black pastel on paper
63.5 x 48
PC
see cat 344

435. *Feeling II*, c.1991
charcoal on paper
48 x 35.5
PC, Blackpool

436. *Threshold*, c.1991
oil on canvas
71 x 61
PC, Blackpool

437. *Bearing the Jars*, c.1991
oil on canvas
68.5 x 61
PC, Blackpool

438. *We Two Are One*, c.1991
oil on canvas
20 x 15
PC, London

439. *Receiving Libation*, c.1991
pastel
63.5 x 48
PC
see cat 344

440. *Help Me!*, 1992
(plate 29)
gouache on paper
211 x 137
COA
Painted in Berlin, in homage to Peter Fechter

441. *Earth/Alter Ego Exhibition*, 1992
monoprint
58 x 48
Part of a suite of four, a co-edition print with Glasgow Print Studio for 'The Alter Ego' exhibition, 1992
see cat 442–444

442. *Fire/Alter Ego Exhibition*, 1992
monoprint
58 x 48
see cat 441

443. *Water/Alter Ego Exhibition*, 1992
monoprint
58 x 48
see cat 441

444. *Air/Alter Ego Exhibition*, 1992
monoprint
58 x 48
see cat 441

445. *It Happened at the Wall: Shaft*, 1992
oil on heavy paper
76 x 56
COA
No.1 in suite of 8 works
see cat 446–452

446. *It Happened at the Wall: Man Searching for a Thread*, 1992
(plate 75)

oil on heavy paper
76 x 56
COA
No.2 in suite of 8 works, see cat 445

447. *It Happened at the Wall: I Spy*, 1992
oil on heavy paper
76 x 56
COA
No.3 in suite of 8 works, see cat 445

448. *It Happened at the Wall:Tooth and Nail*, 1992
oil on heavy paper
76 x 56
COA
No.4 in suite of 8 works, see cat 445

449. *It Happened at the Wall: Moment of Truth*, 1992
oil on heavy paper
76 x 56
COA
No.5 in suite of 8 works, see cat 445

450. *It Happened at the Wall: I Have My Dead Ones*, 1992
oil on heavy paper
76 x 56
COA
No.6 in suite of 8 works, see cat 445

451. *It Happened at the Wall: Run Rabbit Run*, 1992
oil on heavy paper
76 x 56
COA
No. 7 in suite of 8 works, see cat 445

452. *It Happened at the Wall: Don't Look Down*, 1992
oil on heavy paper
76 x 56
COA
No.8 in suite of 8 works, see cat 445

453. *Zimmerstrasse*, 1992
oil on paper
203 x 131
COA
Painted in Berlin.

454. *Ich Habe Hunger I*, 1992
PC
First of a suite of four. I – III were painted in Berlin, and designed to be hung as left, centre and right panels respectively, no. IV added later
see cat 455–457

455. *Ich Habe Hunger II*, 1992
(plate 15)
oil on paper
76 x 56
see cat 454

456. *Ich Habe Hunger III*, 1992
(plate 13)
oil on card
74 x 53
PC, Aberdeen:
see cat 454

457. *Ich Habe Hunger IV*, 1992
oil on heavy paper
76 x 56
COA
see cat 454

458. *Death in a Red Dress*, 1992
(plate 25)
pigment on paper
190.5 x 132
PC, Dunoon

459. *Speak to Me*, c.1992
acrylic
25 x 20
PC, Hong Kong

460. *Zimmerstrasse*, c.1992
gouache on paper
190.5 x 132
Executed in Berlin

461. *Couple*, c.1992
oil on canvas
30 x 25
PC

462. *Performer I*, c.1992
oil on watercolour paper
76 x 56
PC

463. *The Ambiguous Bride*, c.1992
b&w chalk and wash with collage
58 x 48
PC, Ireland

464. *Interlock: Mother and Child*, 1992–93 (suite of four)
oil on paper
all 115 x 88
No.1, 2 and 4: COA; No.3: PC, Aberdeen
Designed to be hung with two above and two below.

465. *The Pity* (diptych), 1993
(plate 12)
oil on canvas
183 x 305
COA

466. *Look and Listen* (diptych), 1993
(plate 7)
oil on canvas
203 x 304
Maclaurin Art Gallery, Ayr

467. *Birthing Blind, Berlin*, 1993
oil on canvas
183 x 152
COA

468. *Over and Above the Wall* (trilogy), 1993
Man Searching for a Thread (LP of trilogy)
Moment of Truth (CP of trilogy)
(plate 30)
Don't Look Down (RP of trilogy)
oil on canvas
each panel 152 x 122
COA/PC, Brechin
Developed from three paintings in an earlier suite of eight

469. *Holding You*, 1993
oil on canvas
96.5 x 96.5
COA

470. *Look and Listen*, 1993
(plate 2)
gouache and pastel drawing
208 x 132
Maclaurin Gallery, Ayr
Executed in Berlin. Cartoon for cat 466

471. *Where Angels Fear to Tread*, c.1993
acrylic and oil on canvas
35.5 x 28
PC, Aberdeen

472. *There Are Angels Everywhere*, c.1993
acrylic on canvas
30 x 25
PC, Aberdeen

473. *Moment of Being*, c.1993
oil on watercolour paper
76 x 56
PC, Aberdeen

474. *Good Times Are Coming Soon*, c.1993
gouache/mixed paints
PC, Nairn

475. *Red Head Holding*, 1993–94
oil on canvas
76 x 66
COA

476. *Babe at Sea-City*, 1994
acrylic on canvas
30 x 25
COA

477. *Four Demons Within: Hunger, Lust, Greed, Desire*, 1994
acrylic on canvas mounted on board
30 x 25
COA
A small version of one painting in the *Witness with Evidence* trilogy, cat 489

478. *Unhappy Womb*, 1994
mixed media construction/collage
12.5 x 10
COA
One of a set of five panels, part of the 'Mary Queen of Scots' series. This and the two below created for exhibition tour, 1994. See also cat 479 and 480

479. *Tragic Distresses*, 1994
mixed media construction/collage
12.5 x 10
see cat 478

480. *Poems and Piety*, 1994
mixed media construction/collage
12.5 x 10
see cat 478

481. *Bride from the East*, 1994
(plate 59)
gouache and feathers
190.5 x 132
PC, Aberdeen
Originally 198 x 127 when made in 1992. Cut down by the artist before sending to an exhibition in Aberdeen, 1994

482. *Bridesmaid I*, 1994
monoprint
58 x 46
PC, Glasgow
One in series of five entitled 'Consuming and Consummation'
see cat 483–496

483. *Bridesmaid II*, 1994
monoprint
58 x 46
COA
see cat 482

484. *Bridesmaid III*, 1994
monoprint
58 x 46
COA
see cat 482

485. *Bridesmaid IV*, 1994
(plate 60)
monoprint
58 x 46
COA
see cat 482

486. *Bridesmaid V (Consummation, Skeletal Bride)*, 1994
(plate 61)
monoprint
58 x 46
COA
see cat 482

487. *Say You Love Me*, 1994
oil on card
74 x 53
PC, Aberdeen

488. *Sweet Desire*, 1994
oil on heavy paper
76 x 56
COA

489. *Witness with Evidence*, 1994
(plate 47)
Trilogy which comprises three paintings and three sculptures. The paintings are the witnesses and the sculptures are the evidence.
Where Were You, God, When I Needed You? (LP of trilogy)
The Near Death of Hope (CP of trilogy)
The Four Demons within: Lust, Greed, Desire, Hunger (RP of trilogy)
oil on canvas
each panel 183 x 152
Charred for Life (sculpture positioned in front of RP)
wood and steel
Repaired to Live (sculpture positioned

in front of CP)
wood
approx. 30 x 91 x 15
Dying to be Born (sculpture positioned in front of LP)
wood with pigment
185 high
all COA

490. *Babe and the Angel Gabriel*, c.1994
30 x 25

491. *Smiling at You Babe*, c.1994
acrylic on canvas
30 x 25
PC, Edinburgh

492. *Succulent Summer*, c.1994
oil
74 x 56
PC, Denmark

493. *Taking the Long Way Round*, c.1994
oil on canvas
30 x 25
PC

494. *Running Wild*, c.1994
oil on paper
74 x 56
PC, Aberdeenshire

495. *Never Ending, Still Beginning*, c.1994
gouache and pastel on canvas
25 x 30
PC

496. *Never Ending, Still Beginning No.1*, c.1994
oil on paper
76 x 56
PC, Aberdeen

497. *Never Ending, Still Beginning No.2*, c.1994
oil on paper
76 x 56
PC

498. *Never Ending, Still Beginning No.3*, c.1994
oil on paper
76 x 56
PC

499. *Never Ending, Still Beginning No.4*, c.1994
oil on paper
51 x 38
PC, Falkirk

500. *Waiting for Love*, c.1994
oil on paper
74 x 56
PC, Aberdeenshire

501. *Free Fall*, c.1994
oil pigment
30 x 25
PC

502. *Free Fall*, c.1994
pigment on canvas
30 x 25
PC

503. *Rope Walker*, c.1994
pure pigment and oil on canvas
183 x 152
COA
Commenced in Berlin, 1992.

504. *I Sent a Letter to My Love*, 1994–95
oil on canvas
30 x 25
PC

505. *Very Human* (trilogy), 1995
(plate 62)
The Greater Spotted Lover (LP of trilogy)
The Sadness of Men Without Women (CP of trilogy)
Speaking in Tongues (RP of trilogy)
oil on canvas
each panel 203 x 127
COA

506. *There is Still a Heartbeat in There*, 1995
oil on heavy paper
76 x 56
COA

507. *Singer with a Change of Heart*, 1995
oil on heavy paper
76 x 56
COA

508. *The Sky's the Limit*, 1995
oil on heavy paper
76 x 56
COA

509. *Heroes All* (trilogy), 1995
Father
Son
Mother and Child
oil on heavy paper
all 76 x 56
COA

510. *Where Have All the Children Gone*, 1995
oil on heavy paper
76 x 56
COA

511. *Wish You Were Here*, c.1995
acrylic on canvas
30 x 25
PC, Hong Kong
Part of a series painted after a visit to Morocco (see cat 512–517)

512. *Maroc Door*, c.1995
oil
29 x 24
PC, Edinburgh
see cat 511

513. *Maroc Blue*, c.1995
oil
approx 30 x 23
PC
see cat 511

514. *Maroc – Bathers*, c.1995
oil on canvas
30 x 25
PC
see cat 511

515. *Maroc – Gateway*, c.1995
oil on canvas
30 x 25
PC
see cat 511

516. *Maroc Dome*, c.1995
oil on canvas and scroll
30 x 25
PC, Edinburgh
see cat 511

517. *Maroc Red*, c.1995
oil on canvas on board
24 x 19
PC
see cat 511

518. *View from Within*, c.1995
gouache on black paper
63.5 x 51

519. *The Transparent Self*, c.1995
gouache on green paper
63.5 x 35.5

520. *N-O-B-O-D-Y*, c.1995
latex plus text on canvas
approx. 169 long
COA
Cast of the artist's body in body bag

521. *Where Did All the Children Go I*, c.1995
monoprint
74 x 56

522. *Where Did All the Children Go II*, c.1995
monoprint
74 x 56

523. *Where Did All the Children Go III*, c.1995
monoprint
74 x 56

524. *Fragile Moments*, c.1995
oil and collage on canvas
63.5 x 56
PC

525. *Between One Thing and Another*, c.1995
oil on canvas on board
24 x 19
PC, Kincardineshire

526. *Moment of Being*, c.1995
oil on paper
76 x 56
PC, Aberdeen

527. *Looking for You*, c.1995
oil on paper
76 x 56
PC, Aberdeen

528. *Somewhere in the City*, c.1995
oil on paper
76 x 56

529. *Better Times are Coming*, c.1995
watercolour
76 x 61
PC, Australia

530. *Ich Habe einen Koffer in Berlin [I Have a Suitcase in Berlin]* (diptych), 1996
(plate 32)
Leiben Lust (LP)
Dead Men Tell No Tales (RP)
oil on canvas
200 x 150
COA
Disjointed diptych with a suitcase. Secondary sense of *Koffer* as a 'special place' is intended.

531. *Suitcase*, 1996
(plate 31)
hard leather suitcase, painted
COA
object accompanying cat 530

532. *Thou know'st that thou hast formed me with passions wild and strong, and list'ning to their witching voice has often led me wrong (No.1)*, 1996
(plate 77)
oil on heavy paper
76 x 56
PC, Brechin
The title comes from a Robert Burns poem 'A Prayer In the Prospect of Death'. Painted for Burns exhibition, Glasgow, 1996

533. *Thou know'st that thou hast formed me with passions wild and strong, and list'ning to their witching voice has often led me wrong (No.2)*, 1996
oil on heavy paper
76 x 56
PC, Perth
see cat 532

534. *Day of the Jackal, March 13 1996 Dunblane*, 1996
(plate 35)
oil on canvas
each panel 180 x 152
COA
This work was already under way when the artist heard news of the Dunblane massacre. It was subsequently inscribed 'March 13 1996 Dunblane'

535. The Jackal, 1996
(plate 36)
collage (derived from an old bicycle seat) on canvas
35 x 30
COA

536. *Who Shot My Child*, 1996
oil on heavy paper
76 x 56
COA

537. *Disturb Not Her Dreams*, 1996
oil on heavy paper
76 x 56
COA

538. *Everyone Has a Cross to Bear: The Printer's Cross*, 1996
oil and pastel on heavy paper
76 x 56
COA
No.1 in series of nine, designed to be hung in a double-cross arrangement (see cat 550–557)

539. *Everyone Has a Cross to Bear: Highlander*, 1996
oil on heavy paper
76 x 56
COA
No.2 in series of nine (see cat 538)

540. *Everyone Has a Cross to Bear: Winter Crossing*, 1996
oil and pastel on paper
76 x 56
COA
No.3 in series of nine (see cat 538)

541. *Everyone Has a Cross to Bear: Border Crossing*, 1996
oil pastels and oil on paper
76 x 56
COA
No.4 in series of nine (see cat 538)

542. *Everyone Has a Cross to Bear: Couple*, 1996
oil and pastel on heavy paper
76 x 56
COA
No.5 in series of nine (see cat 538)

543. *Everyone Has a Cross to Bear: Masonry Tie*, 1996
oil on heavy paper
76 x 56
COA
No.6 in series of nine (see cat 538)

544. *Everyone Has a Cross to Bear: Smokehouses and Ovens*, 1996
oil on heavy paper
76 x 56
COA
No.7 in series of nine (see cat 538)

545. *Everyone Has a Cross to Bear: Island Crossing*, 1996
oil on heavy paper
76 x 56
COA
No.8 in series of nine (see cat 538)

546. *Everyone Has a Cross to Bear: My Grandfather's Shirt*, 1996
oil and pastel on heavy paper
76 x 56
COA
No.9 in series of nine (see cat 538)

547. *Female Nude*, c.1996
unconfirmed media on canvas
12.5 x 9
PC, Stirling

548. *Love Will Keep Us Together*, c.1996
oil
76 x 56
PC

549 *'Tis Never Too Late To Tell Her You Love Her*, 1996–97
mixed media panels with shelf and scroll
183 x 122 (at widest parts)
Installation of 14 mounted panels hung in a T-bar shape with scroll underneath

550. *Hoch Wasser [High Water]*, 1997
oil on canvas
183 x 122
Galerie im Ermelerspeicher, City of Schwedt an der Oder.
Painted in Galerie im Ermelerspeicher to mark the floods there.

551. *Adoring the Fish*, c.1997
acrylic on canvas
30 x 25

552. *Northern Woman*, c.1997
acrylic on canvas
18 x 14
PC, Bridge of Allan

553. *We Come and We Go I*, c.1997
mixed media box construction
53 x 37
COA

554. *We Come and We Go II*, c.1997
oil on canvas and mixed media
30 x 25

555. *We Come and We Go III*, c.1997
oil on canvas and mixed media
30 x 25

556. *Island Mother and Daughter*, c.1997
mixed media on canvas
30 x 25

557. *Love Is Present All the Year Round*, c.1997
mixed media on canvas
30 x 25

558. *Northern Recall*, c.1997
mixed media on paper
76 x 56

559. *Northern Mother*, c.1997
mixed media on paper
76 x 56

560. *Bone of My Bone*, c.1997
mixed media: bone,plastic, wood
box construction.
48 x 43
COA

561. *All That Remains*, c.1997
mixed media: wood, bone, metal
box construction
46 x 43
COA

562. *Ship Ahoy, Ship Ahoy*, c.1997
mixed media: wood, lead, glass
box construction
48 x 43
COA

563. *Monument III*, c.1997
mixed media: wood, plastic
box construction
47 x 39
COA

564. *Heart Speak*, c.1997
mixed media: wood, canvas, jute, paint
box construction
43 x 38
COA

565. *Fleur de Lys*, c.1997
mixed media: bone, wood, stone
box construction
43 x 48
COA

566. *The Angel from Bornholm*, c.1997
objets trouvés, wood and ceramic pieces on canvas board
12.5 x 10
PC, Blackpool

567. *Bone of my Bone (Bone on Bone)*, c.1997
oil
66 x 56 (excl. mount)
PC, Aberdeenshire
Related to box construction *Bone of My Bone* (cat 560)

568. *My Blue Heaven*, c.1997
oil and graphite
76 x 56

569. *Monument I*, c.1997
oil on canvas
30 x 25

570. *Monument II*, c.1997
oil on canvas
30 x 25

571. *Testing the Water*, c.1997
oil on canvas
30 x 25

572. *Always Lovers, Never Friends*, c.1997
oil on paper
76 x 56

573. *Northern Remains*, c.1997
oil on paper
76 x 56

574. *All Heart*, c.1997
oil on paper
84 x 56

575. *The 23rd Psalm: No.1 - Green Pastures ; No.2 - Quiet Waters ; No.3 - The Valley*, c.1997
monoprint and gouache
all 48 x 63.5
COA
Suite of three works designed to be hung vertically

576. *Male Figure*, 1997
acrylic on paper
46 x 33
COA

577. *What Future Remains*, 1997
mixed media panel with bag of plastic discs
30 x 30
PC, Glasgow

578. *Before and After*
oil on canvas on board
127 x
COA

579. *Tulips*
oil or acrylic
17 x 13
PC, Glasgow

580. *Red Queen to Black Knight*
painted collage on canvas
127 x 127
COA

581. *Red Raw Male*
watercolour
20 x 15
PC, Glasgow

582. *Untitled*
watercolour
20 x 15
PC, Glasgow

583. *Bodypiece/Landpiece*, 1998
(plate 22)
oil on canvas
approx 180 x 150

584. *The Sacrifice*, 1998
(plate 23)
oil on canvas
approx 180 x 150

APPENDIX 2

LYS HANSEN – SELECTED REVIEWS, 1966–97

FRENCH PRINTS STEAL THE SHOW (42nd Annual Exhibition of the Scottish Society of Women Artists)

Sydney Goodsir Smith, *The Scotsman*, 28 November 1966

It was announced at the opening that Lys Hansen, Clackmannan, had won the new Anne Redpath award (for her painting, *Interior with Chair*) . . .

Outstanding here, maybe the only painter who could hold her head high in any general, national or international exhibition, is undoubtedly Lys Hansen, whose two large, high-toned, blazing-yellow compositions (*Interior with Chair* and *Boatmaker's Fish Garden*), as well as a brilliant watercolour and a fine drawing, proclaim with a shout that here is a considerable talent moving into the lists.

PORTRAIT OF THE ARTIST AS A YOUNG WOMAN

Lesley Munn, *Glasgow Herald*, 27 May 1978

To be at once a beauty, a distinguished artist and a former 'Housewife of the Future' at the Ideal Home Exhibition might seem an unlikely combination. Lys Hansen is all three.

A slender, raven-haired woman with turquoise eyes set in a blaze of matching eyeshadow, Miss Hansen is far from one's idea of a typical Stirlingshire village dweller. Yet she was born in the county (a sea-faring Danish grandfather who settled in Grangemouth accounts for her unusual name) and has lived much of her life in Blairlogie, that picturesque cluster of whitewashed houses and pocket-handkerchief gardens at the foot of the Ochils.

Today is a special day for the village and its resident artist, for it marks the opening of the annual Crowsteps exhibition in the pantiled village hall. Lys Hansen has been closely involved with organising the exhibition since its inception thirteen years ago, though she gives all the practical credit to a series of dedicated local folk. The exhibitors are mostly professional artists, she explains, 'but we don't question whether a person is professional or amateur'.

Lys Hansen herself belongs firmly to the former category, in terms of both training and achievement.

After a boarding-school education in which her interest in art was kindled by a six-foot-tall teacher with a face like a Murillo Madonna, she went to Edinburgh Art School. Here her teachers included the late Sir William Gillies and Robin Philipson. The transition from boarding to art school was, she recalls, bewildering, with all the excitement of dances and boyfriends and living on one's own in a flat with other students.

Not surprisingly, perhaps, she dropped out for a year – to become a model. 'I was a very good stock size,' she recalls, 'and started to pick up a lot of work as a mannequin.' This is where the Ideal Home Exhibition came in.

As 'Housewife of the Future', she shared her exhibition house with a 'husband' (an opera singer in real life), sporting a silver wig and a remote control bracelet for answering the door. The work paid well but the life of a model wasn't really for her. 'I didn't like trotting round like a dressed-up cabbage.'

So Lys Hansen went back to college and repeated a year. To good effect, for she had acquired a new dedication and did very well, winning both a Prix de Rome (open to all art schools in Britain and enabling her to travel to Italy and study at the British School of Painting in Rome) and a £500 award from Edinburgh Art School.

Travelling on her own she found very exciting. She worked and painted in Aix-en-Provence, then in Germany for a while. She was away two summers consecutively, avoiding Rome the first season because of the Olympics.

A brief period as an au pair girl with the Martel cognac family was interrupted by peritonitis. Back in Scotland, her husband-to-be had his appendix removed at the same time. '*Quel grand amour*,' said the French doctor who treated her.

She went on to do post-graduate work in painting as well as studying fine art at Edinburgh University, earning *en route* a gallant compliment from Stirlingshire Education Authority, who said, 'We don't consider you the bread and butter, we consider you the cake.' Like many another young artist, she did teacher training at Moray House. She now lectures for the Scottish Arts Council.

'Notorious Nudes' is the provocative title of one lecture which she has given as far afield as Orkney and Thurso. (It is in fact a sober study of the female in Western art over the centuries.) 'Being away from your family for a little while is good for them and good for you,' she says. 'They learn to cope – particularly when they're a household of males.'

The men in her life are sons Giles, aged fourteen, Marcus, nine, and husband George Sutherland. Her husband is, she says – relishing the precise definition – 'a Scottish teacher who teaches English.' Fortunately, he's sympathetic to her art. Some husbands say, 'What do you want to paint for anyway?' She adds sadly that few of her contemporaries have continued to paint.

Does she feel any tension between the roles of artist and housewife? Absolutely, she says, but it's no more difficult for her than for thousands of other women coping with career, family and maintaining their own identity. 'I'm quite happy to struggle along with my tensions.'

The Sutherlands' home, a double-storey listed building known as Blairlogie Cottage, reflects her preoccupation with colour. Purple and yellow walls provide the background to a clutter of cultured bric-à-brac. Colour is a thing to be enjoyed like good coffee and the smell of flowers, Lys Hansen says. In quite a lot of her paintings, colour is the first decision.

Her boldly coloured, sometimes disturbing, canvases are obviously rooted in her own particular circumstances and preoccupations. The recurring image is of a female figure (there's something of herself in her nudes, she says – 'I know my own body best') in the setting of a house structure, suggesting at once an area protected or caged, and a landscape. 'The problem is combining these images so that they shift and overlap. Landscapes can filter through you. In painting things don't have to be logical in scale.'

It's no doubt possible to see a Freudian significance in the tree or plant which crops up in many of her paintings, such as the blue nude which dominates the sitting-room wall. The still, enigmatic figure is flanked by a totem-pole-like object – 'A bit phallic, in a way,' comments the artist.

The tree motif, she explains, can provide pictorial interest or a jarring quality. In this painting it is quite fierce and vicious, but it can take on many aspects, sometimes joyful. Take it away and the painting would become rather soft. She mentions Picasso's *Guernica* and says, 'What most artists try to find is a quality not of repulsion or vulgarity but of grit – what's under the skin; what makes you bite.'

The layering, or ambiguity, of images which fascinates her can be seen in a painting in the dining-room. A goose descends out of the sky towards the female. Do we read menace into it, echoes of Leda and the Swan, or does it simply reflect the fact that several well-fed geese inhabit the back garden?

Beyond the giant pear trees in the garden is Lys Hansen's studio – an old shed, splendidly cluttered with paintings in progress. A vase of tulips will find its way into yet another variation on her standard theme. Pots of house paint on the floor raise a momentary eyebrow in the visitor. They are strictly for house painting. For her art work she uses lots of instantly drying PVA paints and acrylics, sometimes finishing off with oils. She also enjoys watercolour with its 'tender, more delicate touch'.

The paintings of this artist, still in her thirties, have been exhibited, among other places, at the Commonwealth Institute, London, and she is a regular contributor to RSA, SSA, RSW and SSWA shows. Bodies like Stirling University and Edinburgh College of Art own her works and they are also to be found in private collections in Canada, Australia and the United States, as well as Britain and Ireland.

Does she regret parting with them? 'Sometimes when they're sold I'm quite sorry. I've got the money for the electricity bill; they've got the painting!'

LYS HANSEN

Cordelia Oliver, *The Guardian*, 22 February 1984

Lys Hansen's new paintings in the Third Eye Centre are very large and, at first sight, more aggressive than most people might expect to find in the work of a woman who is neither old nor unattractive. But this artist is a self-styled 'woman in a hurry'; a wife and mother who, at forty-odd, has at last found the courage to break the mould and employ a welter of bright brash colours and a web of forceful expressionist imagery to release long pent-up emotions and stresses which are more truly female than merely feminine. The difference is far more basic than is usually supposed: many male artists are entirely 'feminine' in the taste and sensitivity they bring to their work.

Hansen's imagery is female, nude and far from passive; a far cry from the voyeuristic nudes of the average male imagination. Most perceptive women would recognise in these paintings a familiar scenario; how it feels to be frustrated, by turns anguished and happy, aggressive and diffident, angry and yet, in spite of everything, capable of being amused at life's obstacles and personal shortcomings.

Here, above all, is someone with real talent, trying to pin down the dual nature of the female make-up; the psychological mystery behind the basic physical reality. Pinning down, though, is maybe not the right phrase to describe the process in question. In these big canvases nothing is clear-cut; as in life and with people, you have to search for, sense and tease out the meanings and relationships.

LYS HANSEN

Clare Henry, *Glasgow Herald*, 24 February 1984

Lys Hansen is one of Scotland's best artists. She also happens to be a woman, and while her work explores the experience of being female, her art is not feminist propaganda in the accepted sense. Rather, she turns the tables and invites us to re-examine and reconsider that archetypal male art subject – the female nude.

There is a Mexican saying: 'Laws are like woman; they're to be violated.' In an age when sexual discrimination and reappraisal of male-female roles is a live debate, her far-from-passive women have much to say. No longer merely an object of male centre-fold perusal, they agitate the canvas with primal vitality; mentally, physically and spiritually torn in numerous directions; trying to be all things to all men – even one man; striving to satisfy themselves, their maternal and sexual instincts – to say nothing of their intellect.

Hansen has wrestled with this theme for some time now, but this exhibition of recent work demonstrates a new violent quality which impresses with its conviction and authority. Gone are the smooth, pale fleshy and voluptuous creatures of the late-1970s and early-1980s to be replaced by more gestural New Image style neo-expressionist pictures. The paint drags and slashes; the colours fight; the painful edge of love and fear is there. In *Reject*, a couple argue; he red and carnivorous, she strident. *Wall of Faces* includes hints of Clemente and Immendorf.

Hansen's work should spark off much reaction during the British Women's Conference which will be held in the Third Eye on 9–11 March.

WOMEN IN THE ROUGH AND TUMBLE

Aidan Dunne, *Sunday Press* (Ireland), 14 April 1985

Lys Hansen is a Scottish painter whose formative influences were international movements like the American Abstract Expressionists and, in Europe, the COBRA Group, as well as the homespun influence of Scottish Expressionism. Her pictures are big, brash, figurative works, full of bright, agitated colours and swirling forms. Her show, 'She is She', at the Project Arts Centre . . .

The figures in Hansen's paintings are fragmented and distorted, but not in a spirit of cruelty. Although there is a great deal of rough and tumble in the way figures balance, embrace, wrestle and merge, the mood is more playful than sinister, even if there is a genuinely aggressive edge to her technique. The women in her pictures, and there are probably more women than men, are often big, stalwart nudes, far removed from passive convention, delighting in their own physicality, their energy and strength.

'Women,' says the artist, 'have been compartmentalised into such a gentle area, either the calm Madonna or the reclining Venus. These are predominantly male views of women, though Picasso and Munch have produced more complex, interesting versions of their experiences of women. I know through my own experience that motherhood, for example, is not a passive role, but a volatile one. So much is demanded of you. So these paintings are partly about stepping from behind the calm façade. Women's sexuality has long been exploited to cater for male fantasies – which I think have to be catered for. I don't really object to the page-three pin-ups in newspapers. But that is just one aspect of a woman.'

The pictures, however, wear these concerns lightly. They avoid complaint and are joyously affirmative. The figures have an almost manic energy, twisting and leaping in impossible angles and contortions. The paint is applied freely, loosely. 'Technique,' says Hansen, 'is getting the imagery to say what you want. You have to marry the idea to the technique. The idea cannot be dominant, because the painting is about visual experience. These paintings are celebrations of energy, love, passion, caring. They are not cool or intellectual. They are done instinctively. I found acrylics too flat on their own, so I used other means as well, like the elements of collage.'

There is a great deal of touching and holding in the pictures and, more than that, figures are often composites, anomalous mixtures of heads, limbs, breasts, torsos, assembled in such a way that all these elements are individually recognisable. Hansen thinks that the blending and merging has to do with pregnancy and birth. 'The child, after all, is a part of you, even afterwards. Physically the cord gets cut but there are strong biological ties. Then, I feel that the body is there to be enjoyed. I don't mean just in a sexual way.'

What of the way the pictures home in on details, like hands? 'Hands are important because they are so expressive. I pick on bits of the body in order to communicate with a kind of body language. It is partly a technical thing. You focus on one bit and dispense with the rest. What you're aiming for is an expressionistic essence. It is limiting to use just the body, but it is good discipline and provides a focus for my ideas.'

Though you can see that women have, in many respects, had a raw deal, Hansen is remarkably free of animosity towards men. On the contrary, she says, 'I'm a great admirer of men, in the way they recognise their own potential and their ability to achieve what they want. I like this honesty and directness. There were no women to serve as role models when I was a student. It was always a man telling you what to do. It's good to help balance things out.'

Summing up what she would like to achieve in her work, Hansen is quite sure and direct: 'I would like a lot of love, a lot of good feelings to come out of it. So much art is about itself, it becomes introverted, and that removes it from everyone. The most exciting thing is painting itself, of course, that you can get so much energy and life in a few colours, so much impact. That is joyous, and the great thing is that you can share it.'

LYS HANSEN: 'SHE IS SHE'

Anne Carlisle, *Circa*, May/June 1985

This exhibition came via the Third Eye Centre in Glasgow and due to its size had to be split when it reached Belfast. Thus, the larger works were shown in the more generous proportions of the Art College, and the smaller drawn and painted pieces were located in the Octagon Gallery. Interestingly, this division of the artist's work emphasised a point which may have been less obvious had the work been all shown together, which is that this artist manages to achieve much more dynamic and resonant images on a small scale than she does in her larger works. Part of the reason for this, no doubt, is that it rescues her work from comparisons with much overblown and bombastic neo-expressionist paintings – it is bad enough having to look at inflated male figures without having to look at big women – but, also, on a smaller scale this artist is capable of a sardonic and biting wit, which really is the strength of much of her work.

Put simply, the work is about relationships: maternal, sexual, combative and fearful. For Hansen, most relationships are a double-edged sword and for this reason her work often treads a borderline between intimacy and aggression, affection and disaffection. Her perspective, which is undoubtedly female, is unsentimental, vigorous and not a little blunt. In a work such as *Love Bites* a deliberate pun is made both upon the title and within the image itself, which is both extraordinarily intimate and also savage as each figure greedily probes and consumes the other. Apparently, she glories in physical as well as psychological exposure. *Mother's Child* is an extremely defensive painting. Here a naked (not nude) woman, arms outstretched, shielding her offspring, compels our gaze as she fiercely, although somewhat fearfully, thrusts her head out over her breasts, her fat belly and thighs set in a posture of defence. As in most of Hansen's paintings the face dominates, heightened by the disproportionately large size of the head. Relentlessly awkward, her figures make few if any concessions to stereotyped women's beauty. Most of the time they look as if they are made from jelly. Many of the figures possess exaggerated limbs, gigantic feet and hands, which look nearly deformed, and although they occasionally border on it, she generally manages to avoid caricature by virtue of the fact that she is seriously attempting to paint something that is both alive and personal to her. Significantly, although the vigorous paint handling and strident use of colour – reds, bright blues and dragged pinks and creams – invite clear comparisons with De Kooning's forceful Woman Paintings, she manages to steer clear of the profound negativism of many of these representations of women. By investing her women with personalities and allowing them to express their emotions, she is attempting to move beyond oppressive definitions of the convention of the female nude, for example, women defining their identities exclusively and reductively through their bodies. At her best, Hansen manages to make a few of her women read as powerful maternal images, but also as women in control of their sexual destiny.

Clearly, her aim is to transform the nude from passive object of contemplation to a fighting symbol. That she does not entirely succeed in this is partly explained by her occasional lapses into ambiguity and her repetitive and almost absent-minded use of male figures. Nowhere is this more clear than in the piece entitled *Red Queen to Black Knight*. Here the heavy-jowled aggressive male figure looms in the foreground, juxtaposed with a rather stupefied, slit-eyed female torso. It is quite unclear where the obvious displeasure on the male's face is directed and what the relationship between the two figures is. In fact, puzzled by the relative closeness of their heads, I was left wondering if it was meant to be an image of affection or aggression. Of course, this obscurity may well have been intended, but to my mind it was an incidence of ambiguity denying meaning. Added to this, the extremely complex combination of collage and energetically applied paint which although interesting enough as painted textural surfaces, functioned more as texture for texture's sake and brought relatively little to the image. In some of the larger works the problem was further compounded by the apparent difficulty that she experienced in sustaining an interesting painted surface; where tightly controlled areas of paint were unhappily juxtaposed with rather flaccid painted expanses.

Generally, however, Hansen was able to make her paintings work for her and not against her. No small part of the impact of these images is the sensation of energy and frenzy that is evident in their making, occasionally resulting in rather raw, even brutal images. The scarcely suppressed shriek of *Drowning* suggests helplessness and tortuous despair, both in its quivering paint and bulging-eyed women. But it should be pointed out that this is not an assertive image, rather it is a reactive image – a human being at odds with the world she inhabits – and in that sense it is as ironically passive as many expressionistic paintings depicting males in similarly convulsive states.

Hansen has set herself a difficult task; her attempt to 'redefine the female torso of her earlier works, which had considered the female in the tradition of Western Art' is effectively an attempt to evolve a counter-culture, where her female figures modify and comment upon official (male) culture in myriad ways. One of the questions which must be asked is to what degree does one affirm received stereotypes by opposing them? This is a crucial question, not only in relation to 'Women's' art, but in this context to the work of Lys Hansen.

CREATION WITHOUT A TRACE OF SHAME

Waldemar Januszczak, *The Guardian*, 6 February 1986

Lys Hansen takes human sexuality as her main theme . . . Her paintings push you right up between the two lovers, so closely you can feel their hot breath on your cheek . . . [They] make a grab for the senses.

The first impression made by her exhibition is of a thick tangle of heads, hands, mouths, feet, torsos, eyes, fingers, all apparently involved in a furious exploration of the human physique. A female hand reaches out and interlocks with the toes of a male foot; it is a painting which seems to circumnavigate the mind entirely and speaks directly to the nerves in your legs.

But such sensuality alone would not have made these paintings as remarkable as they are. The sound of flesh colliding with flesh is common enough in art, witness Rubens on one side, and Utamaro on the other. In Picasso's beach pictures of the 1930s the old rogue showed himself and his outrageously young girlfriend gobbling each other up like a pair of hungry crabs.

What makes these paintings so interesting is that they introduce a note of introspection to the proceedings. This is a woman's view. And however dense the tangle of limbs there always seems to be an eye somewhere in the background, peeping out from between parted fingers, watching, speculating, a thoughtful witness to its own climax.

VISUAL ARTS

Mark Currah, *City Limits*, 21–27 February 1986

Lumped together as part of the Scottish Expressionist bandwagon but deserving attention in [her] own right rather than as part of a movement, Lys Hansen . . . [has] been painting for over twenty years and her experience shows. Lys Hansen's work is the most obviously expressionist . . . the paint is slashed on, her lovers contorted and anxious. *Licking and Biting* is closer to prehistoric warfare than foreplay. There are two breathtaking trilogies of manic colours and grappling limbs, but when the mood lightens the same dynamic lines produce the joyful *Handstand*.

ART: SELECTIONS AND REVIEWS

Sarah Kent, *Time Out*, 20–26 February 1986

Lys Hansen . . . does not get the attention she deserves . . . [She] works in a variety of ways and one is not certain, therefore, where her next step will take her. There are the large pastels, for instance, whose graphic images have a slight archaic quality reminiscent of Clemente's Indian pastels – an uncanny almost mystical calm. Yet her paintings clearly lodge in expressionist terrain. Some demonstrate a strong debt to De Kooning, leaving the uncomfortable feeling that her red-lipped, bright-eyed women are seen voyeuristically, as the subject of ridicule. And whereas one can understand, though not sympathise with, De Kooning's fear of female sexuality, for a woman to distance herself from her own sex enough to portray them as harridans could be interpreted as an act of betrayal rather than of solidarity. On a different plane altogether is her *Divided Self* trilogy, a much more original triptych whose horror has a fierce authenticity that clearly emanates from internal pain. The twisted double face which forms the central panel is also a hand wrenching its own features apart – a powerful evocation of inner conflict and one of the most compelling portrayals of psychic suffering that I have seen for a long time. The kind of bravery required to make a picture that raw should enable Hansen ruthlessly to weed out all (masculine) influences that alienate her from the difficult self that has so much that is valuable to say.

LYS HANSEN

Cordelia Oliver, *The Guardian*, 1 May 1986

If anyone could be expected to make a dent in the rather grim, grey atmosphere of the new 369 Gallery in Edinburgh's Cowgate, it is Lys Hansen, with the force and energy of her best recent work. And so it is with her exhibition now on view there. Hansen is an artist whose work is essentially female, not 'feminine'; whose painting, all furious slashing, smeared and smudged – but seldom uncertain – brushwork, suggests an intensely subjective vision, if not a desperate search for identity.

A lot is talked nowadays about 'new expressionism' with regard to painters who, for all their exaggeratedly violent style, are illustrators if they are anything. But Lys Hansen is an expressionist in the only sense that matters. Her paintings seem to me to express both a wish to hide and a desire to wound; a dichotomy that she tries to resolve in a welter of pigments.

Her recent sojourn in Berlin seems to have given her work a new assurance, a sharpening of focus when compared with what she was doing two years ago when she held an exhibition at Glasgow's Third Eye Centre. The sheer physicality of the act of creating, the struggle with the paint on canvas and the surface tensions which arise in consequence, seem to me to be true painter's equivalents, often effective, sometimes less so, to the naked traumas of being female, vulnerable and at the same time intermittently courageous in a man's world.

LYS HANSEN INTERVIEWED

Wendy Halstead, *Alba*, Summer 1986

WENDY HALSTEAD: *Have you always worked as a figurative painter?*
LYS HANSEN: Yes, always. I'm primarily interested in the figure, that's what intrigues me – the fascination with people.

Where do you get your ideas from? Do you find yourself looking at life and studying people in various situations?
It is an amalgamation of observation and perception – what they do have, they are; the vibrations, gestures, looks they give off. You develop an enlarged vision when you're an artist – a whole gamut of understanding which brings in an understanding of the 'European figurative tradition' – Matisse for colour, Picasso for form and structure and certainly the northern European tradition for content.

Do you work from sketches, drawings or photographic references before you start a painting or do you memorise certain situations?
That, to me, is quite an illustrative way in which to work. Sometimes I prepare large-scale drawings first. Recently, I have been moving towards very considered statements – trying to achieve an intense accuracy of focus – for example, on a fingernail or eye.

I work from the inside out. So I work from feelings, thoughts – far more than external visuals. For example, in some cases, no one figure negates another. Some of my recent works, such as *Trilogies*, are separated onto individual canvases, so there is already separation. The large trilogy, *The Divided Self*, was inspired by a visit to Belfast and Dublin: Belfast a divided city and Ireland a divided country. This is also one of the reasons why I went to Berlin – the political division there.

Do you work from a studio?
Always. My work is about size and space. My studio is a physical representation of my mind. It is important that your mind as an artist has this space in which to work.

Do you have a set timetable? When do you work?
I have very regular hours in which I work. I have a very disciplined approach. Within the discipline, however, I have a unique freedom. I usually work during the evenings and at weekends, although last year I had an Arts Council grant. This meant that I had a lot more time for my work. So then I was able to work every day, seven days a week, and I have always worked full time.

How long have you been teaching?
On and off, all my working life since I graduated from primary right through to teaching adults.

Do you find that whilst you are both teaching and working as an artist, the people around you react differently because you are a woman or do you get more support because of this? Are there any extra pressures upon you to make you feel not so equal?
Well, yes, I certainly feel equal. If you function as an artist, think like an artist, it is a problem for men too, to fulfil all the roles in life. Certainly, for a woman having children, their early years causes a few delays with the nurturing and rearing of children which can be very demanding. But they do eventually grow up.

How did your children affect your life?
I was doing a full-time course at Moray House when my first child was just a few months old. People cope with what they think they are capable of. I am a great believer in doing as much as possible in life. I wouldn't have liked to have been denied the experience of having my children.

What are your opinions on the fact that there are so many female art students and yet so few women art lecturers? Do you agree that women artists are just as good as men but unfortunately lack the same amount of confidence?
Yes, I would agree with perhaps the lack of confidence. It is often more difficult for the woman to negotiate with the world on her own and to have a true focus for herself. This is a basic fundamental of being a female; it must alter in order to become an artist – you must be very, very determined and not be diverted. But that is a woman's problem – an individual decision.

Would you say that it is harder for women art students in art schools due to the fact that they are so male-orientated?
I think if a lecturer is professional and objective then he treats the male and female students as absolute equals – it's simply a young talent in your hands.

Would you agree that there should be more part-time lecturers in art schools and less full-time staff, enabling there to be more part-time and visiting lecturers in order to circulate varied ideas? Do you agree that students would benefit more from part-time lecturers?
It's great to have visiting lecturers who can come and stimulate a constant situation. This can be extremely invigorating for staff and students alike. If lecturers are going to be serious artists then they would welcome a part-time situation which would relieve them and still bring in some money.

In 1985 you had a studio in Berlin. How long were you there for and how big an effect did this have on your work?
I had the studio in Berlin for two months. I had

the amazing experience whilst there of being away from everything that was familiar to me. I was isolated but in a very cultural city and a society that is extremely art-conscious. Being in this situation gives you time to think. It helps to simplify a lot of my painting – to focus, to sit back and really think about what I was doing.

Whilst you were working in Berlin, were you working alongside other artists?

No, I was working on my own but while I was there I did visit other artists' studios. I visited the Cultural Exchange which is an upmarket centre for foreign artists. There I met people from France, England, Ireland and Germany who were taking over the floor of a factory in order to make studios. What I found exciting was the collective force. Grants were not always available so artists had to pool their resources and earn money by working part-time. Some worked in markets. The experience of being in Berlin, having time to myself, was very important. I chose Berlin because it is so culturally alive. There is a tremendous focus on opera and galleries. It is a country of museums with the most amazing collections. Cologne, for example, has over sixty commercial galleries. You have to visit Berlin to appreciate how good some of the collections in the museums there really are.

Berlin is saturated with artists. It is supposed to be easier to get bursaries, awards and travelling scholarships in Germany. How does the position compare with here?

Yes, well, this is an integral part of the German society. You have your opera and your painting just like you have your toast and marmalade for breakfast, or your car. It's very important to be a cultured person. Compared with Britain it leaves us with a terrible dilemma. But then any true artist will survive anyway, whatever. I think in Scotland a lot of energy is diluted. It's like a plant growing in poor conditions – it will still grow but it won't flourish quite so well. However, if one does achieve something, there is a tremendous satisfaction from being an artist.

In the catalogue introduction to your recent exhibition at the 369 Gallery, Judith Macrae states that you have 'chosen the human body as a paradigm for the exploration of emotional and sexual conflict' and describes you as 'giving a disconcerting and difficult vision of our personal and sexual personas, without costumes or props – naked upon the stage of your own choosing, the painting itself'. Could you expand these ideas?

The painting which I think she is specifically referring to is possibly *Stage Fright* which houses many fears and dilemmas about the person and about the sexual persona. I think women are powerful in their profundity. The concept of the all-giving, the all-wonderful mother is something we all experience. The only thing is that some of us *become* mothers as well. The nakedness is not actually about being physically naked but being exposed in an emotional way, psychologically. Painting is really about elements of growth – involvement, fear and the traumas that we must all experience. I think this is as true for men as for women. It's about regrowth, regeneration.

You say that each piece of paint is there for a specific purpose. Are you an artist who constantly repaints and reworks areas, building up a unified surface through a struggle with materials and emotions, or do you arrive at the finished image through a rational process?

Yes I like a piece of paint to have a specific function on the canvas and will study a painting very hard in order to adjust a number of strokes until the painting is going in the right direction. Sometimes the painting works magnificently; other times it's a case of trial and error, readjustment, repainting.

Do you find painting hard? Did you find it hard as a student? Has this changed or is it just the same but on a more advanced level?

There are still problems but, yes, on a more advanced level because you are constantly demanding more from yourself and the work should grow, shall we say, in complexity of meaning, if not in the complexity of the technique. Painting is a dialogue between the painting and yourself.

What made you start painting? Why do you paint?

I suppose my art teacher. She was a very inspiring woman and extremely striking to look at. She was six feet tall and had a head like a Spanish Murillo painting. She fascinated me as opposed to my history and geography teachers. I need to paint, it is a spiritual necessity as opposed to a physical or social necessity. I can look at my thoughts and feelings and put them into some sort of order. I think artists are very aware of their needs and responses. I just have something inside that I must pull out. That's the only way I know how to do it. I find it exciting and challenging.

How do you feel about the art that one sees in galleries today? What are your views on Scottish art and artists?

There is a great energy and vitality. I think they are finding a new confidence. They are painting in a very poignant way which is very relevant. I think things are going well and that the 'Old School' is dying with a new one being born, which is very exciting.

I do believe in sponsorship – getting the work out of the country and having a strong national identity here because Scottish painting has great vigour and shows up extremely well in national comparisons.

What advice would you give to an art student, a keen painter, for example, who is just about to leave art school?

Well, it's a bit like learning to drive. Once you get your driving licence and are on your own, you have to start learning to negotiate problems on your own. This is complex but I think youth is wonderful; it has a wonderful joy and vigour and that is their trump card, really.

Do you think that there should be someone to advise students about all the problems that they are going to come up against once they have left art school, such as how to write up a curriculum vitae, take slides, get an exhibition, how to go about applying for jobs, and so on?

Yes, definitely. There should be specific guidelines about how to present one's work. It is all part and parcel of a professional and serious approach to being organised. But I am sure the information is available either through art lecturers or various magazines such as *Artist's Newsletter*. It is really up to the students to just get it together, get themselves organised and find out just what is available.

A POWERFUL PLEA FOR THE PLANET

Murdo MacDonald, *The Scotsman*, 17 October 1988

These works have been carried out since 1985 and are qualified in their concerns by the trip that Hansen made to Berlin in that year. The journey to this split city sharpens our perception of the barriers inherent in all relationships whether political or personal.

Several of the paintings here (for example, *Blue Lips* and *See All*) are an attempt to develop a sense of the role of the artist in society. For Hansen the responsibility of the artist is to see everything and from that condition to find relevant expression.

She concentrates here on establishing this role and in *Self-portrait, 1987*, a work in charcoal and gouache, she achieves her expressive aim. This is based on a recollection of her three-year-old son, fearful of swimming, clambering up her body and away from the water to find security. The result is a deeply felt image in which her interest in human relationships is fused with her development of a language of gesture through observation of hands, feet and faces.

PASSION IN A CLASH OF COLOUR

Andrew Gibbon Williams, *The Observer*, October 1988

Scotland's record of honouring its first-rate female artists is one in which it can take pride. And it is a fortuitous coincidence that three artists concurrently showing original and mature work in Edinburgh are all women. Of the three, only Lys Hansen has feasted on brash, figurative expressionism; not surprising in the light of her extended sojourns in Berlin.

The artist's exhibition at the City Art Centre in Edinburgh amounts to a major retrospective. Hansen tackles the big issues – man/woman, mother/child relationships, sexual passion, violence, loneliness – peopling her canvases with giant, tumescent, anonymous figures.

They shield their eyes, stagger, rise and clutch, giving the impression they are impatient to escape their medium. Paint is applied with slashing gusto, hallmark of much German painting in the 1980s, and Hansen employs the now almost conventional strident, acidic palette. The latter is her stumbling block, for the colours often clash too capriciously, and the intent to shock – to draw attention to some dislocated limb or torso – is subverted by the ultimately pretty effect.

Consequently, Hansen is at her best where profligacy of colour and texture is denied as in the striking monochrome works, *Allein* and *Signals*. These are wholly original images, as arresting as any by Baselitz, and more memorable than any by British artists.

Incidentally, the artist is to be applauded for the trouble she has taken to explain her aims and technical means. The fascinating personality glimpsed in the catalogue quotations is as intriguing as the work itself.

LYS HANSEN

Geraldine Prince, *The Independent*, 1 November 1988

[Lys Hansen] impressed critics at her London show two years ago, as 'indisputably an important artist . . . positive, spontaneous, fearless'. Back on home ground in Edinburgh . . . Hansen's show of expressionistic paintings and vital drawings reveal increasing artistic maturity, intellectual and stylistic consolidation. Hansen's sources are varied. Ted Hughes's sexual poetry inspired a series of erotic pastels; experience of the divided city of Berlin . . . Massive close-up faces and clutching, straining fingers with the artist's own painted fingernails suppressed speech, both trapping and blocking out sound and vision in *Say Nothing, Hear Everything, See All*. Affected by visits to Belfast and Dublin, as well as Berlin, Hansen deals with 'suppression and powerlessness'. Her vehicle is always the human figure, expressively distorted, communicating directly through vigorously handled paint and personal language of dislocated limbs and torsos.

EXHIBITIONS

William Ferguson, *Times Educational Supplement*, 21 October 1988

Lys Hansen has emerged into full flow since her family grew up. In 1979, she began to paint the female torso using it as a vehicle to express feminine ideas of repression, concealment, emotions unstateable except in body language.

In 1985, Ted Hughes' poem on 'The Bride and Groom' was used to enter more fully into the male experience. A year of study in Berlin had two results; the experience of alienation, and some insight into political reality. The latter appears decisively in a *Berlin Trilogy*, hearing everything, seeing all and saying nothing. Hansen's expressionist colour and gestural technique are the vehicles for her tumultuous emotions.

A MAN'S A MAN FOR A' THAT

W. Gordon Smith, *The Observer*, 1 October 1989

Far and away the most arresting image in the exhibition is an enormous triptych by Lys Hansen. It owes its title to some lines from a sketch inscribed by Burns to Charlie James Fox – 'How Wisdom and Folly Meet Mix and Unite: How Virtue and Vice Blend their Black and their White'. The theme is again duality in the human condition, its dilemmas and conflicts. Virtue and Vice enmesh and intertwine. The poet's head rests on Virtue's breast, his eyes closed in contemplation. The work leaps from the canvas, monumentally raw, straining with energy, wailing with a banshee.

ZWEI EUROPAISCHE KUNSTLER AUS SCHOTTLAND

Joachim Buhler, Direktor, Goethe-Institut Glasgow, Gallerie Broschwitz, Berlin, 1992

Auf dem Gebiet der bildenden Kunst haben die Beziehungen zwischen Scottland und Berlin zu einer Reihe von Austauschprogrammen und gemainsamen Projekten gefuhrt, verstarkt auch dadurch, dass sowohl Berlin wie Glasgow zeitweilig als 'Hauptstadte der Kultur' im Rahmen der Europaischen Gemeinschaft fungierten.

Lys Hansen und Peter Russell – zwei profilierte schottische Kunstler der jungeren Generation, die mit ihrer Ausstellung : IN PLACE OF THE WALL im August 1992 in der Produzenten-Gallerie Broschwitz an die Offentlichkeit treten, haben sich in den vergangen Jahren mehrfach in Berlin aufgehelten und dort gearbeitet.

Beiden gemeinsam ist neben der kunstlerischen auch die kulturpolitische Perspektive: beide sehen in dem europaischen Integrationsbestreben eine grosse Hoffnung fur die Zukunft.

Europaisches Bewusstsein hat in Schottland eine lange geschichtliche Tradition im deutlichen Gegensatz zu England, wo ein mehr insulares Selbstverstandnis die historische Grundlage politischen Handelns war.

Das Goethe-Institut Glasgow misst Initiativen, wie dieser Ausstellung, eine wichtige Bedeutung bei, umsomehr, als die in Berlin entstandenen Arbeiten im Frujahr 1993 in verschiedenen schottischen Stadten gezeign werden sollen.

Den jungen Kunstlern, Lys Hansen und Peter Russell gilt unser Dank und unsere Anerkennung

TWO EUROPEAN ARTISTS FROM SCOTLAND

Joachim Buhler, Director, Goethe Institute Glasgow, Gallerie Broschwitz, Berlin, 1992

In the field of creative art the links between Scotland and Berlin have led to a series of exchange programmes and joint projects, strengthened by the fact that both Berlin and Glasgow have had occasion to be 'Cities of Culture' within the European Community.

Lys Hansen and Peter Russell, two distinguished Scottish artists of the younger generation, whose exhibition 'In Place of the Wall' goes on public view in August 1992 at the Produzenten-Gallerie Broschwitz, have lived and worked in Berlin on a number of occasions in recent years.

The two have a cultural as well as an artistic outlook in common: both see great hope for the future in the efforts towards European integration.

European consciousness has a long historical tradition in Scotland, in marked contrast to England where a more insular attitude formed the basis for political action.

The Goethe Institute in Glasgow attaches great importance to initiatives such as this exhibition, all the more so as the works created in Berlin are to be shown in various Scottish cities in the spring of 1993.

With thanks and acknowledgement to the young artists, Lys Hansen and Peter Russell.

GROSSSTADT IN DER SPRACHE DER KUNST

Hilke Nissen, *Berliner Morgenpost*, 12 August 1992

Zwei schottische Maler und die Berliner Wirklichkeit nach dem Mauerfall

Wie zwei schottische Maler Berlins Wirklichkeit nach der Maueroffnung sehen, is Thema der Ausstellung in der Kreuzberger Produzentgalerie Broschwitz. Beide Kunstler kennen Berlin schon seit veilen Jahren,, und so sind ihre jetzt ausgestellten Arbeiten zwar in den letzten zwei Monaten entstanden, ihre kraftvollen and tiefgrundigen Bildaussagen zeugen aber von einer langern Auseinandersetzung mit dem Thema 'Berlin'.

Lys Hansen und Peter Russell mieteten fur die Monate Juli und August die Raume der Produzentengalerie an, um vor Ort zum Ausstellungsmotto 'In place of the wall' ('Anstelle der Mauer') zu arbeiten.

Peter Russell geht das Thema in seinen kraftigen, grossformatigen Leinwand-Collagen gesellschaftskritisch und satirisch an: Ausschnitte von Finanzzeitungen, Werbeslogans und Comic-Embleme bilden mit kubistisch gebrochen gemalten Grossstadtmotiven wie Hauserzeilen und Baukranen den modern-kritischen Teil des Bildes. Russell ubersetzt hier die vielfaltigen Probleme der Stadt, die Arbeitslosigkeit, Vereinzelung des Menschen und Profitgier im

Immobiliengeschaft in die Sprache der Kunst.

Meist mit Pastell setzt Russell uber und neben diese Textur einen romantischen Bildwert: eine Phonix-Figur oder Stiere, handschriftliche Zitate, zum Beispiel Goethe-Verse. Als optimistisches Motiv kehrt immer wieder die Hibiskusform auf, die als getrocknete Blute uber das Bild verstreut collagiert wird.

Russells pompose Bilderwelt lasst Chaos und Ordnung, Schonheit und Horror, Wirklichkeit und Phantasie zugleich bestehen.

Lys Hansen thematisiert im Gegensatz zu Peter Russell das Private, das Menschliche. Figurative weibliche Korper spuren die Grenzsituationen zwischen Leben und Tod auf. Die madonnen-artigen Frauenfiguren sind weibliche Akte, die uns in einer Welt der Umbruche als Mutter Erde eine positive Erleuchtung geben konnten. Andere Bilder verzerren die menschliche Anatomie bis zue Unkenntlichkeit – hier beruhren sich Gegenstandlichkeit und Abstraktion.

Das wohl eindrucksvollste une zugleich besturzendste Bild zeigt eine gepeinigte, leidende Frau. Stehend, den Kopf hangend, malte sie Lys Hansen in dunklem Rot, der Farbe des getrockneten Blutes, eine Studie des Sterbeus. Nur ein Auge scheint noch funktionstuchtig zu sein, das andere, als underbrochener Kreis gemalt, ist bereit dem Tod geweiht. Der Bildhintergrund wurde mit Erdfarben aufgeraubt, so dass eine Mauer-struktur entstand.

Lys Hansens Malerie auf Papier ist verdichtetes menschliches Leiden. Ihre Arbeiten sind gerade dann von schrecklicher Intensitat, wenn man an die vielen Toten der Berliner Todeszonen erinnernt wird, als die Mauer noch stand.

THE BIG CITY IN THE LANGUAGE OF ART

Hilke Nissen, *Berliner Morgenpost*, 12 August 1992

The way two Scottish painters view the reality of Berlin after the opening of the Wall is the theme of an exhibition on show at the Produzentengalerie Broschwitz in Kreuzberg. Both artists have known Berlin for many years – indeed their works now on display were created within the past two months – however, their powerful and profound statements are evidence of a long period of coming to terms with the subject of 'Berlin'.

Lys Hansen and Peter Russell rented the Produzentengalerie rooms for the months of July and August in order to work at the face, on an exhibition entitled 'In Place of the Wall'.

Peter Russell takes a socially critical, satirical approach to the subject in his vigorous, large-scale canvas collages: cuttings from financial journals, advertising slogans and comic emblems, together with motifs from the city – rows of houses and construction cranes – painted in a cubist style, form the part of the picture critical of the modern day. Russell here translates the city's diverse problems – unemployment, personal isolation and profit greed in the property business – into the language of art.

Russell contrasts this with a romantic portrayal mainly in pastel: a phoenix figure, lizard-like animals or bulls, handwritten quotations, there are for example lines from Goethe. Hibiscus appears again and again as a symbol of optimism, dried blooms scattered as collages over the painting.

Russell's splendid world of paintings allows chaos and order, beauty and horror, reality and fantasy to exist together.

In contrast to Peter Russell, Lys Hansen takes as her theme the private, the human. Figurative female forms trace out the boundaries between life and death. The Madonna-like female figures are female nudes which, as Mother Earth, could give us positive enlightenment in a world of radical change. Other pictures distort human anatomy beyond recognition – here objectivity and abstraction meet.

The most impressive and at the same time most startling picture shows a tormented, suffering woman. Standing, head hanging, Lys Hansen paints her in dark red, the colour of dried blood, a study in dying. Only one eye still seems capable of functioning, the other, painted as a broken circle, is already doomed to death. The background is the colour of clay, creating a wall-like structure.

Lys Hansen's painting on paper is concentrated human suffering. Memories of the many dead of the Berlin death-strips during the time of the Wall give her works a terrible intensity.

DARKER SIDE OF BERLIN

Richard Carr, *The Scotsman*, 19 April 1993

'In Place of the Wall', an exhibition of paintings and drawings by Lys Hansen and Peter Russell at the MacRobert Arts Centre in Stirling, is the result of a month spent by both artists at the Produtzentengalerie Broschwitz in Berlin last summer. They had each been to Berlin twice before and remembered what the city was like before the wall was torn down in 1989. 'In Place of the Wall' reflects on a city that remains divided while embarking on a period of momentous change. . .

. . . Lys Hansen's reaction to Berlin is much more personal. The suffering of those who lived behind – and tried to get through – the wall is shown in a series of simplified, expressionistic figures which are perched precariously on a ledge, or are climbing through a tightly enclosed space, or are hemmed in by massive buildings, or are shielding their faces behind uplifted arms.

The oil paintings, ablaze with splashes of colour – especially reds – that often seem to swirl around a vortex, make direct references to events centred upon the wall . . .

SHOCK TROOPER OF ART

Ann Shaw, *Glasgow Herald*, 19 April 1993

Appropriately, this year's president of the Society of Scottish Artists, a 102-year-old Edinburgh-based organisation formed to represent the more avant-garde and experimental work in Scottish art, is Lys Hansen, a woman who combines Celtic passion with that of a Viking adventurer.

The daughter of an Ayrshire mother – with some Robert Burns blood in her veins – and a Danish father, Lys is one of Scotland's most flamboyant and distinguished artists with her big bold canvases reflecting her Scandinavian heritage.

I first met her at Dollar Summer School. Those of us who have been through the 'Hansen mill' of her life-drawing class have our own favourite clutch of stories. She has a strong theatrical presence and struts around the studio as if it's a stage: 'Why have you put the legs on back to front?' ' Why have you left the hands out?' Flattery is not part of her armoury. 'But if you take a person apart then you've got to be prepared to build them up again.'

Her latest exhibition, 'In Place of the Wall', is currently touring Scotland, having opened recently at the MacRobert Centre, Stirling University. She shares it with another artist, Peter Russell, and it is based on their experiences of Berlin last summer.

Living in Berlin proved a stimulating experience: 'I lived opposite Checkpoint Charlie and I used to bicycle through Berlin, a marvellous way to blend, to observe, and to feel fifteen years old again. Only a short distance from where I stayed was the Prinz Albrechtstrasse 8, the most dreaded address in all Berlin. It was the headquarters of the Gestapo and SS.'

She found it spooky and full of bad vibes. One of the bad memories that remain with her is the sight of teenagers drunk and drugged lying around the steps of buildings. 'Once they were somebody's lovely children.'

Predictably, her twenty-six paintings reflect the turmoil and great social changes going on in Berlin. Her work is always challenging, often disturbing, usually evoking strong reactions. There is no middle ground. She is adamant that art should reflect the age we live in and she is dismissive of those Scottish artists who cling to post-Impressionism with decorative still-lifes and landscapes: 'They have got their heads in a bag. Impressionism was very beautiful and people are reluctant to let go of the past,' says Hansen. 'But our world today is not beautiful. We have made it ugly. Instead of cornfields and poppies we have pollution.'

She sees the environment as the main burning issue facing all young artists today. 'We are lucky in Scotland in that the landscape is still extraordinarily beautiful. This is because it is so wild and cruel. It has grandeur. Men die on it.'

Feminism is an issue she is frequently confronted with: 'I am often asked if I am a feminist artist. I don't think I am. My standard reply is that I am a woman and I paint with a woman's perception and a woman's experience.'

What about nudity? 'Nothing upsets people so much as the human body naked. Even women don't like it unless the female form is delicate, romantic, or even erotically drawn. I want to make my brush like a knife and take out all the things that hurt.'

Looking at the tangled torsos engaged in physical exploration you understand why some people are uneasy when confronted by her work. Her provocative work offers a woman's view on sexuality and the conflicting roles women are expected to play. Certainly it exudes a psychic energy, raw, powerful, reflecting an inner conflict and emotional intensity not often found in British art.

It is both challenging and disturbing in the best European tradition, strongly influenced by German Expressionism, though the artists who have been the greatest influence on her are Edvard Munch and Picasso.

Why no female Picasso? I ask, digging up that hoary old chestnut. 'Women are too busy propping up male egos. They give too much of themselves to too many people. Also, the ego is not so important to them. They get satisfaction from giving to others.'

Combining the triple role of artist, lecturer and mother has left her with little time to become enmeshed in art politics, an area she dismisses as 'men's games', preferring instead to work her lonely furrow in the shadow of the Ochil Hills, allowing her paintings to speak for themselves.

Our art critic Clare Henry describes Lys Hansen as one of Scotland's best artists while another equally distinguished critic, Cordelia Oliver, says she is 'a woman in a hurry', anxious to break the mould, a view reinforced by Hansen herself: 'Rules are there to be broken.'

She lives in a large cottage on the outskirts of Blairlogie, near Stirling, with her husband George, an examiner with the Scottish Examination Board. Now that their two sons, Marcus and Giles, have left home, Lys, freed from the demands of motherhood, is able to put in long hours each day in her WASPS studio, part of a former factory in Menstrie. She also lectures at Glasgow School of Art. The couple's lengthy marriage, over a quarter of a century, is something of a phenomenon in the art world, owing something perhaps to their contrasting temperaments: George is quiet and scholarly while Lys is volatile and extrovert.

Artists' homes are always intriguing and an enriching experience to visit, and Lys's is no exception. It's a colourful cornucopia of paintings, ceramics and richly textured rugs dominated by several of her own large figurative works.

She is a woman of enormous energy and this is reflected in her clutch of academic qualifications. She is a graduate of Edinburgh College of Art, Edinburgh College of Speech and Drama and has a Fine Art degree from Edinburgh University and a teaching diploma from Moray House.

She remembers her student days in Edinburgh during the 1960s: 'It was a different world then, dominated by a precious coterie of Edinburgh artists; pretty girls doing pretty pictures, getting married and having pretty children. They didn't see it as their function to confront difficult issues.' After graduating Lys earned a comfortable living as a model for a year. She describes the experience as 'interesting and exhilarating at first but ultimately boring. You were just a clothes-horse.' The theatre has clearly been a strong influence in her life and if she had her time again she would choose to be a dancer.

Nevertheless many men are clearly at a loss in dealing with her, dazzled by the fatal combination of beauty and intelligence.

Some might find her aggressive, even strident. It is a criticism that annoys her, 'because they are afraid of strong women'.

She is a visiting lecturer at Glasgow School of Art and also the Scottish Arts Council. She has been awarded travelling scholarships to Rome, Berlin and France and held numerous solo exhibitions including major retrospectives in Scotland and London.

Born in Falkirk the daughter of a Danish baker, she grew up in a very practical household. She still remembers her father's shock when she announced that she wanted to be an artist. 'But can you draw? How will you get a job?'

She had in fact been drawing secretly since she was five. 'My first sketch was of a girl whom I disliked in my class. I gave her a square face then obliterated it.'

An extrovert with a strong theatrical streak, she also has a quite contemplative side to her nature, essential in an artist in order to ensure the long lonely hours in a studio necessary if one is to produce a body of work.

'You have to be strong to be an artist. And determined. I feel sorry for young artists today. If they have not made it within two or three years of leaving art college they are written off as a failure. That is a tragedy. Young artists are like plants and need nurturing.' She blames Thatcherism with its emphasis on instant results. Meanwhile her own career continues to mature.

BEYOND THE WALL – LYS HANSEN LOOKS AHEAD IN BERLIN AND BEYOND

Richard Carr, *ArtWork*, April–May 1993

Belfast, Berlin, Jerusalem – cities divided against themselves, separated by walls, by no-go areas, by quarters occupied by people claiming to be different from everyone else.

For Lys Hansen, an artist who has been to these cities and commented upon them in her work, they are physical places full of emotion and searing pain that are no more than metaphors for the human condition itself – the struggle for freedom and self-expression.

Other artists might describe the situation in which they find themselves in other terms: in the haunting poetry of Wilfred Owen or the war requiem of Benjamin Britten. But for Lys Hansen, the response begins where the agony and the ecstasy are felt, in the human body – and, particularly, in the female torso.

This location was chosen in the 1970s, when Lys Hansen began to free herself from the day-to-day demands of bringing up children and building a home – a literal description of what had to be done during the conversion of buildings nestling under the Ochil Hills. There had been an interruption, a break in the progression as an artist begun as a student at Edinburgh College of Art which continued immediately afterwards when Lys Hansen won awards and exhibited her work.

Naturally, demands were made by her husband and children. Other demands were made because of the eighteen years she spent running the Crowsteps in Blairlogie – another building exercise since the gallery and hall were created out of two eighteenth-century cottages which had been given to the village. Crowsteps was used for a month-long summer festival of arts and crafts, and for visits by distinguished people like William Gillies, who had been one of her teachers in Edinburgh.

All this was done at a time when Stirling University and its MacRobert Arts Centre was nothing more than a construction site and the Smith Art Gallery in Stirling was in the doldrums.

Yet another demand was created by teaching art – first at a secondary modern school in Alloa and then part-time and then full-time – at the technical college in Falkirk. Both institutions were situated in another kind of battlefield, in places where traditional industries like coalmining, engineering and textiles had either become run-down or disappeared altogether so that communities lost jobs, social cohesion and even, occasionally, a belief in the future. This belief was also being lost by Lys herself. 'Sometimes,' she told me, 'I used to dream I was dead.' For her, salvation came by returning to her painting and the result was a series of female torsos which were sometimes split down the middle and sometimes bursting apart, but in a way which was much more explosive than the blossoming of a flower.

There was also a concentration on particular parts of the body – a hand or a foot, for example, and later on paintings of heads, hands, mouths, contorted, grabbing, even devouring each other, the individual parts of the body being celebrated for being alive, the heads and their appurtenances expressing the force of inner emotions and the demands of other people.

More recently, this approach to the human form has been given a political dimension so that a figure balancing precariously on a ledge, or a face full of feet, or a triptych of human figures based on the three monkeys who see no evil, hear no evil and speak no evil, expresses the uncertainty, the hunger and the denial of truth that Lys Hansen finds central to the political as well as the human condition.

The character of Lys Hansen's work was brilliantly described by Euan McArthur when he wrote a brief introduction to an exhibition she had in Artspace in Aberdeen in 1986:

> Her works, often large, are figurative, focused primarily on the female body as her site of emotional and sexual conflict.

> Brushwork and colour, massive shifts in space, harsh cropping of figures, unexpected balances add distortions, create explosive images which dissolve the clichés of the conventional 'expressionism' of woman's experience. More than mere simulacra, they possess the authenticity of a reality encountered inwardly and projected into the outer world of shared experience.

And Lys Hansen's own reaction to the outer world has also been expressed in verbal terms. Writing about her visit to Berlin in 1992 – her first was in 1985 – she says: 'Only a short distance away from the street where I live is the Topographie des Terrors. Here was once the most dreaded address in all Berlin: Prinz Albrechtstrasse 8. It was the headquarters of the Gestapo and SS. From this address was planned the persecution of all political enemies and all unwanted social groups, ranging from homosexuals to religious minorities.

'The exploitation and enslavement of millions of people who, next to the Jews, were likewise considered racially inferior, predominantly the Russian and Polish populations.

'Heavily bombed by the Allied Forces, the terrain has now been flattened. Grasses, bushes and wild flowers grow there now and, since 1987, a small museum has been built above and including the interrogation cells. There is now a memorial to all those who died under the Gestapo regime. The visitors are few, faces are pale and voices are hushed as one examines the photographs and documentations of the terrible events that took place here and elsewhere.'

Though the visits to Berlin and other once or still-divided cities seem to mirror Lys Hansen's own persona so exactly, the anger that she expresses is intended to be positive rather than negative. Similarly, she would hate to be labelled a feminist artist despite the nature of her subject-matter and is absolutely clear that her membership of the Society of Women Artists reflected a need for connections beyond Clackmannanshire and not a particular viewpoint.

In fact, she never even considered her own sex as having any bearing on her work as an artist until one male student commented on the fact that she was a woman when she won the Prix de Rome. For her, the sex of an artist is irrelevant: it is the exploration, the search for understanding and truth, 'the things you cannot see but know are there', which matter, as well as her belief that artists can be useful in the world. Here, she acknowledges the value that going on Richard Demarco-led trips to Eire, Holland and Italy had in helping her to put contemporary art into an international context, which was also helped by his conference on housing the arts which was attended by museum curators and gallery owners from around the world.

Lys Hansen's own contribution, apart from her art, now also includes her presidency of the Society of Scottish Artists which she sees as an organisation that, despite its 100 years, remains fresh and innovative in spirit, constantly challenging, willing to take risks and be involved with young people. Among its current aims is the desire to go west – a forthcoming exhibition in Phillips in Glasgow demonstrates this – and to organise small touring exhibitions as offshoots of the annual exhibition, develop the links already being established with artists from abroad, and, at home, promote an educational programme in schools so that children will know that not all artists are dead – that, in fact, artists can be found living and working all over Scotland.

This more managerial side of her work may also be coming through in her work: as she admits, the faces of her figures are becoming androgynous. Is this because she is now playing what has usually been regarded as a more masculine role in life, or is it because her own artistic journey is now revealing a more masculine side to her nature? Or perhaps it is no more than a reminder that each one of us possesses elements of both sexes within our persona.

HERE COMES THE BERLIN BRIDE

John Fowler, *Glasgow Herald*, 28 July 1994

I missed the bride. Wrapped in bubble plastic, she was being strapped on a trailer ready to be driven north. *The Bride from the East* is the larger-than-life-size painting that forms the centrepiece of an exhibition of recent work by Lys Hansen which opened in Aberdeen at the weekend.

At Hansen's studio in the village of Menstrie, near Stirling, she was directing her son Marcus as he stowed cushions under the unwieldy package and secured it behind his car. She was fussing, he was eager to be on the road – and a slight edge was creeping into the mother and son conversation.

Luckily *The Bride* was intact, though it could have been otherwise. Just a few days before, children had broken into the old building where Hansen has her studio. They'd plastered pigments on the floor, damaged some frames, and scrawled a four-letter work on one of the canvases. Hansen discovered the mess when she arrived the following day.

The studio is one of two (the other is used by the artist Peter Russell) on the first floor of a deserted mill building now surrounded by houses. Behind the simple Georgian façade with its clock face stretches an atmospheric, echoing hall where the textile machines used to clatter. Hansen worries about its condition. In the two years since she moved in she's seen the building deteriorate through neglect.

Upstairs she showed me the pictures about to follow *The Bride* to Aberdeen. *The Bride from the East* was gone but her five companion pieces were still to be despatched. They show the same central image – a naked woman with hands (not her own) clasped over her breasts, but on a smaller scale and with significant alterations. These variations on a theme are monoprints – each one a unique image pulled from an original painted on glass.

There is a powerful feeling of brooding unease in the pictures, a sense of violent emotions barely curbed which is a characteristic of Hansen's work – something innate and not imbibed from college teachers like the late Sir William Gillies.

Gillies and Sir Robin Philipson, she says, helped to instil a feeling for colour and painterliness, but she sought something deeper: 'It was as if they were painting with the feminine side of their characters. I had to find my own way.'

Many of her new pictures stem from a six-week exchange visit she made to Berlin two years ago, living and painting in an artists' settlement on the site of Checkpoint Charlie, the famous crossing point between East and West.

She found the experience disturbing. Close by were the museum commemorating the Wall and those who died trying to escape and the Gestapo bunkers redolent of an even grimmer past. Passing along a certain street she felt a vague unease – 'Why did I feel these funny vibrations?' – before realising that it followed the dismantled Wall.

She says that physically East Berlin displays its open wounds. One picture entitled *Death in a Red Dress* was prompted by the distressing figure of a woman drug-addict she saw lying in an alley close to her Berlin studio.

The Bride, too, reflects the Berlin experience directly – it was painted and exhibited there and in a sense symbolises the reunification of the city: 'It's like a marriage where there's been a separation and a coming together again.' But in the painting and its companion pieces there is also a strong feeling of conflicting emotions and ideals.

There has always been a dark element in Hansen's painting. In contrast, some of her new work flames in bright yellows and reds. This is both a reaction to Berlin and a consequence of a workshop on colour she took with students at Glasgow School of Art. Ironically, a sense of place may have influenced both her and the students in that case too. The class took place in an airy, white-walled room filled with light, in contrast to the basement studio where the students had been previously. 'I think they felt the whole weight of Charles Rennie Mackintosh and the Glasgow School of Art pressing down on them,' she says.

A particular place and its mood are also the source of a series of twelve small paintings on show in Aberdeen, though there is nothing specific to link them with Los Angeles, where Hansen spent Christmas visiting an elderly aunt. But the shadowy outline of skewed skyscraper buildings is a common element, implying both imprisonment and escape.

Hansen relates this to her sense of being hemmed in by the sprawling supercity. She recalls how she drove to the Museum of Contemporary Art, parked there, saw the pictures, visited the café, and then drove off without stepping into the outside world: 'I felt confined. Trapped.'

APPENDIX 3: DREAMING FRANKENSTEIN

LIZ LOCHHEAD

For LYS HANSEN, JACKI PARRY and JUNE REDFERN

She said she
woke up with him in
her head, in her bed.
Her mother-tongue clung to her mouth's roof
in terror, dumbing her, and he came with a name
that was none of her making.

No maidservant ever
in her narrow attic, combing
out her hair in the midnight mirror
on Hallowe'en (having eaten
that egg with its yolk hollowed out
then filled with salt)
– oh never one had such success as this
she had not courted.
The amazed flesh of her
neck and shoulders nettled
at his apparition.

Later, stark staring awake to everything
(the room, the dark parquet, the white high Alps beyond) all
normal in the moonlight
and him gone, save a ton-weight sensation,
the marks fading visibly where
his buttons had bit into her and
the rough serge of his suiting had chafed her sex,
she knew – oh that was not how –
but he'd entered her utterly.

This was the penetration
of seven swallowed apple pips.
Or else he'd slipped like a silver dagger
between her ribs and healed her up secretly
again. Anyway
he was inside her
and getting him out again
would be agony fit to quarter her,
unstitching everything.

Eyes on those high peaks
in the reasonable sun of the morning,
she dressed in damped muslin
and sat down to quill and ink
and icy paper.

1983

NOTES ON THE ESSAYS

MIKE BAILEY

1. Maclaurin Art Gallery. The Maclaurin Trust was established in 1971, following a generous bequest by Mrs Mary Ellen Maclaurin. The gallery was given in memory of her husband, for the benefit of the people of Ayr. Funds remaining in the bequest after the building of the gallery have been invested to provide income to support the gallery exhibition programme and the development of a significant collection of twentieth-century art.
2. 'Demarcation' presented by the Richard Demarco Gallery, Edinburgh International Festival, 1984. The exhibition, which formed a component part of the overall 'Demarcation' programme, included work by Ian Hamilton Finlay, Gwen Hardie, David Mach and Fred Stiven
3. See, 'New Glasgow Painting in Context', Ken Currie, *Edinburgh Review*, 1986
4. A title coined by Waldemar Januszczak, then art critic with *The Guardian*. A satirical reference to the comparative maturity and respectability of their predecessors, 'The Glasgow Boys'
5. *Neue Sachlichkeit* (New Objectivity). Most Western countries produced this type of art in the 1920s and 1930s, though its implications varied. In 1925, G.F. Hartlaub, director of the municipal gallery in Mannheim presented an exhibition with this title. The works he selected 'shared an inclination towards realism, . . . [using] . . . traditional skills of hand and eye'. (Lynton, N., *The Story of Modern Art*, Phaidon, Oxford, 1980)
6. 'The Vigorous Imagination', Hartley, K. (1987), *The Green Book*, Vol. 2, No. 7., Bath, The Green Book Press. 'The Vigorous Imagination' was presented at the Scottish National Gallery of Modern Art, Edinburgh, 9 August–25 October 1987. Works were selected by Clare Henry, Henry Meyric Hughes and Keith Hartley.
7. 'Twentieth-Century Scottish Painting', catalogue introduction by Douglas Hall. 369 Gallery, Edinburgh, 25 July–26 September, 1987, and Warwick Arts Trust, London.
8. The 369 Gallery. Founded in 1978 to provide a forum for young artists working in Scotland. In 1985 the gallery acquired three floors of a Georgian warehouse in the Cowgate, Edinburgh, 'for conversion to a living centre for the visual arts in Scotland'. The gallery closed a number of years ago.
9. Camden Arts Centre, Arkwright Road, London. Under the direction of Zuleika Dobson, this became one of the key venues in North London, offering an exciting and varied programme of contemporary art throughout the 1980s.
10. *The Guardian*, 8 February 1986. See Appendix 1. p. 145
11. See 'Women Artists in Glasgow', Lynch, K., MacGregor, S. and Parry, J., in *Visual Arts in Glasgow: Tradition and Transformation*, Third Eye Centre, Glasgow, April 1985
12. Clare Henry, *Glasgow Herald*, 21 October 1988
13. 'For a' That – Contemporary Artists look at Burns'. Contributors were Crawfurd Adamson, Conrad Atkinson, Dorothy Black, Simon Fraser, Lys Hansen, Yvonne Hawker, John Houston, Margaret Hunter, Sandy Moffat, Janet Patterson, June Redfern, Gavin Scobie and George Wyllie. Gracefield Arts Centre, Dumfries, 30 September–29 October 1989, Maclaurin Art Gallery, and Rozelle House, Ayr, 4 November–6 December, 1989.
14. *Address to Edinburgh* (1989), John Houston, oil on canvas, 145 x 152cm
15. See 'Interview', p. 125
16. 'Lys Hansen Paints Burns', Rozelle House, Ayr, 29 March–20 April 1997
17. 'Lys Hansen: Recent Work', City Art Centre, Edinburgh, 15 October–5 November 1988
18. 'Hunter – Husemann – Fioravanti: Three European Artists in Scotland', Maclaurin Art Gallery, 16 June–10 July 1990
19. Press release, Maclaurin Art Gallery, Ayr. Issued December 1989. Quotations from the exhibition catalogue, *Lys Hansen: Recent Work*, published by the City Art Centre, Edinburgh, October 1989.
20. 'In Place of the Wall', Maclaurin Art Gallery, April 1993. Peter Russell and Lys Hansen. Touring to MacRobert Centre, Stirling; Duncan of Jordanstone College of Art, Dundee; and Lillie Art Gallery, Milngavie.
21. Exhibition of Second-Year Student Work. Exhibition originated in association with the Department of Ceramics, Glasgow School of Art, autumn 1987.
22. 'Shopping and More', an exhibition held jointly between members of BBK and SSA; in Scotland entitled 'What is a Suitcase?'
23. 'Lys Hansen Paints Burns', Rozelle House, Ayr, 29 March–20 April 1997
24. *Departure*, Max Beckmann, triptych, 1932–33, oil on canvas, centre panel 159.4 x 115.3cm, side panels 159.4 x 101cm. New York, Museum of Modern Art; *Fish Ride*, Max Beckmann, 1934, oil on canvas, 134.5 x 115.5cm.

METTE BLIGAARD

1. Cited from *Ny Dansk Kunsthistorie, Vol.8*, ed. Peter Michael Hornung, (Copenhagen, 1995), p.65
2. Ibid., p.123
3. *The Divided Self: 'She is She'; 'Grip'; 'Goodbye' (Trilogy for a New Ireland)*, 1985. Collection of the artist
4. *Berlin Trilogy: Say Nothing, Hear Everything, See All*, 1985, Collection of the artist
5. Seamus Heaney, 'Bog Queen', in *North* (Faber and Faber, London, 1975)
6. Hayden Murphy in *She is She* (exhibition catalogue), published by the Octagon Gallery, Belfast, and the Project Arts Centre, Dublin, 1985, p.6

RICHARD CARR

1. 'Towards the Housing of Art in the 21st Century', Presented by the Richard Demarco Gallery in association with the Azienda di Soggiorno, Varese, Italy, and Channel Four Television, 19–21 August 1983, at the David Hume Tower, University of Edinburgh
2. Bill Hare, *Contemporary Painting in Scotland*, pp.86-88
3. This exhibition was entitled 'Zwei europaische Kunstler aus Schottland' ('Two European Artists from Scotland') and took place in Gallerie Broschwitz, Berlin
4. The Kunstlerhaus offers artists a studio, accommodation and exhibition space
5. Letter to Giles Sutherland, April 1998
6. Catalogue note for 'What is a Suitcase?' exhibition, 1996

BILL HARE

1. In English, 'Two Crows'. The ballad invokes the figure of the crow as a symbol of menace and death. Another source of the imagery may be the practice employed by Scottish farmers of hanging the bodies of shot crows in prominent places (fences etc.) in an attempt to scare live birds.

CLARE HENRY

1. The Third Eye Centre, Glasgow. Now the Centre for Contemporary Arts
2. 'Towards the Housing of Art in the 21st Century' (see Carr, note 1, above)
3. Sarah Kent, *Time Out*, 20–26 February 1986

(see Appendix 1, p. ?)
4. Waldemar Januszczak, *The Guardian*, 6 February 1986 (see Appendix 1, p. ?)

JUDITH MACRAE 1

1. The Grange School, Alloa, Clackmannanshire, 1964
2. The Crowsteps annual art exhibitions were held in Lys Hansen's home village of Blairlogie, near Stirling, from 1966 until 1984
3. This exhibition took place in the canteen of the University of Strathclyde, 1968
4. 'In Place of the Wall', Duncan of Jordanstone College of Art, Dundee, 1992. Major exhibition exploring the artists' experience of Berlin (joint project with Peter Russell)

JUDITH MACRAE 2

1. Henderson Gallery, Edinburgh, 1980

HAYDEN MURPHY

1. For full text, see Appendix 3, p.152
2. *The Irish Times*, June 1983
3. Cordelia Oliver, *Lys Hansen: Recent Work* (The Third Eye Centre, Glasgow, 1984)
4. Hannah Arendt, *The Human Condition*
5. John Berger, *Ways of Seeing*
6. 'She is She', University of Ulster, Belfast & Projects Art Centre, Dublin, Hayden Murphy, 1985

CORDELIA OLIVER

1. Cordelia Oliver: 'Lys Hansen: Recent Work', The Third Eye Centre, Glasgow, February, 1984
2. Since its foundation in the late-nineteenth century, the SSA has remained Scotland's most consistently forward-looking art society and Lys Hansen has been a professional member since 1980 as well as its very active president from 1992–95

GILES SUTHERLAND 1

1. *Student*, University of Edinburgh's student newspaper, February 1984
2. *Clanjamfrie*, literary broadsheet. Issues One (1984) and Two (1984) published by Polygon Books, Edinburgh, edited by Giles Sutherland and Duncan McLean; Issue Three (1988) published by Morning Star Publications, Dunblane, and edited by Giles Sutherland. The title is taken from Hugh MacDiarmid's poem 'The Bonnie Broukit Bairn' (1925)
3. For full text, see Appendix 3

GILES SUTHERLAND 2

1. 'Towards the Housing of Art in the 21st century' (see Richard Carr, note 1, above)
2. In *Scandinavian Mythology* by H.R. Ellis Davidson (London, 1982), p.53.
3. The exhibition was entitled 'She is She' and was held in the Octagon Gallery, Belfast/ University of Ulster at Belfast (Northern Ireland Arts Council) and at the Project Arts Centre, Dublin (Irish Arts Council).
4. 'For a' that' – Robert Burns touring exhibition, 1990.
5. *Burns: Poems and Songs*, ed. James Kinsley (Oxford, 1969) p.371.
6. Cyril Gerber is director of the Compass Gallery, Glasgow. The exhibition was entitled 'Compass Celebrates the Life and Work of Robert Burns'.
7. *Burns: Poems and Songs*, p.16.
8. In particular the collection of works entitled *The Love Suite* (1985), based on Hughes' poem, 'Bride and Groom lie hidden for three days'.
9. Emily Ash ran the Ash Gallery opposite the Canongate Tolbooth in the Royal Mile, Edinburgh, from 1990 to 1991. The exhibition was entitled 'Mary Queen of Scots . . . A Feminist Tradition?' and included works by the artists Rose Frain, Helen Flockhart and Jane MacAllister.

LYS HANSEN

1936 Born, Falkirk, Scotland
1962 Married to George Sutherland
1963 Birth of son, Giles
1969 Birth of son, Marcus
1990 Death of parents

EDUCATION

1955-59 Edinburgh College of Art – Diploma of Art
1955-58 Edinburgh College of Speech & Drama – A.L.A.M. Degree
1960 Edinburgh College of Art – Postgraduate Studies in Drawing & Painting
1961 The University of Edinburgh – Fine Art Studies
1963 Moray House College of Education, Edinburgh – Teacher Training Awards
1959 Travelling Scholarship (Andrew Grant Bequest) to France
1960 Abbey Minor Award (Prix de Rome) from British School of Painting in Rome. Three months' study in Italy
1960 Andrew Grant Bequest Scholarship to Holland and Germany
1966 Paintings for Schools
1966-84 Co-Founder and Organiser, Crowsteps Art Exhibition, Blairlogie, Stirling
1967 Anne Redpath Award for Painting
1982 Scottish Society of Women Artists Special Award
1982 Glasgow Lady Artists Trust Award
1984 Scottish Arts Council Major Award
1985 Smith Biennial (Prize Winner)
1985,'86 Studio in Berlin
1992,'96 and'98 Studio in Berlin

MEMBERSHIP

Professional Member of Society of Scottish Artists (President 1992–95)
Professional Member of Society of Artists and Artist Craftsmen
Glasgow Society of Women Artists
Lecturer for the Scottish Arts Council
Part-time lecturer, Glasgow School of Art
Part-time lecturer, University of Stirling
Honorary Member BBK, Berlin

SELECTED SOLO EXHIBITIONS

1994–95 'Mary Queen of Scots', exhibition and installation, touring to:
Cowane Gallery, Stirling
Glasgow Vennel Museum, Irvine
Robson Gallery, Halliwell House, Selkirk
Central Gallery, Lochgelly
1991 The Ash Gallery, 'Mary Queen of Scots . . . A Feminist Tradition?' (poem, painting, sculpture – an installation to commemorate the life and death of Mary Queen of Scots)
1990 Maclaurin Gallery, Ayr
1990 'Windows on the Soul', Glasgow Vennel Museum, Irvine
1988 City Art Centre, Edinburgh
1986 Camden Arts Centre, London
1986 Artspace, Aberdeen
1986 369 Gallery, Edinburgh
1986 Ayling Porteous Gallery, Chester
1985 Octagon Gallery, Belfast/University of Ulster at Belfast (Northern Ireland Arts Council)
1985 Project Arts Centre, Dublin (Irish Arts Council)
1984 The Third Eye Centre, Glasgow
1983 Open Eye Gallery, Edinburgh
1980 Greenock Arts Centre
1980 Henderson Gallery, Edinburgh
1978-80 Stirling Gallery
1977 MacRobert Arts Centre, University of Stirling
1976 University of Stirling
1974 Crowsteps Gallery, Blairlogie, Stirling
1969-78 University of Strathclyde, Glasgow
1962 Commonwealth Institute, Edinburgh
1960 Commonwealth Institute, London

SELECTED GROUP SHOWS

Royal Scottish Academy; Scottish Society of Artists; Scottish Society of Women Artists; Glasgow Group Exhibitions; Perth Festival; Edinburgh Festival Demarcation Exhibition; Richard Demarco Gallery, Edinburgh; Odenwald Gallery; Schwarzwald, Germany; Virginia State Bank, Virginia, USA;

1997–98 'A Patch of Their Own' (Allotments Exhibition – Compass Gallery, Glasgow), touring to:
Smith Art Gallery and Museum, Stirling
Dick Institute, Kilmarnock
Swanson Gallery, Thurso
Lillie Art Gallery, Milngavie
Art Gallery and Museum, Inverness
Iona Gallery, Kingussie
St Fergus Gallery, Wick
'What is a Suitcase?/Was ist ein Koffer?', touring to:
Arts Centre, East Kilbride;
Seagate Gallery, Dundee;
Picture Gallery, Peebles
Glasgow Art Fair
1997 Featured artist, Perth Art Gallery and Museum
'A Sense of Place', The Smith Art Gallery and Museum, Stirling
'Figure This' Featured Guest Artist at McManus Gallery, Dundee
'Hansen Paints Burns', Maclaurin Gallery, Ayr
1996 Glasgow Art Fair
Project: Six Artists Scotland/Six Artists Berlin
Exhibition in Berlin: 'Shopping and More'
Exhibition in Scotland: 'What is a Suitcase?/Was ist ein Koffer?'
'Compass Celebrates the Life and Work of Robert Burns'
Robert Burns Bicentenary Exhibition, The Compass Gallery, Glasgow, touring to:
The Dick Institute, Kilmarnock
Gracefield Art Centre, Dumfries
Rozelle House, Ayr
Glasgow Vennel Museum, Irvine
'Pride and Passion – Robert Burns', Royal Scottish Museum, Edinburgh
1995 '25 Scottish Artists', Print Exhibition, Amsterdam
'3 Scottish Artists', Galerie Wollebrandshof, Culinborg, Holland
1994-96 Annual Invitation Drawing Exhibition, Arts Centre, East Kilbride
1993-95 Society of Scottish Artists Annual Exhibition
1993 'Scottish Painting', Flowers East Gallery, London
1992 'In Place of the Wall' Major exhibition exploring the artists' experience of Berlin (joint project with Peter Russell), touring to:
Francis Cooper Gallery, Duncan of Jordanstone College of Art, Dundee
Maclaurin Art Gallery, Rozelle Park, Ayr
Lillie Art Gallery, Milngavie
MacRobert Arts Centre, University of Stirling

Inverness Art Gallery and Museum
'The Alter Ego' Glasgow Print Studio exhibition, touring to:
Reykjavik, Iceland
Madrid, Spain
Highlands and Islands, Scotland
Binghampton University, New York, USA
'Two European Artists from Scotland' (with Peter Russell), Gallerie Broschwitz, Berlin

1991 'London Art 1991', Business Design Centre, London
'Art 91', London International Contemporary Art Fair, Olympia, London
'Man in the Universe', Richard Demarco Gallery, Edinburgh
International Science Festival Exhibition
'Margaret Gardiner – Thomas Merton: A Correspondence', Richard Demarco Gallery, Edinburgh
Joan Hughson Gallery, Glasgow
Febland Gallery, Blackpool
Gallery Heinzel, Aberdeen (featured artist)

1990 'For a' that' – Robert Burns exhibition (invited artist participating in touring exhibition of Scottish artists considering the poetical works of Robert Burns)
'Art 90', International Contemporary Art Fair, London
21st Anniversary Exhibition, The Compass Gallery, Glasgow
'Glasgow 1990' (City of Culture), Tramway, Glasgow
WASPS Exhibition, Glasgow (Six Tillicoultry Artists)
'The Haldane Connection', Glasgow School of Art
'Four Scottish Artists', Demarco Gallery, Edinburgh
'Burns, Beuys and Beyond', Kelvingrove Art Gallery, Glasgow

1989 SSWA Spring Exhibition, Lillie Art Gallery, Milngavie.
Glasgow Group, Tramway, Glasgow (invited artist)
'State of the Art', Fine Art Society, Edinburgh and Glasgow (A Survey of Contemporary Scottish Painting)
Edinburgh Print Workshop (invited artist)
Glasgow Print Studio (invited artist)

1988 WASPS 1st National Exhibition (touring exhibition) Glasgow Group, McLellan Galleries, Glasgow (invited artist),
Central Regional Artists at Smith Art Gallery and Museum, Stirling
'The First Ten Years', 369 Gallery, Edinburgh
'The Wedding', Mappin Gallery, Sheffield (touring exhibition)
'Crossing Boundaries: Ceramics and Drawings', The Compass Gallery, Glasgow
Tweeddale Museum, Peebles (solo exhibition)
'Bright Light and Sombre Shadows', Smith Art Gallery and Museum, Stirling (a personal selection by Lys Hansen from the Smith's Collection of Paintings)
Glasgow Women Artists, Lillie Art Gallery, Milngavie (invited artist)
Group Exhibition, Los Angeles, USA
SSA, RSA, Edinburgh
SSWA, RSA, Edinburgh
Christmas Exhibition, The Open Eye Gallery, Edinburgh

1987 SSA, RSA, Edinburgh
Contemporary Art Fair, Los Angeles
Christmas Exhibition, Ayling Porteous Gallery, Chester
Blond Fine Art, London (winter exhibition)
'New Acquaintances', Fabian Carlsson Gallery, London
Paisley Drawing Competition
Glasgow Group (invited artist)
RSA, Edinburgh
'Ties That Bind the Family', Collins Gallery, University of Strathclyde, Glasgow (touring exhibition)
'The Self-portrait: A Modern View' Artsite, Bath (major touring exhibition) touring to:
Artsite, Bath
Museum and Art Gallery, Durham
Seven Arts Gallery, Hull
City Museum and Art Gallery, Stoke-on-Trent
Collins Gallery, Glasgow
Hatton Gallery, Newcastle
Glyn Vivian Art Gallery and Museum
Graves Art Gallery, Sheffield
Fisher Fine Art, London
Mostyn Art Gallery, Llandudno
Biennial, The Smith Art Gallery and Museum, Stirling

1986 Selection of Smith Biennial at The Third Eye Centre, Glasgow and at Warwick Arts Trust, London
'Unheard Music', Art Gallery Museum, Stoke-on-Trent

1985 'The First Ten Years', Mayfest Exhibition, The Third Eye Centre, Glasgow
International Arts Fair: London, Bath and Chicago
'Unique and Original', Glasgow Print Studio, Glasgow
SSA – Selection at Glasgow Print Studio, Glasgow
Biennial, The Smith Art Gallery and Museum, Stirling (prize-winner)

WORKS IN PUBLIC COLLECTIONS

University of Stirling
Central Regional Council
Lillie Collection, Milngavie
Scottish Arts Council (now bequested to Glasgow Vennel Museum, Irvine)
City Art Centre, Edinburgh
Kirkcaldy Museum and Art Gallery
Kyle and Carrick Museums
Business Design Centre, London
Maclaurin Trust, Maclaurin Gallery, Ayr
McManus Galleries, Dundee
Paintings in Hospitals
Kelvingrove Art Gallery and Museum, Glasgow
City of Schwedt an der Oder, Germany

WORKS IN PRIVATE COLLECTIONS

Scotland, England, Ireland, United States, Canada, Australia, New Zealand, Papua New Guinea, Holland, Germany, Denmark, Norway, Northern Ireland, Italy, Hong Kong

WORK ABROAD

1998–99 Major solo exhibition (and subsequent tour) at Bornholms Kunstmuseum, Bornholm, Denmark

1998 Invited artist at Internationales Plein Air and Feuchte Arbeiten Exhibition, Szczecin, Poland
Exchange artist work/exhibition at 'Footsteps', Panzerhalle, Brandenburg, Germany

1997 Research visit to Bornholm
Invited artist at Internationales Plein Air and Feuchte Arbeiten Exhibition, Schwedt an der Oder, Germany

1996 Working in Berlin studio/research visit to Bornholm

1993 Study tours to Venice Biennale, Cologne Art Fair, Frankfurt Art Museum

1992 Studio, Berlin (Berlin Project. Living and working in Berlin at Produzentengalerie Broschwitz. Making works and exhibiting. Living in Atelierhaus at Checkpoint Charlie. Final exhibition (with Peter Russell) entitled 'Two Europeans from Scotland'

1991 Study tour to Norway

1988 and 1989 Artist in Residence, Ecole de Peinture, Castelnau de Montmiral, Tarn, France.

1987 Studio, Jerusalem

1986 Studio, Berlin

1986 Visiting Lecturer, Bezalel Academy of Art and Design, Jerusalem

1985 Studio, Berlin; Study tour to Hanover, Cologne, Dusseldorf, Munchengladbach, Essen, Bonn, Dortmund, Bremen, Stuttgart, Munich, Nebüll

Other study tours to Holland, France, Italy, Greece and California

SELECT BIBLIOGRAPHY

PUBLICATIONS

Clanjamfrie (literary broadsheet), Issues One (1984) and Three (1988)

Dreaming Frankenstein, Liz Lochhead (Polygon, Edinburgh, 1984 and 1998)

The Self Portrait – A Modern View (Sarema Press, London, 1987)

Robert Burns, Catherine Carswell (Canongate, Edinburgh, 1988)

Contemporary Painting in Scotland, Bill Hare (Craftsman House, Sydney, 1992)

Scottish Art in the Twentieth Century, Duncan Macmillan (Mainstream Publishing, Edinburgh 1994)

Verkoop je moeder!, Efraim Sevela (Wereldbibliotheek, Amsterdam, 1995)

NEWSPAPER, MAGAZINES AND JOURNALS

Sydney Goodsir Smith, *The Scotsman*, 5 October 1962

Sydney Goodsir Smith, 'French Prints Steal the Show', *The Scotsman*, 28 November 1966

William Ferguson, *Times Educational Supplement*, 1 February 1974

Martin Baillie, *Glasgow Herald*, 1 February 1974

Lesley Munn, 'Portrait of the Artist as a Young Woman', *Glasgow Herald*, 27 May 1978

Sue Innes, *The Scotsman*, 14 March 1983

Hayden Murphy, 'Something Old, Something New', *Irish Times*, June 1983

William Ferguson, 'Exhibitions', *Times Educational Supplement*, 7 October 1983

Cordelia Oliver, 'Lys Hansen', *The Guardian*, 22 February 1984

Clare Henry, 'Lys Hansen', *Glasgow Herald*, 24 February 1984

Iain Finlayson, 'Lys Hansen', *Arts Review*, February 1984

William Ferguson, 'Lion and the Lady', *Times Educational Supplement*, 17 June 1984

Edward Gage, 'Revitalisation of SSA image continues', *The Scotsman*, 24 September 1984

Aidan Dunne, 'Women in the rough and tumble', *Sunday Press* (Ireland), 14 April 1985

Anne Carlisle, 'Lys Hansen: She is She', *Circa* 26, May 1985

William Ferguson, 'Exhibitions', *Times Educational Supplement*, 20 September 1985

Edward Gage, 'Glut of a tiresome tendency', *The Scotsman*, 23 September 1985

Clare Henry, *Arts Review*, 25 September 1985

Cordelia Oliver, 'Fads and Fashions in the Appreciation of Painting', *ArtWork*, December 1985/January 1986

Waldemar Januszczak, 'Creation without a Trace of Shame', *The Guardian*, 6 February 1986

Sarah Kent, 'Art: Selections and Reviews', *Time Out*, 20 February 1986

Mark Currah, 'Visual Arts', *City Limits*, 21 February 1986

Linda Talbot, *Camden Arts*, February 1986

Cordelia Oliver, 'Lys Hansen', *The Guardian*, 1 May 1986

Edward Gage, 'Prints with an eye on the master', *The Scotsman*, 5 May 1986

Wendy Alstead, 'Lys Hansen Interviewed', *Alba*, Summer, 1986

Fabian Carlsson, 'New Acquaintances', *Time Out*, 6 August 1986

Murdo MacDonald, 'A powerful plea for the planet', *The Scotsman*, 17 October 1988

William Ferguson, 'Exhibitions', *Times Educational Supplement*, 21 October 1988

Clare Henry, 'Tackling a new medium brings out pots of talent', *Glasgow Herald*, 21 October 1988

Geraldine Prince, 'The Inside Story', *Scotland on Sunday*, 30 October 1988

Clare Henry, 'Lys Hansen: Edinburgh City Art Centre', *Arts Review*, October 1988

Andrew Gibbon Williams, 'Passion in a Clash of Colour', *The Observer*, October 1988

Geraldine Prince, *The Independent*, 1 November 1988

Clare Henry, 'Artists from Tillicoultry', *Glasgow Herald*, 14 November 1988

Richard Jaques, 'Inventive sculptures steal the exhibition', *The Scotsman*, 11 November 1988

W. Gordon Smith, 'A man's a man for a' that', *The Observer*, 1 October 1989

Pat Gerber, *Glasgow Herald*, 2 July 1990

Clare Flowers, 'Gallery Review', *Scotland on Sunday*, 11 November 1990

Hilke Nissen, 'Großstadt in der Sprache der Kunst', *Berliner Morgenpost*, 12 August, 1992

Richard Carr, 'Darker Side of Berlin', *The Scotsman*, 19 April 1993

Richard Carr, 'Beyond the Wall – Lys Hansen looks ahead in Berlin and Beyond', *ArtWork*, April 1993

Ann Shaw, 'Shock Trooper of Art', *Glasgow Herald*, 19 April 1993

Edward Gage, 'A better world for artists?', *The Scotsman*, 4 October 1993

John Fowler, 'Here comes the Berlin Bride', *Glasgow Herald*, 28 July 1994

Nicki McHarg, 'Lys Hansen, Heinzel Gallery, Aberdeen', *The Scotsman*, 3 August 1994

Tim Pauling, 'Art in '90s Scotland', *The Journal*, 25 March 1995

Edward Gage, *The Scotsman*, October 1995

'Homage to a Tragic Queen', *Dunfermline Press*, 1 December 1995

Clare Henry, *Glasgow Herald*, 15 March 1997

CATALOGUES AND BROCHURES

Cordelia Oliver, *Lys Hansen: Recent Work* (Third Eye Centre, Glasgow, February, 1984)

Hayden Murphy, *She is She* (University of Ulster and Projects Arts Centre, Dublin, 1985)

Waldemar Januszczak, *Biennial* (Smith Art Gallery & Museum, Stirling, 12 September 1985)

Euan MacArthur, *Lys Hansen: Recent Work* (Artspace, Aberdeen, March-April, 1986)

Philip Wright, *New Art from Scotland* (Warwick Arts Trust, London, January 1986)

Andrew Guest, *At the Smith* (Smith Art Gallery & Museum, Stirling, 16 July 1988)

Cyril Gerber, *Crossing Boundaries* (Compass Gallery, Glasgow, 5 October 1988)

Richard Demarco, *Four Scottish Artists* (Demarco Gallery, Edinburgh, 1 November 1990)

Emily Ash, *Mary Queen of Scots . . . a feminist tradition?* (Ash Gallery, Edinburgh, 2 August 1991)

Lys Hansen/Peter Russell: *In Place of the Wall* (touring exhibition, 1992–93)

Elspeth King, *Smith Open* (Smith Art Gallery & Museum, Stirling, 10 December 1995)

Mike Bailey, *Hansen Paints Burns* (Rozelle House Gallery, Ayr, 29 March 1997)

Richard Carr, *What is a Suitcase?* (touring exhibition, 1997)

TELEVISION AND RADIO

The Lunch Party (Profile of Lys Hansen, June Redfern, Jacki Parry presented by Liz Lochhead) BBC Scotland Television, 1984

Tuesday Review, BBC Radio Scotland, 1988

Featured Artist, *MacGregor's Gathering*, BBC Radio Scotland, 1988

Interview by Halla Beloff, BBC Radio Scotland, 1988

Radio Clyde, 1988

Discussion of exhibition and book – *The Glasgow Girls*, BBC Radio Scotland, 1988

Review of 'For a' That', BBC Radio Scotland, 1988

Review of 'In Place of the Wall', BBC Radio Scotland, 1993

Discussion on function of the war artist, BBC Radio Scotland, 1993

NOTES ON THE CONTRIBUTORS

MIKE BAILEY became the first director of the Maclaurin Art Gallery in 1976, where he was responsible for devising an exhibition programme and advising on the development of a permanent collection. Taking early retirement in 1996, he has continued as a freelance exhibition organiser and advisor to the Maclaurin Trust.

METTE BLIGAARD, formerly director of the Museum of Danish National History at Frederiksborg Castle in Denmark, was appointed director of the Danish Cultural Institute, Edinburgh, in 1997. She is an art historian and has written widely on Danish art and architecture.

RICHARD CARR is senior lecturer in the History of Design and Contemporary Studies at Duncan of Jordanstone College of Art and Design, University of Dundee. He is editor of *ArtWork* and writes on architecture, the crafts and design for *The Scotsman*. Formerly design correspondent of *The Guardian*, his publications include *Tartans* (1984), which he co-authored with Ann Sutton.

VERONICA CORDEIRO graduated from the University of Edinburgh in 1997. She has since worked for the São Paulo Biennale and will take up a place at the Royal College of Art studying curatorship in the autumn of 1998.

RICHARD DEMARCO OBE is professor of European Cultural Studies, Kingston University, and director of the Demarco European Art Foundation.

IAIN GALE is art critic for *Scotland on Sunday* and was formerly with *The Independent*. He has written a number of books, including *Corot* (1994) and *Arthur Melville* (1996).

BILL HARE currently works for Edinburgh College of Art, is an associate lecturer with the Open University in Scotland and is head of History of Art with the Centre for Continuing Education at the University of Edinburgh. His publications include *Contemporary Painting in Scotland* (1992). He is the Scottish editor for *Galleries* magazine.

CLARE HENRY FRSA has been art critic of *The Herald* since 1980; Scottish editor of *Arts Review* from 1983; and founder member (1973) and subsequently chairman of the Glasgow Print Studio. She regularly curates exhibitions, including 'New Scottish Prints', New York; Serpentine Summer Show; 'The Vigorous Imagination' for the Scottish National Gallery of Modern Art; 'Scotland at the Venice Biennale', 1990; and 'Critic's Choice', London, 1992, and Glasgow, 1994.

LIZ LOCHHEAD is a poet, playwright and broadcaster. Her works include *Dreaming Frankenstein* (1984), *New Confessions and Old Clichés* (1985) and *Bagpipe Muzak* (1991).

JUDITH MACRAE is an admirer and collector of Lys Hansen's work. She was born in Australia and currently lives in Dunoon, Argyll, where she is Principal Teacher of English at Dunoon Grammar.

HAYDEN MURPHY is a poet, critic and regular contributor to the *Irish Times*. His publications include *Exile's Journal: A Poem Sequence* (1992) and *Wedded Echoes* (1995).

CORDELIA OLIVER is a painter and writer and was formerly *The Guardian*'s art critic in Scotland. She has published numerous works including *James Cowie* (1980), *Joan Eardley* (1988) and *It is a Curious Story: The Tale of Scottish Opera, 1962–87*.

COLIN RUSCOE is a freelance photographer. He has exhibited widely, including the annual exhibitions of the Society of Scottish Artists and the Aberdeen Artists Society. Solo exhibitions have included work on Scottish and French landscape. He has contributed to a number of publications, including *Alberto Morrocco* (1993).

MHAIRI SCOTT graduated from the University of Glasgow in 1995. She has worked as a research assistant on the Eduardo Paolozzi/Dean Centre project for the Scottish National Gallery of Modern Art.

GILES SUTHERLAND has written and lectured on many aspects of art and has been a regular contributor to *The Scotsman*. In 1993 he published *Explorations in Wood: The Furniture and Sculpture of Tim Stead.*

GLOSSARY OF ARTISTS AND WRITERS REFERRED TO BY THE CONTRIBUTORS

Hannah Arendt (1906–75). German-born American philosopher and political theorist.
Sam Ainslie (b.1950). Scottish artist.
Max Beckmann (1884–1950). German expressionist painter and printmaker.
Reinhard Behrens (b. 1951). German artist based in Scotland. President of the Society of Scottish Artists 1988–91.
John Bellany (b.1942). Scottish painetr. Studied at Edinburgh College of Art 1960–65, Royal College of Art, London 1965–68. Represented in the Maclaurin Art Collection
Joseph Beuys (1921–86). German artist.
Pierre Bonnard (1867–1947). French painter.
Constantin Brancusi (1876–1957). Romanian sculptor.
Jack Burnham (b.1905). Critic and commentator. Author of *Suicide of the West: An Essay on the Meaning and Destiny of Liberalism* (1964).
Robert Burns (1759–96). Scottish poet.
Robert Callender (b. 1932). English artist and lecturer at Edinburgh College of Art (1961–92). Attended Edinburgh College of Art, 1954–59.
Jacques Callot (fl. 1630-40, Strasbourg). Published a suite of engravings, '*Les Misères de la guerre*', 1636.
Karin Christiansen (b. 1942). German artist based in Berlin.
John Connolly. Scottish sculptor based in Glasgow.
Victoria Crowe (b.1945). Scottish artist.
James Cumming, RSA (1922–91). Scottish artist. Taught at Edinburgh College of Art, 1950–82.
Ken Currie (b.1960). Scottish artist based in Glasgow.
Alan Davie (b. 1920). Scottish painter.
Kenneth Dingwall (b. 1938), Head of Fine Art, the Cleveland Institute of Art, Ohio, USA. Attended Edinburgh College of Art, 1955–60.
Otto Dix (1891–1969). German painter.
Albrecht Dürer (1471–1528). German painter and etcher.
Joan Eardley, RSA (1921–63). Scottish artist.
John Duncan Fergusson (1874–1961). Scottish painter and sculptor. Along with Cadell, Hunter and Peploe, he was one of the Scottish Colourists.
Beth Fisher (b. 1944) American artist based in Aberdeen since 1976.
Douglas Gifford (b. 1940). Professor of Scottish Literature, University of Glasgow, since 1 October 1995.
Sir William Gillies, RSA, RSW, RA, PPRSW, CBE (1898–1973). Scottish painter. Taught at Edinburgh College of Art, 1925–66.
Francisco José Goya y Lucientes (1746–1828). Spanish artist. Published his suite of etchings, '*Los Desastres de la Guerra*', c.1810.
Germaine Greer (b. 1939). Australian-born feminist writer and lecturer, based in the UK
Richard Hamilton (b. 1922). English painter.
Gwen Hardie (b.1962). Scottish artist based in London.
David Harding (b. 1937). Scottish artist. Head of Sculpture and Environmental Art, Glasgow School of Art, from 1986. Attended Edinburgh College of Art, 1955–59.
Seamus Heaney (b .1939). Nobel Prize-winning Irish poet.
Eric Hilton (b. 1937). Scottish artist working in glass at Steuben Glass, based in New York State, USA. Attended Edinburgh College of Art, 1955–59.
Hermann Hesse (1877–1962). German-born Swiss novelist and poet. Winner of the Nobel Prize for literature in 1946.
Gerard Manley Hopkins (1844–89). English poet and priest.
John Houston (b. 1930). Scottish artist.
Peter Howson (b. 1958). Scottish artist based in London.
Ted Hughes (b. 1930). English poet. Poet Laureate since 1984.
Margaret Hunter (b. 1948). Scottish artist based in Berlin.
Inge X. Husemann (b. 1937). Artist, exhibition organiser and director of Atelier IX, Berlin.
Tadeusz Kantor (1915–90). Polish theatre director and artist.
Omar Khayyám (c.1048–c.1122). Persian poet.
Käthe Kollwitz (1867–1945). German artist. Studied graphics and sculpture. Noted for her graphic works against poverty, injustice and war.
Willem De Kooning (b. 1904). Dutch-born American painter.
D.H. Lawrence (1885–1939). English novelist and essayist.
'Hugh MacDiarmid' was the pen name of Christopher Murray Grieve (1892–1978) Scottish poet and nationalist.
Bruce McLean (b.1944). Scottish artist. Studied Glasgow School of Art 1961–63, St Martins School of Art, London 1963–66. Represented in the Maclaurin Art Collection.
Sir William MacTaggart, RSW, PRSA (1903–81). Scottish artist. Taught at Edinburgh College of Art, 1933–56.
Henri Matisse (1869–1954). French painter.
John Maxwell, RSA (1905–62). Scottish artist. Taught at Edinburgh College of Art, 1929–33; 1935–46; 1955–62.
Paula Modersohn-Becker (1876–1907). German painter.
Edvard Munch (1863–1944). Norwegian painter.
Timothy Neat (b. 1943), author, film-maker and art historian.
Emil Nolde (1867–1956). German painter and printmaker.
Jacki Parry (b. 1941). Australian papermaker and printmaker based in Scotland
Sir Robin Philipson, PRSA, RA (1916–92). Scottish artist. Taught at Edinburgh College of Art, 1947–82.
Pablo Picasso (1881–1973). Spanish painter.
Sylvia Plath (1931–63). American poet.
Charles D. Pulsford, ARSA (1912–89), taught at Edinburgh College of Art, 1947–60.
June Redfern (b. 1951), Scottish painter based in London.
Anne Redpath, RSA, RWA, ARA, OBE (1895–1965). Scottish artist.
Klaus Rinke (b. 1939). German artist.
Theodore Roszak (b.1933). Social commentator. Author of *Masculine/Feminine: Readings in Sexual Mythology and the Liberation of Women* (1969)
Peter Russell (b. 1948). Scottish artist based in Stirling
Peter Stitt (b. 1937). Scottish artist based in Melbourne, Australia. Attended Edinburgh College of Art, 1955–59.
Günter Uecker (b. 1930). German artist.
Richard Waitt (d. 1732). Scottish artist.
Alison Watt (b. 1965). Scottish painter based in London.
Virginia Woolf (1882–1941). English novelist, critic and essayist.

INDEX